HORSE AND HISTORY

FROM ARABIA TO ASCOT

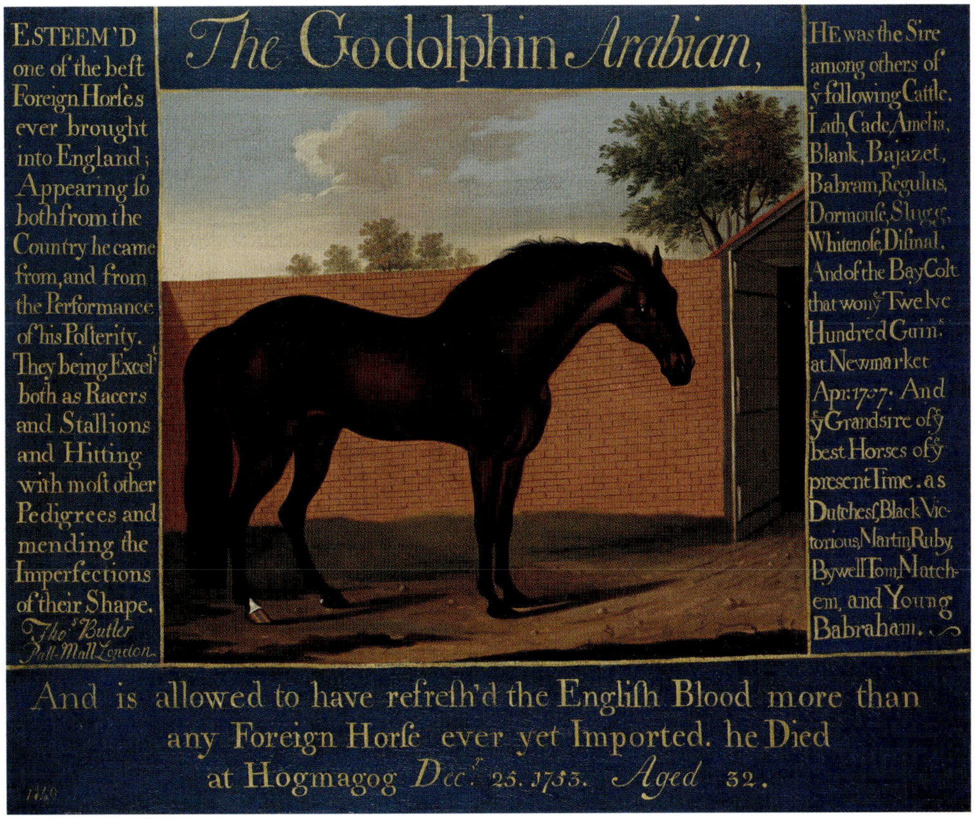

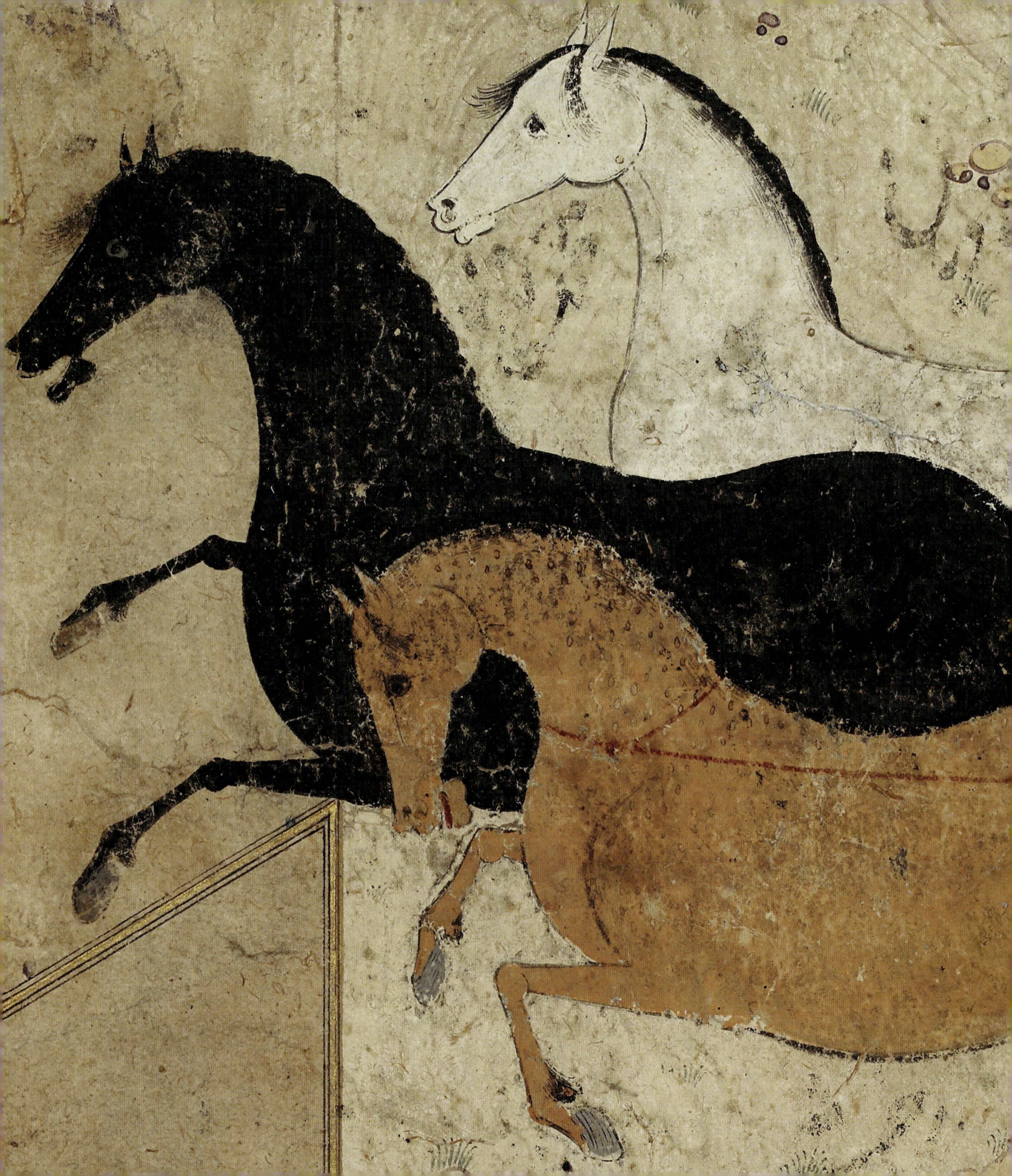

HORSE AND HISTORY

FROM ARABIA TO ASCOT

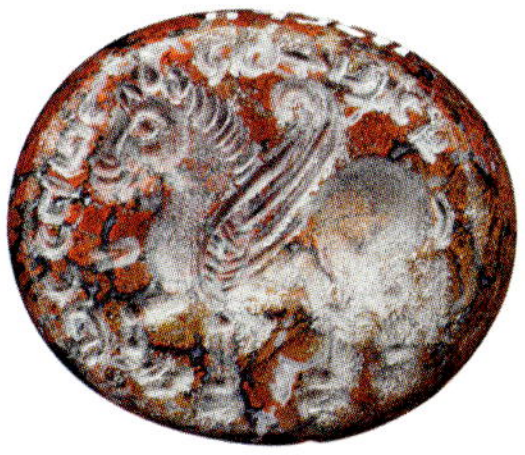

John Curtis and Nigel Tallis
With the assistance of Astrid Johansen

LUND HUMPHRIES

ISBN 978-1-84822-106-2

Published by

Lund Humphries
Suite 420
101 Cherry Street
Burlington
VT 05401-4405
USA

Lund Humphries is part of Ashgate Publishing

www.lundhumphries.com

Library of Congress Control Number: 2012930110

Designed by Price Watkins
Printed in Italy by Graphicom srl

Half-title page: The Godolphin Arabian, Thomas Butler, *c.* 1750–5. See cat. 208.
Frontispiece: Three galloping horses (detail), *c.* 1550. See cat. 152.
Title page: Stamp seal with a winged horse, 4th century. See cat. 126.
Above right: Detail from a ewer with inlaid decoration, *c.* 1232. See cat. 135.
Opposite: Rein-ring decorated with a figure of an ass, *c.* 2600 BC. See cat. 2.
P. 8: Mid-eighteenth century portrait on paper of the grandson of Abul Hasan Qutb Shah (1672–1687), shown riding a richly equipped stallion and carrying a hawk. His grandfather, the last ruler of the Qutb Shahi dynasty of Golconda in India was defeated by the Mughal emperor Aurangzeb in 1687. BM 1974,0617,0.9.

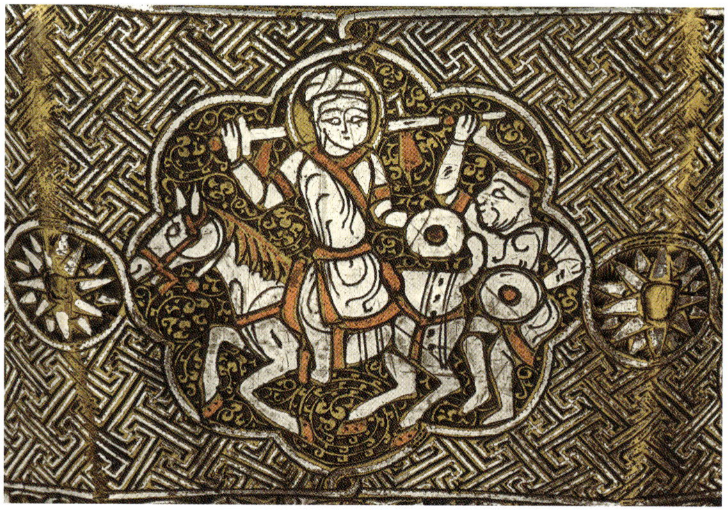

Contents

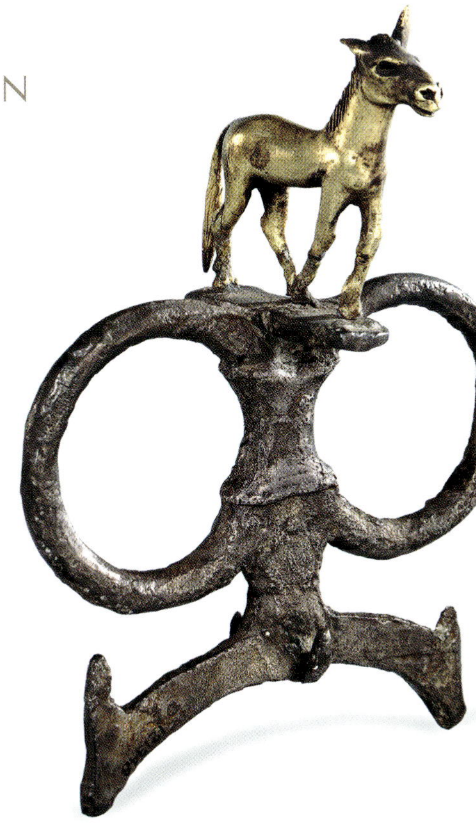

Foreword

IT IS WELL KNOWN that the horse has played a crucial role in the development of civilization, and that a close bond exists between horses and men. This was recognized by the Prophet Muhammad, may peace be upon him, but respect and admiration for horses is not confined to the Muslim region. People all over the world and belonging to many different faiths revere the horse, and it is because of this widespread and deeply rooted interest that it is so important to organize informative exhibitions on the subject. In the long history of the horse Saudi Arabia has played an important role, and the region had given its name to what is now known as 'the Arabian horse'. Important discoveries have recently been made in Saudi Arabia which might shed light on the early history of this horse, and the many rock drawings of horses throughout the kingdom are of absorbing interest. I am proud of the fact that King Abdulaziz al-Saud is sometimes known as 'the last horseman' on account of the fact that he was the last leader in history to unite a country on horseback.

Horses have always been an important part of Arabian culture, and I personally have had a lifelong interest in and association with horses. For many years I harboured an ambition to sponsor some definitive work on horses and horsemanship, and that ambition was realized through two splendid volumes entitled *Furusiyya* published by the King Abdulaziz Public Library in 1996. These volumes, edited by David Alexander, contained a series of authoritative essays about the history of the horse and a list of objects in museums around the world relating to the history of horses. Some of the objects in that catalogue are included in the present exhibition. Following on from the *Furusiyya* volumes it is gratifying that it was possible to organize a major international exhibition on the subject at the International Museum of the Horse in Kentucky Horse Park, from May to October 2010. The exhibition, entitled *A Gift from the Desert: the Art, History and Culture of the Arabian Horse* was accompanied by a beautiful catalogue by Sandra Olsen and Cynthia Culbertson. This comprehensive exhibition proved to be very popular, and made a great contribution to our knowledge not only about the history of the Arabian horse but about the history of horses in general. However, the exhibition did not travel and people in Europe did not have an opportunity to see it. I am therefore very pleased indeed that it has now been possible to arrange an exhibition on a similar subject in London. Of course it does not replicate the exhibition in Kentucky, nor does it cover quite the same ground, but this is a good thing as it gives us an opportunity to look at different aspects of the history of the Arabian horse and the context from which it emerged.

FAISSAL IBN ABDULLAH IBN MUHAMMAD AL-SAUD
Minister of Education
(Chairman of the Board of Trustees of the Saudi Equestrian Fund)

Supported by

الفروسية السعودية
SAUDI EQUESTRIAN

مؤسسة ليان للثقافة
Layan Cultural Foundation

JUDDMONTE

In association with the Saudi Commission for Tourism & Antiquities, the King Abdulaziz Arabian Horse Centre and the King Abdulaziz Public Library.

Foreword

THE COLLECTIONS of the British Museum are renowned around the world for their breadth and depth, which gives visitors an almost unrivalled opportunity to view objects not just in the context of the cultures which produced them but also in the context of other, related societies. Although on the whole the permanent exhibitions are not arranged by theme, many significant subjects and topics which have been of wide significance are well represented across the different departments of the museum. Horses are a case in point, and such is the wealth of the collection that they provide an ideal subject for a special exhibition. Our only concern, in view of the embarrassment of riches at our disposal, has been how to limit the exhibition so that it had a meaningful narrative and could tell in a comprehensible way one part of the very rich history of the horse. Conversations with HH Prince Faissal Ibn Abdullah Ibn Muhammad Al-Saud led us to focus on the story of the Arabian horse, which combines a significant Middle Eastern history with one of the most popular British pursuits.

The result is an exhibition that reviews the history of the horse in the Middle East in the ancient and Islamic periods in order to show the context from which the Arabian horse emerges. We then go on to look at the horse in the Arabian Peninsula itself, and describe how from the seventeeth century onwards many oriental stallions including Arabians were imported into Britain and bred with British and Irish mares to improve the speed and resilience of the native stock. The eventual result of this process was the Thoroughbred horse, and as is well known all modern Thoroughbred horses trace their ancestry back to just three stallions, the Godolphin Arabian, the Darley Arabian and the Byerley Turk. Amongst those involved in the introduction and breeding of oriental horses in Britain were Lady Anne Blunt and Wilfrid Scawen Blunt, and their story is included in the exhibition.

Nowadays in Britain, flat-racing and steeple-chasing are mostly restricted to Thoroughbreds, as opposed to equestrian events, where the competing horses are often Thoroughbreds crossed with other breeds. In addition, purebred Arabian horses are involved in events all around the world. In essence, then, the exhibition describes the history of the horse from its domestication in about 3500 BC down to modern flat-racing and equestrian events which are an important component of the Olympic Games. It is a happy coincidence that this exhibition is taking place in 2012 when the Olympic Games are being held in London.

Many of the objects in this exhibition come from the British Museum's own collection but these have been supplemented by loans from various institutions in Saudi Arabia, the United Kingdom and Switzerland, as well as several private individuals. We are most grateful to all of them for their generosity. We are also indebted to the organizers of the exhibition on the Arabian horse, *A Gift from the Desert,* held in the International Museum of the Horse in Kentucky Horse Park in the summer of 2010. It covered some of the same ground as this exhibition but the overall treatment of the subject is inevitably different. I would also like to pay tribute to the *Furusiyya* catalogue (1996), edited by David Alexander, which gathered a great deal of information about the history of horses and has been a source of inspiration ever since. Finally, we are most grateful to Prince Faissal, HRH Prince Khalid bin Abdullah bin Abdulrahman Al Saud, and organisations in Saudi Arabia for sponsoring this exhibition.

Flat-racing and equestrian events in the United Kingdom have for centuries enjoyed royal support and patronage. HM Queen Elizabeth II has continued this royal tradition with evident enthusiasm and pleasure. This exhibition is offered as a tribute to Her Majesty on the occasion of her Diamond Jubilee.

NEIL MACGREGOR
Director, British Museum

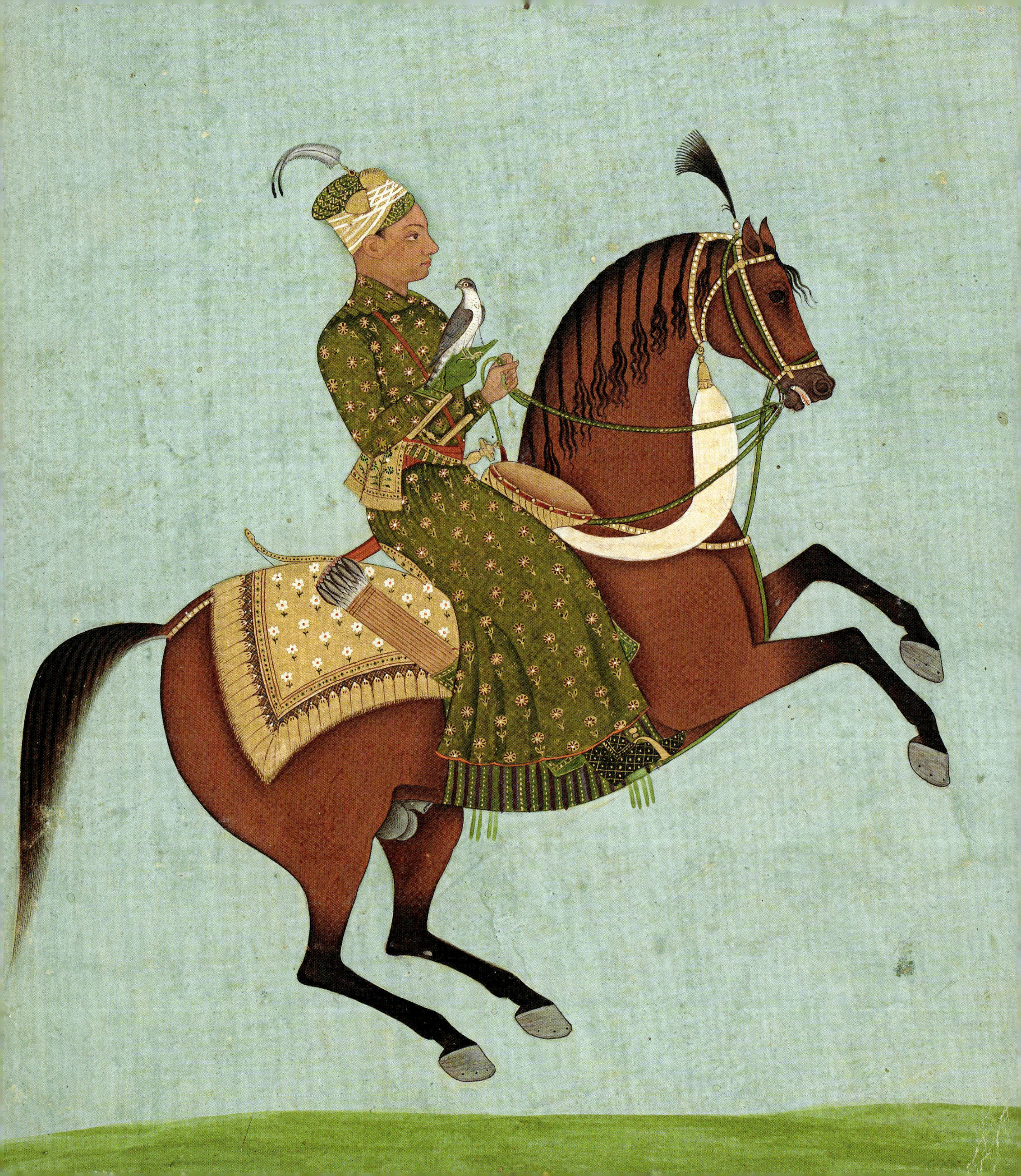

List of lenders

Apart from the British Museum, the objects included in the exhibition *The Horse: from Arabia to Royal Ascot* have been kindly loaned by a number of private and public collections and institutions. The British Museum would like to thank all the lenders for their generosity.

Kingdom of Saudi Arabia

King Abdulaziz Public Library, Riyadh
King Saud University Museum, Riyadh
Layan Cultural Foundation, Jeddah
National Museum of Saudi Arabia, Riyadh

United Kingdom

British Library, London
Fitzwilliam Museum, Cambridge
Jockey Club Estates, Newmarket
Royal Armouries
Royal Collection
Tate, London

Switzerland

Olympic Museum, Lausanne

Individual lenders

HRH Prince Khalid Abdullah
Mrs A.A. Edmunds
Nicholas Knowles
Richard Meade
Peter Upton

Authors' preface and acknowledgements

THE HORSE has played a hugely important part in human history. From its domestication around five and a half thousand years ago, somewhere in the grassy steppe lands that stretch from the Danube to the Altai Mountains, up until modern times, the horse has been an essential element in many of the world's major cultures. Until the age of mechanization, even within living memory, horses were essential for transport, either ridden or pulling vehicles, in warfare, and in industry. Only recently has the emphasis shifted to recreational and sporting activities, including flat-racing, steeple chasing, and equestrianism. In a single exhibition, it would be quite impossible to cover all aspects of the history of the horse, embracing all areas and all periods. We have therefore had to be selective, and this exhibition and accompanying book focus on the Middle East, which is in itself a key area for the development of horses, and describe how oriental horses were brought into Britain from the early seventeenth century onwards and were bred with native British and Irish mares to produce the Thoroughbred horse. An important link in this story is the Arabian horse, in that all modern Thoroughbreds trace their lineage back to two or three Arabian sires, but there were of course in antiquity and still are today many other types of horse in the Middle East. In fact, the further one goes back in time the more difficult it is to recognize particular breeds of horse, and at best one can only point to resemblances to modern breeds. It is not until a relatively late date that one can talk with confidence about particular breeds. The exhibition, then, first looks at the history of the horse in the Middle East from ancient times until the modern period, to see the context from which oriental horses including the Arabian horse emerged. We then look at the evidence for the horse in the Arabian Peninsula, which gives us the opportunity to introduce the GigaPan project. This is an innovative photographic survey of rock drawings featuring horses that will be presented for the first time during the exhibition. Two important individuals in the importation of oriental horses into Britain, although they were active at a time when the Thoroughbred breed had already been established, were Lady Anne Blunt and her husband Wilfrid Scawen Blunt. Nowadays, the Crabbet Stud that they established in Sussex is renowned for its role in preserving the purebred Arabian horse. In Britain, much effort was put into improving the stock of native horses, and by the eighteenth century the Thoroughbred had emerged. The exhibition finishes with a review of modern horse racing, which is restricted to Thoroughbreds, but also touches on modern equestrian events such as the Olympics where the competing horses are not Thoroughbreds but may have the blood of Oriental horses in their veins. Lastly, we point to the continuing story of the pure Arabian horse, which is bred, admired and appreciated around the world, and often takes part in events such as endurance racing, in which it excels.

The British Museum has long wanted to present an exhibition on the horse, and in part this exhibition had its genesis in the two wonderful volumes on Furusiyya (Horsemanship) prepared for the press by David Alexander and published in Riyadh in 1996. These volumes were intended to accompany a large exhibition in Riyadh which in the end did not materialize, but the seeds were sown for a major international exhibition on the horse. Such an exhibition was eventually mounted in the International Museum of the Horse in Kentucky Horse Park in the summer of 2010, under the title *A Gift from the Desert: the Art, History and Culture of the Arabian Horse*. We are most grateful to the curators of this exhibition, Sandra Olsen and Cynthia Culbertson, and the Director of the Museum of the Horse, Bill Cooke, for sharing some ideas with us, and some of the objects shown in Kentucky are included in the present exhibition, but inevitably the end-products are very different.

The core curatorial team has been John Curtis, who was Keeper of the Middle East Department in the British Museum 1989–2011, and is now Keeper of Special Middle East Projects, Nigel Tallis, who is Curator of the Assyrian Collection in the British Museum, and Astrid Johansen, who has been Project Curator for the exhibition since 1 October 2011. Others who have been particularly closely involved in the preparation of the exhibition are Robert Frith (Designer), Claire Edwards (Interpretation Officer), Matt Big (2D designer), Maria Blyzinsky (Project Manager) and Alex Lawson (Development). This group is very grateful to Neil MacGregor and Andrew Burnett of the British Museum Directorate, Joanna Mackle (Director of Public Engagement), Carolyn Marsden Smith (Head of Exhibitions), and Jonathan Tubb (Keeper of the Middle East Department) for their help and support. Other colleagues in the British Museum who have given freely of their expertise, advice and assistance include Ladan Akbarnia, Fahmida Suleman, St John Simpson, Venetia Porter, Sarah Choy and Jane Newson (Middle East), Hugo Chapman and Sheila O'Connell (Prints and Drawings), Neal Spencer (Ancient Egypt and Sudan), Philip Attwood, Thomas Hockenhull and Vesta Sarkhosh Curtis (Coins and Medals), Chris Spring (Africa, Oceania and the Americas), Judith Swaddling (Greek and Roman), Karen Birkhoelzer and Alice Rugheimer (Conservation and Scientific Research), Michael Row and Ivor Kerslake (Photography), David McNeff (Loans Manager), Hannah Payne, Caroline Ingham and Sian Flynn (Exhibitions), Stuart Frost (Head of Interpretation), Hannah Boulton (Communications), Jessica Hunt, Sonia D'Orsi and Ann Lumley (Marketing), Sukie Hemming, Jemma Jones and Clare Tomlinson (Development), and Rosemary Bradley, Roderick Buchanan, Kate Horwood, Angela Pountney, Axelle Russo, Holly Smith and Susan Walby (British Museum Company).

In order to keep this exhibition within manageable proportions, it was decided at the outset to limit the display to objects from the British Museum's own very rich collection supplemented by loans from Saudi Arabia and from various institutions and individuals in the United Kingdom. This we have done, with one exception, a poster from the Olympic Museum in Lausanne. We are extremely grateful to all lenders whose generosity has meant that we have we have been able to assemble such a varied and interesting exhibition. After the names of the lending institutions the names are given in brackets of those who facilitated the loans: the Saudi Commission for Tourism and Antiquities (Ali I. Al-Ghabban); the King Abdulaziz Public Library (HE Faisal Abdulrahman bin Muaammer, Abdul Kareem Al-Zaid, Fahad Al-Abdulkareem); the King Abdulaziz Arabian Horse Centre at Dirab (Sami Suleiman al-Nohait, Guy Rhodes); the Layan Cultural Foundation, Jeddah (HH Prince Faissal bin Abdullah bin Muhammad al-Saud); the Royal Collection, United Kingdom (Jonathan Marsden); the British Library (Colin Baker and Arnold Hunt); the Fitzwilliam Museum, Cambridge (Tim Potts and David Scrace); the Tate Gallery (Sir Nicholas Serota); the Royal Armouries, Leeds (Thom Richardson); the National Horseracing Museum, Newmarket (Chris Garibaldi and Graham Snelling); the Jockey Club, Newmarket (William Gittus); and the Olympic Museum, Lausanne (Frédérique Jamolli). Thanks are also due to the following individuals who have generously lent us material: HRH Prince Khalid Abdullah, Richard Meade, Nicholas Knowles, Mrs A.A. Edmunds and Peter Upton (who also gave us valuable information about the history of the Arabian horse) and Jila Peacock and Afsoon Hayley for donations of their work.

It is a privilege to be able to include in this exhibition some examples of GigaPan photography, and we are grateful to the Director of the project Richard T. Bryant for making this possible. We should also like to thank Kieran Baker for interesting discussions about the making of a documentary film about the life of Lady Anne Blunt.

We have benefited considerably from the combined wisdom of the Advisory Committee, whose members were Saad al-Rashid, David Alexander, Sandra Olsen and Rachel Ward. Dr Saad in particular has been a tower of strength, encouraging us, monitoring progress, and acting as a bridge between ourselves and colleagues in Saudi Arabia. Other individuals who have given generously of their time and advice and sometimes steered us towards important loans include Catherine Wills, James Swartz, John Roche and Ahmed Moustafa. We have also benefited from the advice of the two owners of Arabian horses in the British Museum, Alice Rugheimer and Elizabeth Pendleton.

In Saudi Arabia Khalid H. Tahir, Hany Ahmed Alshuweir and Wedyan Osama Darandary of NCB Capital did much to progress this exhibition, while in London the staff of the Royal Embassy of Saudi Arabia have been extremely helpful, notably the ambassador HRH Prince Mohammed bin Nawaf bin Abdul Aziz al-Saud, Anne Morris and Jennifer Zulfiqar.

This catalogue has been produced in a relatively short period of time, and the credit for this is entirely due to our editor Coralie Hepburn who has been a model of patience and efficiency. We would also like to thank Ray Watkins who did the layout with great skill at short notice. The catalogue entries for the Islamic period objects and the chapter on the horse in the Islamic world were kindly read by our colleague Ladan Akbarnia, who suggested a few amendments, but any faults that remain are of course the responsibility of the authors.

Lastly, the warmest thanks of all are reserved for HH Prince Faissal bin Abdullah bin Muhammad Al-Saud, whose enthusiasm, vision and generosity have greatly helped to bring about this exhibition.

John Curtis and Nigel Tallis

List of maps

Opposite: The western steppe in relation to early Mesopotamian sites mentioned in the text.

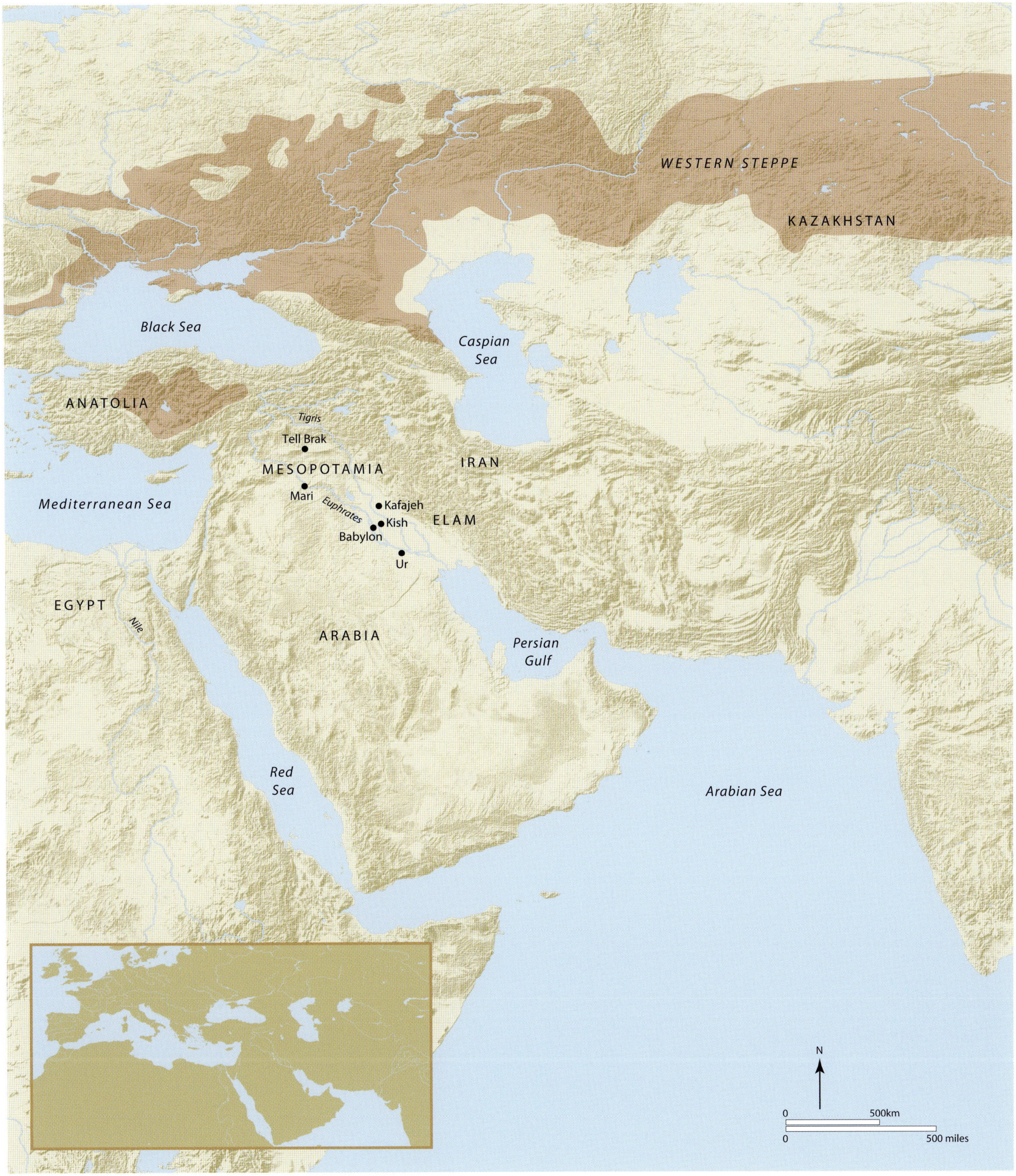
WESTERN STEPPE
KAZAKHSTAN
Black Sea
Caspian Sea
ANATOLIA
Tigris
Tell Brak
MESOPOTAMIA
IRAN
Mari
Mediterranean Sea
Euphrates
Kafajeh
Kish
ELAM
Babylon
Ur
EGYPT
Nile
ARABIA
Persian Gulf
Red Sea
Arabian Sea
N
0
500km
0
500 miles

CHAPTER 1

THE HORSE IN THE ANCIENT NEAR EAST

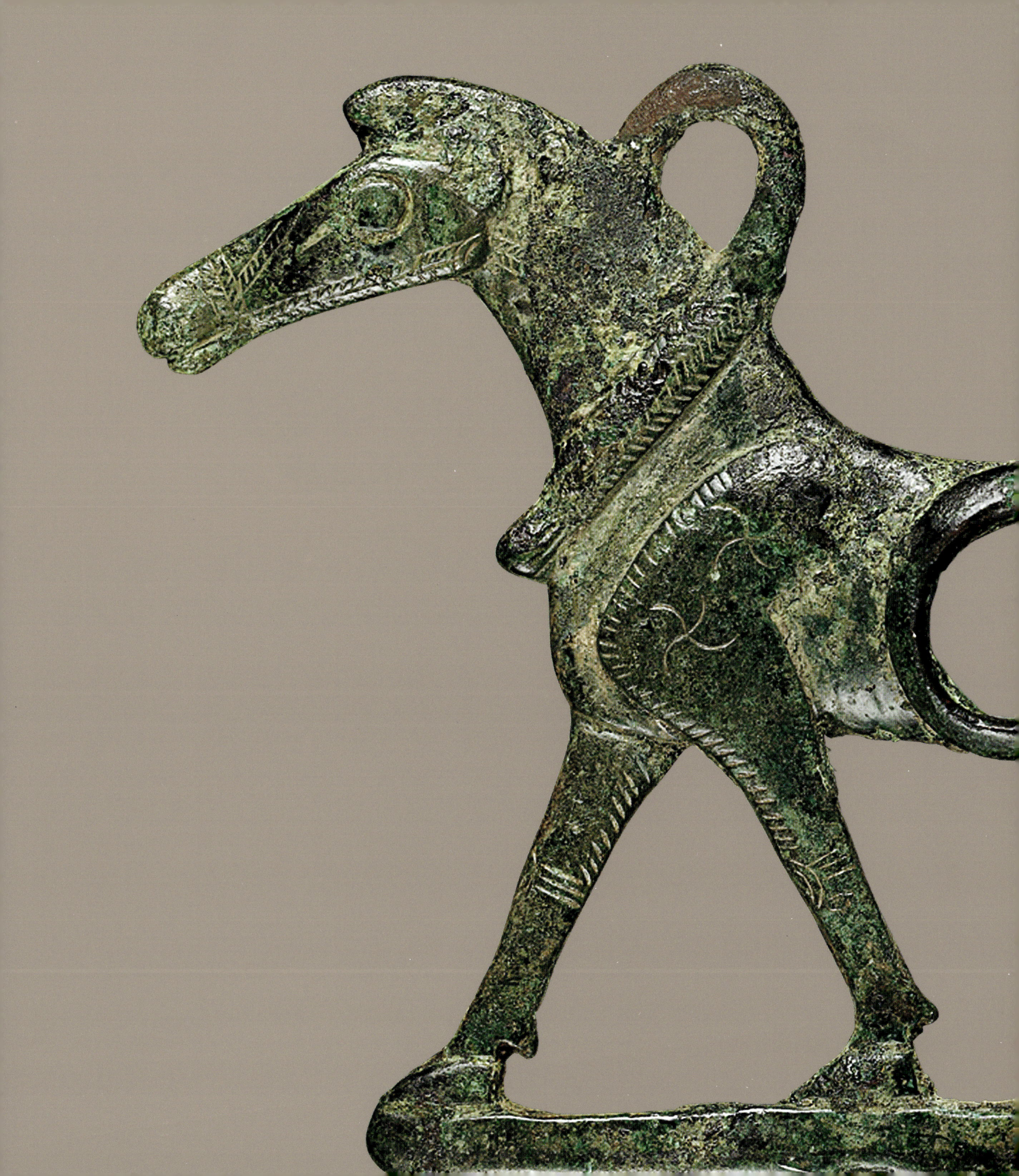

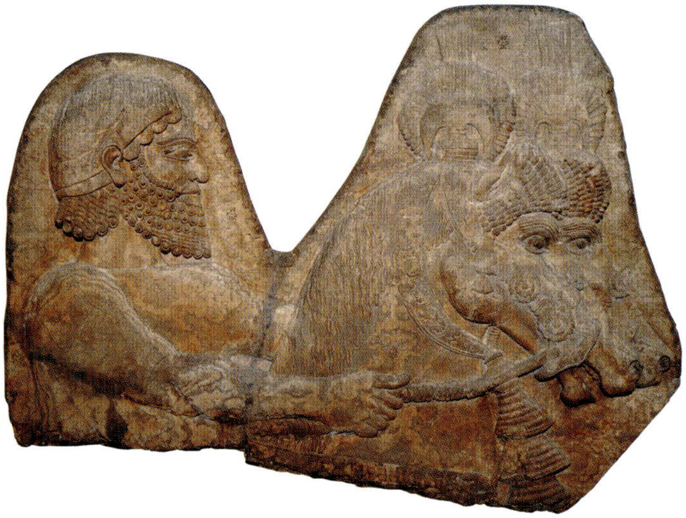

The horse in the Ancient Near East

BEFORE the introduction of the horse, people in the Ancient Near East used donkeys, asses and oxen to pull cumbersome four-wheeled vehicles or sledges. Amongst the earliest depictions of such wheeled vehicles in Western Asia are pictograms on clay tablets from Sumer in southern Mesopotamia, dating from about 3000 BC, which show a roofed cabin mounted on wheels, sometimes with a reed- or basket-work curtain at the side, and with a curved pole or runner at the front. An alternative interpretation is that these are not wheels but numerals indicating numbers of workmen.

The best-known representations of early vehicles, however, are on a so-called 'Standard' found at the Sumerian city of Ur in southern Iraq in a royal cemetery. It dates from around 2600 BC, and is perhaps the sounding box for a musical instrument. It consists of a wooden box covered with bitumen into which is set a mosaic inlay made up of shell and different coloured stones (cat. 1). On one side of the Standard is a scene of farming and banqueting, while on the other is a scene of war. In this representation of a Sumerian army, five war chariots are shown. Each vehicle has a high front to protect the driver, who has a seat, hidden here but visible on clay models, and a platform at the rear on which a man armed with javelins or an axe may stand. The solid wheels are made of

ABOVE
Fig. 1
Part of a stone Assyrian wall panel showing a groom leading a pair of horses, *c.* 710 BC. This relief comes from the Palace of Sargon II at Khorsobad in Assyria (now northern Iraq) and may show tribute being brought to the Assyrian king. The horses wear crescentic crests with elaborate brow cushions and have tassels suspended under their necks.
BM 118828

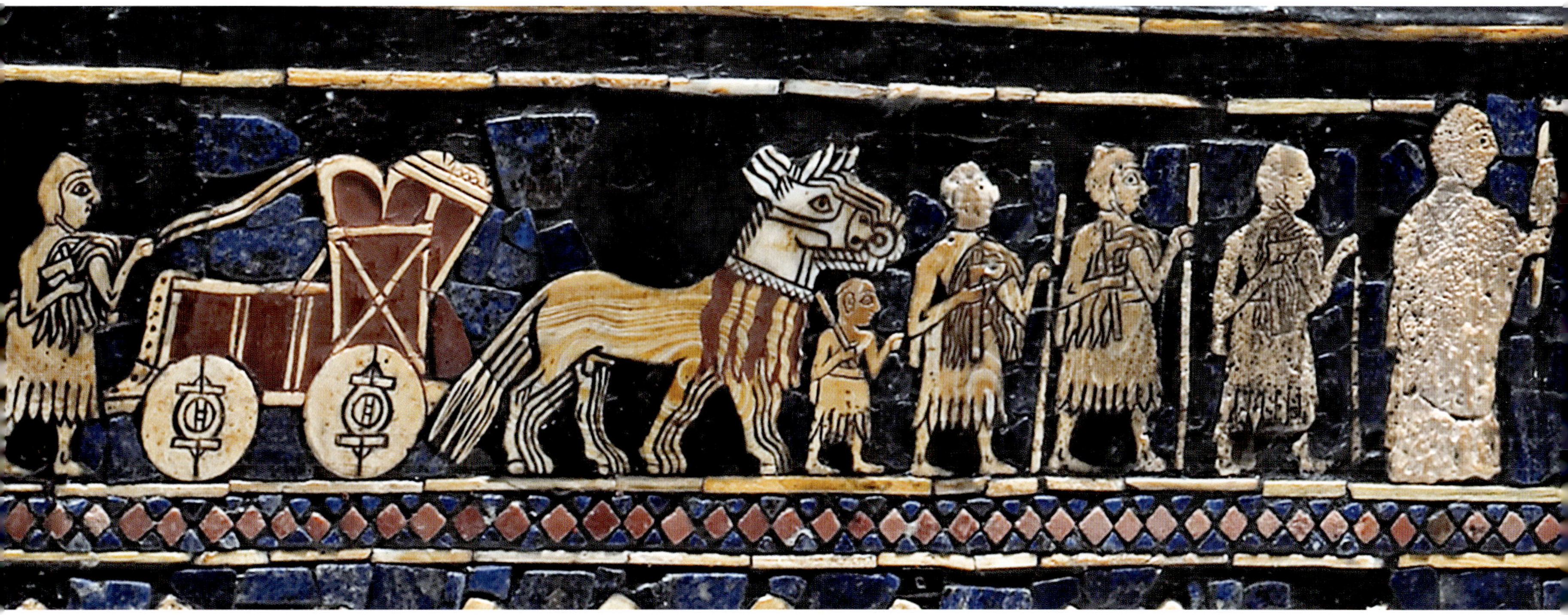

Fig. 2
The ruler and his entourage followed by his four-wheeled chariot, its team of four asses or donkeys held by a groom, shown on the Standard of Ur, *c.* 2600 BC (cat. 1).

three pieces of wood clamped together. The chariot pole is attached to the base of the car and comes up to the shoulders of the four draft-animals. They are controlled by reins which pass through a rein-ring mounted on the chariot pole above a simple yoke to which the animals were attached with collars. These reins are attached to rings through the upper lips of the animals. The purpose of the nose bands, held in place by headstalls, was probably to muzzle the animals (as shown very clearly on other inlays from Kish and Mari), which are apparently crosses from wild asses or donkeys. A similar animal is shown on an electrum rein-ring from Ur.

Models of chariots and representations of them are known from a number of other sites of this date. For example, at Tell Brak in Syria, a seal and a seal impression of the third millennium BC both show a chariot with four solid wheels being pulled by a team of four equids similar to those on the Standard of Ur. In this case they are probably donkeys because the skeletons of six animals have been found that have been identified as donkeys at the same site. They had been ritually sacrificed around 2200 BC and carefully buried in or near a small temple.

These early vehicles were probably fairly speedy (as confirmed by modern reconstructions) but they were difficult to turn and control, and were probably unstable. The

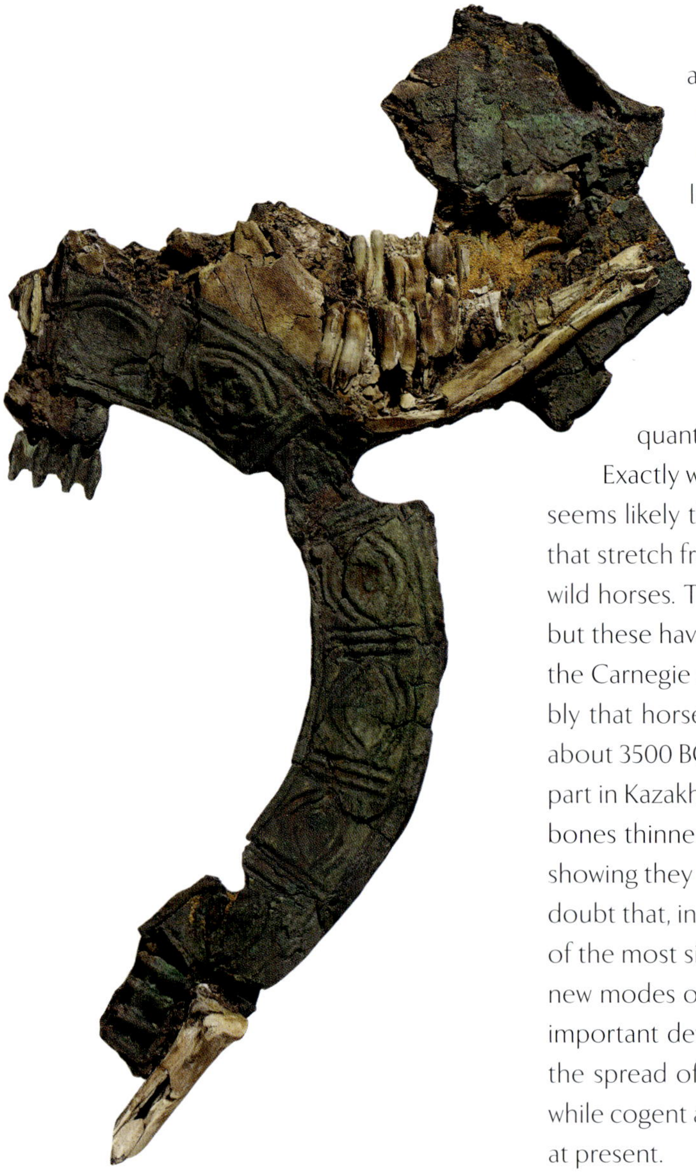

Fig. 3
Bronze or copper breast band (draught collar) with embossed decoration from the Royal Cemetery at Ur in Mesopotamia, dating from around 2600 BC. This collar was worn by one of two oxen pulling a ceremonial sledge. Part of the jaw-bone of the ox is still attached to the collar. Two copper toggles are preserved at each end of the almost intact collar so that it could be fastened to the yoke. The earliest harness collars for asses and horses were based on ox harness.
BM 121480

animals must also have been difficult to handle. Directional control of the team was through a goad (spiked stick) and braking was by reins attached to the nose-ring. The introduction of bits, even for donkeys, was rather later. The earliest certain evidence for the use of a bit in the Middle East is from Tel Haror in Israel, where a donkey skeleton complete with bronze bit has been found in a Middle Bronze Age context (*c.* 1700 BC). There is possibly earlier evidence for metal bits from Tell Brak, but this is as yet inconclusive.

Horses were probably not introduced into the Ancient Near East in any quantity until about 2000 BC, after they had been first domesticated elsewhere. Exactly where and when wild horses were first domesticated is hotly disputed, but it seems likely that it was somewhere on the grassy plains known as the Eurasian steppes that stretch from Eastern Europe to Mongolia, which provided ideal pasture for herds of wild horses. These types of wild horse included the breed known as Przewalski's horse, but these have never been domesticated. Dr Sandra Olsen, Curator of Anthropology at the Carnegie Museum of Natural History in Pittsburgh, Pennsylvania, has argued plausibly that horses were first domesticated in the Botai culture of northern Kazakhstan in about 3500 BC. This is based on findings in archaeological excavations in which she took part in Kazakhstan between 1994 and 2002. The evidence for domestication includes leg bones thinner than those of wild horses and markings on the teeth of horse skeletons showing they had been bridled. Whatever the precise details may have been, there is no doubt that, in the words of Lord Colin Renfrew, 'the domestication of the horse was one of the most significant events in the development of many human societies, ushering in new modes of transport and warfare and generating social and political change'. Other important developments have been linked to the domestication of the horse, such as the spread of wheeled vehicles and even the spread of Indo-European languages, but while cogent arguments have been put forward for these theories they remain unproven at present.

The earliest certain evidence for horses in the Ancient Near East shows them being ridden. For example, there is a Mesopotamian terracotta plaque in the British Museum dating from about 1750 BC that shows a horse with a long hairy tail, possibly exaggerated to show it is not a donkey's tail, being ridden by a man who controls it with reins and a stick. He rides it as one would ride a donkey, far back on the rump, and has no saddle and no stirrups but instead uses a strap around the horse's belly to help keep his seat. However, at this early date horses, nearly always stallions, were mostly used as harness animals in teams of two for pulling chariots. In Mesopotamia and later in Egypt the introduction of the horse led to the development of light, fast chariots with two spoked wheels. From about 1600 BC there was a sweeping change in the nature of warfare and the use of the horse in the Ancient Near East. The fast chariot, which had been known for some two hundred years, now finally reached its full military potential, ushering in what is often known as 'the chariot age'. This came about through the introduction of full defensive armour for horse, vehicle and crew and a complete offensive armament for mounted and foot combat (a powerful composite bow, a large number of arrows, javelins, hand weapons and thrusting spears). Provided and maintained under royal patronage by a military aristocracy, the concept of the 'chariot-system' was to reign supreme throughout the Near East for nearly 1000 years and in modified form was to spread into the Bronze Age Aegean states, India and China. These developments largely came about through a highland people known as the Hurrians, who during the second millennium BC began to form a growing element in the populations of Syria and northern Mesopotamia. By the seventeenth century BC several Hurrian states had formed in these regions and within the following century a confederation of these states between the Euphrates and Tigris, known as the kingdom of Mitanni, had established control over most of Syria and northern Mesopotamia. The skills of horsemanship and chariot warfare were particularly associated with the Hurrians and a high-status class of warriors called 'mariannu'. The influence on contemporary peoples of the Hurrians in equestrian and military matters extended to the powerful Hittites whose capital was at Boğazköy in central Turkey. There are a number of Hittite texts in cuneiform dealing with the training of horses, the best-known of which is the Kikkuli text. This is a chariot horse-training text written in the Hittite language and originally dating from the fifteenth century. It begins: 'thus speaks Kikkuli, master horse trainer of the land of Mitanni.' Pressured by both Egypt, the Hittites and then by Assyria, the kingdom of Mitanni finally collapsed in the thirteenth century BC, but Hurri-Mitannian influence on army organization and equipment was all-pervasive and can be seen in all the Near Eastern states for which we have evidence, from New

Fig. 4
Egyptian wall painting from the tomb of Nebamun at Thebes, *c.* 1500 BC, showing the assessment of crops to establish the payment of tax. Five vertical registers of hieroglyphs on the left side survive. The centre of the fragment is divided into two registers with chariots shown in civil use: the upper register depicts a chariot with a team of two horses, one black and one chestnut, held by the driver, while the lower register shows an indentical chariot drawn by a pair of asses or hinnies with the driver resting in the vehicle. The horses are shown with high tail carriages and arched necks, features that are also present in the later Arabian horse (see cat. 11).
BM 37982

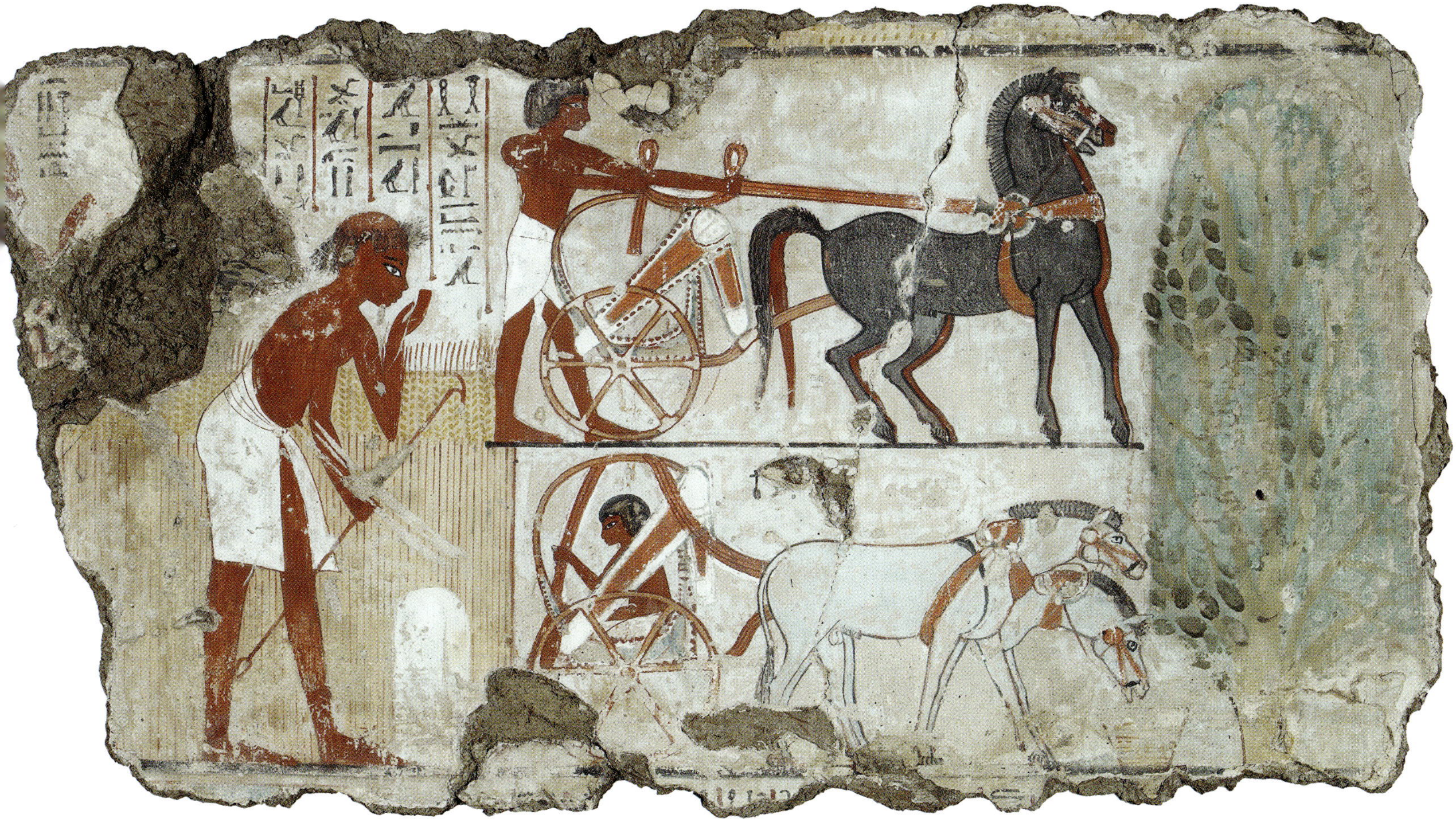

Kingdom Egypt to the Hittites (and even Bronze Age Greece), to the Middle-Assyrian kingdom and Kassite Babylonia.

Horses were much prized, and they were often given as diplomatic gifts in the later second millennium BC, as seen in the Amarna letters. The letters from this archive of royal correspondence with neighbouring kings, found in Egypt but written in the diplomatic language of Babylonian cuneiform, usually begin with an official statement of good wishes for the ruler's 'household, your wives, your sons, your country, your magnates, your horses, your chariots', and commonly include the description of kingly gifts, including five teams of horses from Burnaburiash of Babylon to Amenophis IV or Tutankhamun of Egypt, and long inventories of gifts of horses 'that run swiftly', chariots, harness and equipment, '1 set of bridles, their blinkers of ivory'. It is also in the art of this time, especially in Egyptian tomb-paintings, that we can first see horses with characteristics we now most closely associate with the Arabian breed we know today: for example, a high-arched tail, a short back and prominent eyes.

According to the Bible, Solomon owned a large number of horses. Thus we read in the Book of Chronicles (2 Chronicles 9, v. 25): 'And Solomon had four thousand stalls for horses and chariots, and twelve thousand horsemen, whom he stationed in the chariot cities and with the king in Jerusalem.' We are also told that the horses came from Egypt and Ku'e (possibly Adana in Turkey), and that Solomon's traders also acted as middlemen: 'And Solomon's import of horses was from Egypt and Ku'e, and the king's traders received them from Ku'e for a price. They imported a chariot from Egypt for six hundred shekels of silver, and a horse for a hundred and fifty; likewise through them these were exported to all the kings of the Hittites and the kings of Syria' (2 Chronicles 1, vv. 16–17).

Around 1000 BC horse riding became more widespread, particularly in areas which were suitable for breeding horses. Nowhere was this more evident than the Luristan region of western Iran, where between 1000 and 700 BC there was a thriving culture, perhaps semi-nomadic, which was clearly very dependent on horses. The Luristan culture is renowned for the fine bronze castings that it produced, very often in the form of horse harness and trappings. Many of these have been discovered in the graves of warriors who were buried not only with a set of weapons abut also with a set of horse harness. It seems that horse-bits with associated cheekpieces, the latter often very elaborate, were often placed under the head of the corpse like a pillow.

From their homeland on the River Tigris in northern Iraq, Assyrian armies campaigned widely in the Ancient Near East between about 900 BC and 612 BC. The horses that were needed for this expansion had to be obtained from abroad, as the barren uplands of Assyria were scarcely suitable for raising them. The highland areas to the north and east of Assyria – Urartu, Mannaea and Media – were particularly rich sources. The lush grasslands of the Zagros foothills and the Iranian plateau were ideal breeding grounds. Horses are often listed in the annals of the Assyrian kings among the prizes of war, but they were not only imported as military booty. For example, cuneiform tablets from both Nineveh and Nimrud known as 'horse reports' show that horses were brought to Assyria peaceably from many different parts of the Ancient Near East. Most deliveries were made in the spring, just before the campaign season. Large 'Kushite' chariot horses were even brought from distant Nubia.

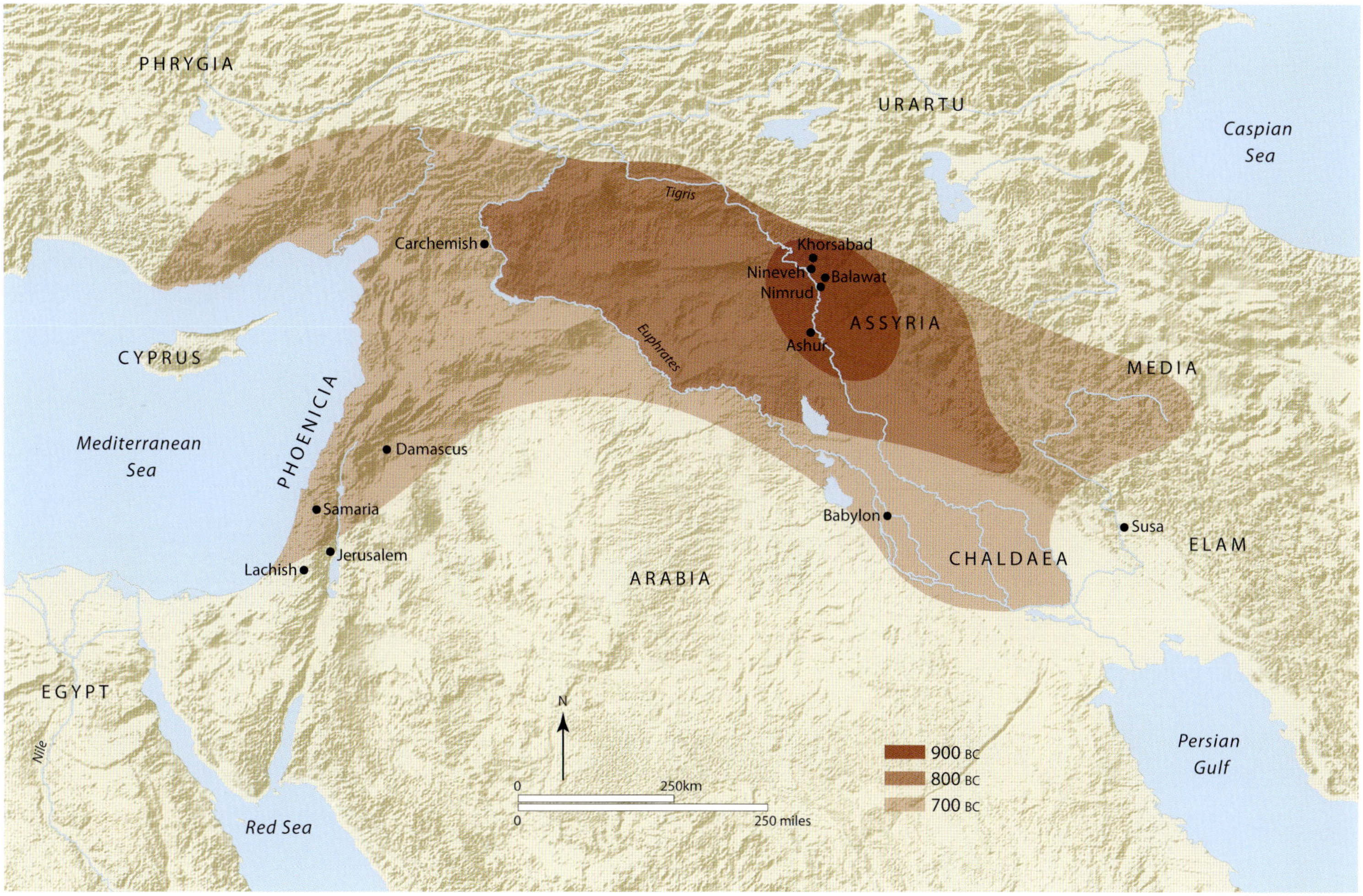

Fig. 5
The expansion of the Assyrian empire between about 900 and 700 BC.

Information about horses and horse trappings comes from contemporary cuneiform texts, the stone reliefs lining the walls of Assyrian palaces, and objects found in excavations at Assyrian sites. Horse bits were made from iron or bronze, and blinkers and nose guards were made of bronze or ivory. Leather bridles and harness straps were decorated with ornaments in bronze, ivory, shell and stone. Some of the elaborate carved ivory harness elements, particularly blinkers and frontlets, were imported from Syria and Phoenicia.

From this evidence a broad picture can be built about the role of the horse in ancient Assyria. Horses were mainly used for pulling chariots in warfare and for hunting dangerous or fast game, particularly lions and bulls. Chariot design and equipment, almost unchanged for nearly 1000 years, evolved rapidly between 900 and 700 BC. During this time chariots became bigger, with the number of horses in the team increased from two to three and finally four, and the number of men they could accommodate increased from two to four. With improved riding skills horse riding itself gradually became more commonplace. Mounted troops were mentioned in texts as early as the reign of Tukulti-Ninurta II (890–884 BC) and they are shown on reliefs in the reign of his son Ashurnasirpal II (883–859 BC) and on decorative gate fittings from his palaces at Nimrud and Balawat.

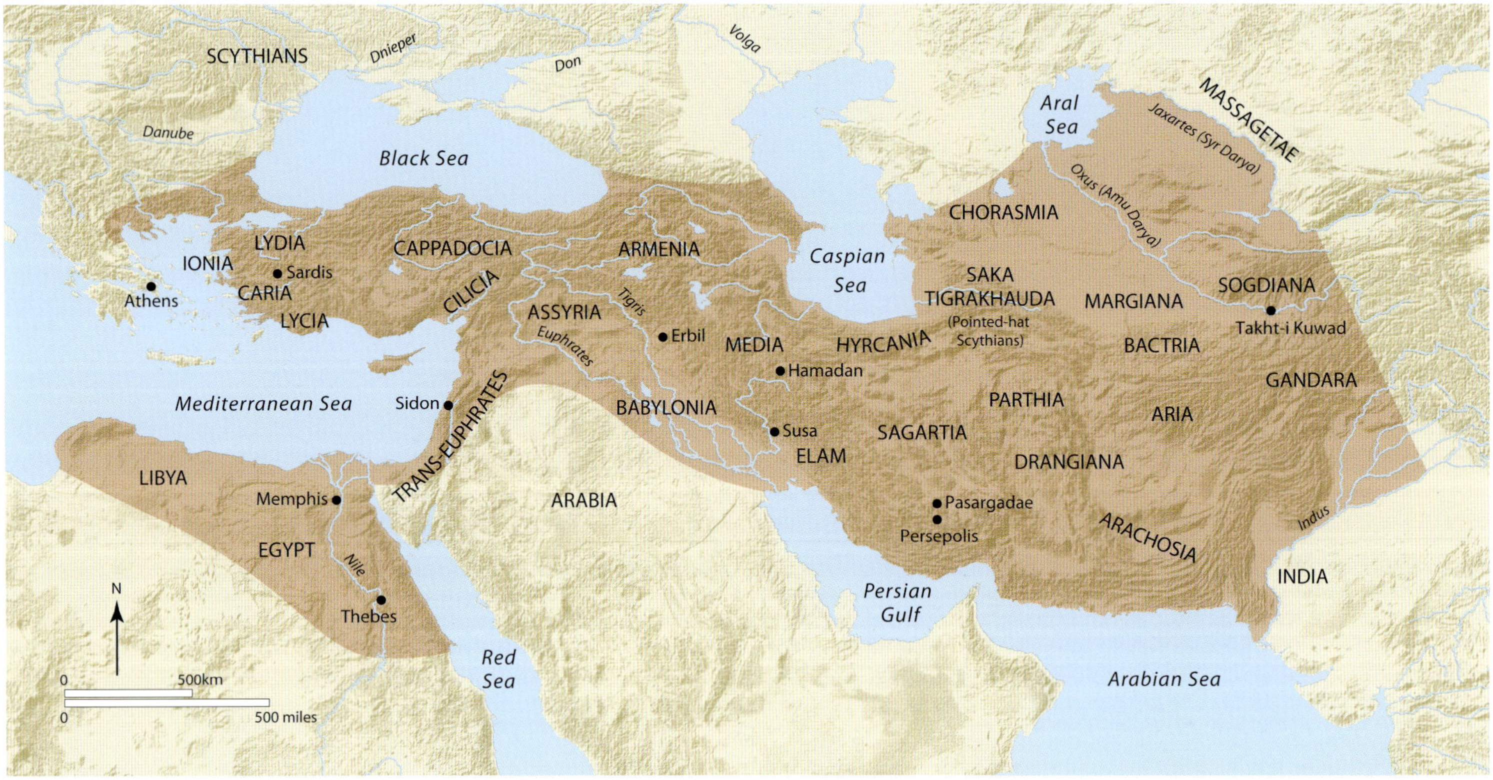

Fig. 6
The Persian empire in the time of Darius (522–486 BC) showing the principal provinces.

During this period the cavalry rode in pairs, with one soldier controlling both horses, leaving the other free to use his bow, acting as a chariot crew but without a chariot. Later, soldiers were able to control their own mounts while fighting with bows and spears at the same time. In the detailed report of the eighth campaign of Sargon II (721–705 BC) it is stated that a cavalry unit, one thousand strong, was always stationed by the side of the king. Increasingly large numbers of cavalry are recorded in Assyrian inscriptions, and by around 650 BC we see for the first time cavalry horses with full armour. Previously only chariot horses had been armoured. Even kings now rode on horses, so that by the time of Ashurbanipal (668–631 BC) the king is celebrated as a master of horsemanship in his hunting reliefs.

The horses seem to have increased in size during the Assyrian period, or at least they are shown as larger, more robust animals, probably because stronger animals were needed as chariot crews increased and cavalry became more heavily armed. There is no appreciable difference between cavalry and draft horses, except in details of harness.

The contemporary kingdom of Urartu, occupying the mountainous areas to the north of Assyria, was also famous for its use of horses, and many splendid bronze horse trappings are associated with this civilization.

Between 539 BC and 331 BC the whole of the Ancient Near East was brought under the control of a Persian dynasty known as the Achaemenids. Horses were an important part of their culture. The Greek historian Herodotus (*c.* 484–425 BC) wrote in his *Histories* that 'the Persians teach their sons, between the ages of five and twenty, only three things: to ride a horse, use a bow and speak the truth.' Darius, one of the greatest of the Achaemenid kings (522–486 BC), recorded in a monumental inscription in the Old Persian language, 'Trained am I both with hands and with feet. As a horseman I am a good horseman. As a bowman I am a good bowman both afoot and on horseback. As a spearman I am a good spearman both afoot and on horseback'.[1] The Persian empire stretched from North Africa to the Indus Valley and from the Caucasus to the Persian Gulf, and to administer this vast area good transport communications were essential. The so-called Royal Road extended from Sardis in Eastern Turkey to Susa in south-west Iran and depended on a system of post horses. Horses were also widely used in the wars with Greece (490–479 BC). The main breed of horse used both for riding and pulling chariots were the 'Great Nisaean' horses said by classical authors to have been bred on the plains of Media in Iran. In addition to these, however, the stone reliefs at the Persian capital of Persepolis show horses being presented to the Persian king by subject peoples from around the empire. The north and east sides of the Apadana Palace which are mirror images of each other show twenty-three delegations bringing presents to the great king. Horses (in all cases stallions) are being brought by six delegations, namely the Armenians, the Cappadocians, the 'pointed-hat' Scythians, the Sagartians, the hauma-venerating Scythians and the European Scythians. It is interesting that all the members of these delegations wear trouser-suits, partly reflecting the Iranian origins of some, but also underlining the clear association of the wearing of trousers with the riding of horses. In

Fig. 7
Detail from a plaster cast made of the Apadana reliefs at Persepolis by the Weld-Blundell expedition in 1892 showing part of a delegation from Cappadocia (central Turkey) bringing a stallion and Median robes as presents for the king of Persia, 5th century BC. This powerful and stocky horse has its forelock tied into a splayed tuft, with long strands of mane arranged on the shoulder and the tail tied in a mud knot – all typical Achaemenid Persian features, as are the details of harness. In some cases these casts now preserve more detail than the originals.
BM C.228.3

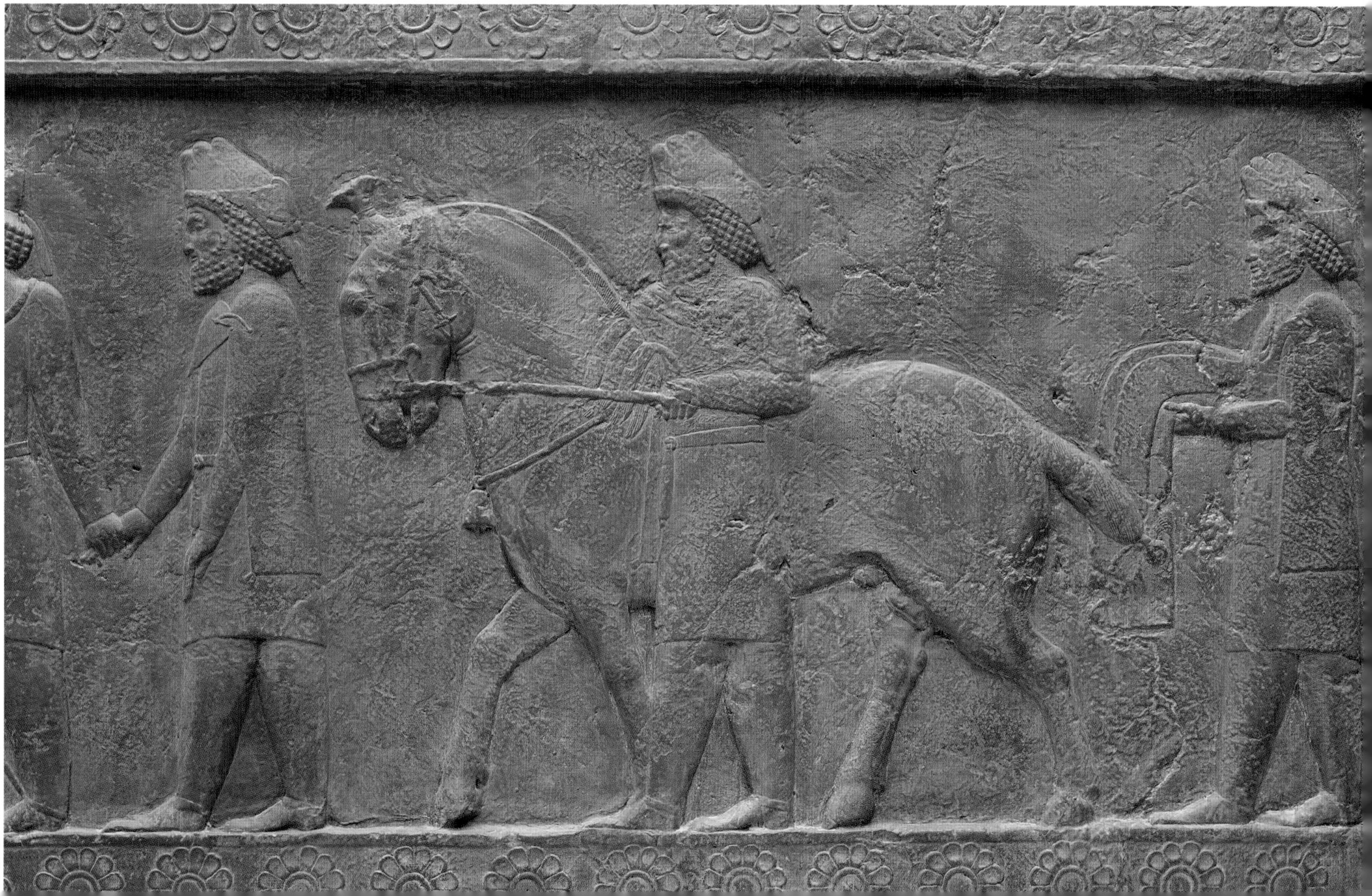

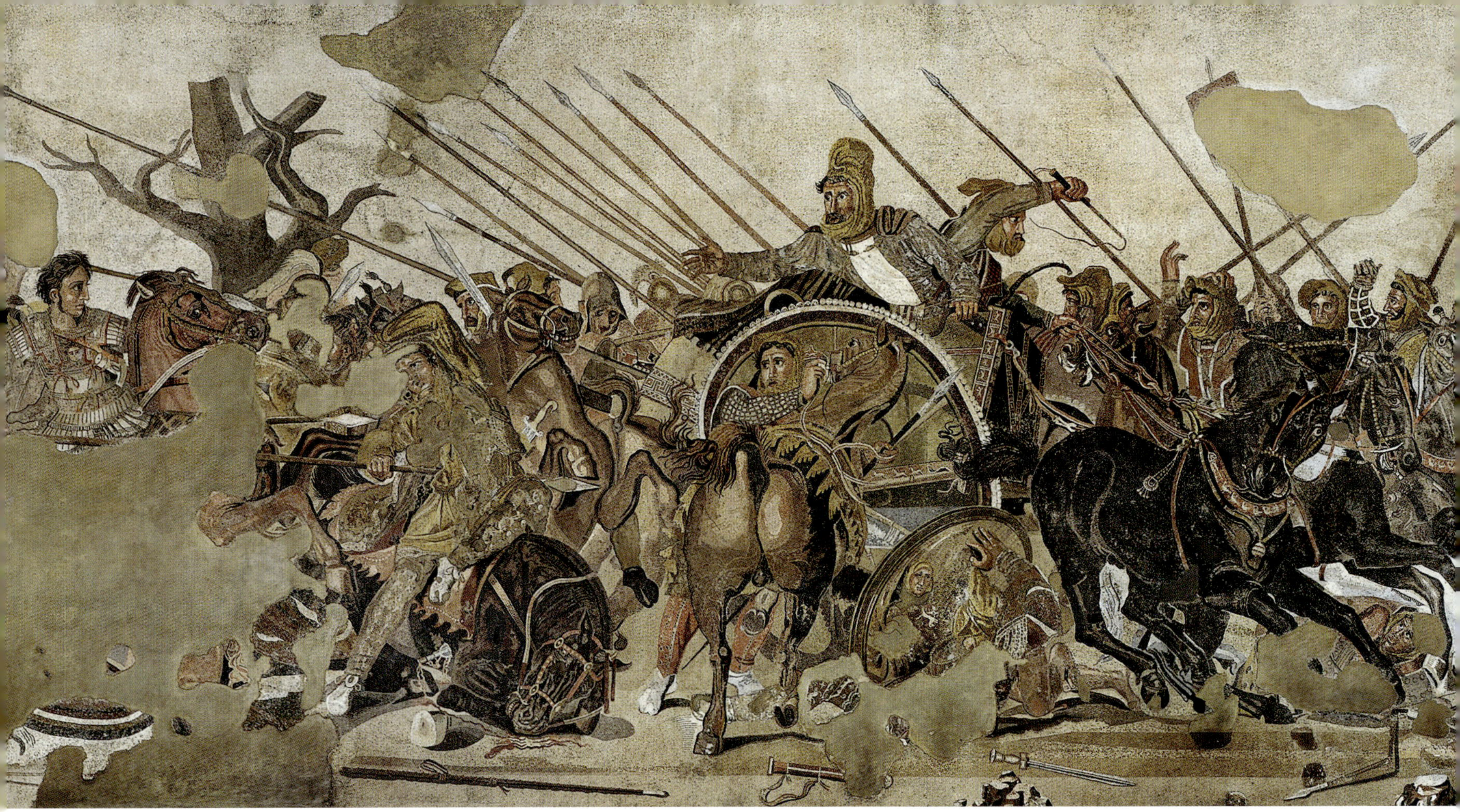

Fig. 8
The Alexander Mosaic was found in the House of the Faun in Pompeii, Italy, and dates from the 1st century BC. It is thought to be copy of a fourth-century BC painting, and probably shows the Battle of Issus in 333 BC. Alexander is shown on horseback on the far left, while Darius III is riding in a two-wheeled chariot in the centre. The chariot is pulled by four black horses and the chariot driver holds the reins in one hand and a whip in the other. The artist, perhaps not knowing Persian harness, has shown Greek bits and harness fittings.
National Archaeological Museum, Naples

addition to the individual horses, horse-drawn chariots are being brought by the Lydians and the Libyans. The Indian delegation brings a donkey. The fact that two delegations bring chariots shows that they were by no means obsolete by this time, but continued as high-status civil vehicles, and this is confirmed by the archaeological record.

The Persepolis reliefs show two-wheeled royal chariots that are especially for the use of the king, and these chariots are of similar design to the model gold chariot in the Oxus Treasure (see cat. 98). The horses pulling the Oxus Treasure chariot are surprisingly small, which has led to suggestions that they might be Caspian horses. This is a breed that was thought to have died out until it was rediscovered in northern Iran in the 1960s by a horse breeder called Louise Firouz. The Caspian is characterized by its small size (11.2 hands at the withers), high work-rate, jumping ability and intelligence. It is certain that in antiquity and in the following Islamic period there were a number of different breeds of horse, and some or all of them may be related to what subsequently came to be called the Arabian.

As well as for ceremonial purposes chariots were also used on occasion in battle, in specialized form in limited numbers as a terror weapon with blades and scythes, and as command vehicles. Thus, the last Persian king, Darius III (336–331 BC), is shown in a chariot in the so-called Alexander Mosaic from a house in Pompeii, which depicts a battle between Alexander's forces and those of the Persians, probably at Issus in 333 BC. Darius is shown in a chariot, while Alexander is shown on his horse Bucephalus.

From around 250 BC onwards the Ancient Near East was invaded by a tribe of Iranian nomads known as the Parthians. They were skilled horsemen and wore trousers, often with the addition of leggings, to facilitate their life in the saddle. The Roman historian Justin, summarizing an earlier work by Pompeius Trogus, wrote that the Parthians 'ride on horseback on all occasions; on horses they go to war, and to feasts; on horses they discharge public and private duties; on horses they go abroad, meet together, traffic, and converse.'[2] The rise to power of the Parthians, and the consolidation of their hold over Iran and Mesopotamia, brought them into conflict with Rome, which was expanding eastwards. They proved to be a powerful adversary for Rome. In his *Roman History* the Latin historian Cassius Dio recorded: 'They are really formidable in warfare (and) even to this day they hold their own in the wars they wage against us ... The Parthians make no use of a shield, but their forces consist of mounted archers and pikemen [lancers], mostly in full armour. Their infantry is small, made up of the weaker men; but even these are all archers. They practise from boyhood, and the climate and the land combine to aid both horsemanship and archery. The land, being for the most part level, is excellent for raising horses and very suitable for riding about on horseback; at any rate, even in war they lead about whole droves of horses, so that they can use different ones at different times, can ride up suddenly from a distance and also retire to a distance speedily; and the atmosphere there, which is very dry and does not contain the least moisture, keeps their bowstrings tense, except in the dead of winter.'[3] In *Antony and Cleopatra*, Shakespeare refers to 'the ne'er-yet-beaten horse of Parthia'.

The main encounter with Rome occurred in 53 BC at the Battle of Carrhae (modern Harran in Turkey) when a force led by Crassus was roundly defeated. On this occasion the light Parthian archers, shooting from horseback, supporting the completely armoured lancers, carried all before them. We know from classical authors that their victory was

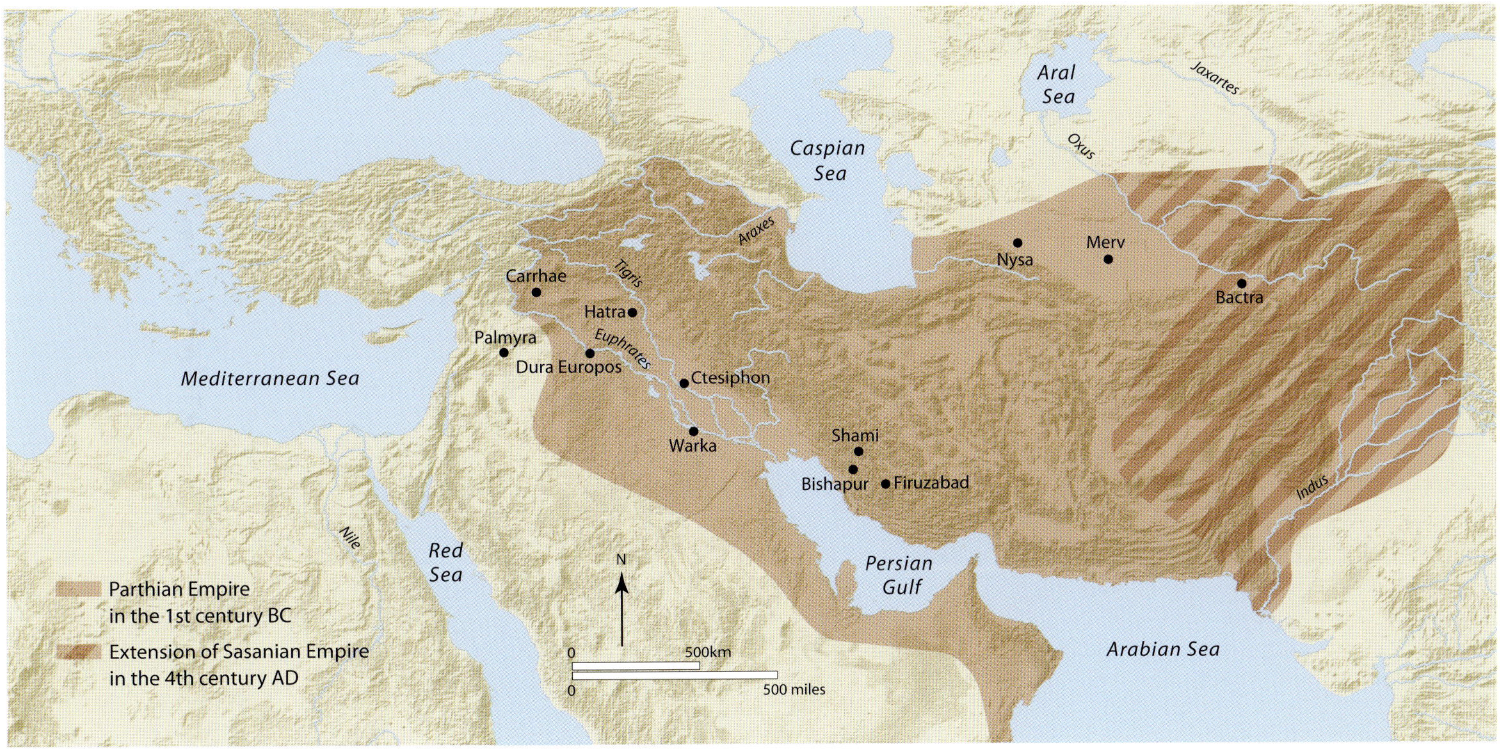

Fig. 9
The Parthian and Sasanian empires.

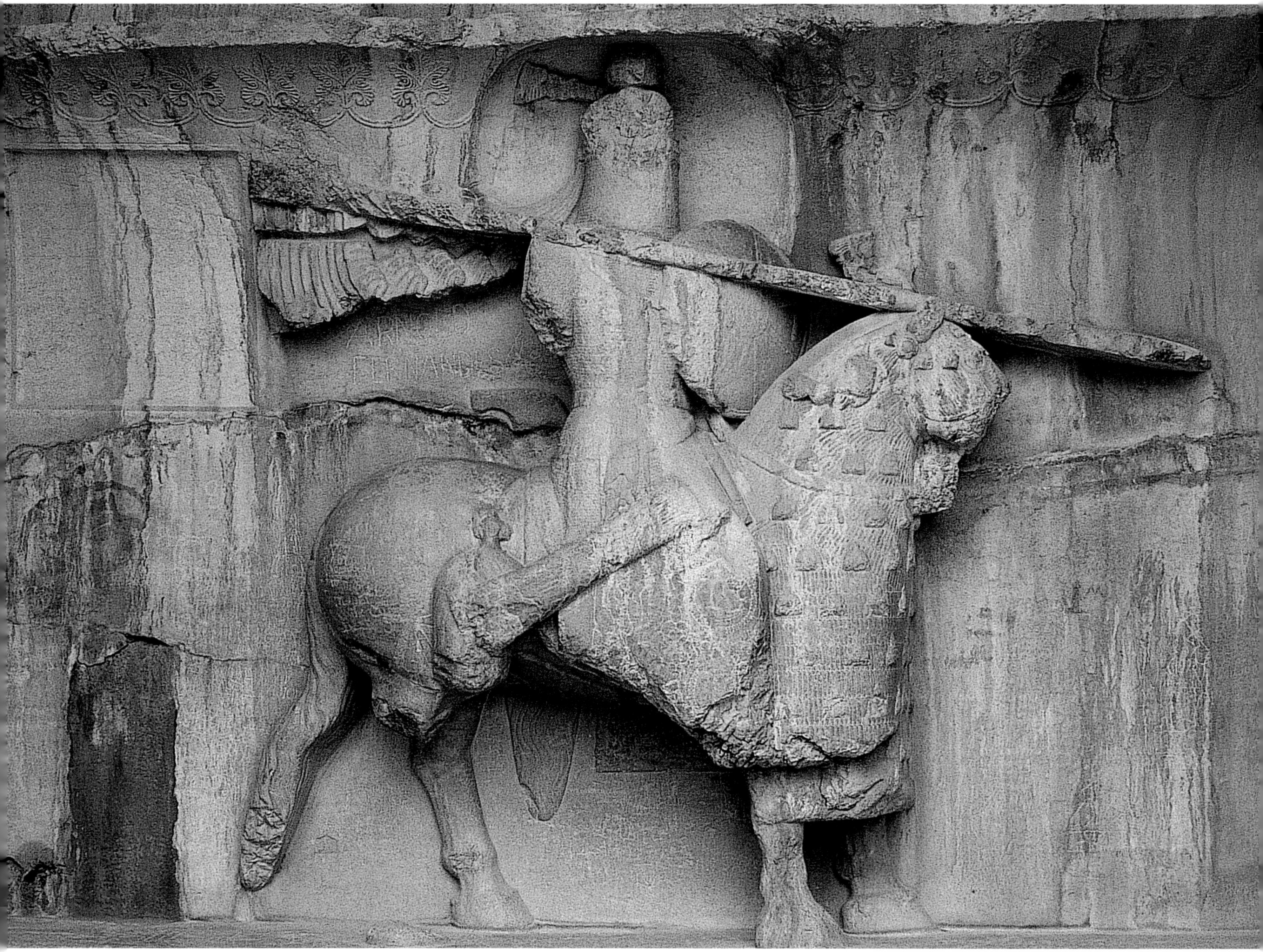

Fig. 10
Rock carving on the back wall of a grotto at Taq-i Bustan, Iran, showing the Sasanian king Khusrow II (Parviz) (AD 591–628) on horseback. Both king and horse are heavily armoured. The side walls of the grotto show a boar hunt and a deer hunt respectively.

partly due to their tactic of shooting backwards from horseback, much feared by the Romans and known as 'the Parthian shot'. This method of fighting is described by both Plutarch and Justin. In his *Life of Crassus*, Plutarch tells us that 'the Parthians threw their darts as they fled, an art in which none but the Scythians exceed them, and it is, indeed, a cunning practice, for while they thus fight to make their escape, they avoid the dishonour of a flight'.[4] According to Justin, 'They fight on horseback, either galloping forward or turning their backs. Often, too, they counterfeit flight, that they may throw their pursuers off their guard against being wounded by their arrows ... In general they retire before the enemy in the very heat of the engagement, and, soon after their retreat, return to the battle afresh; so that, when you feel most certain that you have conquered them, you have still to meet the greatest danger from them. Their armour, and that of their horses, is formed of plates, lapping over one another like the feathers of a bird, and covers both man and horse entirely.'[5]

Some authorities have seen a connection between the Parthian horses and the Arabian horse, but this remains unproven. From the first century AD onwards, by which time the Parthians had become prosperous, there are a number of rock reliefs showing scenes of jousting, a tradition that continued in later periods. In AD 224 the Parthians were replaced by another Iranian dynasty known as the Sasanians, who ruled until the Islamic conquest. In Zoroastrianism, which became the state religion in the Sasanian period, the horse is classed as 'ass-hoofed' (xarpay), one of the beneficent grazing animals. It is also associated with the sun – Mithra – and a chariot pulled by horses. The horse is also one of the three forms of the god Tishtrya (the star Sirius). Sasanian kings hunted lions and other animals on horseback, often apparently in special hunting parks or 'paradise' gardens. The jousting contests known from the Parthian period now became very popular and are shown on a number of Sasanian rock reliefs as symbols of victory. The heavily armoured horses and riders are the forerunners of the European knights of the Middle Ages.

Probably the best known example of an armoured Sasanian warrior on horseback is the stone carving in high relief of the king identified as Khusrow Parviz (the 'victorious') (AD 591–628) at the back of a grotto at Taq-i Bustan near Kermanshah in Iran. The king wears a coat of mail, a helmet with mail face covering, and a quiver, and he carries a shield and a long lance. His horse is also heavily protected, with a coat of armour covering his neck and chest. He sits on a saddle with raised back and sides which stopped him from falling off the horse while fighting. It is usually thought this horse was the famous Shabdiz (meaning 'the colour of night') who featured in later literary epics. In Nizami's *Khusrow and Shirin*, Shabdiz takes Shirin to Khusrow after she has fallen in love with his portrait, and in the Iranian Book of Kings (*Shahnameh*) the minstrel Barbad informs Khusrow of the death of Shabdiz through a song, thereby risking his own life.

Khusrow II is shown without stirrups, as are other Sasanian kings on their rock reliefs, which lends support to the view that rigid stirrups were not introduced into the Ancient Near East until the Islamic period (see below). However, before this time soft stirrups and hook stirrups seem to have been widely known. They were probably intended to be mounting aids for poor riders or the infirm.

CHAPTER 2

THE HORSE IN THE ISLAMIC WORLD

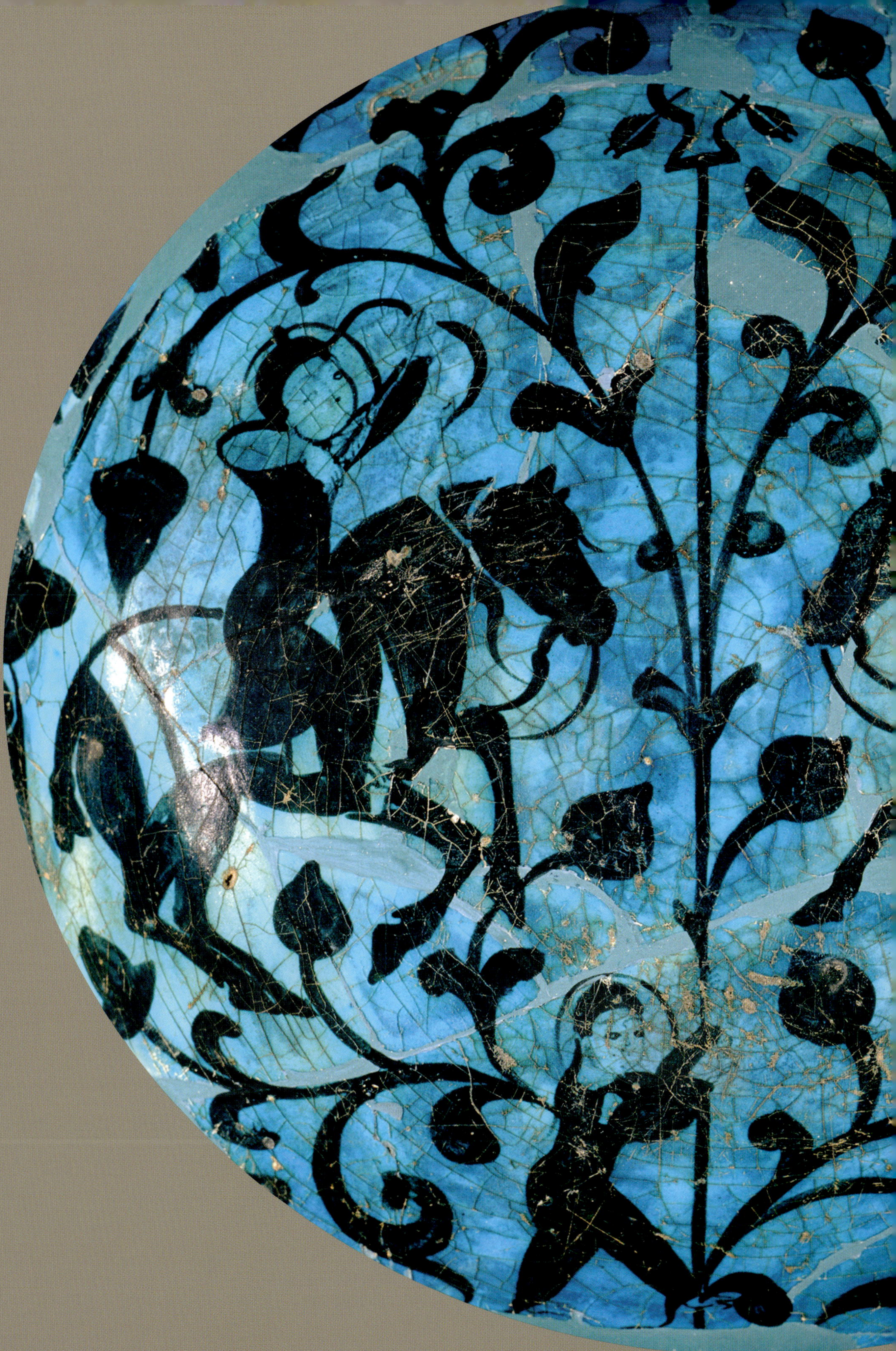

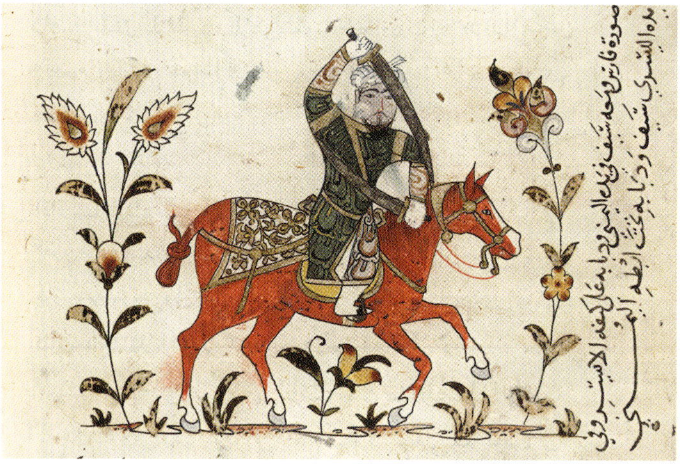

The horse in the Islamic world

ABOVE
Fig. 11
Illustration from the *Furusiyya* manuscript dating from 773 AH/AD 1371 (cat. 134) showing a rider on a red horse brandishing two swords and captioned 'Illustration of a horseman with a sword in his right hand, its blade on his left shoulder and a sword in his left hand whose blade is under his right armpit.' British Library

Fig. 12
Mughal miniature painting from *c*. AD 1790 showing the lovers Baz Bahadur (the last Sultan of Malwa) and Rupmati riding horses by moonlight. Both horses, one dapple-grey and one chestnut, have their lower legs decorated with henna. BM 1913,0617.0.3

THE ISLAMIC conquests in the seventh century AD ushered in religious, political, and social change, a gradual process that was to last several centuries. However, a degree of religious and cultural cohesion was given to a much wider area than before, extending eventually to Spain and into Central Asia, and the seventh century therefore serves as a convenient period in which to introduce a break in our story.

Although in the early stages of the Islamic conquest horses may not have been very plentiful, their worth and value were certainly recognized and they were much prized, indeed by Muhammad himself. This is clear from the references to horses in the Quran where they are referred to as gifts of Allah, and splendid horses are listed among the comforts of life on earth. Thus we read 'He [Allah] has given you horses, mules, and donkeys, which you may ride or use as ornaments; and he has created other things beyond your knowledge' (16.8), and 'splendid horses' are among the comforts of this life (3:14). Horses were also important in spreading the word of the Prophet: 'Let the unbelievers not think that they will escape us. They have not the power to do so. Muster against them all the men and cavalry at your disposal, so that you may strike terror into the enemies of Allah and the faithful, and others beside them' (8:60). They were also

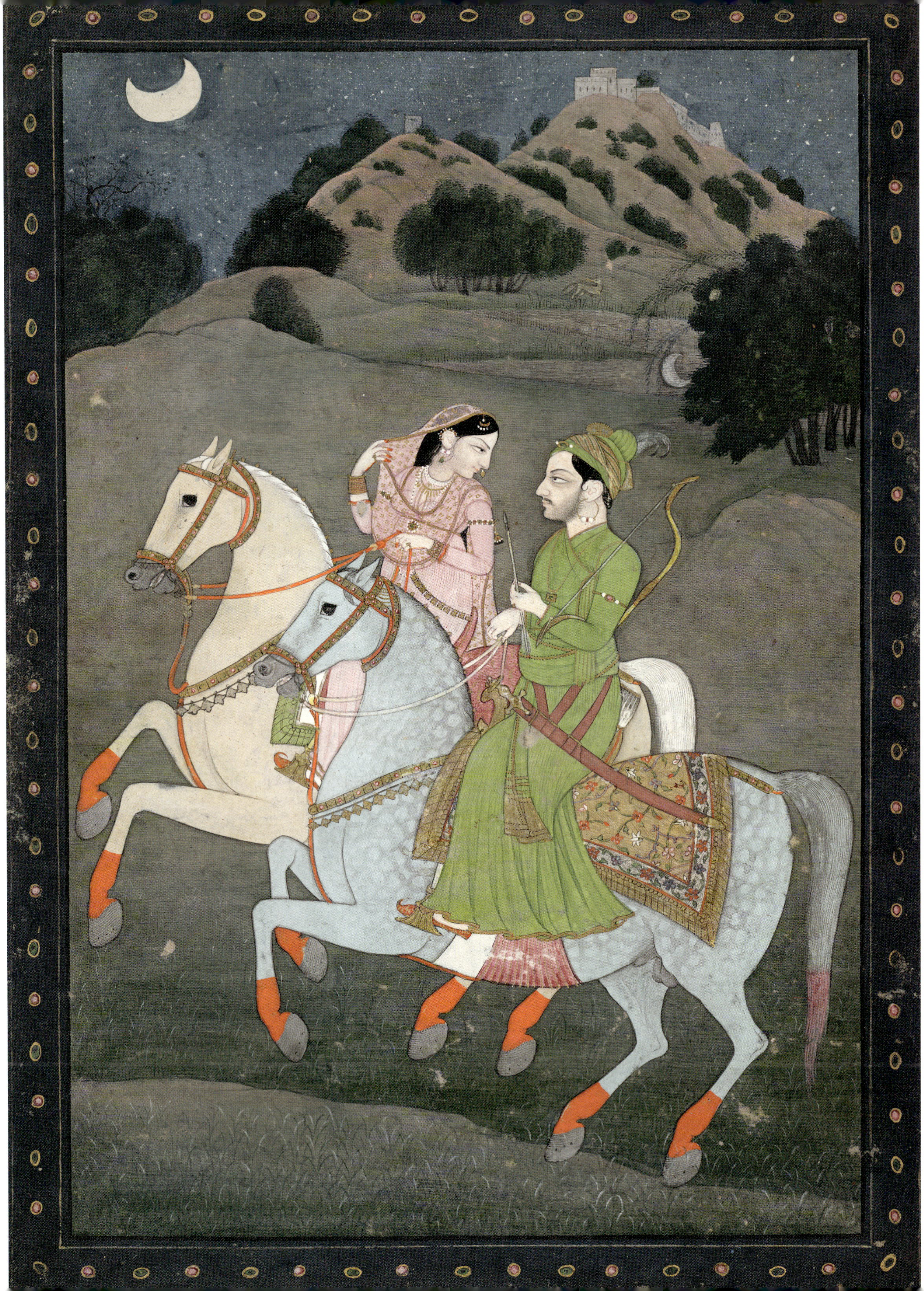

apparently crucial in the intertribal warfare that was prevalent in Arabia before and during the lifetime of Muhammad. Reference is made to 'the snorting war steeds, which strike fire with their hoofs as they gallop to the raid at dawn and with a trail of dust split the foe in two' (100:1–6). Horses had also been important in the time of King Solomon: 'He [Solomon] was a good and faithful servant. When, one evening, his prancing steeds were ranged before him, he said: "My love for the good things of life has caused me to forget my prayers; for now the sun has vanished behind the veil of darkness. Bring me back my chargers!" [after the evening prayers are completed]. And with this he fell to hacking [stroking] their legs and necks' (38:27). There are further indications of the importance of horses in the Hadith, the sayings and beliefs that were attributed to Muhammad and were gathered during the eighth and ninth centuries AD. Thus we are told that horses are kept for three reasons. They may be a source of reward for one man, a 'shelter' (that is, a means of earning money) for another, and a burden (a source of sins against Islam) for a third. The man for whom the horse is a source of reward keeps it for Allah's cause (*Jihad*), and when he tethers the horse in a meadow he will get a reward equal to what it is able to eat and drink.[1] As a special tribute to horses trained for Jihad, Muhammad also said while arranging the forelock of a horse that their forelocks would be blessed until the Day of Judgment.[2] Those who used horses for Jihad were entitled to a larger share of war booty.[3] Last, but by no means least, it was incumbent on everybody, including the Prophet himself, to take good care of horses.[4]

Then also in Islamic tradition there is Buraq (Arabic 'lightning'), the white horse-like creature that transported Muhammad to heaven. It had wings, and was half-mule and half-donkey. It carried Muhammad on his night journey from Mecca to Jerusalem and

Fig. 13
Map of the Islamic world in the tenth century AD.

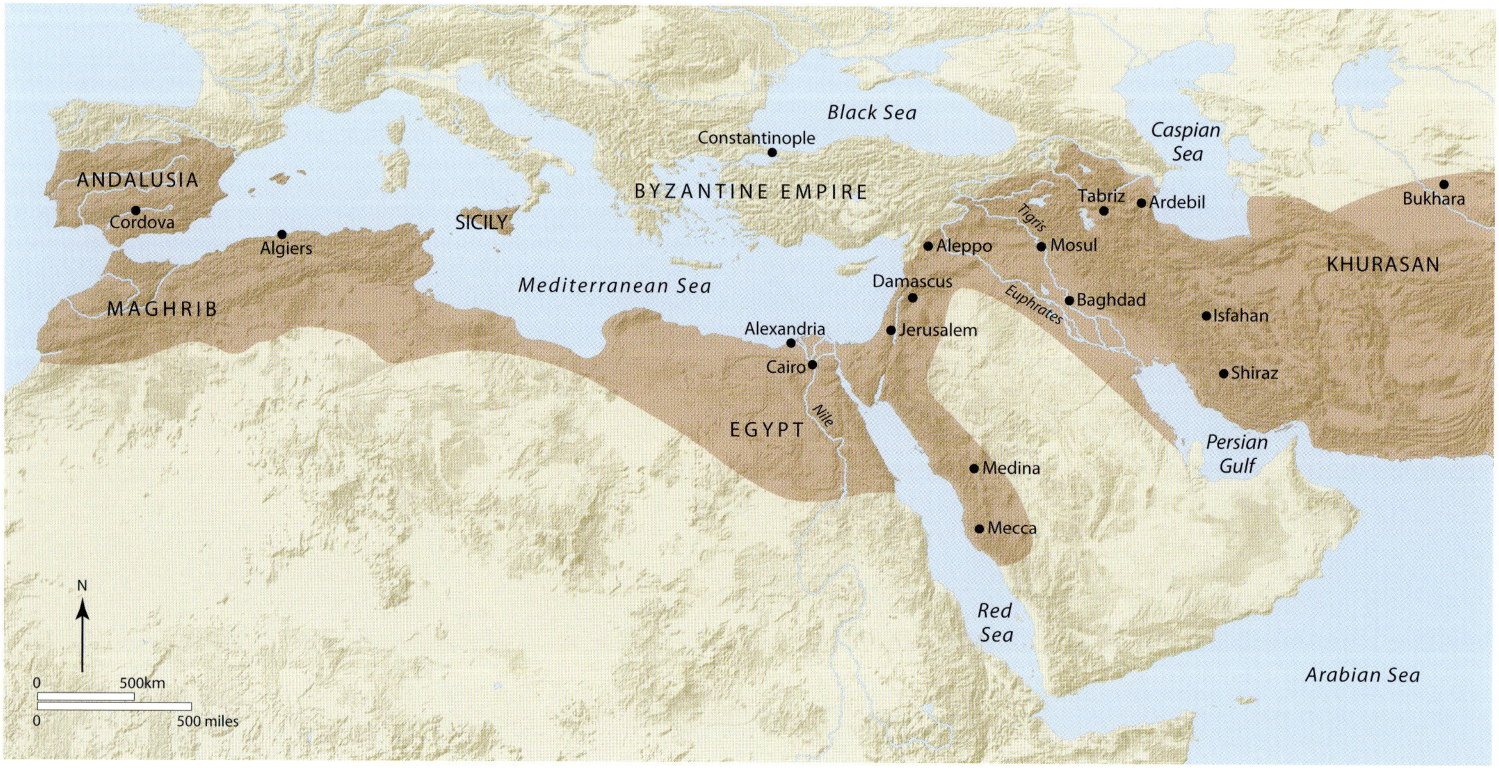

back. In later Persian and Mughal traditions, Buraq was usually portrayed as a horse with a woman's head. In the Shia tradition, Imam Husayn is often depicted on a white horse.

A well-known Arabic legend records that the horse was created by God out of the south wind. The story as recorded in a fourteenth-century manuscript has been translated by Cynthia Culbertson:[5]

> When God wished to create the horse, he said to the South Wind, 'I shall create from thee a new being, and I will make him good fortune for my followers, humiliation to my enemies, and protection for the obedient.' And the wind said, 'Create!' God condensed the wind and made from it a horse. Then he said to his creation, 'I name thee horse and I make thee Arabian. I have bound blessings to thy forelock, and bounty reposes upon thy back, and glory will be with thee, wherever thee may be. I have privileged thee over the rest of the beasts, and I make thee master over them. Thy companions will feel compassion for thee. I make thee to fly without wings'.

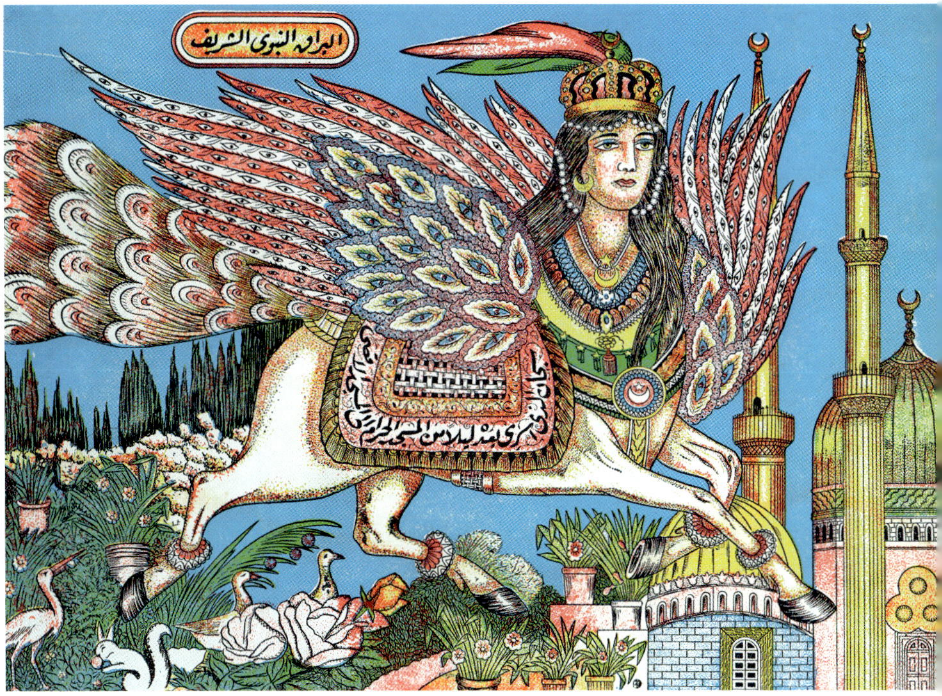

Fig. 14
Modern poster showing the winged human-headed horse Buraq on which the Prophet Muhammad travelled to Jerusalem, represented on the right of the picture. The figure of the Prophet himself is not shown.
Private collection

Belonging to the same tradition as this legend is the Arabic proverb which tells us that 'the air of heaven is that which blows between a horse's ears'. Horses also feature in early Arabic poetry and in epic literature such as the Persian *Book of Kings* (*Shahnameh*). The Arab poet al-Mutanabbi (*c.* 915–965) wrote many memorable lines about horses, including the following:

> Fine steeds, like true friends are few,
> Even if in the eye of the inexperienced they are many.
> If you have seen nothing but the beauty of their markings and limbs,
> Their true beauty is hidden from you.
> (Transl. by Cynthia Culbertson)[6]

There are many famous mythological horses in the Islamic world. We have already spoken of Shabdiz, the horse of Kay Khusrow, and then there is Rakhsh, the legendary horse of the hero Rustam in the Iranian *Shahnameh*. This remarkable horse has 'black eyes, a long tail and hooves like steel. Its light-coloured body has red spots shining like the sun in the sky. Its height equals that of a camel and its strength is like that of an Indian elephant.'[7] Together, Rustam and Rakhsh share many adventures, and among other things Rakhsh saves Rustam from a lion and a dragon. In the *One Thousand and One Nights* there is the story of 'the magic horse' in Edward Lane's translation and 'the ebony horse' in Richard Burton's translation. This enchanted beast, made of ebony and ivory, could soar into the sky, and mounted on it the son of Shapur king of Persia flew to Sanaa in the

Yemen and carried off the king's daughter as his bride. The Egyptian writer Kamal al-Damiri recorded in his *Life of Animals* (*c.* 1371) that there was in Paradise a winged ruby-coloured horse that would fly people wherever they wanted to go.

In the early years of the Islamic conquest, and certainly during the lifetime of the Prophet, there do not seem to have been many horses available to the Muslim forces. The situation changed, however, with the conquests of Syria, Mesopotamia and Iran. As well as large numbers of horses now becoming available, Sasanian heavily armed cavalry also joined the Muslim ranks. In spite of this Sasanian influence, however, early Muslim cavalry were usually lightly armed with a spear or a sword and sometimes also a bow, but they dismounted to shoot the bows. However, heavily armed cavalry in the Sasanian tradition had become an important element in the Islamic army by the end of the Umayyad period in the middle of the eighth century AD. Rigid stirrups, which were absent in the Sasanian period, had also by now become commonplace. The earliest rigid stirrups known are from north-east China in the early fourth century AD, while the earliest rigid stirrups known in Europe are from the late sixth or seventh century AD Avar graves in Hungary. They seem to have reached the Middle East in the early Islamic period. There were also an increasing number of Arabian horses in circulation, as we know from manuscripts dating from the ninth century onwards.

From the eleventh century there was a rapid development in horse-riding skills and military tactics driven by the need to compete with and outclass the invading crusader armies. So successful were these developments that the renowned Salah ad-Din, the founder of the Ayyubid caliphate, was able to recapture Jerusalem from the crusaders in AD 1187. It was during the time of the crusades that western Europeans first came into contact on a large scale with Arabian horses, and they were much admired. Arabian horses also featured in the armies of the Mamluk dynasty which controlled Egypt, Syria and Palestine between 1250 and 1517. It was a Mamluk army led by Sultan Baybars that checked the Mongol advance at Ain Jalut in Palestine in 1260, and as we shall see, Mamluk military prowess was in large part due to their organization and careful preparations. However, it is sometimes suggested that another factor in the Mamluk victory was their use of Arabian horses while the Mongols were dependent on their small steppe ponies that tired quickly in a pitched battle. As the Mamluks were able to match the Mongols in prowess at archery, it may indeed have been their horses that made the difference.

From 1517 right up until the First World War much of the Middle East excluding Iran was under the control of the Ottoman dynasty ruling from Istanbul (former Constantinople). During this Ottoman period, troops on horseback were an important part of the army, and were highly respected by contemporaries. According to Ogier Ghiselin de Busbecq, who was Ambassador of the Holy Roman Emperor at Constantinople from 1554 to 1562, 'The Turkish horseman presents a very elegant spectacle, mounted on a horse of Cappadocian or Syrian or some other good breed, with trappings and horse-cloths of silver spangled with gold and precious stones. He is resplendent in raiment of cloth of gold or silver, or else of silk or satin, or at any rate of the finest scarlet, or violet, or dark green cloth.'[8] He was armed with a bow which was his principal weapon, a light spear, a scimitar and a steel club. What distinguished these Turkish warriors from their predecessors and their contemporaries was their use of fast, wiry, hardy horses and their considerable riding skills which enabled them to use bows to maximum effect while on horseback. Surprisingly, Arabian horses did not feature largely in the Ottoman army. According to the Italian soldier and naturalist Luigi Ferdinando Marsigli, who wrote a book about the Ottoman war machine in 1732, Arabian horses were not popular because they could not stand gunfire (in fact, firearms were adopted at a relatively late date by the Turks) and were difficult to handle on the battlefield. Instead, Ottoman troops preferred above all horses bred on the Çukarova Plain on the southern slopes of the Taurus Mountains in south-east Turkey. This is in contrast to the Persians, who under Nadir Shah (1736–1747) preferred Arabian horses for their cavalry.

Although Arabian horses may not have been highly esteemed by the Ottoman army, they were in great demand amongst other sections of Ottoman society. In the nineteenth century, for example, they are found throughout the Ottoman empire, and were often admired and commented upon by European travellers. One such traveller was William Heude, who journeyed from India to England in 1817, and whom we shall encounter again in the next chapter. He wrote that the Arabian horse 'is trained very early to submission, to abstinence, and fatigue ... In a march of thirty hours which we made across the small desert between Mosul and Nissibin, though we rode almost continually during that time, our horses had no sustenance whatever, besides a few handfuls of an inferior kind of barley, and the dry stubble they could snatch up in their unremitting course ... It is in this facility of subsistence, and in their hardiness, no less than in their beauty and docility, that the pure Arabian of the desert may be distinguished from every other race.'[9] He went on to say that the traveller and diplomat John Macdonald Kinneir (1782–1830) once rode a young Arabian horse for ninety miles without stopping.

Another admirer of Arabian horses was Austen Henry Layard, the excavator of the Assyrian sites of Nimrud and Nineveh, who in the course of recounting an expedition to the River Khabur in north-east Syria in 1850, describes the Arabian horses he encountered there:[10]

> The Arab horse is more remarkable for its exquisite symmetry and beautiful proportions, united with wonderful powers of endurance, than for extraordinary speed. I doubt whether any Arab of the best blood has ever been brought to England. The difficulty of obtaining them is so great, that they are scarcely ever seen beyond the limits of the Desert. Their colour is generally white, light or dark grey, light chestnut, and bay, with white or black feet. Black is exceedingly rare, and I never remember to have seen dun, sorrel, or dapple. I refer, of course, to the true-bred Arab, and not to the Turcoman or to Kurdish and Turkish races, which are a cross between the Arab and Persian ... Although docile as a lamb, and requiring no other guide than the halter, when the Arab mare hears the war-cry of the tribe, and sees the quivering spear of her rider, her eyes glitter with fire, her blood-red nostrils open wide, her neck is nobly arched, and her tail and mane are raised and spread out to the wind.

Such horses were also to be found near Mosul, as noted by Humphry Sandwith, an English doctor who visited Layard in 1850. In his memoirs he describes an encounter with a tribal

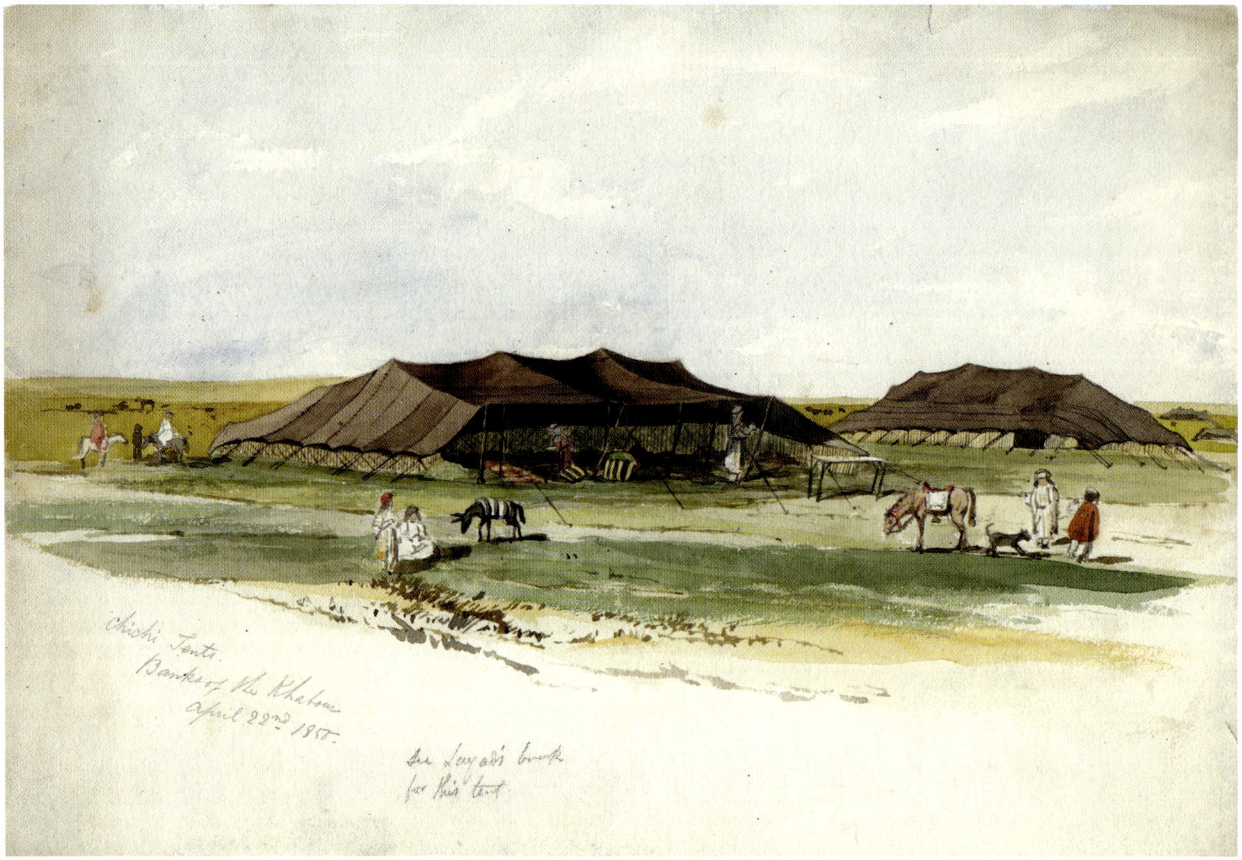

Fig. 15
Watercolour by Frederick Charles Cooper dated 22 April 1850, showing a Bedouin encampment on the banks of the River Khabur in north-east Syria. Both horses and donkeys are visible here. Cooper accompanied Austen Henry Layard on his second archaeological expedition to Assyria (now in northern Iraq) in 1849–50, and between 21 March and 5 May 1850 the members of the expedition journeyed to the River Khabur in search of archaeological sites.
BM 2010,6001.7

leader near Khorsabad: 'He was superbly mounted on a dark chestnut, which he managed to perfection. His horse had all the beauties of the Arab – a small, intelligent head, a bright eye, a soft, silky mane and tail, and the general symmetry which is obvious to the most untutored eye.'[11]

In the Islamic world there was great interest in the different breeds and different types of horses, as evidenced by the large number of words in the Arabic language for horses with different characteristics and at different stages of development. Layard describes how the Bedouin of northern Mesopotamia knew the lineage of every horse in their possession, assigning each to one of the five races of horse descended from the five favourite mares of the Prophet. In addition to the interest in the breeding of horses in the Islamic world, great importance was also attached to the care and training of horses. There are a number of veterinary treatises describing in great detail the physiognomy and anatomy of horses, and recommending treatments for sick animals. Probably the earliest preserved Arabic text on this subject is the *Kitab al-furusiyya wal-baytara*, by Ibn Akhi Hizam, dating from the second half of the ninth century AD and now in the Topkapi Museum in Istanbul. By his own admission, the author draws on Arabic, Persian and Indian sources. The first half of the book is a collection of information about horses, including advice on how to train them and ride them, and the second half is about medical treatments. Some of these treatments were advanced for their time, showing how far Islamic medicine in general was ahead of its European counterpart, but other veterinary treatments of the time seem bizarre by modern standards. For example, a treatise on hippology (the study of horses) in the Bibliothèque Nationale in Paris, dating from the mid-fifteenth century but copied from an earlier text, describes what to do if a horse has been bitten by a rabid dog. 'Every animal bitten by a rabid dog will develop rabies and show the following symptoms: the head drooping, the glance dim, the throat clogged, the eyes red; it has its tail between its legs and an erratic walk, and it bites everything it meets. The treatment consists of giving it, at the onset of the illness, black hellebore (a plant), then boiling some squirting cucumber in wine, sprinkling it with tamarisk, and administering this to the animal several times. If it pleases God, it will cure.'[12]

There are also texts exclusively about *furusiyya* (horsemanship), dealing with the care of horses, training and military tactics and strategy. From the eleventh century onwards there was an increasing amount of this Arabic military literature, probably inspired by the need to compete with the invading crusader armies who were better equipped and better trained. The manuals are based in part on earlier traditions going back as far as the pre-Islamic Sasanian period. Such treatises were certainly used by the Ayyubids, who ruled Egypt and Syria in the twelfth and thirteenth centuries, but they mostly date from the time of the Mamluk dynasty, which controlled Egypt, Syria and Palestine between 1250 and 1517. As we have seen, a Mamluk army was victorious over the Mongols at Ain Jalut, and their military preparations and organization were largely informed by military literature on horsemanship, archery and military tactics. Outstanding among these works is the British Library manuscript commonly known as *Furusiyya* or Horsemanship. This manuscript is dated to AD 1371, and was probably copied in Syria or Egypt. It contains eighteen coloured paintings showing mounted warriors undertaking exercises with swords, lances and bows, sometimes singly and sometimes in groups of four. These group activities evolved into organized games that quickly became a popular spectator sport. As in Europe where medieval knights participated in jousts and tournaments, there was a close connection between sport and military training. The paintings in the *Furusiyya* manuscript are an important source of information for the harness arrangements at this date and for the type of horses being used. The horses are of various colours, and although small are powerfully built with solid bodies and quite short legs. It has been suggested they are Barbs or Barb crosses, originally from North Africa. It was presumably this type of horse – rather than, say, an Arabian – that was best suited to Mamluk military tactics.

Horse racing is attested in Islam from earliest times, and is considered an essential part of military horse-training. Although gambling is forbidden in Islam, an exception is made for horse racing where betting is permitted. In the Early Abbasid period horse racing was particularly popular, and at the Abbasid capital of Samarra, on the east bank of the River Tigris in Iraq, built by Caliph Al-Mutasim in AD 836 and abandoned by Caliph Al-Mutamid in AD 892, there are traces of no fewer than four racecourses. The most famous of these is known as the cloverleaf

Fig. 16
A page from the *Furusiyya* manuscript dating from 773 AH/AD 1371 (cat. 134) showing a rider mounted on a black horse spearing a boar with a special type of short lance.
British Library

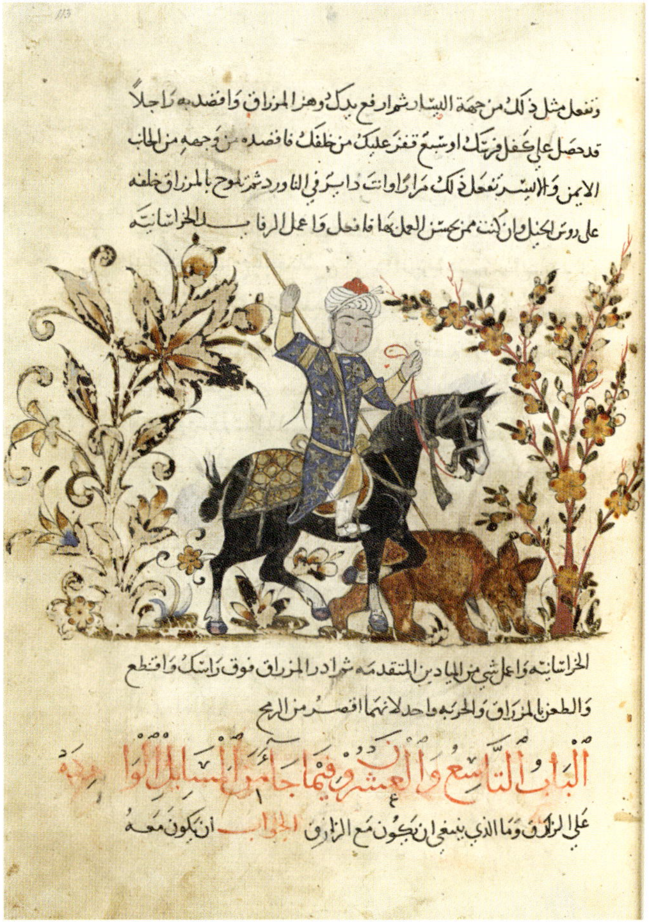

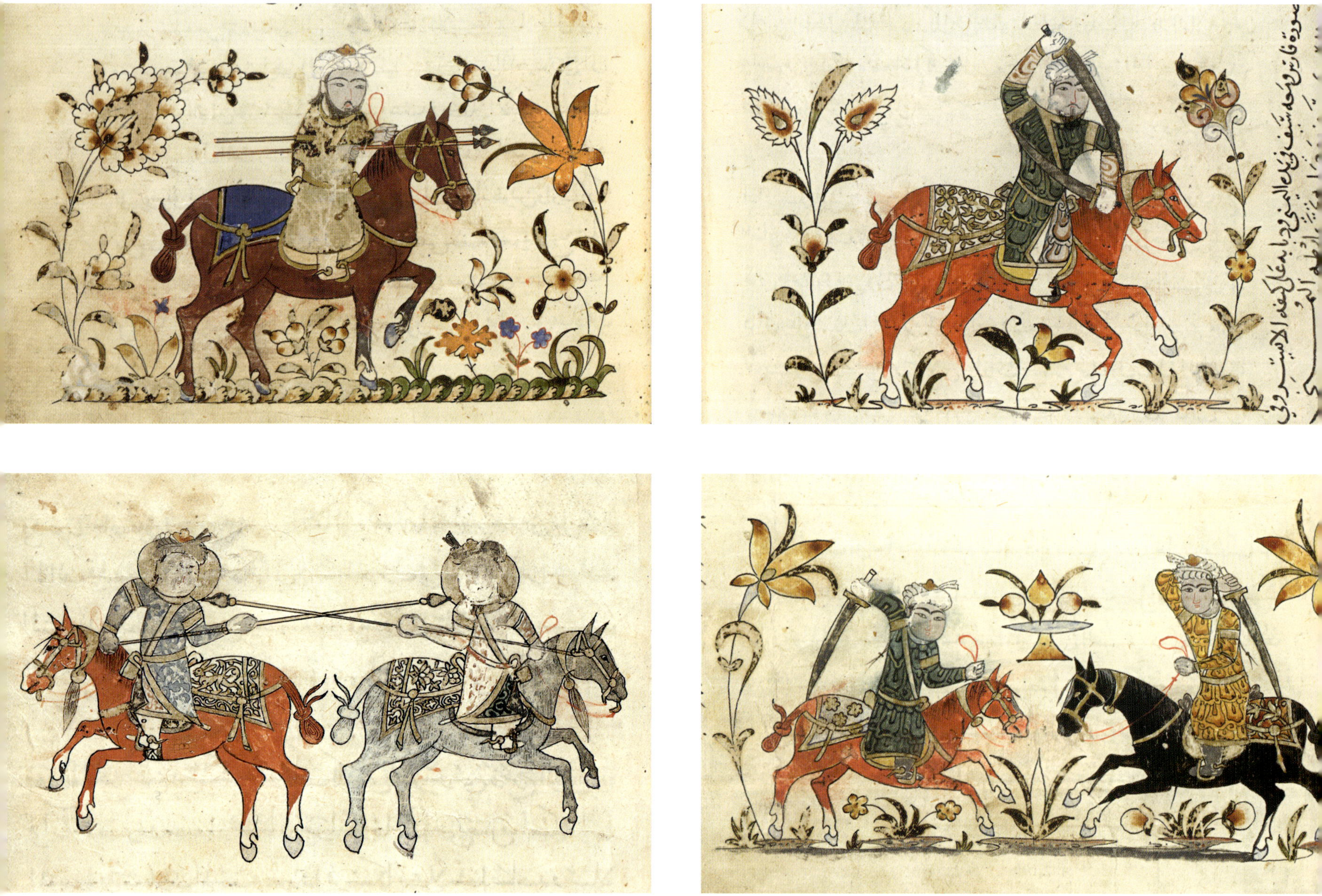

Fig. 17
Illustrations from the *Furusiyya* manuscript dating from 773 AH/AD 1371 (cat. 134) showing men on different coloured horses engaging in military exercises involving lances and swords. Not every painting in the manuscript has a caption, but the lower two shown here are (left to right): 'Illustration of two horsemen whose lance-heads are between each other's shoulder-blades' and 'Illustration of two horsemen wheeling round, with a sword in each one's hand on the horse's back.'
British Library

course, and consists of four circles joined in the centre. Preparations for horse races in the Islamic period were taken very seriously, and before the race, horses had to undergo a period of forty to sixty days of special training and diet known as 'tadmir' or 'idmar'. Any excess weight was sweated off under blankets.

Reflecting the high value placed upon them in Islamic societies, horses, invariably with riders, are often depicted on high-quality prestige objects. The riders are usually princes or nobles and are mounted on the finest horses with expensive and beautifully made harness and trappings. The objects themselves are made of various materials such as metal, glass and pottery. This tradition is well demonstrated by three splendid pieces in this exhibition, all dating from the thirteenth century AD but made from different materials. They are a ceramic dish with *sgraffiato* painted decoration showing a mounted warrior, a glass pilgrim flask with polychrome enamel decoration that includes representations of mounted huntsmen, and a brass ewer with silver and copper inlaid decoration showing various scenes including a warrior on horseback. Horses are also shown in Arabic, Persian, Mughal and Turkish miniature paintings. The horses in Persian miniature paintings often appear in association with legendary figures such as Rustam in the *Shahnameh*, whose horse Rakhsh was invested with magical powers. The miniature paintings of the Mughal period in North India (sixteenth to nineteenth centuries AD), which were heavily influenced by Persian art and culture, are a particularly rich source for illustrations of horses.

As well as horses in the Islamic world, armour for both horses and men was highly regarded in the West from an early period. Consequently, both horses and armour were highly prized. For example, the gifts presented by Louis the Pious to Charlemagne from the spoils of a victory over the 'Saracens' of Barcelona in *c.* AD 795 included 'a fine horse, a fine coat of mail and an Indian sword'. In the nineteenth century in some parts of the Islamic world horse armour made of cloth was developed as a less expensive and lighter alternative to metal, and this was no less admired in the West than the steel armour with Damascene decoration. A suit of horse cloth armour was brought to England as one of the spoils of war after the Battle of Omdurman in 1898 when a Sudanese army was defeated by Lord Kitchener. Fabric was also widely used in many parts of the Middle East and still is today for brightly coloured harness ornaments, often with attractive designs and these are much admired and sought after by museums and collectors.

In this account of horses in the Islamic world, the Arabian horse has flitted in and out of our story. At this point a word of caution is necessary. As several authorities have pointed out, 'Arab' was sometimes a generic term and was probably used indiscriminately to refer to all Middle Eastern horses, including Arabs, Barbs, Turkmens, and Kurdish and Persian breeds. Nevertheless, some of the horses described above were clearly Arabs on the basis of their physical characteristics, and we will move on now to discuss the Arabian horse in the Arabian Peninsula itself.

Fig. 18
Ivory chess piece in the form of a chariot pulled by a pair of horses with two riders. This is similar to chess pieces excavated at Afrasiab near Samarkand and dating from around the eighth century AD. This piece corresponds to a rook (Persian *rokh*) or castle.
BM 1991,1021.1

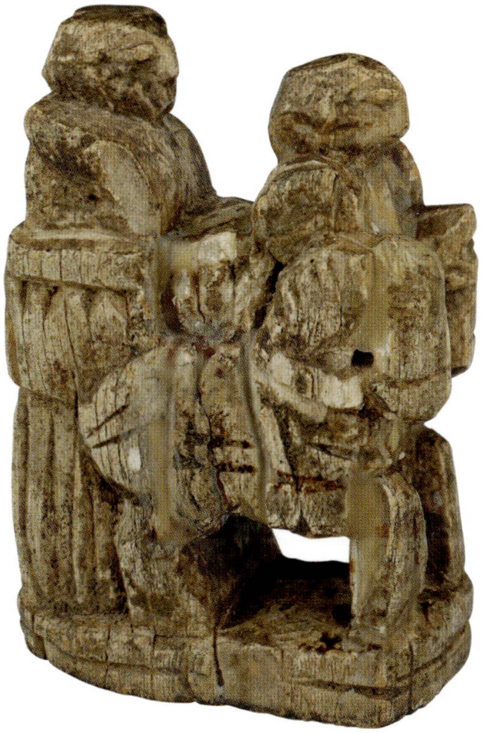

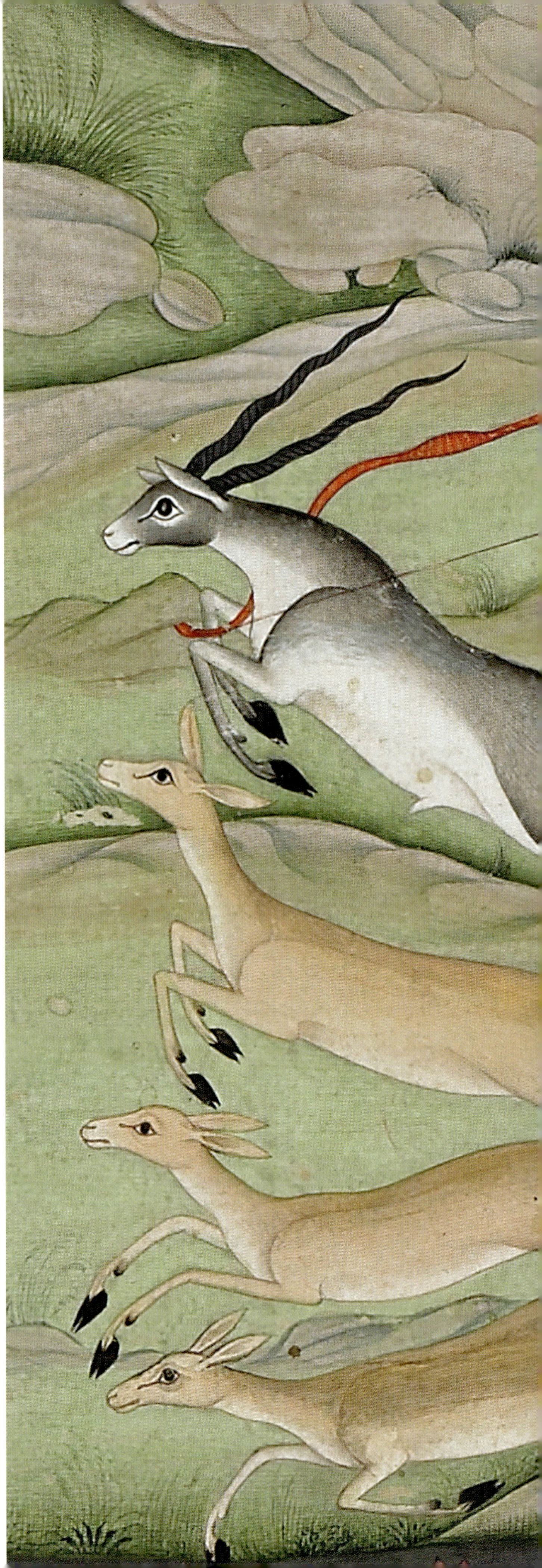

Fig. 19
Detail from a Mughal miniature painting, *c.* AD 1650–1750, showing Akbar hunting on horseback (cat. 149).

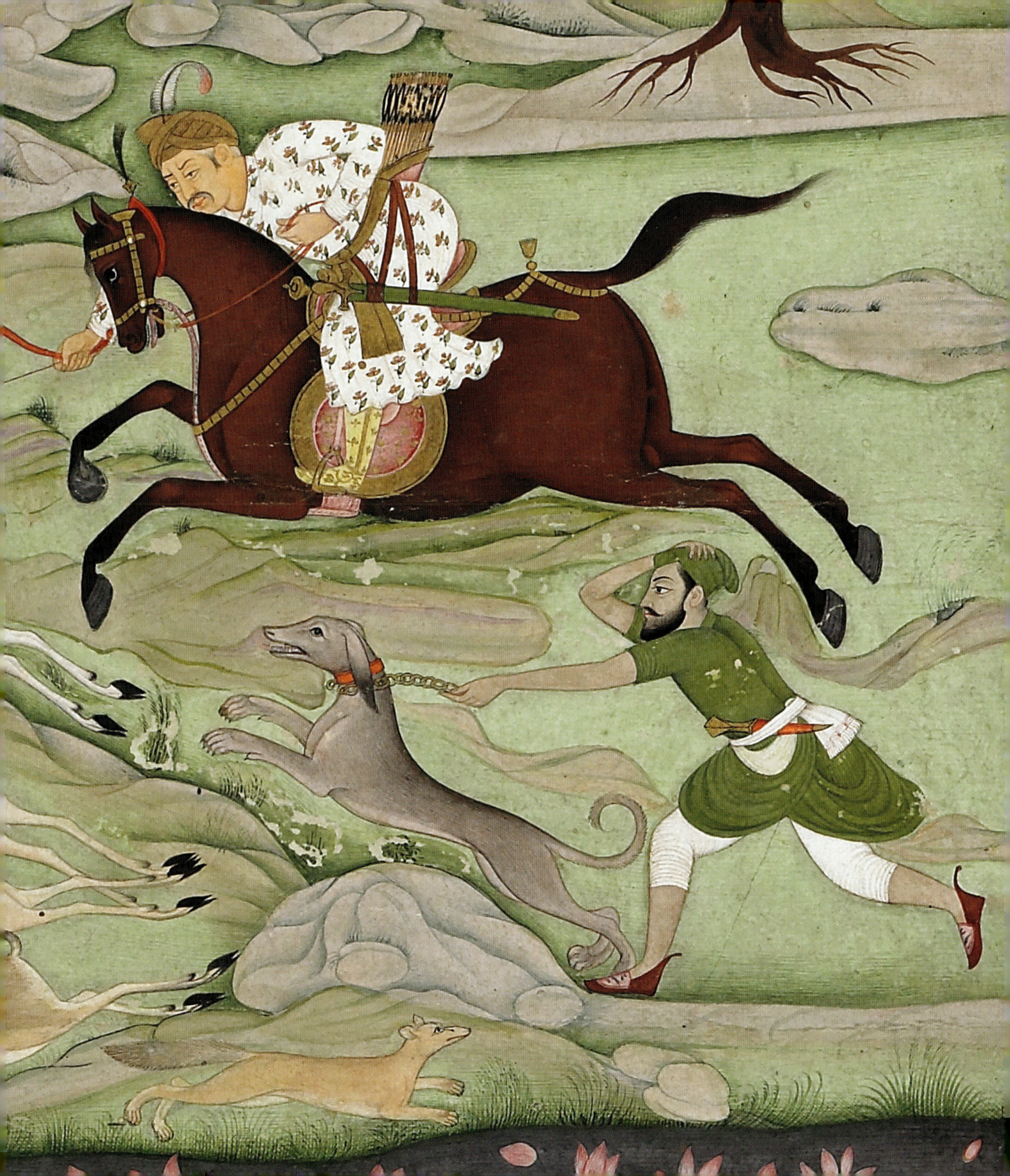

CHAPTER 3

THE HORSE IN ARABIA

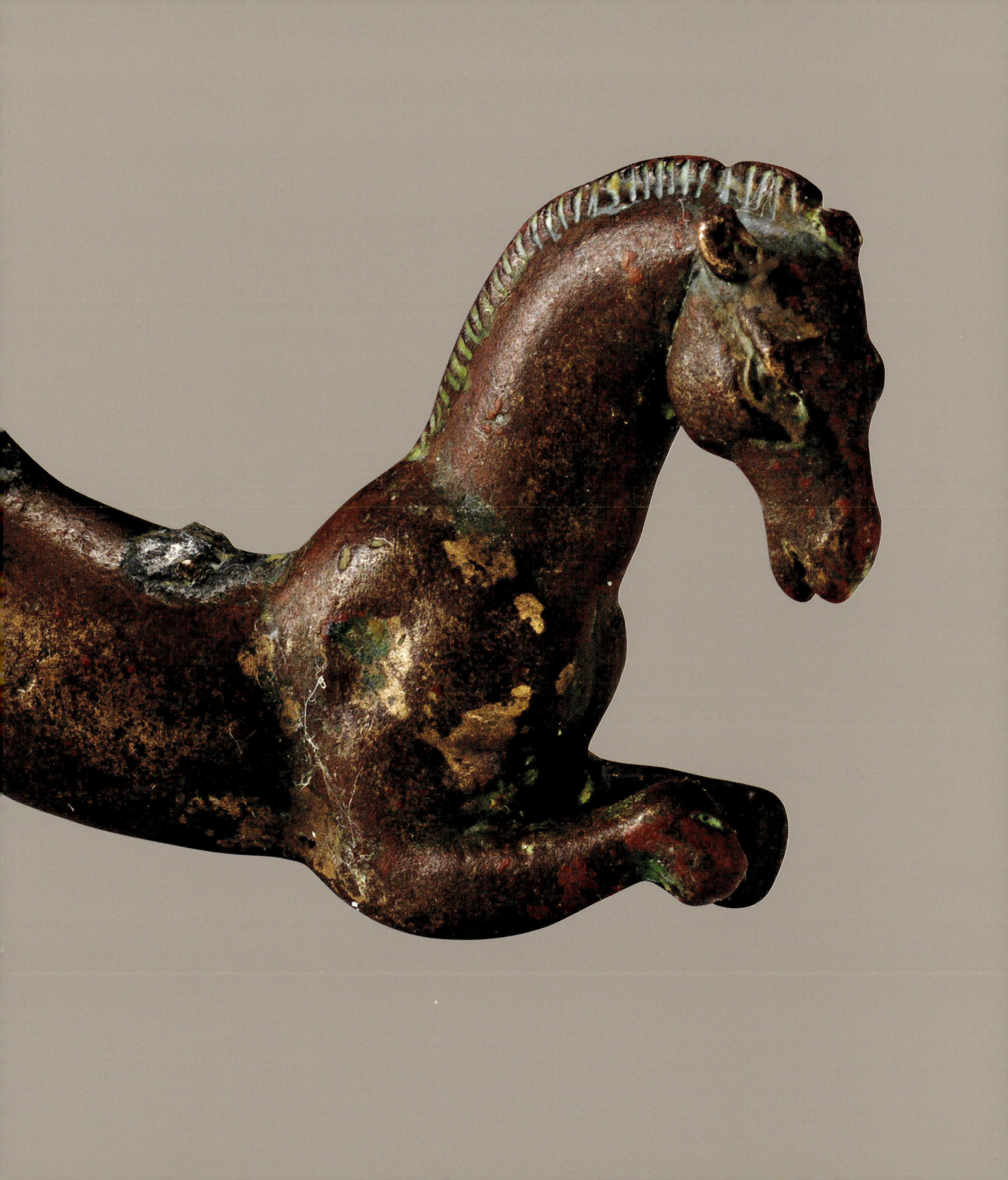

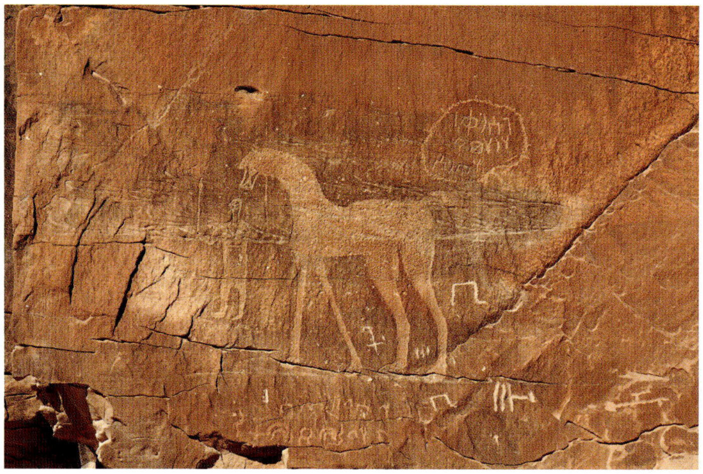

The horse in Arabia

IN the Middle East, in Arabia in particular, the centrality of the horse in society was a cultural phenomenon widely noted by travellers. Together with falconry and hunting with salukis, the horse was an inseparable part of the traditional Bedouin way of life and its concepts of honour and chivalrous behaviour. The Arabian Peninsula is central to the development and preservation of the Arabian breed of horse. Prevailing wisdom, however, has long dictated that the horse was unknown there before about 200 BC. The Greek author Strabo was able to write in his *Geography* that 'The extreme parts towards the south, lying opposite to Ethiopia, are watered by summer rains and are sowed twice ... The country is in general fertile, and abounds in particular with places for making honey; and with the exception of horses and mules and hogs, it has an abundance of domesticated animals; and, with the exception of geese and chickens, has all kinds of birds.' Strabo himself was actually writing in the late first century BC or the early first century AD, but he borrowed the above passage from an earlier author, Eratosthenes of Cyrene, who died in about 195 BC. Even in Strabo's day, the situation may not have been very different. Describing the ancient Nabataean kingdom, that embraced Sinai, the northern Hijaz and southern Jordan, he wrote: 'the country does not produce horses'. Further, two of the greatest experts on the dated inscriptions of Southern Arabia, Jacques Ryckmans and Christian Robin, are agreed that those inscriptions mentioning horses all date from the Christian era. However, other experts, for example, Michael Macdonald, point to evidence for the horse from the fourth

ABOVE
Fig. 20
Rock drawing at Al-Naslaa, Saudi Arabia, showing a led horse.

century BC onwards, if not in what is now Saudi Arabia at least in adjoining regions. This evidence takes the form of clay horse figurines from the island of Failaka, from Bahrain, and from Petra in Jordan, the capital of the Nabataean kingdom. Bronze bowls showing horses from Samad in Oman and Mleiha in Sharjah in the United Arab Emirates are dated between the fourth and third centuries BC. Even if the horse was introduced into Arabian Peninsula in the fourth century BC, however, this would still be very late compared with other parts of the Middle East. There are emerging now, however, two sources of evidence that may oblige us at least to re-examine the traditional view. Firstly, there is a new discovery made in 2011 by a team of archaeologists working in the south-west part of Saudi Arabia, near a village called al-Maqar. The site apparently covers a wide area and is in a *wadi* not far from the main arterial north-south road. Here were found about thirty stone objects carved in the round. The most significant of these (cat. 165) appears to show the head and foreparts of an animal resembling a horse, possibly complete with a halter. This object is large, being 86 cm in length. There is also a smaller horse-like figure represented by head and shoulders only, the head of a bird of prey that could be an eagle or a falcon (cat. 166), and the head and chest of a dog with a pointed nose bearing some resemblance to a modern saluki (cat. 167). Other figures retrieved from al-Maqar include what appear to be a fish, the neck and head of an ostrich and two sheep or goats. At the same site, archaeologists have found bifacial flint arrowheads with tangs and barbs (cats 168–72) and flint scrapers (cats 173–7) that date from the Neolithic period, the fifth millennium BC. Samples from the same site that were subjected to radiocarbon analysis have also given dates in the Neolithic period. If the stone figures are definitely associated with the arrowheads and the radiocarbon samples,

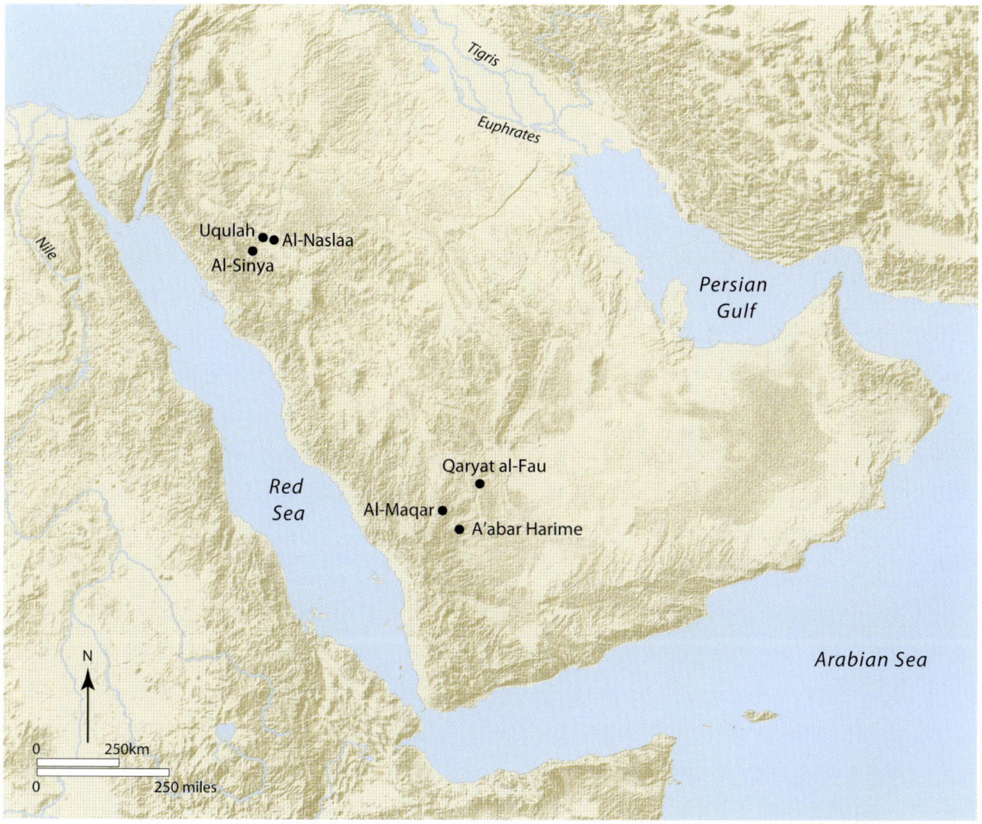

Fig. 21
Map of the Arabian Peninsula showing the location of sites mentioned in the text.

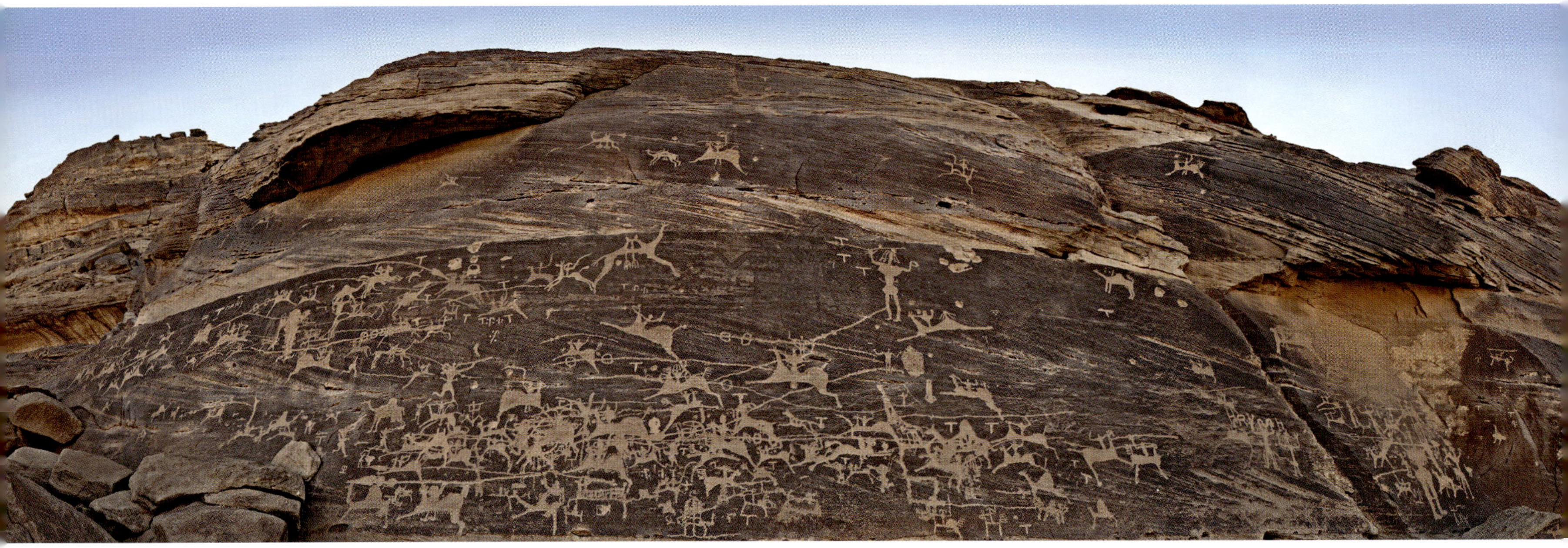

Fig. 22
Rock drawings at A'abar Harime, Saudi Arabia, showing mounted horsemen in scenes of raiding and battle.

and if they definitely show horses as suggested, we would have evidence for the existence of horses in Saudi Arabia at a very early date. However, the relationship between the stone figures and the arrowheads and radiocarbon samples is not yet clear, and research is continuing on this matter. These investigations include further archaeological excavation and survey at al-Maqar. The results will be eagerly awaited by the archaeological community. At the moment we can only conclude that little is known about early members of the horse family in Arabia, although there is evidence for domesticated goats, sheep and cattle and for wild asses in the Neolithic period about six to eight thousand years ago.

The second source of possible new evidence about the introduction of the horse into Arabia is the rock art that is to be widely found throughout Arabia and the Syrian desert on boulders and rocky outcrops. We are fortunate here in that a wealth of new evidence has recently come to light as a result of a new and innovative programme of GigaPan photography of many of the rock drawings. This project, directed by Sandra Olsen and Chris Beard and with photography by Richard Bryant, has brought to light many previously unknown drawings and they can now be studied in much greater detail than was previously possible. Typically, incised rock drawings show scenes of hunting, herding and warfare. They appear to range in date from the Neolithic to the present. It is difficult to date them exactly, but some have associated inscriptions in local scripts which allow dating on philological grounds or sometimes through people or events mentioned. Horses feature very prominently in this art, either as rather rare large-scale portraits of horses, or as the mounts of huntsmen and warriors. A few scenes show chariots, and the majority of these can be dated from the design of the vehicle to the Iron Age, probably the Achaemenid period, although some could be earlier. Other than these few horses in harness, most representations of horses show them ridden, often charging with the rider holding a characteristic long lance horizontally above his head. Some rock drawings, then, would already appear to push the history of the horse in Saudi

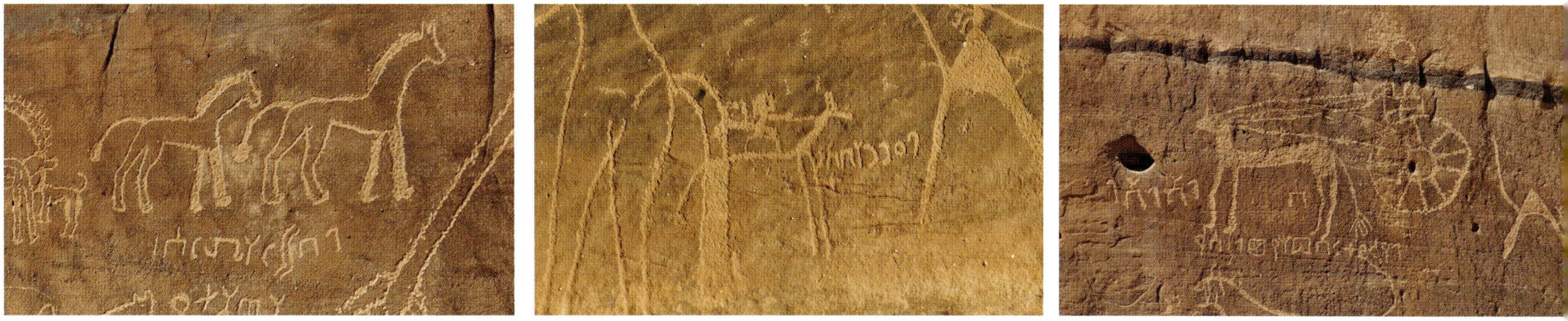

Fig. 23
Rock drawings at Uqulah (left and centre) and Al-Sinya (right), Saudi Arabia, showing horse figures and a chariot with a large, multi-spoked wheel. The form of the vehicle possibly suggests a date in the Achaemenid period (5th–4th century BC) for the drawing at Al-Sinya.

Arabia back beyond the fourth century BC, but further research is needed on this interesting material. Thanks to the GigaPan photographs, this will now be possible.

It is likely, then, that further research on the rock drawings and possibly on the new discoveries at al-Maqar will oblige us to push back the date of the introduction of the horse into the Arabian Peninsula, but at the moment certain evidence for the horse does not go much further back than the fourth century BC. From this time onwards, however, corresponding to the Hellenistic and Roman periods beyond the region, there is increasing evidence for horses. This is not surprising, as Arabia was not an empty land: it was the source of products such as frankincense and myrrh, of immense value and traded over great distances. Coastal, highland and oasis areas were home to settled communities, towns and kingdoms that prospered on trade. With the domestication of the camel even the great deserts were open to long-distance trade and to semi-nomadic tribes who sought grazing for their herds and ranged over wide areas in the Middle East. The art of the later Arabian kingdoms that are founded on this prosperity shows many influences from the ancient Greek and Roman worlds. The importance and status of horses in society is reflected in Arabian art of this time. This is nowhere exemplified better than at Qaryat al-Fau, an ancient caravan city on the edge of the Empty Quarter in southern Saudi Arabia. The site was occupied between the second century BC and the third century AD, and many of the items from here, including the frescoes and the bronze horse that are in the exhibition (cats 181–3), show evidence of Roman influence.

Arab literary sources are also informative about horses. Ancient South Arabian inscriptions record royal horsemen in war, and later Arab poets praise the horse in deeply expressive verse:

> Early in the morning, while the birds were still nesting, I mounted my steed.
> Well-bred was he, long-bodied, outstripping the wild beasts in speed,
> Swift to attack, to flee, to turn, yet firm as a rock swept down by the torrent,
> Bay-coloured, and so smooth the saddle slips from him, as the rain from a smooth stone,
> Thin but full of life, fire boils within him like the snorting of a boiling kettle;
> He continues at full gallop when other horses are dragging their feet in the dust for weariness.
> (*Imru' al-Qais*, sixth century)[1]

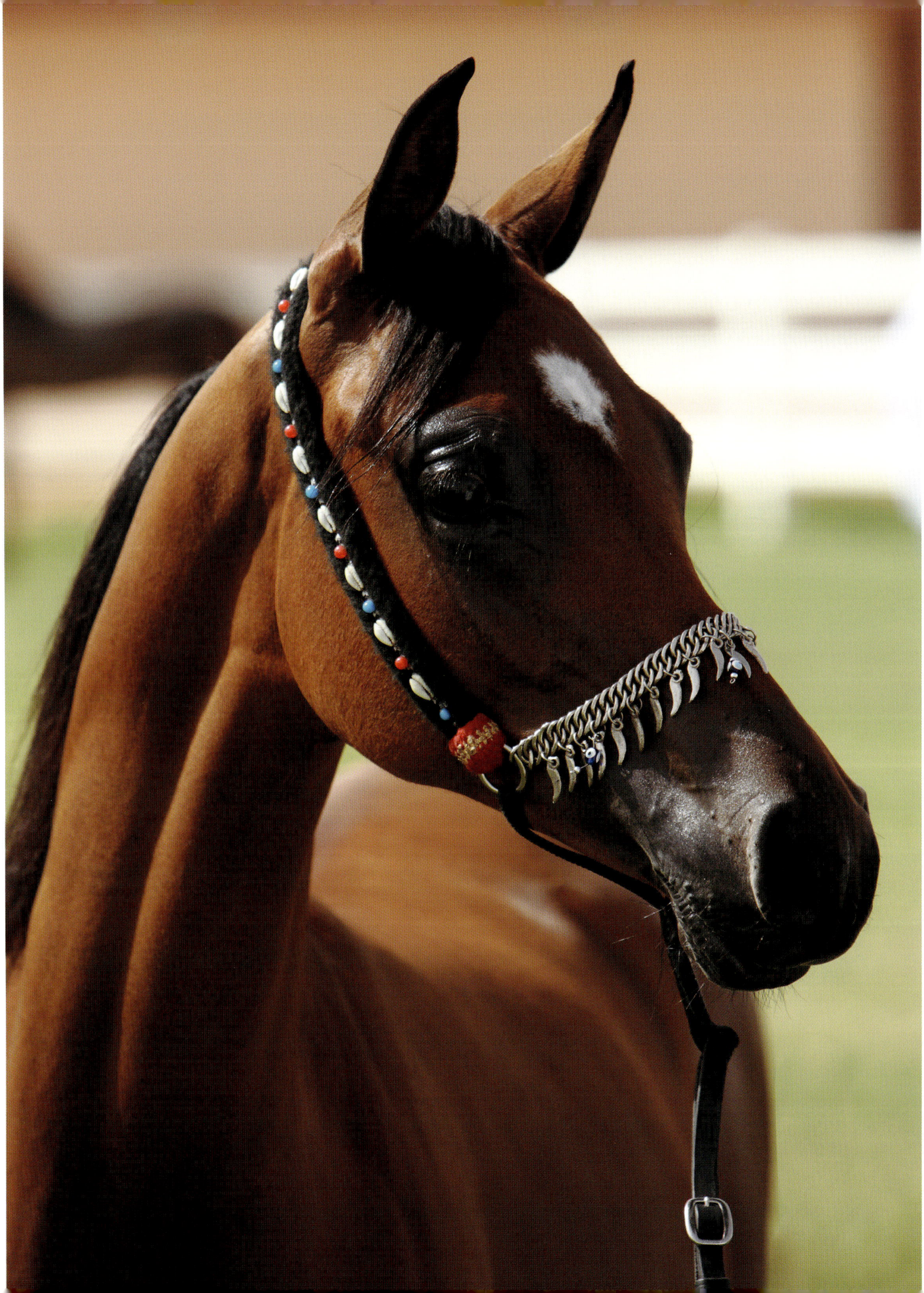

The origins of the Arabian breed of horse are not clear. Modern breeds of horses are creations of sometimes many hundreds of years of human intervention. Breeds will therefore change over time, either because of such intervention, or the lack of it, or even vanish completely as human requirements and needs change. Today, the Arabian horse has special characteristics of speed and hardiness but above all of stamina, endurance and temperament. The Arabian breed has a unique and easily recognizable appearance, or conformation, in the shape of the head (with a dished nose and large eyes) and a high arched bearing of the tail. As has been mentioned in earlier chapters, similar physical characteristics are clear in some ancient representations of horses, particularly, for example, in Ancient Egyptian art, while Roman and Byzantine texts describing Arab horsemen often stress the speed and agility of their horses, characteristics which would have been essential for the fluid *karr wa farr* or 'hit and run' warfare which was their speciality.

We see this in the history of Ammianus Marcellinus, a military bureaucrat in the Late Roman administration writing in the fourth century AD. Writing of the *saraceni*, the 'Saracens', Arab warriors who played a major role in the affairs of the Roman East, he says:

> all the men are warriors of equal rank; half naked, clad in coloured cloaks down to the waist, overrunning different countries, with the aid of swift and active horses and speedy camels, alike in times of peace and war.[2]

Ammianus takes most of this digression almost word for word from much earlier authors, but his comment on the speed and agility of Arab horses can be compared with other accounts to show that this at least was probably based on experience rather than literary cliché alone. It is from the close observation of later Byzantine writers that we can most clearly see what was perceived to be the special virtues of Arab horses. The Byzantine emperor Leo VI (886–912), whose compendium on military tactics, the *Taktika* (which, in Arabic translation, was by far the favourite military manual in the Islamic world), noted that Arab Bedouin horses were better than the Byzantine's own. Leo advised that in battle his archers should target the Arab horses,

> for in this manner, with their horses, the so-called *pharia*, being shot at ... they will quickly rush off in flight. They will do this for two reasons, namely because of their desire to save their horses, which are highly prized, and not easily procured, and because they want to save themselves as well through saving the horses.[3]

The word *pharia* is of course clearly derived from *faris*, the Arabic for horse (and in western Europe at the same time we similarly find *alfaraces* is used in Latin texts to describe horses captured from the Arabs in Spain). The Byzantine emperor Nikephoros Phokas (963–969) described in detail in his own book of military tactics the remarkable speed of Arab horses and the impossibility of catching them in pursuit:

> The *Arabitai* [Bedouin] will encircle our four-sided [square] formation in a swarm, as they usually do, confident in their horses. There is no need for the

Fig. 24
Photograph by Abdullatif al-Obaida of a modern Arabian horse showing its characteristic profile. The dished face, large eyes and curled ear-tips typical of the breed are clearly visible.

> [Byzantine] cavalry to head off in pursuit of them because of the speed of their horses, for when pursued they are not overtaken and, aided by the speed of their horses, they quickly counterattack and strike against our men. It does no good at all to go chasing after them.[4]

A century later, another Byzantine commentator described the Bedouin 'emboldened as ever by the ability of their horses to run very quickly', but notes significantly, given that modern Arabians are above all known for their endurance, that 'although the Arab horses can run very swiftly for a time, they do not bear up well over a long distance'.[5]

Of course, not keeping a regular formation would give the Bedouin horsemen a speed advantage over the Byzantines, whose military doctrine stressed a steady advance, keeping formation and battle discipline, and Byzantine horses may have been selected for stamina over speed alone, but there is clearly agreement in all these texts that the Arab horses were fast and nimble. Indeed, the Byzantines attributed these remarkable advantages specifically to the horses of Arab semi-nomadic horsemen, something they do not note for any of their other opponents – even other Islamic opponents.

The mythical origins, abilities and training of the Arabian horse were well-established by modern times and the reports of European travellers all agree on the essentials:

> 'Whether it be owing to this extreme care in the breeding, or to the climate which is generally thought favourable, they are certainly very beautiful creatures; although a pure Arabian is seldom of any superior height, yet for docility, form, hardiness, and speed, a rival is difficult to be found. Bred in the tents of the Bedooin, like children, they feed at his hand; and follow their master's steps in his wanderings; or when he falls in battle, remains immovable by his side. With an arched, commanding crest; nervous, straight, compact limbs; the shoulder of a racer, and a spreading open chest; the Arab, when provoked to speed, displays an open nostril that snuffs the wind, an eye of fire, and the action, if not the speed, of the antelope. He scarcely feels the ground, or leaves a print behind; whilst his spirit but seems to rise and display itself with the continuance of the chace [*sic*] ... The finest [horses] come from the province of Najd, and the Bedooins preserve with a superstitious care the memory and descent of their purest blood; tracing these various breeds to five original sources, which have each given their name to some peculiar race, and are acknowledged as the parent stock. From one or other of these families, the most celebrated Arabians derive their descent through their dam.'[6]

It is said that during the reign of Imam Saud Ibn Abdul Aziz (1803–1814) some 1500 Arabian horses were stabled in al-Dariyah, which was the capital of the first Saudi state (now 20 kilometres from the centre of Riyadh). Al-Dariyah is now a World Heritage Site with a museum on the Arabian horse planned to open in 2013. The gentleness in breaking and training compared to the harshness of European methods was noted by Palgrave, who saw the royal stables of Faisal ibn Saud (1785–1865) at Riyadh on his expedition to Arabia of 1862–3. Palgrave's 'picturesque paragraphs which have since been constantly quoted'

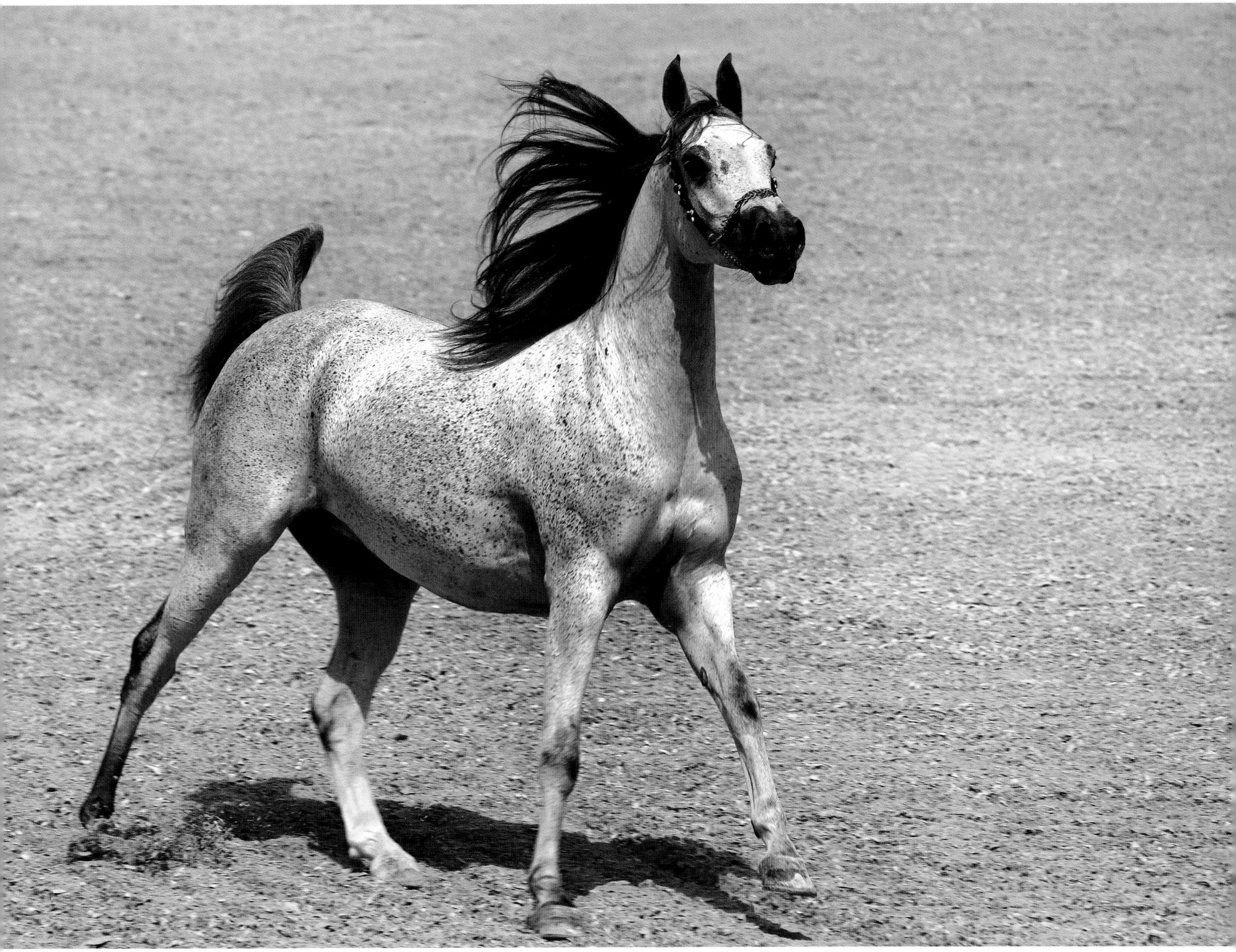

Fig. 25
Photography by Abdullatif al-Obaida of a modern Arabian horse with tail held high and flared nostrils.

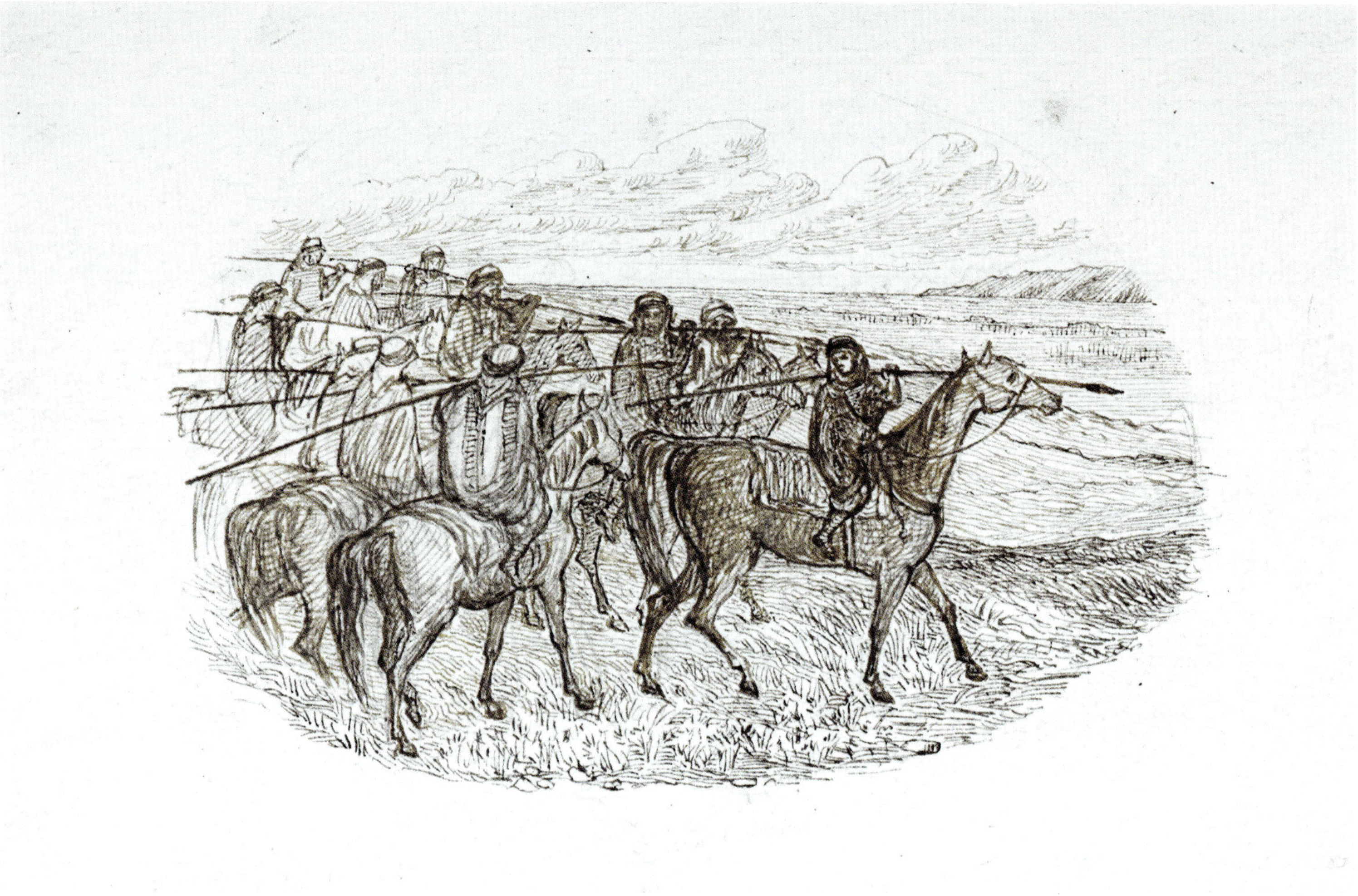

Fig. 26
Sketch by Lady Anne Blunt showing Arab horsemen on a raid, a loose leaf from her diary of 16–24 April 1878. This is the classic pose of the Arab lancer as captured in rock art, with a long and flexible cane lance balanced over the shoulder or held over the head in both hands. Even in the nineteenth century the Bedouin horseman disdained the use of saddle and stirrups (and even bits, unless absolutely necessary, using halters as shown here), preferring to rely on skill and horsemanship.
British Library

(as noted by the Blunts) have often to be treated with caution, but his eyewitness account of Faisal's stables at their height reveal an impressive establishment:

> 'They cover a large square space, about 150 yards each way, and are open in the centre, with a long shed running around the inner walls; under this covering the horses, about 300 in number when I saw them, are picketed during night; in the daytime they may stretch their legs at pleasure within the central courtyard. The greater number are accordingly loose; a few, however, were tied up at their stalls; some, but not many, had horse-cloths over them ... About half the royal stud was present before me, the rest were out at grass, Feysul's entire muster is reckoned at 600 head, or rather more.'[7]

Of Faisal's fine horses, Palgrave thought, 'their appearance justified all reputation, all value, all poetry'. Faisal's territorial ambitions led eventually to his imprisonment in Egypt where he became a friend of the grandson of Muhammad Ali, Abbas Pasha I (1813–1854), the Viceroy of Egypt. Abbas Pasha's greatest passion was the Arabian horse, and he assembled the most famous Arabian stud of the time. The detailed records kept by his representatives of the pedigrees of the horses he acquired, full of vivid anecdotes and histories of their exploits and past owners, forms the unique Abbas Pasha manuscript (cat. 189), which is an essential document for the history of the Arabian breed. Following Abbas Pasha's assassination in 1854, the stud was partly dispersed but Ali Pasha Sherif, the son of the governor of Syria, acquired a significant number of the finest horses.

Johann Ludwig Burckhardt (1784–1817), the Swiss scholar who travelled extensively in the Middle East, noted that 'It is a general but erroneous opinion that Arabia is very rich in horses; but the breed is limited to the extent of fertile pasture-grounds in that country, and it is in such parts only that horses thrive, while those Bedouins who occupy districts of poor soil rarely possess horses. It is found, accordingly, that the tribes most rich in horses are those who dwell in the comparatively fertile plains of Mesopotamia, on the banks of the river Euphrates, and in the Syrian plains. Horses can there feed for several of the spring months upon the green grass and herbs produced by the rains in the valleys and fertile grounds, and such food seems absolutely necessary for promoting the full growth and vigour of the horse. We find that in Najd horses are not nearly so numerous as in the countries before mentioned, and they become scarce in proportion as we proceed towards the south.'[8]

Two generations later, Lady Anne Blunt similarly commented that 'Whatever may have been the case formerly, horses of any kind are now exceedingly rare in Nejd. One may travel vast distances in the peninsula without meeting a single horse, or even crossing a horse-track. Both in the Nefud and on our return journey to the Euphrates, we carefully examined every track of man and beast we met; but . . . not twenty of these proved to be tracks of horses. The wind no doubt obliterates footsteps quickly; but it could not wholly do so, if there were a great number of the animals near. The Ketherin, a true Nejd tribe and a branch of the Bani Khalid, told us with some pride that they could mount a hundred horsemen; and even the Muteyr, reputed to be the greatest breeders of thoroughbred stock in Nejd, are said to possess only 400 mares. The horse is a luxury with the Bedouins of the Peninsula; and not, as it is with those of the north, a necessity of their daily life. Their journeys and raids and wars are all made on camel, not on horseback; and at most the Sheikh mounts his mare at the moment of battle. The want of water in Nejd is a sufficient reason for this. Horses there are kept for show rather than actual use, and are looked upon as far too precious to run unnecessary risks.'[9]

Nowadays, the purity of the Arabian breed is carefully preserved. In the kingdom of Saudi Arabia, for example, all purebred Arabian horses are registered at the King Abdulaziz Arabian Horse Centre at Dirab, 35 kilometres south-west of Riyadh. Each horse is issued with a registration certificate, a passport and a pedigree chart. There are currently nearly 10,000 Arabian horses registered in the Kingdom. The King Abdulaziz Centre is a member of the World Arabian Horse Organization which is concerned with the registration of Arabian horses around the world and has its headquarters in London. The King Abdulaziz Arabian Horse Centre also breeds Arabian horses and there are around 170 horses, comprising stallions, mares and foals there at any one time. King Abdulaziz had a herd of desert-bred warhorses for fighting. These horses typically had larger lungs and stronger bones than European-bred Arabian horses. This unique herd still exists and a number are based at the Centre.

CHAPTER 4

THE ARABIAN HORSE AND THE BLUNTS

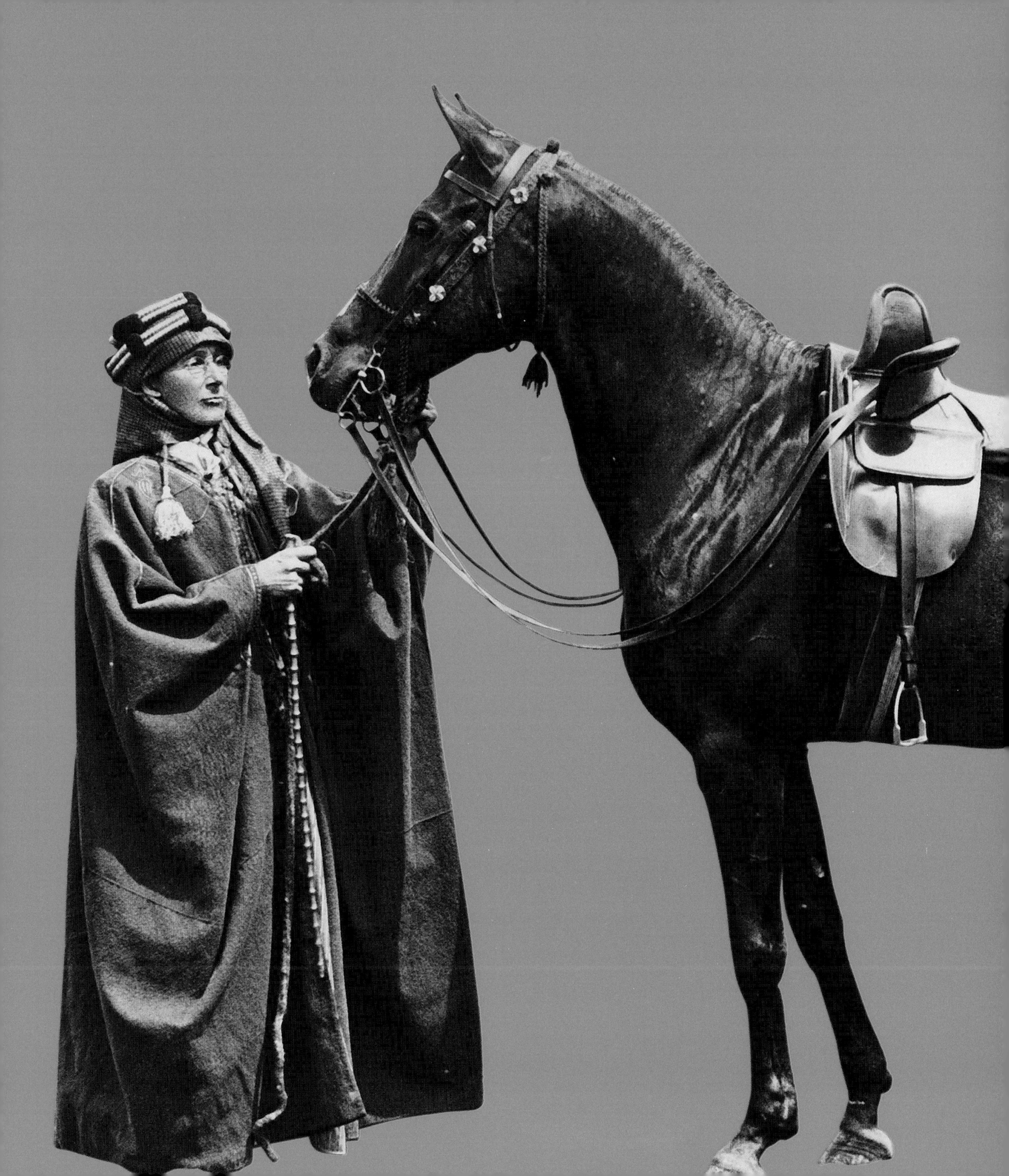

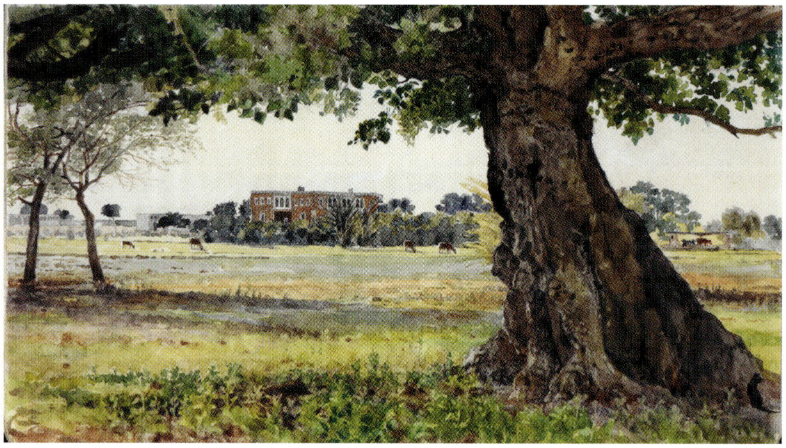

The Arabian horse and the Blunts

TO-DAY, all day, I rode upon the down,
With hounds and horsemen, a brave company,
On this side in its glory lay the sea,
On that the Sussex weald, a sea of brown.
The wind was light, and brightly the sun shone,
And still we galloped on from gorse to gorse.
And once, when checked, a thrush sang, and my horse
Pricked his quick ears as to a sound unknown.

I knew the spring was come. I knew it even
Better than all by this, that through my chase
In bush and stone and hill and sea and heaven
I seemed to see and follow still your face.
Your face my quarry was. For it I rode,
My horse a thing of wings, myself a god.

St Valentine's Day, Wilfrid Scawen Blunt[1]

ABOVE
Fig. 27
Watercolour sketch by Lady Anne Blunt showing the 'Pink House' at Sheykh Obeyd near Cairo in 1900. The Blunts had this house built in 1891 for the use of guests, and Lady Anne spent her last years here from 1906.
British Library

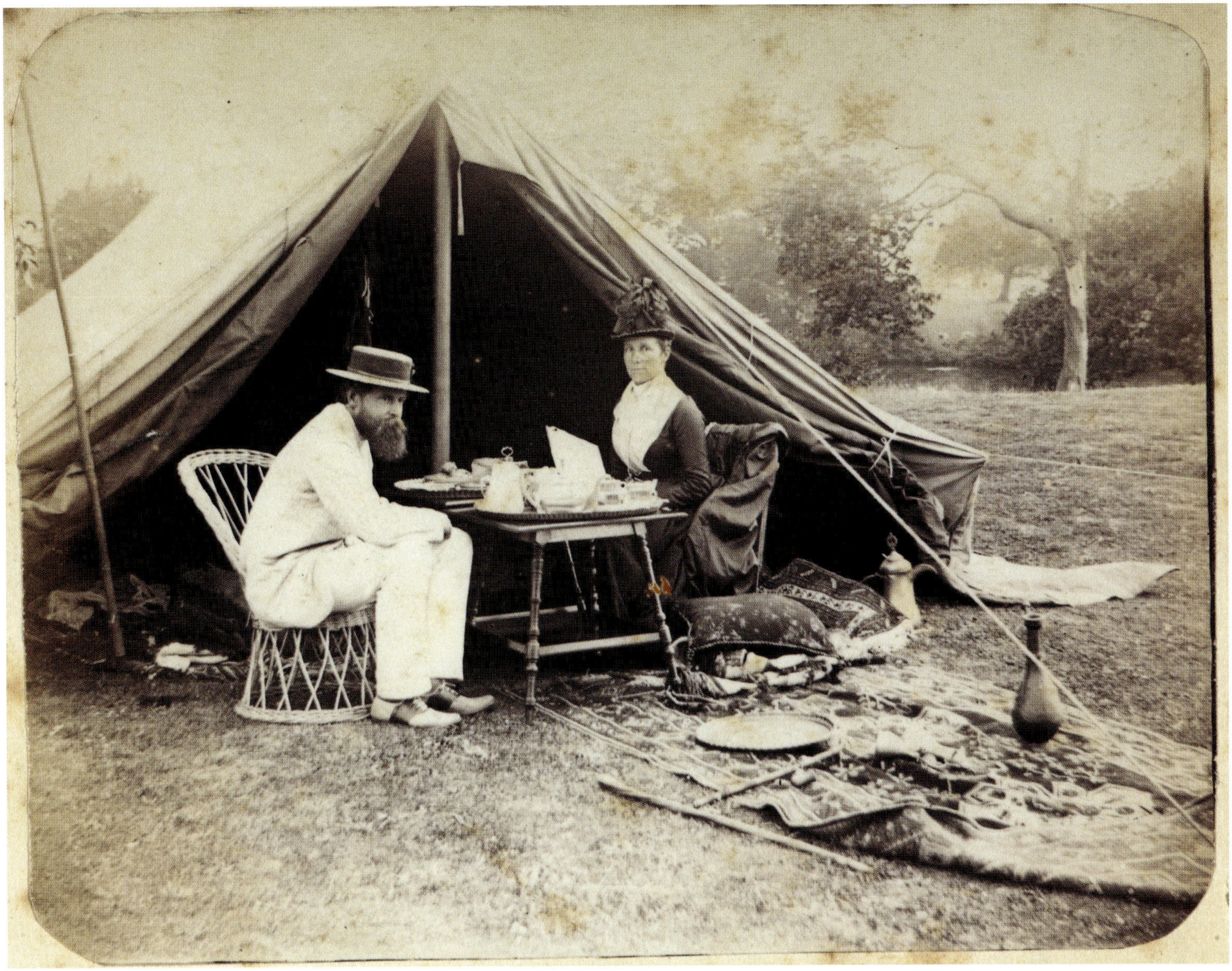

Fig. 28
The Blunts kept their travelling tent pitched at Crabbet Park where, called the 'Desert', it was equipped with Middle Eastern carpets, coffee pots, lances, armour and other accoutrements, where they might receive guests in traditional Eastern style. Wilfrid said: 'Some people laugh at me for keeping it so, but it would astonish you what a reputation it has got. I have had the Bedouins in Asia ask me about it.' In this photograph, Wilfrid and Lady Anne take tea and cake outside the Desert.
British Library

The heyday of the importation of Arabian or oriental horses into modern Britain was in the seventeenth and eighteenth centuries, but the bridge between Middle Eastern horses and horses in Britain is nowhere better encapsulated than in the story of the Blunts. Although they were operating in the nineteenth century, the Blunts made it their life's mission to, as they saw it, preserve the purity of the Arabian horse.

Fine Arabian horses had always been highly prized and sought after in the Middle East, and their pedigree and purity was of great importance. In Britain, interest in the Arabian was mostly confined to the improvement of the Thoroughbred, but it was the preservation of the Arabian breed which eventually became the life's work of Wilfrid Scawen Blunt (1840–1922) and Lady Anne Blunt (1837–1917), daughter of William King, 1st Earl of Lovelace and Ada King, Countess of Lovelace (and so the granddaughter of Lord Byron). The mercurial Wilfrid, now known more for his scandalous liaisons and poetry

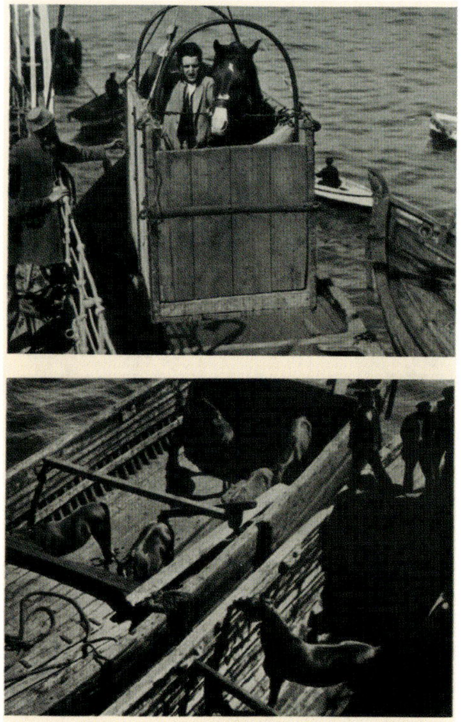

Fig. 29
Arabian horses being taken by boat to Europe. The photographs were taken by Carl Raswan just after the First World War and reproduced in his book *Drinkers of the Wind* (London, 1938). Transport of horses aboard ship had changed little since the Blunts' time.

and forthright, if forlorn, anti-imperialist political interventions for the causes of Home Rule for Ireland and Egyptian nationalism, was in many senses a wayward contradiction. An aristocrat who revelled in the country-house life and country pursuits of all kinds, he nevertheless described, for example, William Morris, the artist, pioneer of the Arts and Crafts movement and socialist, as the greatest man he ever met. Wilfrid had been a junior diplomat in Constantinople and a number of European capitals for some years before his marriage to Lady Anne in 1869. As far as Wilfrid was concerned, it was scarcely a love match. His description of her, although not unkind, was hardly flattering and is distinctly lacking in warmth. 'She thought herself plainer than she was, and had none of the ways of a pretty woman, though in truth she had that sort of prettiness that a bird has, a redbreast or a nightingale, agreeable to the eye if not aggressively attractive. Her colouring, indeed, I used to think was like a robin's, with its bright black eyes, its russet plumage and its tinge of crimson red.'[2] In later life, Wilfrid remembered her as 'an unobtrusive quiet figure', unfashionably dressed (characteristics not shared by Wilfrid), but they had more in common than was at first apparent. Both had had a dislocated European childhood, and Wilfrid's aspirations to be recognized as a poet responded to Anne's Byronic heritage: Wilfrid had some success, and Oscar Wilde was to declare that by imprisoning Wilfrid over his Home Rule politics 'Mr Balfour must be praised ... [he] has converted a clever rhymer into an earnest and deep-thinking poet'; surviving photograph albums pose portraits of Anne and Byron on opposing pages. They also shared a keen interest in the natural world and art. He had been tutored in art by G.F. Watts, Anne had been taught drawing by Ruskin. Most importantly, both were totally fearless, well travelled and with fluency in a number of languages. Wilfrid would say of Anne that 'There was never anybody so courageous as she was. The only thing she was afraid of was the sea.' Together they travelled widely in Spain, North Africa and the Levant and, both keenly interested in horses, from 1877 they made several expeditions in the Middle East, meticulously recorded and illustrated in Lady Anne's journals and in her letters to her daughter Judith (Judith Anne Dorothea Blunt-Lytton, 1873–1957), to buy the best Arabian horses available. At first their idea had been the commonly advanced British attitude to improve the English Thoroughbred through another infusion of eastern stock, but quickly this was abandoned in favour of the preservation of the Arabian breed itself.

Lady Anne's books, derived from her detailed diaries, were revised and edited with Wilfrid's heavy-handed collaboration and illustrated with her sketches. *Bedouin Tribes of the Euphrates* (1879) and notably *A Pilgrimage to Nejd* (1881) recorded their journey to the heart of Arabia and describe their travels in areas then very little known by Europeans and rarely if ever visited by European women. Unlike other Europeans who had made similar journeys, they travelled openly by horse and camel as the wealthy British aristocrats and gentry they were, unescorted but with local attendants, guides and servants. Despite occasional adventures and skirmishes with raiders (Wilfrid survived at least one lance thrust merely due to the thickness of his cloak) they were largely received with great friendship and as equals by the sheikhs of the tribes amongst which they travelled. Both eventually became proficient in spoken Arabic while Lady Anne, with her usual careful and exhaustively methodical approach, acquired considerable knowledge of the written language, translating two volumes of Arabic poetry with great success: *The*

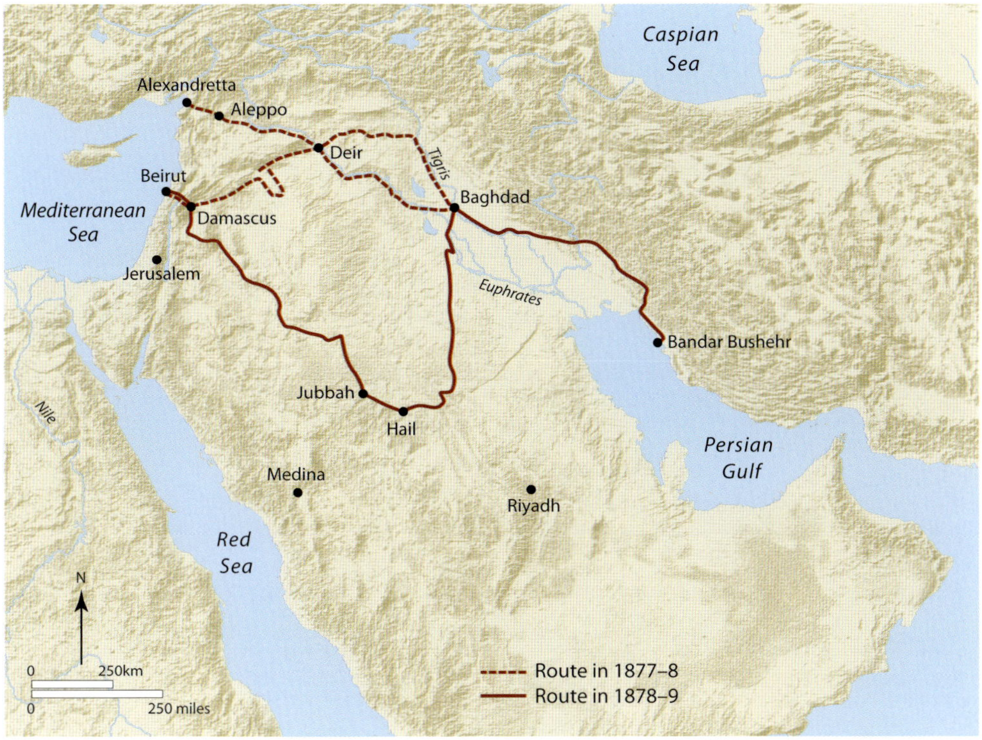

Fig. 30
Map of the Blunts' expeditions to acquire Arabian horses in 1877–8 and 1878–9.

Celebrated Romance of the Stealing of the Mare (1892) and *The Seven Golden Odes* (1903).

Their first expedition, from November 1877 to April 1878, began in earnest at Aleppo after a voyage from Marseilles to Alexandretta. Lady Anne, writing to her daughter every few days (and regularly chiding the poor four-year old 'BeeBee' for her lack of replies), had explained that they were to journey from there to Baghdad as 'people tell us that the best Arab horses are to be got at Baghdad', but they soon changed their plans. Foul weather delayed them at Aleppo for a month and they quickly realized that their enterprise was not to be so simple. There James Henry Skene, the British Consul, encouraged them in their project, gave much valuable advice and assisted them in their first purchases of horses and, most importantly, secured the permits for their export. Anne wrote to BeeBee on 17 December that 'Papa has now arranged a plan to go to a place called Deir on the river Euphrates, & to buy some horses there to bring home ... The Arabs we want to see at Deir are probably not yet there and we must wait to hear when they are coming & also when it is convenient to Mr Skene to start.'

After reaching Baghdad in February they received letters of introduction to important sheikhs of the Shammar tribe, one of whom, Faris, became a great friend of the Blunts and Wilfrid's sworn brother. After travelling widely in the Euphrates valley among the tribes of the Anazeh and the Ruwalla, the Blunts reached Damascus in April and shipped the horses they had purchased, and those bought with the assistance of Skene, to England.

The first horses, the mares Dajania, Hagar, Jerboa, Wild Thyme and Burning Bush with the stallion Kars, arrived in England in July. They were the foundation of the Blunts' Arabian stud at Crabbet Farm near Three Bridges in Sussex. This modest property was

photographed by Mr. T. Ellis

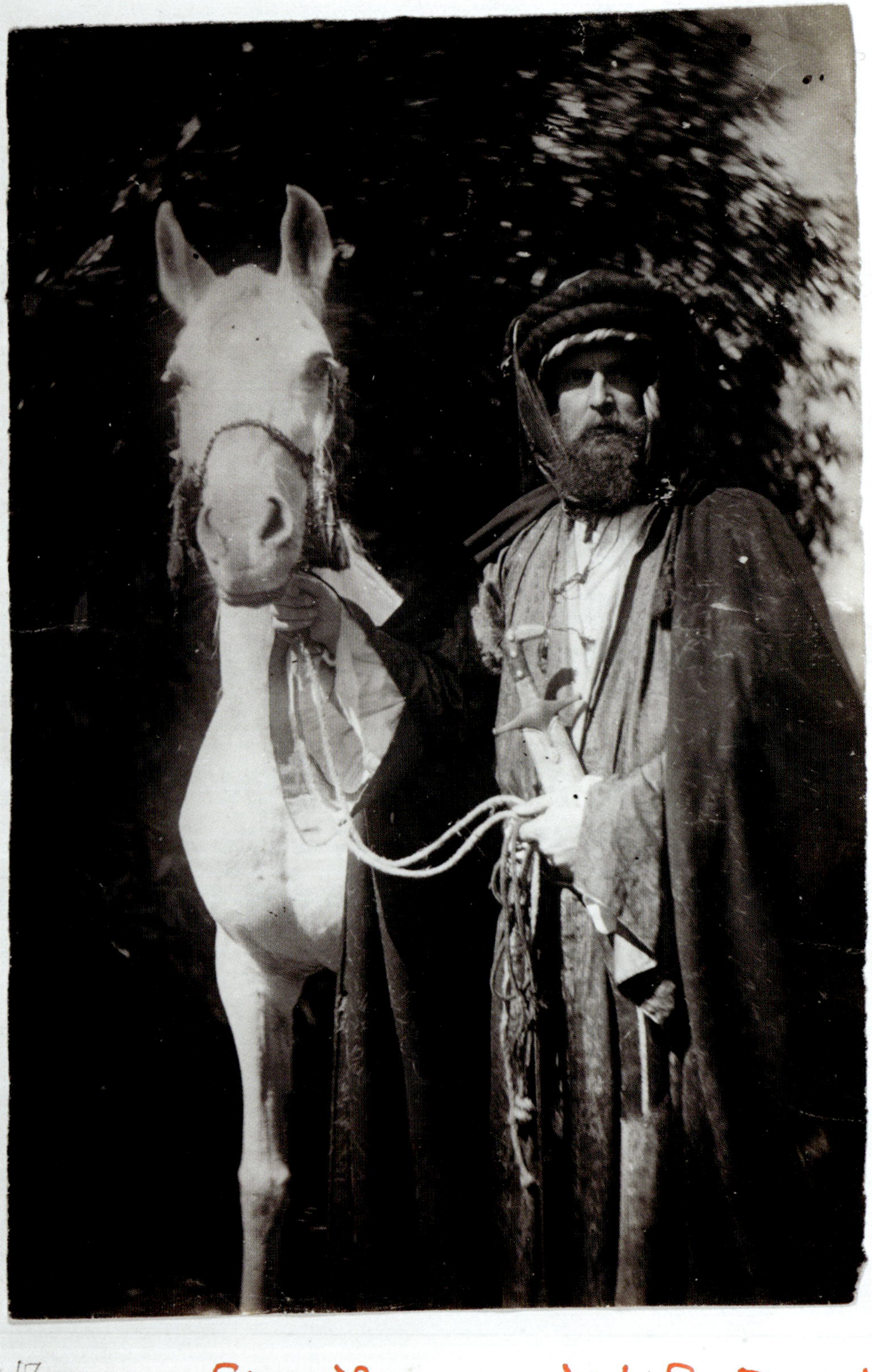

17 Sherifa W. S. B. 1883.

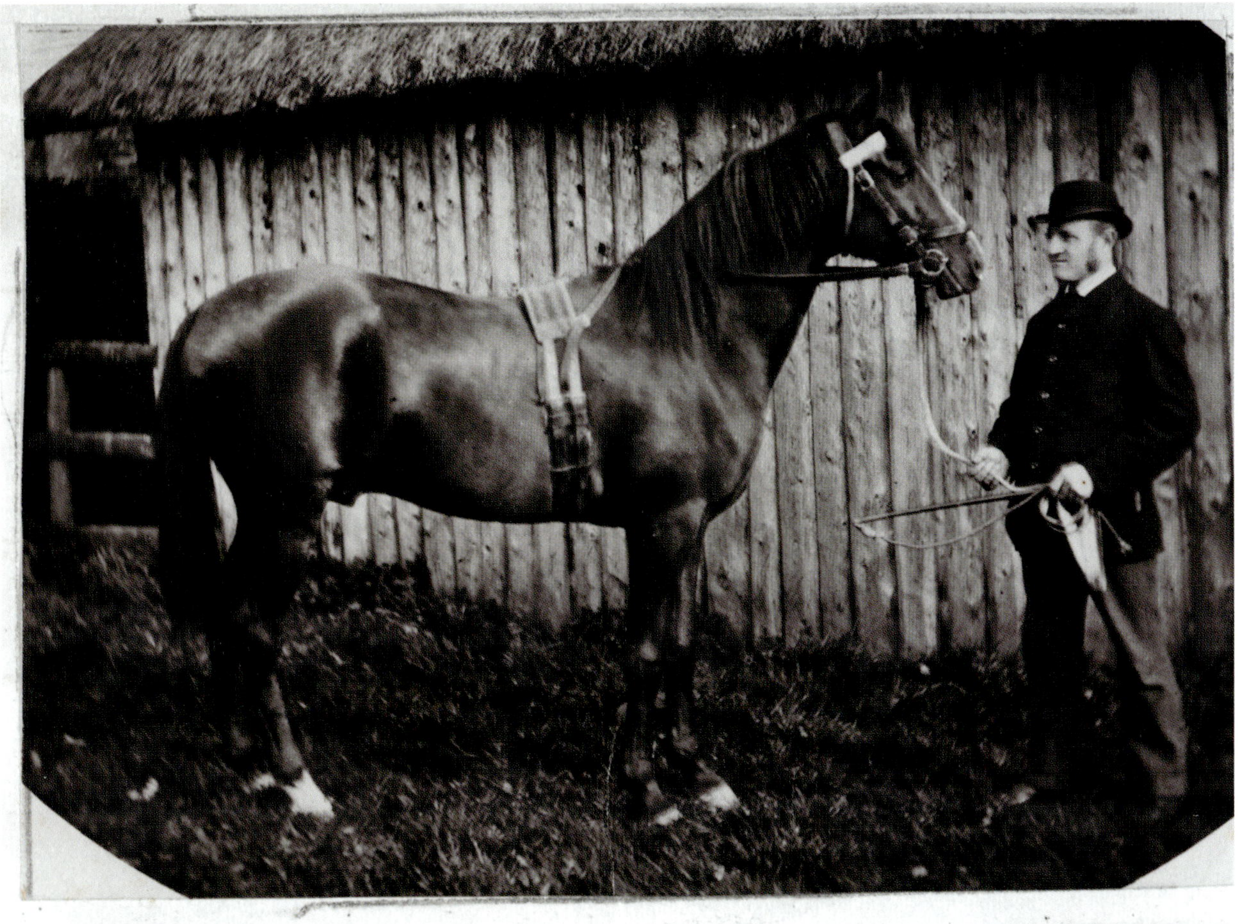

part of Wilfrid's inheritance following the death of his brother in 1872, and the Blunts had already established a small stud there before they had decided to breed pure Arabians.

Lady Anne kept her own accounts for the estate at Crabbet and her diaries are full of scribbled lists with calculations of feed (oats, hay, bran), straw and shoeing, harness, veterinary bills and labour. Perhaps as was to be expected of the daughter of the brilliant mathematician Ada Lovelace, she calculated every expense – so, in 1877, she noted that each horse or mare cost them seventeen shillings and fourpence-halfpenny per week in upkeep. Her exhaustive summaries of farm expenses included details of every kind, including monthly milk accounts with her pencil notes of consumption of butter cream and milk by dining room, nursery, kitchen, housekeeper's room and servants hall, and purchases of tools and equipment, all carefully itemised in her own hand. Naturally, the same minute attention to detail, essential as her money subsidised Wilfrid, was to be applied to recording the bloodlines of their Arabian horses and it was this which was to prove crucial in establishing the authenticity of the Crabbet stock for the future.

By the end of the year the stud numbered two stallions, nine mares and a foal.

Fig. 32
The dark bay colt Pharaoh with a groom. Pharoah was one of the Blunts' most important early acquisitions, and is shown here in 1881 shortly before his sale and export to Poland the following year.
British Library

Fig. 31
Wilfrid Scawan Blunt in Arab dress with his favourite horse, Sherifa, at Crabbet Park in 1883. Sherifa was a mare from the Nejd, purchased at Aleppo in 1878. Like many of their horses, she bore the scars of battle, in this case the mark of an old spear wound on her near quarter.
British Library

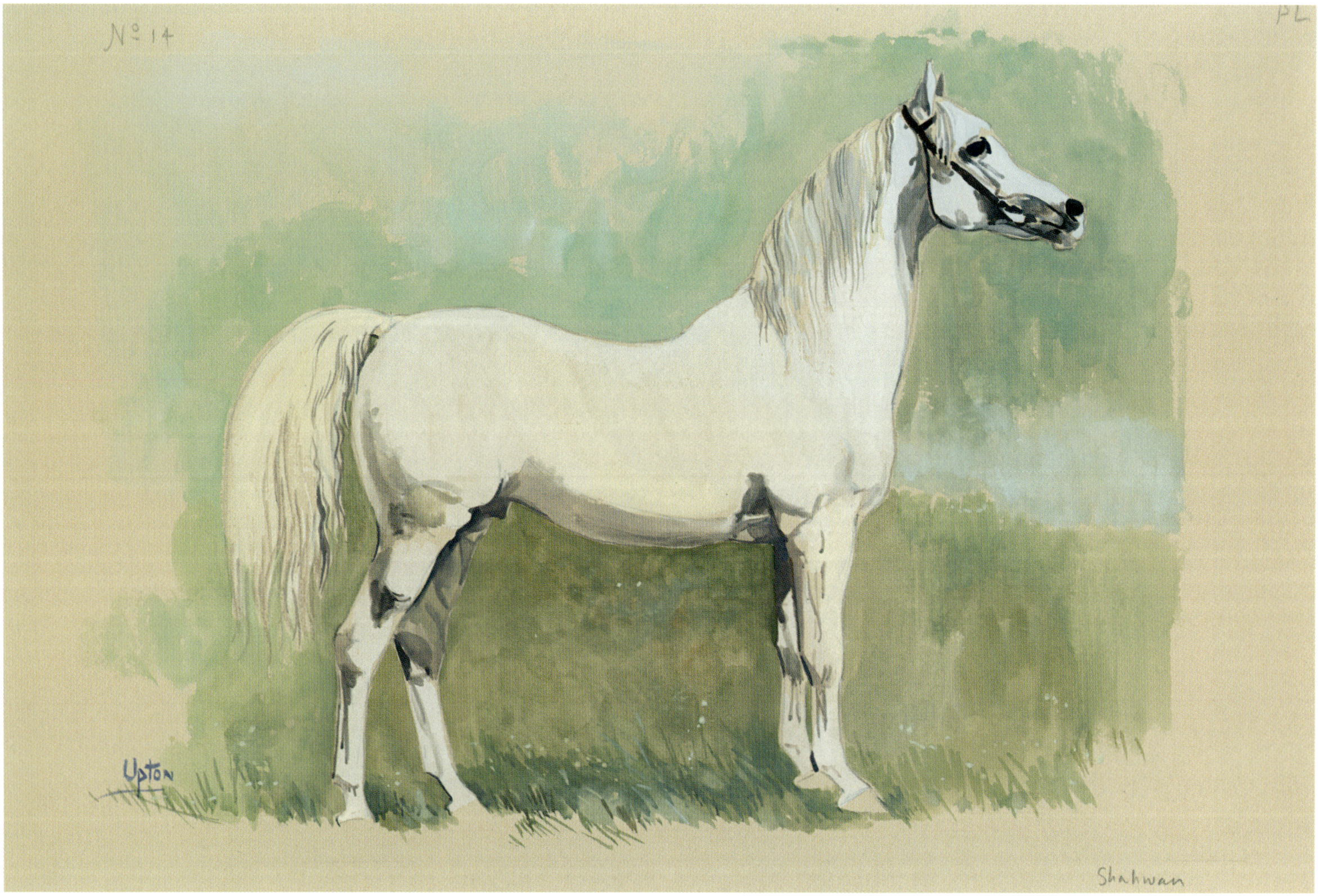

Fig. 33
Modern watercolour painting by Peter Upton of the grey horse named Shahwan by the Blunts. This product of the stud of Ali Pasha Sherif was bought in 1892. Lady Anne said it was the 'event of the day and indeed of the winter', and the horse had the 'unmistakable Ali Pasha Sherif stamp, so fine in all ways, beautiful shoulders with excellent action, tail erect in the air.'

The total cost of the purchase and transport of these first acquisitions was a little less than £2000. As Lady Anne later wrote:

> My view in having a stud of Arabians that it is a good action to preserve that pure blood somewhere else than in Arabia where as time passes it is more and more surrounded by dangers, and as to Egypt hitherto breeding has always fallen through. Though it need not.

All the initial mares were from the tribes of the Anazeh, except for Sherifa, a Nejd mare which had belonged to Saud ibn Saud, the emir of Riyadh. The Blunts were rigorous, ruthless in fact, in only breeding from the best of the descendants of their stock and in 1897, Wilfrid noted that they had preserved descendants from only five of the original mares of 1877–8 (Queen of Sheba, Basilisk, Dajania, Jerboa and Sherifa).

The Blunts recorded their stock in great detail, and the 'Old Stud List' includes details of the all-important pedigrees:

> Pharaoh bay colt (foaled in 1876) a Seglawi Obeyran of the Ibn Ed Derri purchased from Neddi Ibn Ed Derri of the Resallin (Sebaa Anazeh), his sire a Kehilan Ajuz of the Gomussa (Sebaa Anazeh) his dam's sire a Seqlawi Jedran of Obeyd el Belasi of the Roala (Ruwalla tribe). This strain of blood is considered the best now remaining to the Sebaa.

Pharaoh was one of the most important of the Blunts' early purchases. The transaction was arranged through Skene and made near Palmyra in 1878. The stallion's price was an astonishing £275, reflecting his evident quality. In 1882, when he was six, Pharaoh was sold at the first Crabbet auction when eleven Arabians were sold. He was bought by Count Potocki for 525 guineas, who took him to Poland, and in 1885 Pharoah was sold to the Imperial Russian state stud at Derkoul.

The Blunts' second expedition to the Middle East was to be far more ambitious. This was to the highlands of Nejd in the heart of Arabia itself, said to be the home of the finest Arabian horses and as Wilfrid wrote, 'in the imagination of the Bedouins of the North, is a region of romance, the cradle of their race, and of the ideas of chivalry by which they still live'. They started from Damascus in December 1878 and concluded at Bandar Bushehr in April 1879. At this date the Emir of Hail, Muhammed Ibn Rashid, was paramount in the Nejd and had the finest horses in his stables, many from the stud of Faisal ibn Saud, now displaced as overlord. The winter nights in the desert were cold and the way was hard and unforgiving though ample game of grouse, gazelle and camel gave Wilfrid opportunity to hunt. It was at this point they were attacked by raiders who broke Wilfrid's own gun over his head and struck Lady Anne with a lance before realizing they were under the protection of their ruler. Muhammed Ibn Rashid had a reputation for cold ruthlessness, but the Blunts were well received at Hail as guests of the emir in January 1879. There they stayed several days, finally seeing the famous horses from the royal stud, after some tantalizing delay, with Anne 'almost too excited to look' at the forty fine mares, eight stallions and their foals. Their objective achieved, and before their welcome should pale, they departed northwards with Persian pilgrims returning from Mecca to Meshed and then alone to Baghdad. From Baghdad, having received an invitation to visit Lord Lytton the Viceroy of India, they travelled the dangerous route overland to the Persian Gulf, overcoming brigands and sickness, before sailing to Karachi, only returning to Britain in July 1879. A single mare was bought on their second expedition, in Baghdad, but, failing the Blunt's rigorous criteria of quality, it was not kept beyond a few years.

Following these two initial expeditions, the Blunts travelled in Egypt in the winter of 1880, where they first saw the stud of Ali Sharif Pasha, Lady Anne recording the horses, anecdotes and pedigrees in great detail in her journal. A visit to Arabia had to be curtailed when Wilfrid fell ill at Jeddah, and following his recovery they made for Sinai and Syria, buying some more horses from the Anazeh tribes. Although already noting that there were far fewer good mares than they had seen before, one of their purchases was the mare Rodania, from which Wilfrid later said that, 'nearly everything of the best at Crabbet' was descended.

They returned to Crabbet in May 1881 and in February the following year they purchased the small walled garden of some thirty-seven acres with the tomb of Sheykh

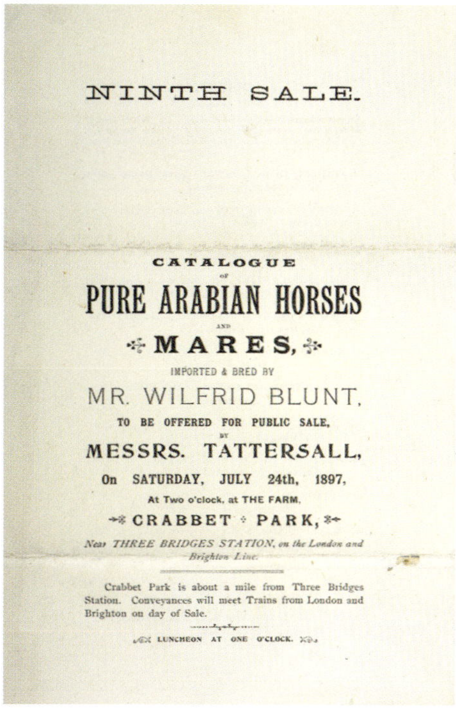
NINTH SALE.

CATALOGUE OF PURE ARABIAN HORSES AND MARES,

IMPORTED & BRED BY

MR. WILFRID BLUNT,

TO BE OFFERED FOR PUBLIC SALE, BY

MESSRS. TATTERSALL,

On SATURDAY, JULY 24th, 1897,

At Two o'clock, at THE FARM,

CRABBET PARK,

Near THREE BRIDGES STATION, on the London and Brighton Line.

Crabbet Park is about a mile from Three Bridges Station. Conveyances will meet Trains from London and Brighton on day of Sale.

LUNCHEON AT ONE O'CLOCK.

Fig. 34
Catalogue for the sale of pure Arabians at the Crabbet Stud in 1897. These were held every two years, with most of the sales going abroad. Wilfred's finances were often precarious, but Lady Anne susidised Crabbet's running costs and so the sales were not important for the money they raised. They were instead great social occasions which received considerable publicity, raising the profile of both the stud and the Arabian breed.
British Library

Obeyd on the edge of the desert nine miles north-east of Cairo, plus an extra fifteen acres outside the walls and a steam engine for irrigation for £1500. Here they planned to create a small Arabian stud in the Middle East itself but, typically, Wilfrid's outspoken support for the perceived outsider and for his own interpretation of anti-imperialism led him to agitate for the Egyptian nationalist cause. For this he was banned from Egypt for four years. After this, however, Sheykh Obeyd became their second home where they stayed most winters, receiving guests in Arab dress. Wilfrid and Lady Anne's last desert expedition together was launched from there in 1896, when they travelled between the Nile and Suez.

In Britain, Arabians were only valued for what they could contribute to other breeds and their own unique qualities were little appreciated. Even Captain Nolan, now known, if at all, as the doomed courier of the infamous confused order prompting the charge of the Light Brigade in the Crimea in 1854, but who was also the author of clear-sighted and influential works on horsemanship, thought Arabians of lesser practical use. So, though the Blunts' Arabian imports were widely noted, even appearing in *The General Stud Book* of 1881, the comment was only that 'A recent importation of Arabians from the believed Desert strains will, it is hoped, when the increase of size has been gained by training, feeding and acclimatization, give a valuable new line of blood from the original source of the English thorough-bred'.

The Blunts' work at Crabbet was of worldwide importance in maintaining the integrity of the Arabian breed. As Wilfrid emphasized, Crabbet's outstanding feature was that all of its original stock was of known pedigree and the majority of purebred Arabians today trace their lineage to the Crabbet stud. The Blunts would not buy any horses, no matter how fine, unless they could determine their exact breeding.

In this they followed in the footsteps of Muhammed Ali (1769–1849), Viceroy of Egypt, who had built up the Arabian stud later inherited by his successor Abbas Pasha I (1812–1854), the viceroy from 1848 to 1854. Abbas Pasha had sought the finest Arabian horses he could find, partly through the help of Faisal ibn Saud, and formed the most renowned Arabian stud of the time. According to the Blunts, writing in 1897, 'he ransacked the desert of Arabia and broke down, by the enormous prices he offered, the traditional refusal of the Bedouin breeders to part with their best mares'. Even a generation later, Lady Anne could still find Bedouin who well remembered these impositions: 'Salah ibn Rashid, a Bedouin Shammar spoke to me in Jan 1879 of how [he] made 3 journeys to Cairo with mares for Abbas.' The stud was partly dispersed following Abbas Pasha's assassination in 1854, but Ali Pasha Sherif, the son of the governor of Syria, acquired many of the horses and the stud still survived in the 1880s from which the Blunts eventually managed to obtain some of their most significant stock. The desert-bred horses originally acquired by the Blunts were eventually crossed with the stock purchased from Ali Pasha Sherif, the first of which came to Crabbet in 1891: the stallions Mesaoud and Merzuk and mares Sobha, Safra and Khatila. Additional stock was purchased in 1897, 1898 and 1904 (another three stallions and eight mares, with the descendants of the stallion Shahwan kept for breeding), with Ali Pasha Sherif mares kept both at Crabbet and at Sheykh Obeyd.

Wilfrid's tempestuous character and his constant, destructive affairs and indiscretions led finally to the Blunts' separation in 1906, with Lady Anne keeping Crabbet Park

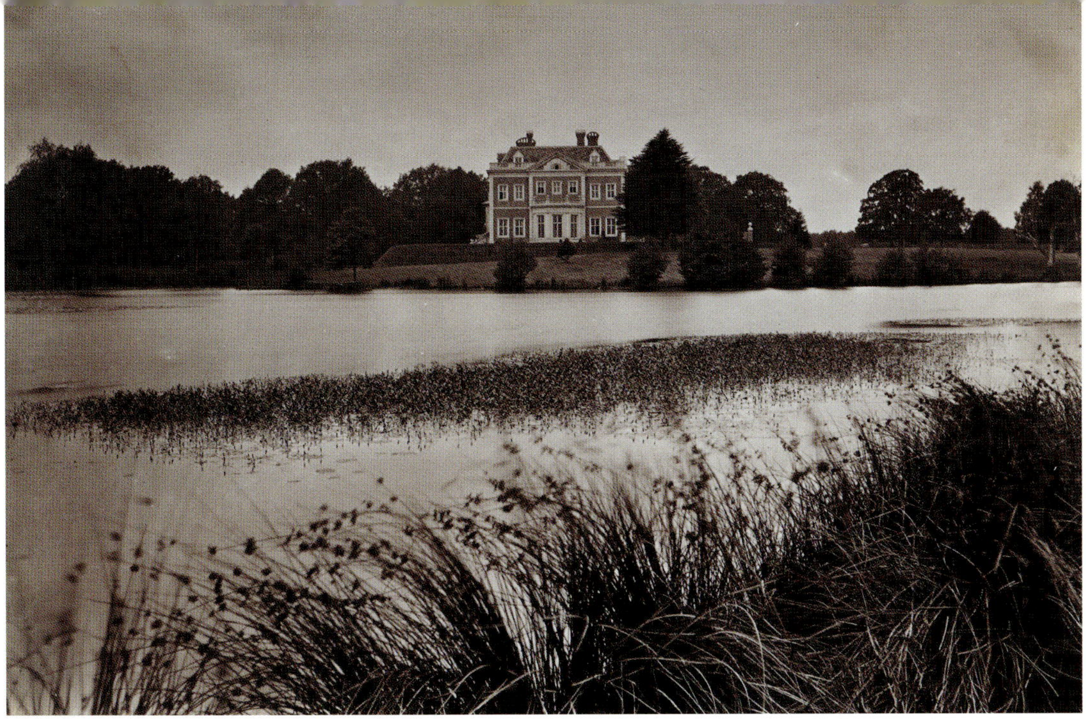

Fig. 35
The rebuilt Crabbet House near Crawley in Sussex, home of Wilfrid Blunt and Lady Anne Blunt. In this photograph, taken in 1876, the house is seen from the east across the lake in Crabbet Park. The house has now been converted into offices.
British Library

and half the horses, following which she retired to Sheykh Obeyd in Cairo, where she died in 1917. Their only child, Judith Lady Wentworth, inherited the Crabbet stud after a bitter legal dispute with Wilfrid. Until her death in 1957 the stud thrived as never before – some ninety per cent of purebred Arabians today trace their lineage to Crabbet Park and it was of worldwide importance in maintaining the integrity of the breed. A charming account of life and work at Crabbet Park House and Arabian Stud during this time is given in the dictated memoirs of Fred Rice who started work there just after the First World War and rose to become head groom. It emerges that Lady Wentworth was much admired by her staff and greatly respected for her knowledge of horses (though perhaps lacking Lady Anne's scholarly depth). Upon Lady Wentworth's death in 1957, the stud passed to her manager, Cecil Covey and then to his son, who ran Crabbet until 1971, when the building of a motorway divided the property and finally forced its closure.

There is no doubt that the Blunts made a significant contribution to the history of horse breeding in Britain. They were also successful in promoting the Arabian breed and preserving its purity. At this distance in time, it is difficult to say which of the couple deserves the greater credit for these achievements. The picture is also obscured by Lady Wentworth's fierce championship of her mother at the expense of her father: 'Her devotion to this brilliant but wayward being is a record of self-sacrifice and self-effacement which will be dealt with one day ... His tyranny and spirit of discord eventually alienated him from his family, from most of his friends and from several countries.' Although she was clearly biased, however, it has to be admitted that by all accounts Wilfrid Blunt was a complex, self-centered and overbearing man, at times extremely difficult, ruthless and unpleasant. Perhaps for an evaluation of their respective contributions, we should leave the last word to Lady Anne's biographer Howard Winstone: 'In her [Lady Anne's] command of languages, her assessments of Arab notables and the oral history of the tribes, and her marshalling of facts and sources of information on horse genealogy and breeding, she was vastly his [Wilfrid's] superior and was greatly assisted by single-mindedness and the absence of preconceptions.'[3]

CHAPTER 5

THE HORSE IN MODERN BRITAIN

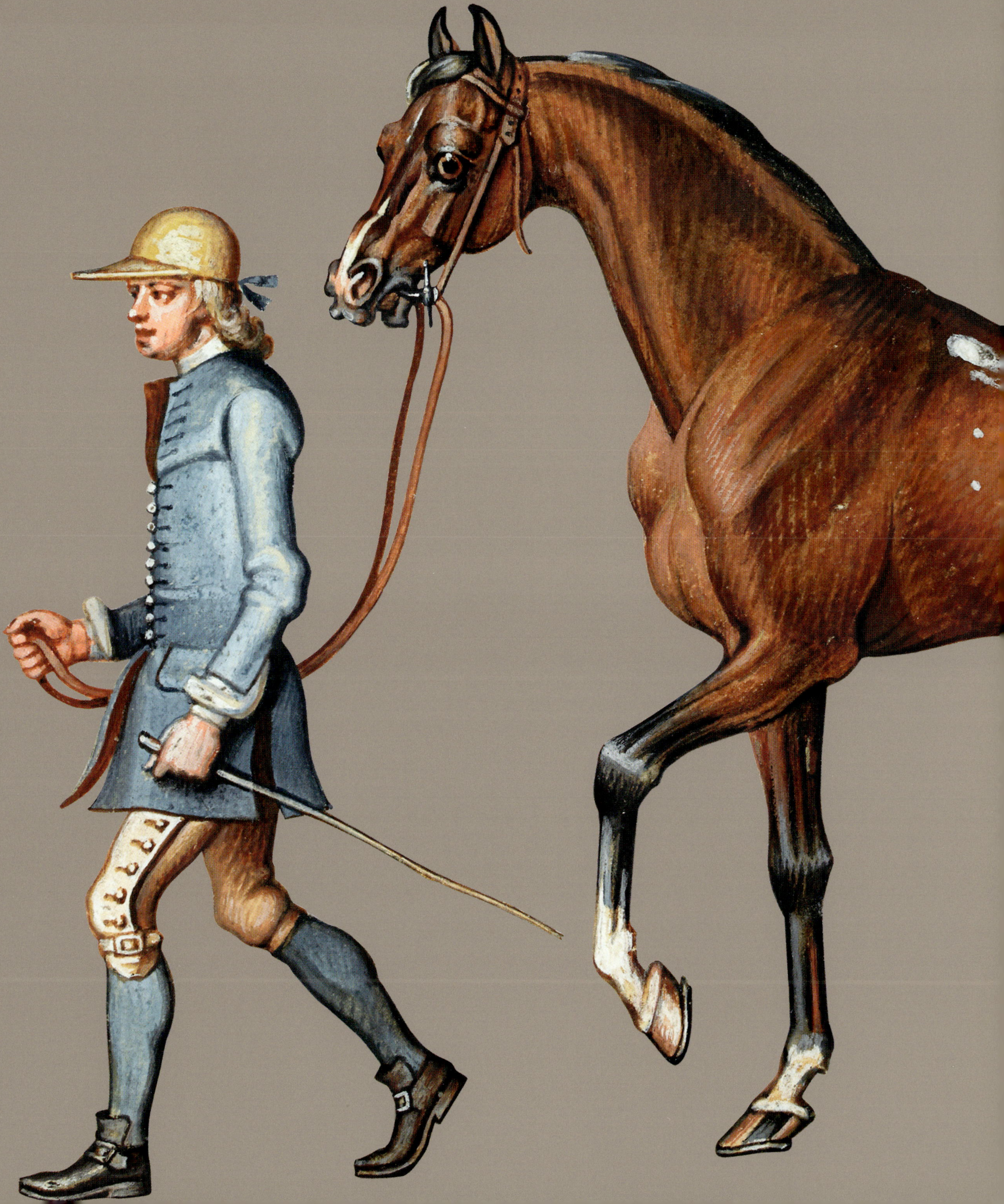

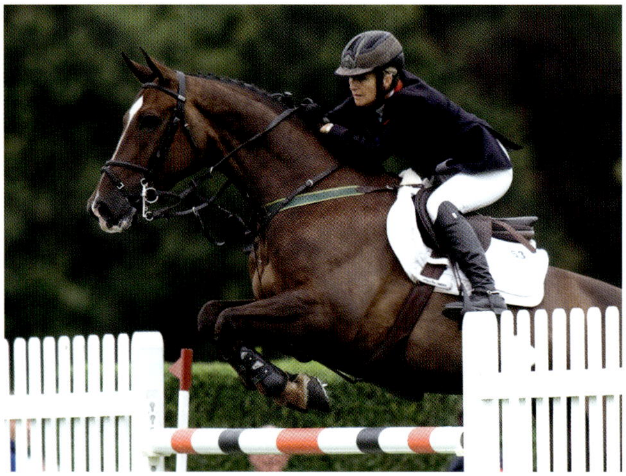

The horse in modern Britain

ABOVE
Fig. 36
Tina Fletcher riding Hallo Sailor as part of Great Britain's winning show jumping team in the Meydan FEI Nations Cup during the Longines Royal International Horse Show at Hickstead, England, on 30 July 2010.

Fig. 37
Painting by Sir Anthony Van Dyck dated 1633 and entitled *Charles I with M. de St Antoine*, a preparatory sketch for which is cat. 201. This fine equestrian portrait was commissioned by Charles himself and was on an unprecedented scale. The king is shown on a magnificent grey horse, with a fine head and flowing mane. Skilled horsemanship has long been regarded as the embodiment of excellence. Beside the king is Pierre Antoine Bourdin, Seigner de St Antoine, who was a master in the art of horsemanship.
The Royal Collection

SO FAR, we have reviewed the history of horses in the Middle East and in Arabia to establish the context from which the Arabian horse emerged. Our intention now is to describe the introduction of the Arabian horse into Britain from the seventeenth century onwards and the role it played in the creation of the Thoroughbred. But first, by way of background, it may be useful to consider briefly the importance of the horse in British military, social and economic history since the Norman Conquest.

The importance of horses in warfare in England was first recognized at the Battle of Hastings in 1066, when Norman knights on horseback finally broke through the wall of shields surrounding King Harold. The military significance of the mounted soldier remained undiminished until the age of mechanization and the introduction of artillery and the machine gun. Already in the reign of Edward I (1272–1307) there was a royal stud importing horses from Spain.

By the end of the medieval period changes in military technology, particularly the development of firearms, meant that the focus of breeding shifted from heavy, powerful warhorses to lighter, more nimble animals. From the reign of Henry VIII onwards there were many government instructions aimed at breeding suitable horses for warfare. As

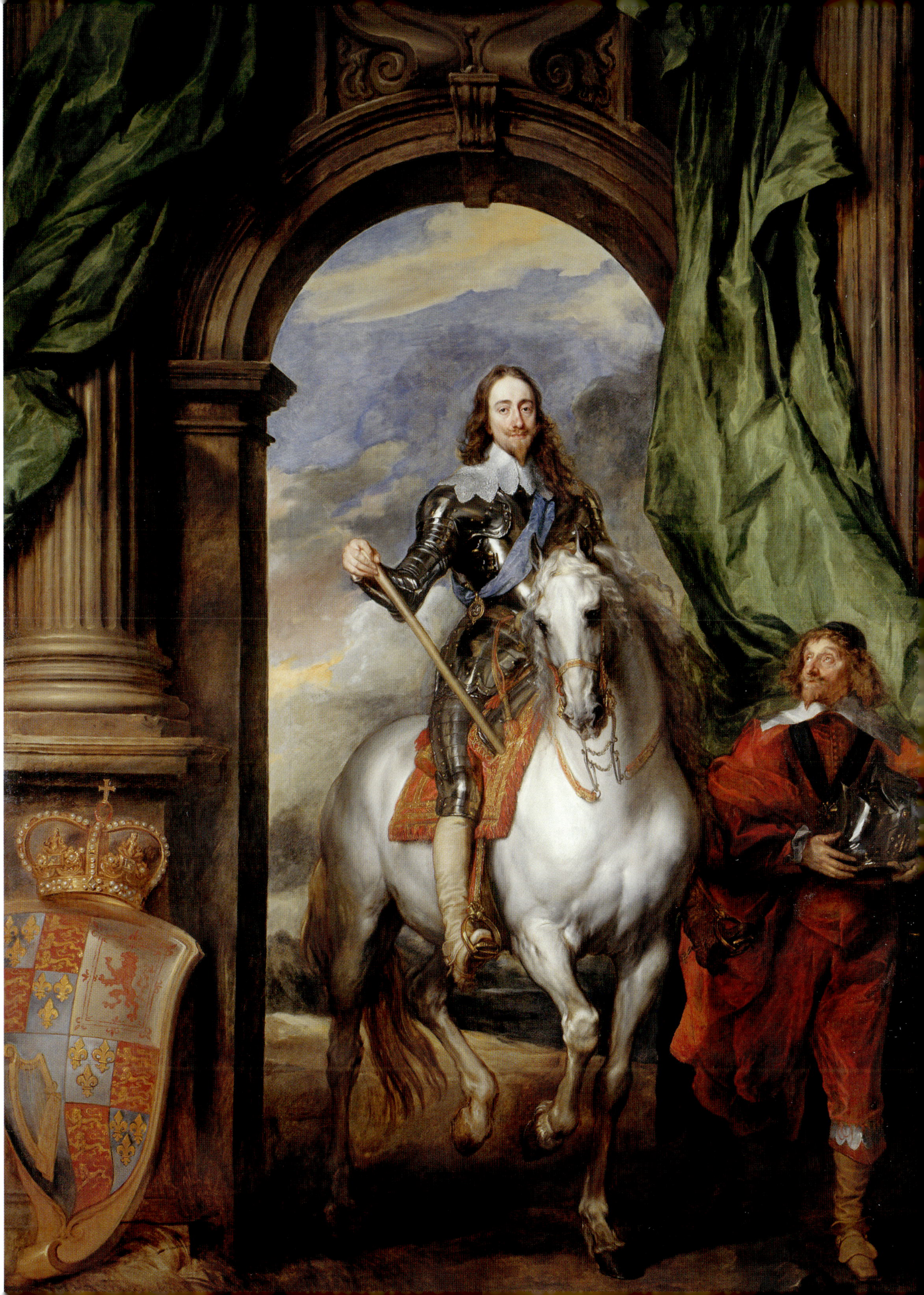

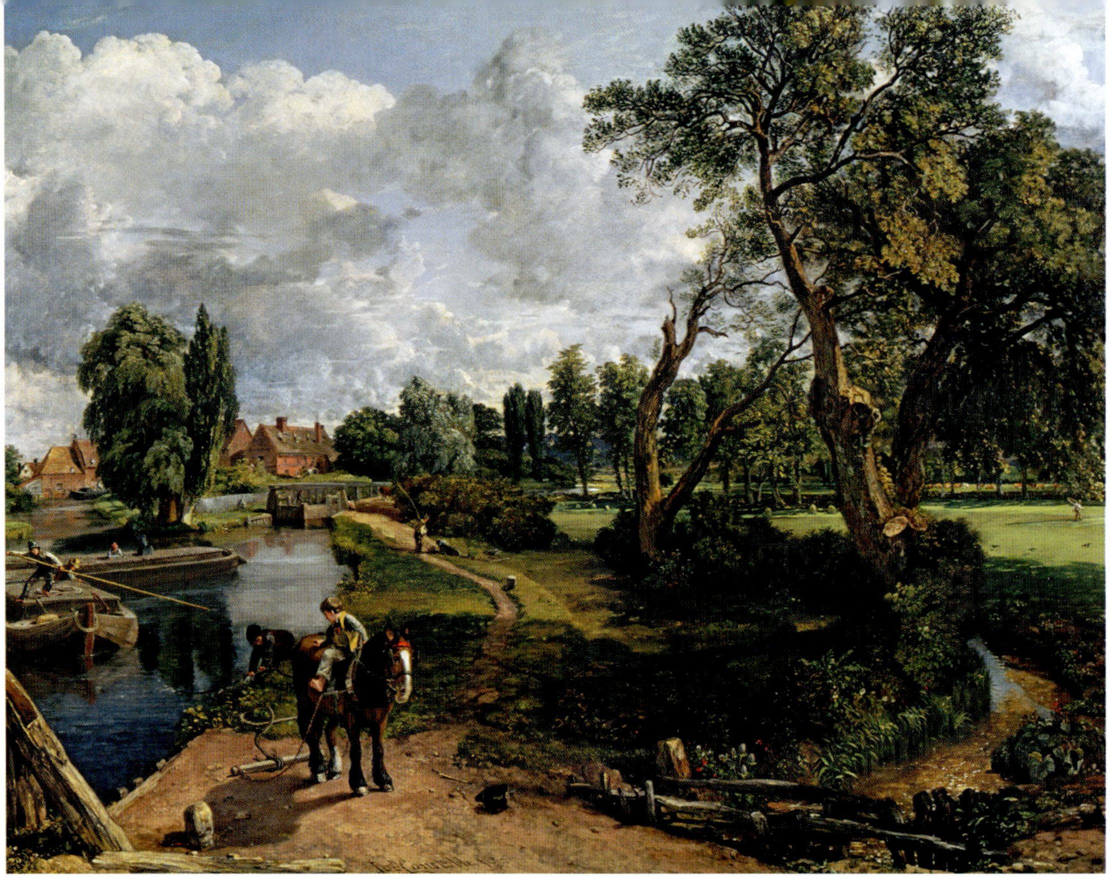

Fig. 38
Flatford Mill (Scene on a Navigable River), a bucolic scene painted by Constable in 1816–17, shows a pair of barges being pulled along the canal by a towing-horse. The barges are about to be disconnected so that they can be poled under Flatford bridge. Horses, ponies and mules were all used to pull barges and narrow boats along canals throughout Britain. This was very much more efficient that pulling carts via roads, but after the Industrial Revolution barges were widely replaced by the use of railways and steam-powered boats. Despite this, horses were still used to tow boats commercially until well into the twentieth century.
Tate Britain

well as importing breeding stock from Europe, Henry established royal studs at Hampton Court, Eltham, Tutbury and Malmesbury. Much of this progress was lost with the dispersal of the royal studs during the English Civil War, but in the Commonwealth and later during the Restoration, official efforts were made to import horses from the Middle East. Britain could never match the sheer quantity of cavalry forces of the European powers with their expansive areas of land for grazing, but British horses were of high quality and for the most part ably supported British infantry through the wars of the eighteenth and early nineteenth centuries. At the Battle of Waterloo in 1815, for example, a charge by two British cavalry brigades was instrumental in holding up the advance of the French infantry at a crucial moment in the confrontation. In the nineteenth century, cavalrymen particularly in India were encouraged to improve their skills through 'sports' such as horse racing, polo, tent-pegging, pig sticking and fox hunting. The close link between equestrian sports enjoyed by young country gentlemen and what might be required in a war are well demonstrated in Siegfried Sassoon's classic book *Memoirs of a Fox-Hunting Man* (1928). It is estimated that in the First World War about six million horses were used by both sides, but by this time they were mainly employed to transport supplies and ammunition and haul guns. The fictional life of one such horse, requisitioned for war service, is portrayed in the book *War Horse* by Michael Morpurgo (1982), now adapted as a very successful stage play and more recently as a film by Steven Spielberg. Although 'Joey', the subject of the story, was repatriated to Britain after the war, many others were left behind, sometimes in appalling circumstances. This led to the foundation of charities such as The Brooke, a charity for working horses, donkeys and mules that was started in Egypt in 1934 by Dorothy Brooke to rescue horses including Thoroughbreds that had been left behind in Egypt after the Palestine campaign and were working in harsh conditions. Other existing charities also came to the aid of these abandoned horses, such as the Royal Society for the Prevention of Cruelty to Animals (RSPCA) founded in 1824 and the Blue Cross Animal Charity (originally called 'Our Dumb Friends League') founded in 1897 to help working horses in London.

From an early period horses were also an important means of transport, whether for armies or for individuals. Great distances could actually be covered surprisingly quickly on horseback. For example, Sir Robert Carey was able to ride from London to Edinburgh (with changes of horses) in three days to inform James VI of Scotland about the death of Elizabeth I in 1603. Stage coaches were introduced from the middle of the sixteenth century onwards, but because of the poor state of the roads they were generally unreliable until the early nineteenth century. In towns and cites, horses pulled omnibuses and cabs, and the rise in the number of harness horses seemed inexorable by the late nineteenth century.

In agriculture, horses displaced oxen for ploughing and were used extensively to pull carts and wagons, and for carrying loads, and increasingly from the Elizabethan period onwards, horses were used in industry. For example, in coal mines pit ponies were used underground, and horses pulled canal barges. So great was the need for horses with the burgeoning economy in the nineteenth century that the number of horses in Britain increased from just over one million in 1811 to over three million in 1901.

Activities involving the horse were so varied that different qualities were required for each of them. For example, farm horses had to be big and powerful, while racehorses had to be swift and sleek. This led to the introduction of selective breeding programmes and the importation of horses, from Europe, the Middle East and North Africa.

In view of their importance for military, economic, and social purposes, it is scarcely surprising that horses should feature largely in the literature of the sixteenth and seventeenth centuries, both in terms of describing the ideal horse and extolling its virtues. Thus, in *Venus and Adonis*, Shakespeare described the ideal horse as follows:

> Round-hoof'd, short-jointed, fetlocks shag and long,
> Broad breast, full eye, small head, and nostril wide,
> High crest, short ears, straight legs and passing strong,
> Thin mane, thick tail, broad buttock, tender hide:
> Look, what a horse should have he did not lack,
> Save a proud rider on so proud a back.

Admiration for the horse is also expressed by the Dauphin in *Henry V*:

> I will not change my horse with any that treads.
> He bounds from the earth;
> When I bestride him, I soar, I am a hawk.
> He trots the air; the earth sings when he touches it.
> The basest horn of his hoof is more musical that the pipe of Hermes.
> He's of the colour of the nutmeg and of the heart of the ginger.
> He is pure air and fire, and the dull elements

of earth and water never appear in him,
but only in patient stillness while his rider mounts him ...
His neigh is like the bidding of a monarch,
and his countenance enforces homage.

Sometimes this eulogizing of the horse is taken to ridiculous lengths, as noted by Shakespeare in *The Merchant of Venice*: 'He doth nothing but talk of his horse' (1.2.10).

This close bond with the horse is all the more remarkable in that before the eighteenth century in England there was little if any concern for animal welfare in general. The horse was an exception largely because he was indispensable. Admiration for the horse continued unabated after the time of Shakespeare. In his poem 'Retirement' published in 1782 William Cowper (1731–1800) wrote of 'poor Jack' who 'Lived in the saddle, loved the chase, the course,/And always, ere he mounted, kissed his horse'. This love affair with the horse was taken to extreme lengths in the nineteenth century with sentimental works such as *Black Beauty* by Anna Sewell (1877).

In the eighteenth century, the thriving economy and increasing amount of leisure time for the well-off meant that wealthy landowners could indulge their passions for hunting, recreational riding and horse racing. Horses became an indicator of social status, and there was much competition to own the most and the best horses. Hand in hand with this development came a desire to record these horses, their setting and their owners for posterity. Foremost amongst the painters whose services were in much demand was George Stubbs (1724–1806). His careful studies of the animal, reflected in his *Anatomy of the Horse*, published in London in 1766 with eighteen plates engraved by Stubbs from his own drawings (cat. 217), set him apart from other contemporary painters. However, it is only in the last forty years that his true genius has been recognized. In the 1790s Stubbs enjoyed the patronage of the Prince of Wales, and painted a number of portraits of people in his circle with their horses, including Lady Lade on a rearing horse (cat. 204). Her husband, Sir John Lade, was renowned as the fastest four-in-hand driver between London and Brighton.

Horse racing had in fact been popular from at least the late Elizabethan period onwards, and its patronage by the royal family led to its becoming known as 'the sport of kings'. The Stuart kings James I (1603–1625), Charles I (1625–1649) and Charles II (1660–1685) were all interested in horse racing, and it was during their time, particularly in the reign of Charles II, that the town of Newmarket in Suffolk became a centre for horse racing. The Newmarket racecourse known as the Rowley Mile is named after Charles II's favourite black stallion Old Rowley. At first the races often involved just two horses, but with the formation of the Jockey Club in 1750 sets of rules were drawn up and modern horse racing gradually came into existence. In Britain there are five so-called 'classic' races, the St Leger Stakes (founded Doncaster 1776), the Oaks Stakes (1779) and the Derby (1780), both run on Epsom Downs, and the 2000 Guineas (1809) and the 1000 Guineas (1814), both run over the Rowley Mile at Newmarket.

The desire to produce champion racehorses led to the development of a horse breed known as the Thoroughbred. This breed was developed in seventeenth- and eighteenth-century England when imported oriental stallions were bred with native mares. The great contribution to the Thoroughbred of these native British and Irish mares has

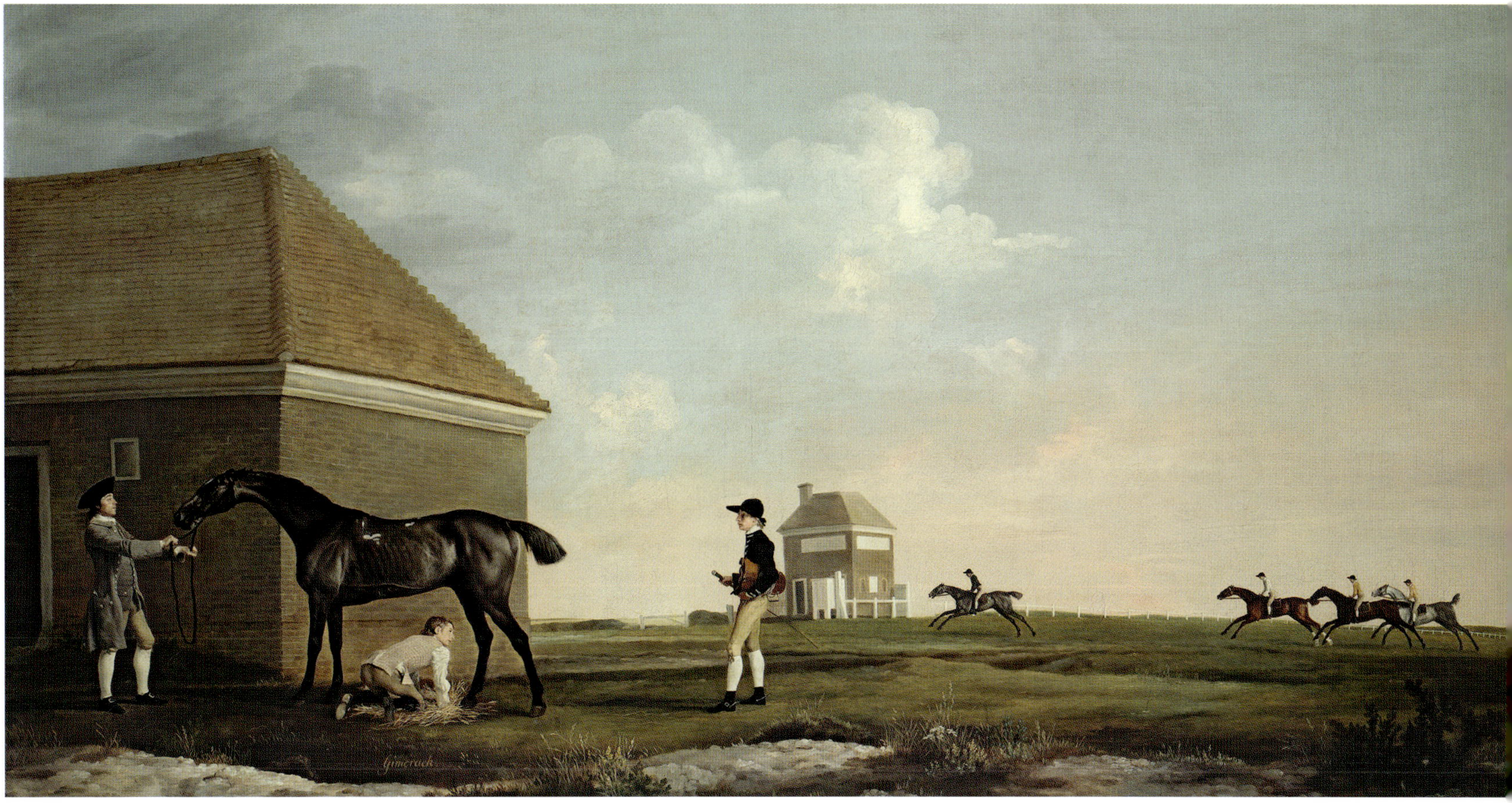

recently been confirmed by DNA analysis. It has even been suggested (although not yet conclusively proved) that the speed gene present in the Thoroughbred may have derived from the Shetland pony. However that may be, the combination of oriental stallions with native British mares proved to be unbeatable. After the development of the breed, Thoroughbreds were exported all around the world, including to Europe and the USA. Only Thoroughbred horses are allowed to take part in Thoroughbred horse racing.

It is sometimes claimed it was James I (1603–1625) himself who had the idea of covering native mares with imported oriental stallions to produce better racehorses. This story is probably apocryphal, but oriental horses (mostly stallions) were certainly already being imported in his time. In fact, more than two hundred oriental horses (called variously Arabians, Barbs and Turks) are listed in the ancestry of the British Thoroughbred between 1614 and 1815. However, all modern Thoroughbreds trace their pedigrees back to just three stallions known as the foundation sires, two of which and possibly all three were Arabians. They are the Byerley Turk, the Darley Arabian and the Godolphin Arabian. The dark brown stallion known as the Byerley Turk (d. 1706) was named after Captain Robert Byerley. According to one tradition, the horse was captured from Ottoman troops at the Battle of Buda in Hungary in 1686 between Turkey and the Holy League. It is equally possible, however, that the horse was purchased by Captain Byerley in London after it had been imported following the relief of Vienna in 1683. However that may be, the horse was used by Byerley when he fought for William of Orange at the Battle of the

Fig. 39
Gimcrack on Newmarket Heath, with a Trainer, a Stable-Lad and a Jockey, by George Stubbs, dates from 1765 and depicts the famous racehorse Gimcrack in two scenes. On the left he is shown outside one of the rubbing-down houses at Newmarket, while on the right he is seen winning a race. The horses are shown galloping with all four of their legs outstretched, a common artistic inaccuracy before the true gait of horses was revealed through photography. This painting was sold at auction in 2011 for £22.4 million, a record for a Stubbs painting.
Private collection

Boyne in Ireland in 1690. In 1697 the Byerley Turk was retired to stud at Goldsborough Hall in North Yorkshire. Although relatively few modern Thoroughbreds trace their line back to the Byerley Turk, the famous eighteenth-century stallion Herod, also known as a founding sire, is descended from him.

The Darley Arabian (d. 1733) was a bay horse bought in Aleppo in Syria in 1702 by Thomas Darley (b. 1664), British consul to the Levant. Writing home to his brother in England, Darley described the horse as 'immediately striking owing to his handsome appearance and exceedingly elegant carriage'. He never raced, but covered mares at Aldby Park in Yorkshire between 1705 and 1719. Amongst the descendants of the Darley Arabian was the famous horse Eclipse (1766–1789), not only unbeaten in nineteen races but also a notable sire. His success on the racecourse gave rise to the phrase 'eclipse first and the rest nowhere'. He is another of the later foundation sires. Amongst the progeny of Eclipse was Pot-8-os, another very successful racehorse. It is estimated that around ninety-five percent of modern Thoroughbreds can trace their blood-lines back to the Darley Arabian, due in large part no doubt to the unrivalled success of Eclipse.

The Godolphin Arabian, a 'gold-touched bay', was imported from France in 1729 by Edward Coke (*c.* 1701–1733) of Longford Hall in Derbyshire. The earlier history of this horse is not clear, but according to one tradition he was originally brought from Syria to

Fig. 40
Simplified chart showing a selection of bloodlines traced back to the Darley Arabian, one of three founding sires of the Thoroughbred breed. The majority of Thoroughbreds today trace their line back to the Darley Arabian, whose descendants include the famous Eclipse.

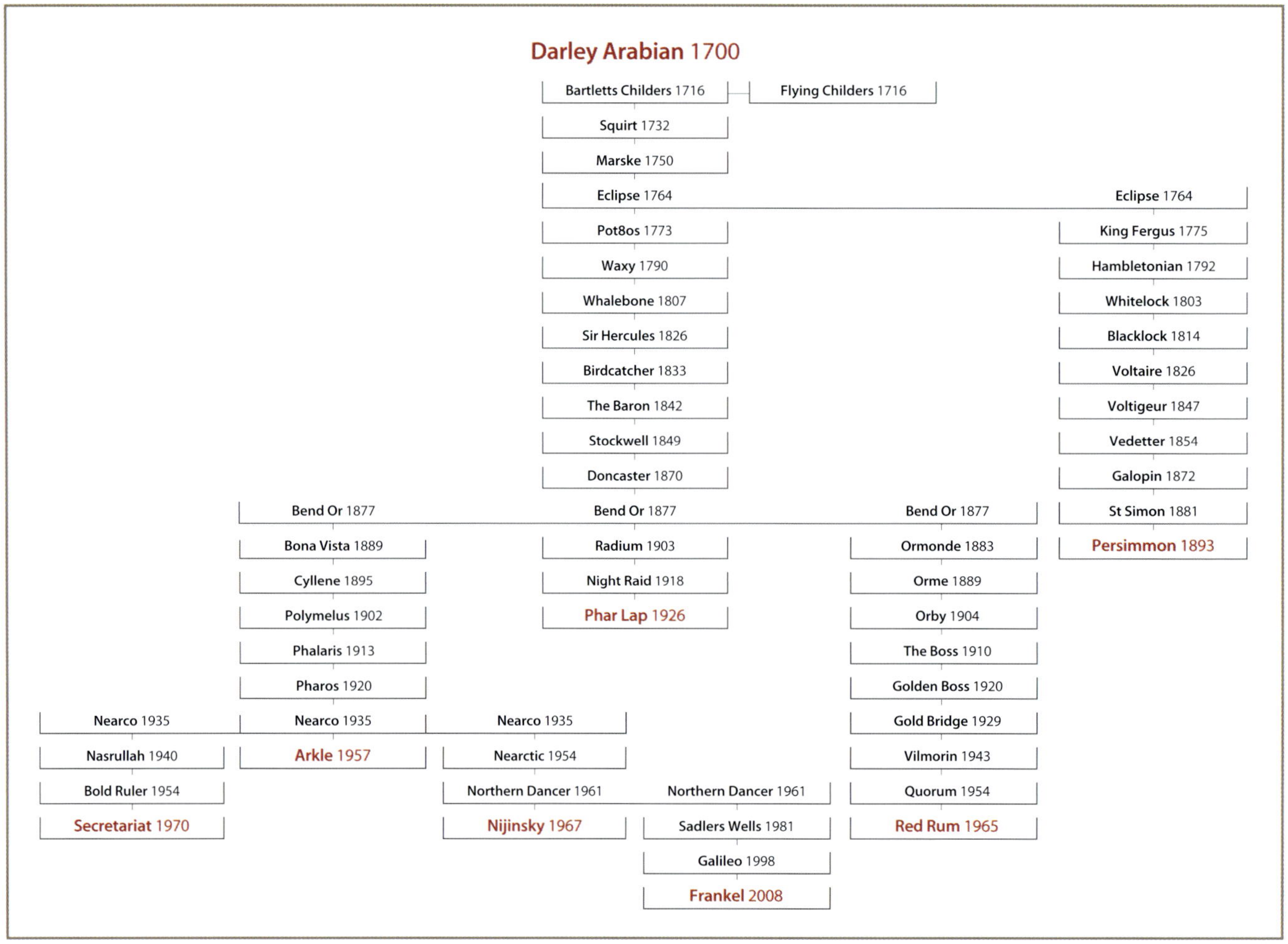

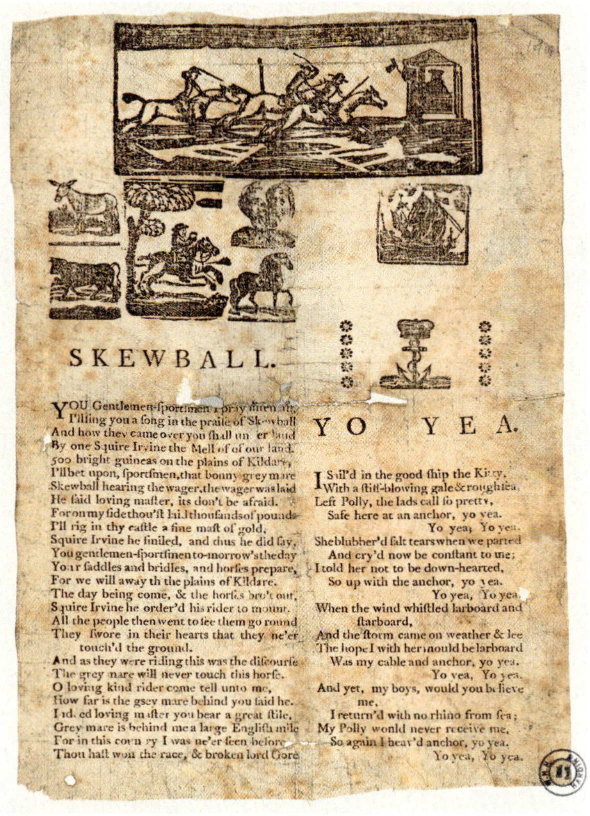

SKEWBALL.

YOU Gentlemen-ſportſmen I pray liſten all,
I'll ſing you a ſong in the praiſe of Skewball
And how they came over you ſhall under ſtand
By one Squire Irvine the Mell of of our land.
500 bright guineas on the plains of Kildare,
I'll bet upon, ſportſmen, that bonny grey mare
Skewball hearing the wager, the wager was laid
He ſaid loving maſter, its don't be afraid.
For on my ſide thou'ſt laid thouſands of pounds
I'll rig in thy caſtle a fine maſt of gold,
Squire Irvine he ſmiled, and thus he did ſay,
You gentlemen-ſportſmen to-morrow's the day
Your ſaddles and bridles, and horſes prepare,
For we will away th the plains of Kildare.
The day being come, & the horſes bro't out,
Squire Irvine he order'd his rider to mount.
All the people then went to ſee them go round
They ſwore in their hearts that they ne'er
touch'd the ground.
And as they were riding this was the diſcourſe
The grey mare will never touch this horſe.
O loving kind rider come tell unto me,
How far is the grey mare behind you ſaid he.
Indeed loving maſter you bear a great ſtile,
Grey mare is behind me a large Engliſh mile
For in this country I was ne'er ſeen before
Thou haſt won the race, & broken lord Gore

YO YEA.

I Sail'd in the good ſhip the Kitty,
With a ſtiff-blowing gale & rough ſea,
Left Polly, the lads call ſo pretty,
Safe here at an anchor, yo yea.
Yo yea, Yo yea.
She blubber'd ſalt tears when we parted
And cry'd now be conſtant to me;
I told her not to be down-hearted,
So up with the anchor, yo yea.
Yo yea, Yo yea.
When the wind whiſtled larboard and
ſtarboard,
And the ſtorm came on weather & lee
The hope I with her ſhould be larboard
Was my cable and anchor, yo yea.
Yo yea, Yo yea.
And yet, my boys, would you believe
me,
I return'd with no rhino from ſea;
My Polly would never receive me,
So again I heav'd anchor, yo yea.
Yo yea, Yo yea.

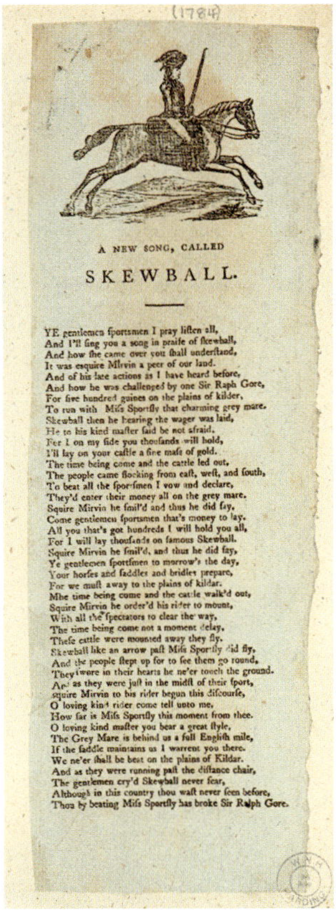

(1784)

A NEW SONG, CALLED

SKEWBALL.

YE gentlemen ſportsmen I pray liſten all,
And I'll ſing you a song in praiſe of ſkewball,
And how ſhe came over you ſhall underſtand,
It was esquire Mirvin a peer of our land.
And of his late actions as I have heard before,
And how he was challenged by one Sir Raph Gore,
For five hundred guines on the plains of kilder,
To run with Miſs Sportſly that charming grey mare.
Skewball then he hearing the wager was laid,
He to his kind maſter ſaid be not afraid.
For I on my ſide you thouſands will hold,
I'll lay on your caſtle a fine maſe of gold.
The time being come and the cattle led out,
The people came flocking from eaſt, weſt, and ſouth,
To beat all the ſportſmen I vow and declare,
They'd enter their money all on the grey mare.
Squire Mirvin he ſmil'd and thus he did ſay,
Come gentlemen ſportsmen that's money to lay.
All you that's got hundreds I will hold you all,
For I will lay thouſands on famous Skewball.
Squire Mirvin he ſmil'd, and thus he did ſay,
Ye gentlemen ſportſmen to morrow's the day,
Your horſes and ſaddles and bridles prepare,
For we muſt away to the plains of kildar.
Mhe time being come and the cattle walk'd out,
Squire Mirvin he order'd his rider to mount,
With all the ſpectators to clear the way,
The time being come not a moment delay.
Theſe cattle were mounted away they fly.
Skewball like an arrow paſt Miſs Sportſly did fly,
And the people ſtept up for to ſee them go round,
They ſwore in their hearts he ne'er touch the ground.
And as they were juſt in the midſt of their ſport,
squire Mirvin to his rider begun this diſcourſe,
O loving kind rider come tell unto me,
How far is Miſs Sportſly this moment from thee.
O loving kind maſter you bear a great ſtyle,
The Grey Mare is behind us a full Engliſh mile,
If the ſaddle maintains us I warrent you there.
We ne'er ſhall be beat on the plains of Kildar.
And as they were running paſt the diſtance chair,
The gentlemen cry'd Skewball never fear,
Although in this country thou waſt never ſeen before,
Thou by beating Miſs Sportſly has broke Sir Ralph Gore.

Fig. 41
Broadsheet featuring a song about Skewball. The new breed of Thoroughbred was not only widely feted in the visual arts, through portraiture, sporting print and graphic satire. Famous horses and races also featured in popular song in the eighteenth century. These broadsides, cheaply printed sheets of songs, here decorated with stock woodcuts, celebrate Skewball (sired by Godolphin Arabian in 1740) and his famous victory at the Curragh in Kildare, Ireland. The race was already a generation past by the time the sheets were printed, but the song evidently remained popular, crossing the Atlantic as 'Stewball', and survived in Britain as a folk song until the present day when taken up again in the folk revival of the 1960s.
Bodleian Library

Fig. 42
George IV when Prince of Wales (1791) by George Stubbs shows the Prince of Wales (later George IV) riding in Hyde Park, looking over the Serpentine towards Apsley House and Westminster Abbey. The prince rides a magnificent chestnut horse preceded by two dogs. He wears a blue frock coat on which is pinned the Start of the Garter, with buff breeches and a tall hat. This painting was commissioned by the Prince of Wales himself.
The Royal Collection

Tunis, where he was presented to the King of France by the Bey of Tunis. He is also known as 'the Godolphin Barb', reflecting his possible origins in or passage through Tunisia on the Barbary Coast. After the death of Edward Coke in 1733, he was taken to the stud of the 2nd Earl of Godolphin at Babraham, Cambridgeshire, where he remained until his death in 1753. He was described by the veterinary surgeon William Osmer, writing in 1756, in the following glowing terms: 'There never was a horse … so well entitled to get racers as the Godolphin Arabian … his shoulders were deeper, and lay farther into his back, than those of any horse yet seen. Behind the shoulders, there was but a very small space ere the muscles of his loins rose exceedingly high, broad, and expanded, which were inserted into his quarters with greater strength and power than in any horse I believe ever yet seen of his dimensions, viz fifteen hands high.'[1] It had not been intended to use the Godolphin Arabian for breeding purposes, but a union with the mare Lady Roxana, after she had rejected another stallion, led first to the famous colt Lath and then in turn Cade and Regulus. All became champion racehorses, and sired many horses. Amongst them were Matchem, a son of Cade, who is also regarded as one of the later foundation sires.

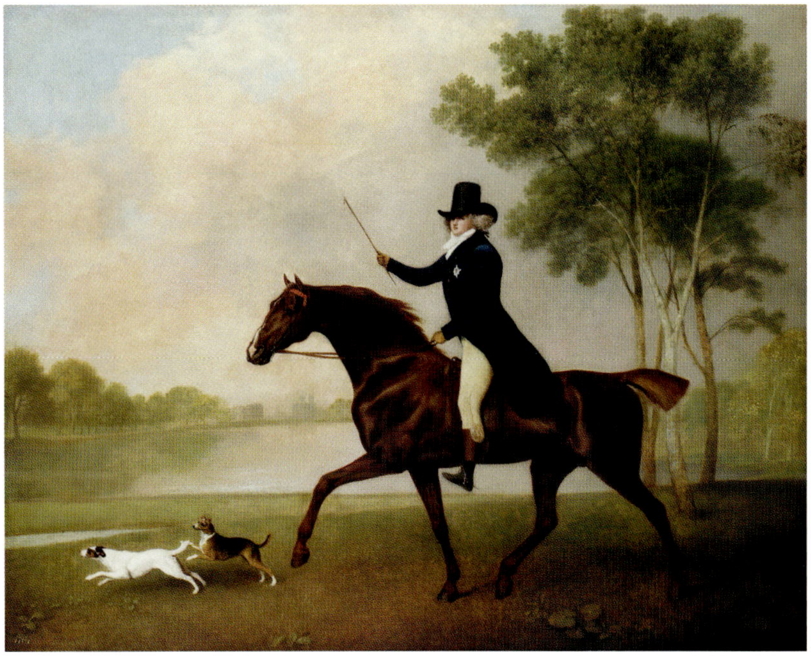

Although our purpose here is to trace the history of the horse in modern Britain, and the development there of the Thoroughbred, it should be noted that in France, too, there was much interest in the possible benefits of covering native mares with oriental stallions. This is hardly surprising as the merits of the oriental horse were known to both countries from the time of the crusades onwards. Napoleon was a great admirer of oriental horses, and himself often rode a grey Arabian named Marengo that was brought to France from Egypt as a six-year-old in 1799. He served Napoleon until the Battle of Waterloo in 1815, after which he was captured and brought to England. His skeleton is now preserved in the National Army Museum in Chelsea.

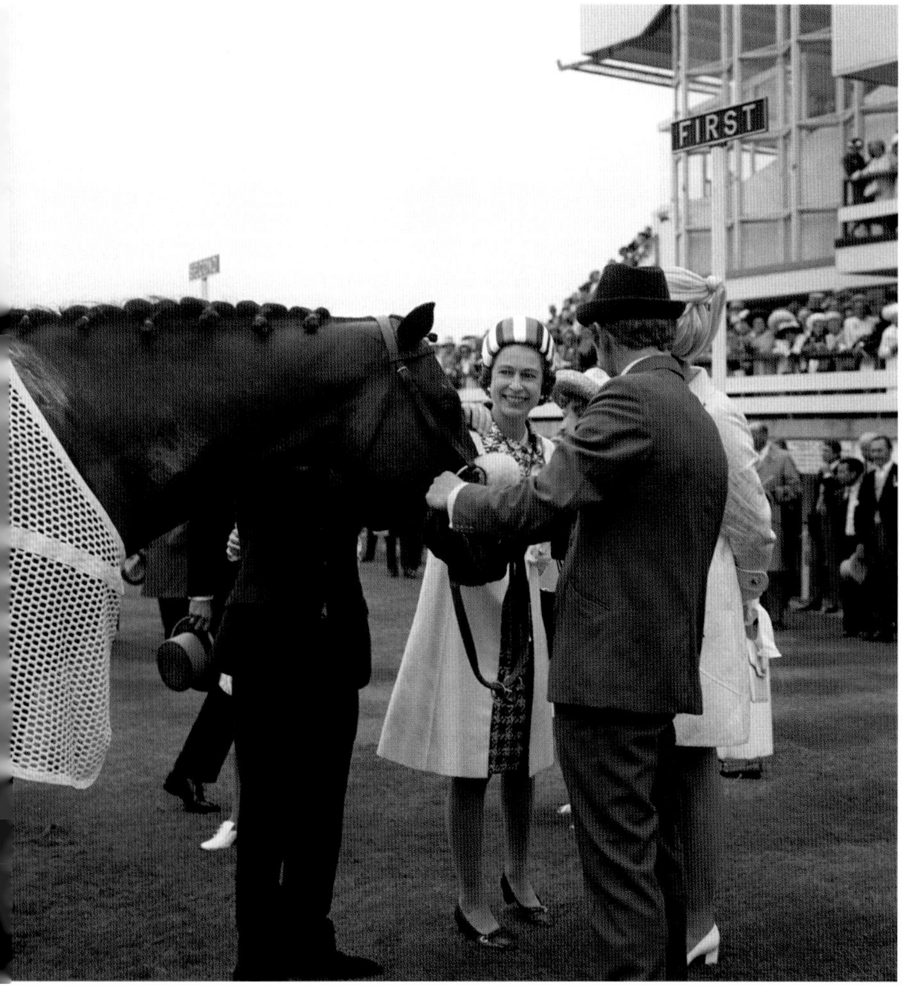

Fig. 43
HM Queen Elizabeth II with her horse Magna Carta after it had won the Ascot Stakes on 16 June 1970. The Queen has attended the Royal Ascot races every year since 1945 and has had a number of winning horses.

As so much importance was and still is attached to the pedigrees of Thoroughbred horses in Britain, it was necessary to record in exact detail their lineage. This was first done by James Weatherby in 1791 in The General Stud Book, which records the pedigrees of over 350 mares, all of which were descended from Herod, Eclipse or Matchem. In the United Kingdom this book is still regularly updated by the Jockey Club, and stud books are kept by appropriate regulatory bodies in other countries. The American stud book was started in 1868. Thoroughbred horses are now bred all around the world, especially in Ireland and Kentucky, USA, and Thoroughbred races are run in many parts of the world. In addition to those noted in the UK, we might mention the Kentucky Derby, the Prix de l'Arc de Triomphe in Longchamp, France, and the Dubai World Cup in the United Arab Emirates. In the United Kingdom, Ireland and France, Thoroughbred horse racing takes two forms, flat racing, which we have already discussed, and national hunt racing. National hunt racing is the official name given to horse racing where the horses are required to jump over hurdles or fences. The main annual events in the UK are the Grand National at Aintree near Liverpool and the Cheltenham Gold Cup.

Although Thoroughbreds are mainly used nowadays for racing, they are also sometimes used in other equestrian sports such as show jumping, dressage and polo. Very often, however, Thoroughbreds are crossed with other breeds of horse to produce horses that are best suited for the event in question, such as jumping. This is possible because unlike racing other equestrian events are not restricted to Thoroughbreds. As a result, many of the horses competing in these events are not Thoroughbreds but many will have the blood of the Arabian horse in their veins, and it is remarkable how just one breed of horse has come to have such a major influence on the breeding of horses around the world.

Equestrian events feature in the Olympic Games, having been introduced in the second Summer Olympics in Paris in 1900, but they did not become a permanent feature until the 1912 Games in Stockholm. Nowadays, Olympic equestrian events include dressage, eventing and jumping, for each of which individual and team medals are awarded. Show jumping is also one of the five disciplines in the modern pentathlon. Outside the Olympics, in

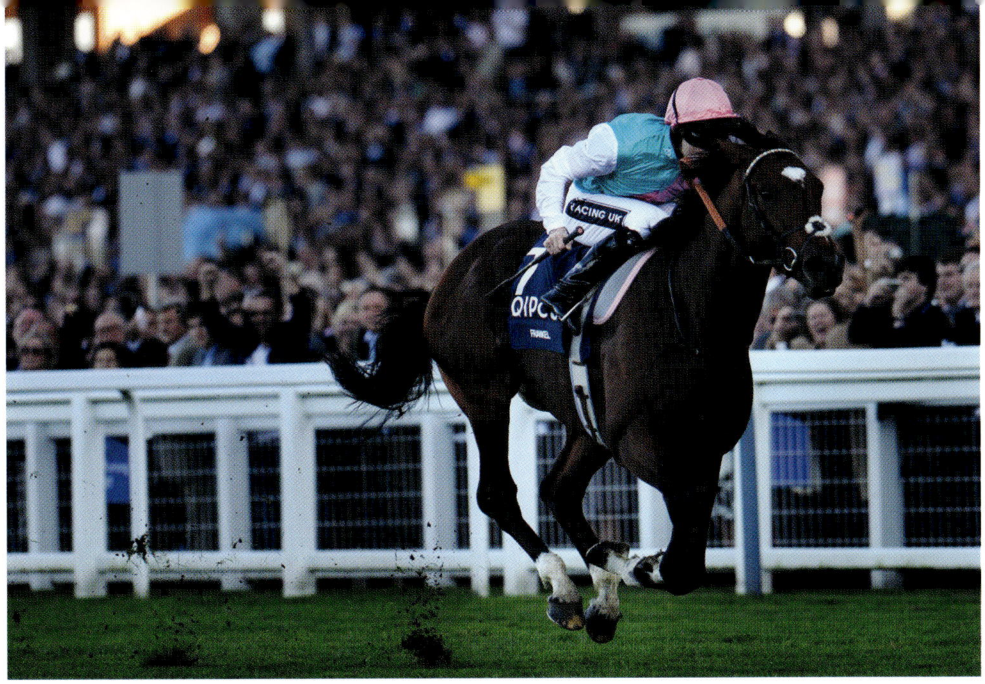

Fig. 44
Frankel, ridden by Tom Queally, goes on to win the Queen Elizabeth II stakes at Royal Ascot racecourse on 15 October 2011. The victory led to Frankel being named as the best horse in the world in 2011, according to the World Thoroughbred Racehorse Rankings. He is owned by HRH Prince Khalid bin Abdullah of the Kingdom of Saudi Arabia.

modern Britain, horse shows (for example, the Windsor Horse Show and the London International Horse Show), horse trials or eventing (for example Badminton), dressage (training) competitions, show jumping and gymkhanas are all very popular, as they are in many parts of the world.

Horses are no longer essential in our modern age, but horse riding and sporting events involving horses are still very popular. According to the British Equestrian Trade Association there were 1.35 million horses in the UK in 2006. Foremost amongst the horse owners in the UK is HM The Queen, who owns several stud farms including the Royal Stud at Sandringham, and has bred many winners. Throughout the UK there are many clubs and societies devoted to horses, notably the Arab Horse Society based in Marlborough in Wiltshire. Their principal activity according to their website is 'to encourage the breeding and importation of pure bred Arabian horses and to encourage the introduction of Arab blood into light horse breeding.' Similar organizations are thriving in many countries in the world, all members of the World Arabian Horse Organisation, a body that gives its stamp of authority to national breeding stud books. This has ensured the purity of the Arabian breed, so that in the UK for example the Arabian horse is one of the categories in the annual Horse of the Year show. Lastly, it may be noted that the racing of purebred Arabian horses as opposed to Thoroughbreds, already popular in Saudi Arabia, the United Arab Emirates and the USA, is a fast growing activity. There are also endurance events for Arabian horses, for which they are particularly well suited.

As we have seen in this survey, the Arabian horse not only thrives today in its own right but it played a major role in the development of most types of modern horse, particularly the Thoroughbred. The climax of the British flat racing season is now Champions Day at Ascot, the racecourse near Windsor Castle founded by Queen Anne in 1711. Champions Day was first staged at Ascot on 15 October 2011 and the most prestigious race, the Queen Elizabeth II stakes, was won by Frankel, widely regarded as the greatest racehorse of modern times. From our point of view, it is of particular interest that Frankel's ancestry includes both the Darley Arabian and the Godolphin Arabian, thus taking our story full circle from the Middle East and the Arabian Peninsula to Royal Ascot.

THE CATALOGUE

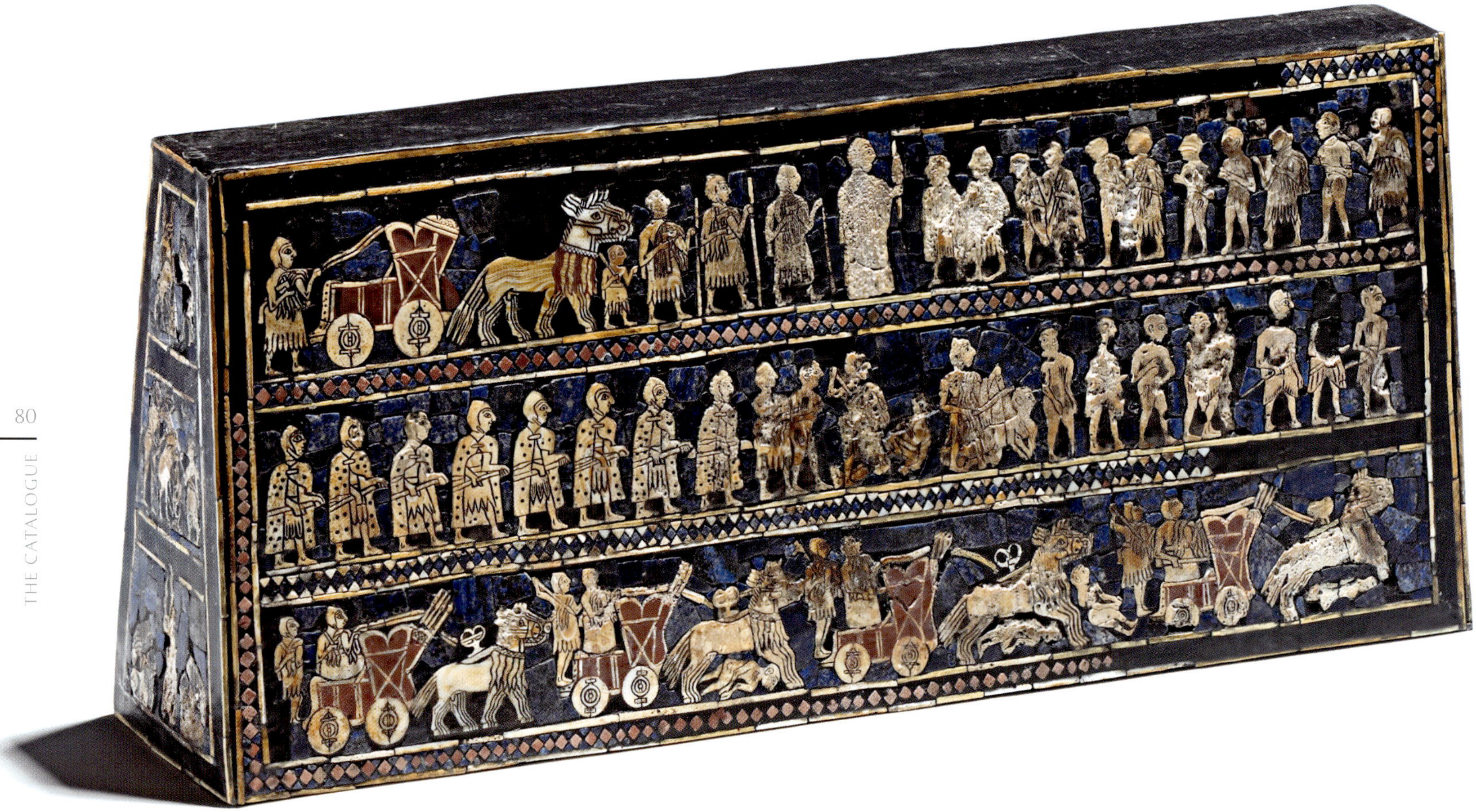

1

Standard of Ur

c. 2600 BC, Sumerian
PG 779, Royal Cemetery, Ur, Mesopotamia
Shell, lapis lazuli, red limestone and bitumen
W 21.6 cm, L 49.5 cm, D 4.5 cm (end, base), D 2.5 cm (end, top)
BM 121201

The 'Standard of Ur' is a small tapered box, originally of wood, decorated with figural scenes in an inlaid mosaic of shell, lapis lazuli and red limestone set in bitumen, discovered by Sir Leonard Woolley during his excavations in the Royal Cemetery at Ur. Its original purpose is uncertain, but it may have been the sounding box of a musical instrument. The two main side panels feature an important figure shown slightly larger than the others, probably the king, in scenes of war and feasting.

One of the two main panels shows the conclusion and aftermath of a battle. In the centre of the upper register is the largest figure, with a spear and wearing a high status dress of fleece, as also worn by the charioteers, and a helmet. Behind him is a procession of three men, armed with axes and staves (possibly once spearshafts, the heads now missing), and a four-wheeled vehicle like a wagon. This is one of the earliest types of chariot, now sometimes called a battle-car. It has a framework perhaps of wood backed with red leather, with a high protective front (shown twisted to the side as if facing the viewer) from which hang a pair of long quivers for javelins, and low sides which typically conceal a bench seat for the driver. One of the quivers is partly concealed behind the vehicle and only the lower end is visible. The wheels are not a single plank but are composite, made of three shaped pieces bound together, as it was possible to make a larger, stronger, faster wheel this way. The battle-car is harnessed to a team of four male asses or donkeys (made clear by the number of ears) by a yoke on a single draught-pole. A charioteer is shown standing behind the vehicle holding the reins which pass through a double rein-ring (see cat. 2). In front of the central figure, victorious soldiers parade bound enemy captives, stripped of their clothes and armour.

The second register shows on the left an ordered file or rank of marching soldiers with levelled spears and wearing helmets and protective capes. On the right, soldiers in fleecy dress, perhaps officers and charioteers, are executing some enemy captives while herding the remainder to their commander.

The lower register shows the elite charioteers in four chariots, each drawn by a team of four asses or donkeys, and carrying a crew of two: a driver and a soldier both identically dressed. The leftmost team is only walking and the driver is seated, but the others are charging. Here the drivers are standing and the second crewman is shown either with javelins or an axe. Victory is signified by the stripped bodies of the enemy dead, covered with wounds, shown lying beneath the animals' hooves.

The teams have decorated breast bands (draught-collars) with long decorative or protective fringes in front. With this type of vehicle only the central pair were yoke animals, while the outer two were 'outriggers' probably to help in turning. All four were controlled by the driver by long goads and by reins which were attached to the asses with nose rings (carefully shown on the Standard). The reins run from the team to the driver, being threaded through plain rein-rings or terrets. Similar, but richly decorated terrets were recovered in the excavations of the Royal Cemetery.

The ends of the box are decorated with crossed animals and stylised scenes while the other side of the Standard shows feasting and music together with the bringing of produce and animals, sheep, asses or donkeys: perhaps tribute and the fruits of victory.

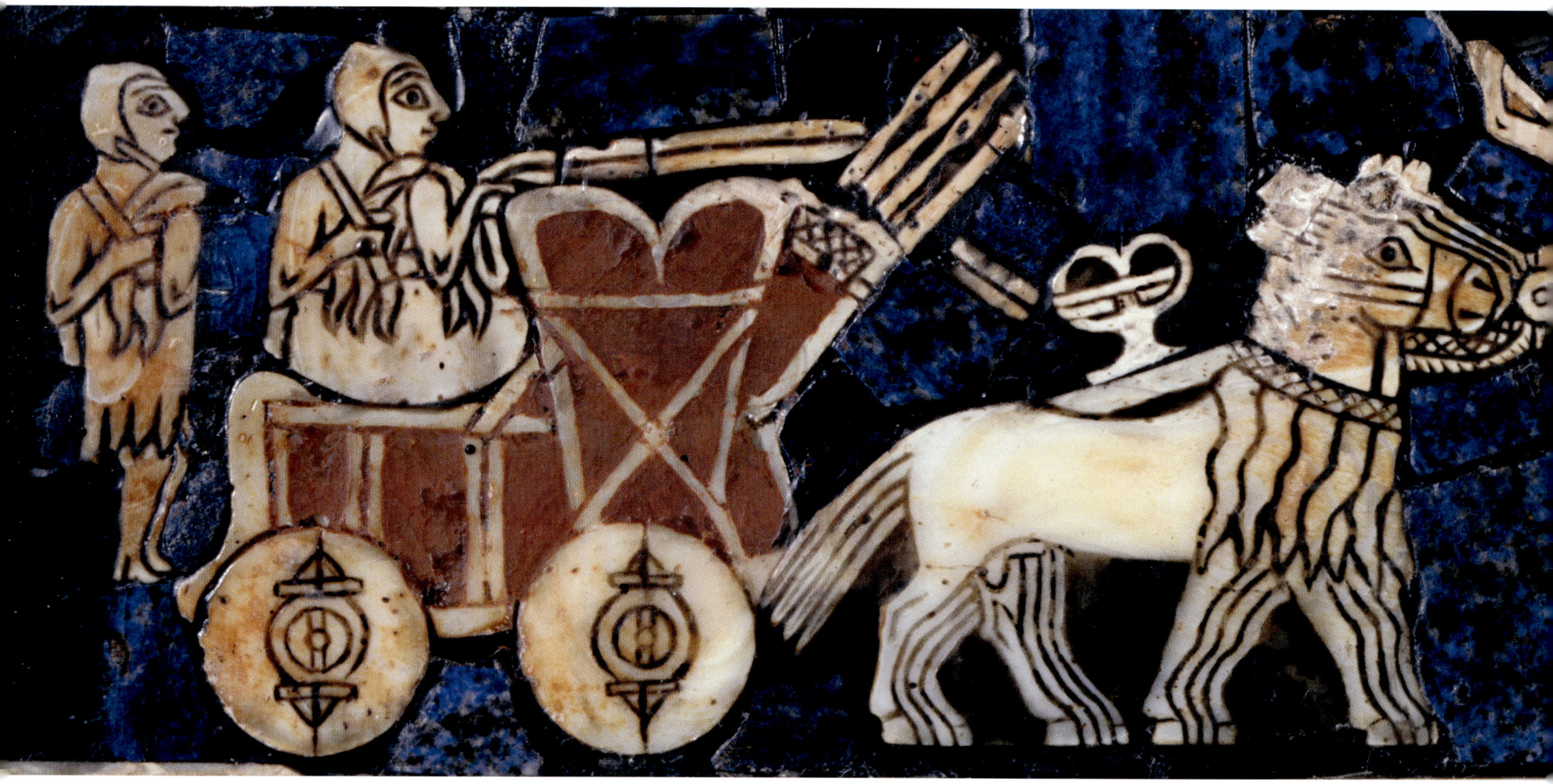

This is the first chariot or battle-car shown on the lower register of the Standard of Ur. Here, the team is shown walking and the driver is clearly seated. The rein-ring, or double terret, is very is very prominent, as are the reins and nose-ring.

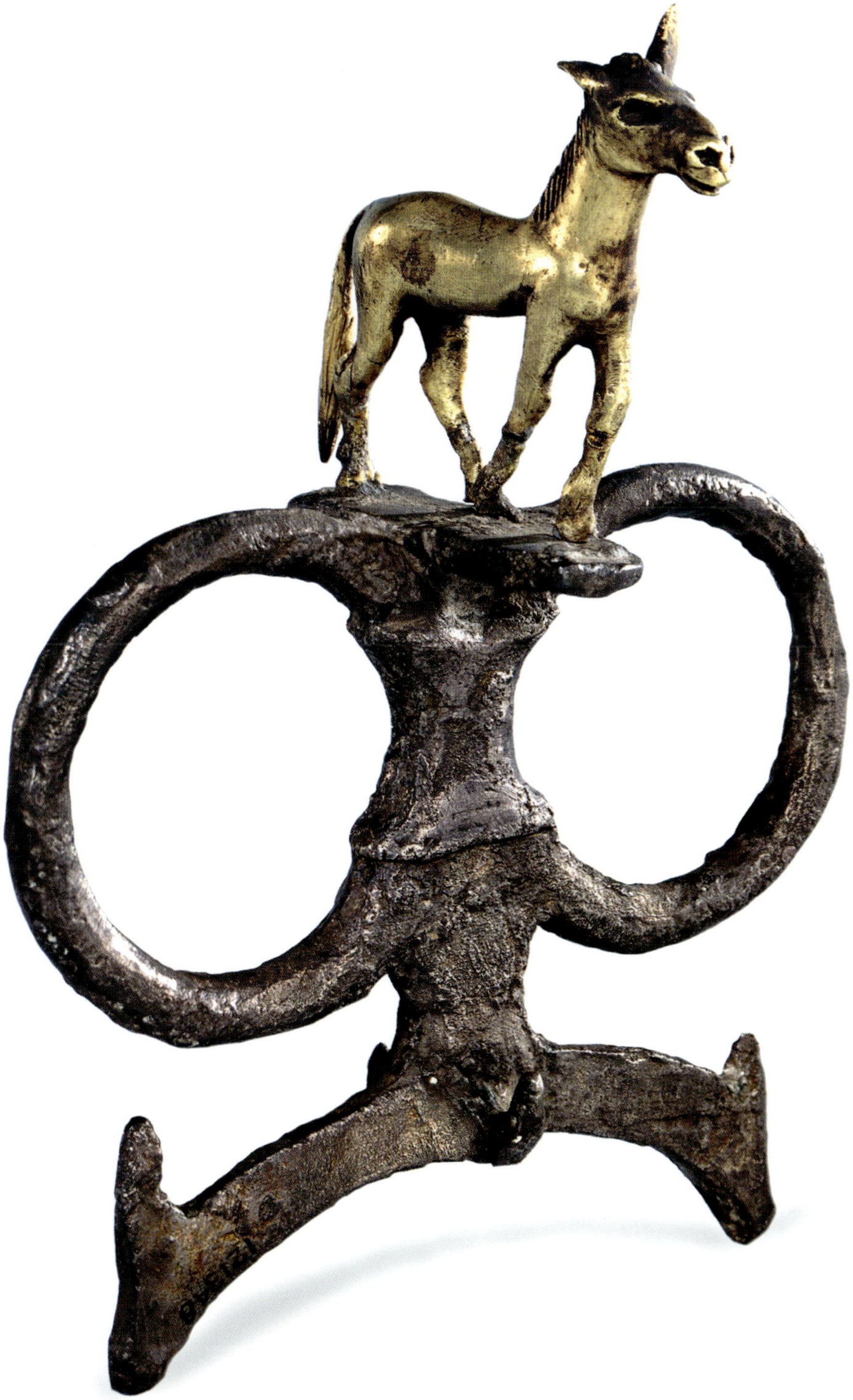

2

Rein-ring decorated with a figure of an ass

c. 2600 BC
PG 800, Royal Cemetery, Ur, Mesopotamia
Silver, electrum
H 13.5 cm, W 10 cm, Th. 5.7 cm
BM 121348

This silver rein-ring, or double terret, was found at Ur in the tomb of queen Pu-abi (PG 800), where it was once fixed on the draught-pole of what the excavator believed to be a richly decorated ceremonial sledge pulled by an ox.

The terret is of silver decorated with a figure of an ass in electrum (a gold-silver alloy) mounted on top. It would have been attached to the pole and secured with straps wrapped over the prongs on both sides. It was used to separate and organize the reins, which were probably used for braking rather than directional control. The reins held by the driver would have passed through these rings to a small ring through the nose of the ox.

A similar elaborate silver terret decorated with a figure of a bull was found in a nearby tomb (PG 789).

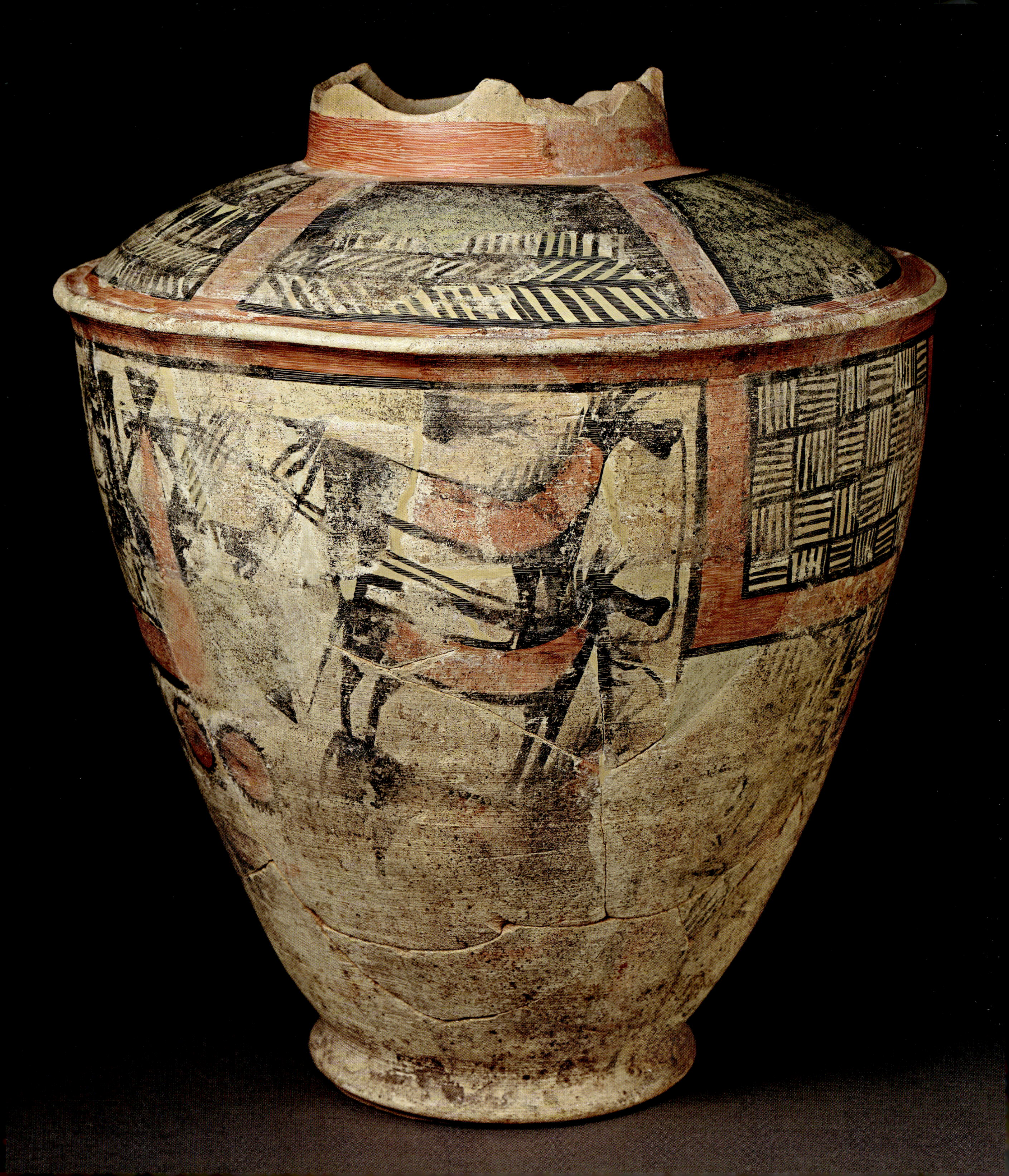

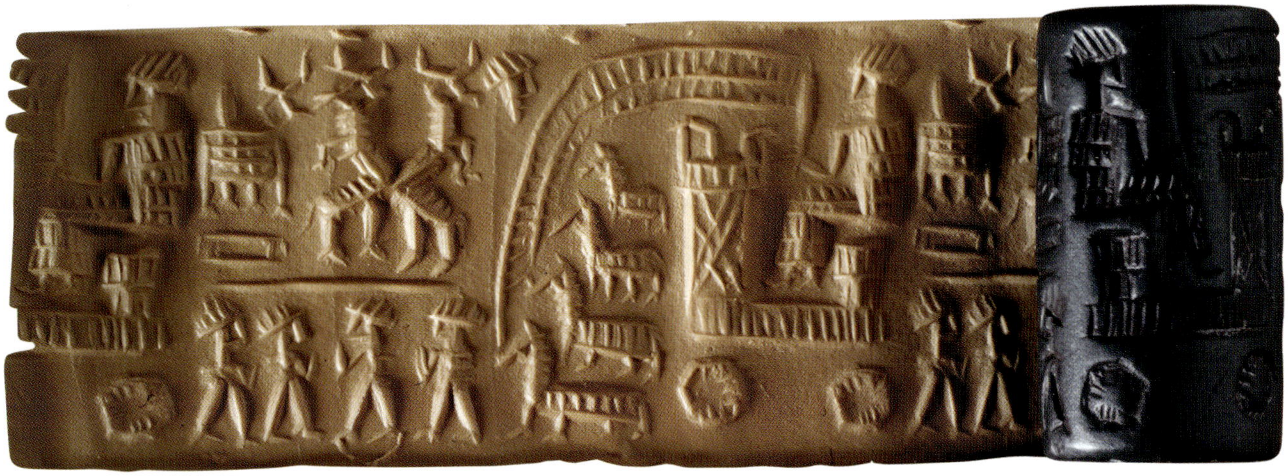

3

Painted pottery jar

c. 2800–2600 BC
Khafajeh, Mesopotamia
Ceramic
H 34.3 cm, Diam. 30.5 cm
BM 123293

This polychrome jar is decorated with red and black paint on a white slip. It shows one of the earliest representations of a four-wheeled early chariot, or battle-car, drawn by four asses, as shown on the later Standard of Ur. As on the Standard there are also scenes of feasting and music, a goat, a bird and a figure holding two goats or gazelles.

The driver is a small figure behind the larger, more important figure in front. This shows that the main personage was actually the leading figure in the vehicle, with the seat.

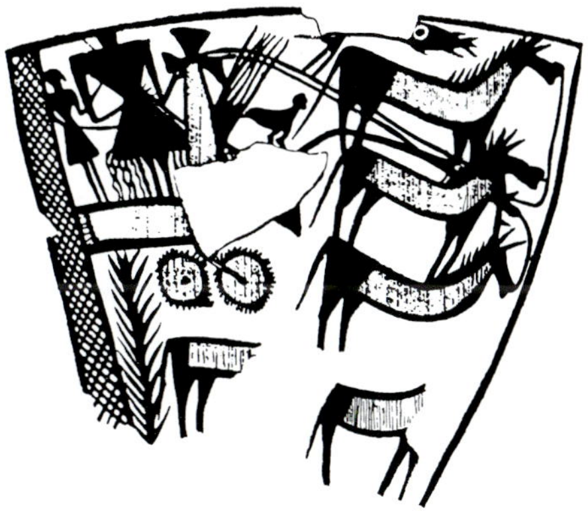

4

Cylinder seal showing a charioteer in a four-wheeled vehicle

c. 1920–1740 BC, Old Assyrian
Provenance unknown, probably Mesopotamia; acquired 1825
Black haematite
L 2.5 cm, Diam. 1.3 cm
BM 89774

This Assyrian cylinder seal shows a figure seated in a four-wheeled chariot or battle-car, by this later date more a form of ceremonial transport than a practical or battlefield vehicle, though still probably drawn by a team of four asses rather than horses. The treatment of the wheels is unclear and could suggest that either a solid wheel with a metal tyre or a more advanced cross-bar wheel or a four-spoked wheel is intended (both types were known by now). The remainder of the scene shows what might be a bull-shaped stand or altar, a pair of crossed bulls and a human head, above four small striding figures.

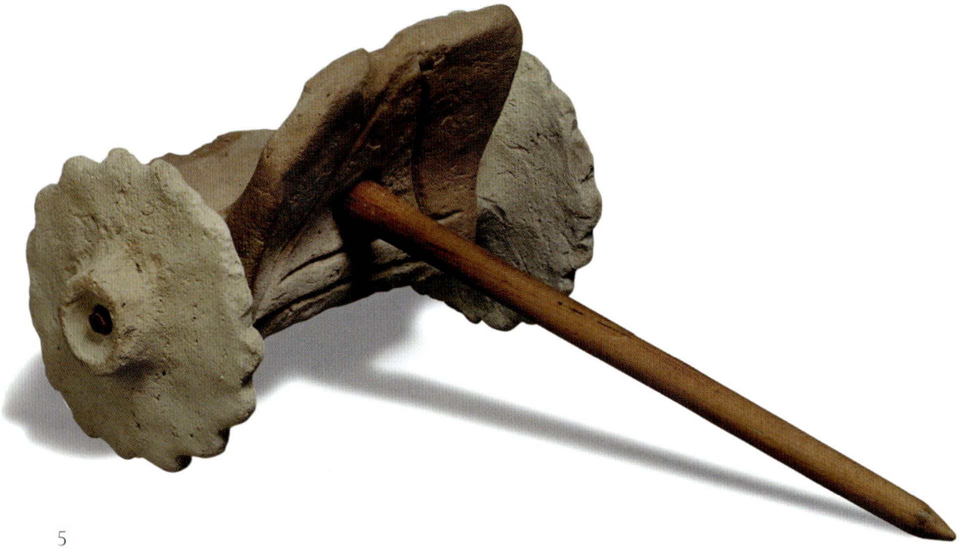

5

Model chariot

c. 2500–1800 BC
Ur, Mesopotamia
Clay
H 6.2 cm (without wheels), L 7.4 cm, W 5 cm
BM 116863

Small clay models of vehicles with either four or two wheels are common in this period. Faster, more manoeuvrable two-wheeled vehicles driven by a single rider seem to have been developed in parallel with or slightly after the wagon-like battle-cars. Two types are known: 'straddle-cars', where the rider rode astride an extension of the draught-pole, rather like riding an ass, and 'platform cars' (like shorter battle-cars) which are the ancestors of the true fast chariot. Here this 'platform car' has the back part with the seat broken away. The wheels have studded edges representing a leather or bronze tyre held on with nails.

Assembled with a modern wooden pole and with two related wheels.

6

Model chariot

c. 2000–1800 BC
Ur, Mesopotamia
Clay
H 5.1 cm, L 8.7 cm, W 7.1 cm
BM 129386

Many of these model vehicles appear to be votive. This example, with an intact seat, has stylized divine imagery in relief on the inside of the high front. Divinities are often associated with chariots and texts describe their special teams and the appearance and manufacture of divine vehicles.

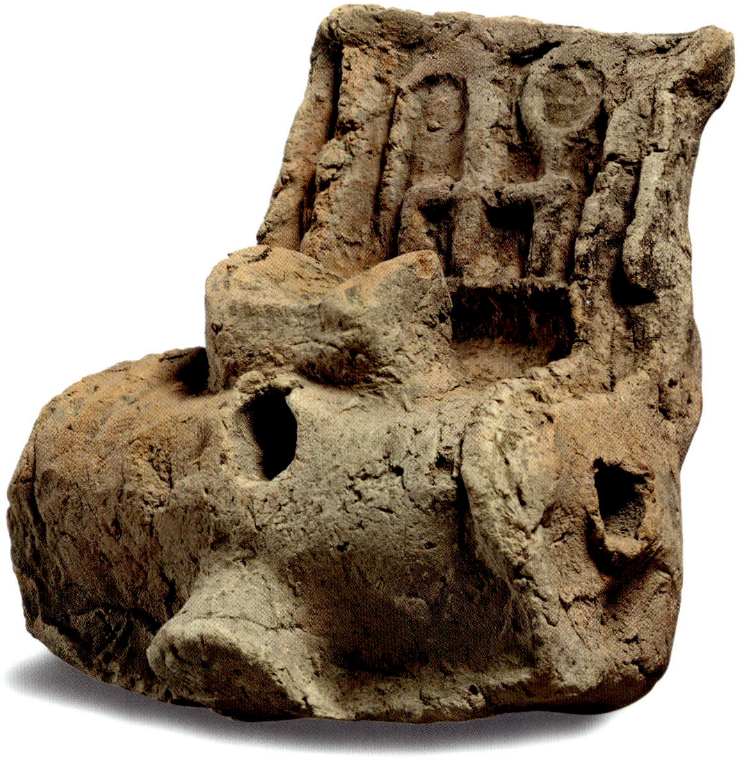

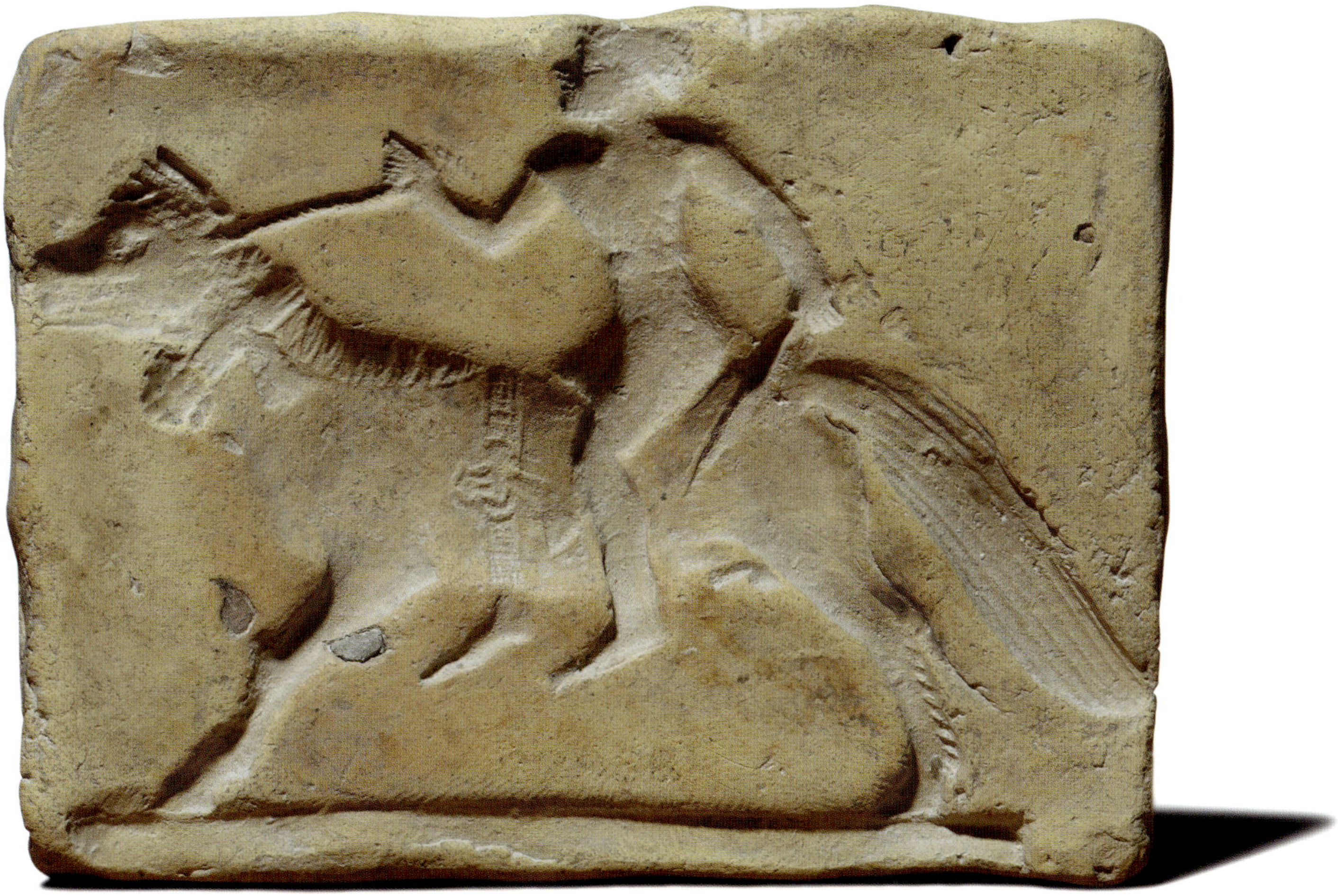

7

Plaque mould depicting a youth riding a horse

c. 2000–1800 BC, Old Babylonian
Provenance unknown, probably Southern Mesopotamia; acquired 1897
Baked clay
L 9.8, W 7.3 cm
BM 22958

This mould for making small clay plaques shows one of the earliest representations of horse riding, probably dating from around the end of the Third Dynasty of Ur to the early Old Babylonian period, around the beginning of the second millennium BC.

It shows a young male rider with a rein in his left hand and a stick in his right. He is poised far back on the animal's rump, where one would sit to avoid an ass's high vertebrae and narrow withers, a position known as the 'donkey seat', but the animal's clearly exaggerated long and flowing hairy tail shows it is a horse. Around the horse's neck is a collar, which sometimes appears to have a tassel or bell on other examples, and while there is no saddle or saddlecloth there is a broad strap around the belly for the rider to grip with his knees or free hand.

Horses appear in the written record at around the same date as this plaque or a little earlier. King Shulgi of Ur likens his running to that of a stallion and there are mentions of messengers on horseback.

8

Clay tablet case with seal impression of horse-drawn early fast chariot

1779 BC, Reign of Hammurabi, Old Babylonian
Provenance unknown, probably Southern Mesopotamia; acquired 1892
Clay
H 4.5 cm, W 7 cm, Th. 3.3 cm
BM 16815a

This important sealing is dated by the inscription to the fourteenth year of Hammurabi, king of Babylon (1779 BC). It shows an evolved type of 'platform car'. This has a lower front, though there are still low sides and a seat, but the most important change is in the draught team: the vehicle is apparently pulled by horses. This is shown by the shape of their tails and by the large tassel visible above the shoulder. The tassel likely indicates a yoke-saddle, a new adaptation where a wooden element in the shape of an inverted Y is attached to the yoke and sits along the animal's shoulders. This transmits the energy of the animal to the vehicle and so avoids the choking effect of the earlier simple neck collar.

The wheels have either four spokes or are solid wheels, but with a representation of cast bronze tyres with attachment lugs (as known from excavation in Iran and elsewhere). The vehicle therefore captures the transition between the old two-wheeled platform cars and the new technology and 'engine' which were shortly to revolutionize warfare and transport as the true, fast chariot.

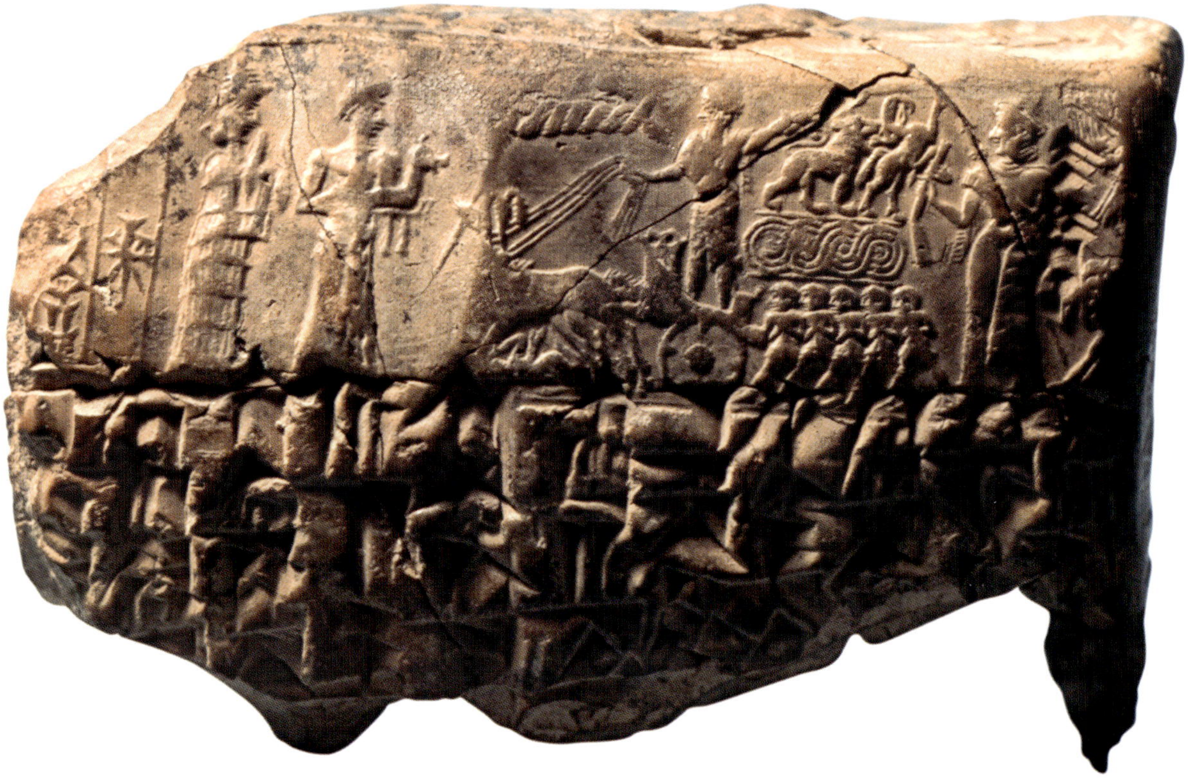

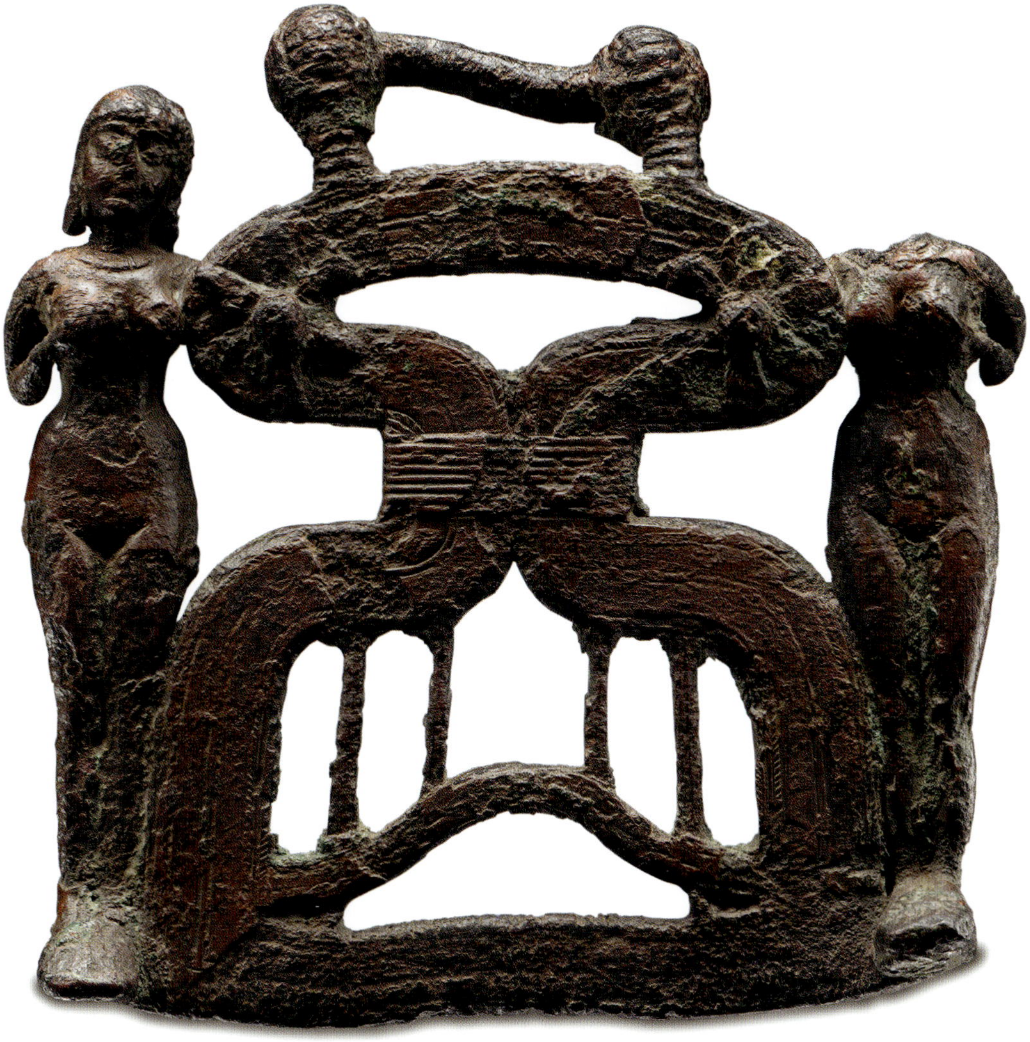

9

Harness fitting

2000–1000 BC, Babylonian
Said to be from Mesopotamia
Bronze
H 11.5 cm, W 11.5 cm
BM 123899

This object is possibly a rare example of an early harness fitting, perhaps a strap terminal. It is decorated with two nude female figures standing on either side.

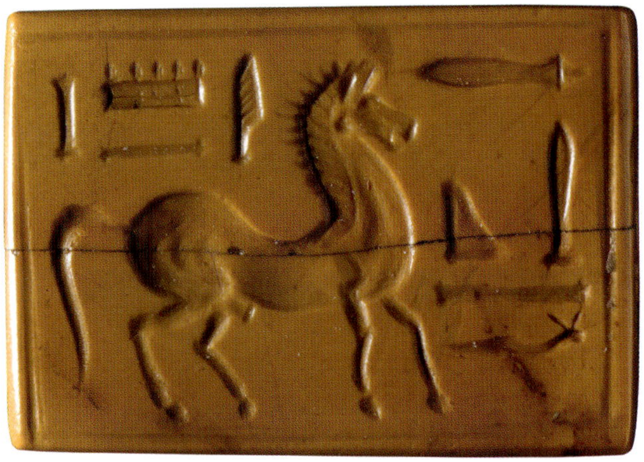

10

Plaque from a finger ring engraved with a horse

c. 1550–1298 BC, 18th Dynasty, New Kingdom, Egyptian
Provenance unknown, Egypt; acquired 1840
Jasper
H 1.8 cm, Th. 0.6 cm, W 1.3 cm,
BM 4077

This finely engraved yellow jasper ring stone or bezel is on one side inscribed with an engraving of a horse which shows some of the features of the modern Arabian breed, in the arched tail and short back, together with Egyptian hieroglyphs that include the name of Amun and the words 'great' and 'he is strong'. On the other side is the prenomen of the Egyptian king Amenhotep II, with the hieroglyphs for 'steadfast of heart', and a representation of a bull.

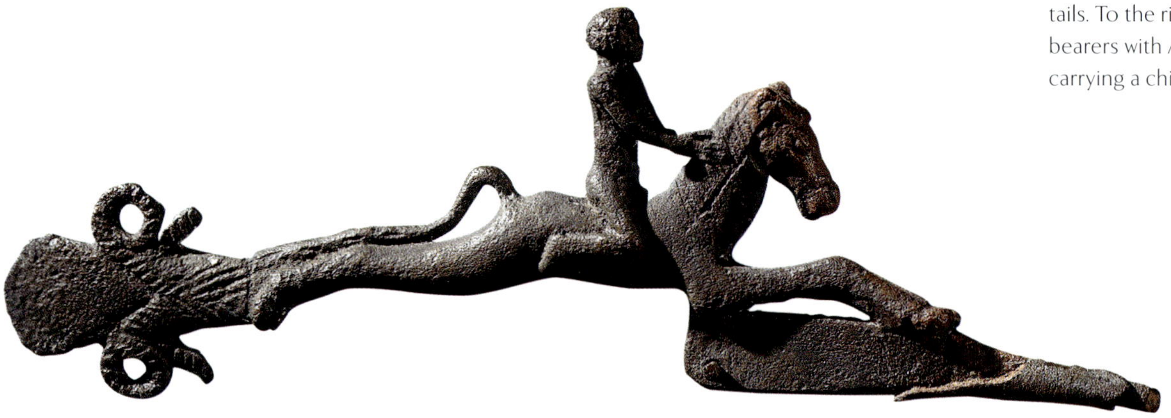

11

Wig-curler in the form of a horse and rider

c. 1550–1069 BC, New Kingdom,
Egyptian
Provenance unknown, Egypt; acquired 1920
Bronze
H 3.6 cm, Th. 0.8 cm, L 11.6 cm
BM 36314

Horses and riders are relatively common subjects in ancient Egyptian art, appearing on weapons, wall reliefs and in objects like this wig-curler. The artists clearly revelled in the horses' sinuous appearance when galloping and in representing their fine, expressive features.

12

Egyptian wall painting of Asiatic tribute-bearers with horses and a chariot

c. 1400 BC, 18th Dynasty, New Kingdom, Egyptian
TT63, Thebes, Egypt; aquired 1852
Plaster, mud
L 60 cm, W 58.5 cm
BM 37987

This fragment of wall painting is probably from the tomb of Sobekhotep at Luxor, who was an important treasury official in the reign of Thutmose IV (*c.* 1400–1390 BC). One of his duties was probably to oversee foreign gifts brought to the king. The tomb wall from which this fragment came almost certainly showed Sebekhotep receiving rich tribute and luxury gifts from the Levant and Africa, which he then presented to Thutmose IV.

In this fragment from the tribute scene we have gifts including a chariot, vessels and possibly servants. The felloes (rims) of chariot wheels are just visible at the bottom left-hand corner, followed by a team of two fine horses, with their reins possibly tied to the back of the chariot. They both have some of the distinct features we know today in the Arabian horse, with their gracile limbs, bearing and high-arched tails. To the right of the horses are two tribute-bearers with Asiatic hairstyles and dress, one carrying a child.

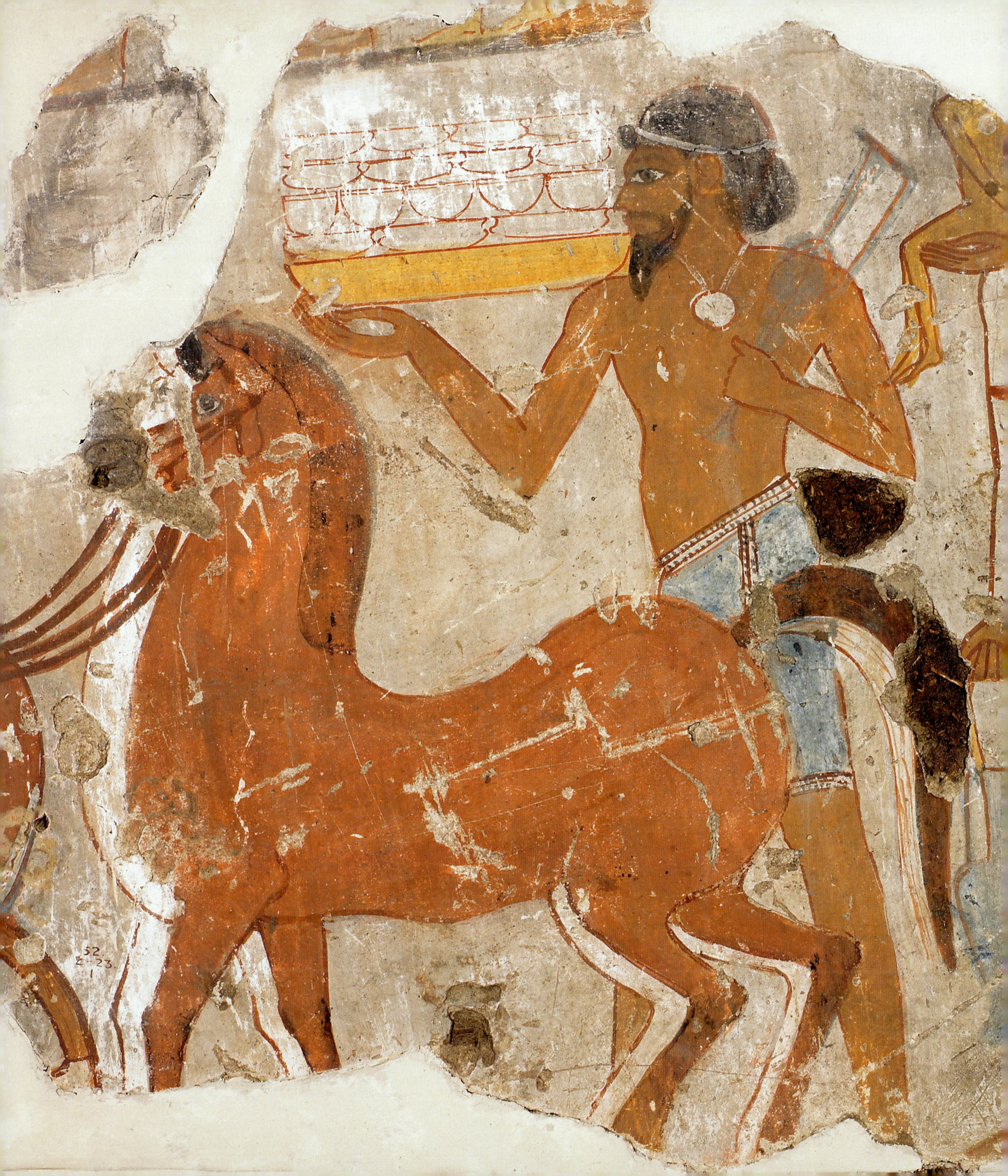

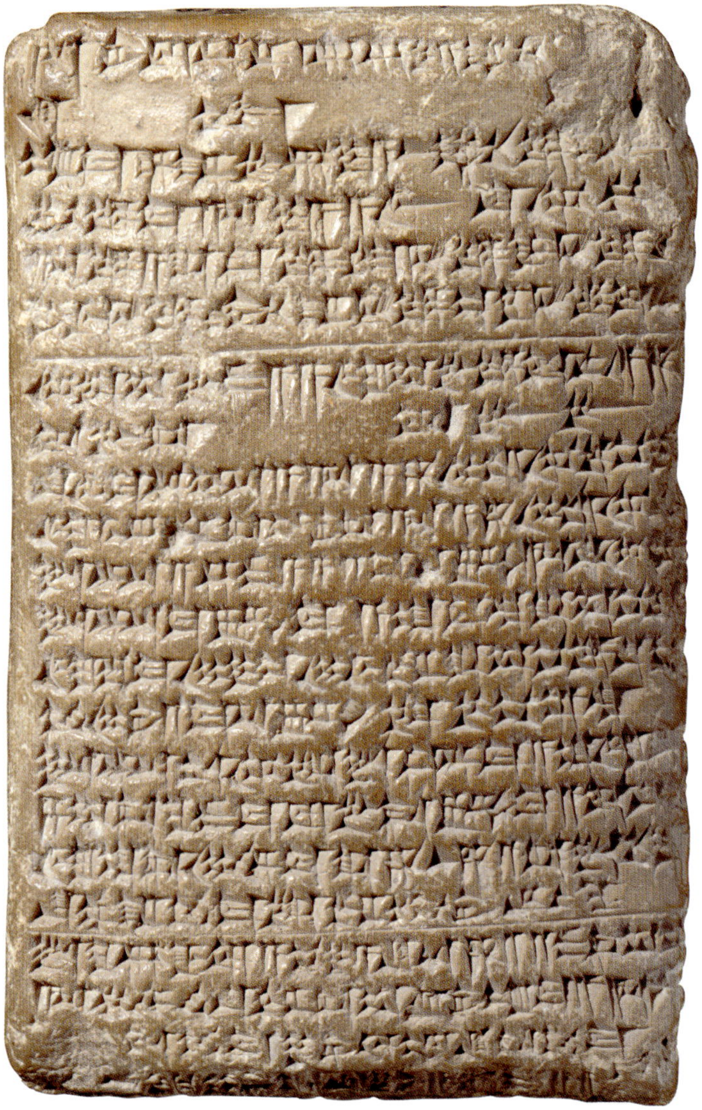

13

Letter from king Burnaburiash II to Amenhotep II

c. 1350, Middle Babylonian
el-Amarna, Egypt; acquired 1888
Clay
L 11.4 cm, W 7.3 cm
BM E29785

The Amarna letters were discovered in 1887 by a local village woman who was digging ancient mud-brick to be used as a fertilizer. This remarkable find is largely an archive of diplomatic and other correspondence sent to Amenhotep III and his son Akhenaten, with a few addressed to Tutankhamun, from subject rulers and brother kings in the Middle East. Some 380 letters survive, generally written in Babylonian Akkadian cuneiform on clay tablets. They provide invaluable details of the international relations between Egypt, Babylonia, Assyria, Mitanni, the Hittites, Syria, Canaan and even Alashiya (Cyprus).

This letter to Akhenaten from Burnaburiash II, the Kassite king of Babylonia (reigned 1359–1333 BC), concerns luxury gift exchanges, with lapis lazuli and horses sent to the Egyptian king in return for expectations of gold.

Early in his reign, relations between Burnaburiash II and Akhenaten were cordial and even included plans for a marriage alliance. As time passed, the association weakened considerably, especially when the Assyrian king Ashur-Uballit I was received in Akhenaten's court. Burnaburiash took personal offence, since he regarded the Assyrians as his vassals.

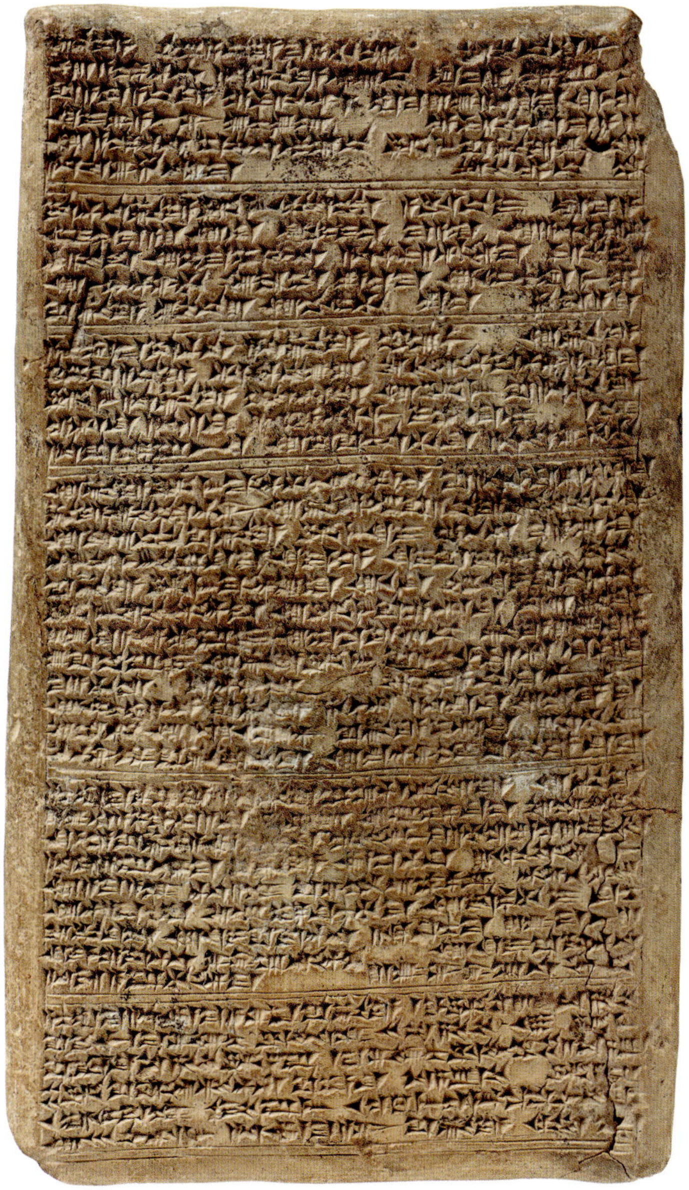

14

Letter from Tushratta of Mitanni to Amenophis III

c. 1400 BC, Mittanian
el-Amarna, Egypt; acquired 1888
Clay
L 22.2 cm, W 12.7 cm
BM E29791

The horse was introduced to Egypt in the seventeenth century BC and several tomb paintings of the New Kingdom feature gifts from Asia of horses and chariots, together with harness and equipment, helmets and coats of armour. Here, Tushratta, the king of Mitanni, sends gifts including no fewer than ten chariots with their teams of horses. Amenophis III belonged to the Egyptian 18th Dynasty.

In addition to representations in Egyptian art, chariot equipment and armour for man and horse are described in great detail in texts from the northern Mesopotamian town of Nuzi.

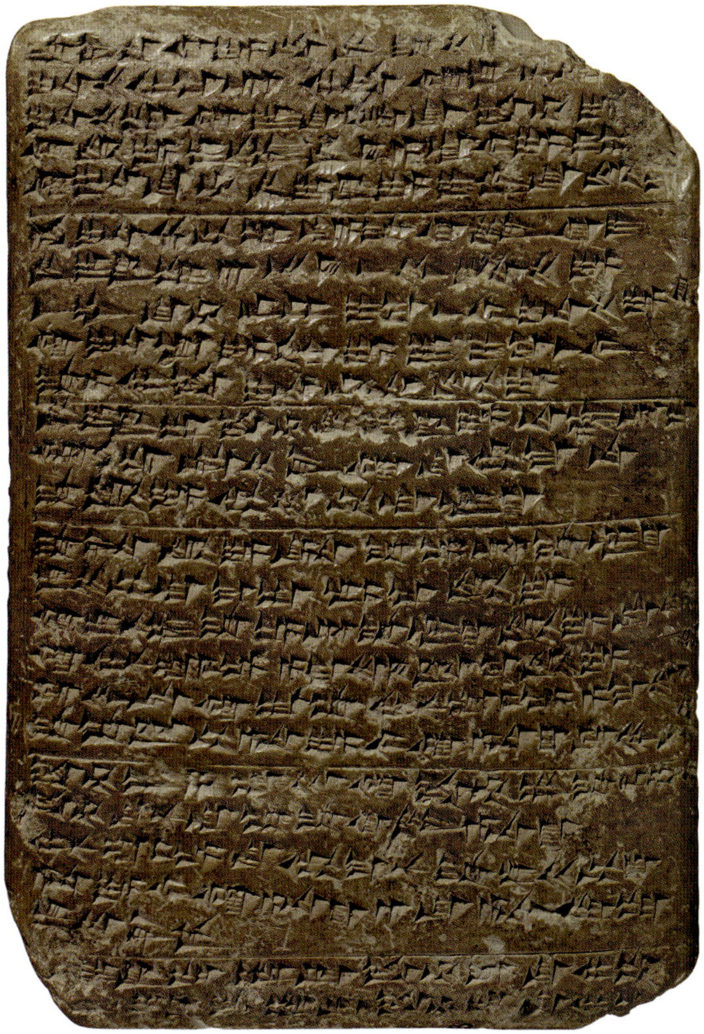

15

Letter from the King of Alashiya to the King of Egypt

c. 1375 BC, Middle Babylonian
el-Amarna, Egypt; acquired 1888
Clay
L 14.6 cm, W 9.8 cm
BM E29788

The possession of chariots and horses was a key indicator of power and status in the international world of the Late Bronze Age. Here, in the standard greeting format between kings of equal standing, the king of Alashiya (Cyprus) begins by reporting that his house, horses, chariots and land are well and hopes the same is true for the king of Egypt.

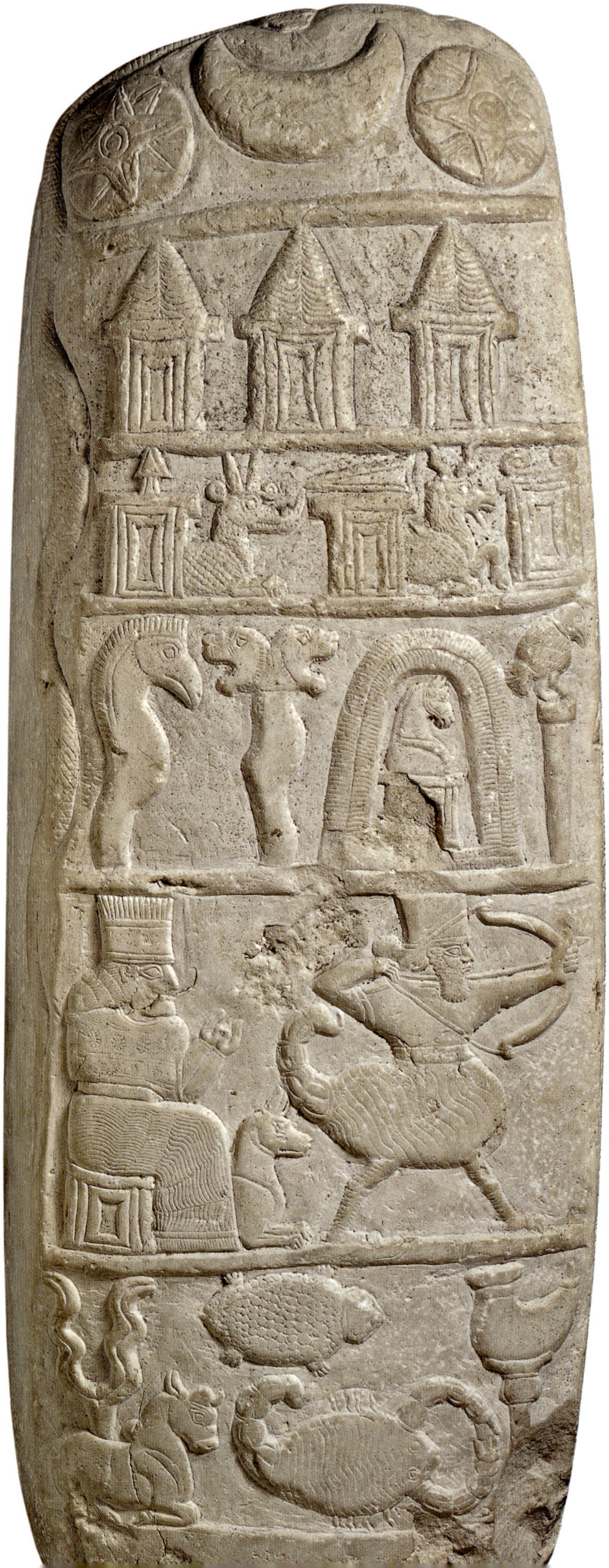

16

Stela, or kudurru, of Nebuchadnezzar I

c. 1100 BC, Middle Babylonian
Sippar, Mesopotamia
Limestone
H 64 cm, L 21 cm, W 18 cm
BM 90858

This very fine limestone stela, kudurru, or 'boundary stone' is sculptured in relief with symbols of deities and supernatural figures arranged in registers and columns of inscription concerning a declaration of Nebuchadnezzar I (1125–1104 BC), the king of Babylon. The figures include the goddess Gula seated upon a shrine with a dog lying beside her, and a horse's head, neck and shoulders within a double arch on a raised base or shrine.

The inscriptions record the granting of land and privileges by Nebuchadnezzar to Ritti-Marduk, the commander of his chariots, in reward for his heroic services in gaining the victory in a battle fought against Elam on the River Ulai. It describes vividly the arduous campaign, fought in the summer months, the suffering of the horses with no water in the wells, and the storm, confusion and dust of battle.

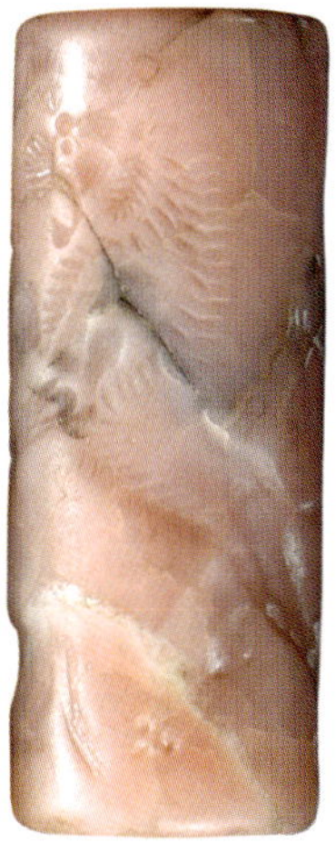

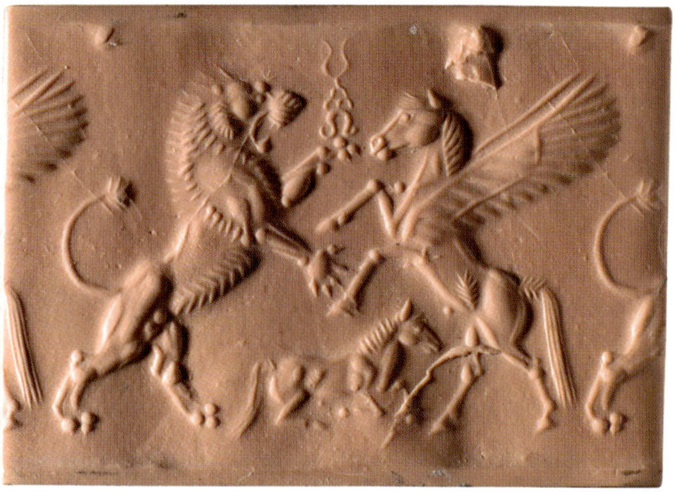

17

Cylinder seal showing a lion attacking a winged horse

1250–1200 BC, Middle Assyrian
Provenance unknown, probably Mesopotamia; acquired 1945
Pink chalcedony
H 4.1 cm, Diam. 1.6 cm
BM 129572

This seal, probably dating to the reign of the Assyrian king Tukulti-Ninurta I (1243–1207 BC), shows a supernatural battle between a rearing lion and a spirited winged horse. A wingless foal stands between them below an uncertain device.

18

Rein-ring with goats

12th–11th century BC, Middle Elamite
Said to be from Harsin, western Iran; acquired 1931
Bronze
H 16.5 cm, W 8.4 cm, Th. 2.2 cm
BM 122700

This rein-ring is surmounted by a pair of goats with their front feet resting on a tree. It has provision for two reins or two sets of reins like the famous silver rein-ring from Ur (cat. 2).

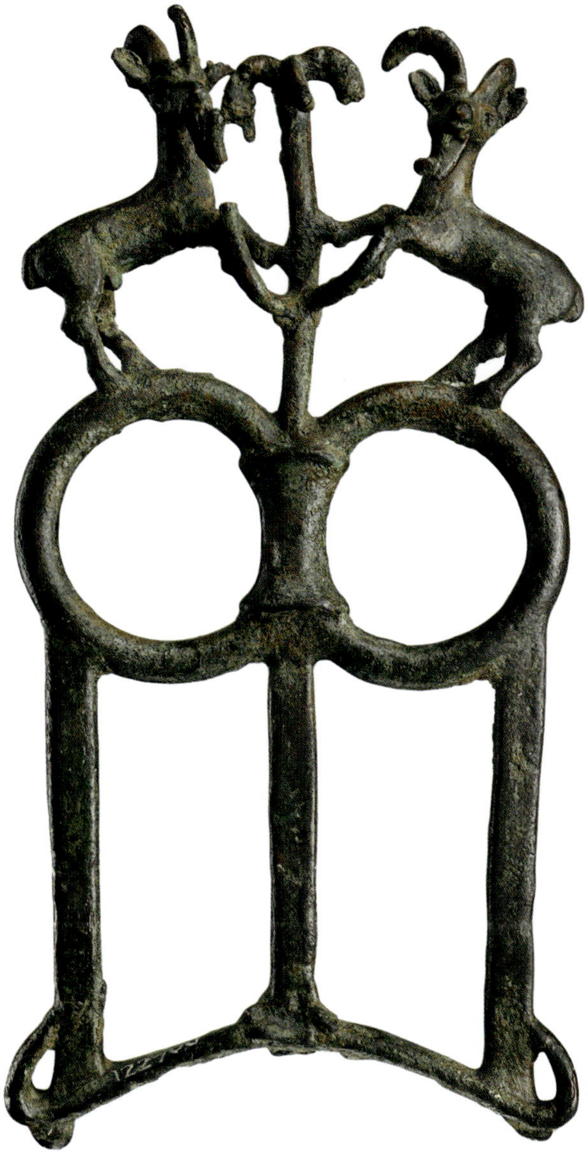

19

Horse cheekpiece in the form of a horse and rider

10th–7th century BC, Luristan
Provenance unknown, probably Luristan, Iran; acquired 1967
Bronze
H 11.8 cm, L 11.7 cm
BM 134927

The horse is a stallion and has a long tail reaching to the ground. He wears a headstall with brow-band and is being controlled by reins of twisted rope. The horse stands on a base-line and there is a hole in its body for the mouthpiece and rings above the head and the rump for the straps of the headstall. The rider, who has been represented at a very small size in comparison with the horse, wears a belted tunic and a large beehive-shaped hat. A bronze cheekpiece in the Metropolitan Museum of Art in New York is probably the companion piece to this example.

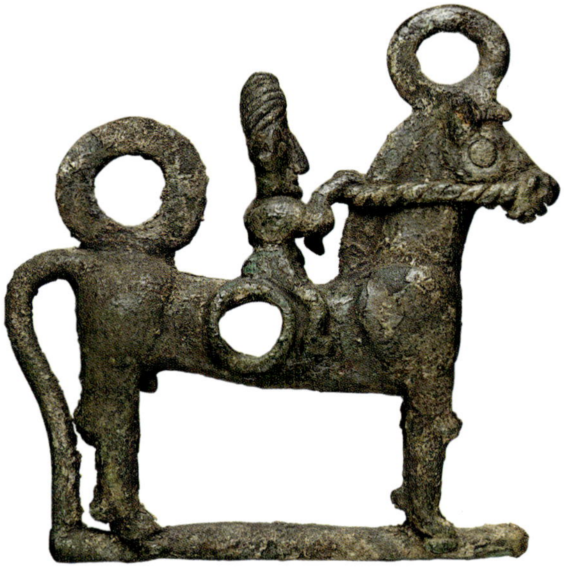

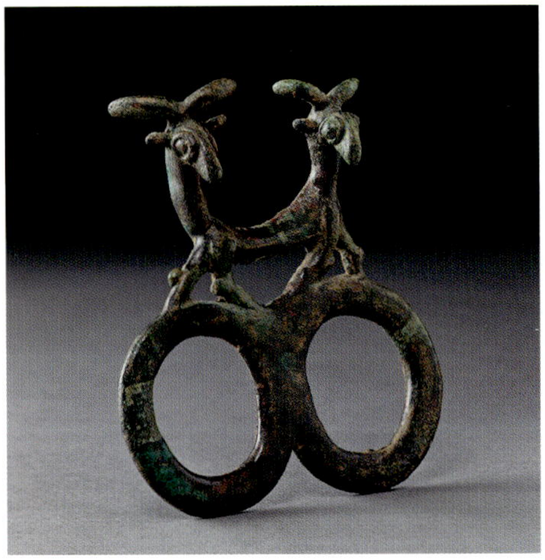

20

Horse harness-rings with goat's heads

10th–7th century BC, Luristan
Provenance unknown, probably Luristan, Iran; acquired 1930
Bronze
H 8.8 cm, W 3 cm, Th. 1.9 cm
BM 122918

A double harness-ring surmounted by the foreparts of two animals, possibly goats, joined back-to-back. The goat's heads are turned to face the front. Harness-rings such as these are thought to have been fitted to the headstalls of horses. They were probably largely decorative.

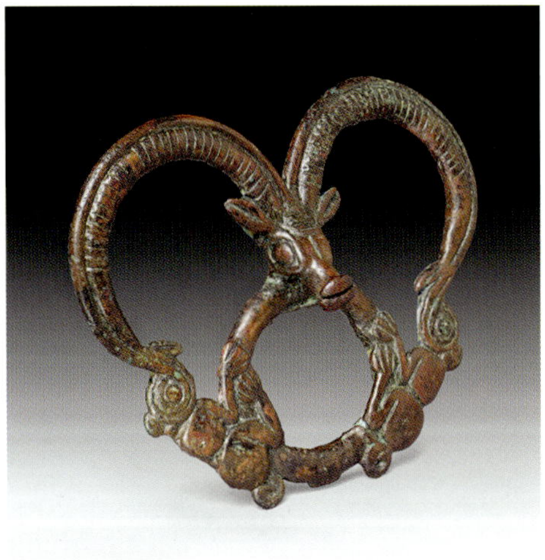

21

Horse harness-ring with head of a mouflon

10th–7th century BC, Luristan
Provenance unknown, probably Luristan, Iran; acquired 1934
Bronze
H 7.1 cm, W 8.9 cm, Diam. (central aperture) 2.4 cm
BM 123542

This consists of a ring surmounted by the head of a mouflon, a type of wild sheep with very large curled horns that was indigenous to western Iran. At the bottom of the ring, touching the tips of the mouflon's horns, are two stylized animals with curled tails, probably lions.

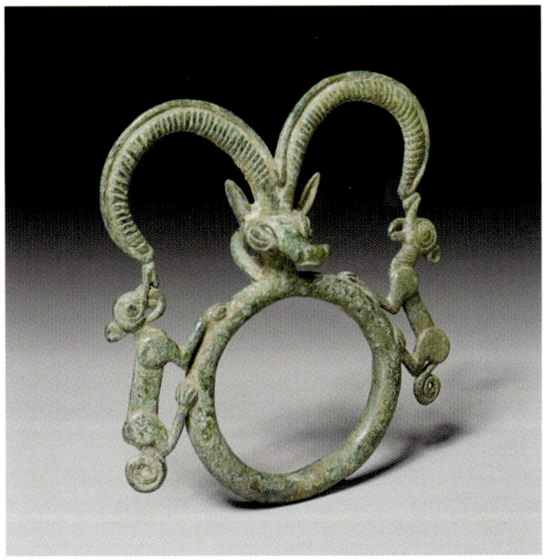

22

Horse harness-ring with head of a mouflon

10th–7th century BC, Luristan
Provenance unknown, probably Luristan, Iran; acquired 1930
Bronze
H 9.4 cm, W 8.4 cm, Th. 0.5 cm
BM 122917

A bronze harness-ring similar to cat. 21.

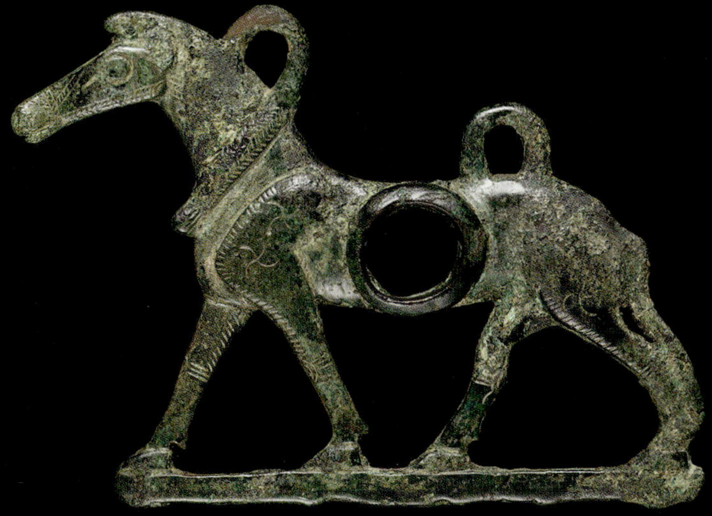

23

Horse cheekpiece in the form of a horse

10th–7th century BC, Luristan
Provenance unknown, probably Luristan, Iran; acquired 1924
Bronze
H 10 cm, L 13.9 cm
BM 135972

This horse stands on a base-line. It has a long, narrow nose and a long tail and wears a bridle and a collar around its neck. There is a hole in its body for the mouthpiece and two rings on the back for the straps of the headstall.

A bronze cheekpiece in the form of a running horse has been found at Nimrud and cheekpieces in the form of running horses can be seen on Assyrian reliefs dating from the reigns of Sennacherib and Ashurbanipal. Examples, possibly of Assyrian origin, are also known from the island of Samos. The Assyrian examples are not exactly the same as the Luristan examples, lacking a base-line and represented at the gallop, but it seems likely that the Assyrian cheekpieces were inspired by those of Luristan. It is even possible that Sennacherib saw these cheekpieces during his campaign in Luristan in 702 BC and that they were copied on his return to Assyria.

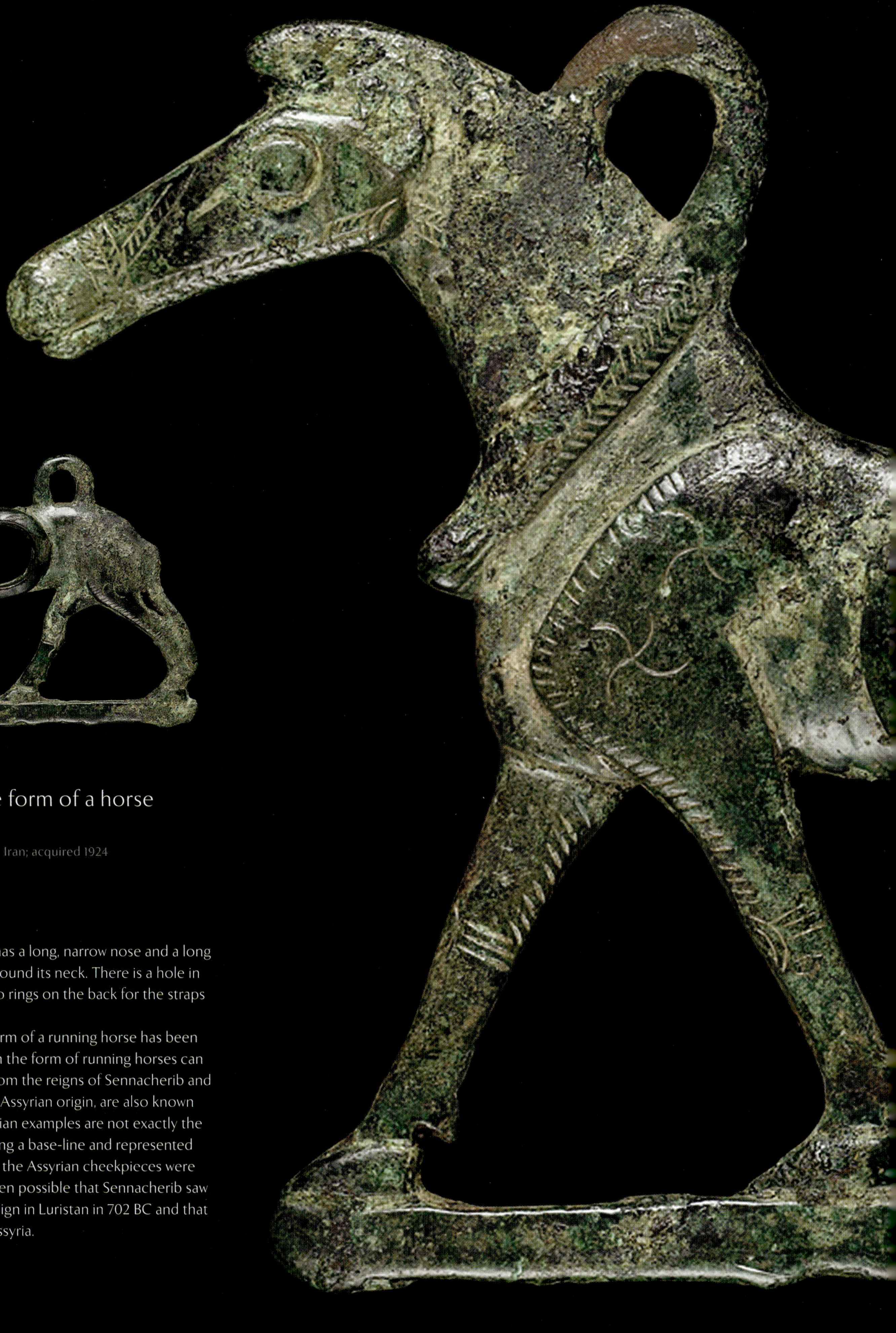

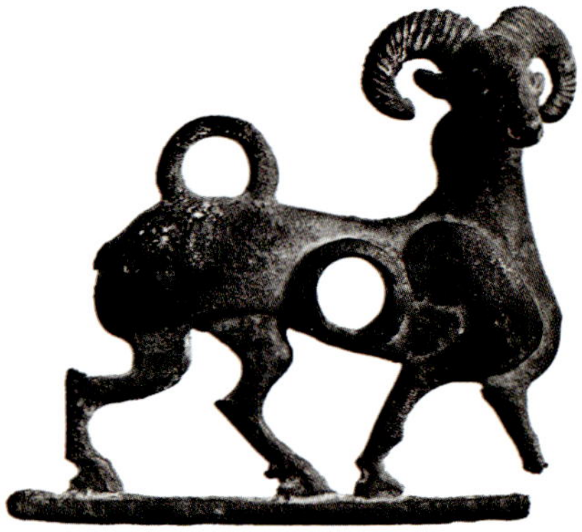

24

Cheekpiece in the form of a goat

10th–7th century BC, Luristan
Provenance unknown, probably Luristan, Iran; acquired 1924
Bronze
H 9.6 cm, L 10.5 cm, Th. 3.2 cm
BM 123273

The goat has curved horns and stands on a base-line, the end of which is broken away. There is a hole in its body for the mouthpiece and rings behind the neck and above the rump for the straps of the headstall. There are spikes on the inside of the cheekpiece that would have bitten into the horse's face when pressure was applied.

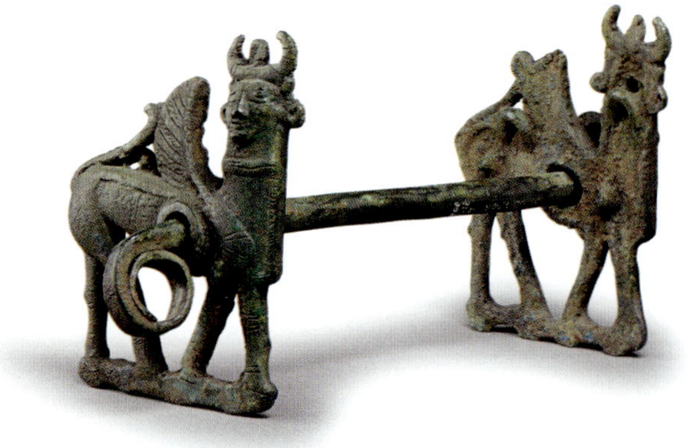

25

Horse bit with cheekpieces in the form of hybrid animals

10th–7th century BC, Luristan
Provenance unknown, probably Luristan, Iran; acquired 1946
Bronze
Cheekpiece 1: H 9.7 cm, L 8.5 cm; cheekpiece 2: H 9.6 cm, L 9.2 cm; W 18.1 cm
BM 134746

The bit itself is formed from a single bar with loops at either end. The cheekpieces are in the form of winged animals with human heads wearing horned headdresses. These human figures have locks of hair on either side of the head, and wear torcs or chokers. The animals have the hooves of horses or bulls, and long tails that are held high. There are two rings on the inside of each cheekpiece for the straps of the headstall, and single spikes that may have helped to control the horse.

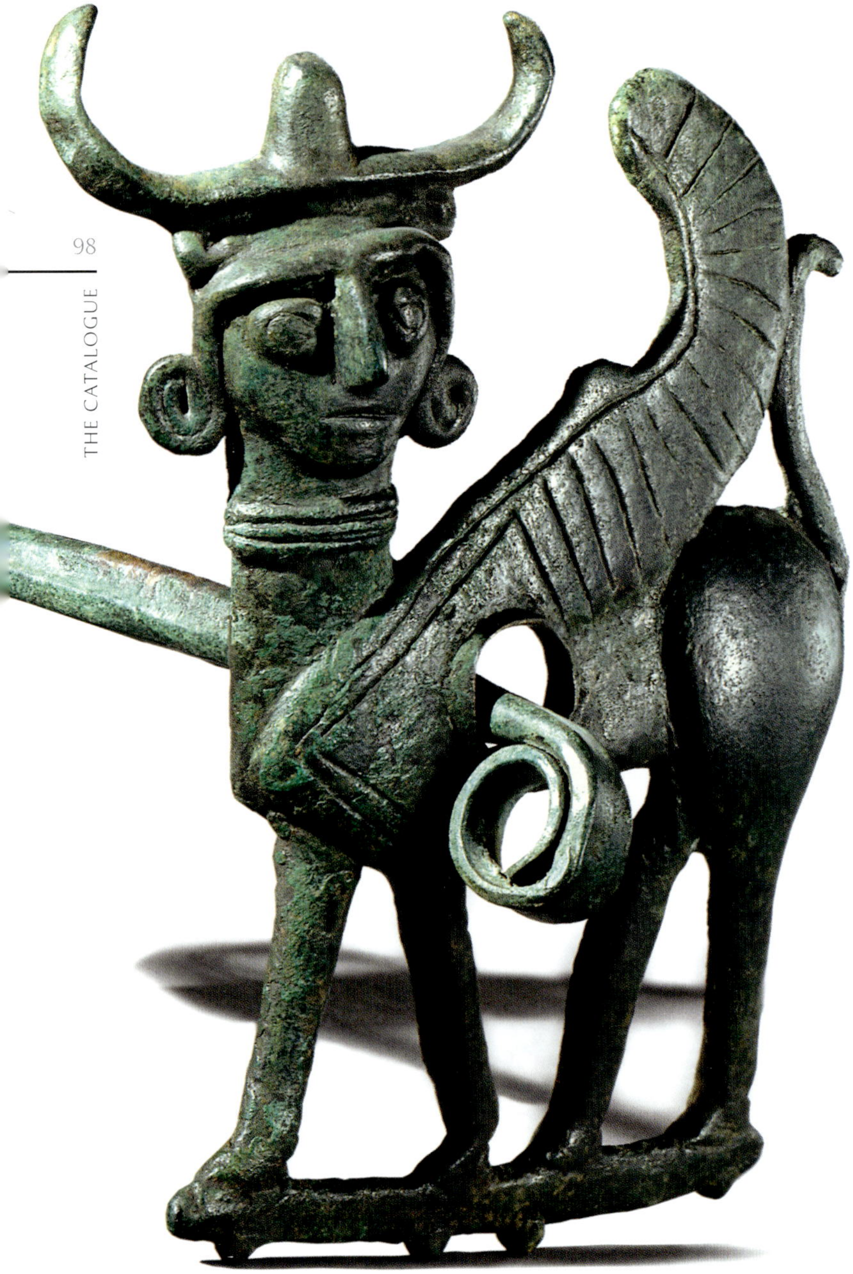

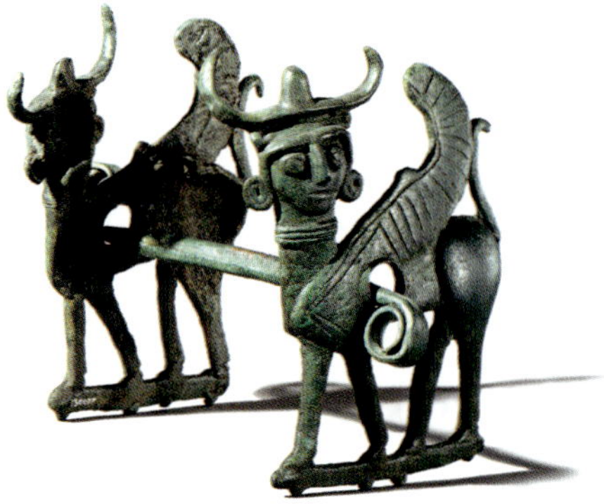

26

Horse bit with cheekpieces in the form of hybrid animals

10th–7th century BC, Luristan
Provenance unknown, probably Luristan, Iran; acquired 1945
Bronze
H 18.5 cm, L 16 cm (cheekpieces), W 12.5 cm
BM 130677

The bit itself is formed from a single bar with loops at either end. The cheekpieces are in the form of winged animals with human heads wearing horned headdresses.

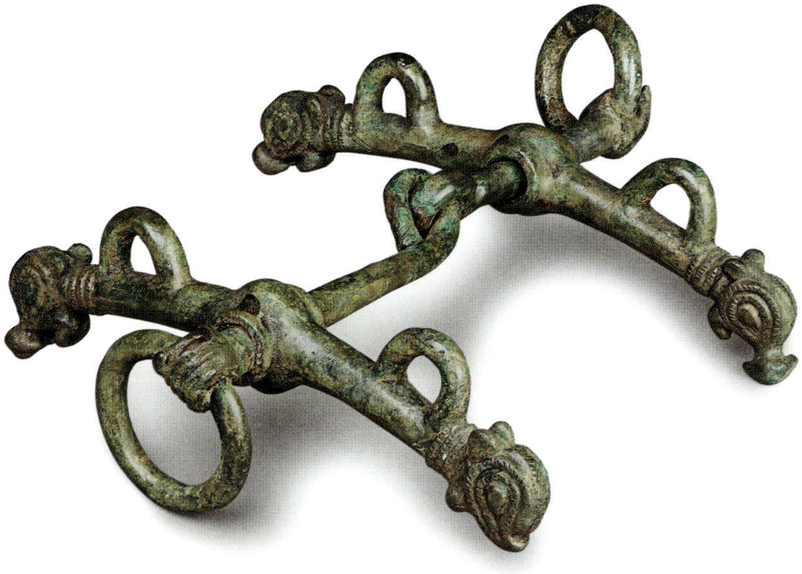

27

Horse bit with cheekpieces in the form of stylized lions

10th–7th century BC, Luristan
Provenance unknown, probably Luristan, Iran; acquired 1945
Bronze
L 16.8 cm (cheekpieces), W 21.5 cm
BM 130675

The bit is in two parts joined in the middle forming what is known as a snaffle bit. When the reins are pulled the bit arches and presses into the roof of the horse's mouth, helping to control it. The ends of the bit are in the form of human fists that grip the rings that would have been attached to the reins. The cheekpieces have loops on top for the straps of the headstall, and end in the heads of stylized animals that are probably lions.

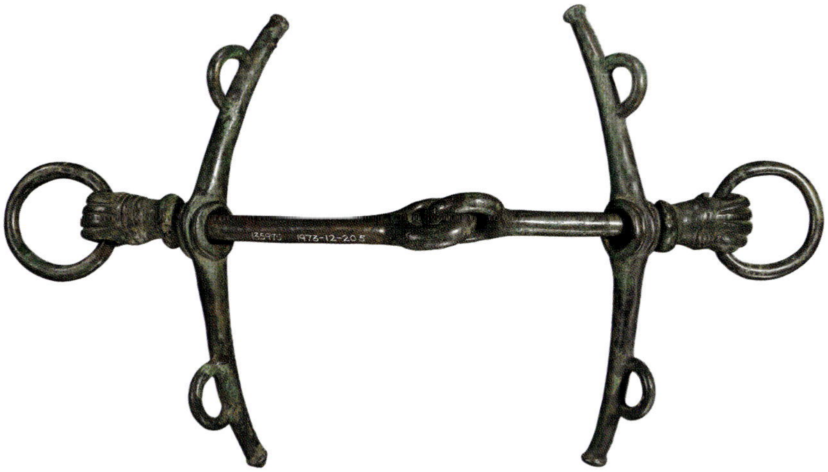

28

Horse bit with bar-shaped cheekpieces

10th–7th century BC, Luristan
Provenance unknown, probably Luristan, Iran; acquired 1973
Bronze
L 13.5 cm (cheekpieces), W 17.5 cm
BM 135975

Bronze snaffle bit consisting of a jointed mouthpiece with the two ends terminating in fists which hold the rein-rings. The two bar-shaped cheekpieces are curved and each has two loops on the top for the attachment of the headstall straps.

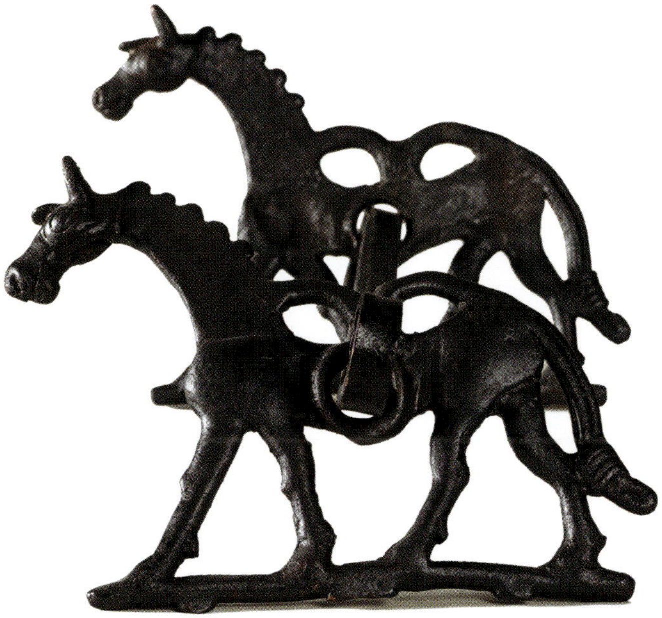

29

Horse bit with cheekpieces in the form of horses

10th–7th century BC, Luristan
Provenance unknown, probably Luristan, Iran; acquired 1930
Cheekpiece 1: L 11.4 cm; cheekpiece 2: L 8.3 cm;
W 16.5 cm
BM 122928

The bit has a single bar with loops at either end. The cheekpieces are in the form of horses standing on a base-line. The horses have arched necks, bulbous noses and shaggy manes. There is a hole in the body of each horse for the bit, and two loops on the back of each horse for the straps of the headstall.

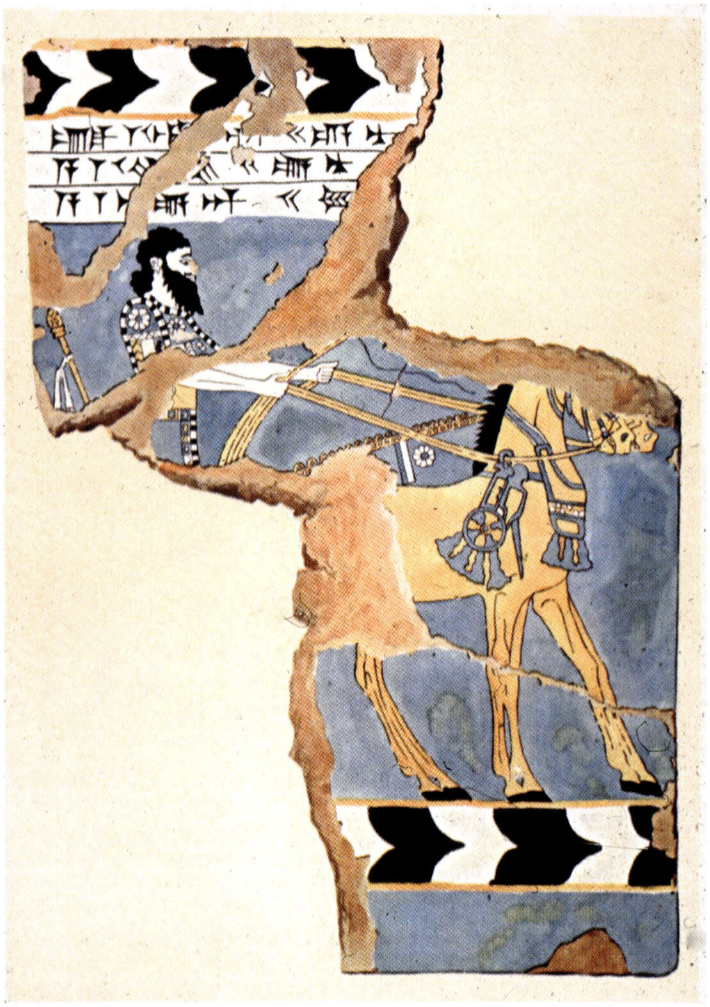

Fig. 45
Watercolour by Walter Andrae of cat. 30 at the time of excavation.

30

Painted tile

890–884 BC, Assyrian
Ashur, Mesopotamia, excavations of W. Andrae 1903–14
Baked clay
H 66.5 cm, W 46.5 cm, Th. 6.5 cm
BM 115705

A large incomplete tile with painted decoration showing a bearded man wearing an elaborately decorated tunic standing in a chariot and holding the reins of the two horses that are pulling it. The nearside horse has breast and shoulder ornaments from which tassels are suspended. At the top and bottom of the tile there are bands of chevron decoration, and a cuneiform inscription that gives the name of Tukulti-Ninurta II (890–884 BC). The decoration is in black, brown, blue and white paint.

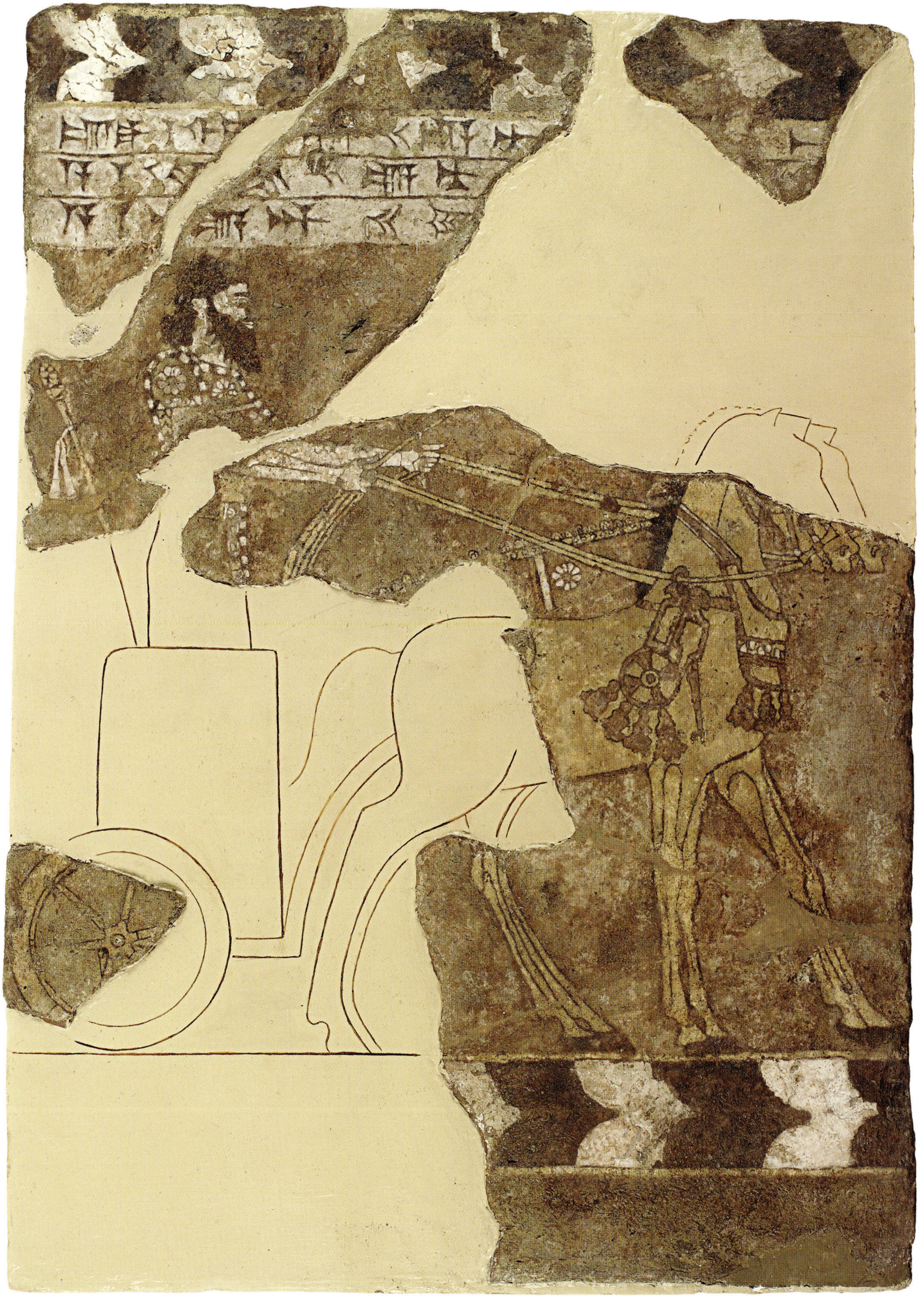

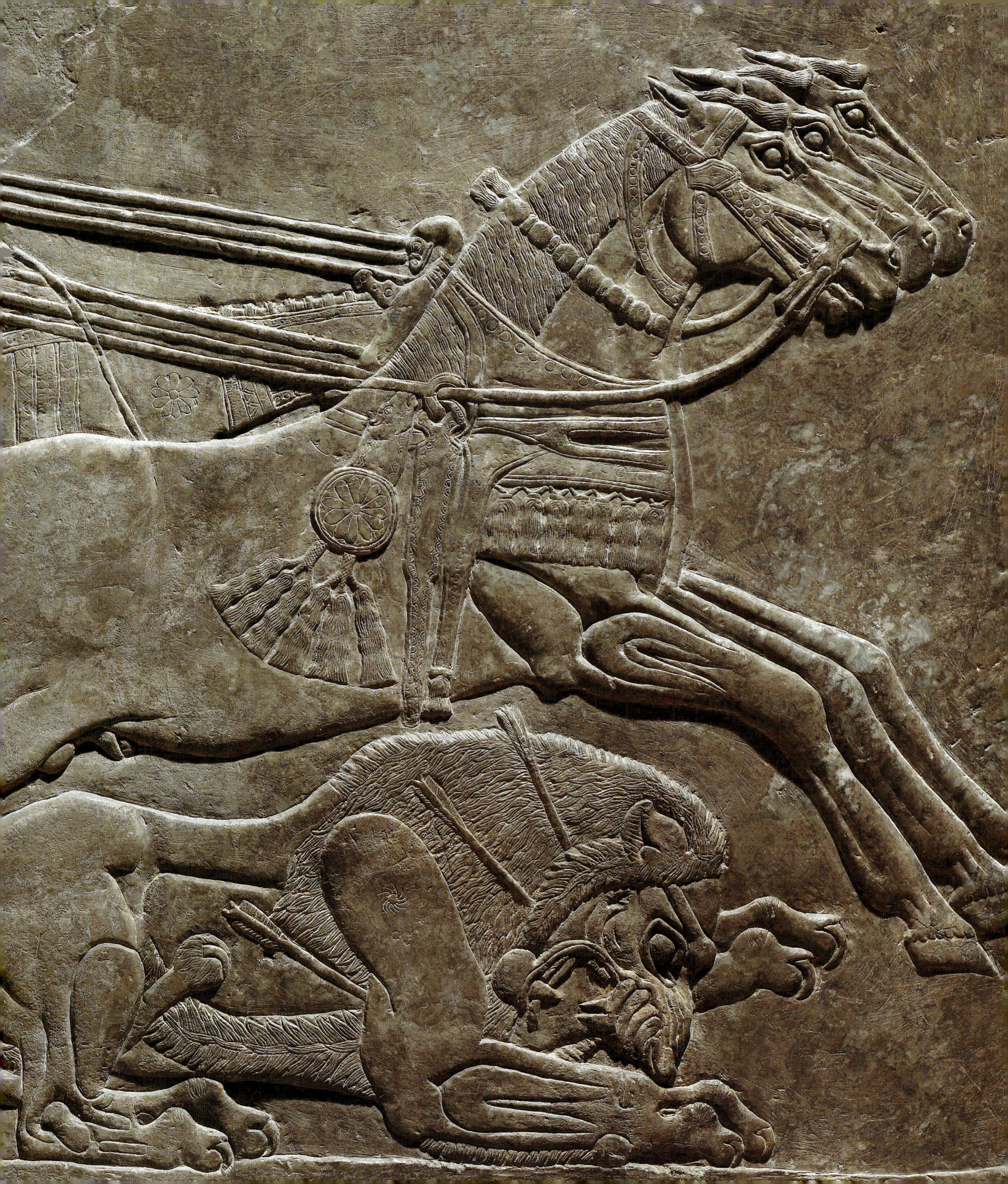

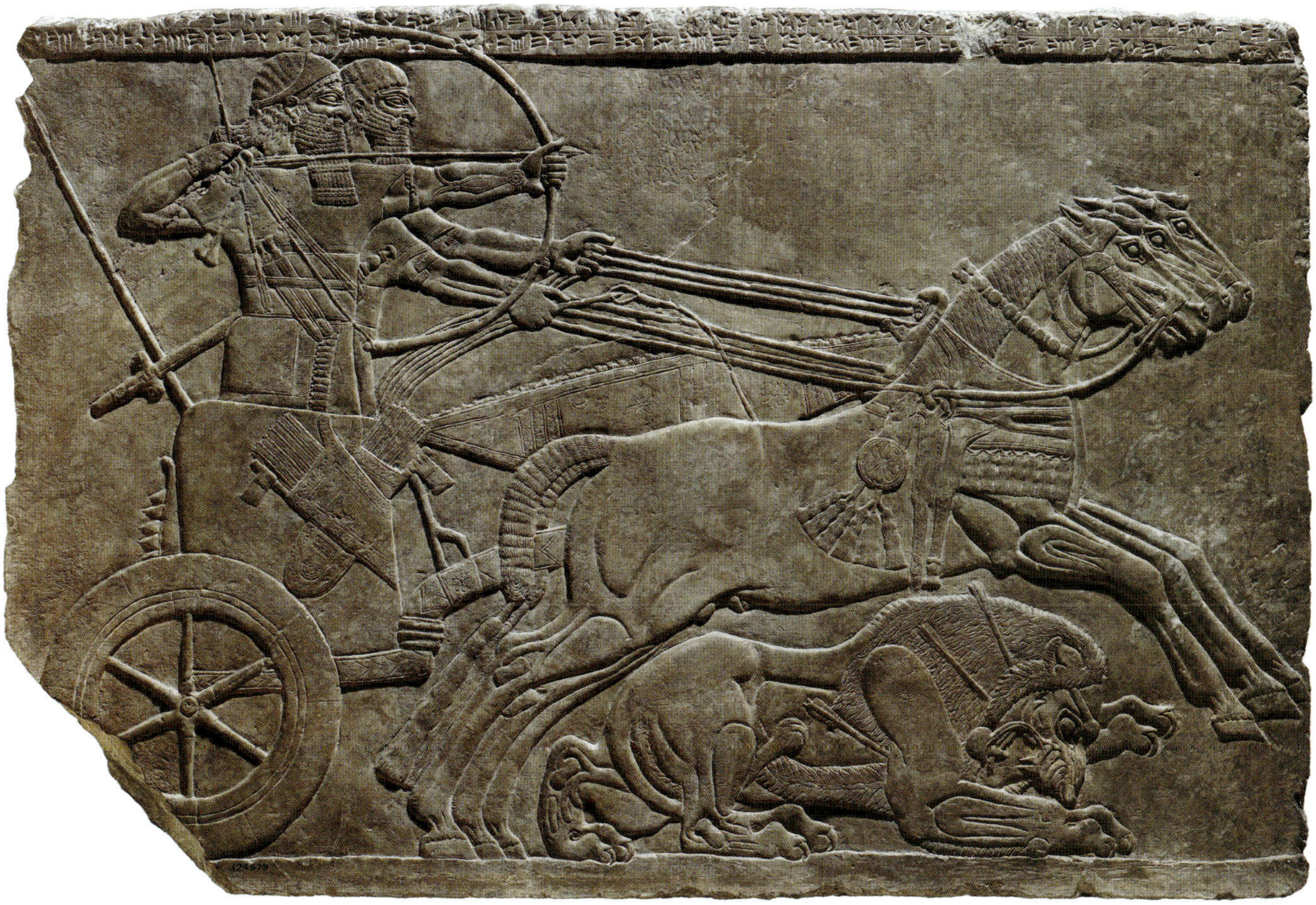

31

Assyrian wall relief showing a lion hunt

c. 875–860 BC, Assyrian
Nimrud, North-West Palace, West Wing, from excavations of A.H. Layard, 1845–51
Gypsum
H 98 cm, W 139.5 cm, Th. 23 cm
BM 124579

This panel shows two men in a light chariot hunting lions. The figure drawing the bow is wearing a diadem (headband) knotted at the back of his head with the two ends hanging down. This is probably King Ashurnasirpal II (883–859 BC) although the king is usually shown wearing a tiara with a flat top. A wounded lion, pierced by two arrows, lies beneath the hooves of the horses. Lions were still to be found in Mesopotamia until the nineteenth century AD, usually living in reed thickets by the side of rivers. The chariot is pulled by three horses who are controlled by the driver; he holds three pairs of reins and a whip in his hands. The horses wear headstalls decorated with small bosses and they are fitted with spade-shaped blinkers. The horses have bits with large cheekpieces in a 'bow-tie' shape. Known examples of this type are sometimes barbed. This relief is carved from a type of gypsum known as Mosul marble.

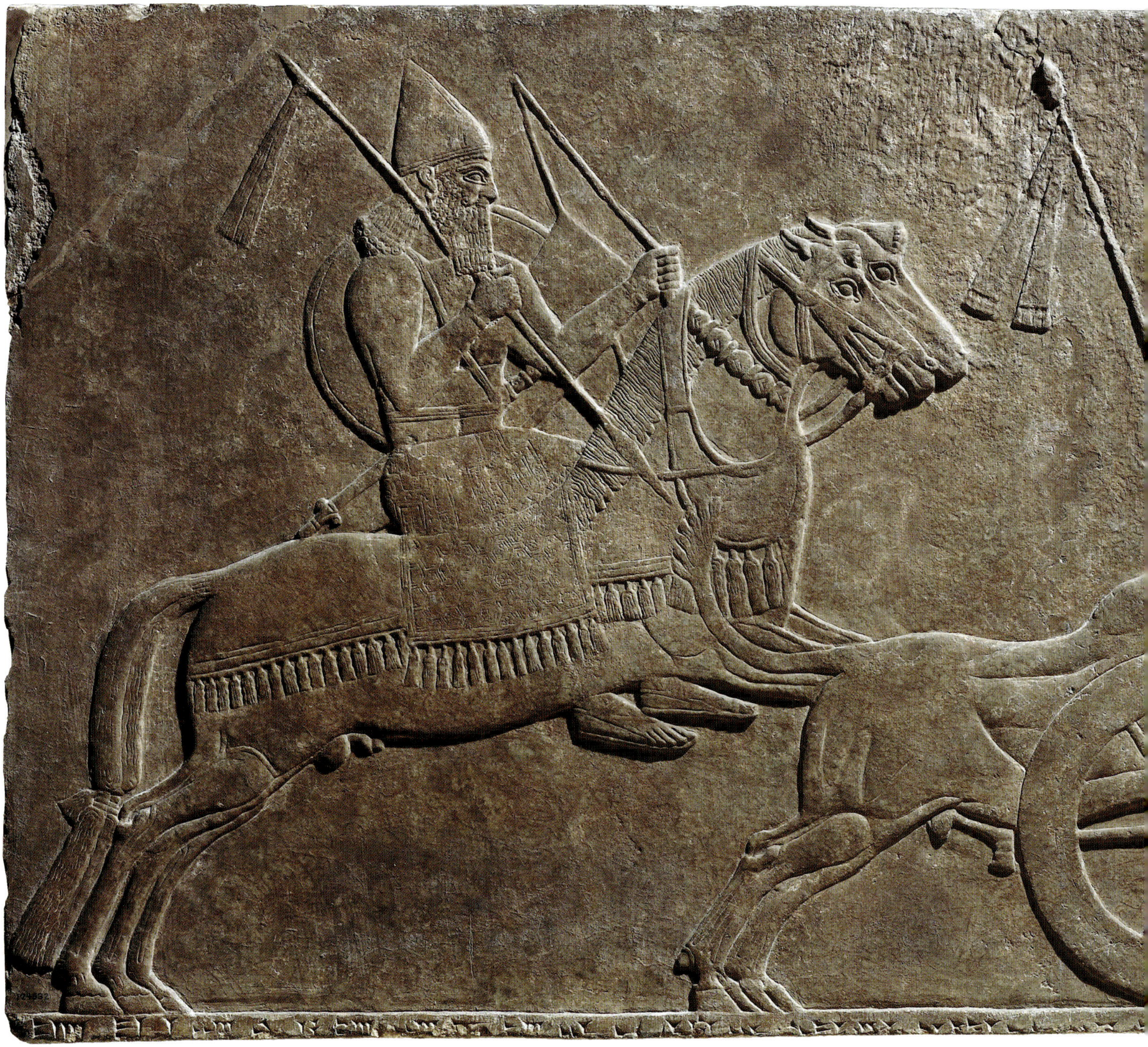

32

Assyrian wall relief showing a bull hunt

c. 875–860 BC, Assyrian
Nimrud, North-West Palace, Room B, from excavations of A.H. Layard, 1845–51
Gypsum
H 93 cm, W 225 cm, Th. 9 cm (extant)
BM 124532

This panel shows the Assyrian king Ashurnasirpal II riding in a chariot while hunting bulls. One bull lies dead or dying, riddled with arrows, beneath the hooves of the chariot horses, while another bull charges the chariot from behind. The king turns, and while holding it by the horn thrusts a dagger into its neck. The chariot is being pulled by three horses wearing elaborate harness and it is being driven by a charioteer who holds three sets of reins and a whip in his hands. Behind the chariot is a horse and rider leading another horse with a richly decorated saddle-cloth with tassels, which may be a mount for the king.

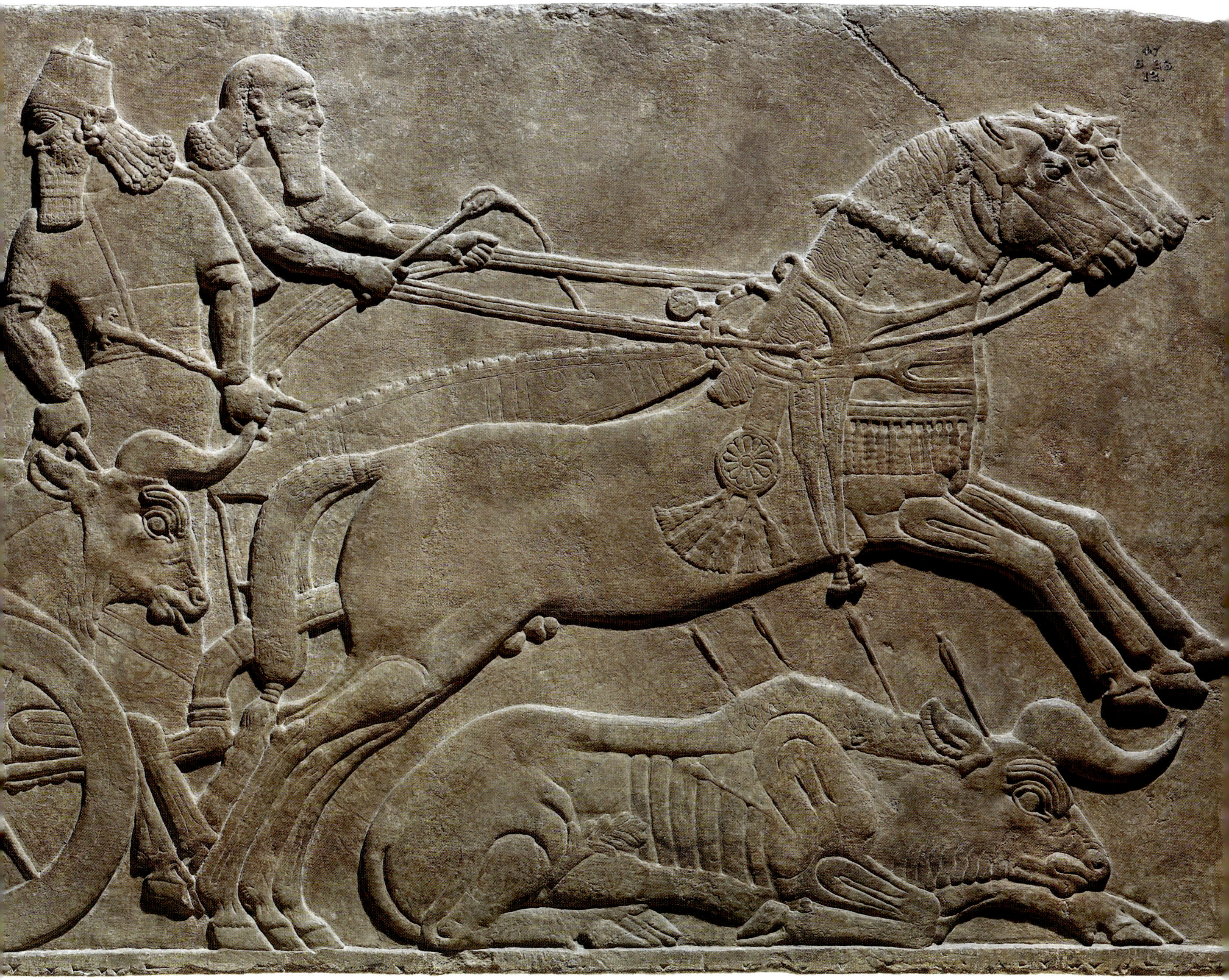

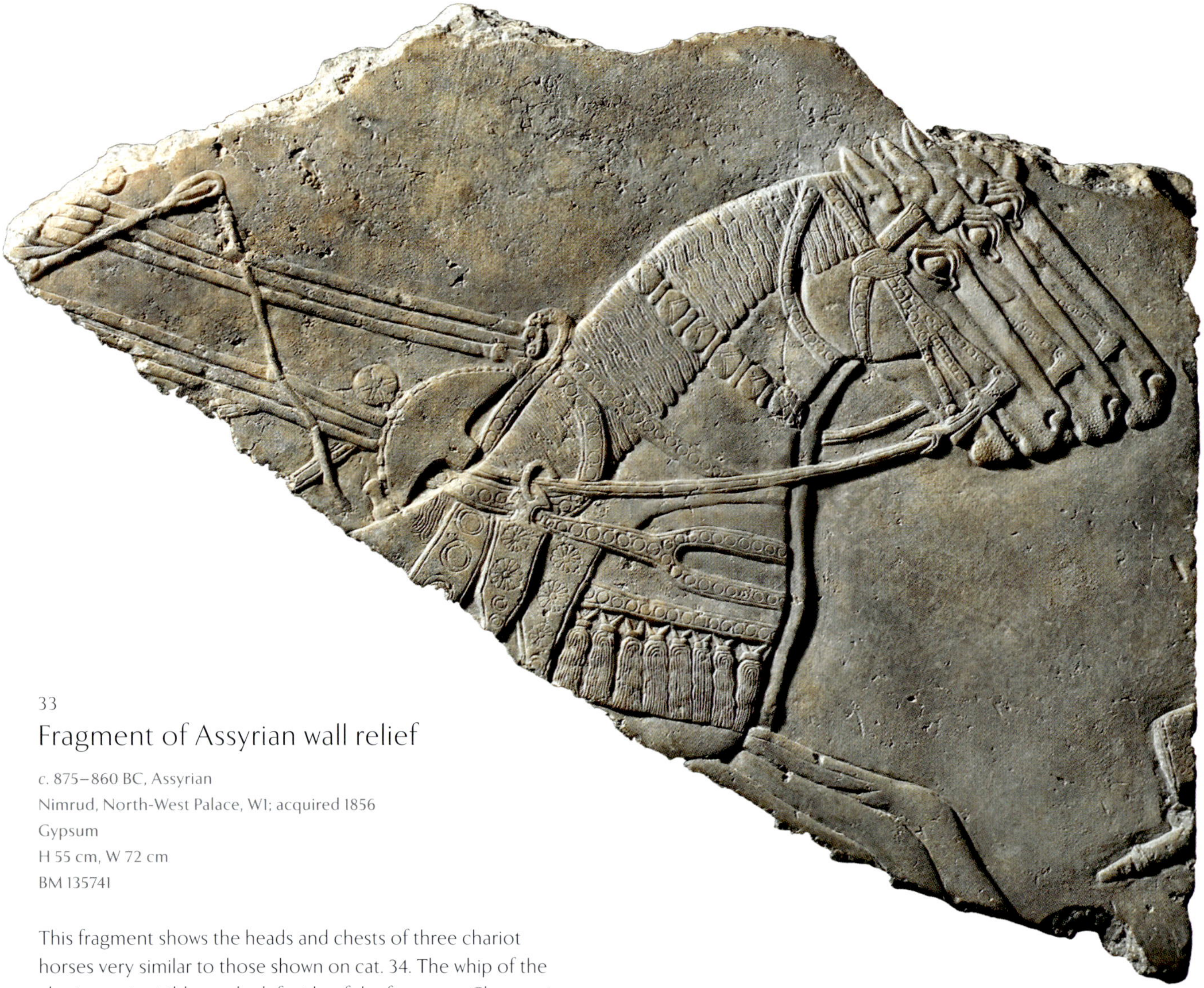

33

Fragment of Assyrian wall relief

c. 875–860 BC, Assyrian
Nimrud, North-West Palace, W1; acquired 1856
Gypsum
H 55 cm, W 72 cm
BM 135741

This fragment shows the heads and chests of three chariot horses very similar to those shown on cat. 34. The whip of the charioteer is visible on the left side of the fragment. Changes in chariot design led to larger crews and teams of three and four horses. At this time only two were under the yoke; the others were 'outriggers'.

34

Assyrian wall relief showing the king riding in a chariot

c. 875–860 BC, Assyrian
Nimrud, North-West Palace, West Wing; acquired 1856
Gypsum
H 101 cm, W 86 cm, Th. 20 cm
BM 124557

This panel shows King Ashurnasirpal II, a driver and an attendant riding in a chariot. The eight reins probably indicate that there are four horses, although only three heads are shown. The king himself wears a flat-topped tiara with a small spike in the middle, and stands in the near side of the chariot. He holds in his hands a bow and a pair of arrows. The charioteer holds the reins and a whip, and the third man holds a parasol over the king's head. The three visible chariot horses wear crests surmounted by horse hair and are decorated with trappings that include tassels on their chests and on their flanks. A soldier at the front guides the team of horses over what is evidently rocky terrain, indicated by the scale pattern at the bottom of the relief. There is also a river or stream in the vicinity, indicated by wavy lines with spirals. This scene is probably part of a military campaign, with the king passing by a mountain stream.

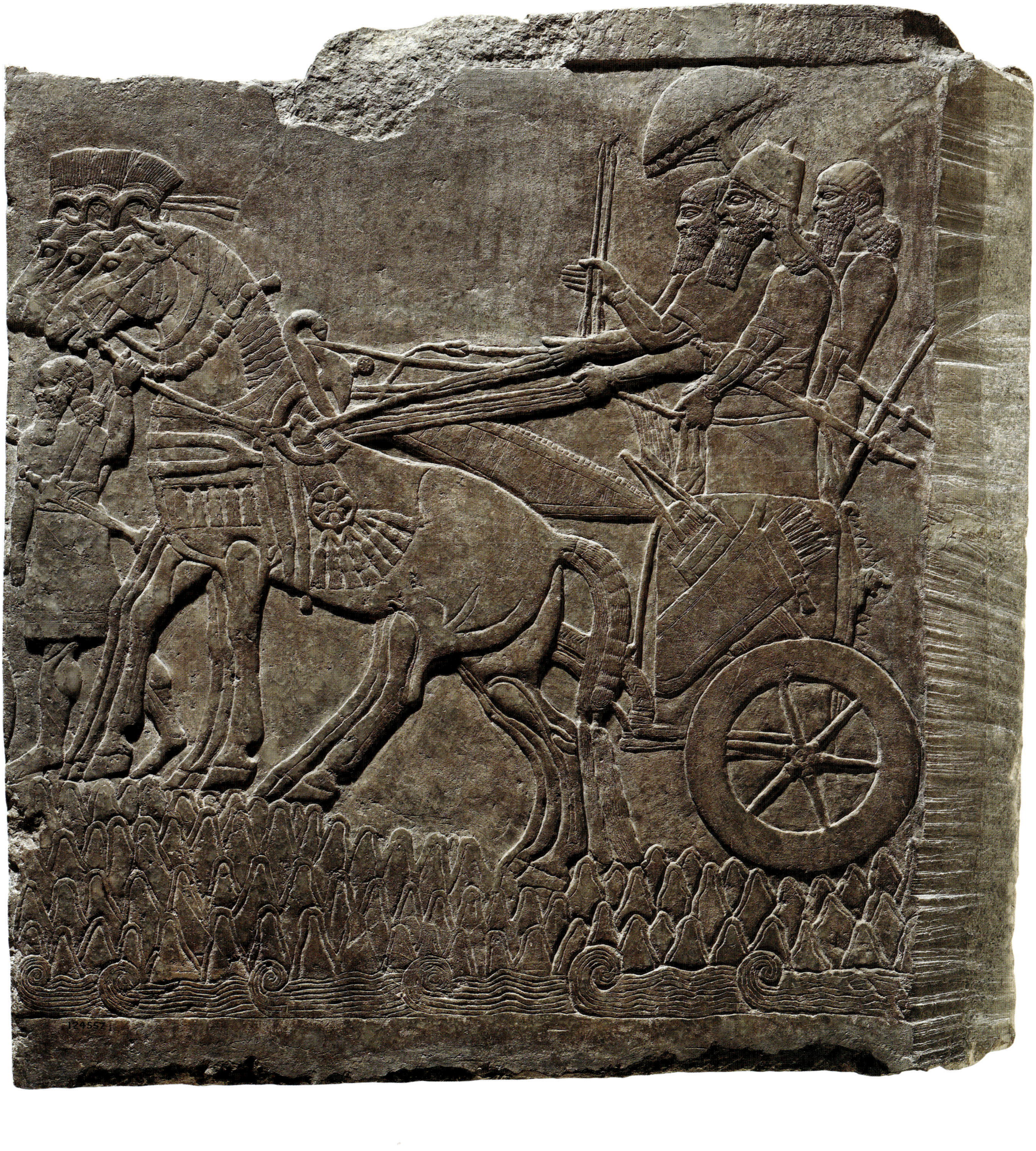

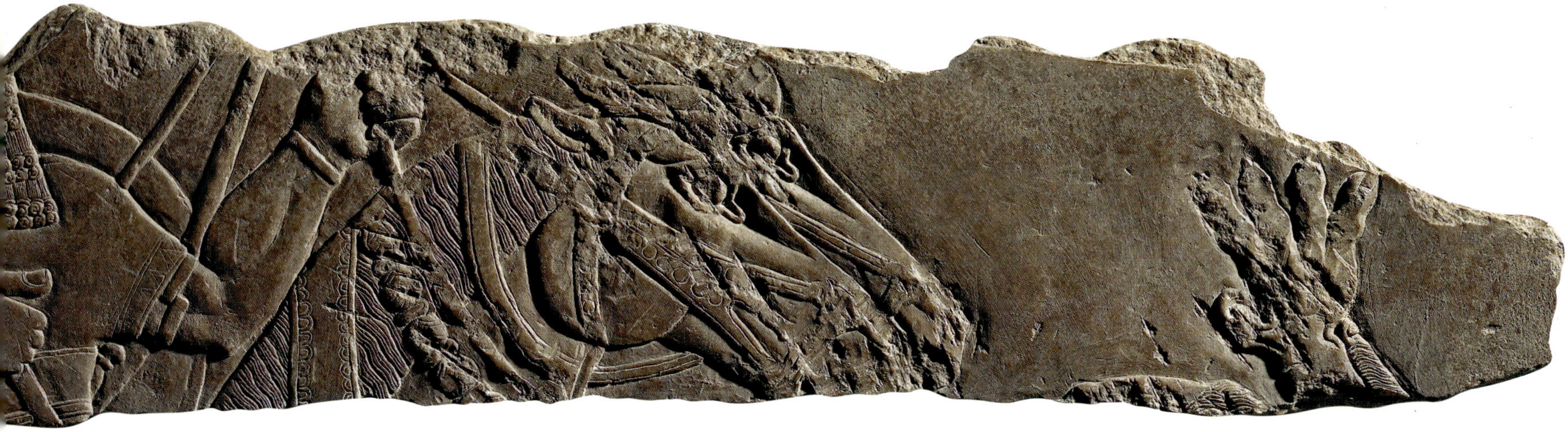

35

Fragment of Assyrian wall relief showing horses and a lion

c. 875–860 BC, Assyrian
Nimrud, North-West Palace, Room W1; acquired 1856
Gypsum
H 77.8 cm, W 20.7 cm
BM 135742

Shown on this fragment are the heads and necks of two horses, apparently being controlled by a bearded man. At this time it was standard practice for a single rider to control two horses, as if he was a charioteer, leaving any fellow rider free to use his bow or spear. In this case, the second horse might be for the king, as seen in the relief, cat. 34. In front of the horses are the head and claws of a rampant lion, so the scene being shown is evidently a lion hunt, which was a royal preserve. The horses wear harness that is typical of the ninth century BC.

36

Painted sherd

9th–8th century BC, Assyrian
Provenance unknown
Pottery
H 13 cm, W 11.5 cm
BM 122083

Part of a large pottery vessel with decoration in dark brown paint showing an archer on horseback pursuing another mounted rider who is largely missing. The rider has a beard and helmet in the Assyrian style. In accordance with standard Assyrian practice, a second horse can be observed which is presumably been ridden by the man who controls the archer's horse. The horse wears a crescentic breast ornament from which are suspended bells or tassels. Assyrian texts begin to list cavalry as well as chariotry in the reign of Tukulti-Ninurta II, and they are shown widely in the art of his son Ashurnasirpal II and grandson Shalmaneser III.

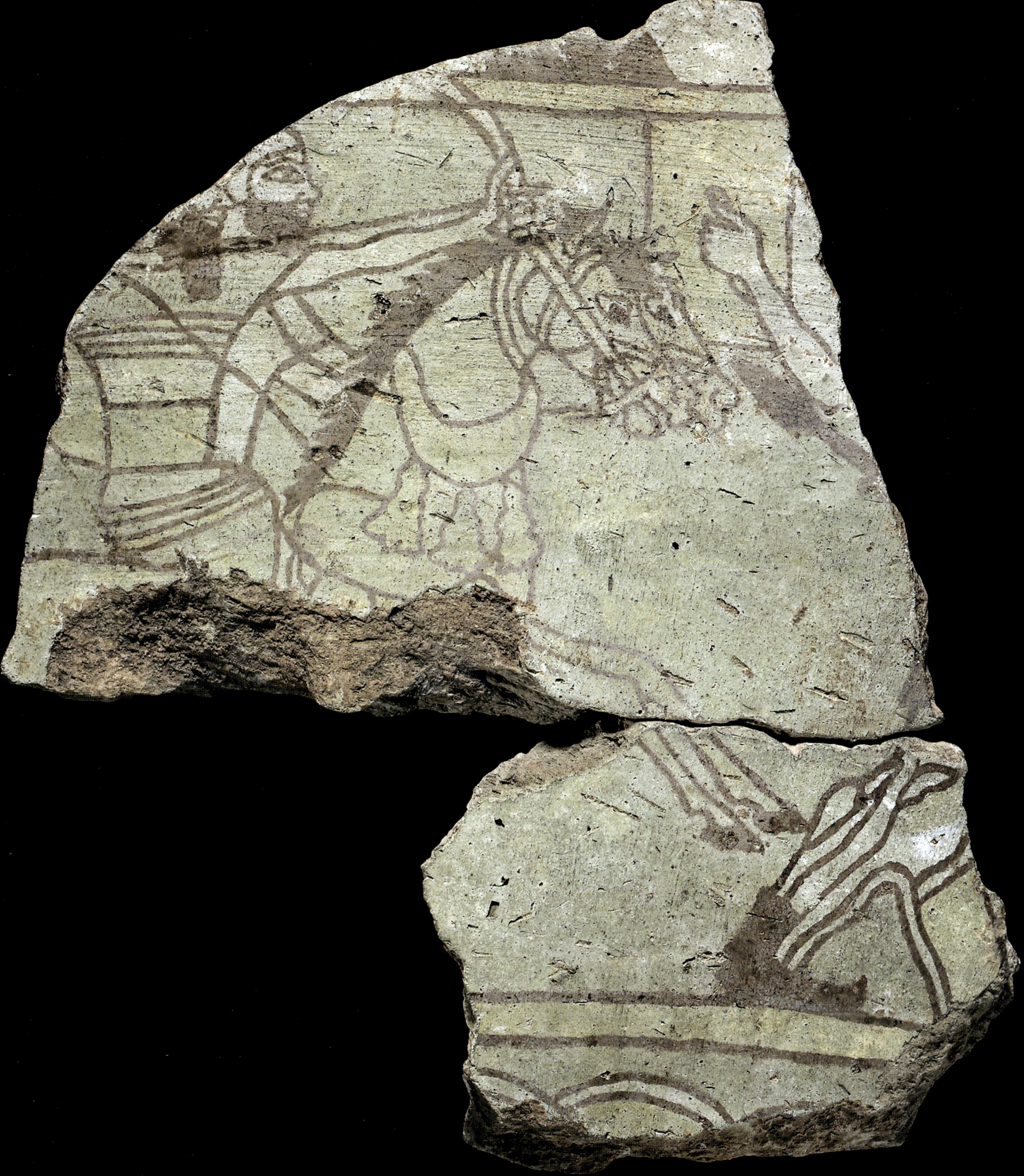

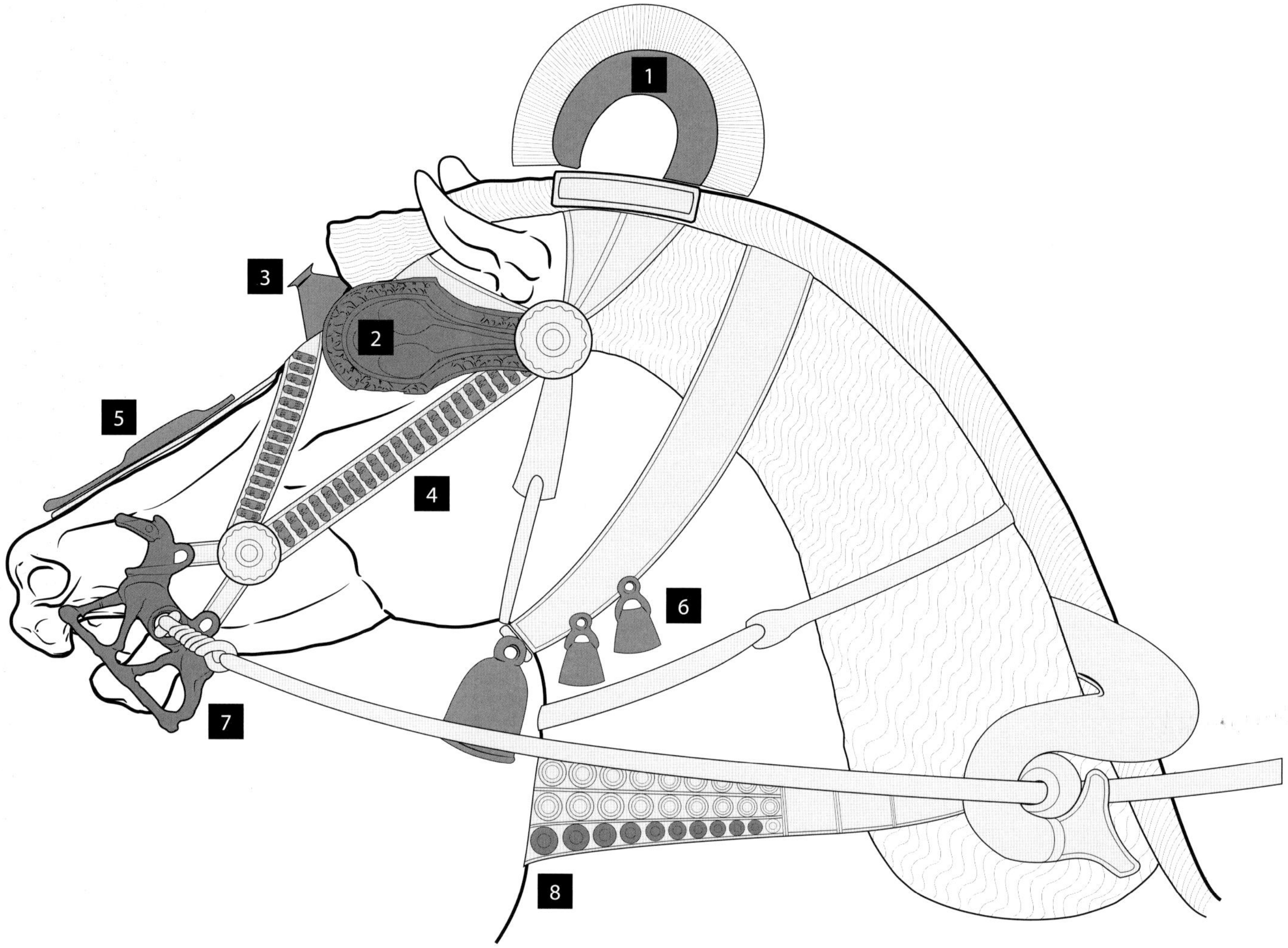

37
This diagram shows a simplified arrangement of bridle and yoke harness elements for an Assyrian chariot horse keyed to actual examples. This particular form of harness dates to the seventh century BC, though some of the actual pieces used here are earlier in date.

1 Crest holder (cat. 59).
2 Blinker (cat. 48). Blinkers are used so a harness horse can see ahead but not to the side or behind, to avoid sight of the vehicle and to prevent bickering. They are often reduced in size or omitted completely in Assyrian art, perhaps for supernatural reasons to avoid hiding the horse's eye.
3 Frontlet boss (cat. 57).
4 Bridle studs (cat. 70).
5 Frontlet (cat. 59).
6 Bells suspended from a nape strap (cat. 60–66).
7 Cheekpiece in the form of a horse (cat. 23). The cheekpieces held the mouthpiece of the bit in place and sometimes have spikes to exert extra control. This example is from Luristan, but very similar horse-shaped cheekpieces are shown used by some Assyrian horses.
8 Harness studs on the neck strap (cat. 68). The neck strap held the yoke in place.

38
Fragment of Assyrian wall relief showing a horse's head

721–705 BC, Assyrian
Khorsabad, Mesopotamia, Palace of Sargon II; acquired 1847
Gypsum
H 45.7 cm, W 33 cm
BM 118831

This fragment shows the head of a horse, probably part of a chariot scene. On the top of the horse's head is an elaborate crest, furnished with horse hair or wool, and the headstall is decorated with *phalerae* (embossed metal discs). The horse wears a brow cushion, and suspended around its neck is a series of large tassels. Around the chest of the horse is a wide band decorated with toggle-shaped (?) ornaments (see cat. 70). Scientific examination has revealed traces of red and blue paint on this relief, although they are difficult to see with the naked eye. Originally, all Assyrian reliefs were brightly coloured.

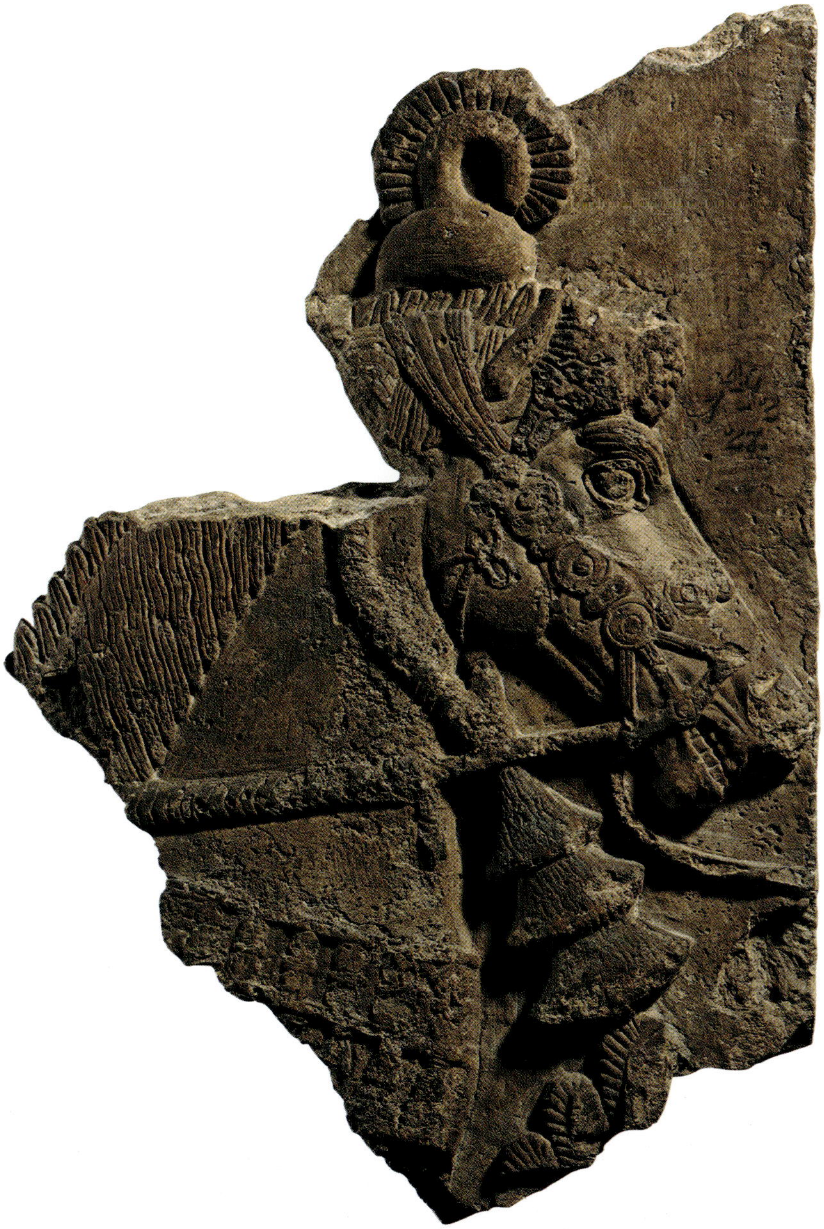

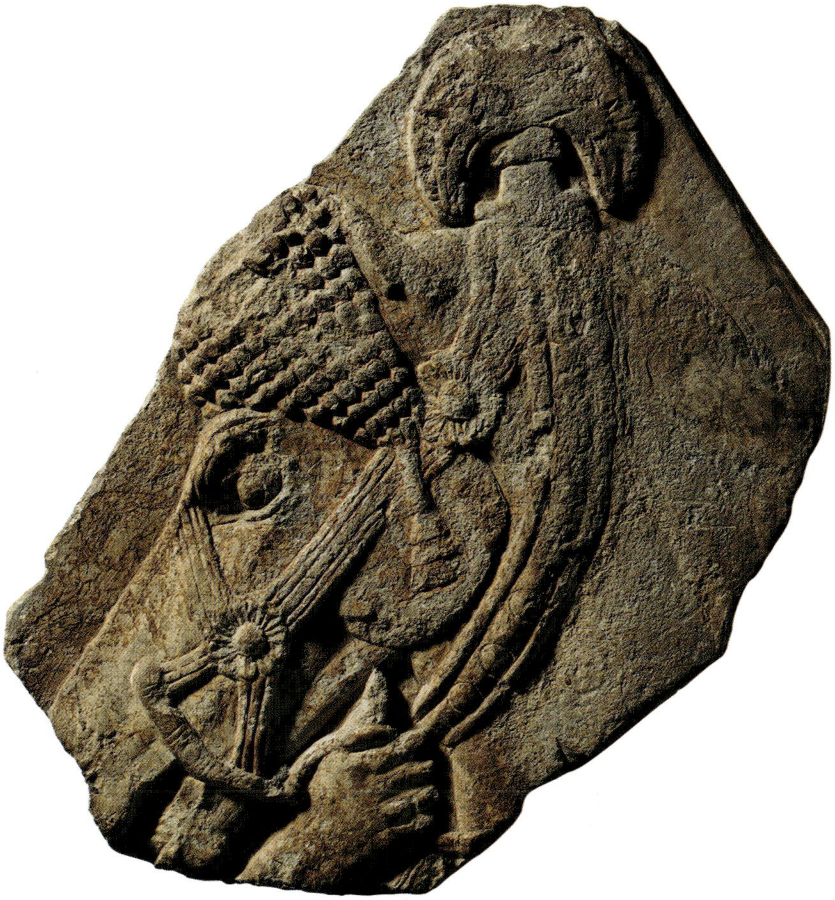

39
Fragment of Assyrian wall relief showing a horse's head

721–705 BC, Assyrian
Khorsabad, Palace of Sargon II; acquired 1847
Gypsum
H 49 cm, W 38 cm, Th. 10 cm (mounted)
BM 118833

This fragment shows the head of a horse being led by a groom, whose hand is visible holding the reins. The horse wears a curved, tapering cheekpiece that probably represents a reproduction in metal of a bone or antler cheekpiece, a padded brow cushion and a crescentic crest on top of its head. The headstall is decorated with rosettes, and tassels or corrugated metal caps (see cat. 67) hanging from the end of the brow cushion. This relief dates from the reign of Sargon II (721–705 BC).

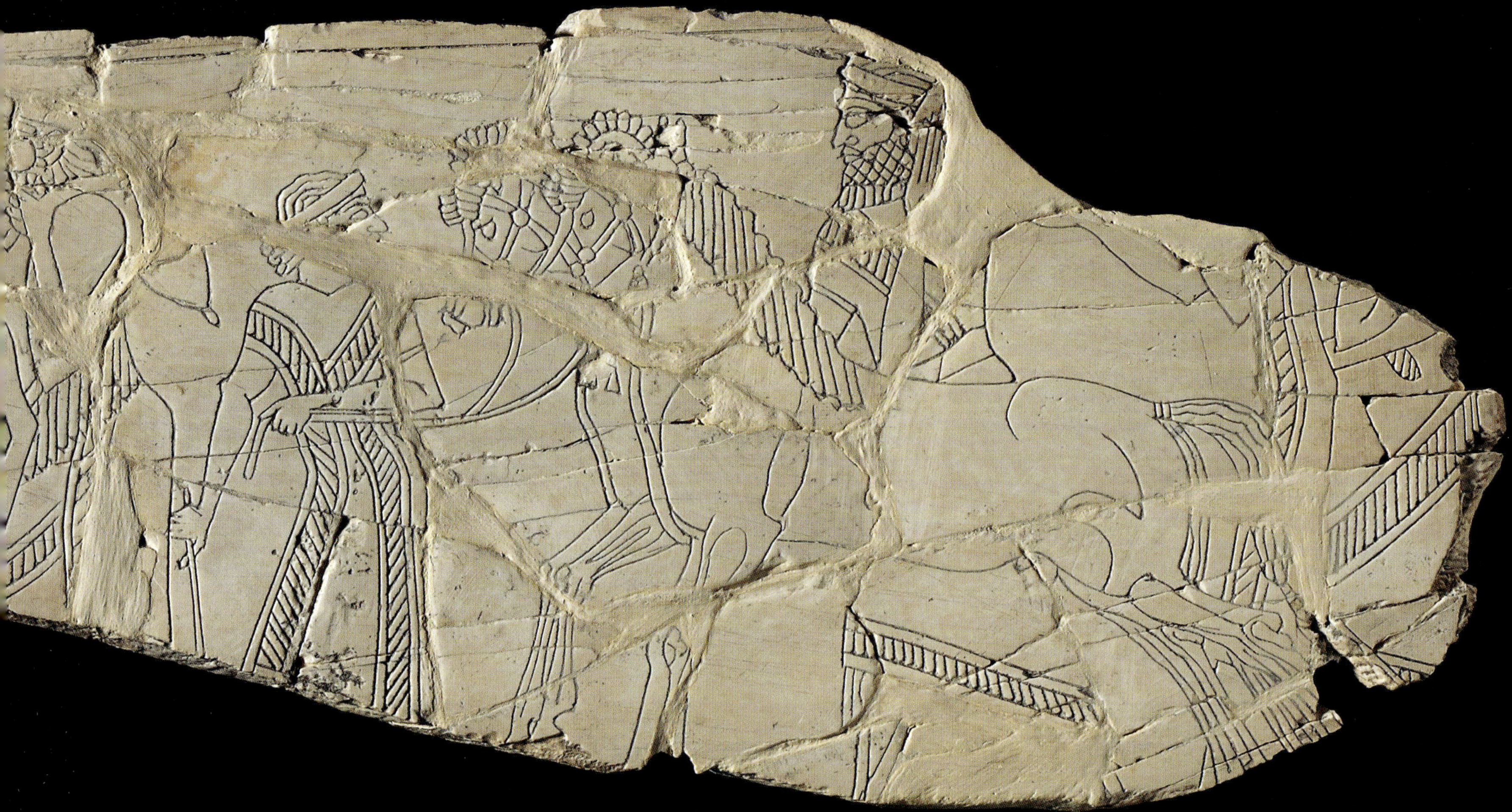

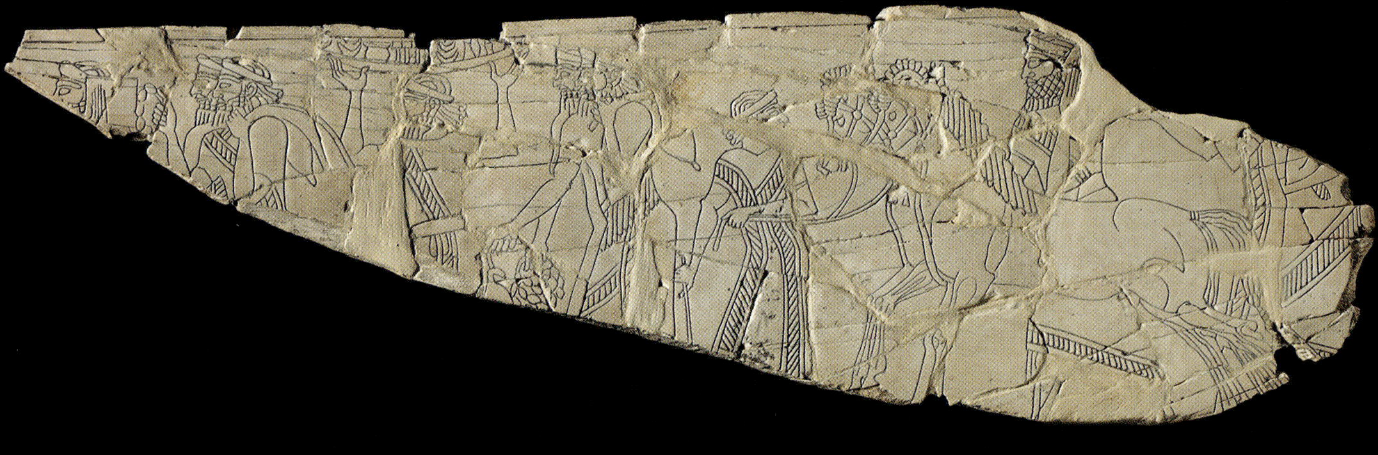

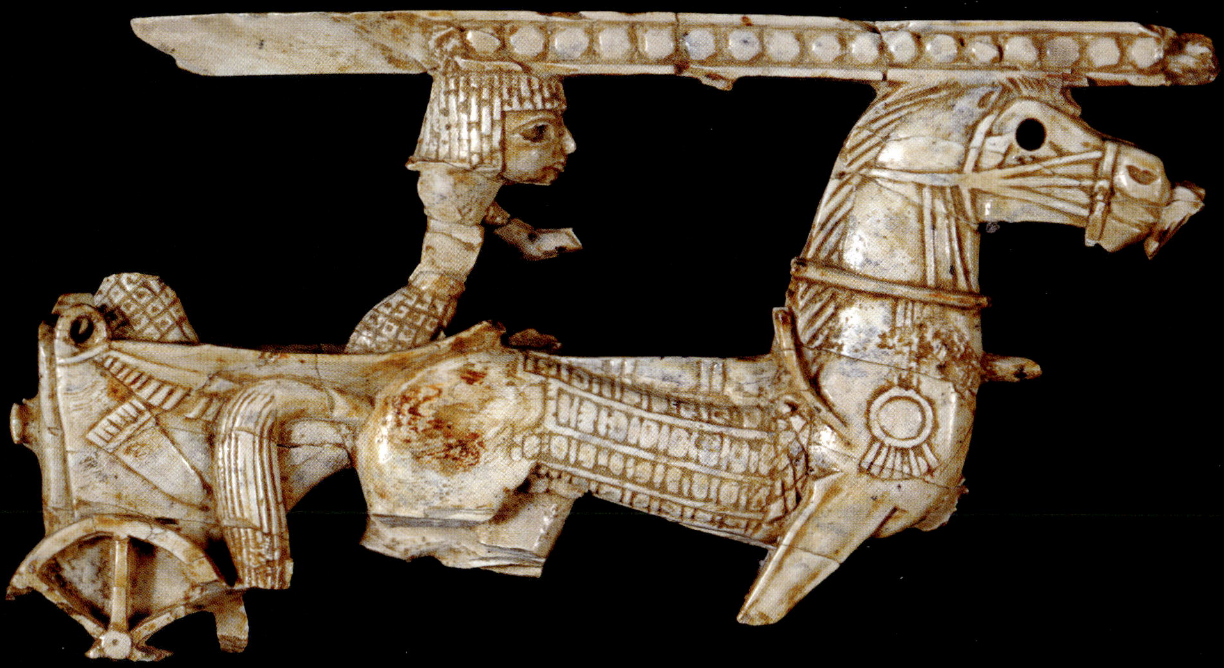

40

Ivory panel with procession of tributaries

8th–7th century, Assyrian
Nimrud, North-West Palace, excavations of W.K. Loftus, 1854–5
H 8 cm, L 26 cm
BM 118099

This fragmentary panel has incised decoration showing presents being brought for the Assyrian king, although he is not shown on this plaque. The tributaries are dressed in long fringed robes and headbands and come from the western part of the Ancient Near East. They bring various presents, including fruits and a pair of horses. The horses have arched crests topped with horse-hair and are being led by a tributary holding their reins. This plaque is in Assyrian style and was probably made in Assyria.

41

Ivory plaque showing a horse and chariot

9th–8th century BC, Syrian or Phoenician
Nimrud, Fort Shalmaneser, Room SW 37, excavations of British School of Archaeology in Iraq (BSAI), 1949–63 (ND 10316)
Ivory
H 6 cm, L 11 cm
BM 132939

This fragmentary ivory plaque was originally part of a larger composition, a veneer attached to a piece of wooden furniture or a box. It shows a horse pulling a chariot in the front of which stands the driver or charioteer. Traces of a passenger can be seen at the back of the cab. The chariot has a six-spoked wheel and a quiver hanging on the side. The charioteer has an Egyptian hairstyle, or wig, and a patterned tunic similar to that of the missing passenger. The horse also wears a patterned trapper, and has a large medallion hanging on his shoulder. It was suggested in the catalogue of the *Gift of the Desert* exhibition (2010) that this horse 'has many Arabian attributes, including a concave facial profile, a strong vertical neck, and arching tail'.

Many ivory plaques of this type were brought to Assyria as tribute or booty from cities in Syria or Phoenicia (Lebanon) where they were made. It is likely that this plaque comes from a Syrian centre.

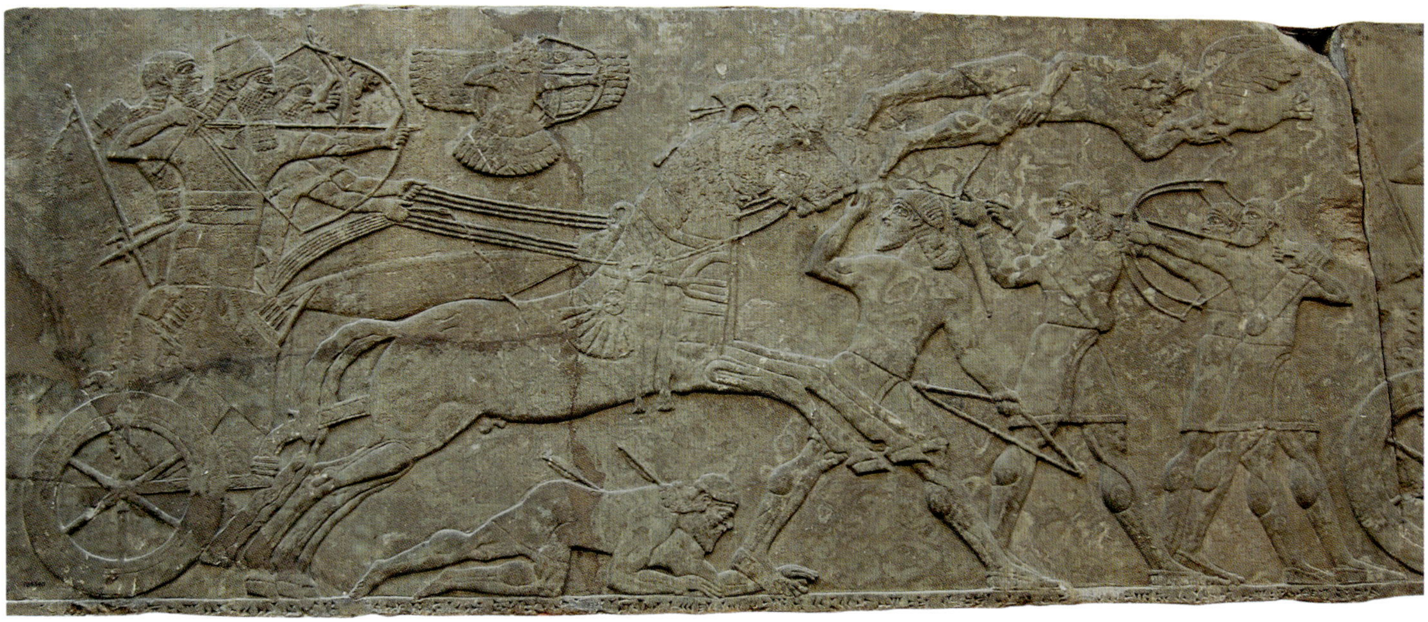

Fig. 46
A brand in the shape of a stylized running lion is shown on the hindquarters of this chariot horse on a relief from the North-West Palace of Ashurnasirpal II at Nimrud.
BM 124540

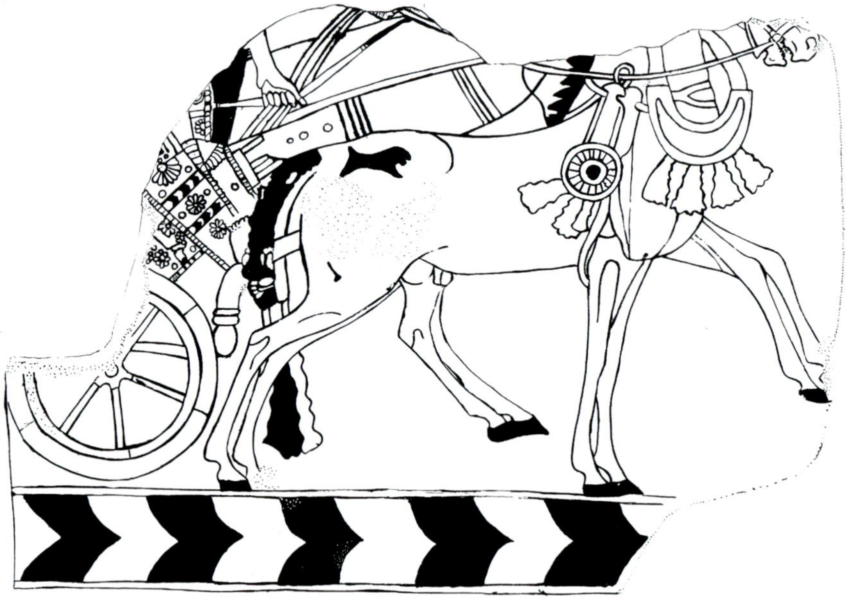

Fig. 47
This drawing shows a painted brick with a chariot from the palace of Ashurnasirpal II at Nineveh. The mark of a running lion is very clear on the horse's hindquarter.

42–6

Bronze branding-stamps

9th–7th century BC, Assyrian
Nimrud, from excavations of A.H. Layard
Bronze
BM 124598 H 2.9 cm, W 5 cm, L 4.8 cm
BM 135465 H 2.8 cm, W 5.1 cm, L 5.7 cm
BM 135466 H 2 cm, W 3.8 cm, L 6.3 cm
BM 135467 H 2 cm, W 3.1 cm, L 4.9 cm
BM N.507 H 2.5 cm, W 4.1 cm, L 2.5 cm (not illustrated)

These five metal stamps are in the shape of running lions and at the back of each is a Y-shaped attachment that would have fitted into a handle, probably of wood. Because of the existence of clay bricks stamped with similar designs at Khorsabad in Assyria and at Susa in south-west Iran these objects have traditionally been identified as brick-stamps. However, it is also possible, and perhaps more likely, that they were stamps for branding horses. Designs of the same shape made by stamps can be clearly seen on a relief of Ashurnasirpal II and on a painted tile from Nineveh. Horses were valuable and this lion symbol may have denoted royal ownership.

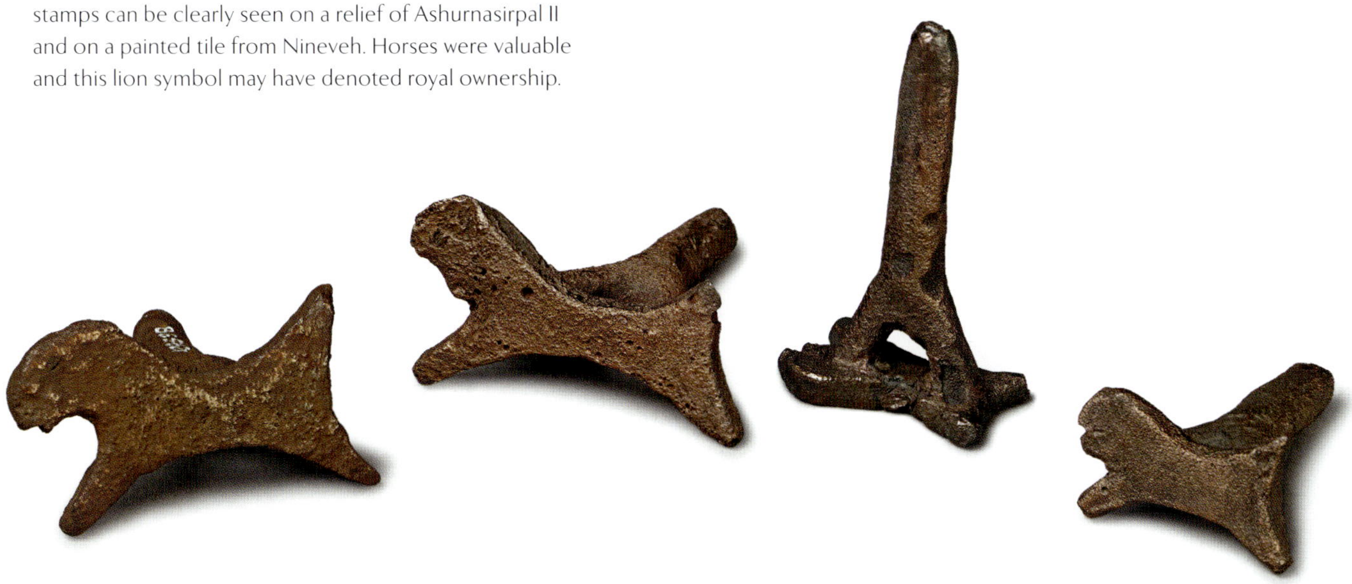

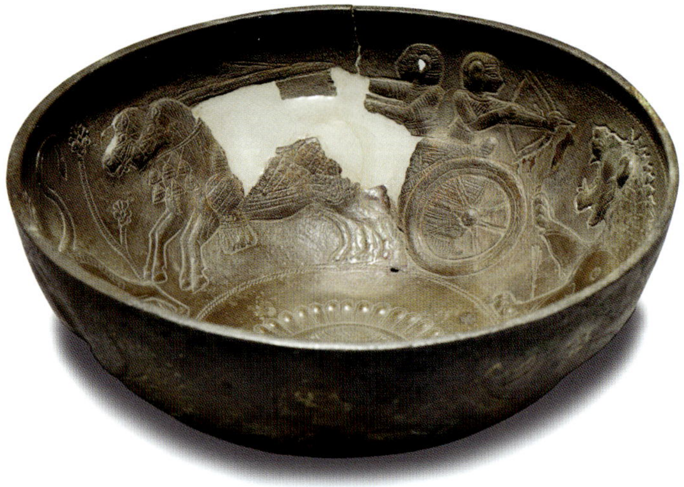

47

Bronze bowl showing a lion hunt

9th–8th century BC, Syrian or Phoenician
Nimrud, North-West Palace, excavations of A.H. Layard, 1845–51
Bronze
H 7.5 cm, diam. 21.5 cm
BM 118780

A deep bronze bowl with embossed and chased decoration showing a lion hunt. A large lion, already wounded by an arrow through its leg, is facing towards a retreating chariot, from which an archer is facing backwards and shooting an arrow at the lion. Both the archer and the driver of the chariot wear belted tunics and have Egyptian hairstyles. The driver holds the reins and a whip or goad in his hands. The chariot, with eight-spoked wheels, is being pulled by two horses wearing spade-shaped blinkers. The nearside horse is wearing a trapper decorated with a cross-hatched design and a large circular ornament on its shoulder, again with a cross-hatched design, from which are suspended feathers. Behind the lion is a bearded man armed with a spear, also with an Egyptian hairstyle. The scene is completed by a falcon between the lion and the spearman, and a winged sphinx with a woman's face and a lion's body between the spearman and the horses.

In January 1849 A.H. Layard discovered a hoard of about 140 bronze bowls in the so-called 'Room of the Bronzes' in the North-West Palace at Nimrud. Some of the bowls had embossed and chased decoration in Syrian or Phoenician style, like the present example, suggesting that these bowls were brought back to Nimrud by one of the Assyrian kings following a campaign in the west.

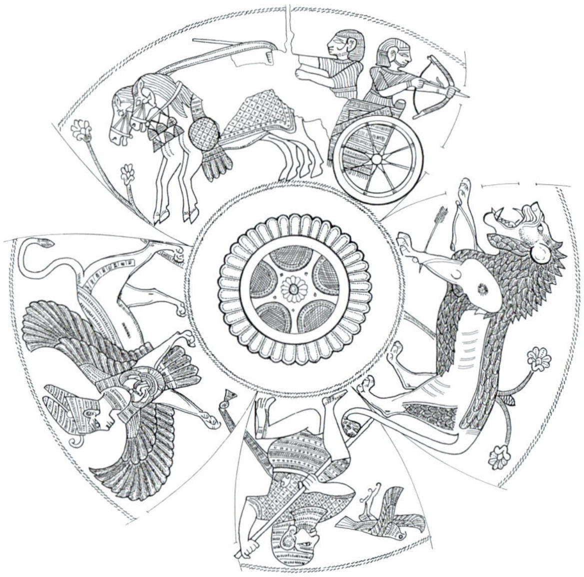

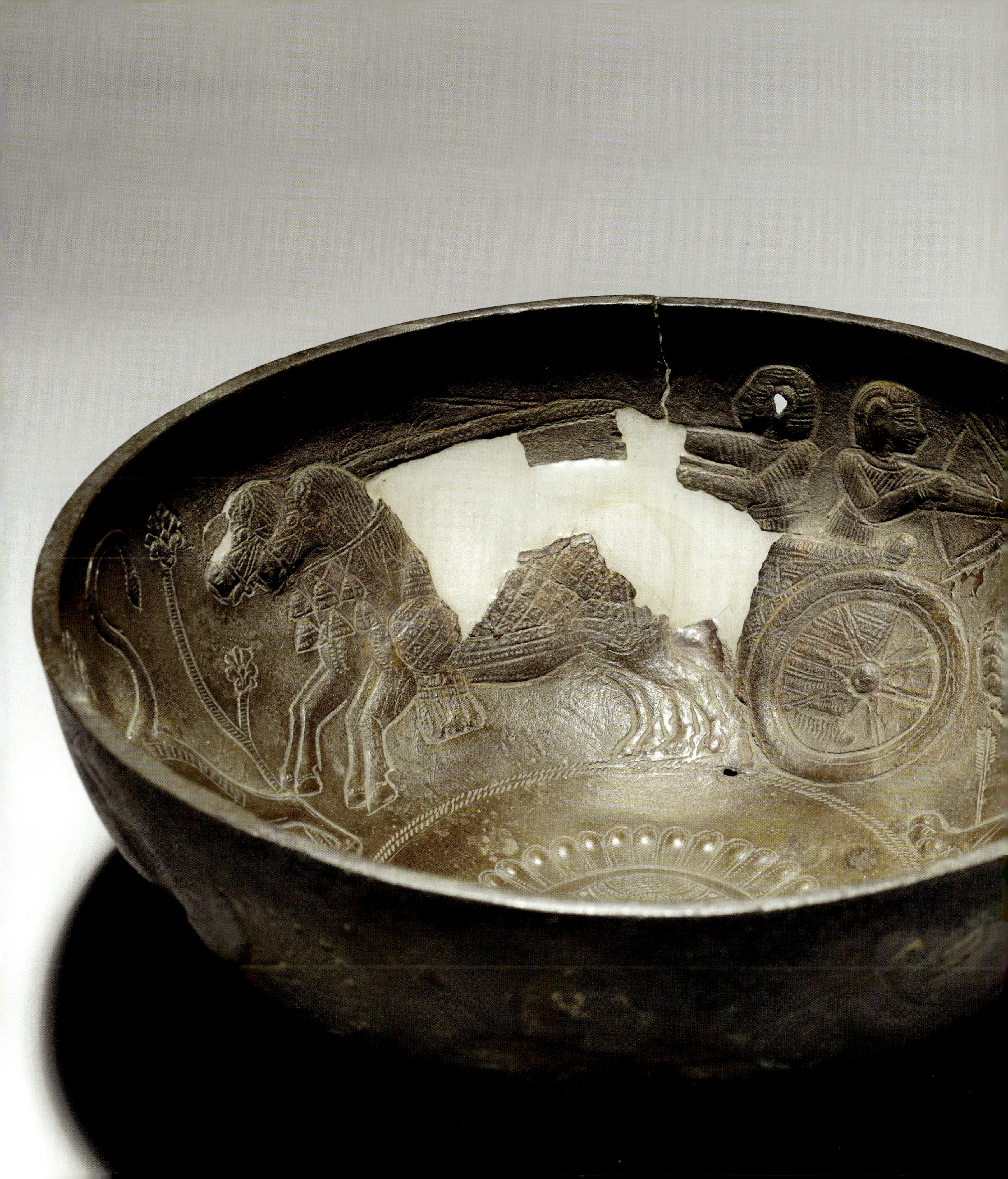

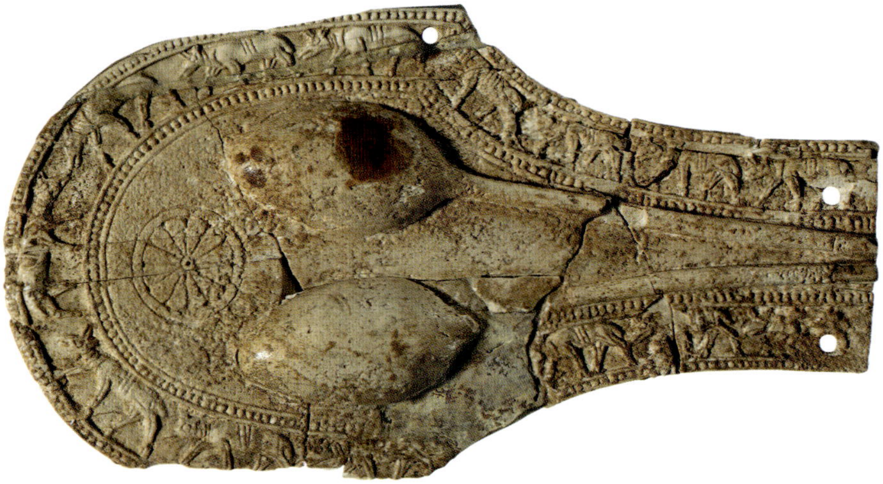

48
Horse's blinker ornament

9th–8th century BC, Syrian or Phoenician
Nimrud, Fort Shalmaneser, Room SW 37, excavations of BSAI, 1949–63 (ND 10752)
Ivory
L 16.1 cm, max. W 8.7 cm
BM 134960

Spade-shaped blinker ornament in carved ivory showing in the middle two lotus buds with long stems in high relief and an incised rosette, and around the edge of the plaque two friezes of animals, probably goats, set between two bands of dotted decoration. The plaque was fixed to a backing by means of four holes around the edge.

49
Horse's blinker ornament

9th–8th century BC, Syrian or Phoenician
Nimrud, Fort Shalmaneser, Room SW 37, excavations of British School of Archaeology in Iraq 1949–63 (ND 10802)
Ivory
L 8.2 cm, W 6.1 cm
BM 2011,6001.745

Shield-shaped blinker ornament in carved ivory with decoration that includes an Egyptian *wedjat*-eye (eye of Horus) and a human arm and hand with bangles on the upper arm. There are holes along the base of the plaque for attachment.

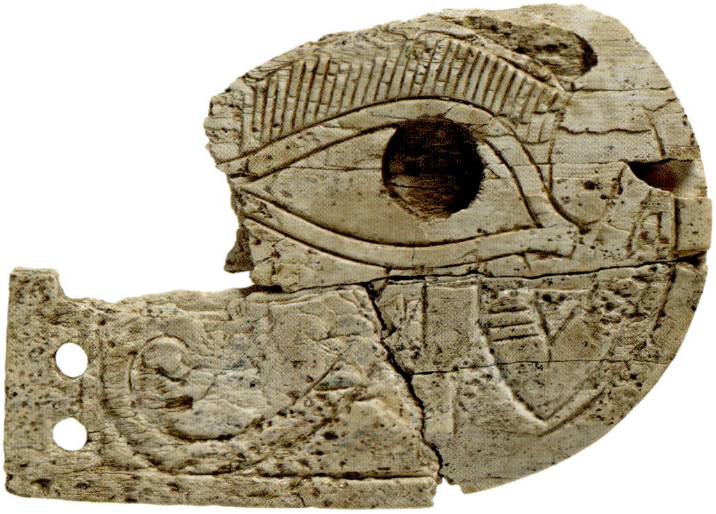

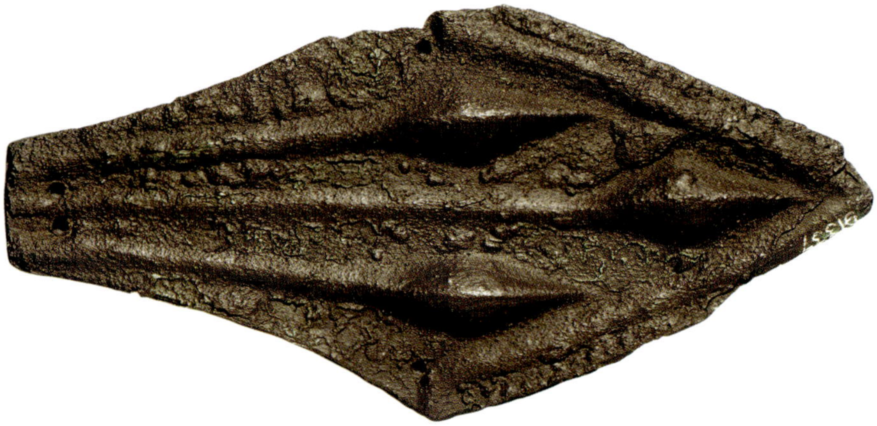

50
Blinker ornament

9th–8th century BC, Syrian or Phoenician
Possibly from Nimrud
L 16.8 cm, max. W 8 cm
BM 91337

Spade-shaped blinker ornament in bronze with embossed decoration showing three lotus buds on long stems in the centre. Two embossed ribs repeat the outline of the plaque at the front, and there are four holes for attachment.

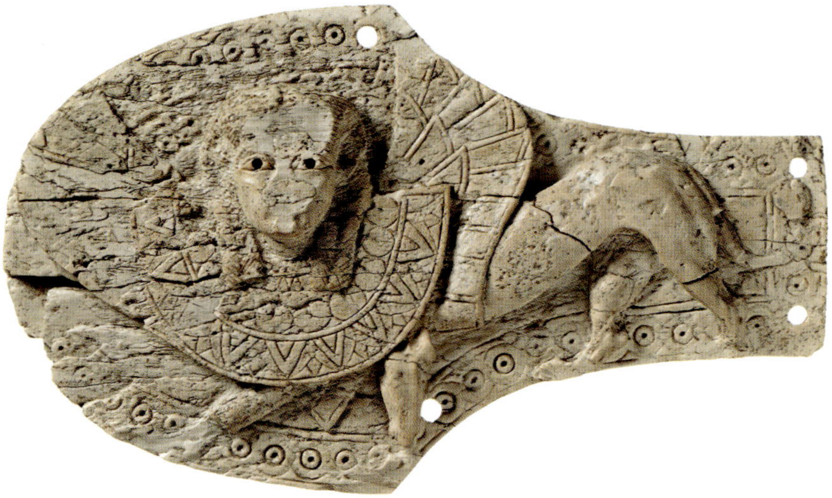

51

Horse's blinker ornament

9th–8th century BC, Syrian or Phoenician
Nimrud, Fort Shalmaneser, Room SW 37, excavations of BSAI, 1949–63 (ND 10495)
Ivory
L 12.8 cm, W 7.6 cm
BM 2011,6001.637

Spade-shaped blinker ornament in carved ivory showing a sphinx with a woman's head and lion's body wearing a large collar. There is a border of guilloche ornament around the outside of the plaque, and there are four large holes for securing it to a backing. The Egyptian style of the sphinx shows that this plaque was made in Phoenicia (Lebanon) or Syria.

52

Horse's blinker ornament

9th–8th century BC, Syrian or Phoenician
Nimrud, Fort Shalmaneser, Room T 10, excavations of BSAI, 1949–63 (ND 11200)
Gypsum
L 11.3 cm, W 7.9 cm
BM 132997

Spade-shaped blinker ornament with a large bud in high relief in the centre. Two faint lines below the bud are probably meant to indicate the stem. There is a sunken border around the edges of the plaque in which are holes for attachment.

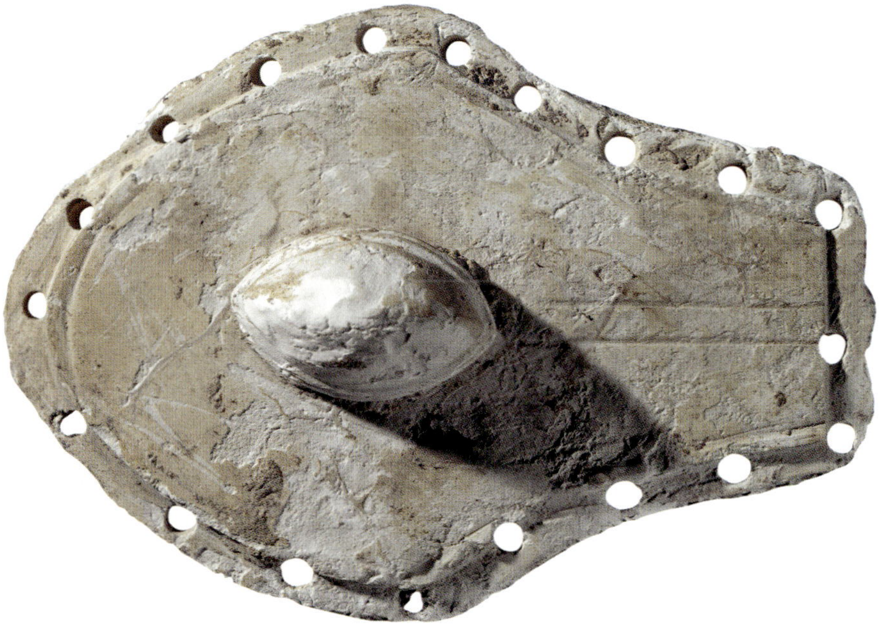

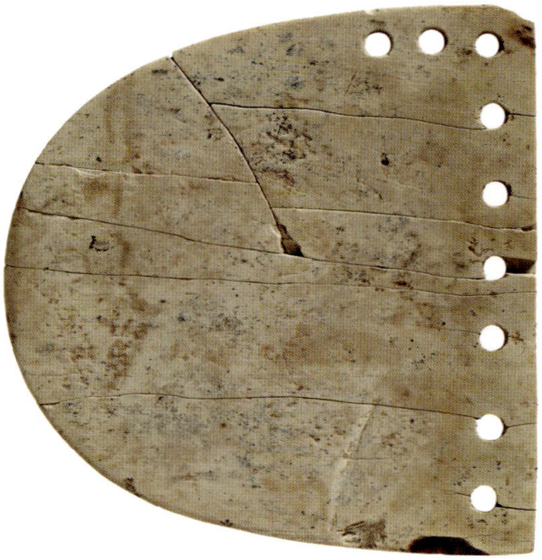

53

Horse's blinker ornament

9th–8th century BC, Syrian or Phoenician
Nimrud, Fort Shalmaneser, Room SW 37, excavations of BSAI, 1949–63 (ND 9449)
Ivory
L 6.8 cm, W 7.1 cm
BM 2011,001.472

Plain shield-shaped blinker ornament with large holes for attachment along the base and for a short distance along one side.

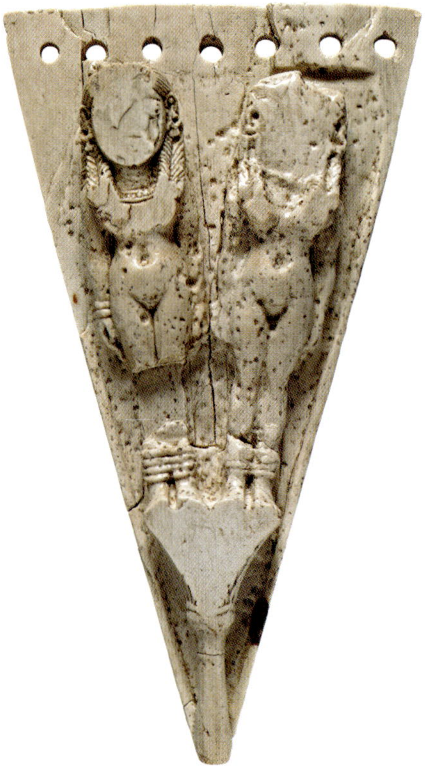

54
Horse's frontlet ornament

9th–8th century BC, Syrian or Phoenician
Nimrud, Fort Shalmaneser, Room SW 37, excavations of BSAI, 1949–63 (ND 10511)
Ivory
H 10 cm, W 5.6 cm
BM 2011,6001.643

Triangular-shaped horse's frontlet or face-piece ornament in carved ivory decorated with two naked women standing on a lotus flower. They wear bangles on their wrists and ankles. There is a row of large holes at the top of the plaque for attachment.

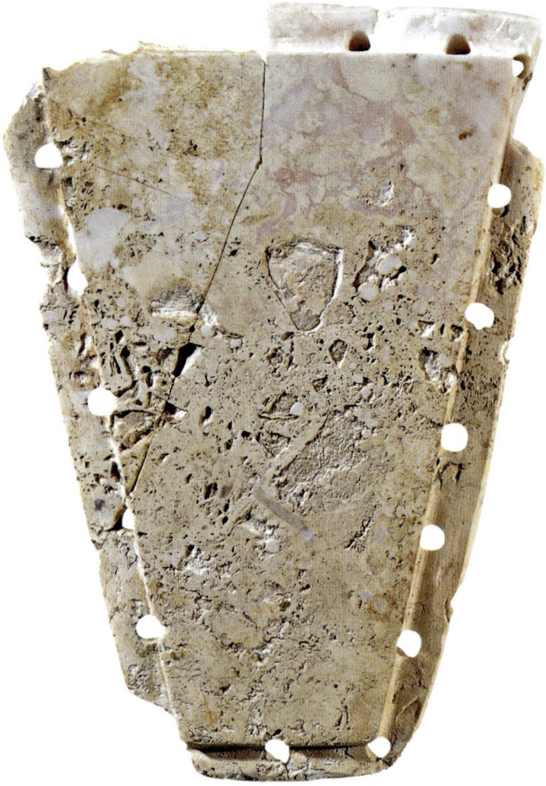

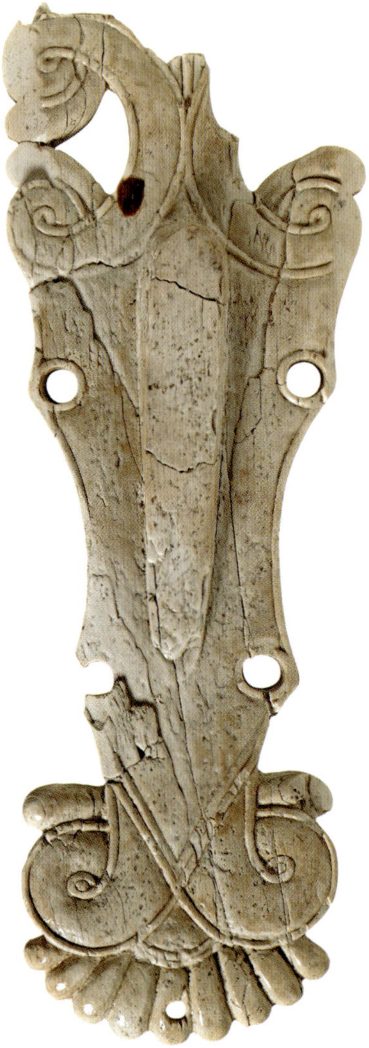

55
Horse's frontlet ornament

9th–8th century BC, Syrian or Phoenician
Nimrud, Fort Shalmaneser, Room SW 37, excavations of BSAI, 1949–63 (ND 10515)
Ivory
H 15.0 cm, W 5.3 cm
BM 2011,6001.644

Horses frontlet or face-piece ornament in carved ivory with double volute ornaments at the top and a palmette combined with a lotus flower at the bottom. There are four holes for attaching this ornament to a backing.

56
Horse's frontlet ornament

9th–8th century BC, Syrian or Phoenician
Nimrud, Fort Shalmaneser, Room T 10, excavations of BSAI, 1949–63 (ND 12503)
White stone
H 11.1 cm, W 7.9 cm
BM 140417

Horse's frontlet or face-piece ornament in white stone of quadrilateral shape tapering towards the bottom. There is a sunken border around the edges of the plaque in which are holes for attachment.

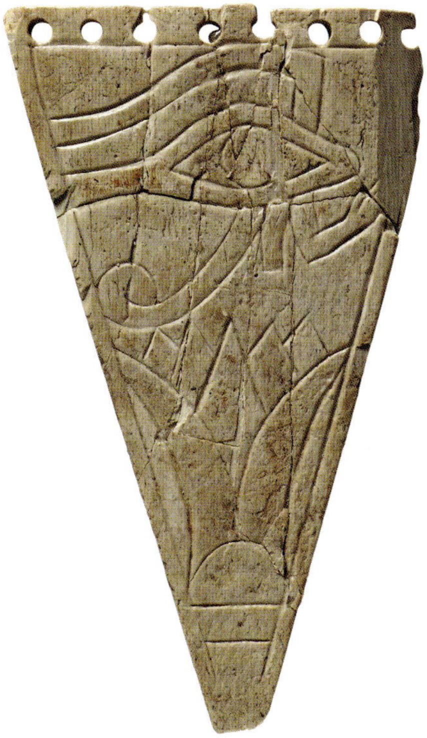

57

Horse harness boss

8th–7th century BC, Assyrian
Nimrud, Iraq, excavations of A.H. Layard, 1845–51
Bronze
H 3.5 cm, W 6.3 cm
BM N.116

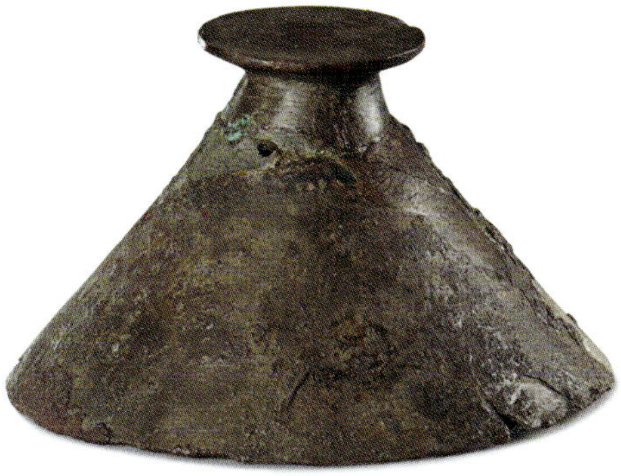

Hollow bronze boss with flared sides, a flat top and a ring fastener inside for attachment. Such bosses can be seen on Assyrian reliefs mounted on the horse's forehead above the frontlet. Alternatively, elaborate bosses are sometimes mounted on the headstall.

58

Horse's frontlet ornament

9th–8th century BC, Phoenician or Syrian
Nimrud, Fort Shalmaneser, Room SW 37, excavations of BSAI, 1949–63 (ND 10435)
Ivory
H 10.2 cm, W 5.9 cm
BM 2011, 6001.620

Horses frontlet or face-piece ornament in carved ivory. The decoration includes a *wedjat*-eye (eye of Horus), a human arm and hand and a lotus flower. There is a row of large holes at the top of the plaque for attachment.

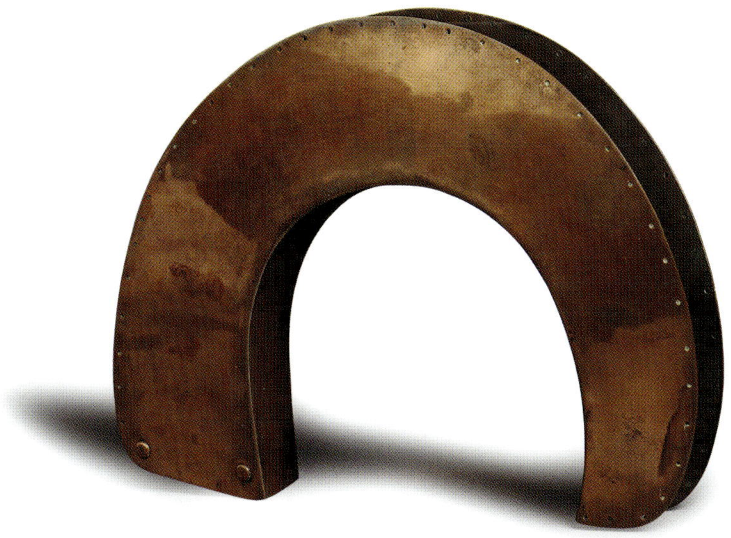

59

Bronze replica of horse harness crest

This is a copy of a bronze object found in the Assyrian destruction level at Lachish dating from 701 BC, when Sennacherib attacked the city. The original is now in the Rockefeller Museum in Jerusalem. It has been variously interpreted as a helmet crest or a horse harness crest. The object is crescent-shaped and hollow, and would have held an upstanding crest made from textile or horse hair. Such crests can be seen on Assyrian reliefs worn on the top of horse's heads.

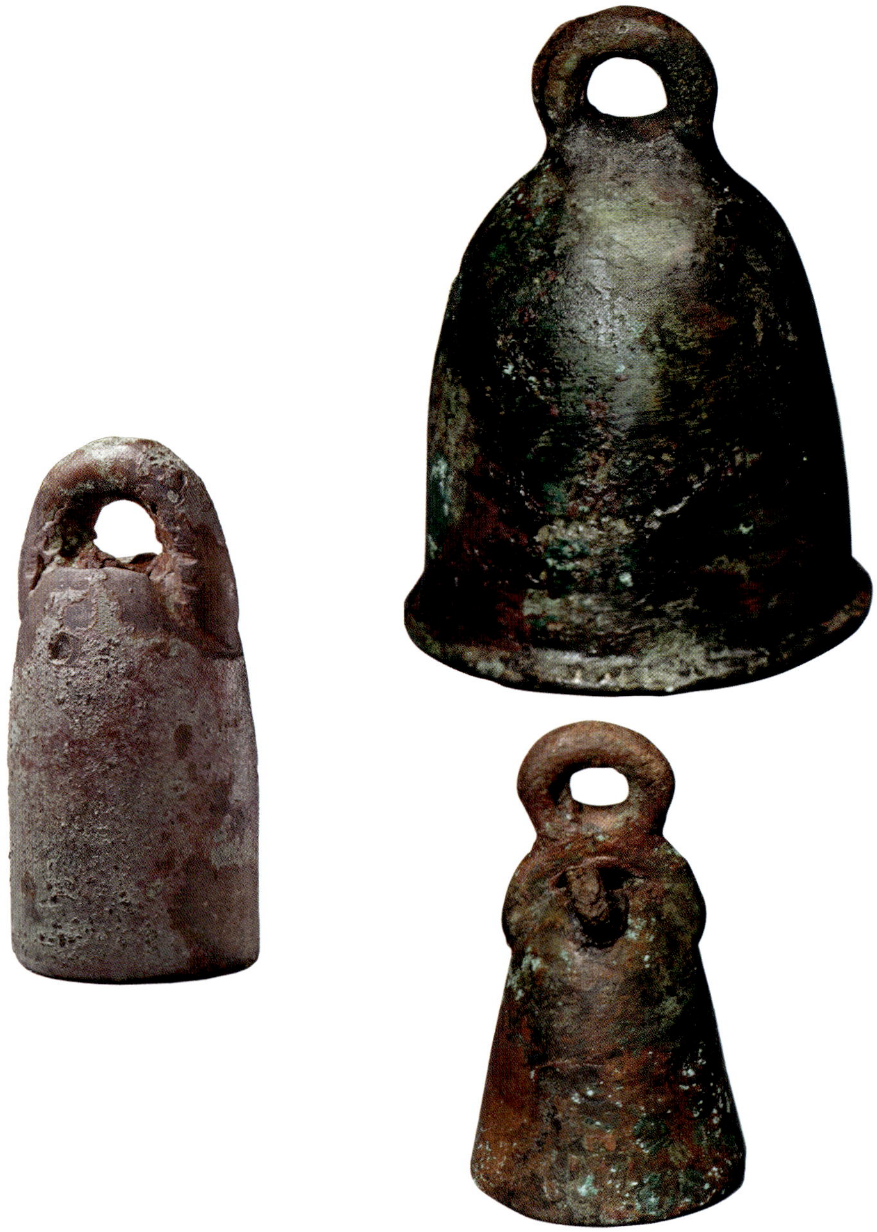

60–66

Horse harness bells

9th–7th century BC, Assyrian
Nimrud, North-West Palace, Room AB, excavations of A.H. Layard, 1845–51
Bronze
H from 4.85 cm to 8.2 cm
BM N.157, N.182, N.177, N.155, N.199, N.193, N.215

In two cauldrons in the 'Room of the Bronzes' (AB) in the North-West Palace at Nimrud, Layard found what he rightly identified as 'ornaments of horse and chariot furniture'. Amongst them was a large collection of nearly eighty bells which are now in the British Museum. They include large examples with rounded shoulders, a ring at the top and a flange at the bottom, smaller straight-sided examples with loop holders at the top, and bells with straight flaring sides and a figure-of-eight holder at the top. A noticeable feature of all these bells is that they have clappers in the form of thick iron rods. These clappers sometimes survive intact, but are mostly missing.

The Assyrian reliefs clearly show that bells were suspended around horses' necks. From the time of Tiglath-pileser III (744–727 BC) onwards, bells or tassels sometimes hang from a band or strap, sometimes of plaited leather and usually referred to as a nape strap. Both draught and cavalry horses are shown wearing bells, the purpose of which seems to have been both decorative and to intimidate the enemy with their noise. Large numbers have been found in Urartu, the Caucasus and western Iran, suggesting that the fashion for using them as horse trappings comes from those areas. It is interesting that these are the same regions, to the north and north-east of Assyria, which also bred horses.

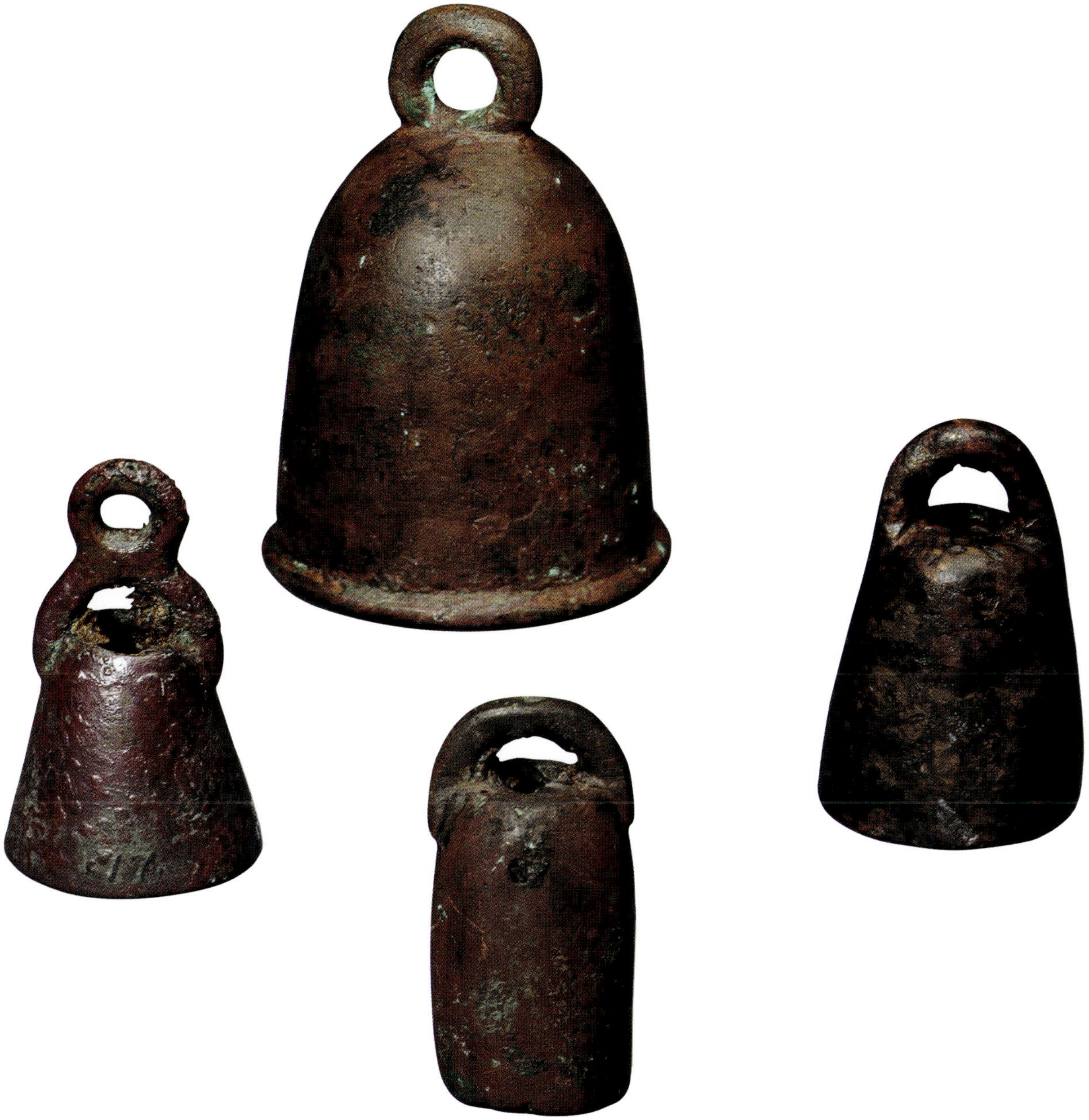

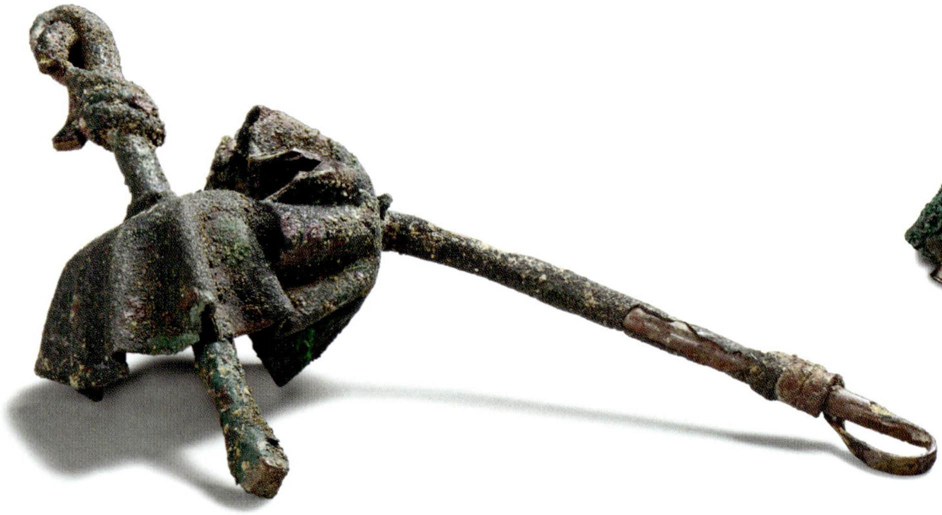

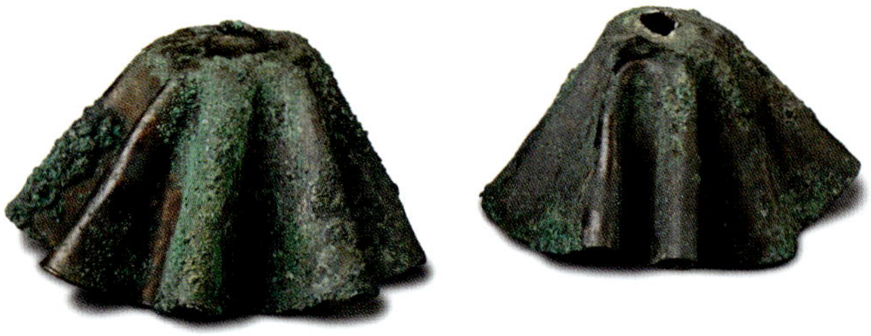

67

Tassel-holder, part of horse harness

8th–7th century BC
Nimrud, North-West Palace, Room AB, excavations of A.H. Layard, 1845–51
Bronze
Max. L 10.16 cm, max. diam. 4.5 cm
BM N 281, N 282, N 546

Bronze caps with corrugated sides and a hole in the top, for fixing to a metal rod. The rods have a loop at the top for attachment and a stop at the bottom to keep the cap in position. Sometimes three of these caps are suspended from a small holdfast. They are either harness ornaments in their own right or they are meant to be tassel-holders.

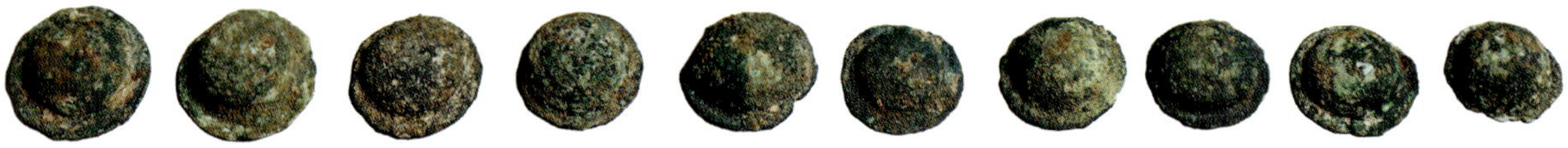

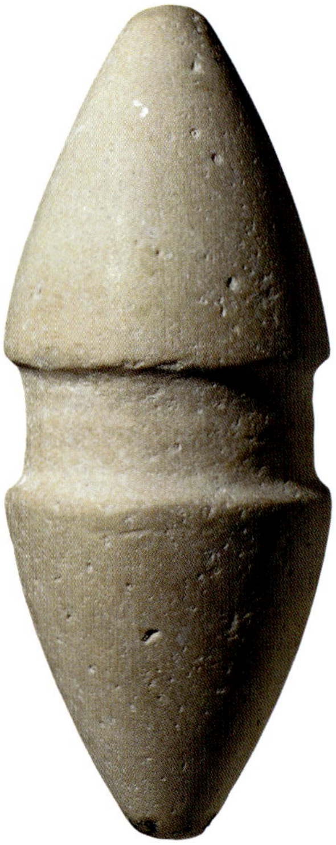

68

Harness studs

9th–7th century BC
Nimrud, excavations of BSAI, 1949–1963
Bronze
Diam. 1.1 cm
BM 1984,0205.266

Small bronze bosses used for decorating a horse's harness. These are hammered from sheet-metal and inserted into leather harness straps.

69

Toggle

9th–7th century BC
Nimrud, Fort Shalmaneser, Room SE 11, excavations of BSAI, 1949–63 (ND 7814)
White stone
H 12 cm, max. diam. 4.5 cm
BM 140336

Oval stone toggle with a groove around the centre. Toggles are shown in various contexts on Assyrian reliefs, but in connection with horses they are used to fix securely the trappers or horse-blankets sometimes worn by cavalry and draught horses. This is particularly clear on reliefs of Ashurbanipal (668–631 BC).

70
Harness ornaments

9th–7th century BC
Nimrud, North-West Palace, Room AB,
excavations of A.H. Layard, 1845–51
White stone
L 2.4 cm, W 0.9 cm, Diam. 1.2 cm
BM N 2081

Elongated oval studs with rib decoration and a projection underneath with two holes, for fixing to a background. Such ornaments are to be seen on breast straps and other elements of harness.

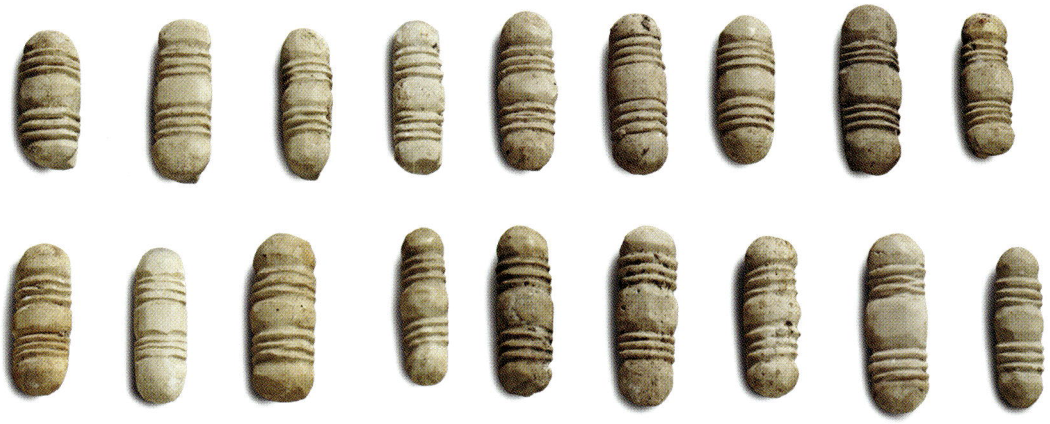

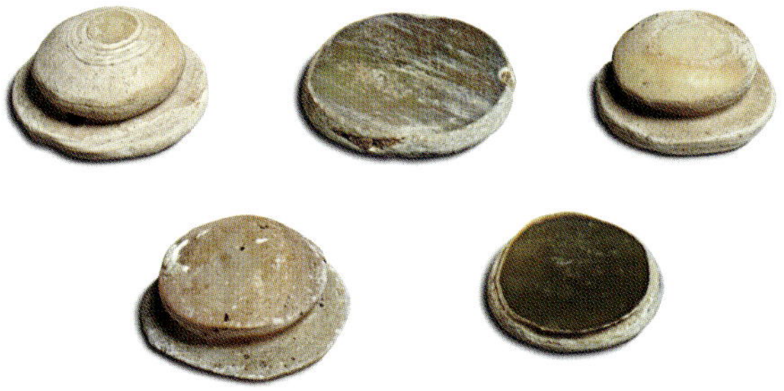

71
Harness studs

9th–7th century BC
Nimrud, North-West Palace, Room AB, excavations
of A.H. Layard, 1845–51
Shell
Diam. c. 1–1.5 cm
BM 140345, 1994,1105.129

These studs have a flanged base and a domed top. They would have been used to decorate leather straps and items of harness.

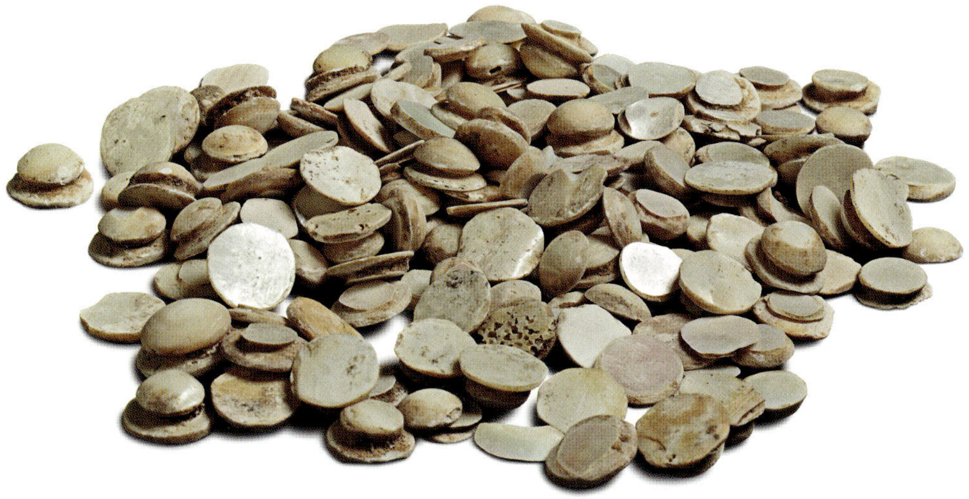

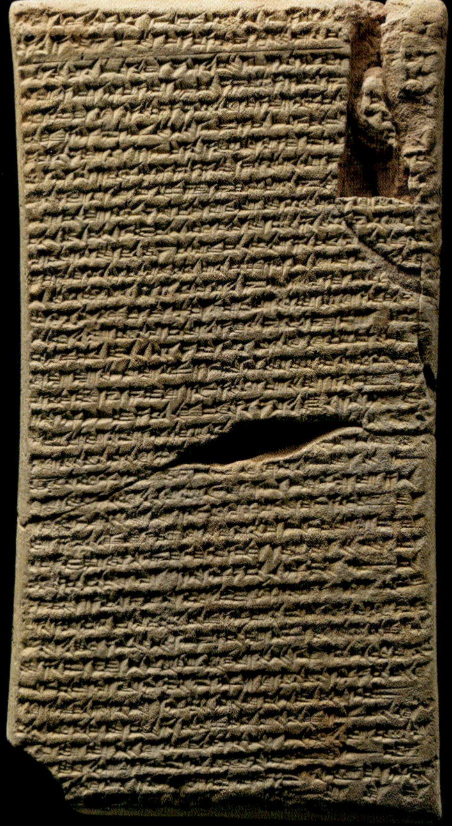

72

Cuneiform tablet

7th century BC, Assyrian
Nineveh, Mesopotamia; acquired 1882
Baked clay
L 16.2 cm, W 8.6 cm
BM 1882,0323.1

This tablet contains an inscription describing an elaborate ritual to avert headache, plague and pestilence affecting the royal horses or soldiers.

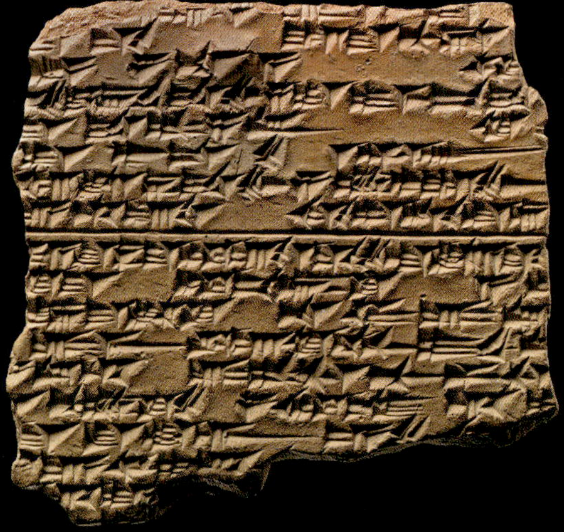

73

Cuneiform tablet

7th century BC, Assyrian
Nineveh, Ashurbanipal's Library
Baked clay
L 5.7 cm, W 5.7 cm
BM K.8197

This tablet describes the fable of the ox and the horse and details a dispute over their relative merits. Here, the horse expounds on itself. The tablet is part of a library of cuneiform tablets believed to have been collected by or for King

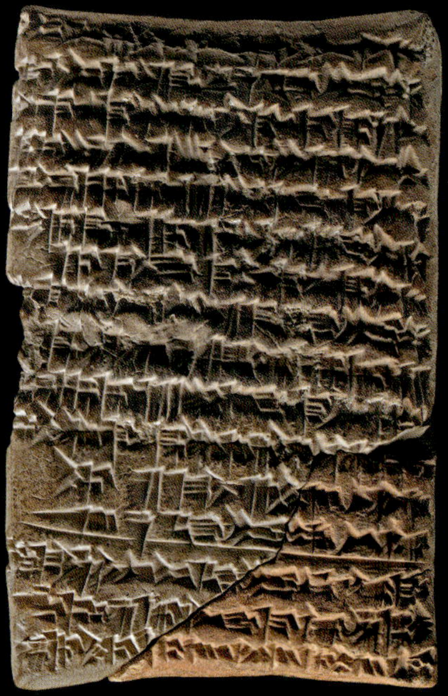

74

Cuneiform tablet

7th century BC, Assyrian
Nineveh, Ashurbanipal's Library
Baked clay
H 7.7 cm, W 4.8 cm
BM K.6163

Part of a clay tablet, containing the question to the gods about the suitability of a particular horse to pull the chariot of Marduk, the patron god of Babylon. It includes a short hymn to the horse and an incantation to be spoken into

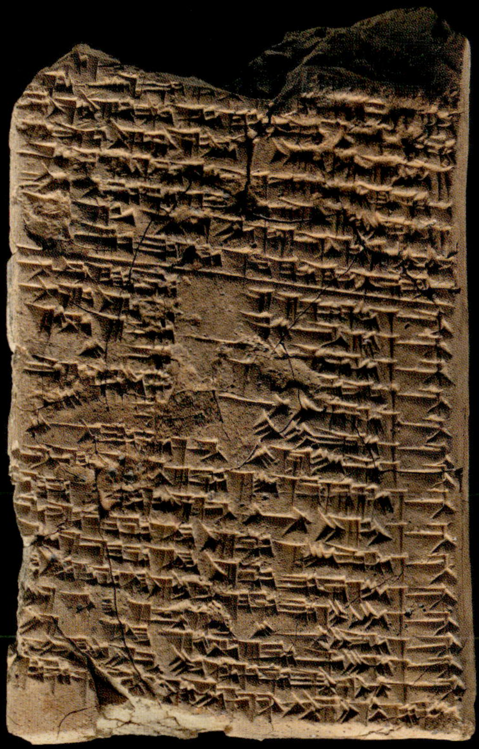

75

Cuneiform tablet

7th century BC, Assyrian
Nineveh, Ashurbanipal's Library
Baked clay
H 11.5 cm, W 7.5 cm, Th. 3 cm
BM K.324

This tablet is part of a private contract, concerning the purchase of a village. The penalty for default includes giving white horses to Ashur. It is dated December to January, 663–662 (?) BC.

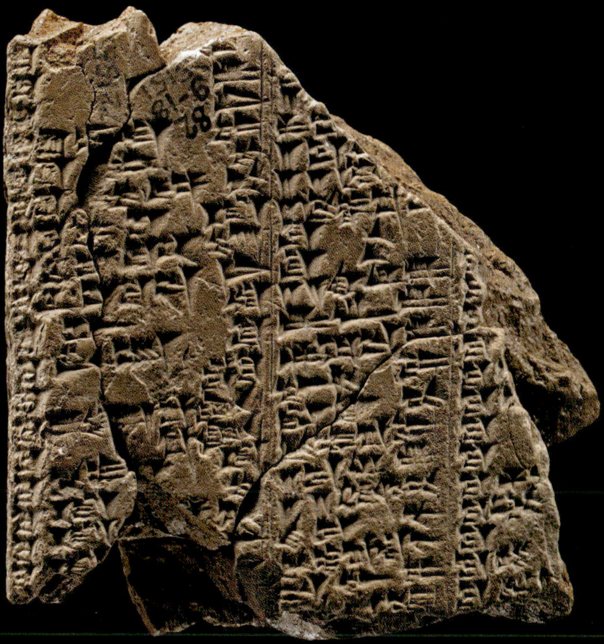

76

Cuneiform tablet fragment

7th century BC, Late Babylonian
Sippar, Southern Iraq; acquired 1882
L 6.4 cm, W 7.6 cm
BM 93080

The tablet contains a lexical list of equids.

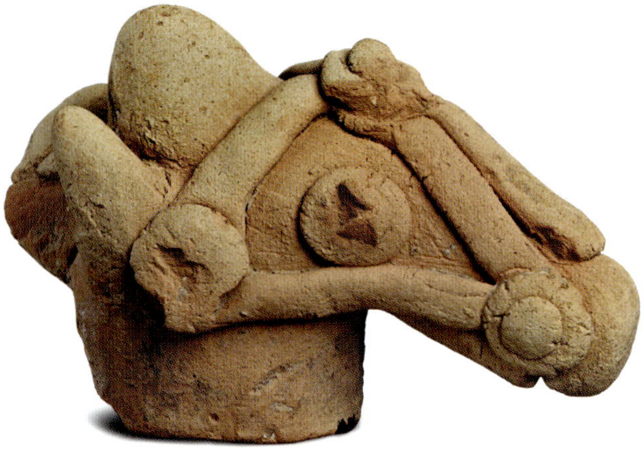

77

Figurine of horse

8th–7th century BC, Neo-Hittite
Carchemish region; acquired 1913
Baked clay
H 6.2 cm, W 10.2 cm
BM 105096

Crude model of an animal with legs missing, recognizable as a horse through its mane. There is a band around the neck, but no other signs of harnessing.

78

Figurine of a horse's head

8th–7th century BC, Neo-Hittite
Carchemish region; acquired 1913
Baked clay
H 3.3 cm, W 5.3 cm, Th. 2.6 cm
BM 105038

The head only from the model of a horse. The horse wears a frontlet on its nose and a headstall decorated with *phalerae* (decorative metal bosses). The harness has been indicated by adding strips of clay to the surface.

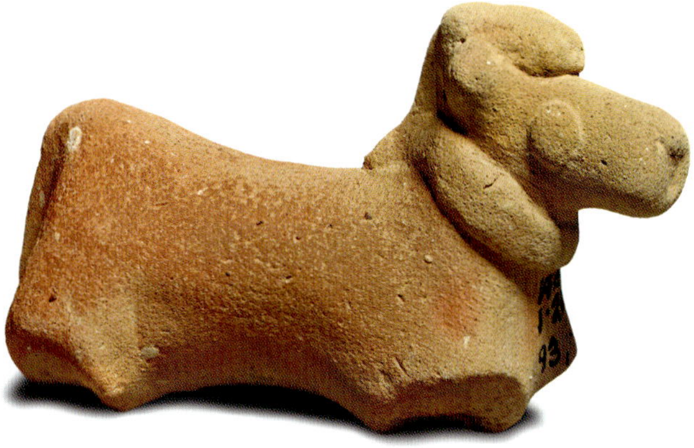

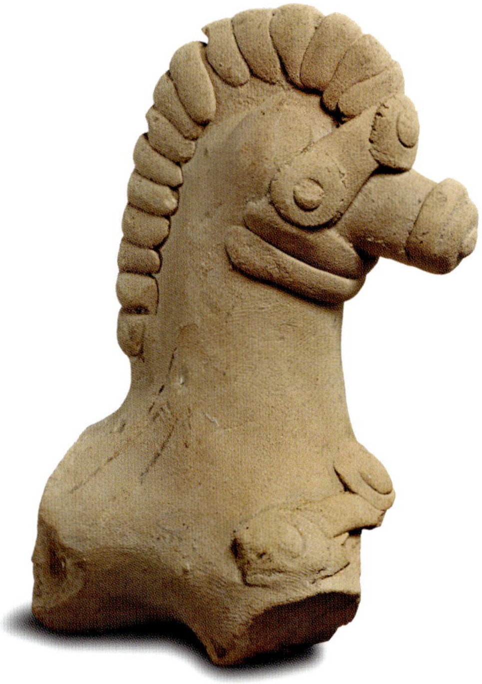

79

Figurine of horse's head and chest

8th–7th century BC, Neo-Hittite
Carchemish region; acquired 1913
Baked clay
H 9.5 cm, W 6.8 cm, Th. 4.8 cm
BM 105029

Head and chest of a horse model. The headstall and other harness are decorated with *phalerae*. The horse has an erect mane. The mane, eyes and harness have been indicated by applying small pieces of clay.

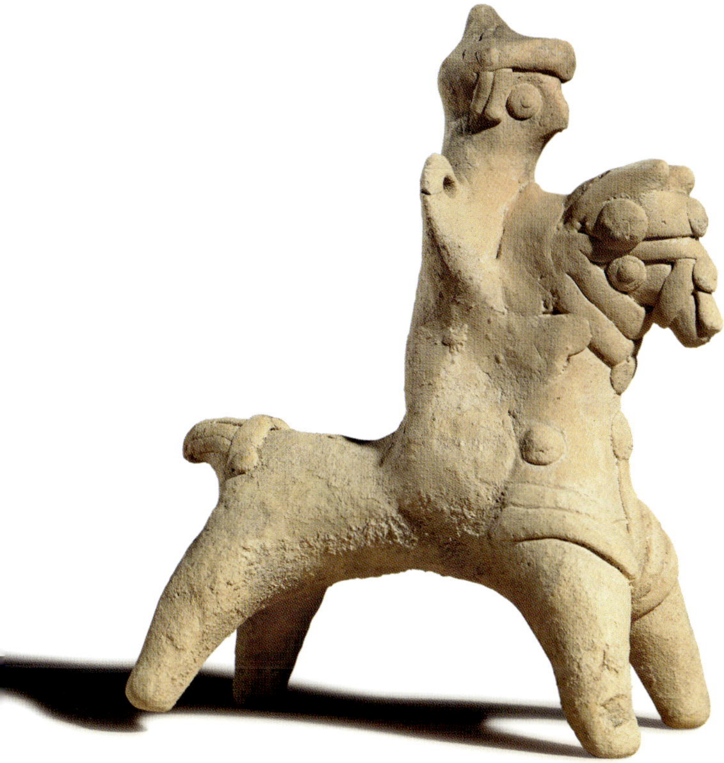

80

Figurine of horse and rider

8th–7th century BC, Neo-Hittite
Carchemish region; acquired 1913
Baked clay
H 13.5 cm, L 10.8 cm, W 5.7 cm
BM 105006

Model of a horse and rider. The rider sits well forward on the horse, and clutches its neck. The headdress of the rider and the headstall and chest harness of the horse have been indicated by strips of clay, and the eyes of both horse and rider have been shown with applied dots. This is a characteristic feature of Syrian figurines of this date.

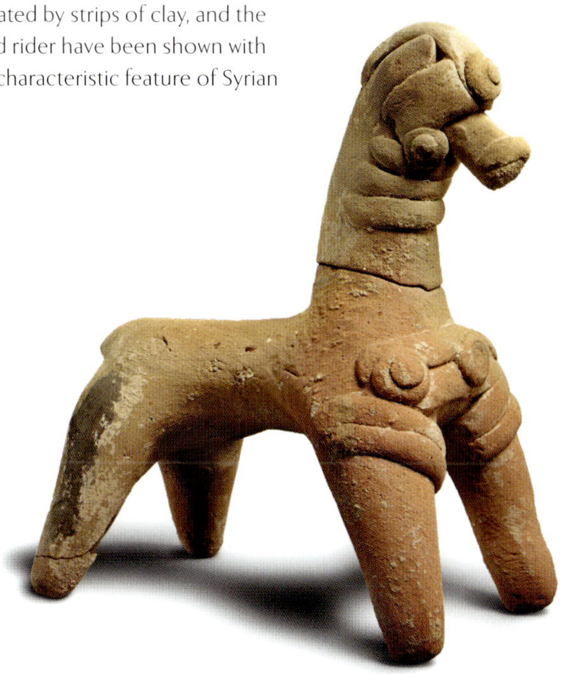

81

Figurine of horse and rider

5th century BC
Tyre, Lebanon; acquires 1884
Painted baked clay
H 14.5 cm, W 9 cm
BM 939092

The horse stands on a base and has a plaited necklace from which is suspended a large tassel or bell. The bearded rider wears a Median-style headdress. There are traces of red and black paint on this figurine.

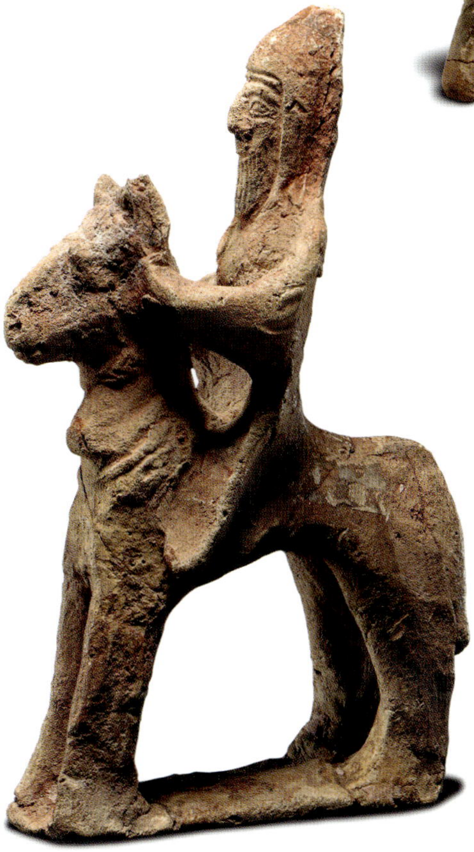

82

Figurine of a horse

8th–7th century BC, Neo-Hittite
Carchemish region; acquired 1913
Baked clay
H 10.2 cm, W 9.6 cm
BM 105007

Model of a horse with elaborate headstall and harness decorated with *phalerae*. Details have been added by applying pieces of clay.

83

Statuette of a horseman

6th–5th century BC
Sanctuary of Apollo, Phrangissa, Cyprus; acquired 1910
Limestone
H 45.7 cm
BM 1910,0620.17

This fine limestone statuette of a horseman from Cyprus shows features of harness derived from Mesopotamia and Iran. The frontlet and tasselled brow-pad on the horse's head are of earlier Assyrian inspiration, as is the long tassel on a strap around the neck, but the curved cheekpieces of the bit and the elaborate stepped saddle-cloth can be compared with Achaemenid examples.

Interestingly there are plaques on the headstall and at the top of the tassel which resemble either the Pazuzu demon, or more likely, Bes masks (see cat. 98). The horse itself resembles Persian horses in the shape of the head.

The horseman's dress also reflects costume, particularly the style of hat, known widely in Syria. There is a Cypro-syllabic sign incised above his right knee.

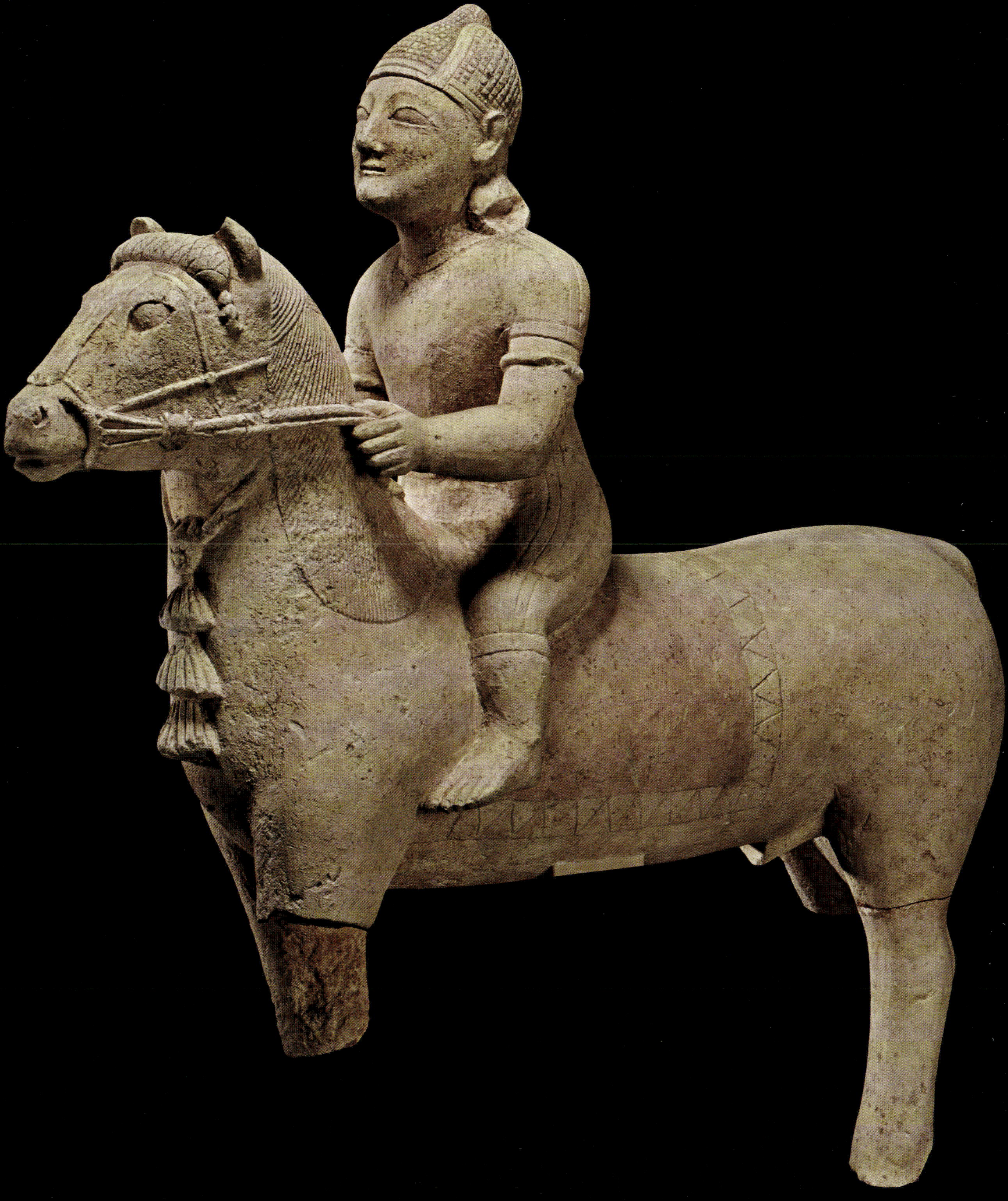

84

Fragment of stone relief showing a charioteer

6th–5th century BC, Achaemenid
Persopolis, Iran, from the top register of the east wing of the northern staircase of the Apadana; acquired 1817
Limestone
H 56 cm, W 88 cm
BM 118843

The figure is standing in a chariot box, the front part of which is preserved. It has rosettes around the edge. There is a quiver on the front of the box and another (only the top of which is visible) is mounted on the side. The charioteer holds a stick and reins that pass over the backs of two horses and run through a terret or rein-ring that is set on the yoke. There is a fan-shaped yoke ornament above the terret and a tassel hangs down from the yoke.

The heads of the horses are preserved on a fragment that is now in the Miho Museum in Japan. This fragment was found with the main piece at Persepolis in 1811 but was apparently given to Sir Gore Ouseley and became part of his collection. It passed to his son Sir Frederick Ouseley who founded a school called St Michael's College in Tenbury, England. After the school closed down in 1985 the relief was sold at auction and was eventually purchased by the Miho Museum. A cast of this piece is shown in the exhibition. Originally this relief would have been part of a scene that showed a procession of Persian guards followed by an usher and four grooms carrying whips, saddle-cloths and a stool, then an usher with three horses and grooms, and finally another usher with two royal chariots.

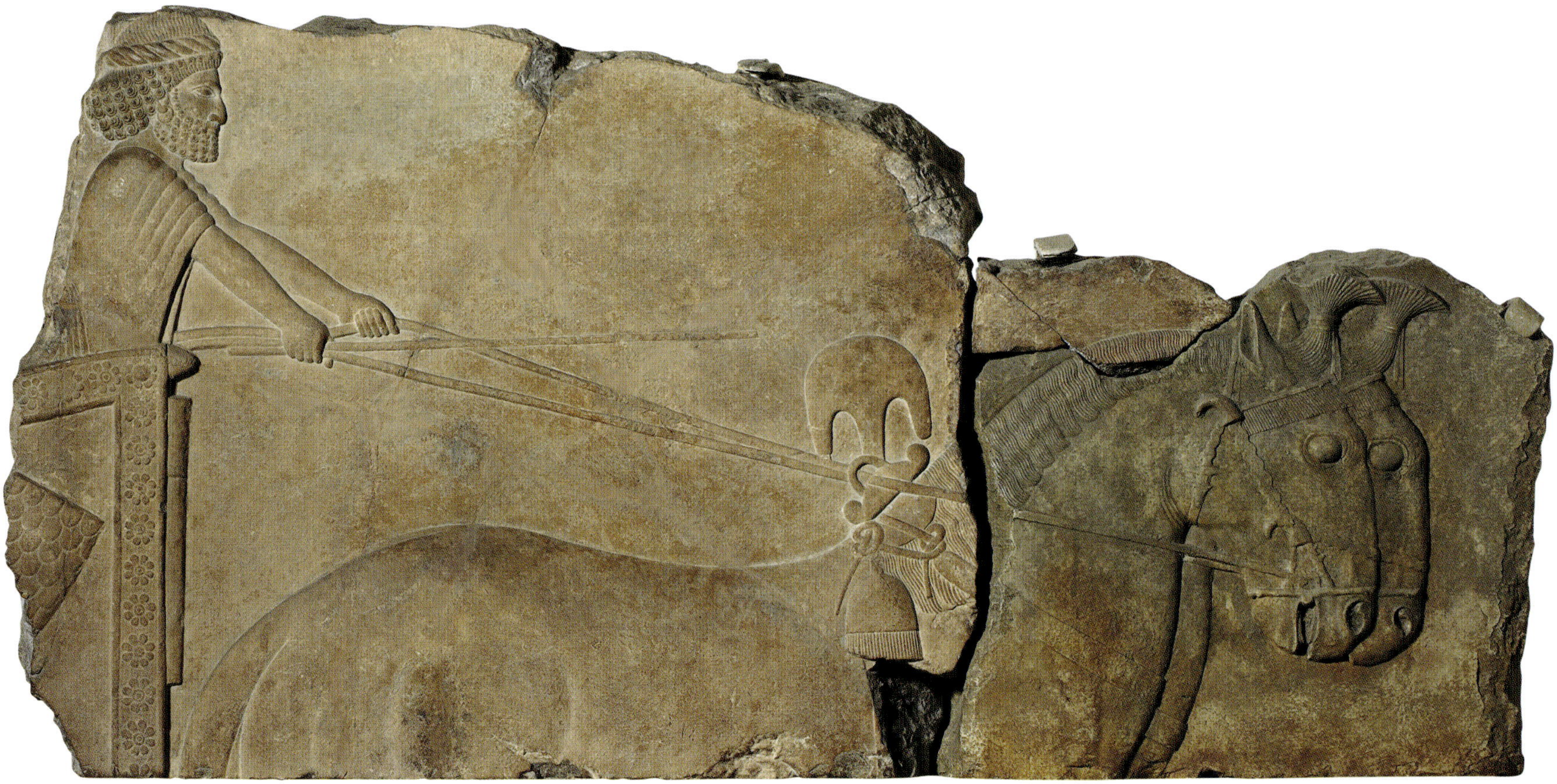

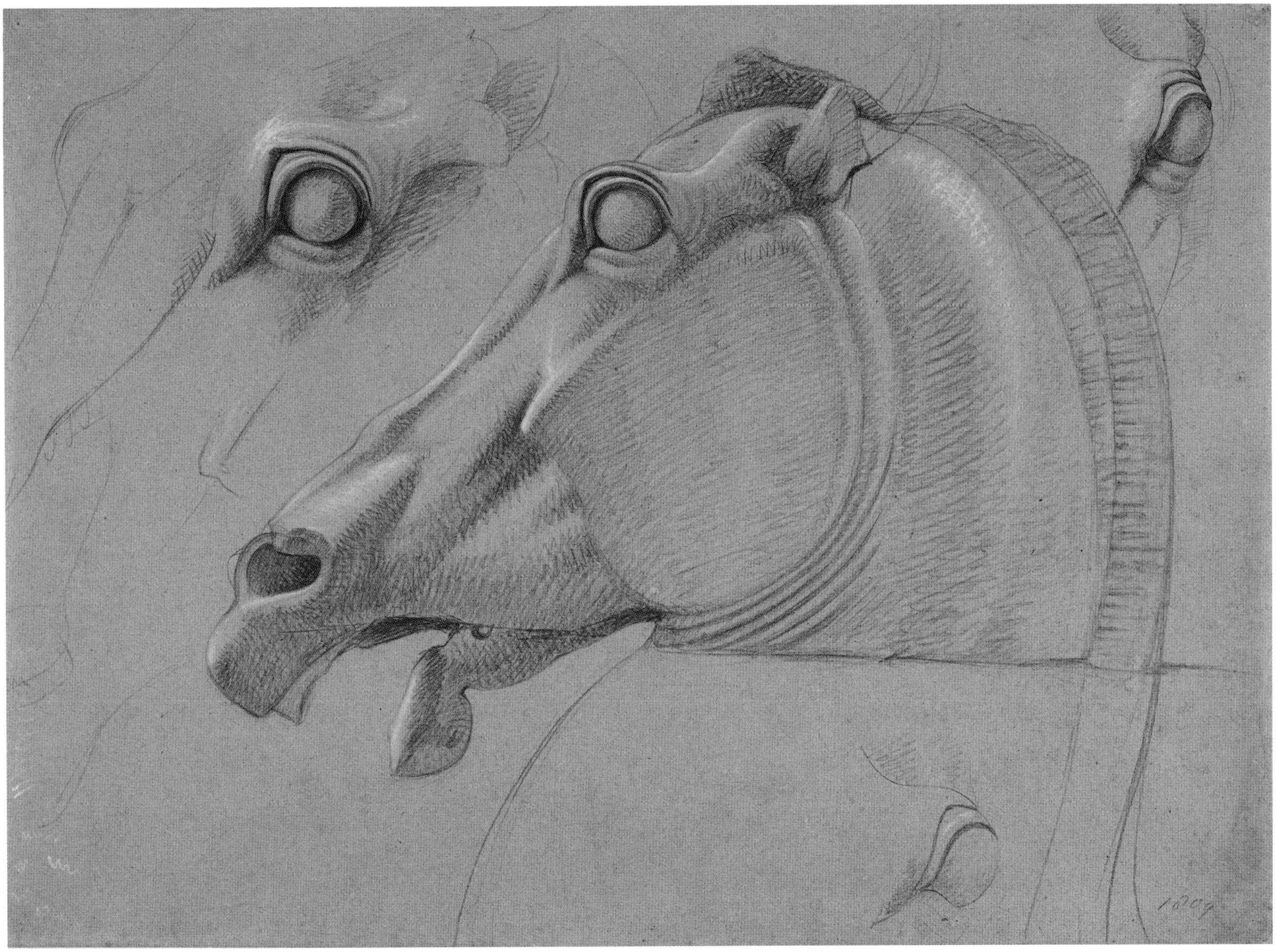

85

Drawing of the head of the horse of Selene, from the east pediment of the Parthenon

Benjamin Robert Haydon
Dated 1809; acquired 1881
Drawing, black chalk, heightened with white, on grey paper
H 55.4 cm, W 75.9 cm
BM 1881,0709.346

This striking head of the horse of Selene, in profile to left, with separate studies of the eye, is by Benjamin Robert Haydon and is taken from the east pediment of the Parthenon.

The horse was one of the best preserved of the Parthenon sculptures at Athens and Haydon was fascinated by its realism and vigour. The understanding of the eye in particular convinced him that the Greeks had made anatomical dissections, and he followed his study of their work with his own dissections, later building the practice into his own teaching.

It is sometimes suggested that the horse of Selene has some of the characteristics of the Arabian horse.

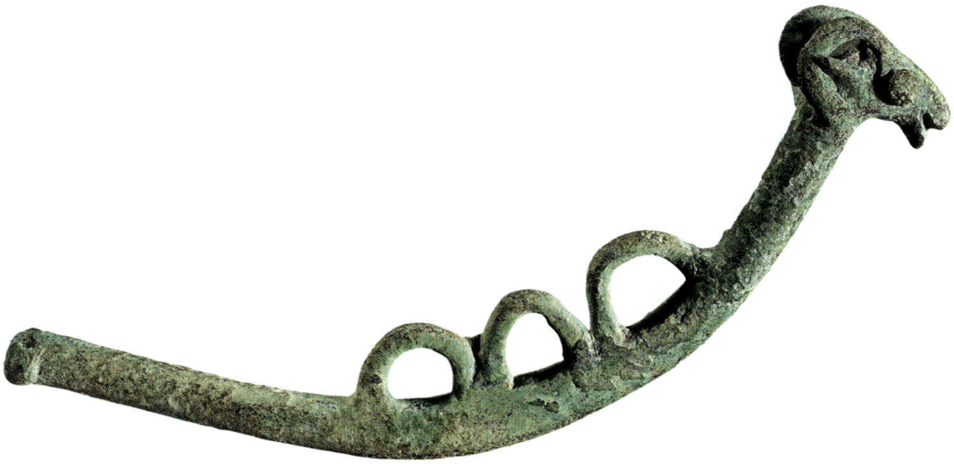

86

Horse cheekpiece with ibex or mouflon head terminal

Late 8th–7th century BC, Scythian
Provenance unknown, probably Iran or the Caucasus; acquired 1964
Bronze
L 13.9 cm
BM 134365

Bronze bar cheekpiece from a horse bit in the form of a curved rod with three loops inside the curve and an ibex or mouflon head at one end and a stylized animal's hoof at the other.

Cheekpieces with animal heads are found in both bone and bronze. Most bone examples are found in the Pontic and north Caucasian steppes associated with the Scythians, an Iranian nomadic steppe people of the seventh to fifth centuries BC. Bronze examples like this are often unprovenanced but also belong to the world of the Scythians.

87

Horse cheekpiece with goat's head terminal

8th–7th century BC, Scythian
Provenance unknown, probably from north or north-western Iran/Caucasus; acquired 1964
Bronze
L 17.6 cm
BM 134363

This bronze cheekpiece from a horse bit is a flat strip of metal with three circular holes in the centre and a stylized animal's head, possibly a goat, at one end.

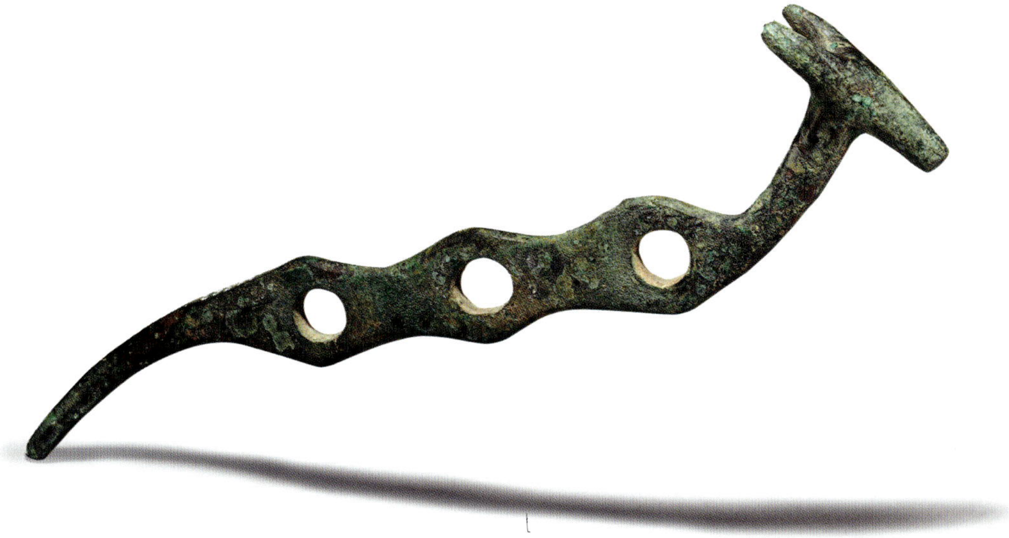

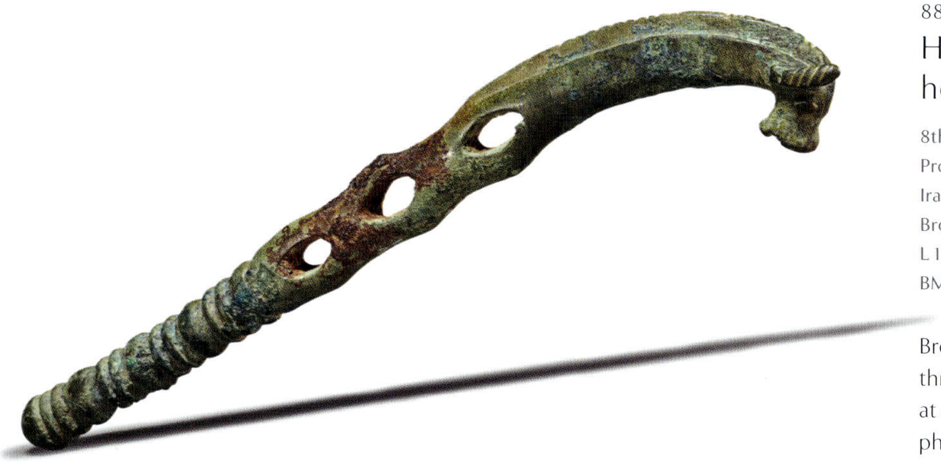

88

Horse cheekpiece with a horse's head terminal

8th–7th century BC, Scythian
Provenance unknown, probably from north or north-western Iran/Caucasus; acquired 1964
Bronze
L 15.2 cm
BM 134362

Bronze bar-shaped cheekpiece from a horse bit with three oval-shaped holes and a stylised horse's head finial at one end and bead and reel mouldings terminating in a phallic shape at the other. There are remains of iron staining around two of the holes.

89

Snaffle bit

5th century BC, Achaemenid
Probably from Deve Hüyük, Syria; acquired 1913
Bronze
Cheekpieces: L 21.6 cm, 25.4 cm; canons: W 21.6 cm
BM 108759

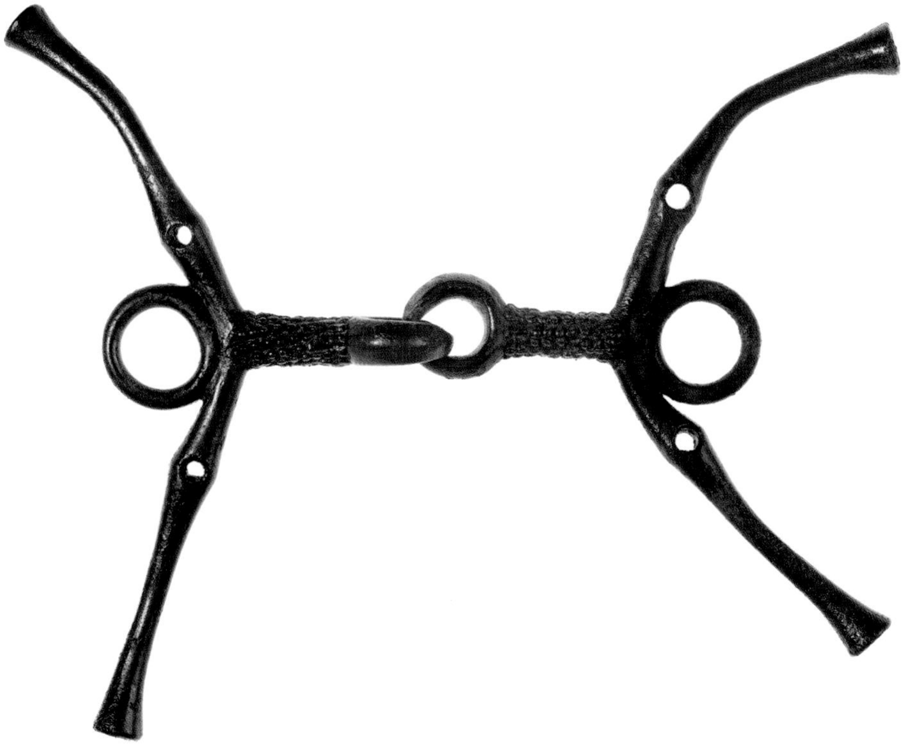

This snaffle bit has curved cheekpieces with plain, flattened, slightly swollen terminals. Each cheekpiece has double circular perforations for the ends of the cheek strap, and integral round rein-attachments. It has a jointed mouthpiece and the canons are barbed.

Achaemenid Persian draught and riding horses were controlled by a simple bitted bridle. The commonest known form is a bronze snaffle with jointed canons, or mouthpiece, cast in one piece together with the usually curved or angular, rod- or bar-like cheekpieces and rein attachments. The attachments are ring-shaped or rectangular, while the cheekpieces, often with decorated terminals, have two holes to take the ends of the bifurcated cheek straps. Significantly, the canons are usually studded or barbed, which is a device to improve a rider's control by increasing the effect of the bit on the horse's mouth. This suggests a military context, where a horse will be operating in an unusual and frightening environment and where extra control is required.

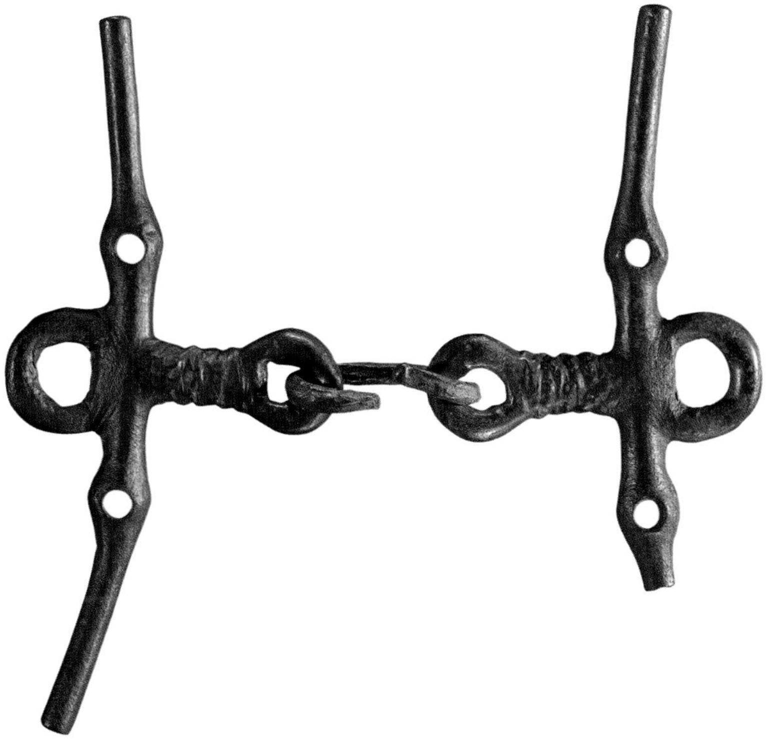

90

Snaffle bit

c. 5th century BC, Achaemenid
Warka, Mesopotamia, excavated by W.K. Loftus; acquired 1856
Bronze
L 15.24 cm (cheekpiece)
BM 91187

This example has slightly curved bar cheekpieces, swollen around double perforations for the cheek strap, and with slightly swollen terminals. The canons are joined by a separate ring, a rare variant of the standard type, and are barbed.

91

Horse harness strap-divider

c. 5th century BC, Achaemenid
Provenance unknown; acquired 1891
Bronze
H 2.3 cm, W 4.1 cm, Th. 1.7 cm
BM 1891,0513.2

A bronze plaque showing a recumbent boar in low relief facing left. On the back, which is flat, is a hollow 'junction box' pierced by four lateral holes.

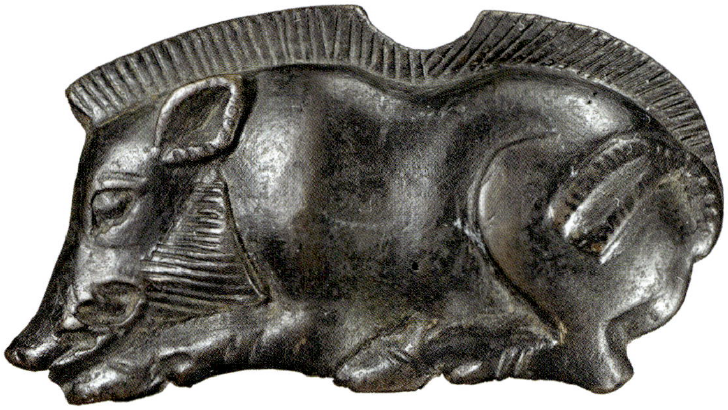

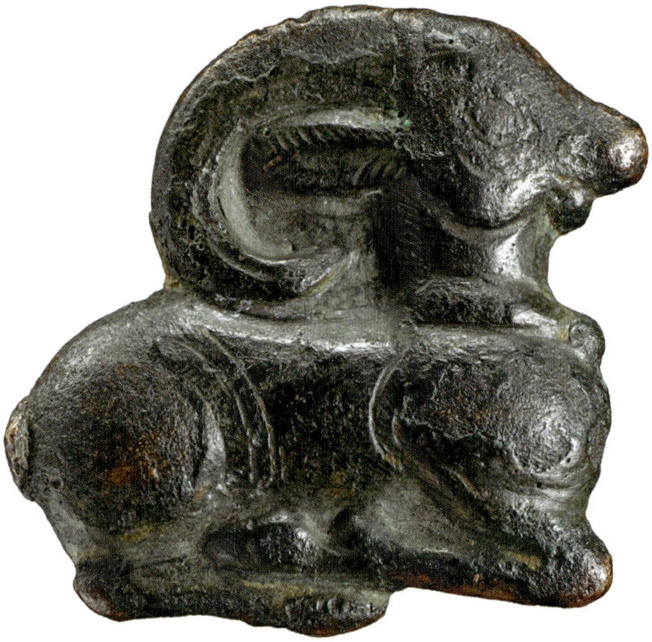

92

Horse harness strap-divider

c. 5th century BC, Achaemenid
Provenance unknown; acquired 1888
Bronze
H 3.14 cm, W 3.18 cm, max Th 1.55 cm
BM 1888,0512.12

This bronze strap-divider is in the form of a goat or ibex.

93

Horse harness strap-divider

6th–5th century BC, Achaemenid
Provenance unknown; acquired 1956
Bronze
H 2.9 cm, W 3.4 cm, max. Th. 1.8 cm
BM 132120

In the form of a bronze plaque showing a recumbent goat or ibex in low relief. Two loop-fasteners are mounted on the back, which is flat.

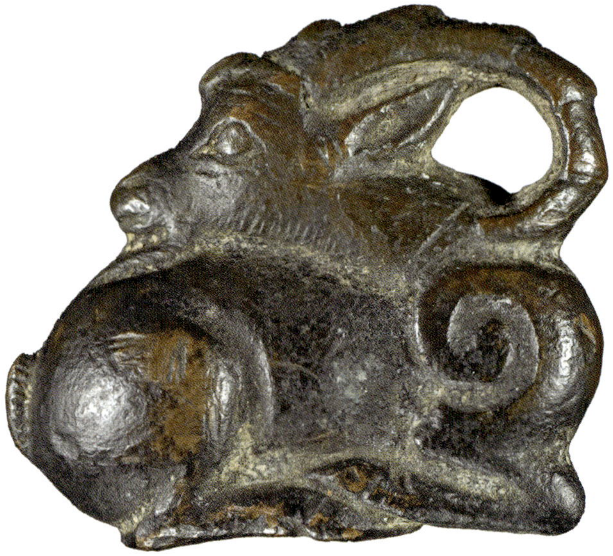

94

Figure of a horse, probably a bridle fitting

5th–4th century BC, Scytho-Achaemenid
Provenance unknown; acquired 1995
Bronze
H 5.2 cm, L 4.5 cm
BM 1995,0223.2

This bronze attachment is in the form of a horse protome with a square projection at the back pierced vertically and horizontally. The horse's legs are folded beneath its chest and it has a swept-back forelock. The mane is pulled but has long strands on the lower neck in Persian style.

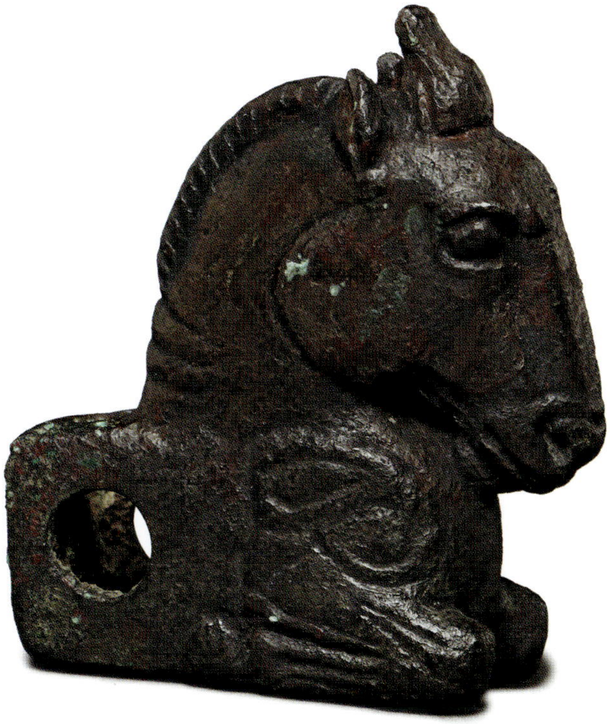

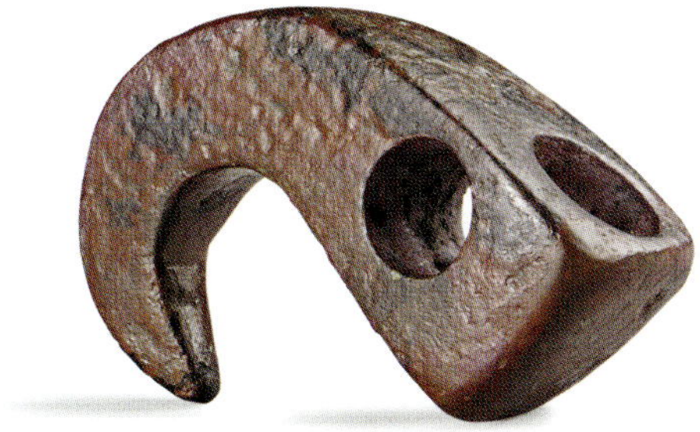

95

Horse harness strap-divider

6th–4th century BC, Achaemenid
Provenance unknown; acquired late 19th–early 20th century
Bronze
H 3.3 cm, W 3 cm
BM 1999,1201.17

This strap-divider is made of bronze, in the form of a boar's tusk. It is square in section and tapers to a point. The other end is hollow and is pierced on four sides with interconnecting holes. The end is closed.

These horses' bridle ornaments are thought to have originated from bone attachments associated with the nomadic steppe peoples and with Iranian tribes such as the Cimmerians and Scythians. Other examples are known in white stone.

96

Strap-divider, probably a bridle fitting

5th–4th century BC, Achaemenid
Oxus Treasure; A.W. Franks bequest 1897
Gold
Diam. 2.4 cm
BM 124049

A plain disc with a flat top, at the back of which is a hollow 'junction box' with four openings at right angles to each other.

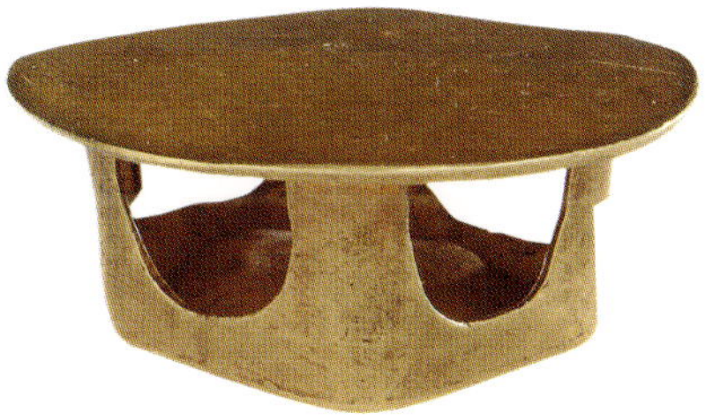

97
Model chariot

5th–4th century BC, Achaemenid
Oxus Treasure; acquired 1957
Gold
L 8.4 cm, W 4.7 cm
BM 132256

This chariot contains a driver and a now-headless seated figure. There is only a single surviving gold model horse. The vehicle has a long body with a central box-divider and seat, and with added wire stiffening for the top edge of the sides and to form two open loop handgrips at the rear of the box. The axle is formed by gold wire and is placed at the rear edge of the box. The wheels are missing. There are two draught-poles as with the model above, but made of a flat gold strip, and, unlike that model, there are two two-horse yokes, each originally fitted with two terret rings for reins (only one of which survives).

98
Model four-horse chariot

5th–4th century BC, Achaemenid
Oxus Treasure; A.W. Franks bequest 1897
Gold
L 18.8 cm
BM 123908

The chariot box or cab is open at the back. It has an irregular square front, wider at the top than the bottom, ornamented with two incised bands, probably representing diagonal bracing struts as shown on the seal above. These bands are decorated with triangles and have a Bes head at the intersection. The floor is covered with cross-hatching, most probably representing a flooring of interlaced leather thongs. The two large wheels each have eight or nine spokes, and the running surfaces are studded with small pellets to represent the bulbous heads of large stud-like nails which in the full-size original would have secured a tyre and felloe-sheathing of bronze. A seat, in the form of a narrow strip of gold, runs from the front to back of the interior. On this is seated the principal figure. He wears a long robe reaching to the ankles, the sleeves of which appear to be empty. On his head is a hood or cap and around his neck is a gold wire torc.

The driver wears a similar cap without a fillet, a short girded tunic and a wire torc; his legs are also formed of wires. The two human figures are fixed to the chariot by wires.

The chariot is pulled via a pair of draught-poles fixed to four horses under a single four-bay yoke. On the yoke above each horse is a large loop, representing the terrets, through which the wire reins pass; alternating with these loops were originally four crescentic fan-shaped yoke ornaments. The bits have large rings at the sides as rein attachments, and each animal has duplicate representations for its neck strap and backing-element, the former with a pendant tassel, punched into the metal.

The horses are small, pony-sized animals, but otherwise have the appearance of ram-headed Nesaeans. Their tails are tied up in mud-knots and the hair of the forelock is pulled back, as shown on the Darius seal (cat. 107), but not tied in a splayed tuft as shown on the Persepolis reliefs and elsewhere. Only nine legs of the horses survive and the spokes of one wheel are imperfect.

The profile of the cab or box and the general appearance of the wheel match representations of Achaemenid chariots on the sculptured facades of the Apadana at Persepolis and on the so-called Darius seal above. The use of a Bes head on the Oxus chariot model is compatible with it having been made for a child or as a votive offering, as Bes was regarded as being a protective deity of the young, and was popular throughout the Persian empire (see cat. 83).

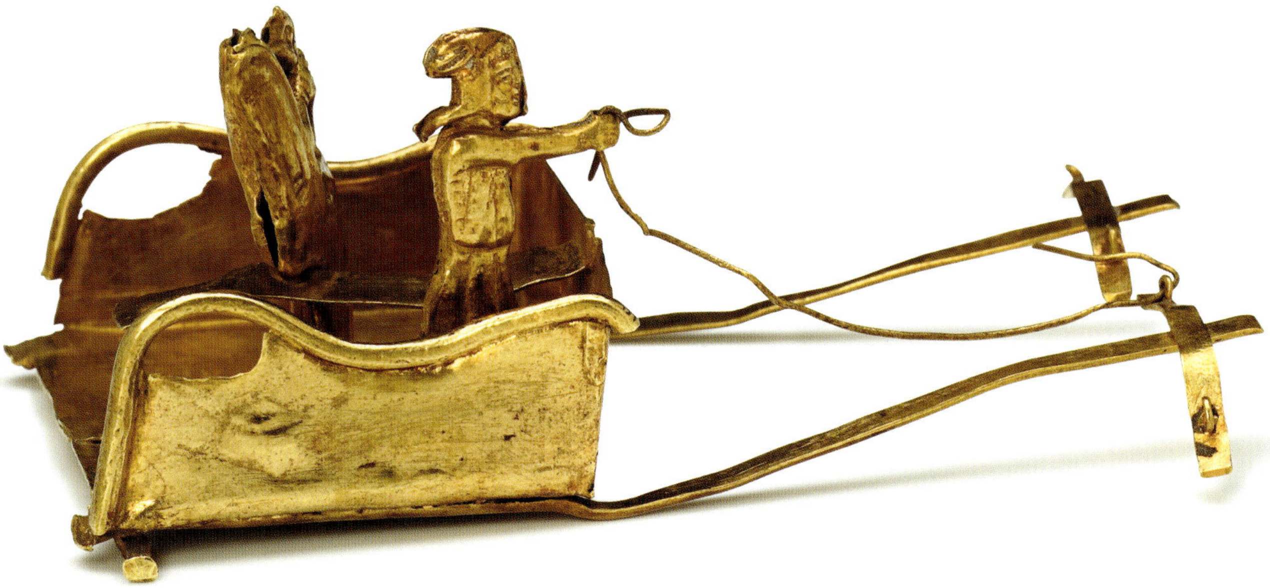

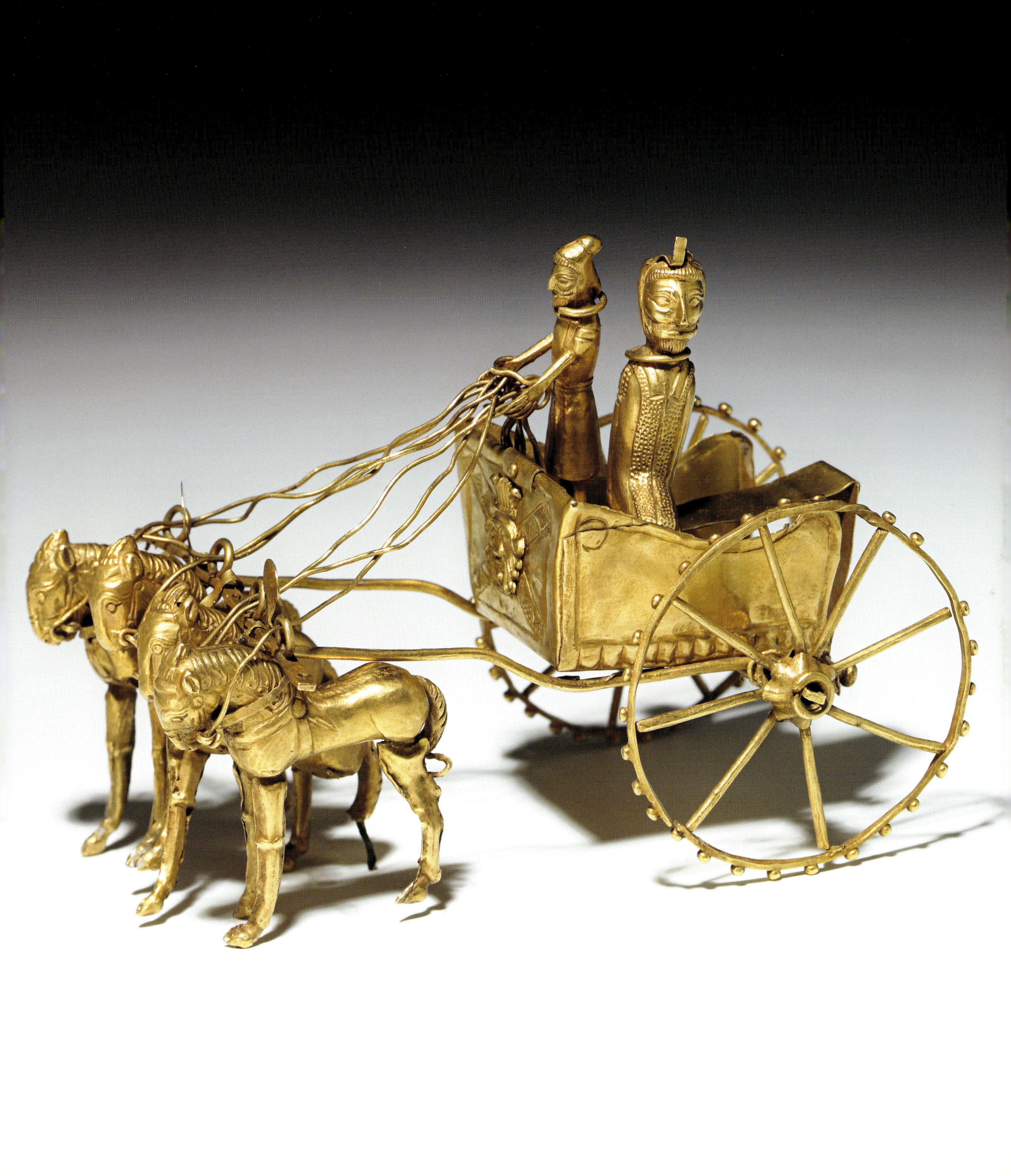

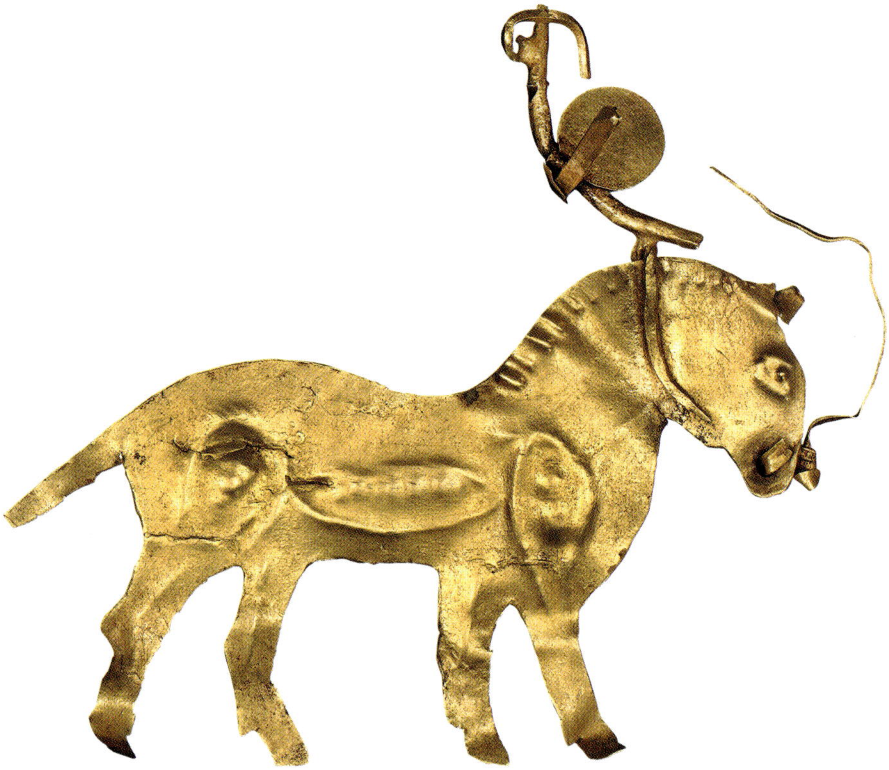

99

Gold sheet cut-out figure of a horse

5th–4th century BC, Achaemenid
Oxus Treasure; A.W. Franks bequest 1897
H 3.4 cm, L 5.3 cm
BM 123946

With punched and embossed details. There are the remains of an attached yoke with a circular yoke-standard and a short length of rein. This must originally have been a draught horse for a model chariot, possibly also made of metal sheet.

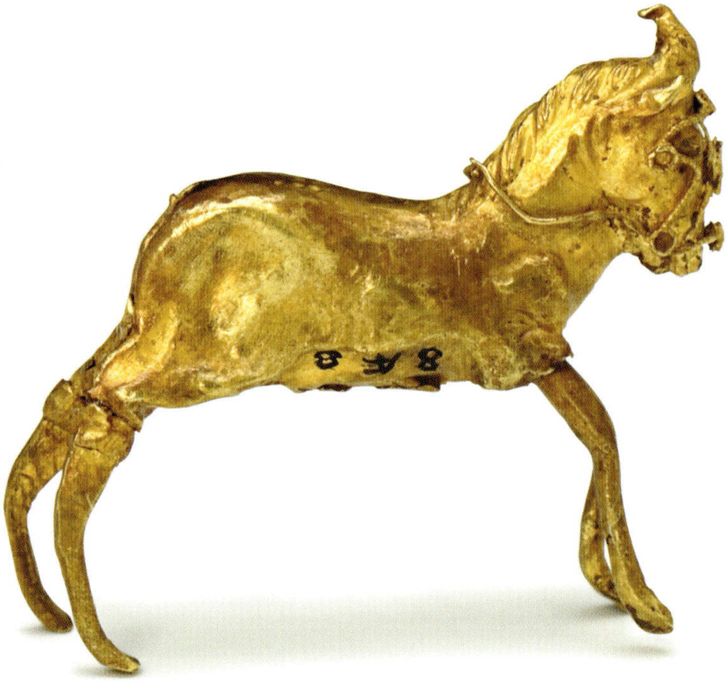

100

Figure of a horse

5th–4th century BC, Achaemenid
Oxus Treasure; A.W. Franks bequest 1897
Gold
L 4.3 cm
BM 123909

The horse has a highly detailed headstall made of gold wire, which includes a frontlet consisting of a central diamond joined to two upper and lower rings, probably intended to represent circular plaques or *phalarae* as found on a bridle from Barrow 5, at Pazyrk in the Altai region.

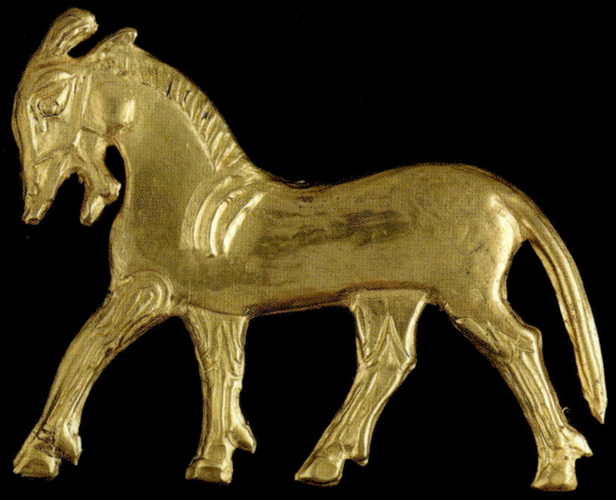

101

Gold sheet cut-out figure of horse

5th–4th century BC, Achaemenid
Oxus Treasure; A.W. Franks bequest 1897
Gold
H 2.8 cm, L 3.6 cm
BM 123945

Gold sheet cut-out figure of a horse, embossed with muscles indicated by punching, forelock swept back and mane pulled but long at the neck in typical Achaemenid style.

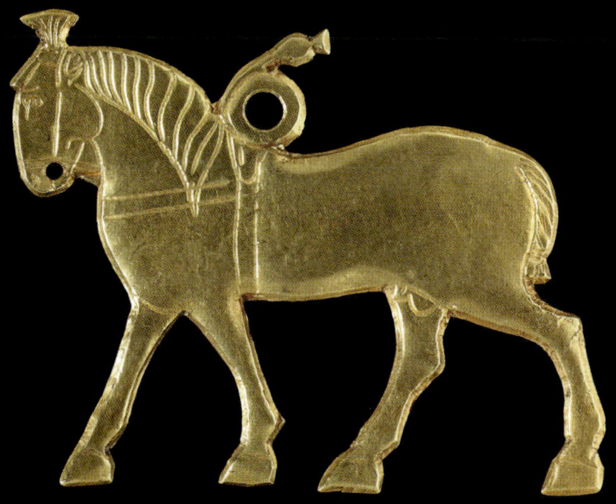

102

Gold sheet cut-out figure of a horse

5th–4th century BC, Achaemenid
Oxus Treasure; A.W. Franks bequest 1897
Gold
H 4.2 cm, L 5.5 cm
BM 123947

The horse, possibly intended to be a Nesaean, is more finely finished than the above, with punched and incised details of harness, mane (though not dressed in typical Persian style) and tail. The mouth is pierced, probably for wire reins now missing. The forelock is shown tied into a splayed tuft on the poll and there is a loop on the horse's back, probably for a wire yoke. If so, then this is a draught horse for another chariot model.

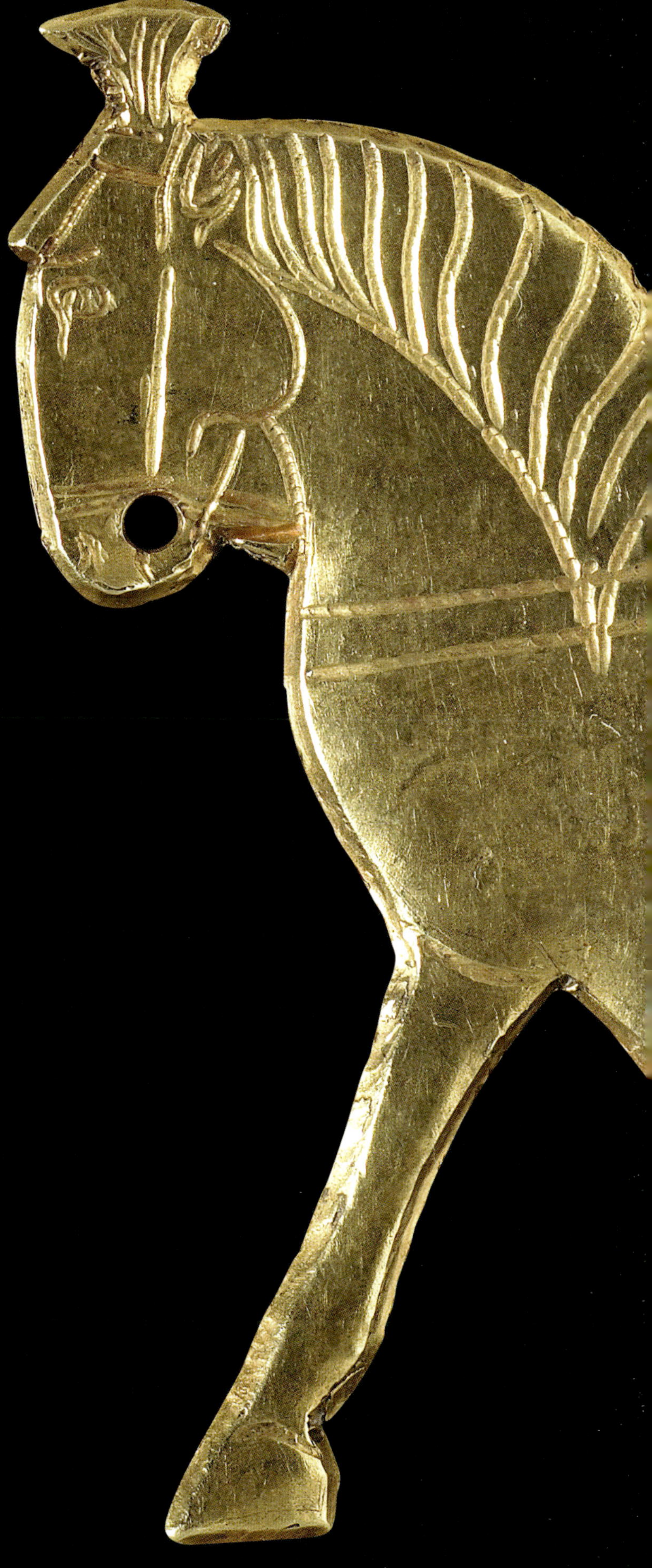

103

Horse harness ornament or shield-boss

5th–4th century BC, Achaemenid
Oxus Treasure; A.W. Franks bequest 1897
Silver, gold
Diam. 9.7 cm
BM 123925

This ornament contains a hunting scene involving three riders on horseback. It consists of a circular disc with gold overlay and an embossed centre pierced by five holes. There is a guilloche pattern around the edge. The hunters are wearing Median dress with caps and ornate trouser-suits. They ride without stirrups, which were not known at this time. The horses wear patterned saddle-cloths secured with a breast strap and fringed at the back, and their tails are tied in mud-knots with bows. Two of the horsemen converge on a pair of ibexes, one of which has already been struck by a spear. One of these horsemen is armed with a spear and the other with a bow and arrow. The third horseman, again armed with a spear, pursues two deer, one of which has a broken spear sticking into it. In front of the ibexes is a hare. The figure-of-eight or waisted shield types at Persepolis are sometimes represented with similar circular fittings in the centre, but the similarities are not close, so it is more likely that this piece is a harness ornament, or *phalera*.

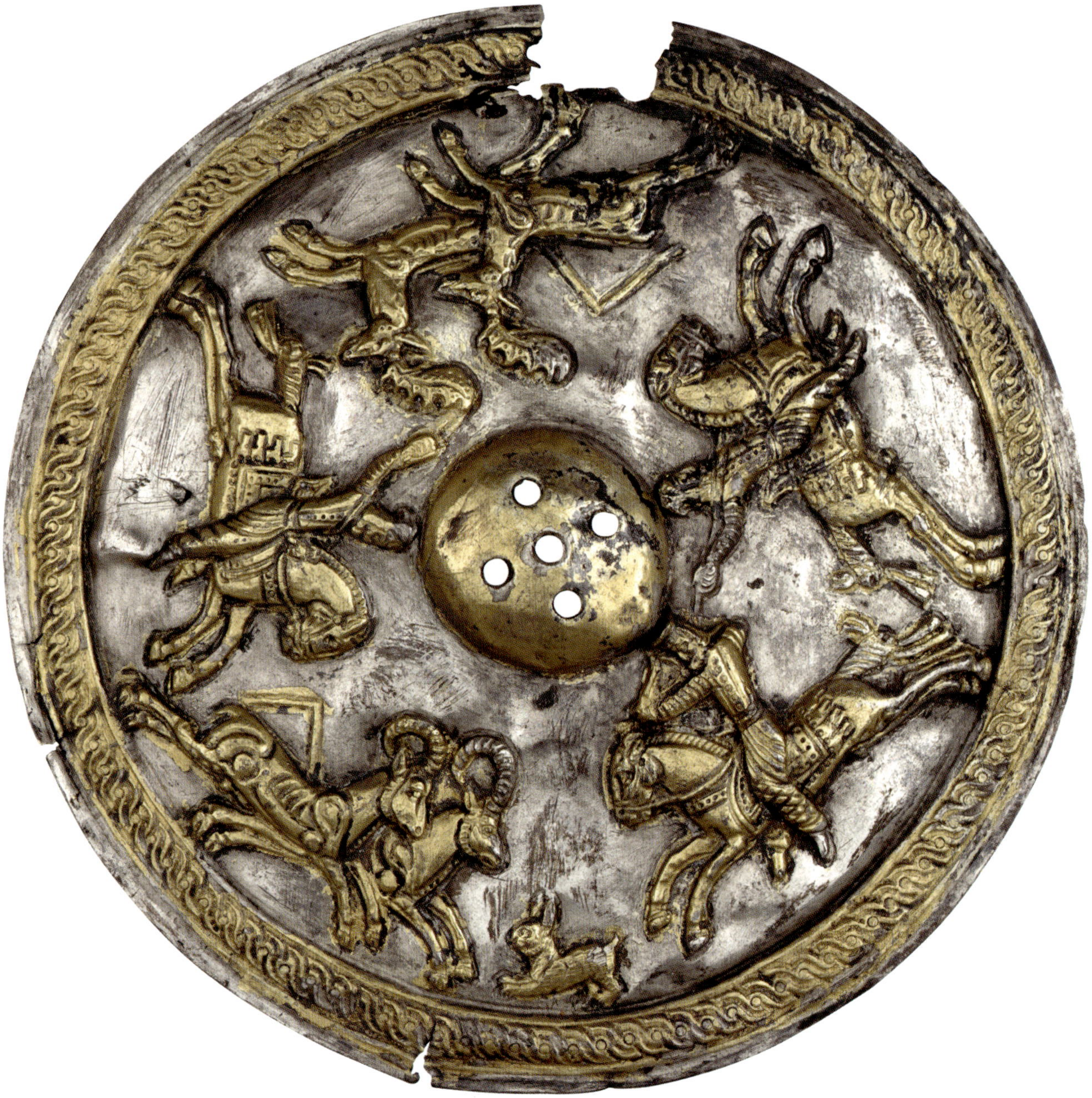

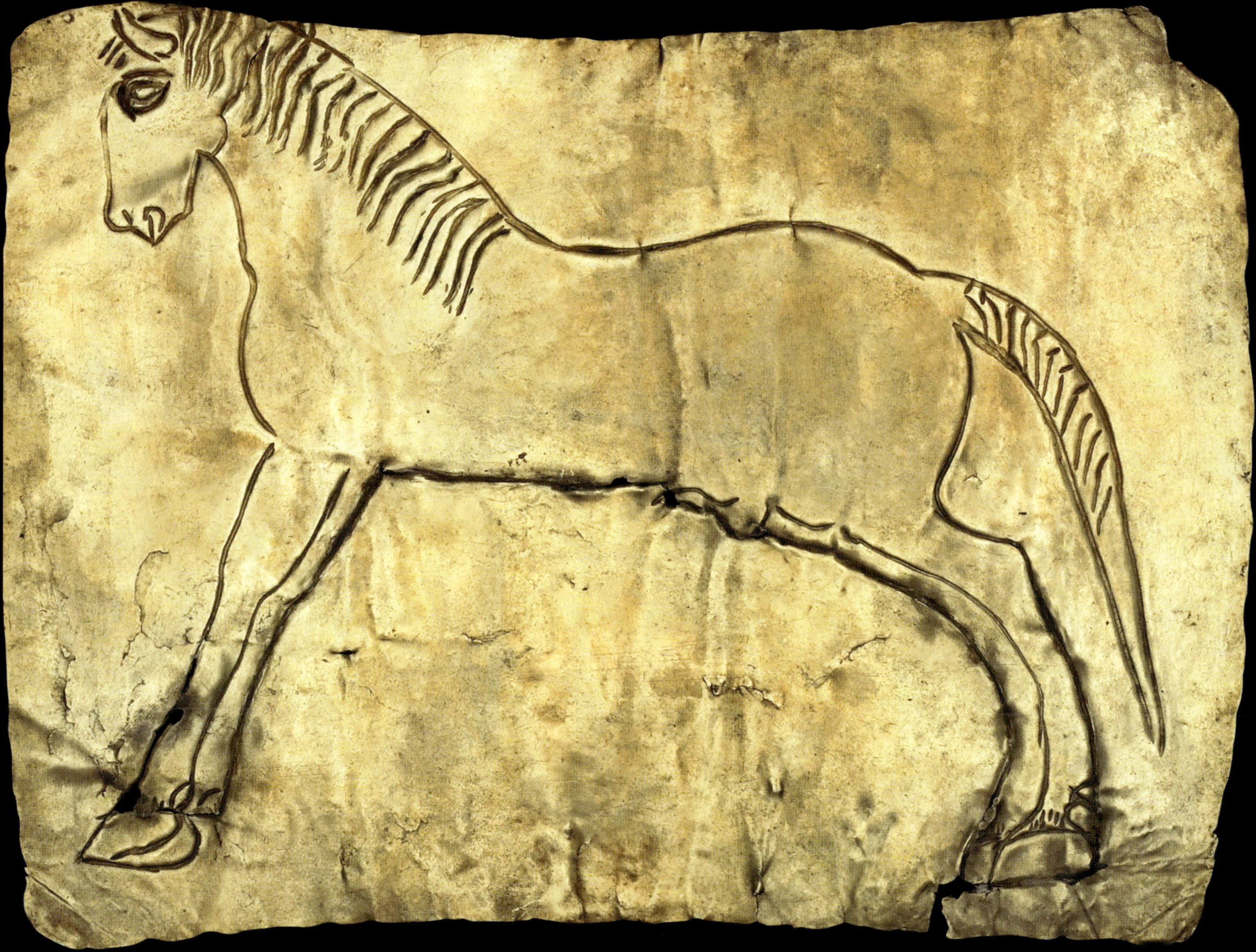

104

Plaque with chased decoration showing a horse facing left

5th–4th century BC, Achaemenid
Oxus Treasure; A.W. Franks bequest 1897
Gold
H 9.4 cm, W 12.5 cm
BM 124000

In the Oxus Treasure are fifty-one gold plaques whose purpose is generally assumed to be votive. It is likely that all the plaques were dedicated to a temple.

All have representations of human figures except for three plaques with representations of animals and one that is plain. This plaque shows a horse, others show an ass or donkey and a camel.

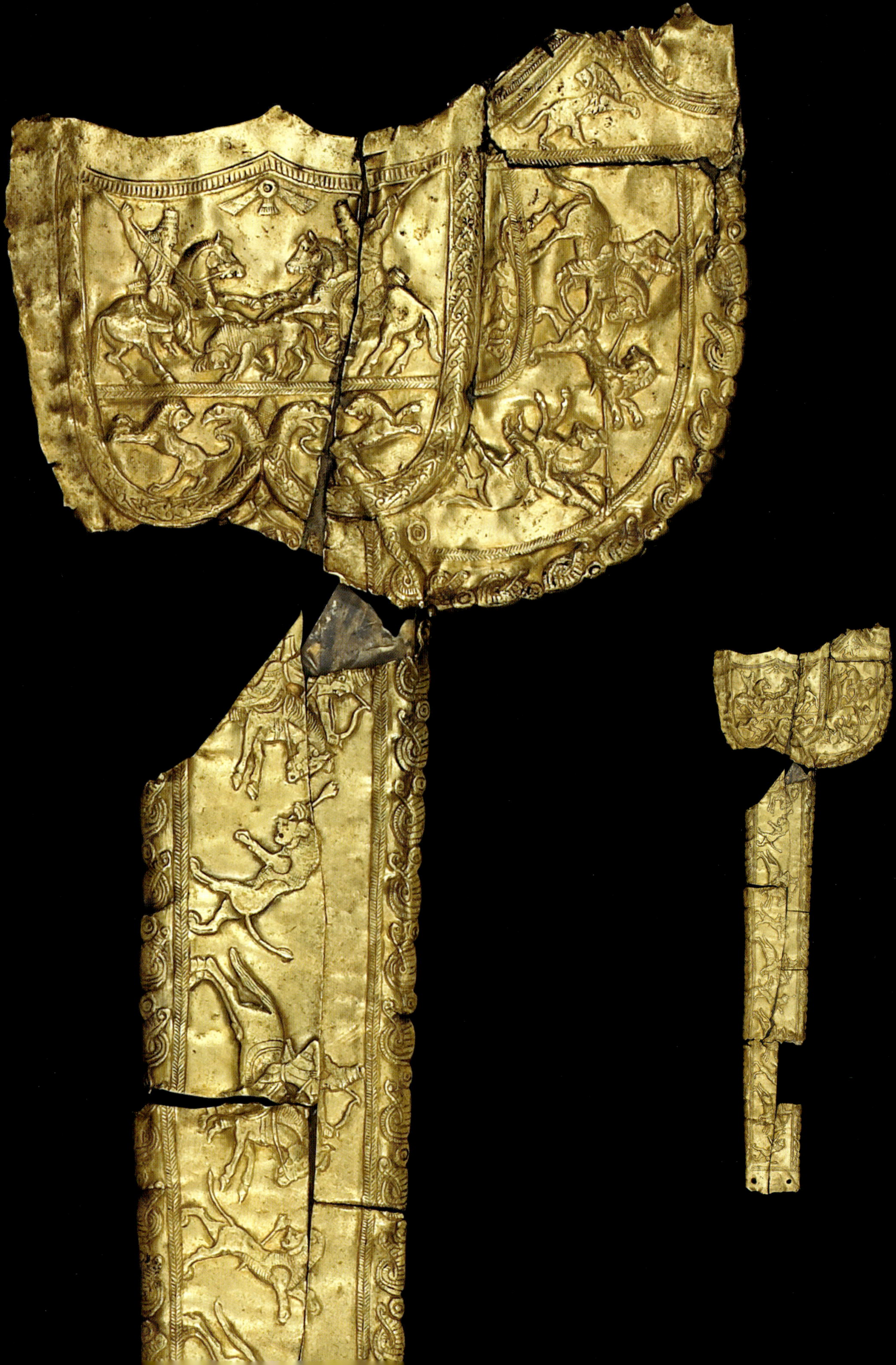

105

Scabbard for an *akinakes*

5th–4th century BC, Achaemenid
Oxus Treasure; A.W. Franks bequest 1897
Gold
L 27.6 cm
BM 123923

An akinakes is a type of short sword specialized for use by horsemen and closely associated with ancient Iranian riders. This exceptional scabbard has embossed decoration of hunting scenes. It was originally overlaid onto a wooden or leather sheath with a double-convex profile, with a separate chape, or point, now missing. The reverse was plain. The wide upper part shows four riders on horseback, armed with long spears and attacking lions, within herringbone-pattern and serpentine borders. There is a winged disc above one pair of horsemen. The riders wear belted decorated dresses and tall hats, and are apparently barefoot. They are seated on rounded saddle-cloths, the surfaces covered with small punched circles, the edges finished with decorative borders or fringes. The long narrow part of the scabbard has a further five horsemen and lions arranged in a line. At the top of the scabbard on the back is a strap-fitting by which the scabbard was partly suspended. It has been restored from seven fragments.

This scabbard has sometimes been compared with Assyrian art of the seventh century BC because of the lion hunt theme and the tall fez-like hats of the riders; however, the horse harness is not Assyrian and has Scythian parallels, particularly with the rounded saddle-cloths. It has been suggested, partly because of the form of the winged disc, that this scabbard cannot be earlier than the reign of Darius and possibly dates from the reign of Artaxerxes II (404–359 BC).

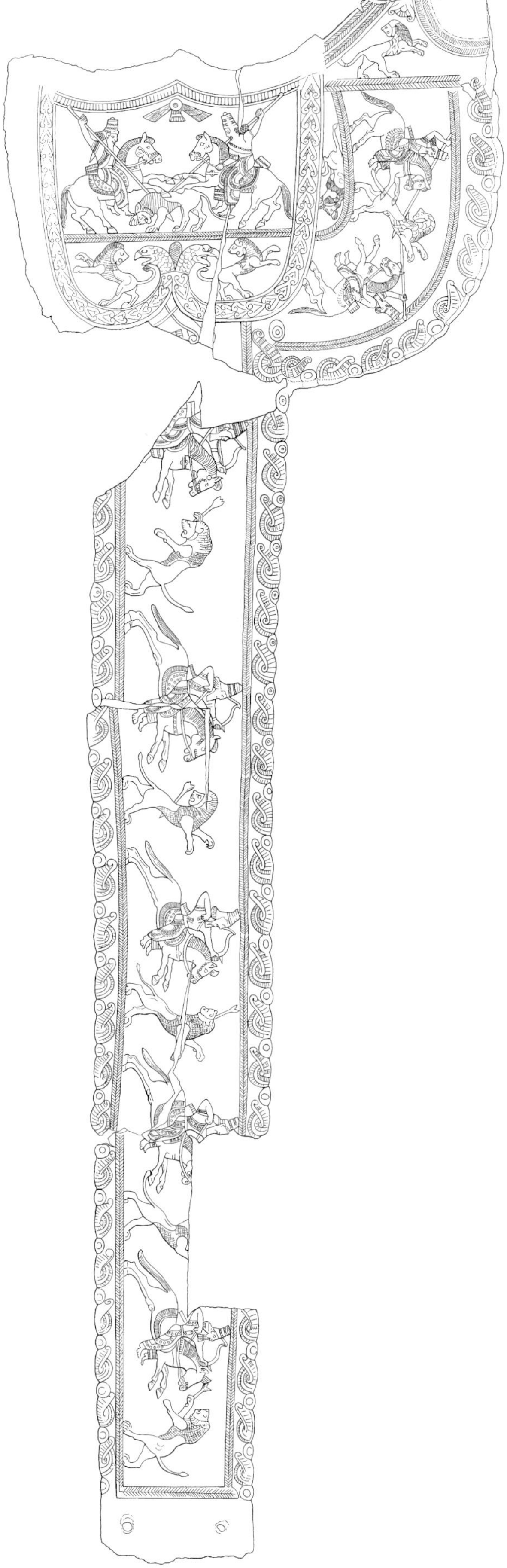

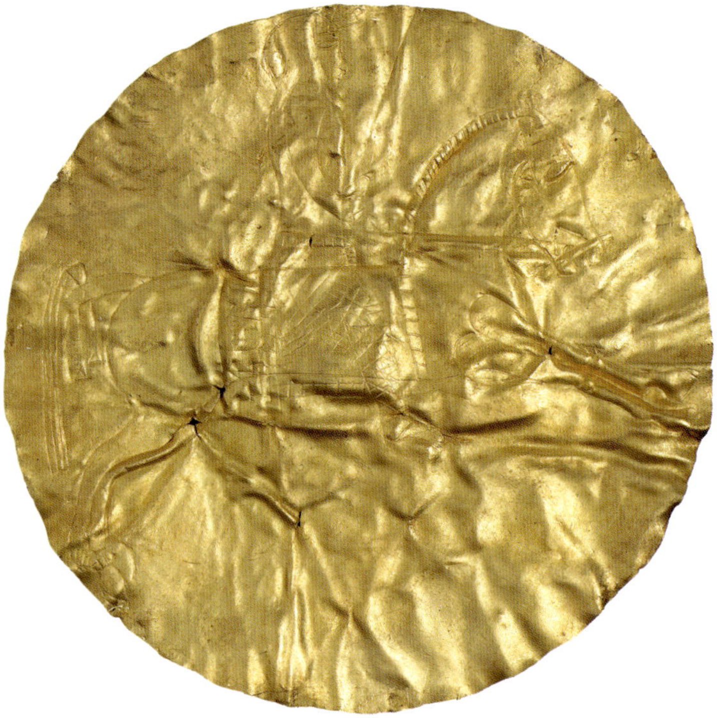

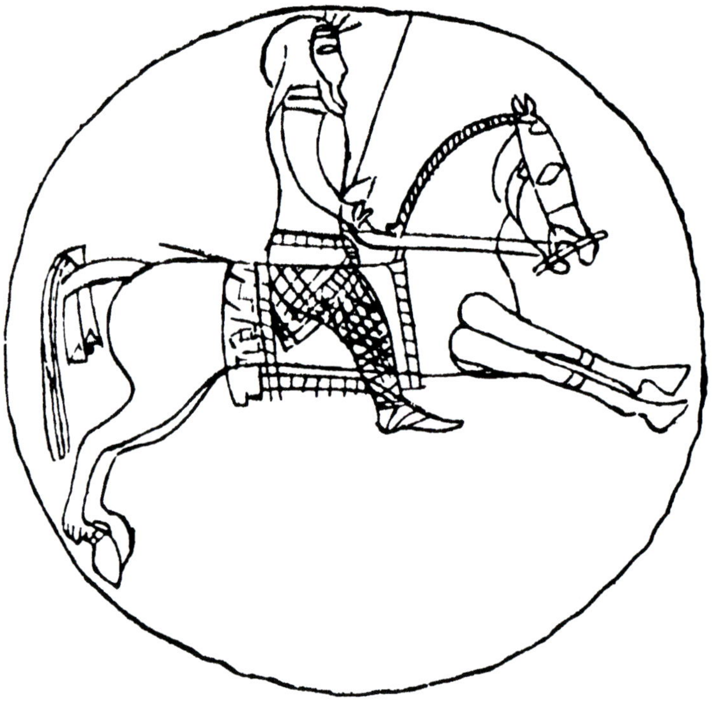

106

Gold disc clothing appliqué

5th–4th century BC, Achaemenid
Oxus Treasure; A.W. Franks bequest 1897
Gold
Diam. 4.8 cm
BM 123937

This example of luxury clothing decoration shows a horse and rider in punched outline. The rider is in riding dress of a trouser-suit and wears a hood or cap, while the horse is shown with a saddle-cloth.

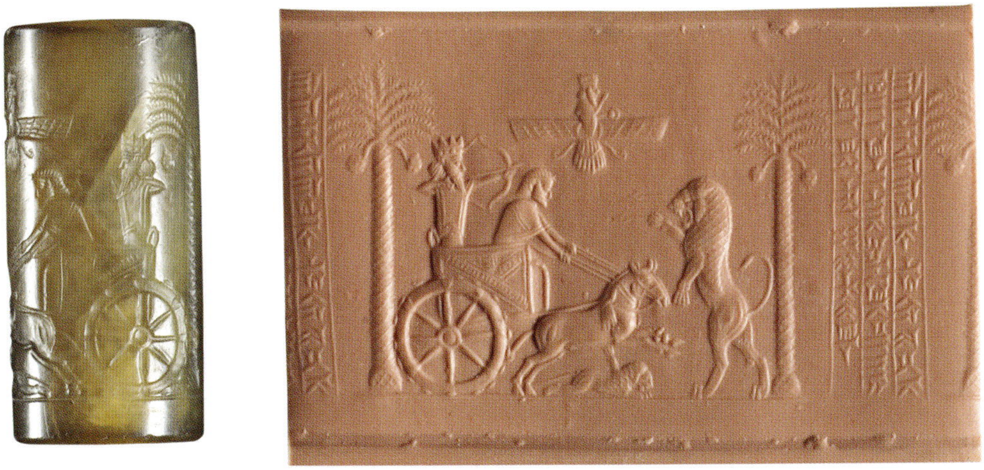

107

Cylinder seal

6th–5th century BC, Achaemenid
Said to have been found in Lower Egypt; acquired 1835
Green and grey-brown clouded chalcedony
H 3.7 cm, diam. 1.7 cm
BM 89132

The king stands in a chariot driven towards the right, and aims a third arrow at a rampant wounded lion. The two horses are leaping over the body of a fallen lion. Above, there is a figure in a winged disc. The scene is flanked by palm trees between which is a trilingual cuneiform inscription in Old Persian, Elamite and Babylonian: 'I (am) Darius, Great King'. This was probably a seal of office.

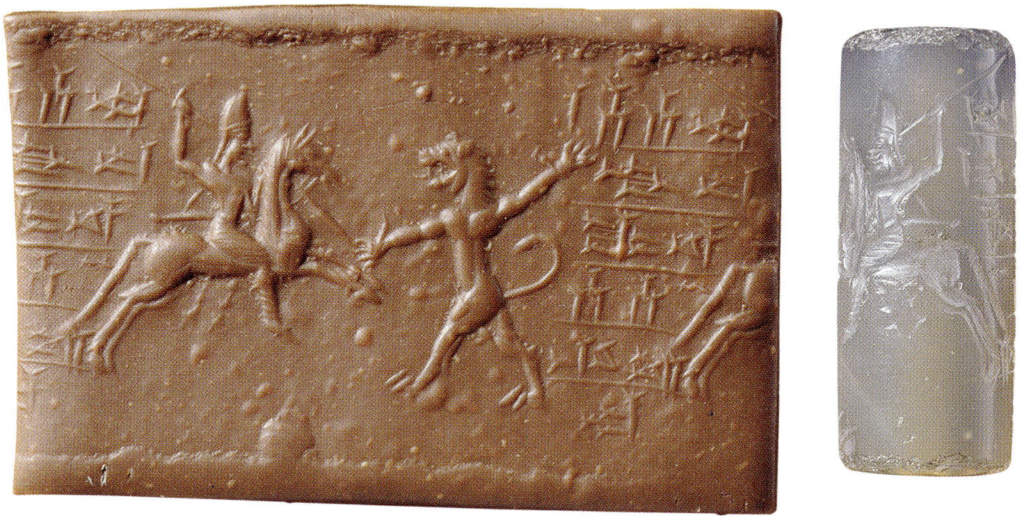

108

Cylinder seal showing a rider in Median dress

6th–4th century BC, Achaemenid
Provenance unknown; acquired 1841
Grey-blue chalcedony
H 3.5 cm, diam 1.4 cm
BM 89009

The rider gallops to the right and aims a spear at a rampant lion. There is a six-line inscription in Elamite, reading 'Ainakka son of Fraitish'. The horse has a slender frame with a long neck, full mane and short forelock. The tail is tied spirally at the upper end, but hangs loose below. Two tassels hanging under the horse's belly may indicate a saddle blanket.

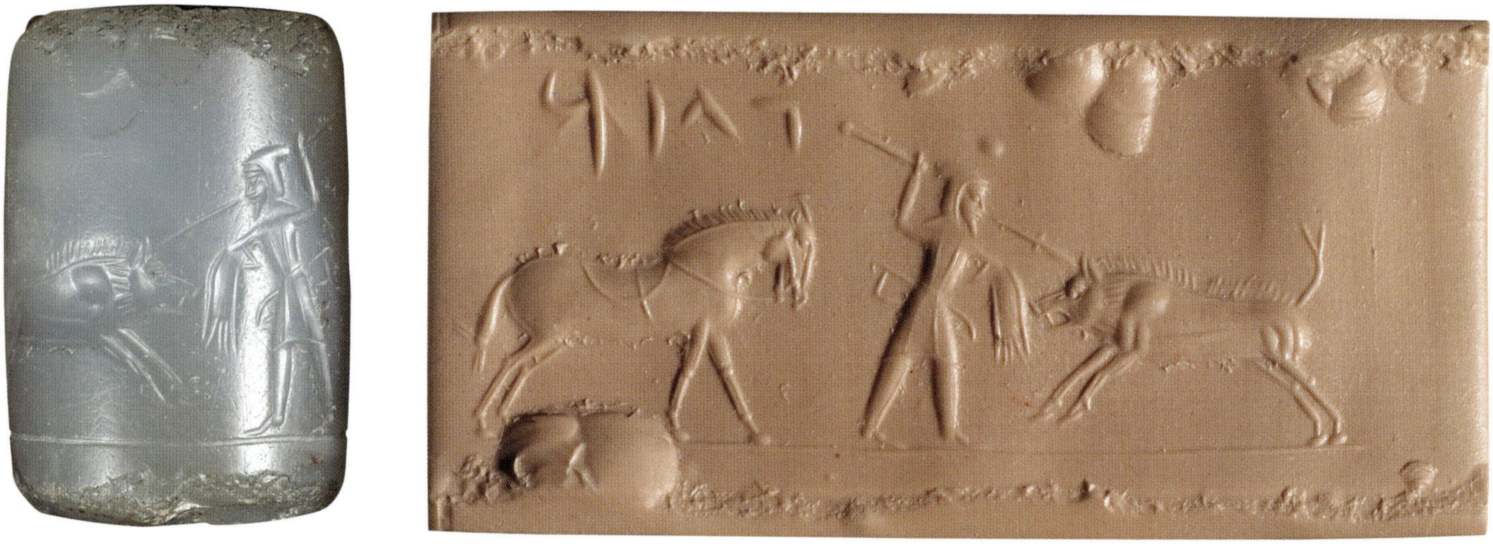

109
Cylinder seal

6th–4th century BC, Achaemenid
Provenance unknown; acquired 1846
Mottled blue and grey-blue chalcedony
H 3.3 cm, diam. 2.2 cm
BM 89144

A horse stands facing right. The dismounted rider in Median dress spears an advancing boar. The reading of the name, written in Aramaic above the horse, is uncertain, but it is probably of Iranian origin.

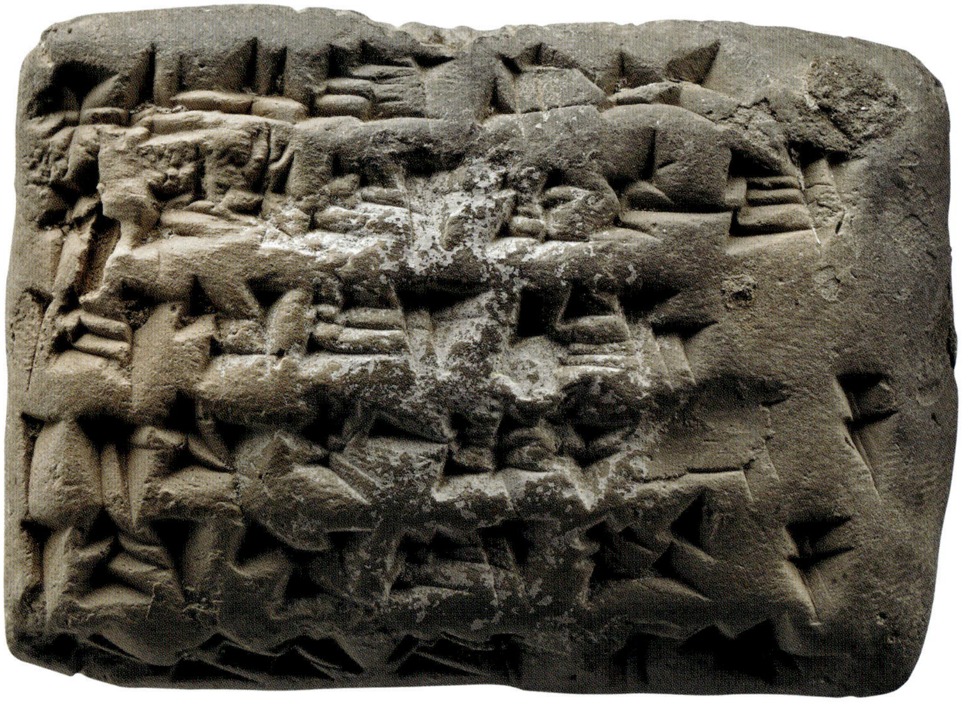

110
Clay tablet, gift of a horse to the Ebabbar temple in Sippar

516 BC
Sippar, Iraq
Clay
L 5.1 cm, H 3.5 cm
BM 56781

This complete clay tablet, written in cuneiform, is a Late Babylonian receipt for a horse given to the Ebabbar temple in Sippar. It was written during the reign of Darius I, when Mesopotamia was part of the Achaemenid empire.

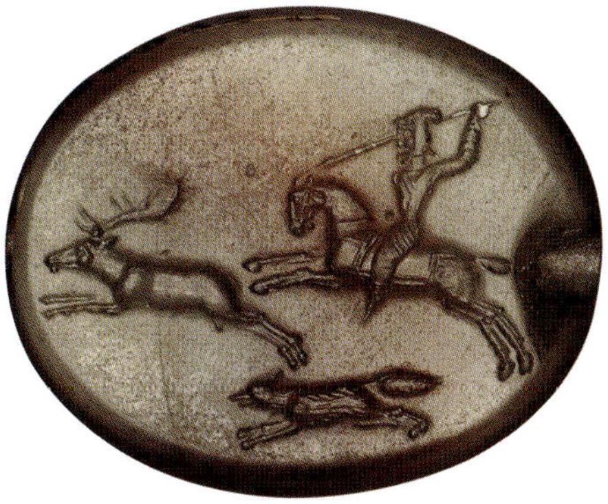

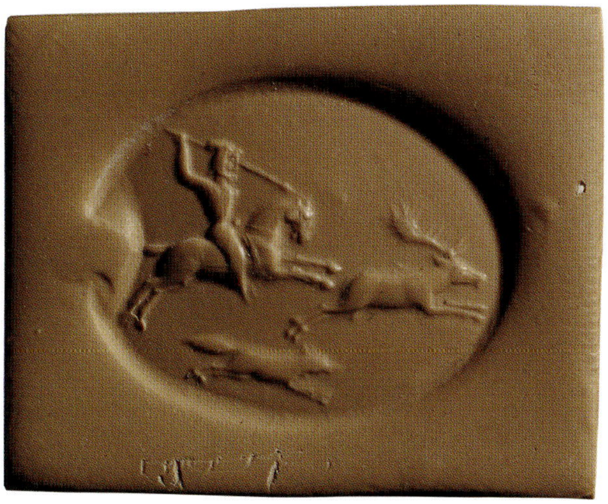

111

Scaraboid stamp seal engraved with a rider in Median riding dress

5th–4th century BC, Achaemenid
Provenance unknown
Agate or chalcedony
H 1.7 cm, W 2.1 cm, Th. 1.8 cm
BM 120332

This pink and grey agate or chalcedony scaraboid stamp seal has an oval base and a convex top. It has a hole pierced through longitudinally. The seal is engraved with a scene of a horseman in Median riding dress and armed with a spear or javelin in chase of a stag or deer together with his hunting dog.

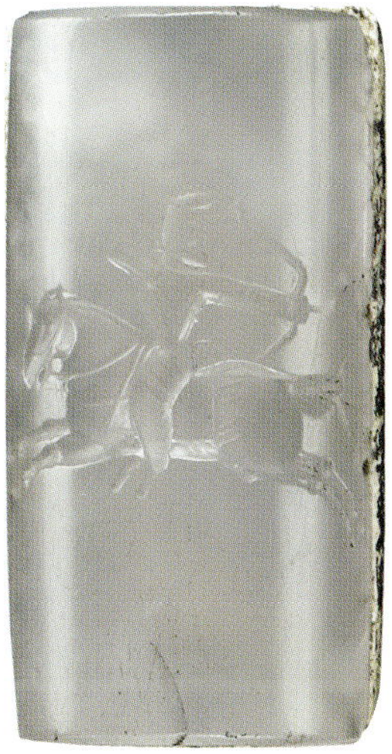

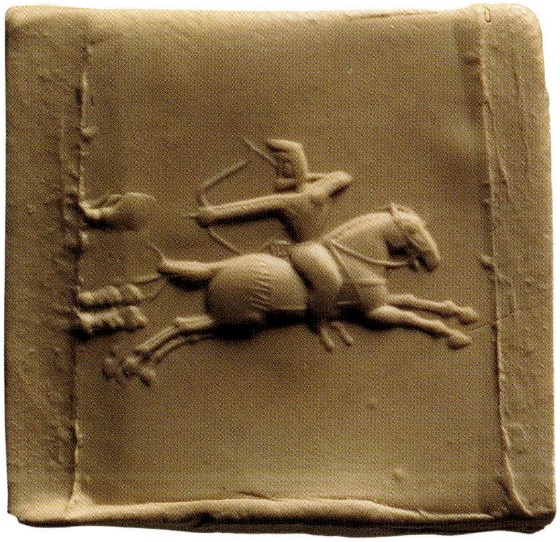

112

Seal showing a rider in Median dress hunting a lion

c. 5th century BC, Achaemenid
Provenance unknown; acquired 1869
Pale-blue chalcedony
H 2.6 cm, Diam. 1.4 cm
BM 89816

On this cylinder seal, of which only half remains, a rider in Median dress gallops towards the right and turns back in the saddle to aim an arrow from a double-recurved bow at a leaping lion. Only the nose and forepaws of the lion remain. This is an example of the so-called 'Parthian shot', first known in the Near East from eighth- or ninth-century Assyrian depictions: a skirmishing technique of the highly skilled horse-archer later made famous by the Parthians in the wars against Rome. The rider sits on a saddle-cloth, with tufts along the rear edge, secured by a breast strap.

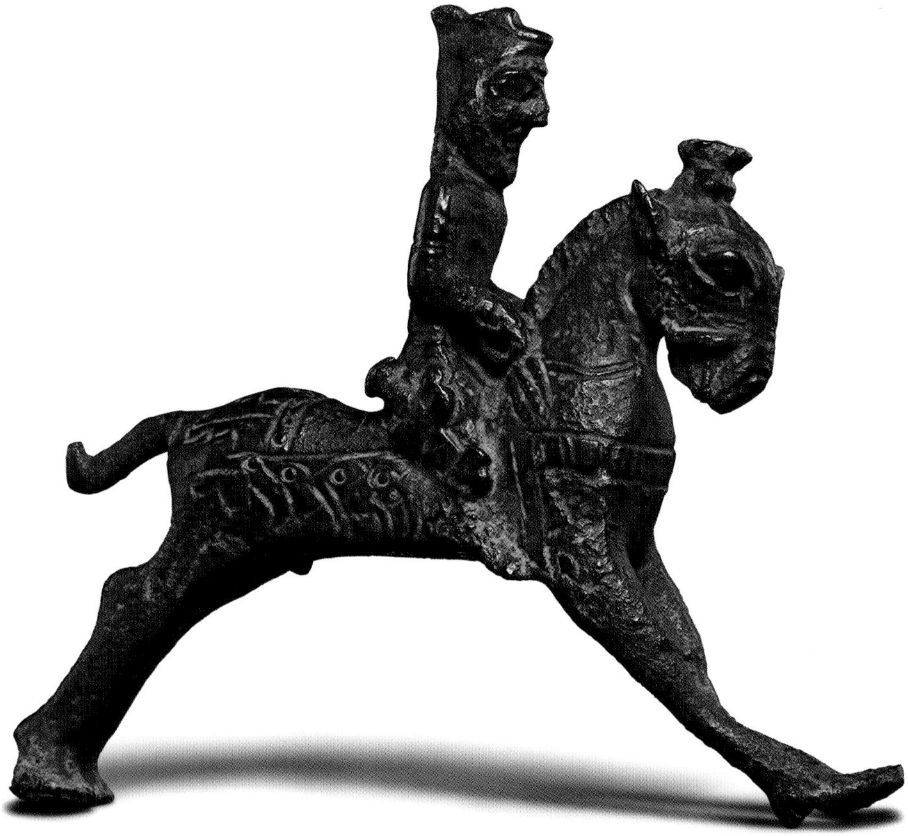

113

Figurine of a horse and rider

c. 5th–4th century BC, Achaemenid
Provenance unknown; acquired 1890
Bronze
H 8.5 cm, L 10.1 cm
BM 117760

The rider is wearing Median riding dress with a soft cap and an *akinakes* suspended from a waist belt on his right thigh. His tunic has edge decoration and he wears bracelets. The horse has a rectangular saddle blanket with edging tufts along the lower edge and stepped lappets at the rear. There is a strap below the blanket to secure either it or a pad-saddle and a breast strap. The mane is pulled but has long strands on the lower neck, and a forelock is tied up into a splayed crest on the poll (top of the head) – all of which are distinctively Achaemenian features. The horse is shown in a fast gallop, and the pairs of fore and hind hooves are joined together for attachment to an element now missing (perhaps a vessel). Similar riders are shown as border decoration in a pile hanging or carpet from barrow 5 at Pazyryk in Siberia; a decorated saddle blanket of felt with stepped lappets in Achaemenid style was recovered from the same barrow.

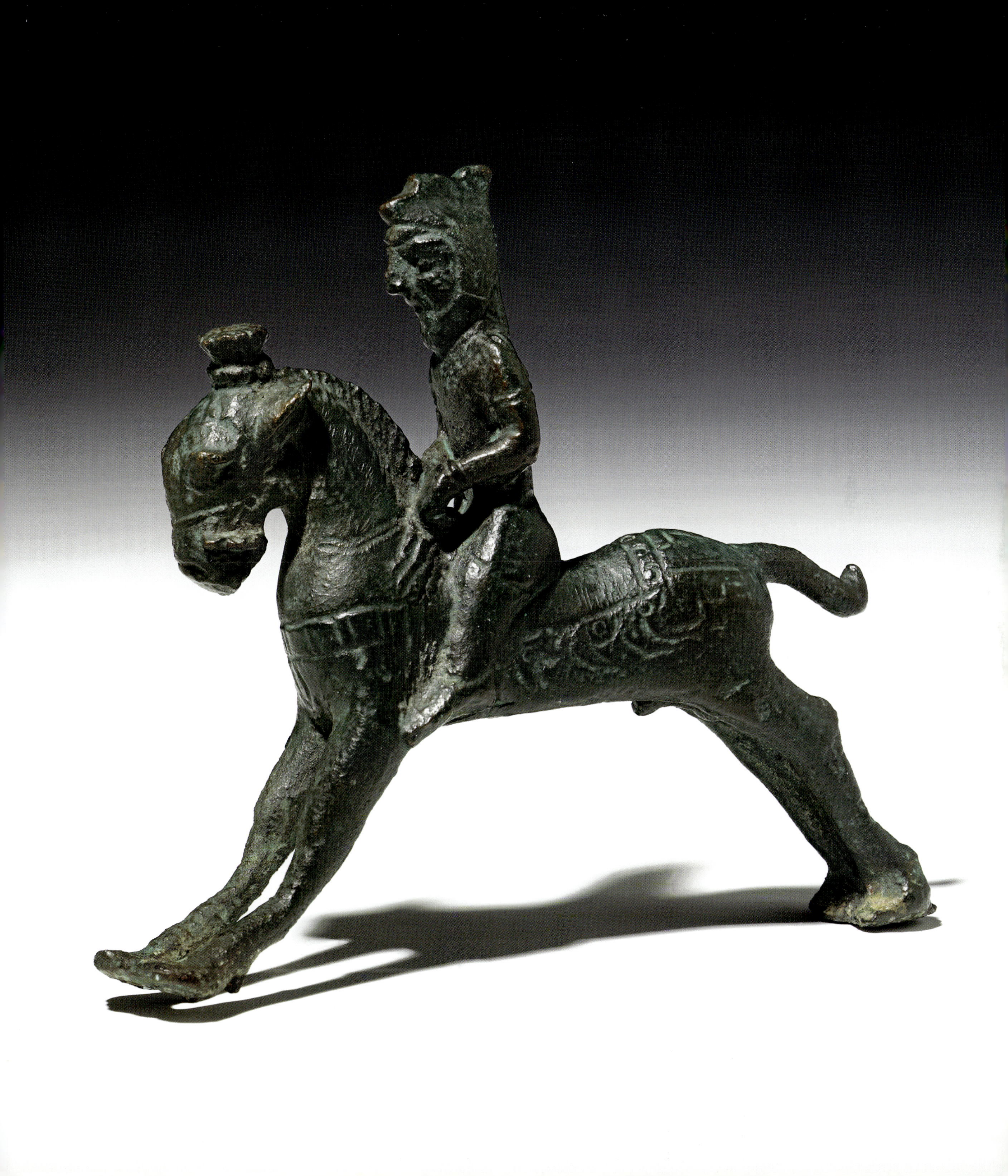

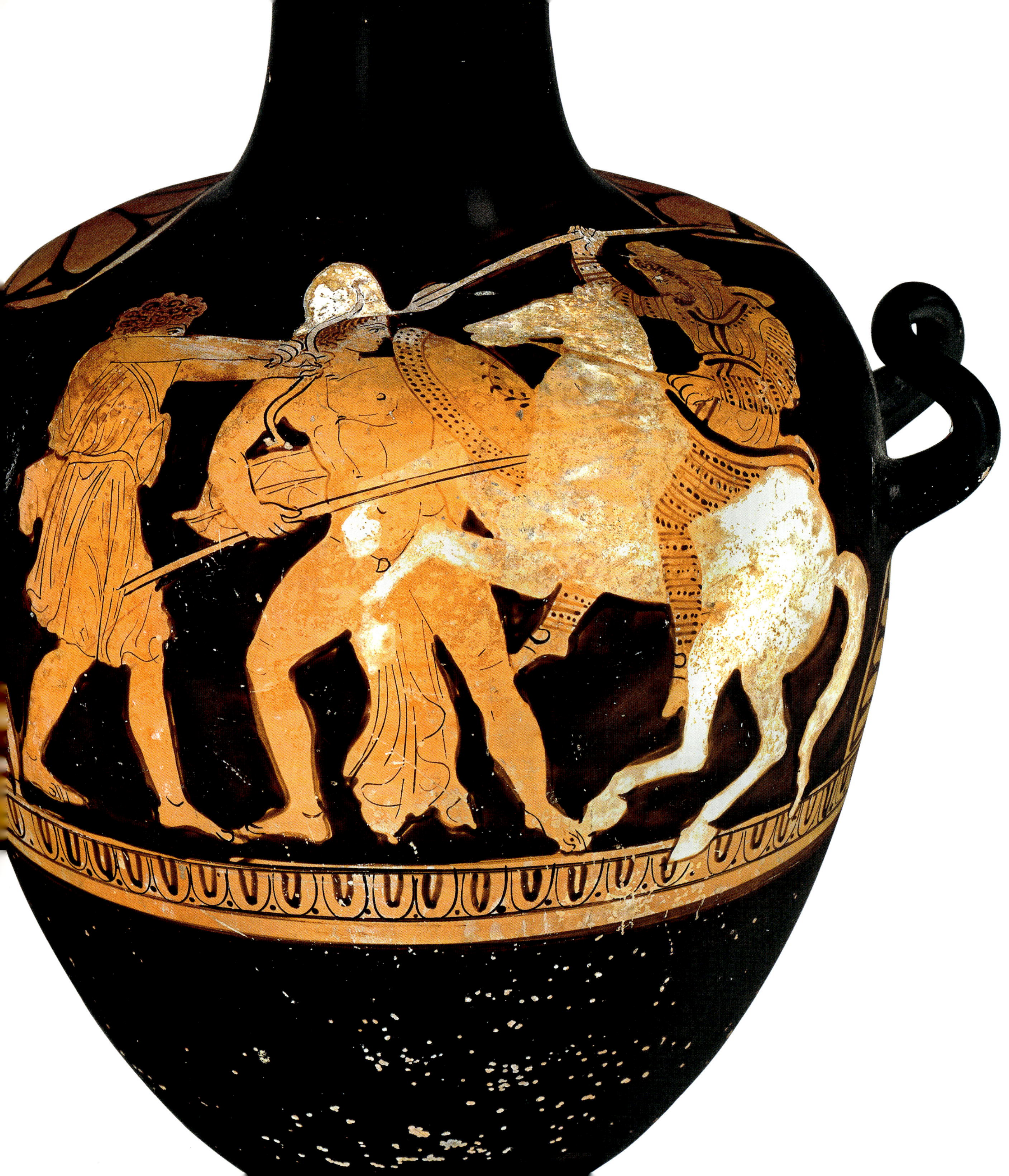

114

Athenian red-figured *hydria* (water-jug) with two Greeks fighting a mounted Persian

c. 360–330 BC
From Cyrenaica (Libya); acquired 1866
Ceramic
H 29.5 cm
BM 1866,0415.244

On the right a bearded Persian is mounted on a rearing white horse and aims a spear or javelin at a Greek warrior on foot. The Persian wears a soft skin hat (*kidaris*) with its long ear-flaps hanging down, an oriental trouser-suit, and soft shoes. The young warrior is equipped with a white *pilos*-style helmet, circular shield and a *chlamys* round his back. He thrusts up with his long spear at the Persian. On the left a wavy-haired archer, wearing a short chiton and with a quiver at his hip, aims his bow at the Persian while sheltering behind his companion's shield.

This is one of the latest red-figured Athenian vases to show a fight between Greeks and Persians.

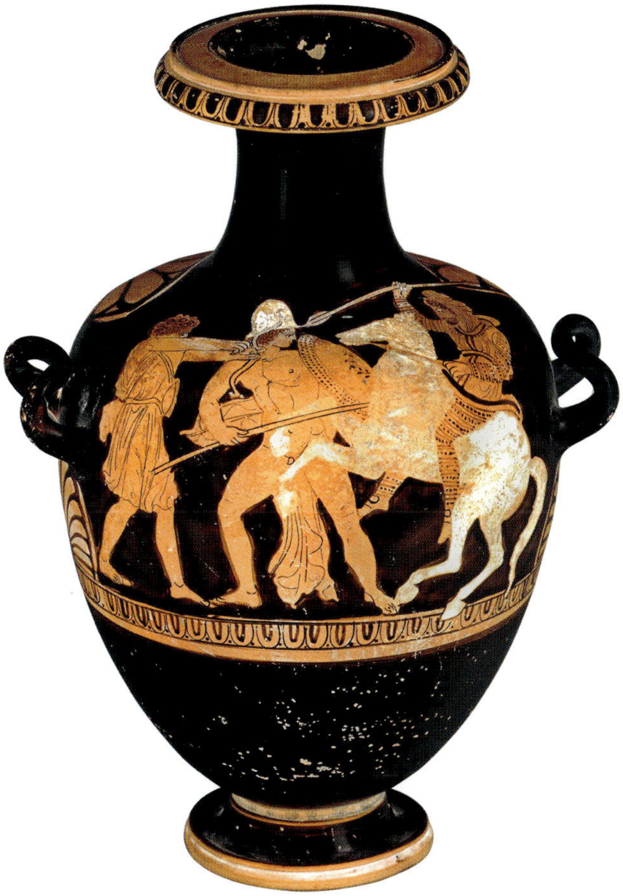

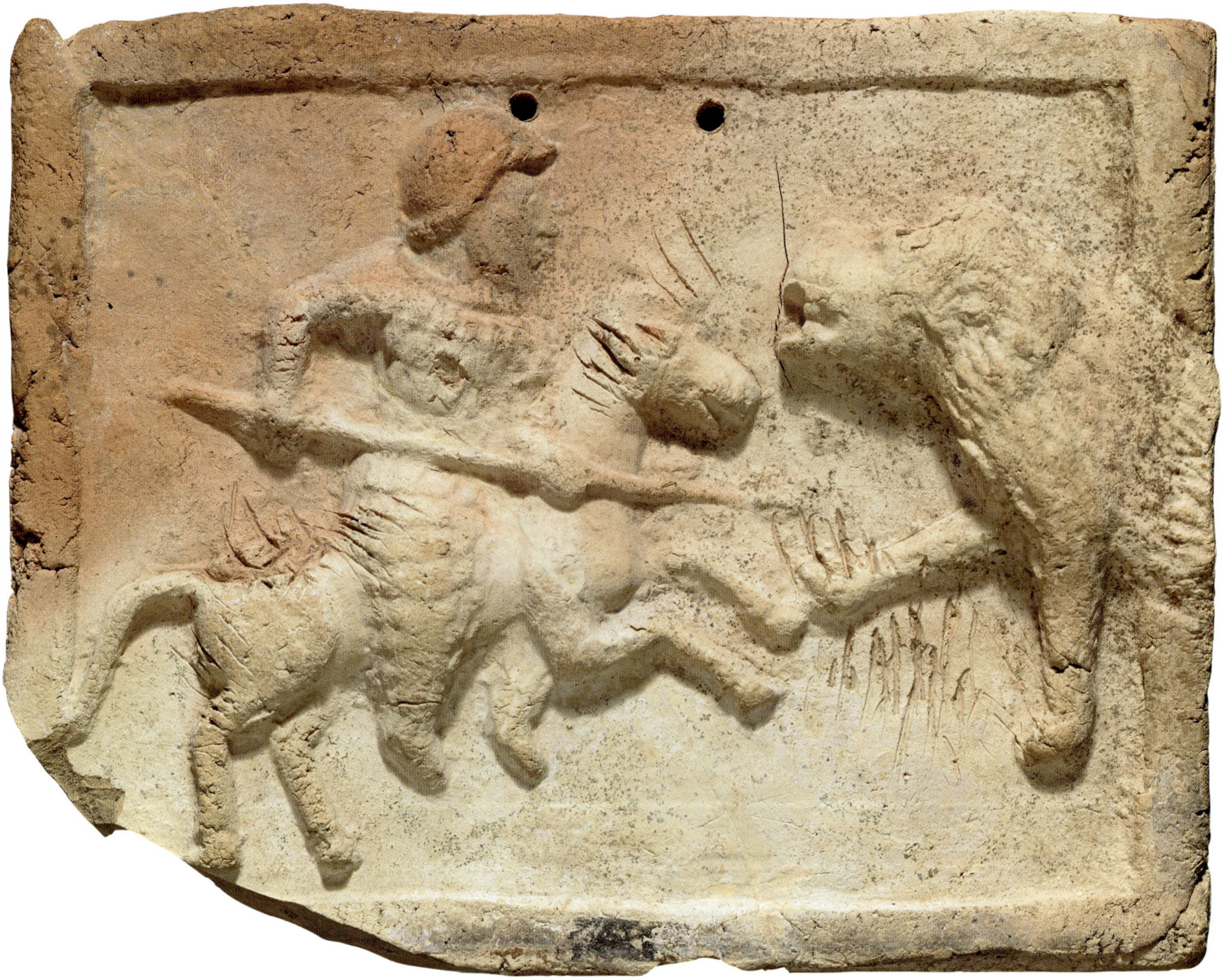

115

Plaque showing a mounted cataphract

3rd–2nd century BC, Late Hellenistic or Early Parthian
Mesopotamia; acquired in 19th century
Baked clay
H 15.2 cm, W 19 cm, Th. 2.3 cm
BM 91908

A warrior seated on a rearing horse, wearing a round helmet with a rim at the bottom and a suit of scale or lamellar armour, holds a long spear with which he is fighting a lion. The horse wears a bridle and has a bushy tail. The plaque is pinkish-cream in colour and has a border all around the edge. There are two holes at the top of the plaque to hang it up or to fix it to a background.

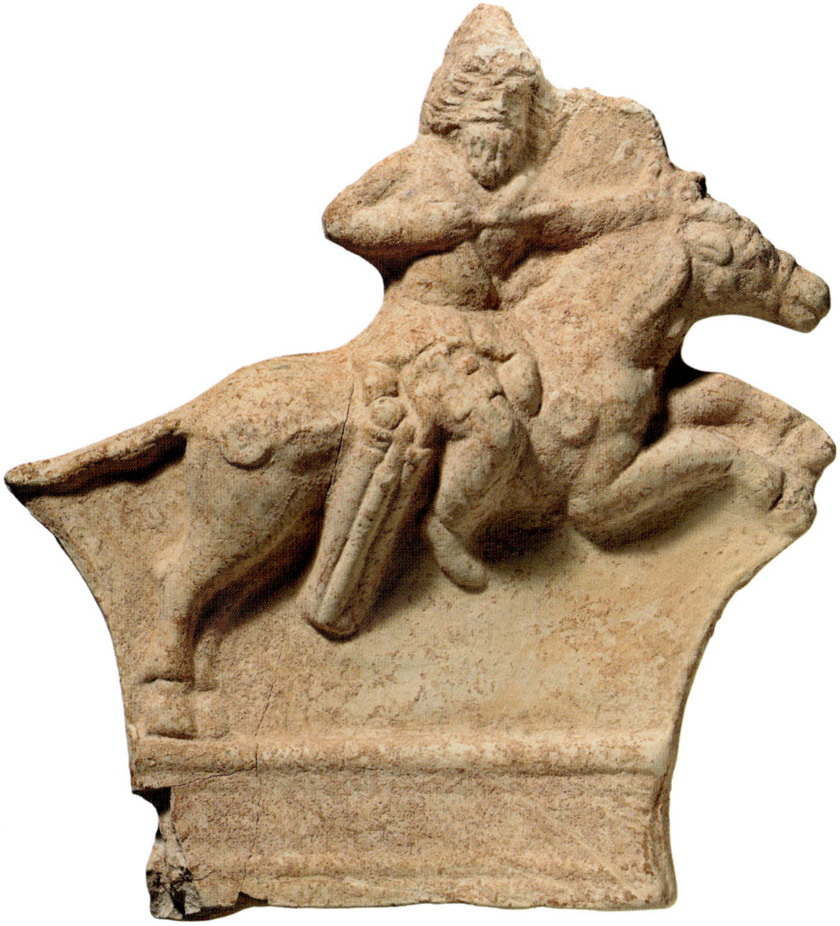

116

Plaque with archer on horseback

1st–3rd century AD, Parthian period
Provenance unknown; acquired 1972
Baked clay
H 17 cm, W 15.6 cm, Th. 4 cm
BM 135684

Hollow moulded plaque showing a Parthian archer on horseback. He is bearded and wears a hat together with a belted tunic and trousers. He sits on a horned saddle. There is a quiver behind his leg and he draws a composite bow. This plaque has been made by moulding the front and back sides separately and then joining them together. It was probably originally brightly painted. The harness is decorated with two large *phalarae*.

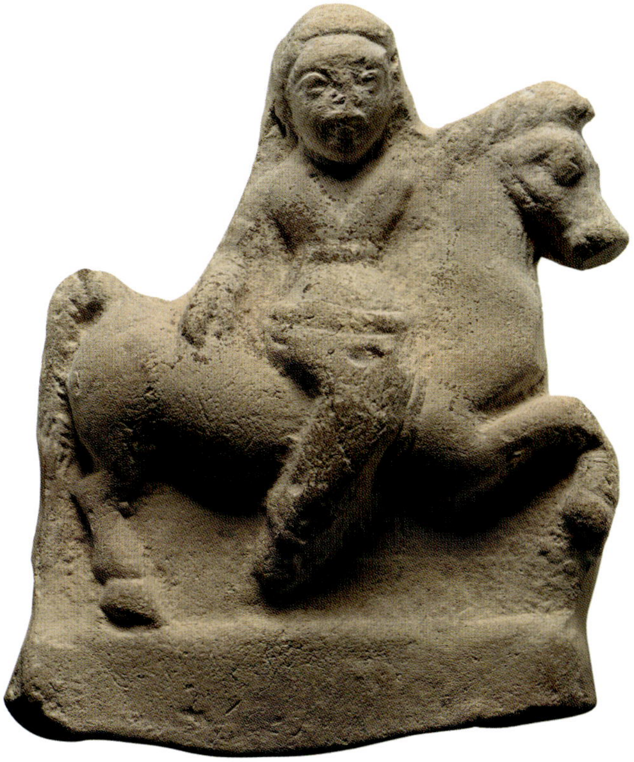

117

Hollow plaque showing a horse and rider

1st–3rd century AD, Parthian
Provenance unknown; acquired 1914
Baked clay
L 10.5 cm, W 4.5 cm, H 8.9 cm
BM 113178

The rider is a beardless youth or a woman and is apparently shown as bare-headed, wearing a crossed-over belted jacket and trousers or leggings. The rider's head and upper body are turned to face the front. The horse wears a bridle, but no reins are visible. It has an upright mane, which was probably clipped, nose with concave sides, large eyes and a bushy tail with high carriage. Because of these features it has been suggested that the horse may be an Arabian type.

118

Hollow plaque showing a horse and rider

1st–3rd century AD, Parthian
Nineveh, Mesopotamia; acquired 1856
Baked clay
L 11.8 cm, H 15.9 cm
BM 1856,0903.122

The rider is a beardless youth wearing a rounded helmet or cap and a long-sleeved belted tunic and trousers with a flowing cloak. He is probably also wearing leggings. He sits on a saddle which is mounted on a rounded saddle-cloth. The horse has an upright mane and a *phalera* on its shoulder. Hollow plaques of this kind were made by pressing the front and back sides into moulds and joining the two sides together while the clay was still wet.

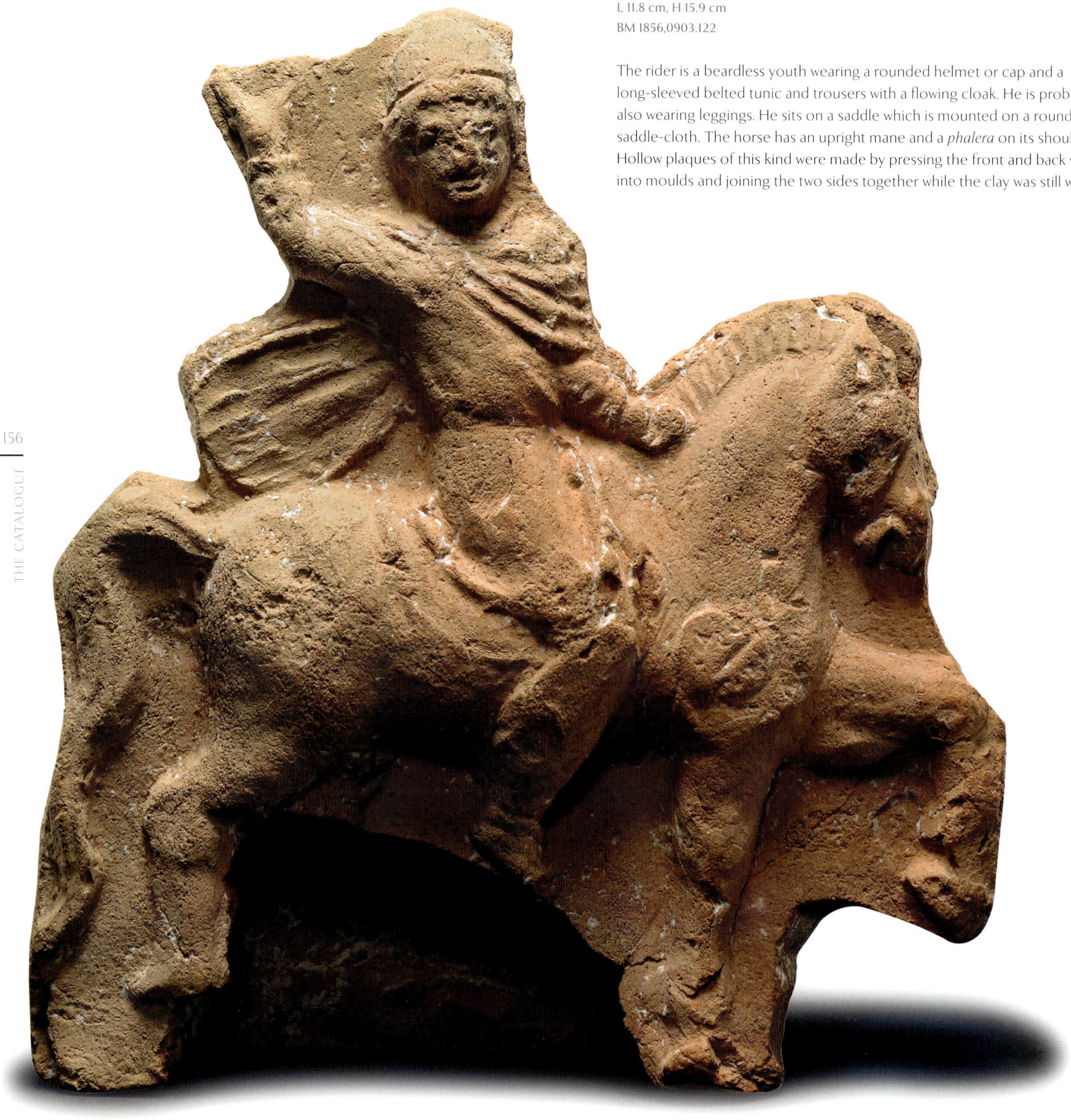

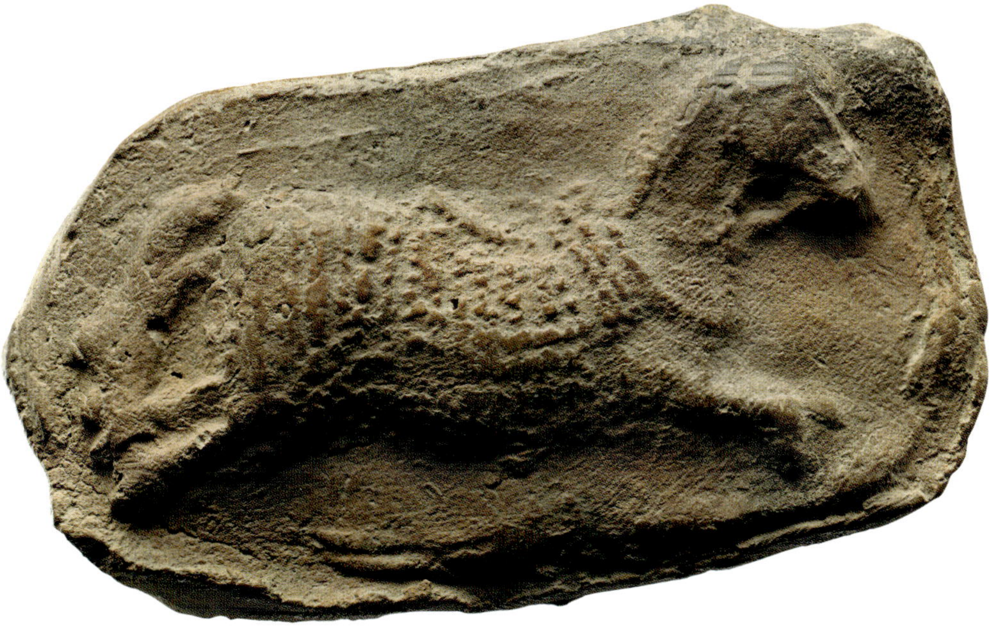

119

Plaque showing a galloping horse

c. 3rd century AD, late Parthian or early Sasanian period
Mesopotamia; acquired 1965
Baked clay
L 7.8 cm, H 4.4 cm
BM 134643

This plaque shows a horse at full gallop wearing a suit of scale or lamellar armour, together with a saddle. The bridle and reins are clearly depicted. Fully armoured horses of this kind are a characteristic feature of the early centuries AD.

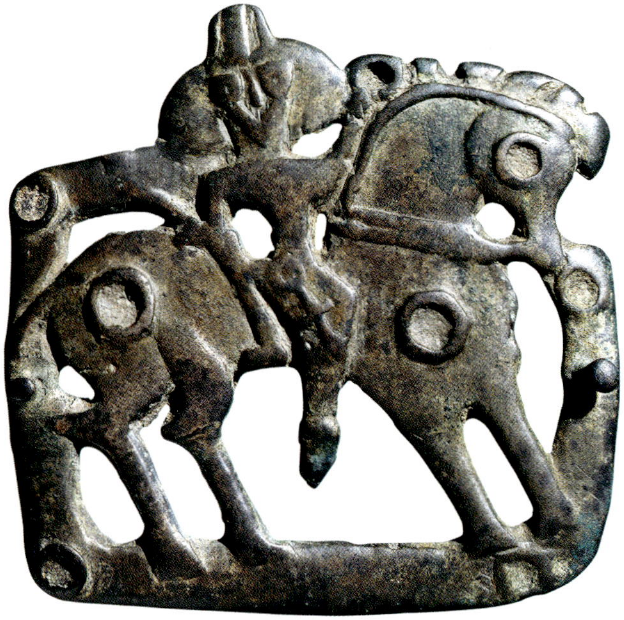

120

Openwork belt buckle showing a horse and rider

1st–3rd century AD, Parthian
Provenance unknown; acquired 1981
Bronze
H 7.2 cm, W 7.1 cm, Th. 0.7 cm
BM 139205

The rider wears a helmet and belted tunic and trousers, and a dagger rests on his thigh. There are bunches of hair on either side of his face. The hairstyle and the costume are typical of the Parthian period. There are embossed circles on the outer frame of the buckle and on the horse. The rider's head and upper body are turned to face the front. The horse has a thin nose with concave sides. There are lugs on either side of the buckle to fix it to the belt.

121

Openwork belt buckle showing a horse and rider

2nd–3rd century AD, Parthian
Provenance unknown, acquired 1992
Bronze
H 8.1 cm, W 8.2 cm, Th. 1 cm
BM 1992,0125.1

The bearded rider wears a helmet, a belted tunic and tight trousers, and a dagger. There is a large bunch of hair at the back of his head, which is shown in profile. There are embossed circles on the outer frame of the buckle and on the horse. The horse has pricked ears, a thin nose with concave sides and an arched tail. There are lugs on either side of the buckle to fix it to the belt.

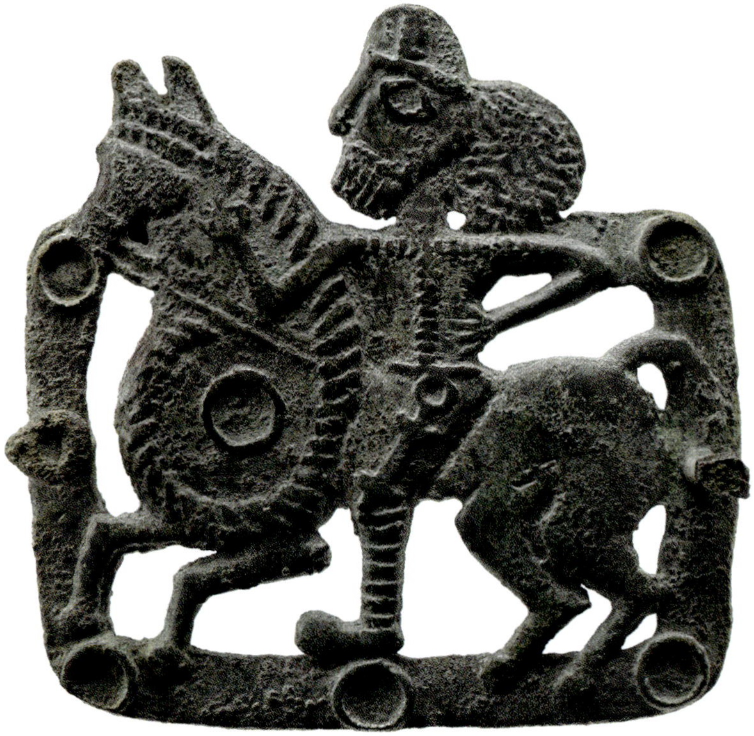

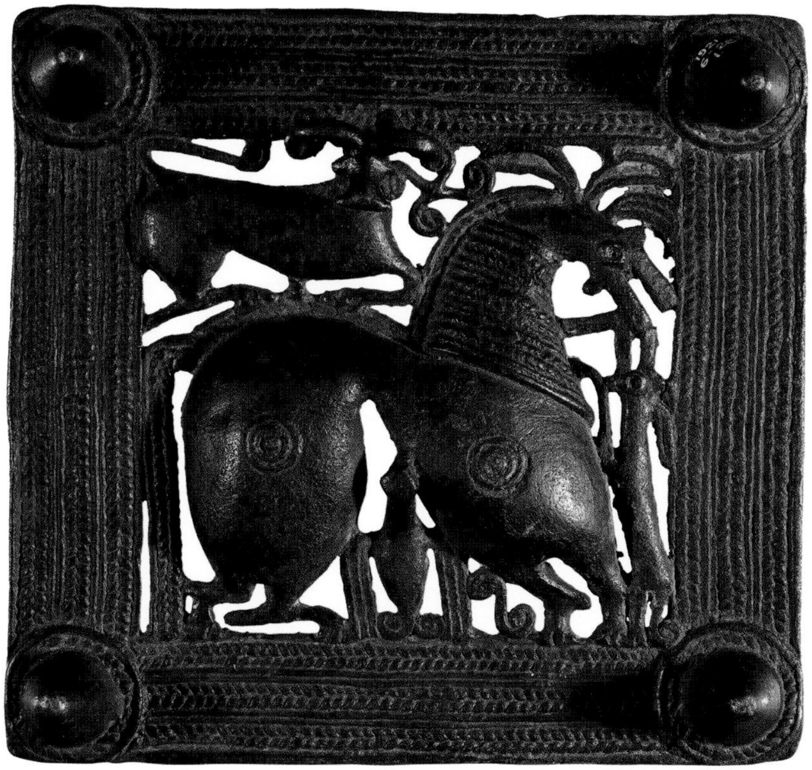

122

Openwork plaque showing a horse

1st–2nd century AD, Georgian
Provenance unknown; acquired 1921
Brass
H 13.2 cm, W 14 cm
BM 1921,0628.1

This cast brass plaque shows a stylized horse with a covering on its neck and the top part of its chest. It has concentric circle decoration on its haunches. There is an ox above the horse and a bird below, while in front of the horse, standing on its hind legs, is a dog(?) On the flat border around the plaque there is plaited decoration. There are hollow conical bosses at the corners of the plaque, and on the back there is a ring on one side and a hook on the other. Many openwork plaques of this type have been found in graves in Georgia in the Caucasus region. The central figure consists of a stylized animal, generally a stag with antlers, a horse or a goat. These animals have wasp-like waists and exaggerated fore- and hind-quarters. These plaques are usually identified as belt clasps or belt fittings, but a recent article suggests they may be chest ornaments or armour. They are approximately the same date as the Parthian belt clasps (cats 120–1), and may be distantly related to them, but stylistically and culturally they are very different.

123

Openwork plaque showing a horse

1st–2nd century AD, Georgian
Collected in the Caucasus by W.J. Meyers (1858–1899); acquired 1994
Leaded bronze
H 12.3 cm, W 11.8 cm
BM 1994,0409.2

This cast leaded bronze plaque, parts of which are missing, shows a stylized horse with bands around its neck, its chest and its middle. Its legs are curled at the end. It has a long mane and tail each of which ends in a spiral. The central design is set within a double border each containing spirals within bands of plaited decoration. The borders are separated by short pegs with moulded decoration. On the back a hook is preserved on one side. This plaque is of the same type as cat. 122 above.

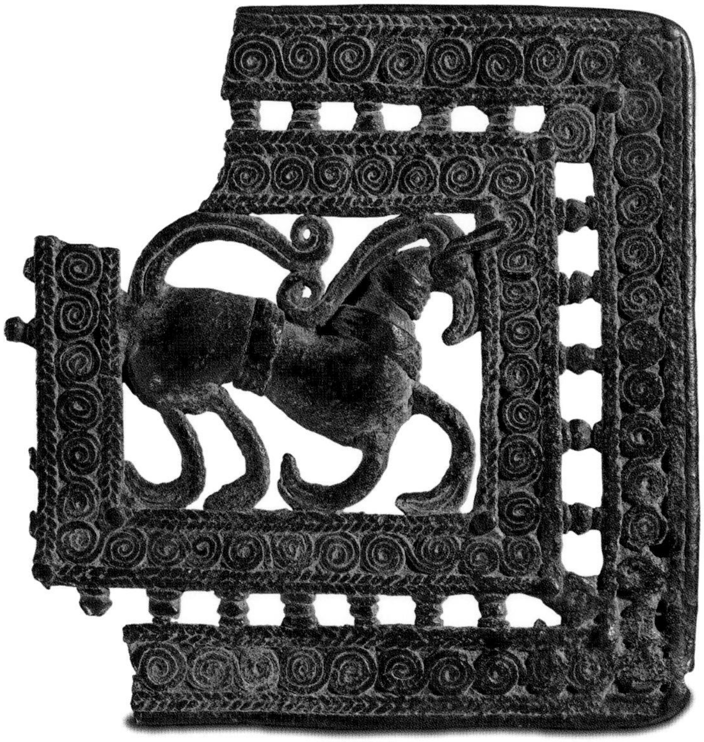

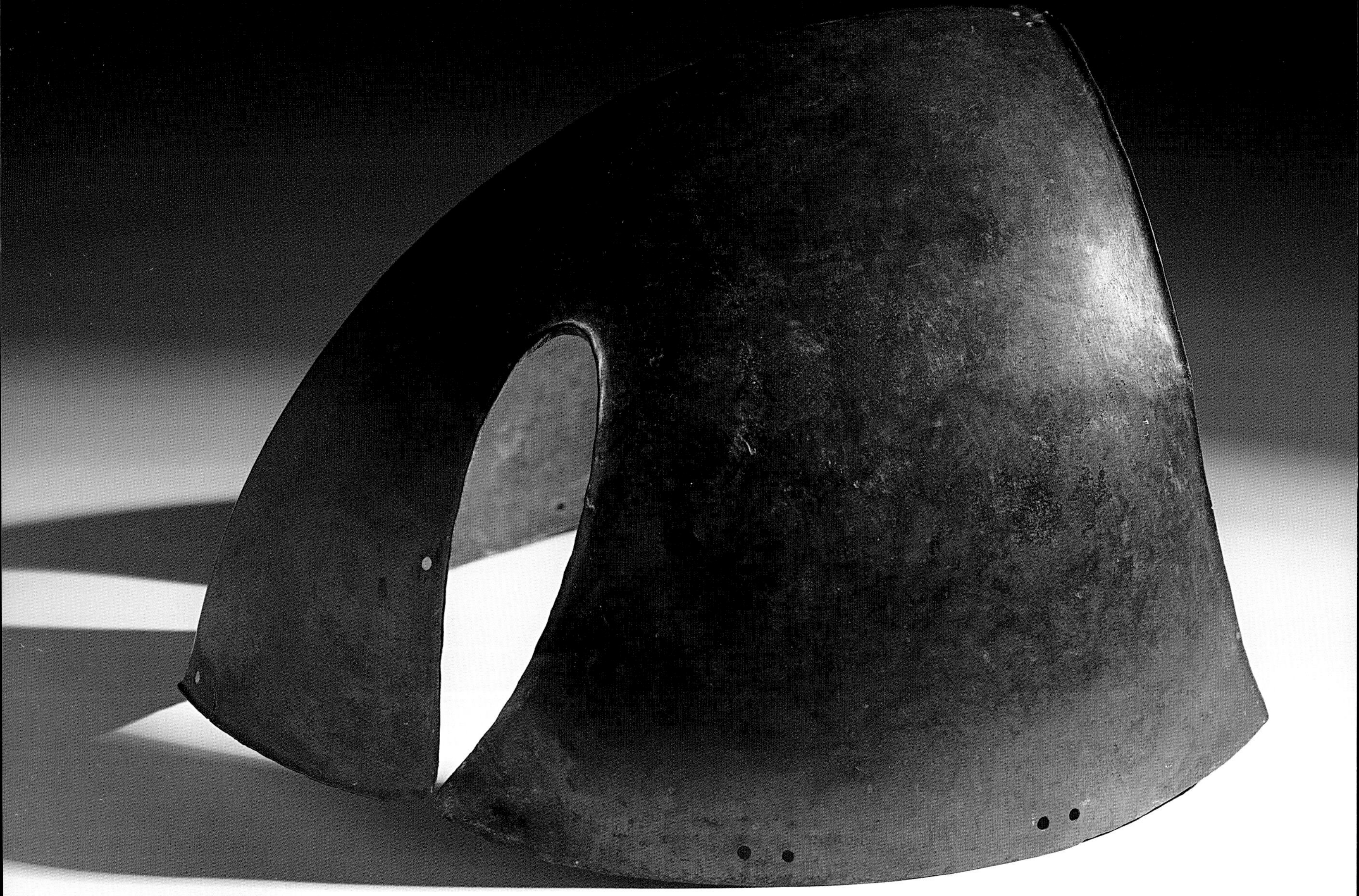

124

Horse's helmet

3rd–7th century AD, Sasanian
Provenance unknown; acquired 1970
Bronze
L 29.5 cm, W 19 cm
BM 135437

Helmet or head-covering made from sheet bronze with two large holes cut out for the ears. There are pairs of holes around the edge of the helmet showing that it was fixed to a backing of cloth or leather. Experiments with replica pieces have shown that it was designed to fit the head of a small horse, probably a pony. The date of this piece is uncertain, as there are no exact parallels in the archaeological record or amongst ancient representations, but as there was a strong tradition of arming horses and riders in the Sasanian period it has been tentatively ascribed to this era.

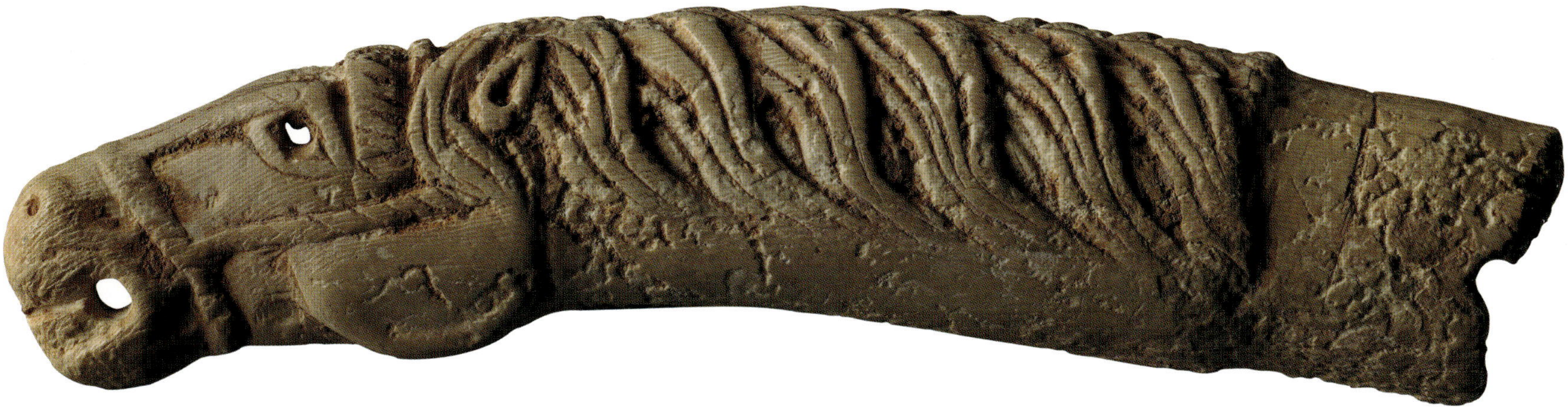

125

Handle in the form of a horse's head

1st–2nd century AD, Parthian, Ptolemaic or Roman
Provenance unknown; acquired 1972
Bone
L 9.8 cm, W 2.7 cm, Th. 1.3 cm
BM 135718

Length of bone, hollowed out in the middle, carved in the form of a horse's head and neck. The horse wears a headstall and brow-band, and has a long and flowing mane. There are holes at either end of this handle, one of which must be to fix it in position.

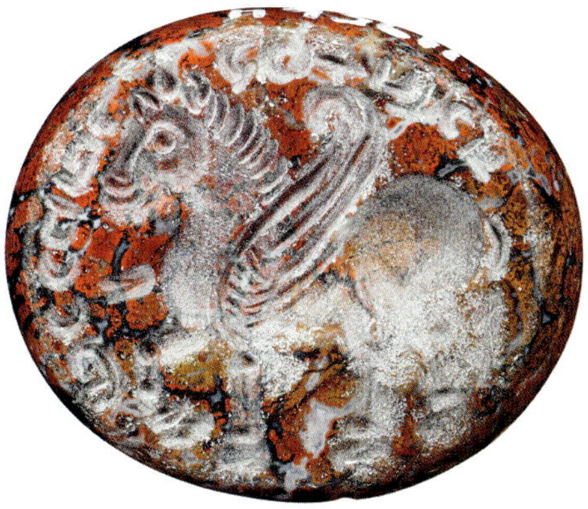

126

Stamp seal with a winged horse

4th century AD, Sasanian period
Provenance unknown; acquired 1841
L 1.9 cm, W 1.6 cm
Jasper
BM 119564

This domed stamp seal has an engraved design showing a winged horse (Pegasus) surrounded by an inscription in Pahlavi letters. The Pahlavi script was used to write inscriptions in the Middle Persian language.

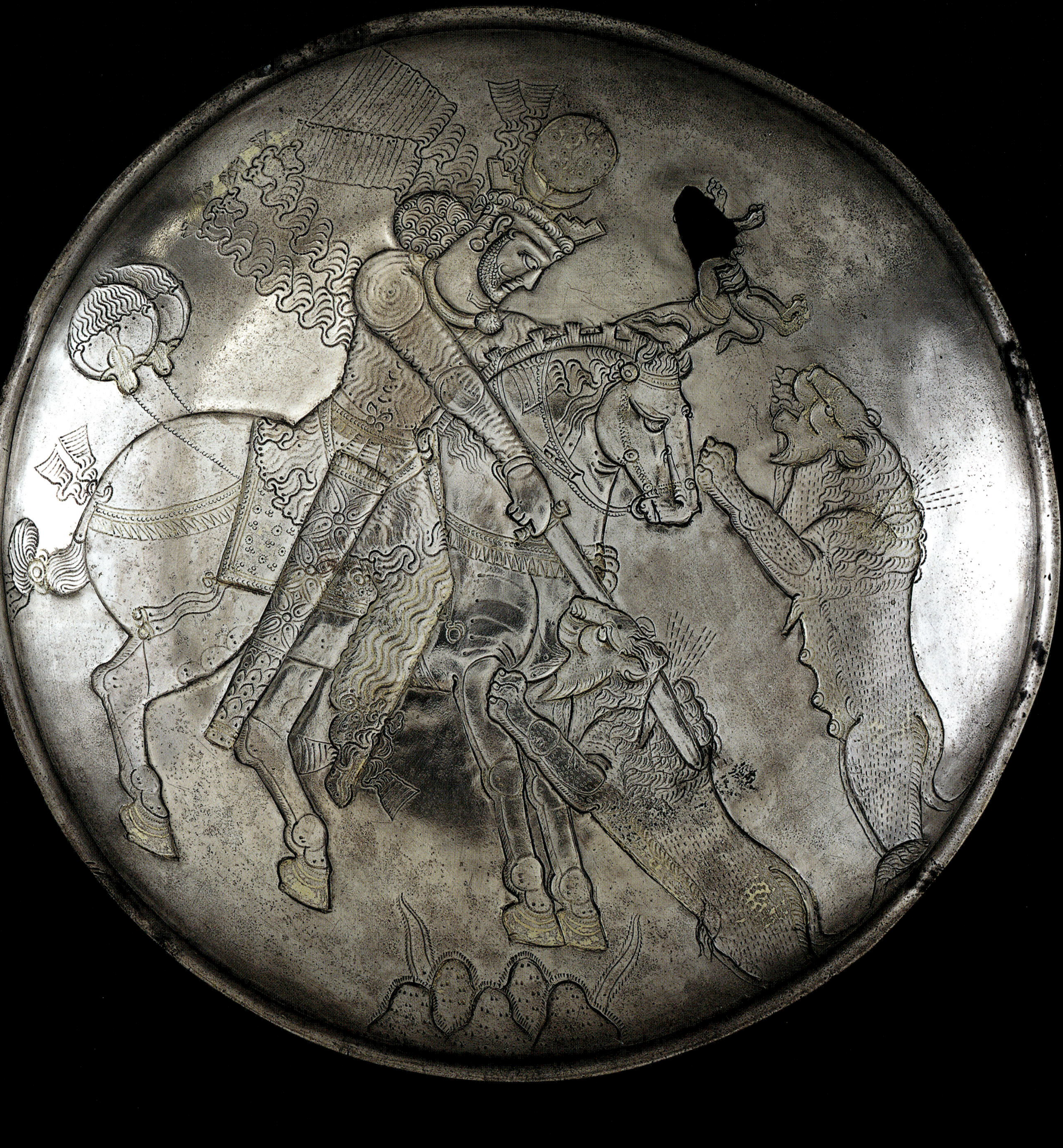

127

Silver gilt plate with hunting scene

5th–7th century AD, Sasanian
Provenance unknown; A.W. Franks bequest 1897
Silver with traces of surface gilding
Diam. 27.6 cm, max. H 5 cm
BM 124092

This plate shows a Sasanian king on horseback hunting lions. He holds a lion club in his left hand, and slashes at a lion with a sword held in his right hand. Blood spurts from the wound inflicted on the lion. A lioness leaping up in front of the horse has already been wounded in the same place on the back of the neck. The lion and lioness are probably the parents of the cub being held by the king. The scales at the bottom of the scene indicate the action is taking place in rocky or mountainous countryside. The king is identifiable as Bahram V (421–439) through his crenellated crown with a crescent and a globe that is also found on coin portraits of this reign. The king wears an elaborate belted tunic, probably of silk, and leggings over his trousers. A richly decorated quiver is suspended from his belt. The diadem ties (ribbons) attached to the king's crown, shoulders, shoes, and the horse's rump, are all symbols of the monarch's kingly glory (*khwarna/farr*). The king sits on a patterned saddle cloth with his feet hanging loose, not supported in stirrups. The horse has a bridle decorated with *phalerae* and wears tasselled bands around breast and rump. The two 'balloons' attached to the back of the horse are sometimes thought to be fly-whisks. The plate has a ring foot and the decoration is engraved and chased. Although the plate depicts Bahram V, it may have been made later than his reign, possibly in Afghanistan or north-west India.

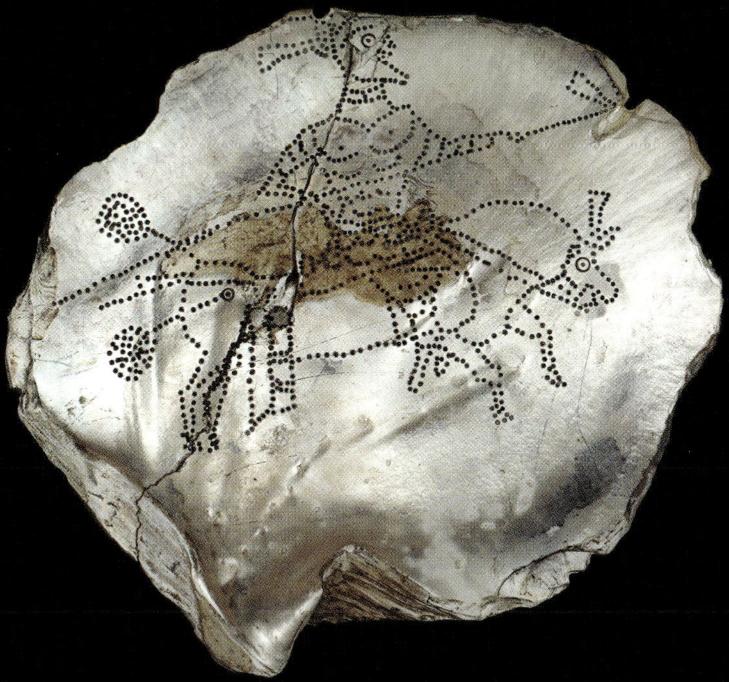

128

Oyster shell showing horse and rider

5th–7th century AD, Sasanian
Provenance unknown; acquired 1996
Shell
H 13.1 cm, W 13.7 cm, D 1.5 cm
BM 1996,1001.1

The decoration on this oyster shell has been made with incised dots. The bearded rider wears a cuirass and holds a long lance. He sits on a saddle-cloth and behind him is a quiver. The diadem ties (ribbons) on the rider's headdress, the lance and the horse's head show that the rider is a king. Floating behind the horse are two 'balloons' or fly-whisks. The diadem ties and the fly-whisks are characteristic features of Sasanian art and can be found on the silver plate, cat. 127. This shell is probably of similar date.

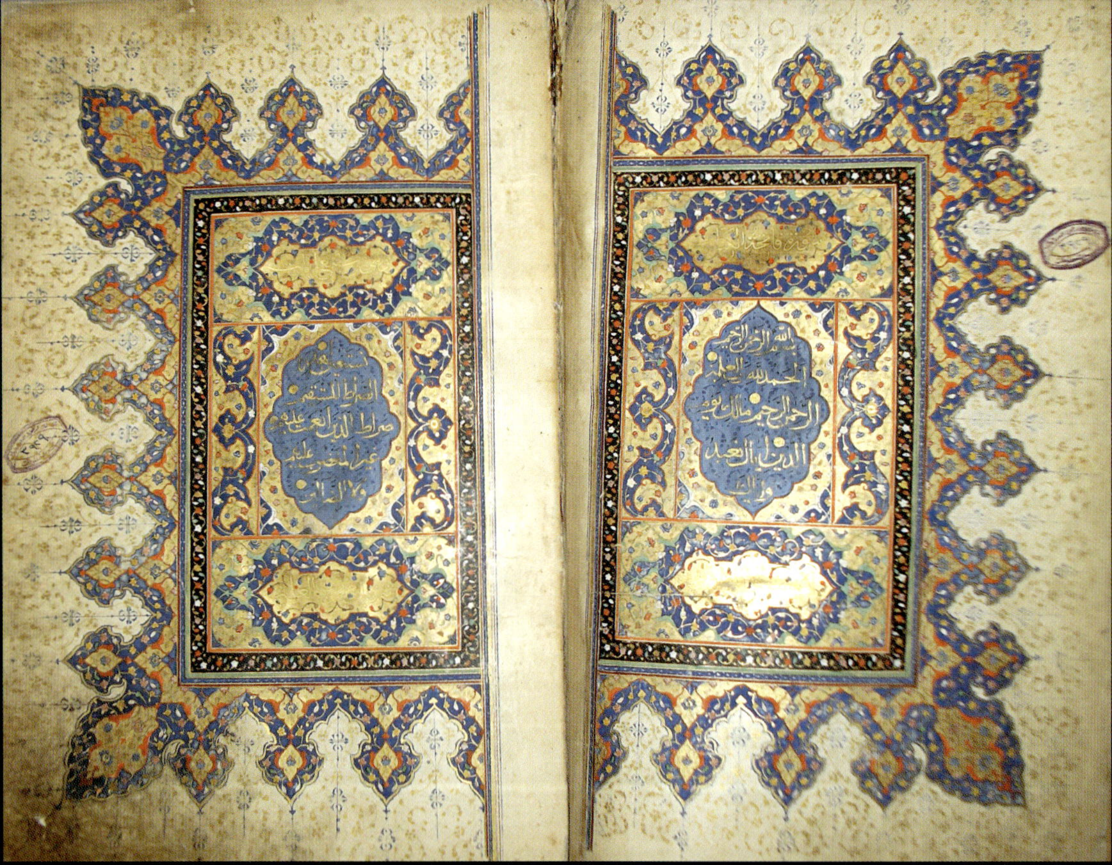

129
Complete Holy Quran

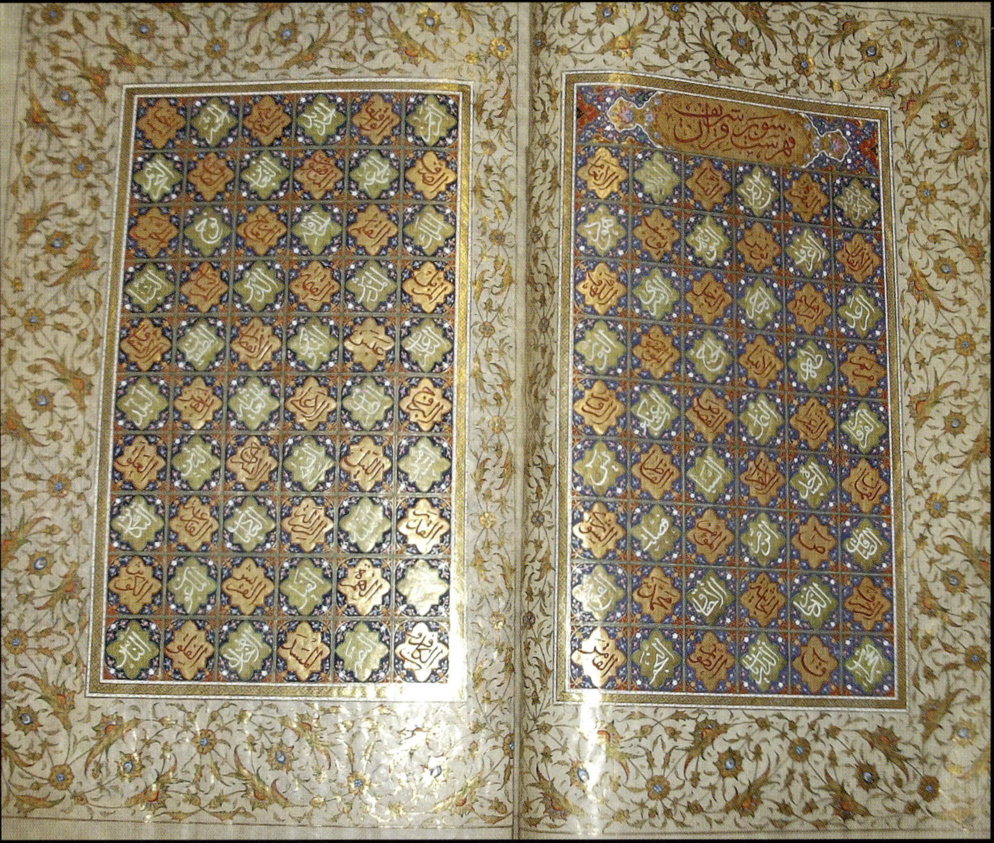

130

Complete Holy Quran

19th century AD
H 35 cm, W 22 cm (closed), 40 cm (open)
King Abdulaziz Public Library, 2332

This complete *mushaf* from Surah Al-Fātihah to Surah Al-Nās is written in black ink with diacritical marks, inside golden, green, red and blue coloured borders. The footnotes of the first and last pages are embellished with gold-leaf botanical designs. Inside the ruler margins are impressions in the shape of Islamic decorations. The blue colour was extracted from turquoise that lends a beautiful appearance to the decoration. At the beginning of the *mushaf*, an index of the *surahs* (chapters) was written in italics inside small squares by the famous Iranian calligrapher Muhammad Sharif Afshar, in Jumādā Al-Awwal 1270 AH (AD 1853). This manuscript is deemed to be from the imperial manuscripts, which are written for a ruler with great care and precision over a long period. It is bound with impermeable Persian leather. Paper extracted from rice husks was placed in between the manuscript's pages to prevent the colour from overlapping.

131

Complete Holy Quran

17th century AD
Saudi Arabia
H 18 cm, W 11 cm (closed), 24 cm (open)
King Abdulaziz Public Library, 1600

This complete *mushaf* from Al-Fātihah to Surah Al-Nās is written in black ink, with diacritical marks, inside red and blue ruled margins. It was written during Ramadan in 1025 AH (AD 1616), in Mecca in front of the Holy Ka'bah, and was compared to a copy written by the noble scholar Al-Mulla Ali Al-Qari who died in the year 1014 AH.

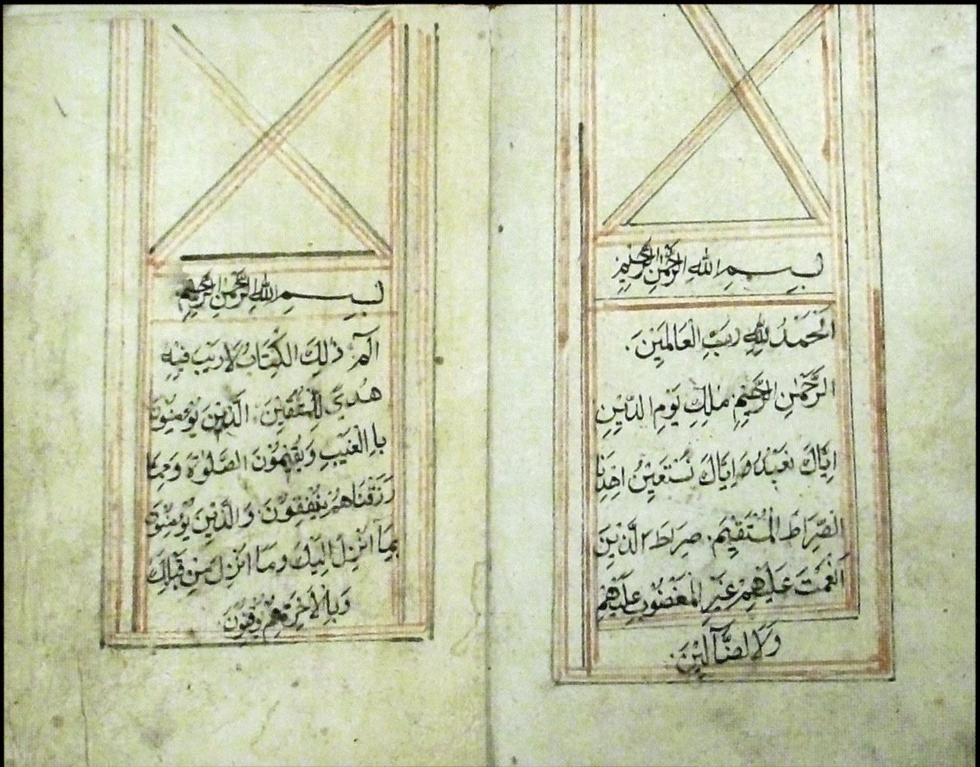

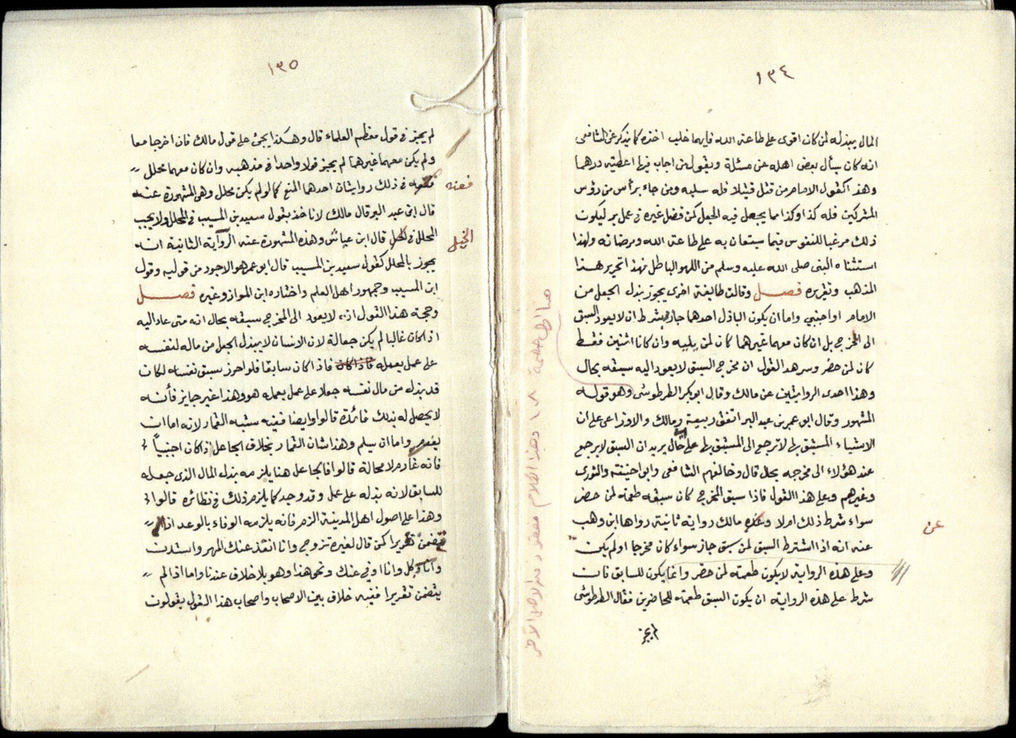

132

Al-Furusiyya ah-Hemmareh

20th century AD
Saudi Arabia
Manuscript
H 21 cm, W 15 cm
King Abdulaziz Public Library, 5871

This is a modern copy of a manuscript by Mohammed ibn Abu Bakr ibn Ayoub ibn al-Qayyim al-Joziah written before the author's date in 751 AH/AD 1350. The copy was verified by Sheikh Abdul Qadir Hamza who died in Mecca in 1352 AH/

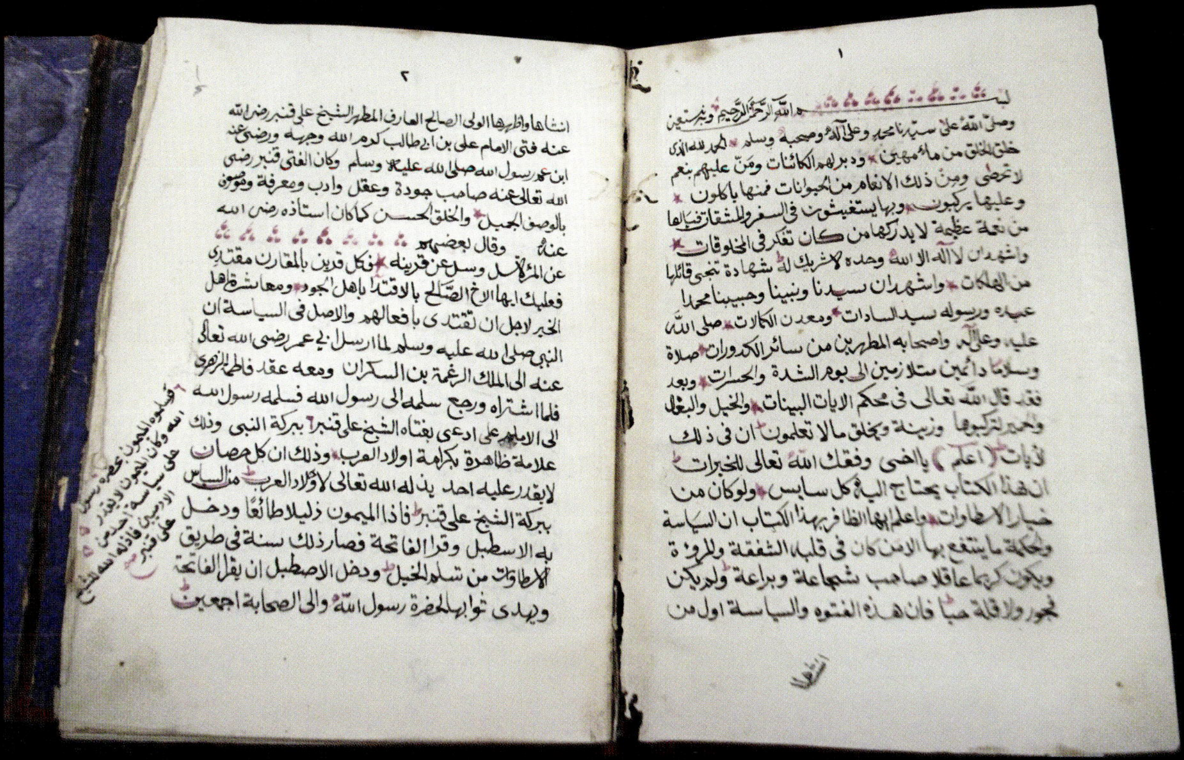

133

Horse manuscript

19th century AD
Egypt
H 23 cm, W 16 cm (closed), W 33 cm (open)
King Abdulaziz Public Library, 5899

This group of manuscripts is comprised of three books about horse care and hippiatrics. The author of the first book is unknown. The book is divided into chapters. Among them, one deals with what is needed in order to become a professional horse keeper; another discusses the characteristics of horses. There is also a chapter on the study and treatment of diseases of horses (hippiatrics). The manuscript has sixteen pages and was copied in 1301 AH (AD 1883) in Cairo.

The second book is a treatise on horse care. The author of this book is also unknown. The author says in his introduction, after invoking the name of Allah, 'To proceed: This treatise is about equitation and horses, the signs that indicate their superiority or inferiority, and the advantages and disadvantages of their riders. It is from the treasures of kings, so do not give it except to one who deserves it.' This treatise has nine pages, and was copied in Cairo in the year 1301 AH (AD 1883).

The third book, *Isbāl Al-thayl fee Thikri Ajyād Al-Khayl*, is written by Muhammad ibn Khairuddeen ibn Ahmad Al-Ramly Al-Shafi'ee, who died around 1121 AH (AD 1709). He wrote this book to fulfil the request of Prince Mustafa Agha. He cited in this book the Qur'anic Verses and Prophetic Traditions that indicate the virtue of horses and horsemanship, in addition to mentioning some issues related to horse care. The book is forty-seven pages, and was also copied in Cairo in the year 1301 AH (AD 1883).

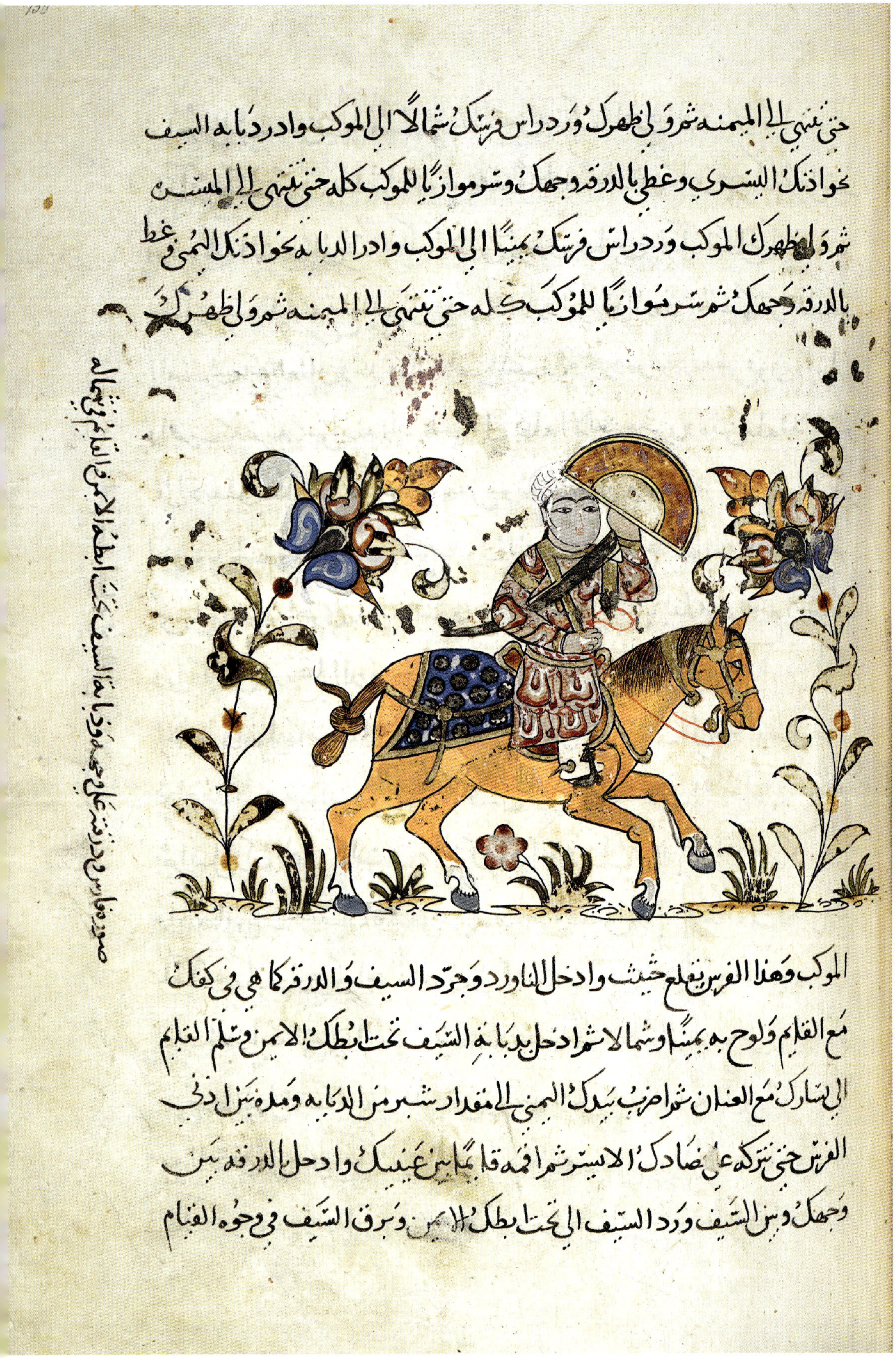

134

Furusiyya manuscript

Copied 773 AH/AD 1371, Mamluk
Syria or Egypt
W 13 cm, H 20.5 cm
British Library, Add MS 18866

The full title of the famous Arabic manuscript in the British Library commonly known as *Furusiyya* is 'An end to questioning and desiring [further knowledge] concerning the learning of the different exercises of horsemanship'. As the title implies, the text is a manual of horsemanship primarily for the training of Mamluk cavalrymen. The text is accompanied by eighteen coloured paintings showing mounted horsemen engaged in various exercises, most of them with a clearly military purpose, and by diagrams showing formation manoeuvres. The opposing folios displayed in the exhibition show respectively a warrior armed with a sword and a hide shield which he holds in front of his face (captioned, 'illustration of a horseman with a hide shield over his face, the sword edge under his right armpit and the hilt on his left'), and a warrior armed with bow and arrow, sword and small shield riding on a dappled horse (captioned, 'illustration of a horseman with a small shield round his neck and a sword in his hand which he brandishes to left and right').

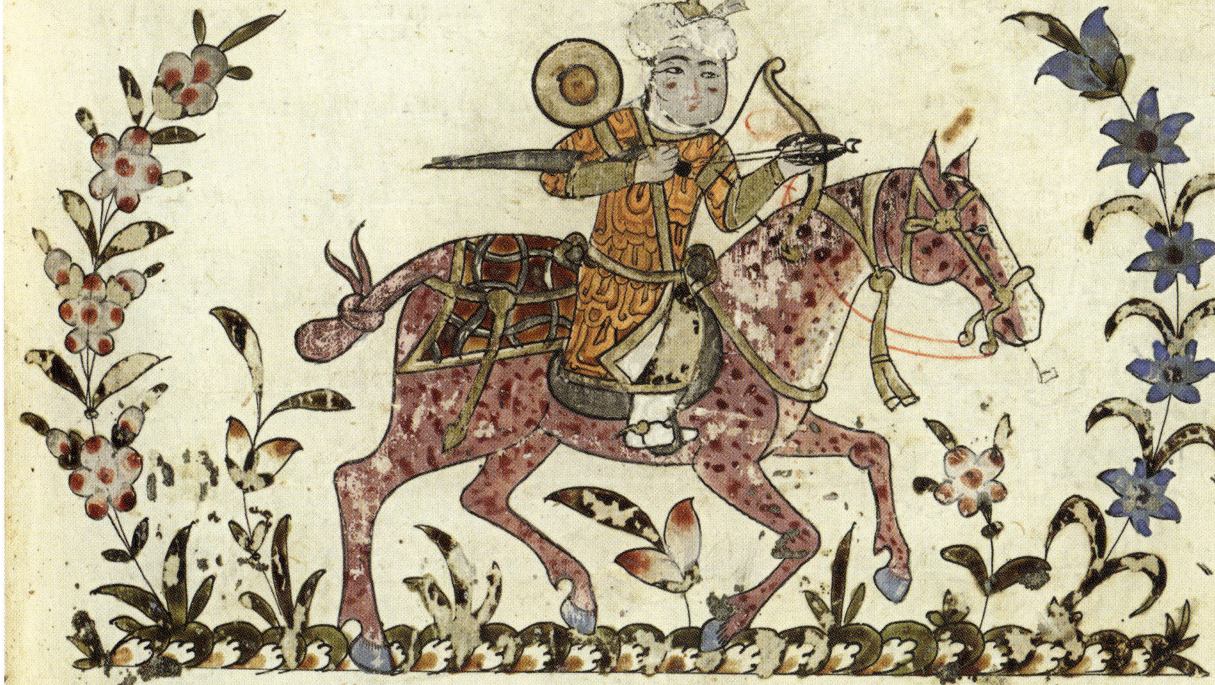

صورة فارس يتقلد بدرقه صغيره ويلعب بسيف يلوح به يمينا وشمالا

الى شمالك مع العنان ثم اضرب بيدك اليمنى الى على ذبابته ومده بين اذني الفرس حتى توكا على
قصادك الايسر ثم ادخل يدك اليمنى الى مقبض الدرقه فمكن اصابعك الثلثه السبابه والوسطى
والبنصر من المقبض ثم اخرجها من تشميرتك وشمر حتى توافي ازاي المبسم ثم اضرب بيدك
اليمنى والدرقه فيها الى قايم السيف وجرده واعقد به من فوق راسك بغوصة مليحه بحت
السيف ثم شد يدك وغطي بالدرقه وجهك وانظر من تحتها والسيف معارض ذبابته
نحو اذنك اليسرى ودر داس فرسك شمالا وسر بازاي الموكب حتى تنتهي الى ازاي الميمنه
ثم ادر ذبابة السيف نحو اذنك اليسرى والدرقه بين عينيك تغطي بها وجهك ودر داس
فرسك يمينا وسر بازاي الموكب كله حتى تنتهي الى ازاي الميسره ثم اعبر الى الموكب وادر
ذبابة السيف نحو اذنك اليمنى وغطي بالدرقه وجهك ودر داس فرسك وسر موازيا للموكب كله

حتى

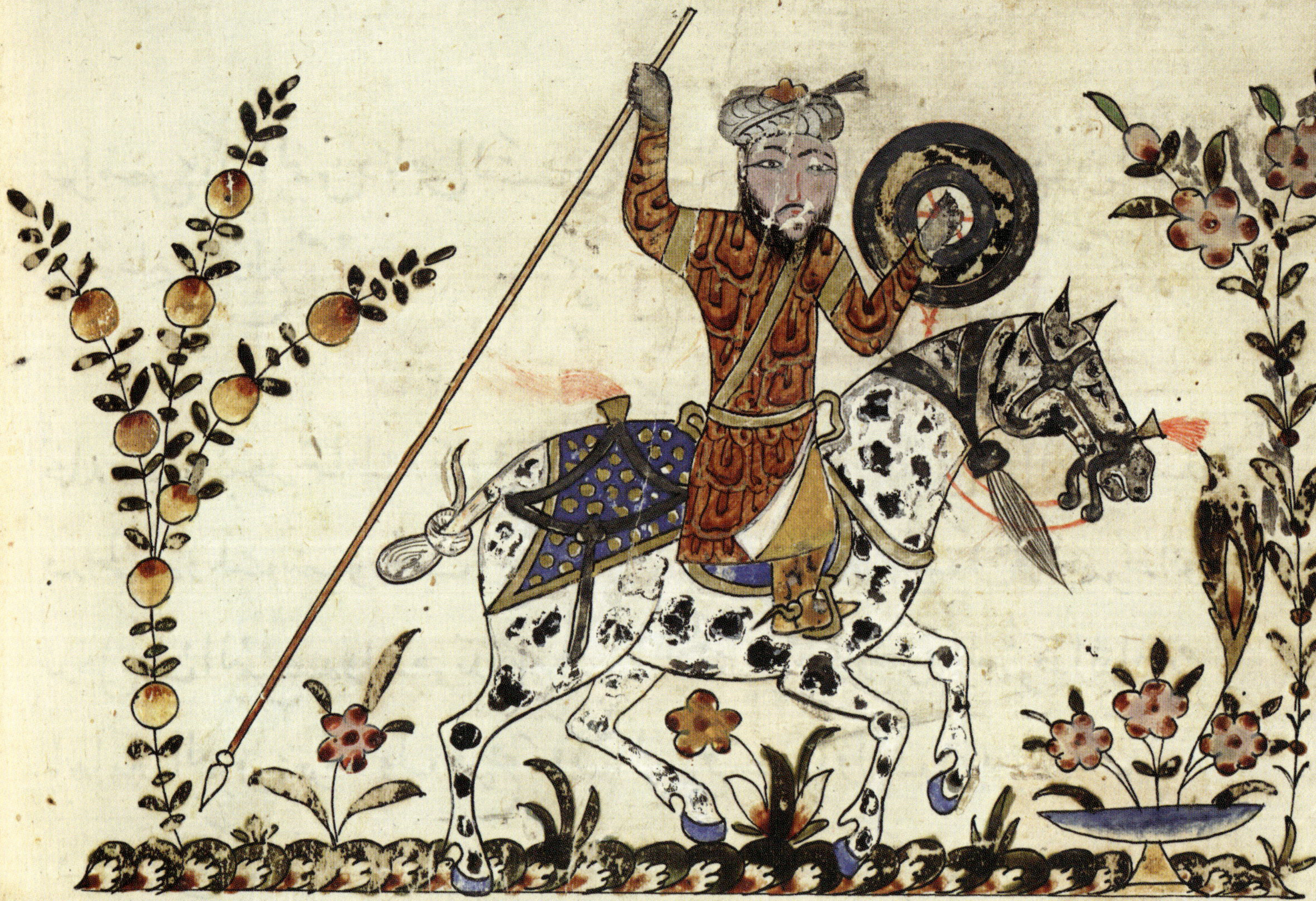

صورة فارس بيده رمح محجوره وراه وفي يده الاخرى ترس

فيحصل عقبه في يمينك وهو مطروح على ساعدك الايسر فتحبا نفسك بالترس وتغمز
الى الموكب وتشد يدك في السبور كلها فاذا طعنت فاطرح نحو المبسن ثم جر الرمح
على الارض وشل يدك بالسبر الذي في ابهامك حتى تسلم عقب الرمح الى يسارك
وتدير الترس نحو يمينك ورد راس فرسك يمنا واغمز على الموكب بغوصه في الترس
تفعل ذلك ما اخترت من الدفعات ثم تدخل الىا ورد على اي جانب شيت ويكون
سنان الرمح من داخل ويدك غايص في ترسك حتى اذاجيت الى اصحابك ودرت

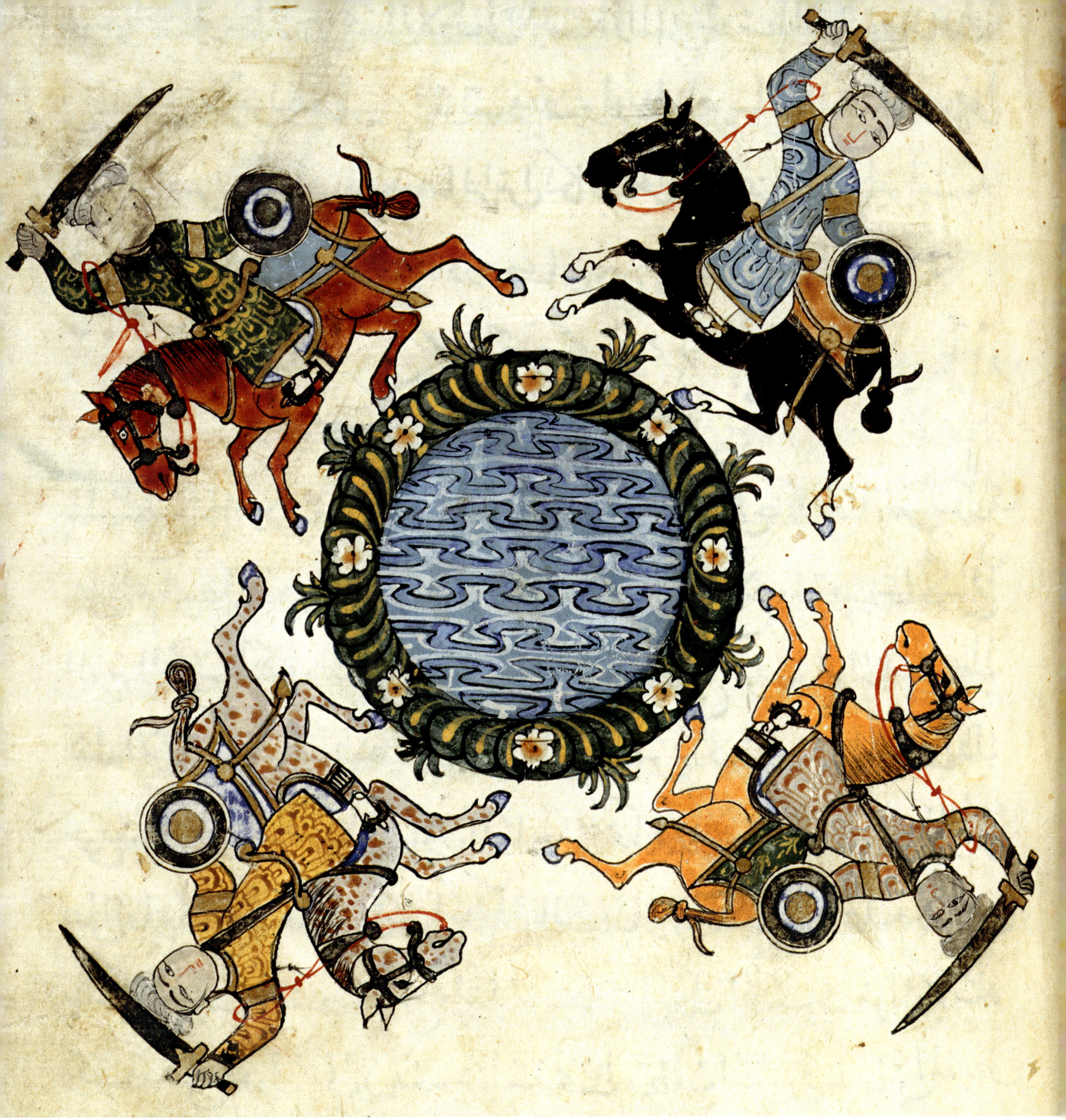

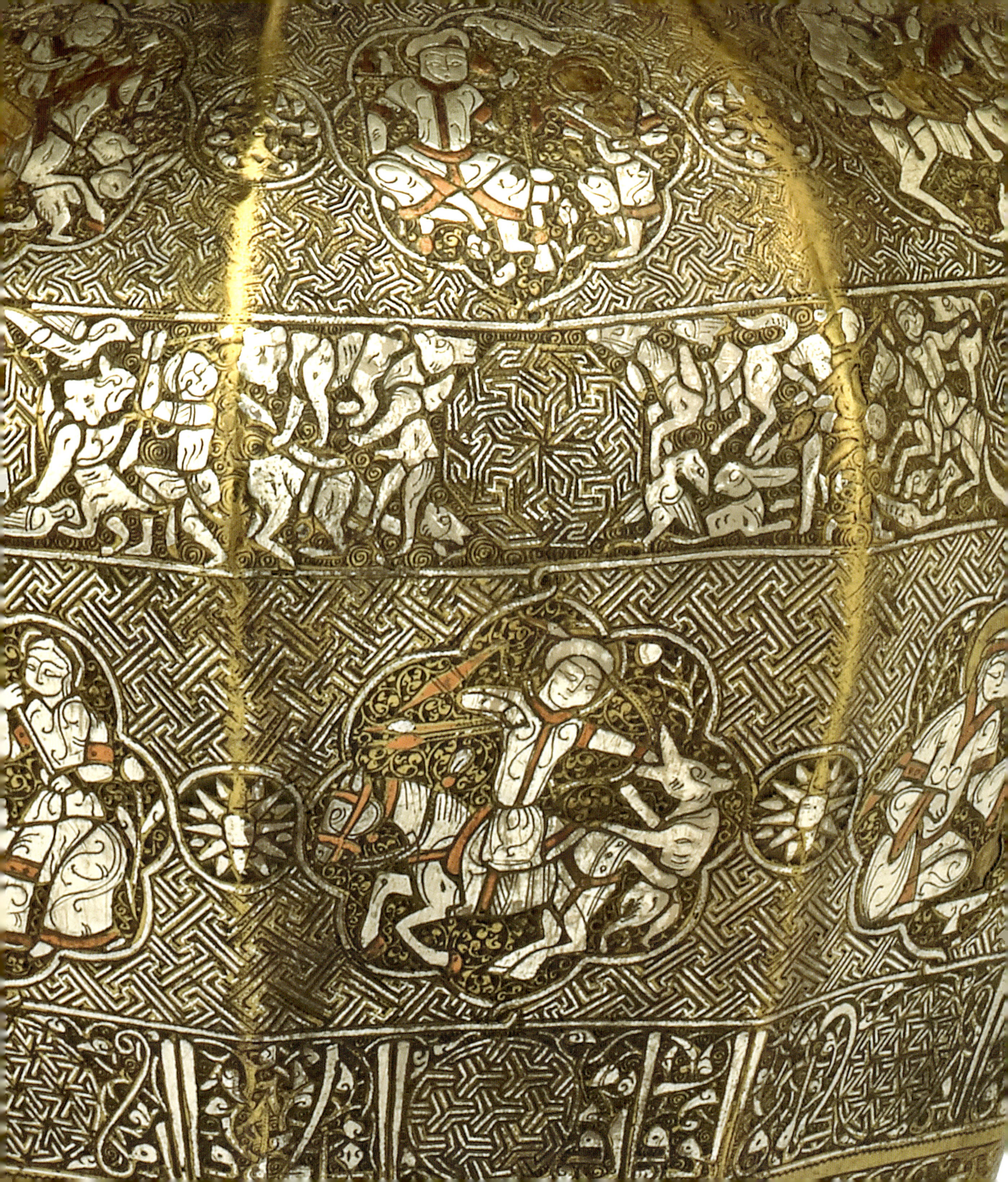

135

Ewer with inlaid decoration

c. AD 1232
Mosul, Iraq
Brass inlaid with silver and copper
H 30.4 cm, W 22 cm, D 21.5 cm
BM 1866,1229.61

This splendid ewer, made of hammered sheet brass and engraved and inlaid with silver and copper, is celebrated as one of the finest and most important examples of Islamic metalwork, carrying information about its maker and place of production. This identification, inscribed in Arabic around the neck of the ewer, states that the object was decorated by Shuja ibn Mana al-Mawsuli ('of Mosul', in modern Iraq) in Rajab 629 AH/April AD 1232. It is also commonly known as the Blacas Ewer, after the Duke of Blacas, a nineteenth-century French Ambassador to the Kingdom of the Two Sicilies whose collection was acquired by the British Museum in 1866. Although missing its spout and foot, the ewer's body and neck are richly decorated with a series of scenes, many of them contained within medallions. Scenes showing horses include a mounted warrior with a sword and shield fighting with a soldier on foot, a horseman out hunting with a feline creature (possibly a cheetah) seated on the rump of his horse, and an archer on horseback shooting at what appears to be a boar jumping up at the back of his horse. A benedictory Arabic inscription circling the lower body of the vessel reads: 'Glory, long life, and ease, (God's) sympathy, blessing, health, felicity, victory over enemies, superiority, and (God's) protection forever for its owner.'

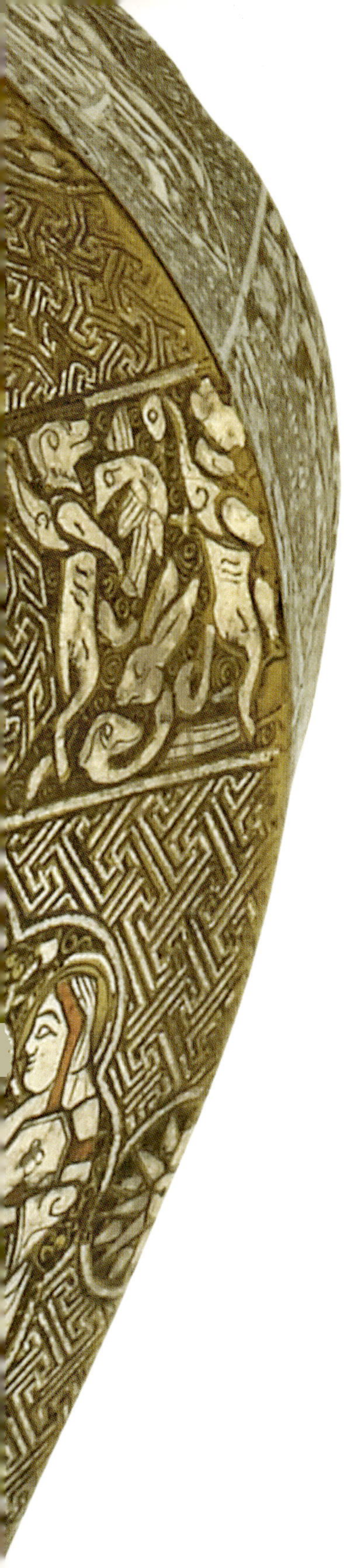

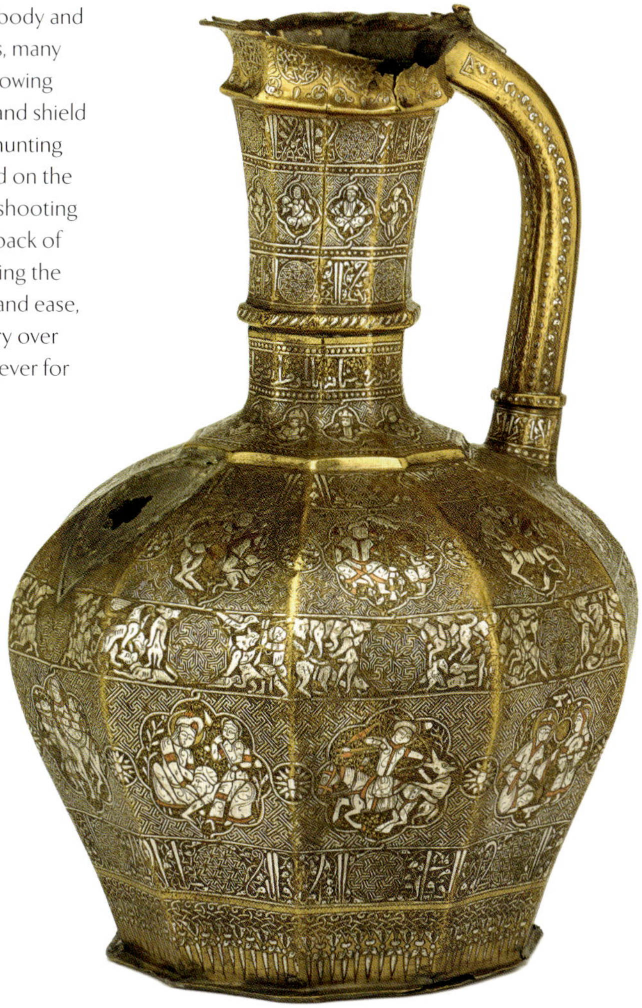

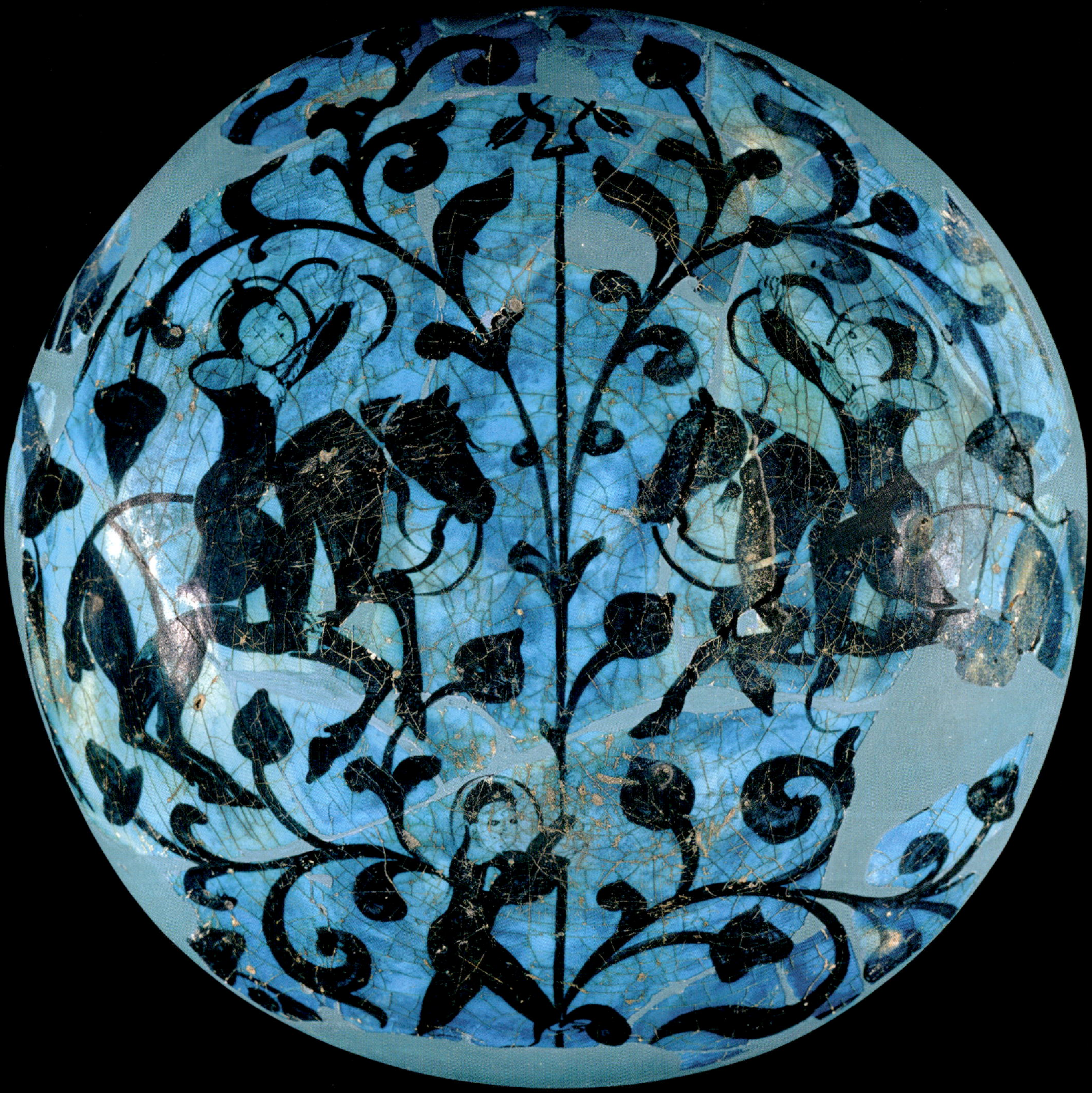

136

Boss depicting archers

Late 12th–early 13th century AD
Kashan, Iran
Ceramic with underglaze painted decoration
Diam. 28 cm
BM 1964,1013.2

The scene on this boss, painted in black under a transparent turquoise glaze, shows two mounted archers shooting arrows at a target mounted on a tall pole. This may be an early representation of a sport known as *qabaq* in which archers aimed at a gourd mounted on top of a pole. Such activities played an important part in developing equestrian and archery skills. The purpose of this boss is unknown.

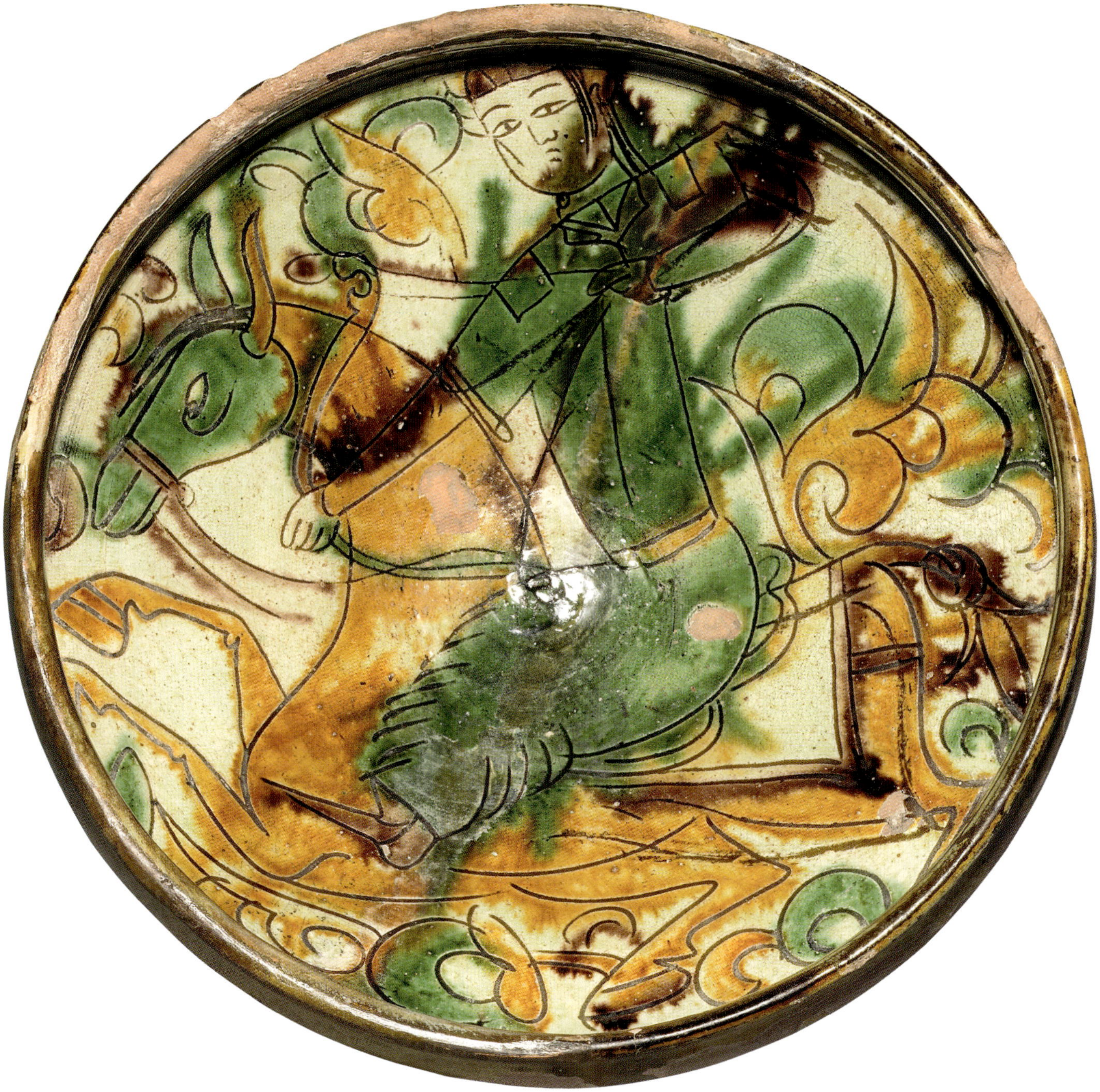

137

Sgraffiato bowl depicting a mounted archer

c. 1250
Aleppo, Syria
Ceramic with underglaze, incised and painted decoration
Diam. 26.3 cm, H 11.7 cm
BM 1931,0716.1

This bowl shows a helmeted warrior on horseback drawing a bow. He wears a belted tunic with ornamental bands on the sleeves. He sits on a saddle that is mounted on a plain saddle-cloth. The reins appear to be hanging loose, so the rider was presumably controlling the horse with his knees. The technique known as *sgraffiato* involves incising a design into a slip on the surface of the vessel before firing. After firing, the scene is then painted, in this case green, brown and purple, and covered with a clear glaze.

138

Pilgrim flask

c. 1250–75, Mamluk
Egypt or Syria; Slade bequest, 1869
Enamelled glass
H 23 cm, L 23 cm, W 16.2 cm
BM 1869,0120.3

Glassmakers active in Egypt and Syria during the thirteenth and fourteenth centuries were known for their fine work in the production of mosque lamps, bottles, beakers and flasks. Some scholars suggest that Syrian glassmakers were the first to use the technique of enamelling and gilding on glass beginning in the late twelfth century.

This object is modelled after a pilgrim flask and was skilfully painted in red, white, blue, green, yellow, mauve and greyish-black enamels, with the design executed in gold outlined in red. One side is decorated with a large palmette filled with a scrolling foliate design. The other two sides depict a seated banqueter and seated femail lutenist, each with a mounted rider shown above. The riders, dressed in long tunics and flowing cloaks, are identified as Christian both by their clothing and their rounded broad-brimmed 'kettle' helmets associated with the Crusader infantrymen. One impales a wolf or a bear with a couched lance, the other shoots a lion (?) with a crossbow – both western weapons. Their horses, a grey and a chestnut, are wearing bridles with curb bits, decorated neck bands, breast bands and striped saddle-cloths.

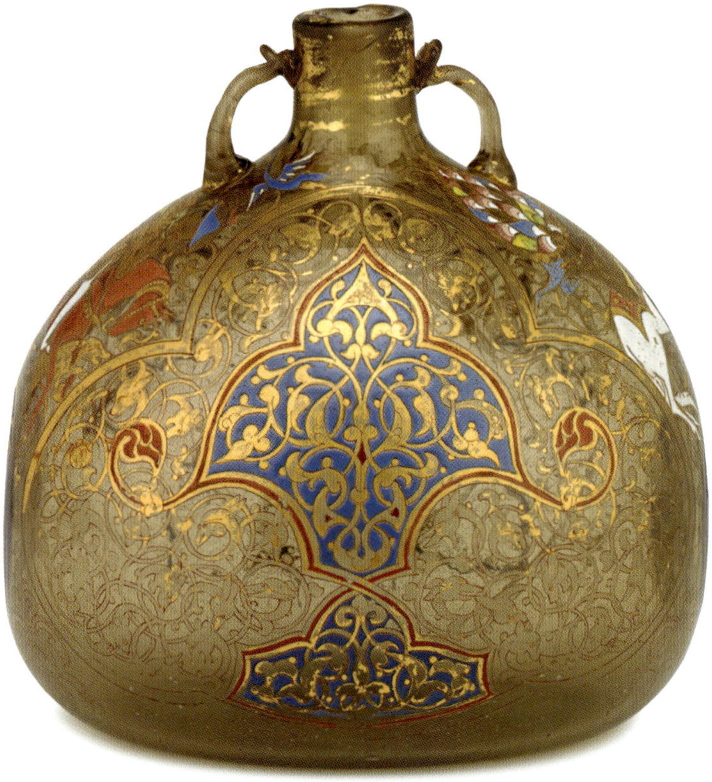

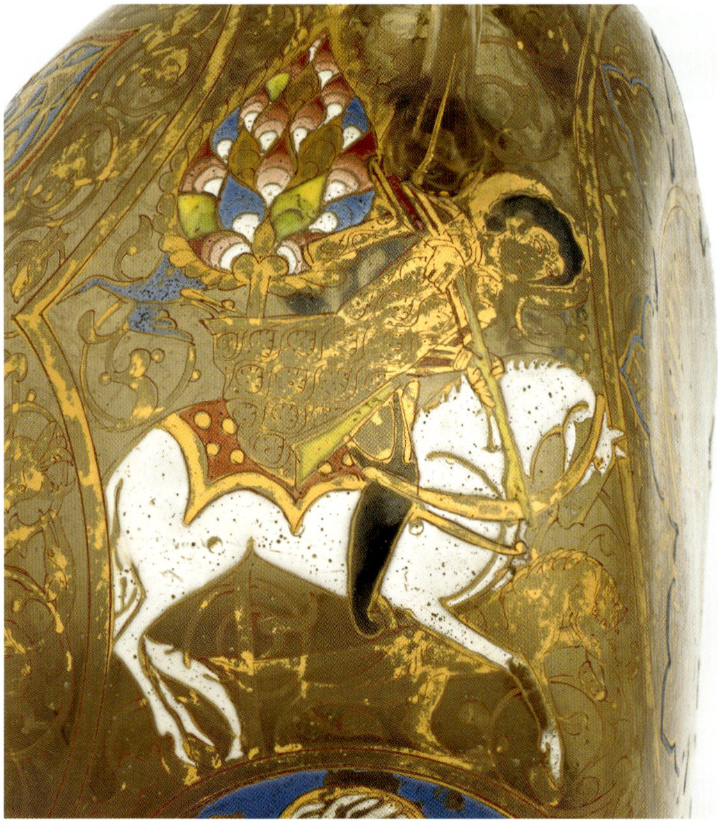

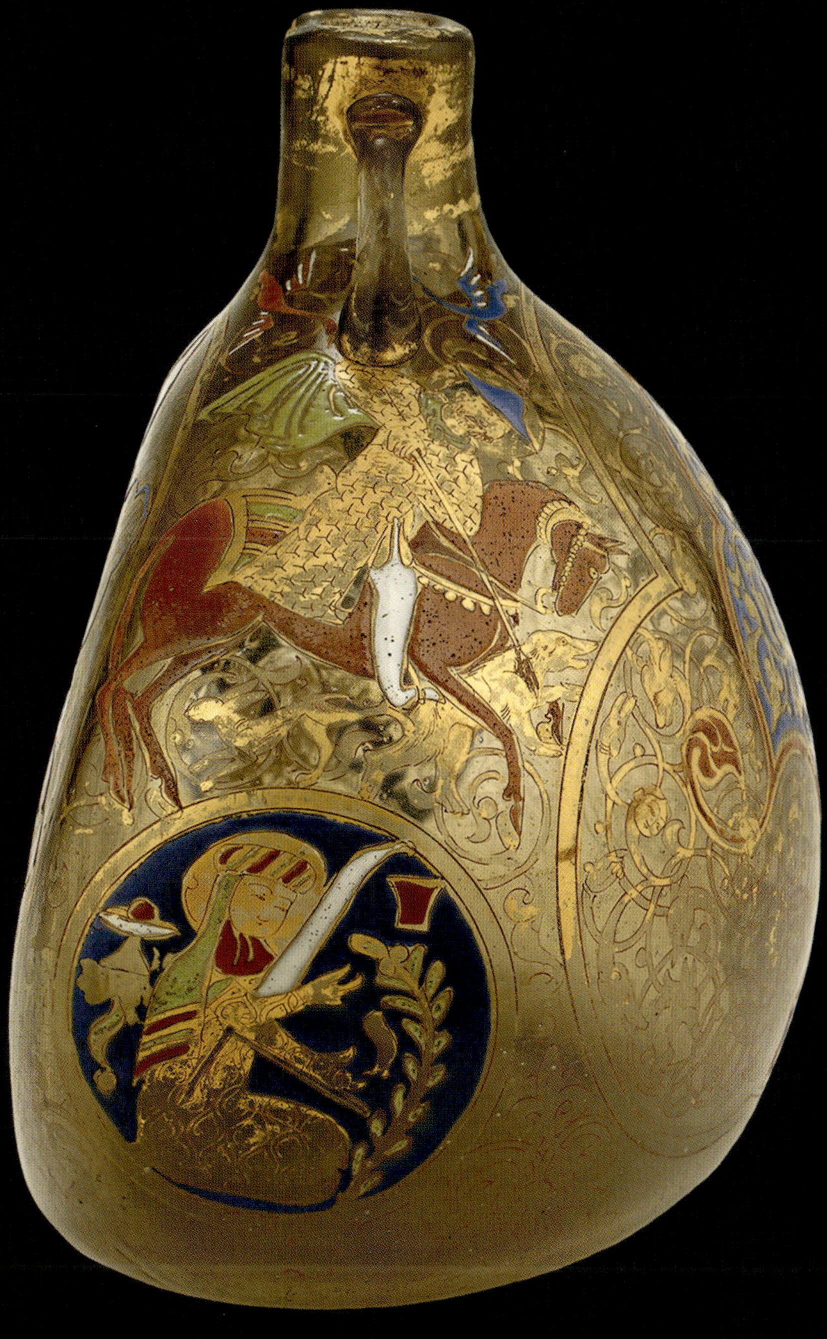

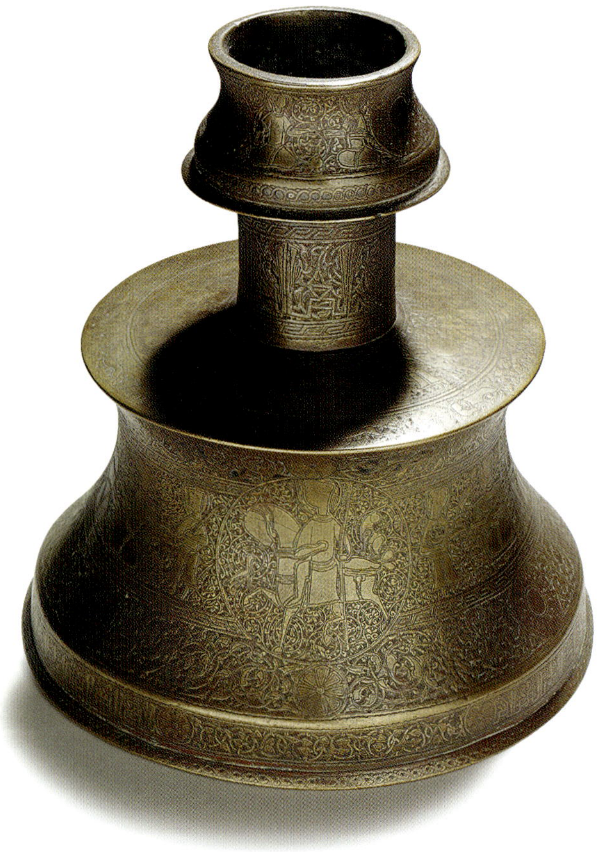

141

Candlestick holder

13th–14th century AD
Konya, Turkey; acquired 1955, gift of P.T. Brooke Sewell
Brass engraved and inlaid with silver
H 20.3 cm
BM 1955,0214.1

This candlestick holder is made of cast brass inlaid with silver and gold. On the body of the candlestick the decoration includes a medallion showing a horseman slaying a lion with a sword. On the socket there are representations of musicians.

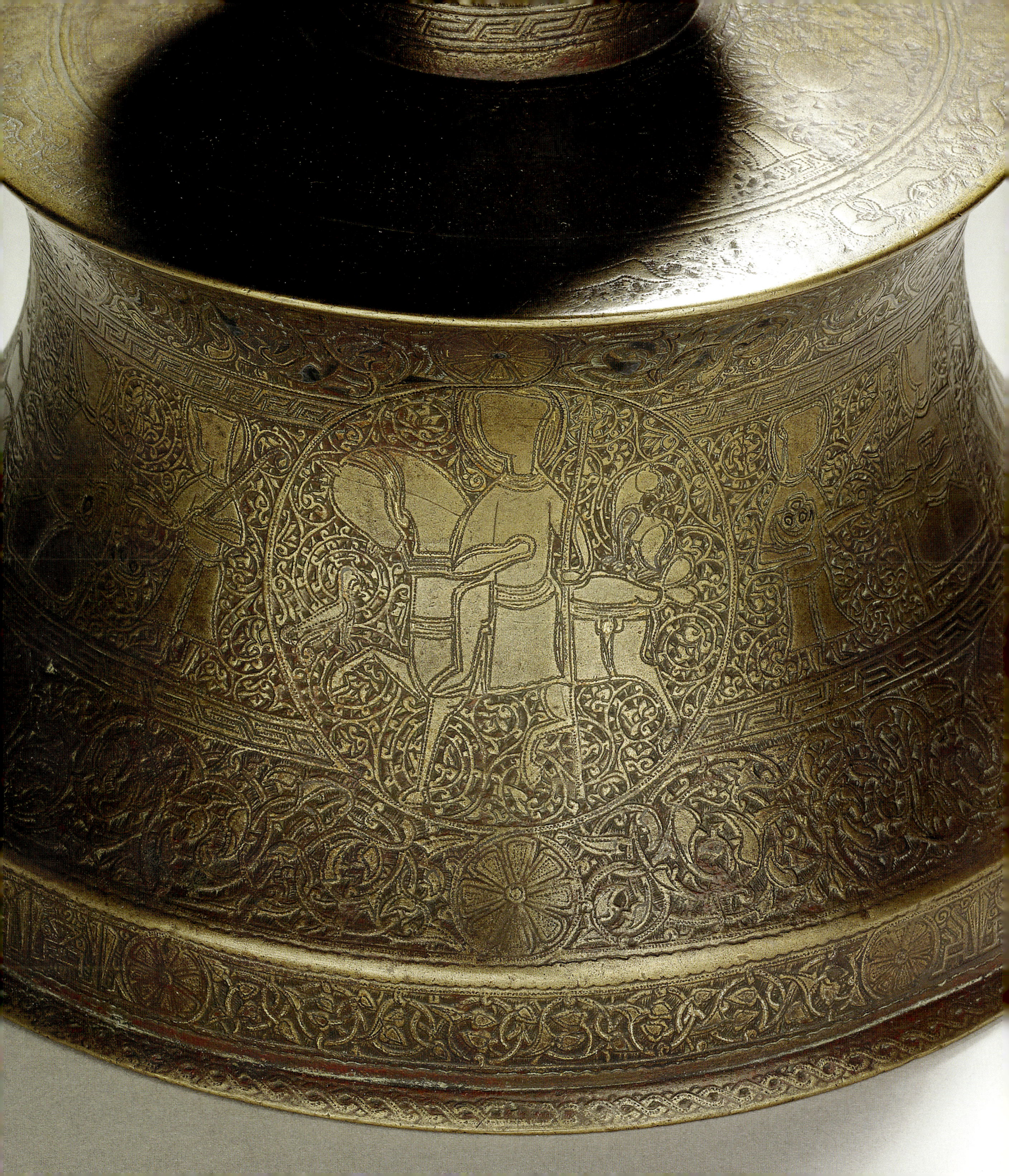

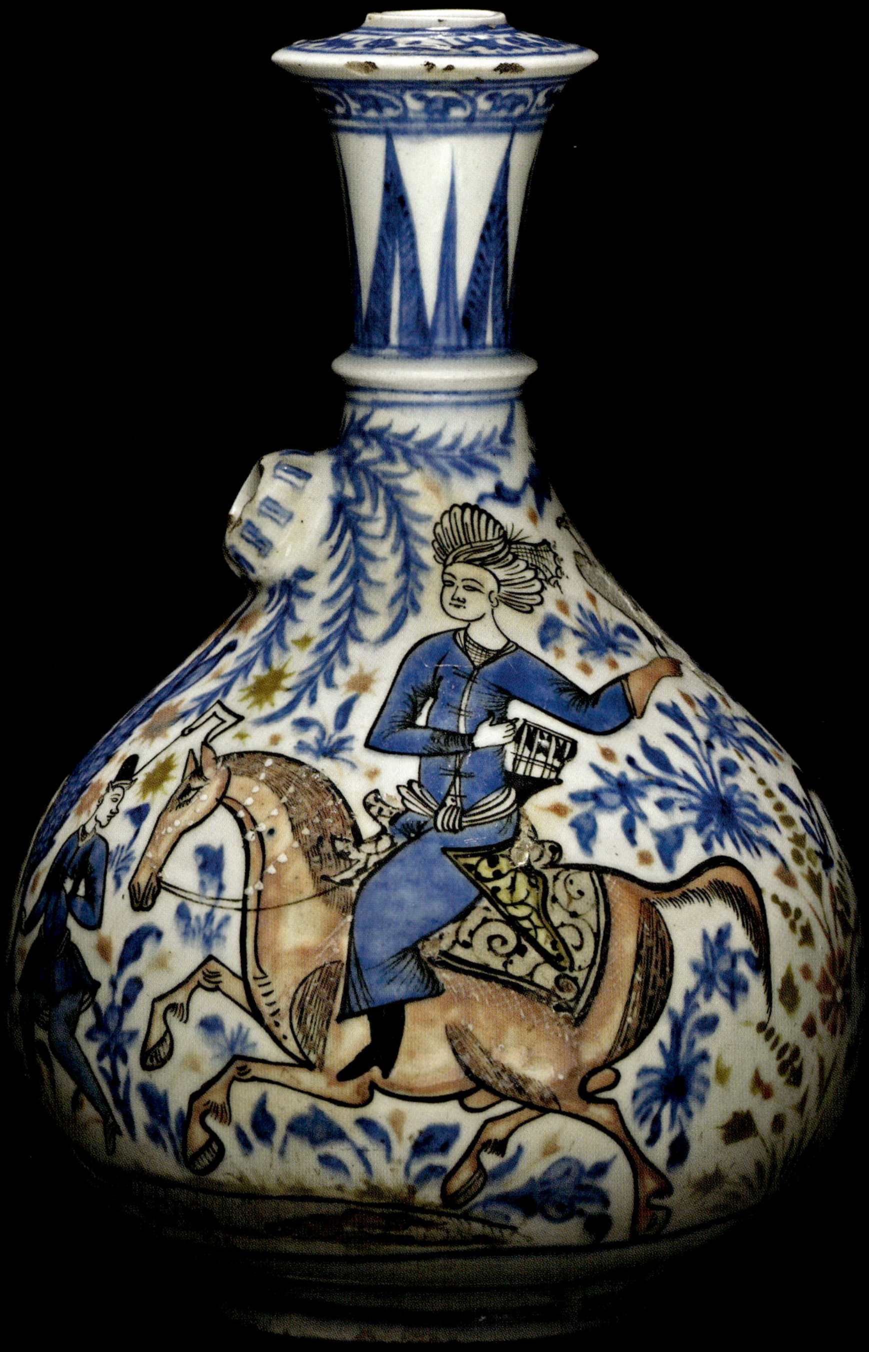

142

Base of a waterpipe or *galiyan*

17th century AD
Kerman, Iran; presented by A.W. Franks in 1890
Stone-paste ceramic with underglaze painted decoration
H 29.3 cm, Diam. 18.7 cm
BM 1890,0517.13

This is the base of a *huqqa*, or waterpipe, known as a *galiyan* in Persia. Tobacco smoke is passed through water in this container before being inhaled. The polychrome painted decoration shows scenes from the story of Khusrow and Shirin immortalized by the twelfth-century Persian poet NIzami. The story is based on the life of the Sasanian king Khusrow II. In one scene Khusrow is shown out hunting on horseback, with a quiver behind him and a falcon perched on his gloved hand. In another scene, a semi-naked Shirin is bathing in a stream, but Khusrow does not realize she is the beautiful Armenian princess his vizier has described to him.

Glazed tile showing a polo match

c. AD 1850, Qajar
Tehran, Iran; Godman bequest, 1983
Stone-paste ceramic with underglaze painted decoration
H 30.6 cm, W 30.6 cm
BM G.314

The scene on this tile is from the Persian epic the *Shahnameh* and shows a polo match between Siyavash and Afrasiyab. Siyavash had fled to the court of Afrasiyab (King of Turan) after a dispute with his father, the king of Iran. The story is described in a Persian inscription around the edge of the tile. The cartouches at the top contain the name of the potter, Muhammad Ibrahim.

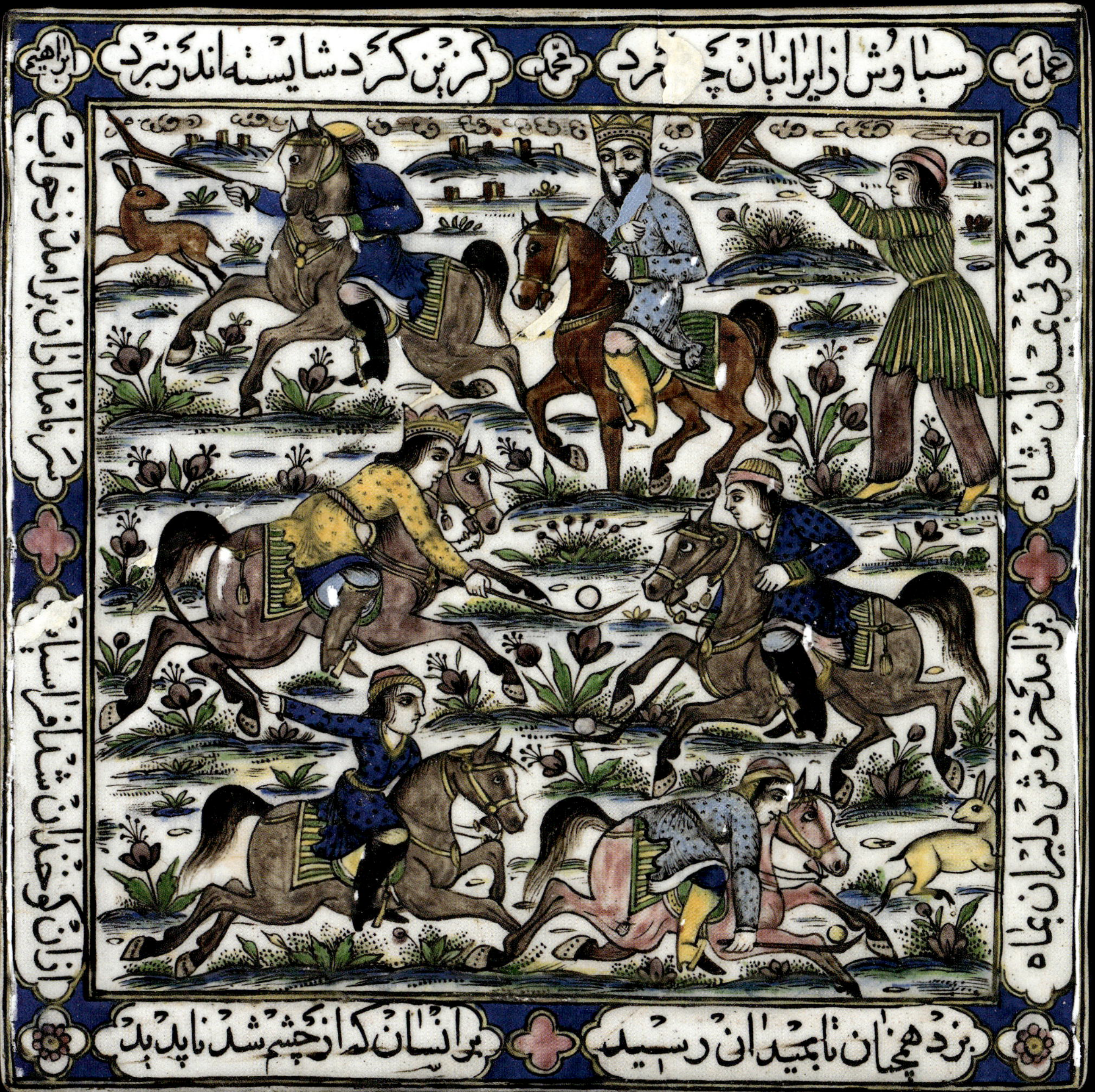

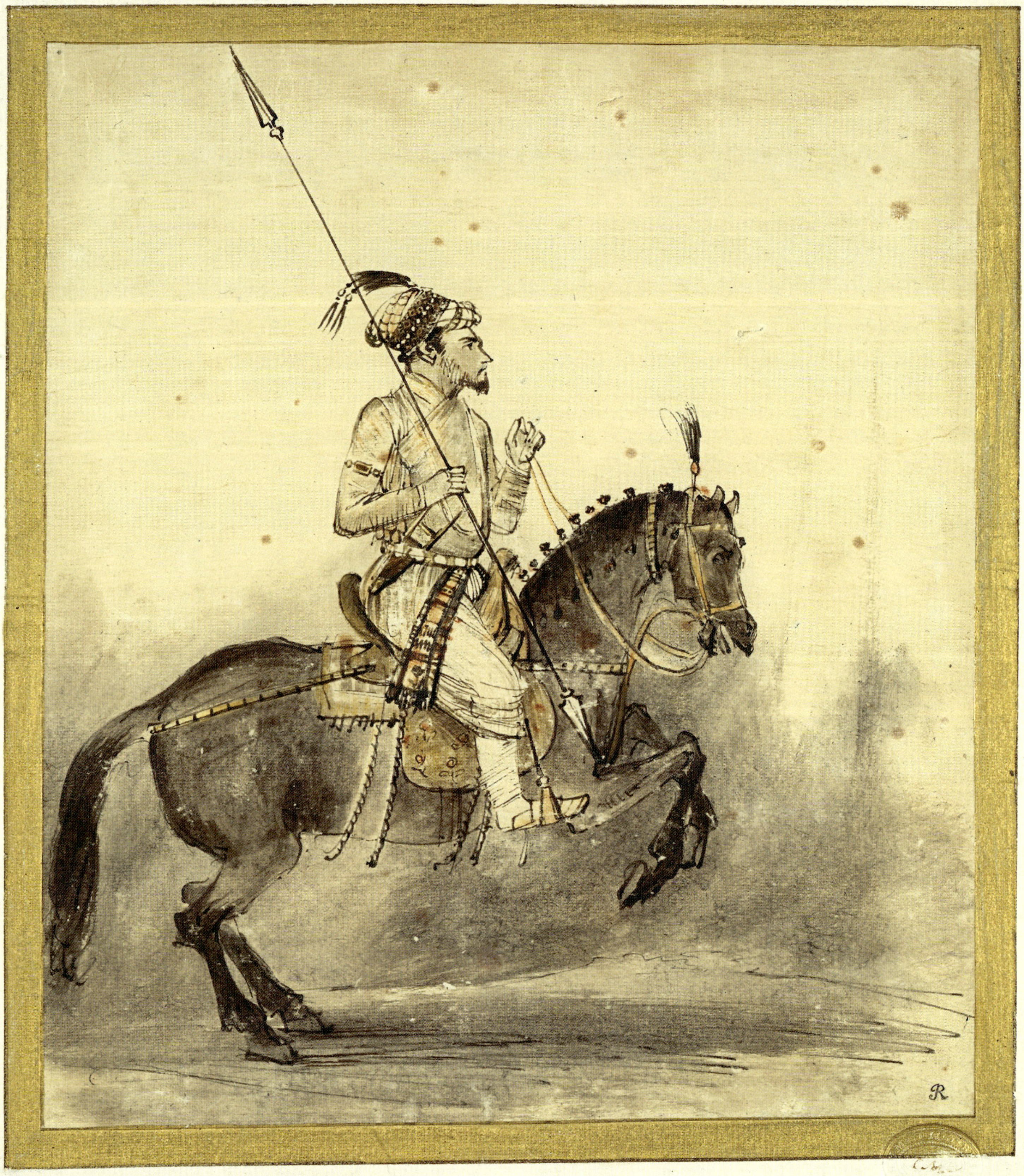
R

144

A Mughal nobleman on horseback

Rembrandt van Rijn (1606–1669)
c. 1656–61; Mordaunt Cracherode bequest, 1799
Ink on paper
H 20.5 cm, W 17.7 cm
BM Gg.2.262

Rembrandt was known to have produced a series of twenty-one drawings inspired by Mughal miniatures, many of which originally came from the court of Shah Jahan (reigned 1627–1658). Several of his drawings are similar to the Mughal vignettes found on the walls of the 'Million Room' at Schönbrunn Castle, Vienna.

This drawing shows a Mughal nobleman, probably Shah Jahan, on horseback, holding the reins in his left hand and a lance in his right. It is unclear where Rembrandt copied this drawing from, but as with most of his Mughal images, he has not drawn a background and has probably left out some details, such as the tassel that would have hung from the horse's neck strap (as seen in cats 145, 146, 151).

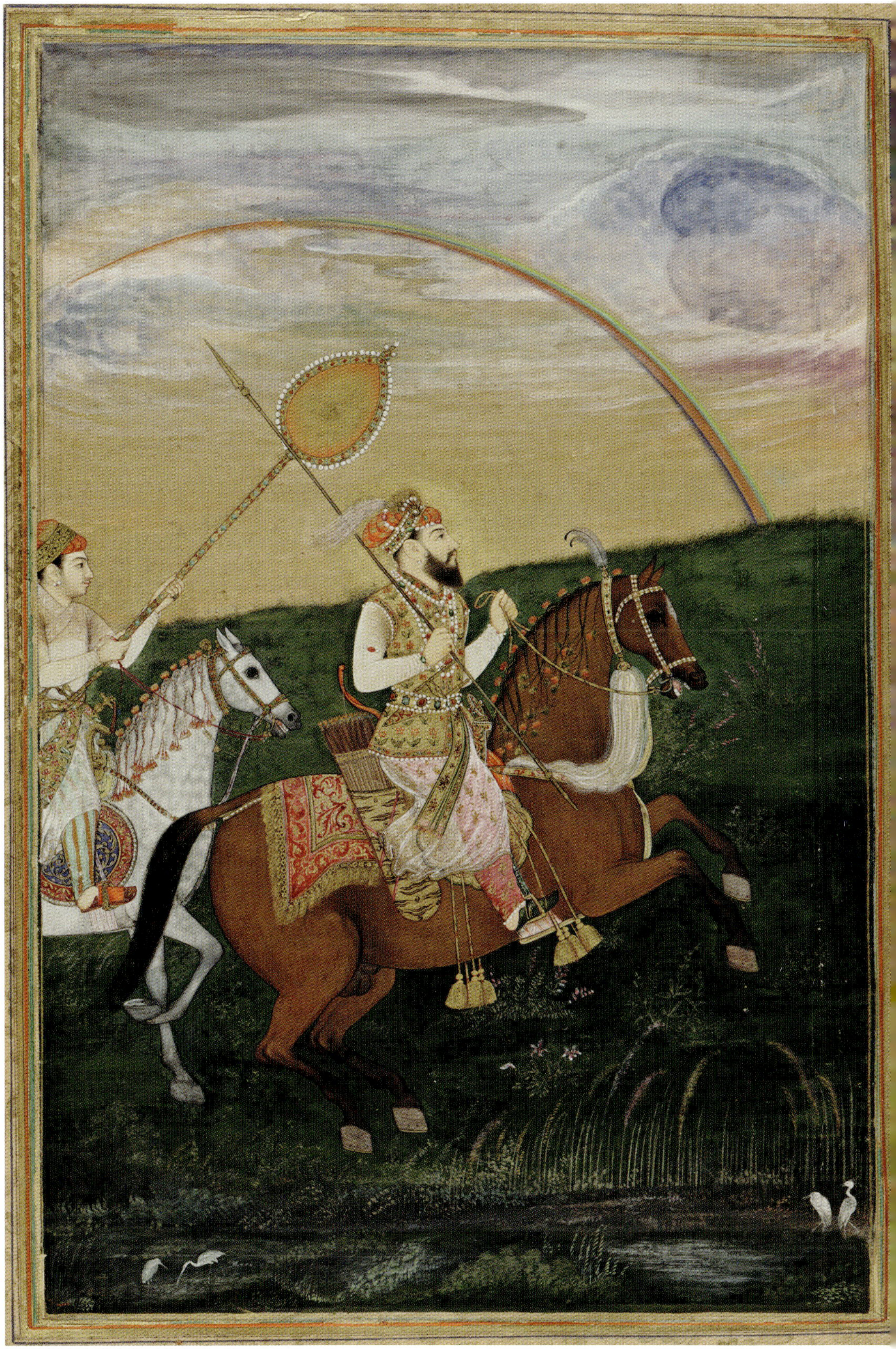

145

Copy of miniature painting in the Bodleian Library

1630
H 26.3 cm, W 17.2 cm
Bodleian Library, MS. Douce Or. a.1: fol. 25.a

This miniature shows Shah Jahan riding his horse and holding a lance, much like the figure shown in Rembrandt's drawing. In this example one can see the details that have been left out of Rembrandt's work, such as the horse's neck-strap tassel. While this work has not been identified as that which influenced Rembrandt, it demonstrates that his drawing would have been inspired by an existing Mughal piece.

This image is from an album of forty-one Indian paintings, chiefly from the Shah Jahan period (1627–1658).

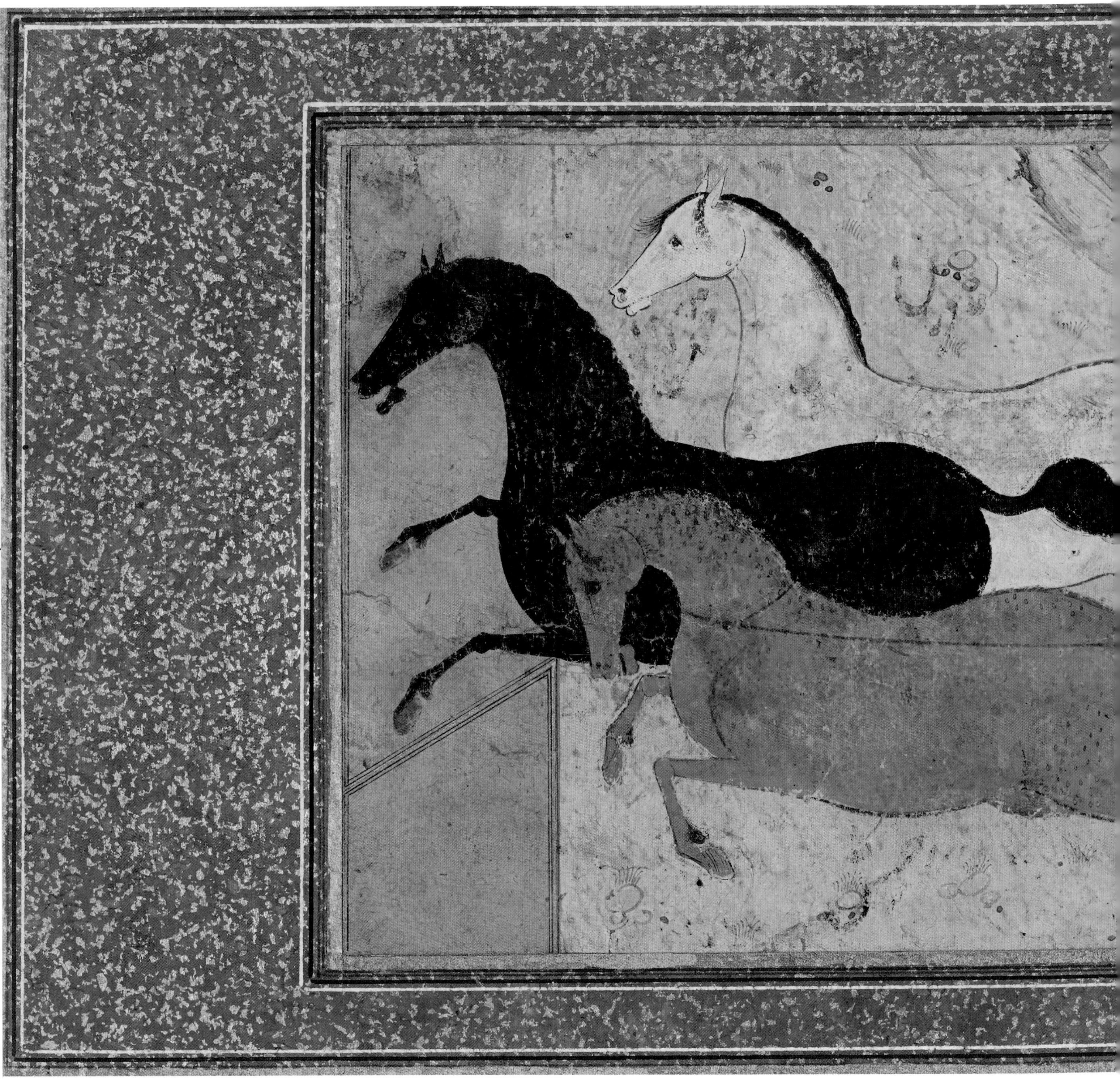

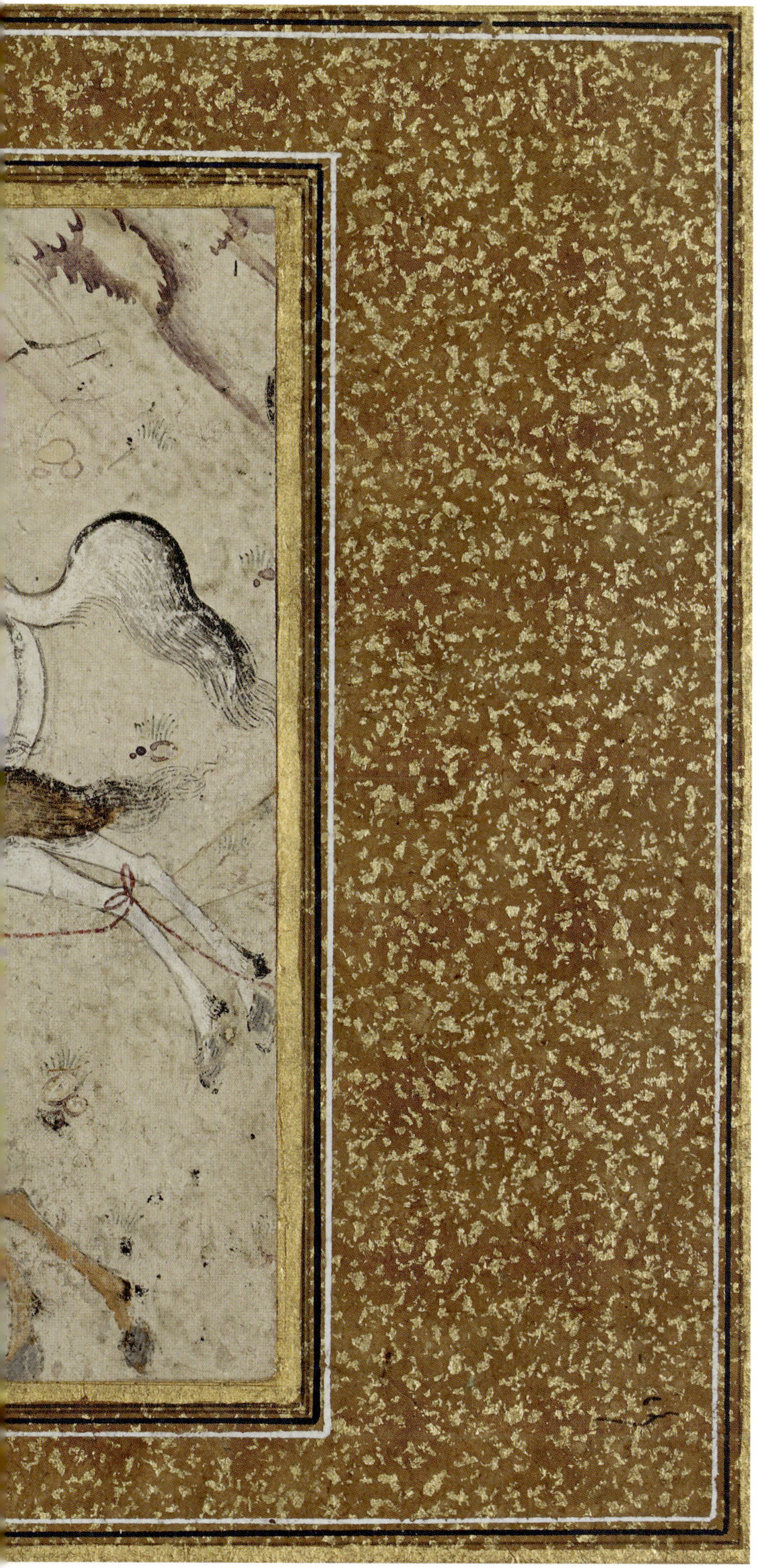

152
Three galloping horses

c. 1550, Safavid
Iran
Ink, opaque watercolour and gold on paper
H 13.7 cm, W 22 cm
BM 1930,0607,0.10

This painting depicts three galloping horses: a light chestnut, a black and a grey. The horse in the foreground has a lasso around its neck that is knotted to the hind leg of the grey horse in the background. The lasso suggests that this page is from a manuscript of the *Shahnameh* and depicts the capture of the stallion Rakhsh by Rustam.

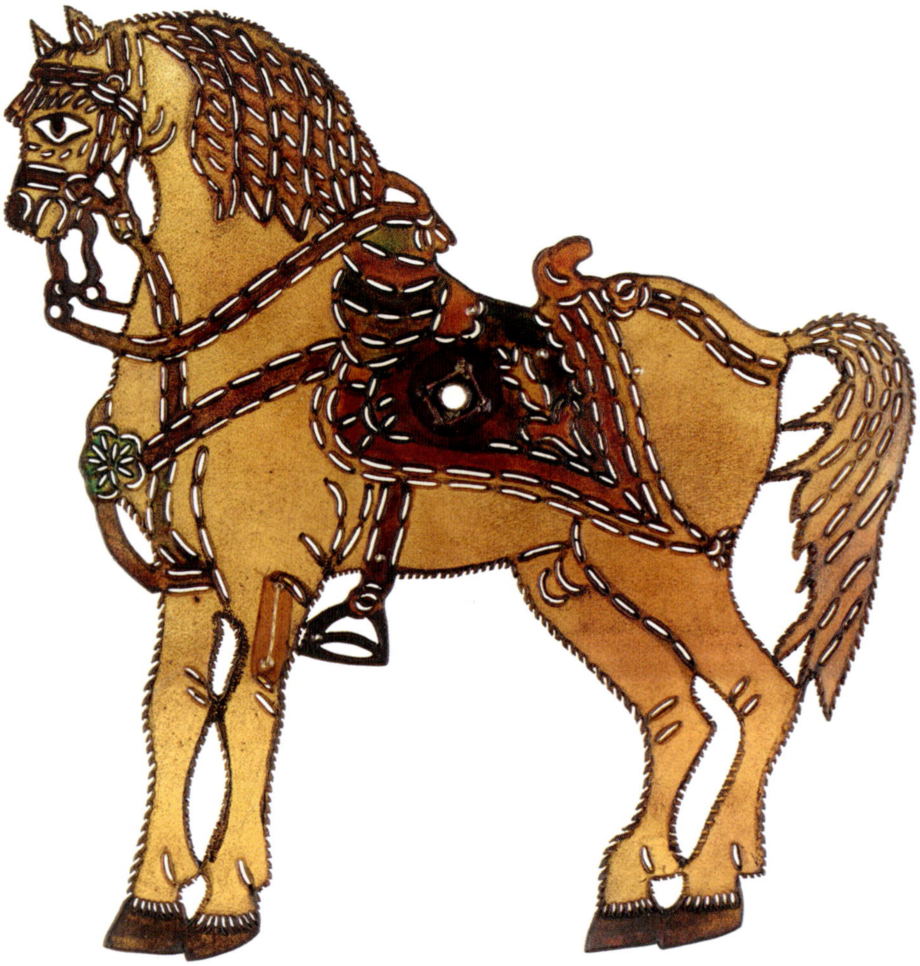

153
Shadow puppet

1970s
Istanbul, Turkey, made by Metin Özlen
Leather and pigments
H 22.5 cm, W 23 cm
BM 1980,09.16

Leather shadow puppet in the shape of a horse with a saddle and full harness. Shadow puppetry is an ancient form of storytelling and entertainment using articulated puppets in front of an illuminated backdrop to create the illusion of moving images. Although originating from China, shadow theatre became a deeply rooted genre of literature and entertainment in medieval Arab culture. The earliest Arabic references to shadow theatre (*khayal al-zill*) date to the eleventh century in Fatimid Egypt and attest to the performance of shadow plays in both popular and courtly spheres. However, the oldest surviving leather puppets and scripts date from thirteenth-century Mamluk Egypt. From Egypt, the tradition of shadow theatre was transferred to Ottoman Turkey.

154
Horses

2012
Afsoon
Print on Somerset paper of a watercolour and paper collage
H 42 cm, W 29 cm
BM 2012,6008.1

This print is from a series called 'Persian Expressions, Say Flower Hear Flower'. The composition shows horses being presented to a woman seated on a couch, who seems uninterested in the gift. The Persian inscription on the side corresponds roughly to the English proverb 'Don't look a gift-horse in the mouth'.

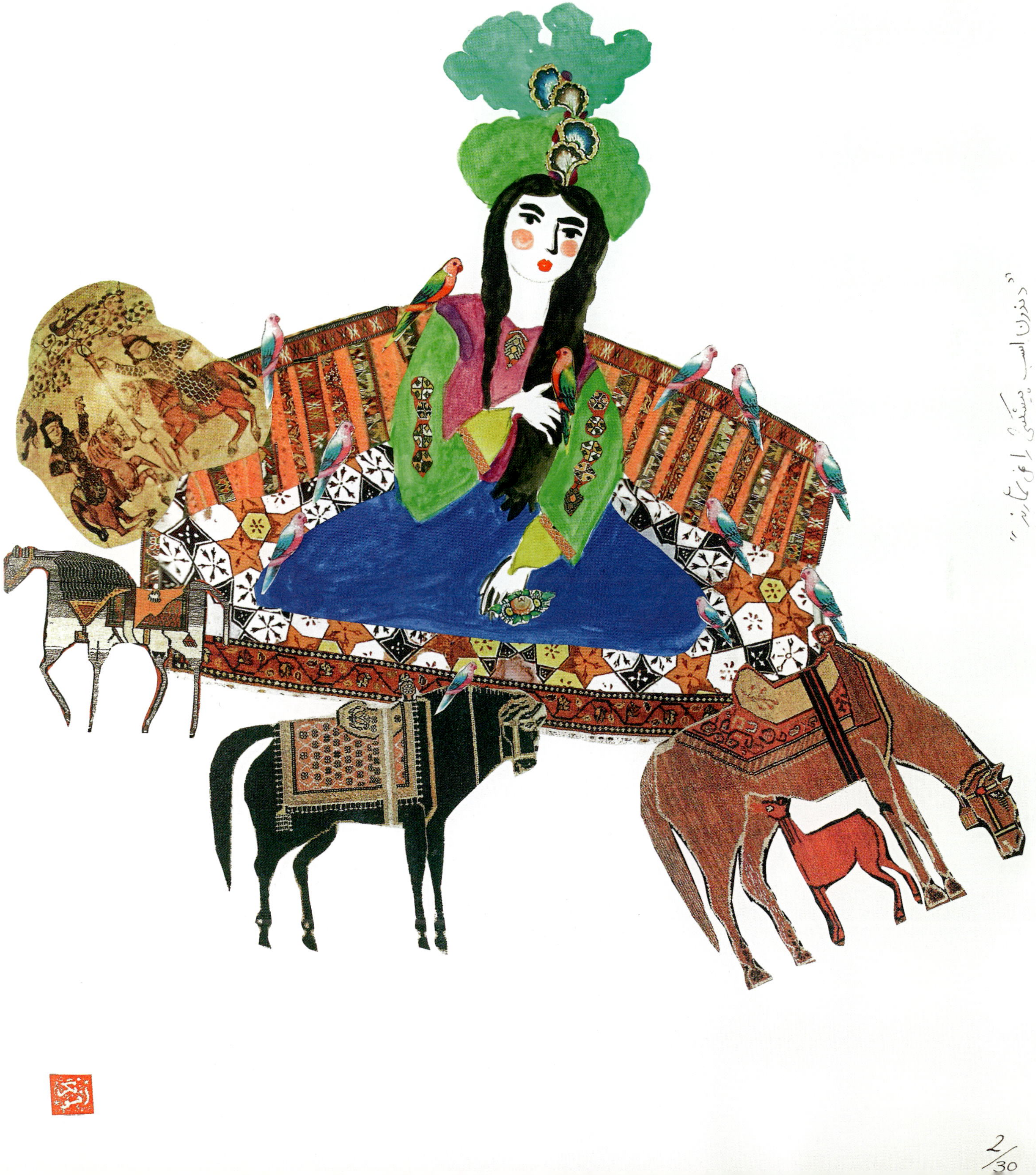
2/30

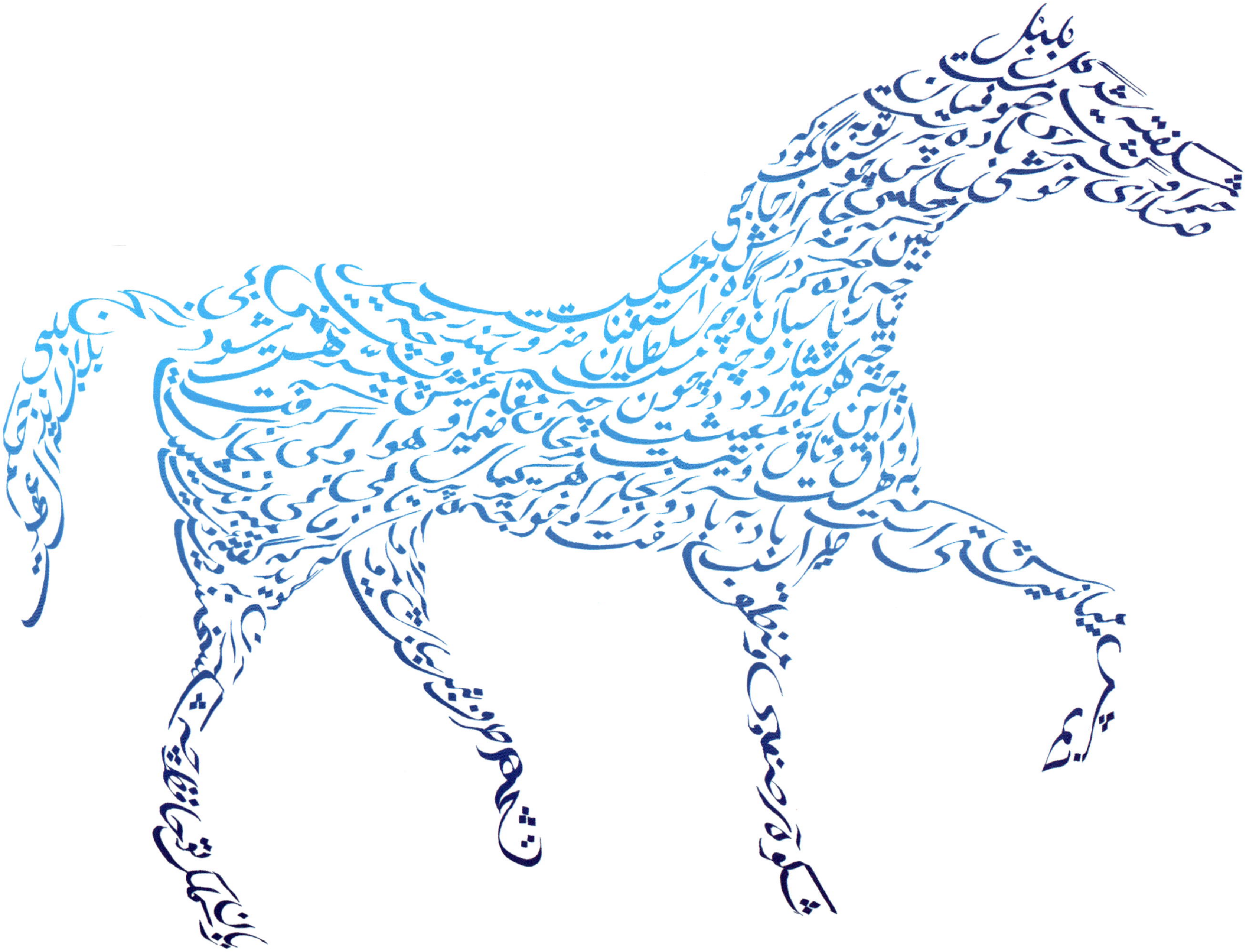

155

Horse

Jila Peacock
2012
Silkscreen blend on Somerset satin paper, with pearlescent ink
H 29.7 cm, W 42 cm
BM 2012,6011.1

Following the tradition of zoomorphic calligraphy which became particularly popular in Iran and Turkey in the nineteenth century, Jila Peacock has used the poems of Hafez, the fourteenth-century lyric poet of Shiraz, to create images of animals mentioned in the poems, such as the horse illustrated here. This piece is formed from the words of ghazal (poem) 20:

> The rose opens crimson
> For the drunken nightingale.
> Happy news, you revelling Sufis,
> For the rock of your resolve is
> Shattered by the crystal chalice.
>
> Bring wine to the throne of Heaven,
> For when the time of parting comes
> From this tavern of two doors,
> Sentry or sultan, wise man or fool,
> Lofty or low through worldly gain,
> All must pass through.
>
> Even Assef's pomp and splendour,
> The horse of the winds,
> And the language of birds
> Are lost with the wind, a worthless void.
>
> So follow the path not the plumage
> For powerful arrows soar a while
> And then descend to dust.
>
> Our time of joy comes tied to care,
> For life was bound to loss at time's dawn.
> Quit the struggle with being and non-being
> And love life now,
> For oblivion completes all design.
>
> O Hafez, rejoicing in the beauty of your pen,
> We pass your precious words from heart to heart!

Translation from Persian by Jila Peacock

156
Quilted horse armour

19th century
Sudan; acquired 1899, gift of M. Maxse
Cotton, fibre, wood
H 135 cm, W 84 cm, L 170 cm
BM 1899,1213.2

Quilted horse armour with diamond patchwork design, comprising four pieces sewn together. This armour is made of textile (cotton) and fibre padding, with wooden toggles and rope ties.

In the armies of the great empires in the savannah regions to the south of the Sahara, horses were equipped with heavy, often brightly coloured, garments of quilted cotton cloth. Several pieces of cloth were sewn together and stuffed with kapok, the wool-like strands that surround the seeds of the silk cotton tree. In full battle armour the war-horse would also have worn mail or pieces of leather across the flanks. A chamfron, or headpiece, of metal and cloth completed the outfit.

However, these colourful horses did not always go into battle. Instead they often formed the bodyguards for the Emir in the field. The armour was also worn at grand military parades. Today these fabulous costumes are worn only on ceremonial occasions. This particular horse armour was probably taken during or shortly after the Battle of Omdurman (2 September 1898), which ended the Mahdist state in Sudan. This was founded in 1885 by Muhammed Ahmad, the Mahdi, and fully established by his successor, the Khalifa, whose forces were defeated by General Kitchener at Omdurman.

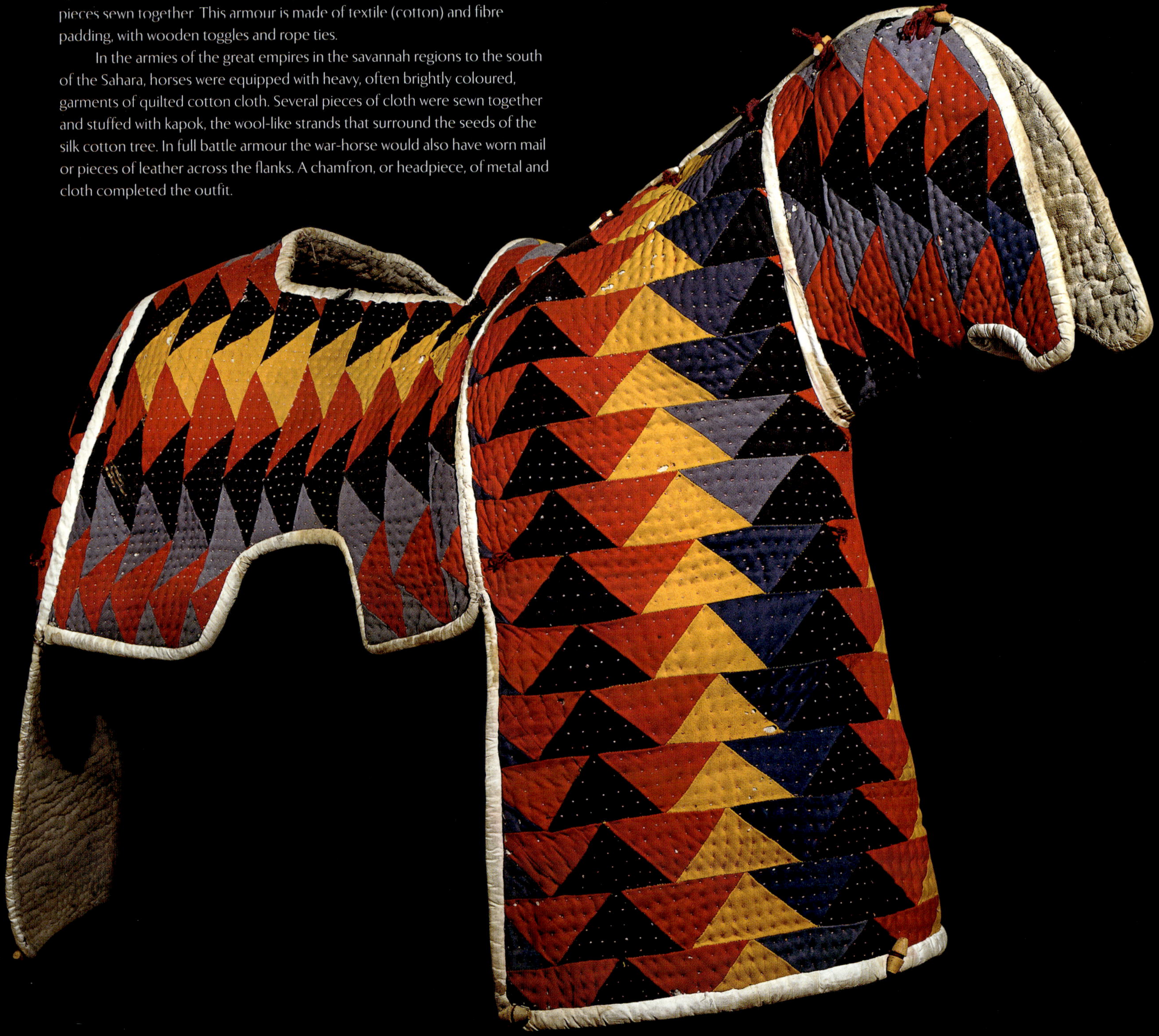

157

Helmet (*çikaç*)

Turkish, 16th century, modified for use in Sudan, late 19th century
Bequest of Dr R. Williams, 1974
H (of skull) 28.7 cm, H (overall) 52 cm, Diam. (of skull) *c.* 23.5 cm
Steel and textile
Royal Armouries, XXVIA.119

The faceted conical skull of this helmet is elegantly engraved with scrolling foliage. Its original peak has been lost and replaced with a later one, at the same time as the threaded bracket for the lost nasal defence was replaced. The quilted textile lining is typical of those fitted to Sudanese helmets, and the mail aventail (hood), which was most likely fitted at the same time as the lining, is European, cut from a fifteenth-century mail shirt.

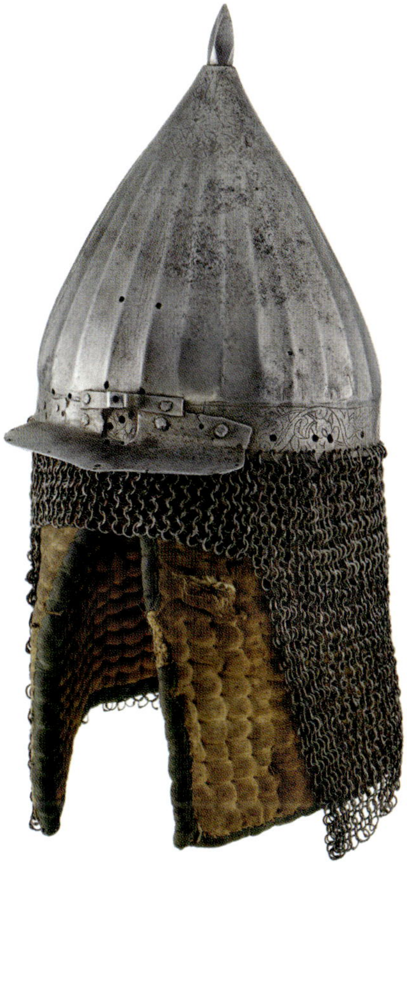

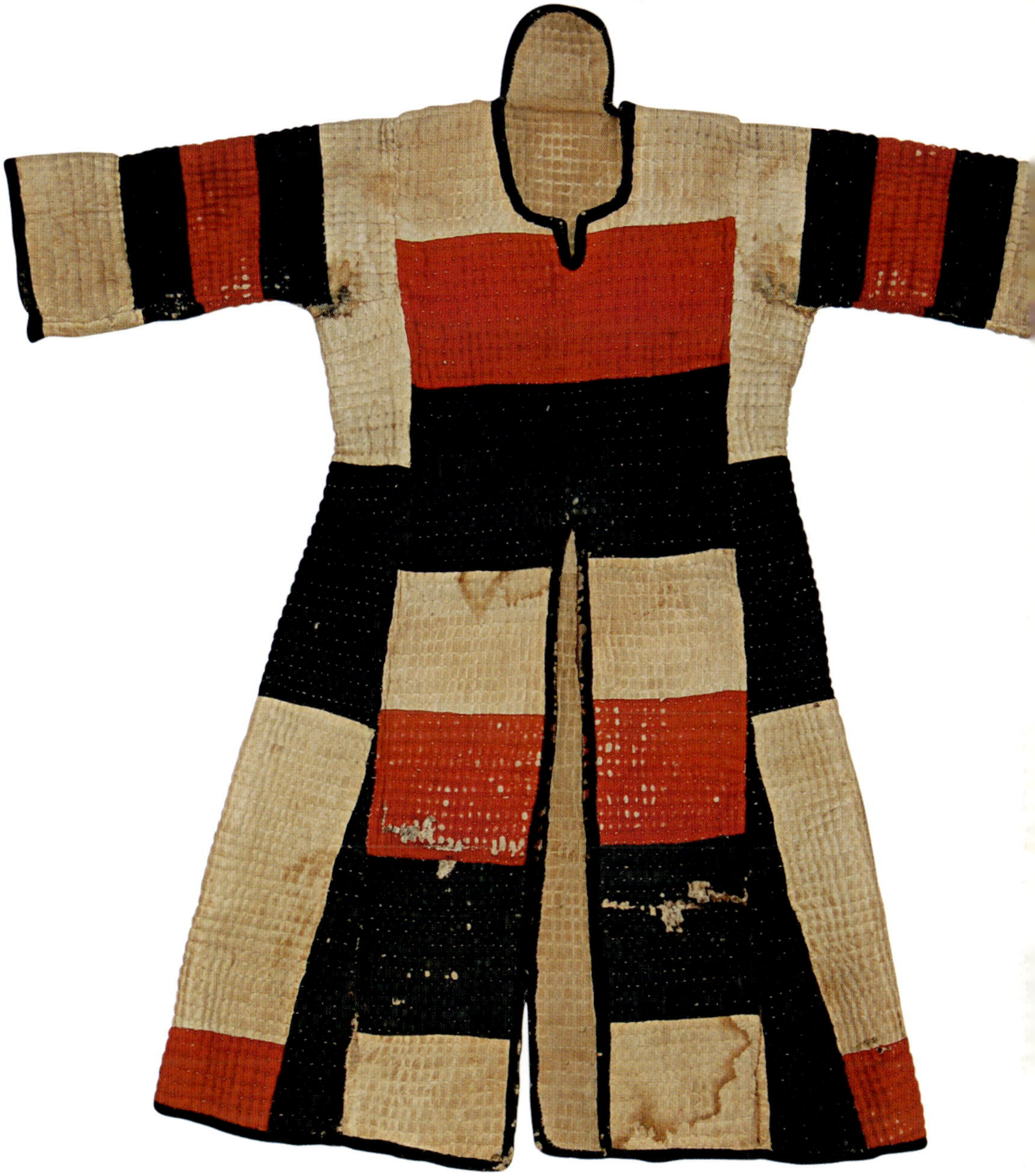

158

Quilted suit of armour

19th century
Sudan; acquired 1899, gift of M. Maxse
Cotton, fibre
L 138 cm, W 130 cm
BM 1899,1231.1

Suit of quilted textile armour worn by a horseman (probably a Dervish warrior), with bands of red and dark blue colour on a natural ground and black edging.

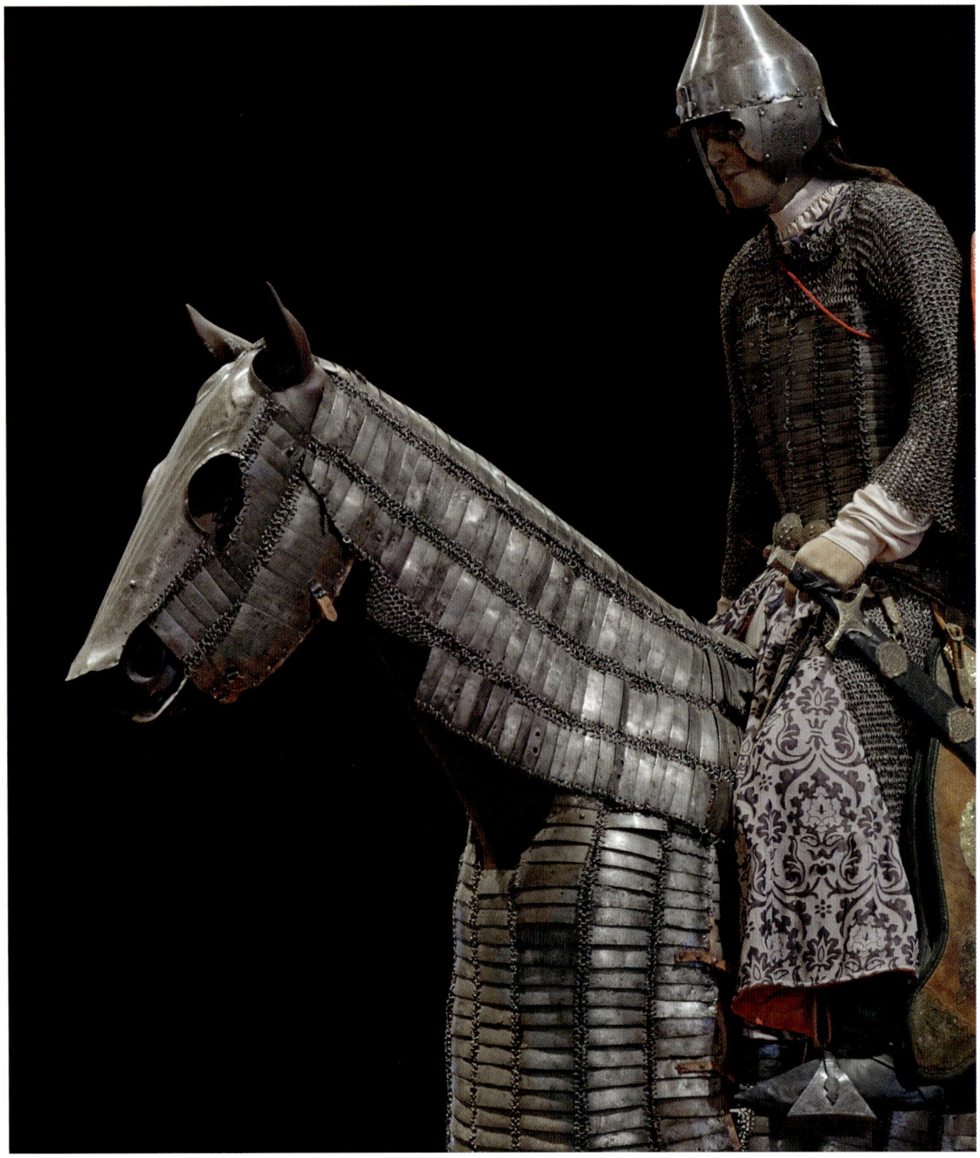

159

Armour for horse and rider

Late 15th century, Turkish
Original pieces all from Hagia Irene, Istanbul (Helmet purchased, 1841; coat on loan to the Royal Armouries from the Royal Collection; horse armour purchased 1992, formerly in the collection of Frank Gair Macomber)
Steel
Royal Armouries, XXVIA.116, XXVIA.222, XXVIH.33–5

Mail and plate armour for man and horse became the standard type of equipment for the heavy cavalry under the Timurids (1370–1506), the Mongol successor empire which ruled from Samarkand, and under the Ottoman Turks. Such heavy cavalry, armed with bow, sword and sometimes lance, were the main component of all the medieval Islamic armies.

Horse armours of mail and plate appear relatively common among Islamic cavalry of the fifteenth century, judging by artistic representations, but this example is one of only seventeen to survive today. It and the mail and plate armour for the man (*zirh gomlek*) lack all the quilted textile linings with which they were originally fitted. The helmet is probably south Russian, modified into a Turkish *çikaç* with additional neckguard and cheekpieces. The armour is supplemented by modern replicas of sword (*kılıc*) and scabbard, bow, bow-case and quiver, and shield (*kalkan*) to give a vivid impression of heavy cavalry equipment.

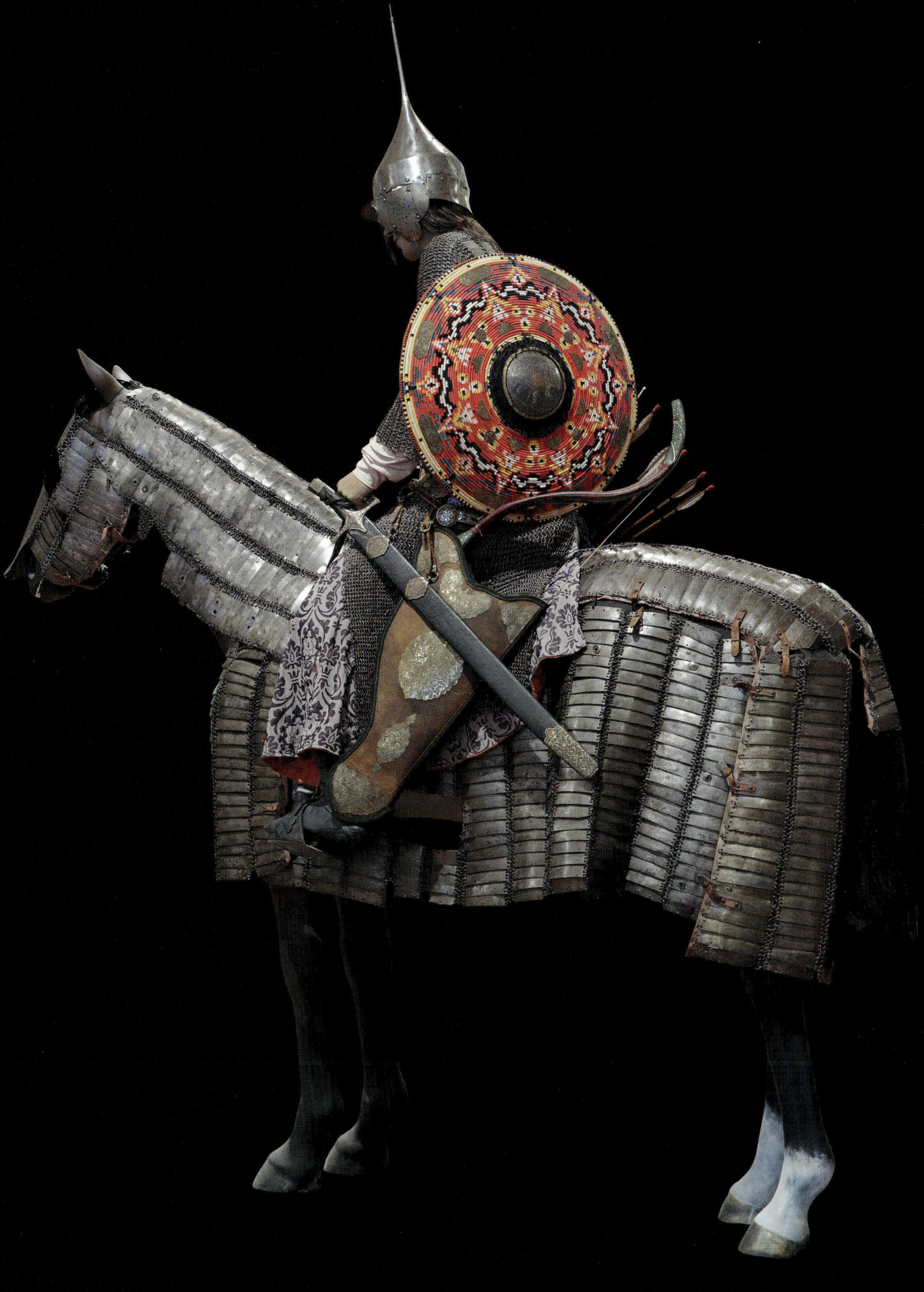

160

Horse headstall with suspended tassels

20th century
Ankara, Turkey
Dark red cotton with silver-coloured metal-wrapped thread
L 73 cm
BM 1968,10.55

This horse's decorative headstall has a flat (tabby) woven strip with ten tassels suspended from the bottom edge. The end of each tassel has a tiny copper bead attached. A single tassel is suspended from two longer braided cords in the centre. Attached to the upper edge of the strip is a circular disc with an eleven-pointed star embroidered onto black leather. Five further tassels are fixed to it.

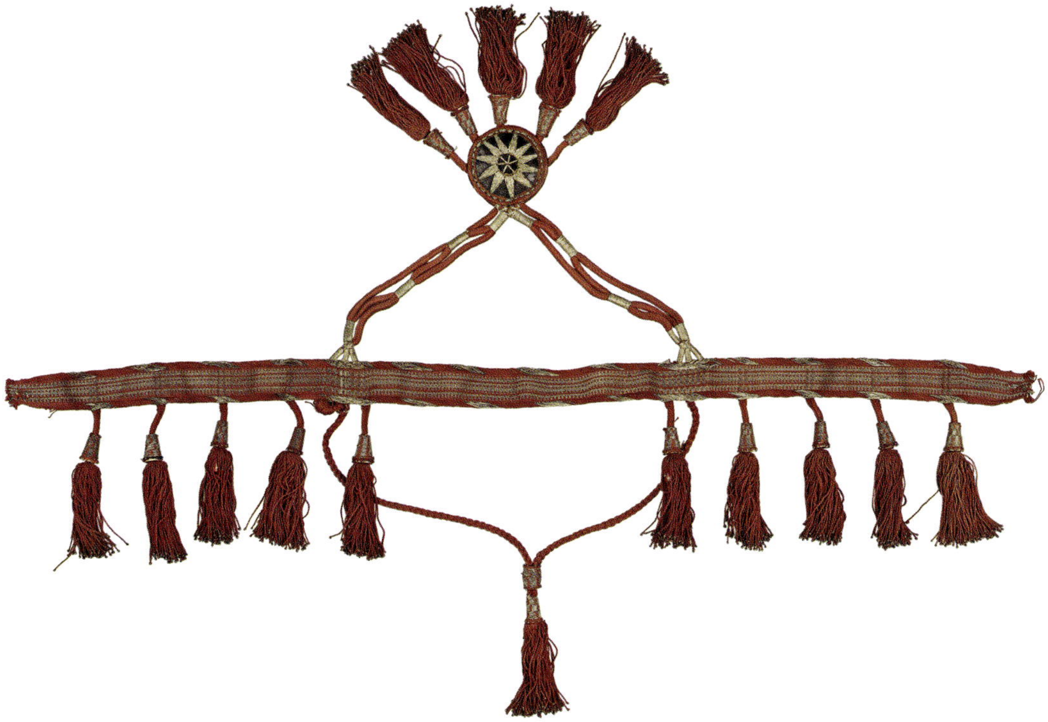

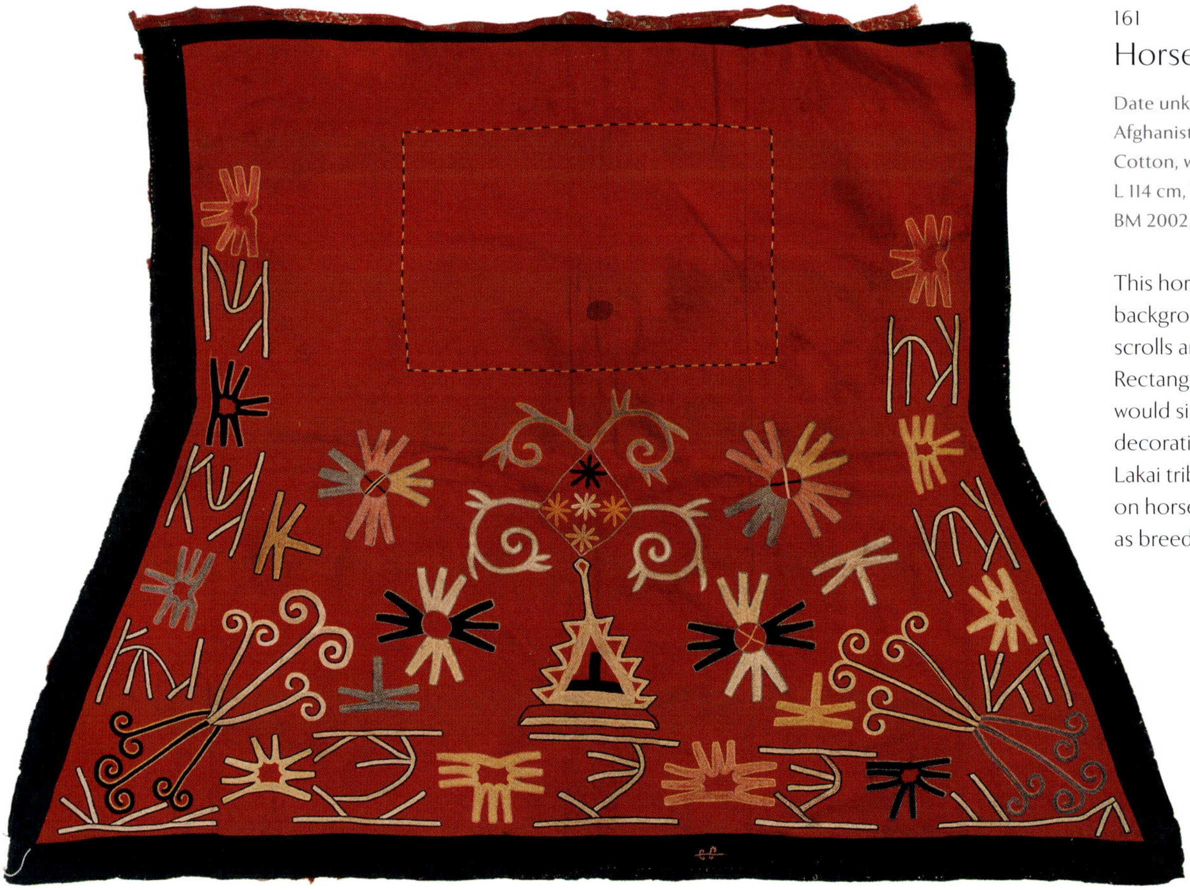

161

Horse cover ('Da-our')

Date unknown, Uzbek (Lakai tribe)
Afghanistan
Cotton, wool, and silk with embroidery
L 114 cm, W 156 cm
BM 2002,03.43

This horse cover (trapper) or 'Da-our' has a red background, with motifs of star or sun shapes, scrolls and lines, and an outer navy-coloured border. Rectangular in shape and fanning out at base, this would sit underneath the horse's saddle, with the decorative embroidery visible. The way of life of the Lakai tribe of the Uzbeks in Central Asia was based on horsemanship, initially as horse raiders and then as breeders.

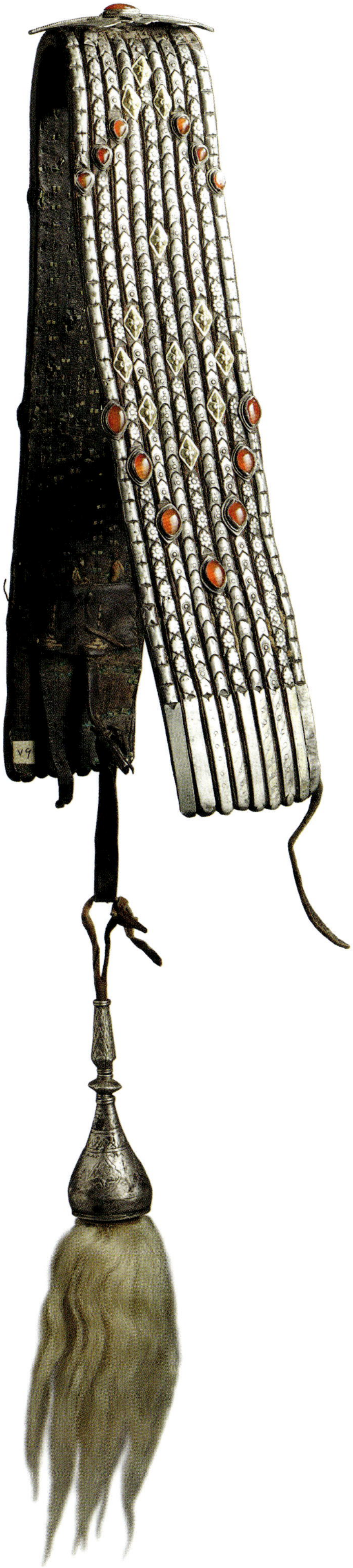

162
Neck-strap

Date unknown, Turkman
Iran
Leather, silver, gilt (?), gold (?), stone (agate?) and wool
Max. W 10.5 cm, max. L 83 cm (excl. tassel), L 38 cm (tassel only)
BM 1979,08.21

This decorated leather neck strap is of a similar type to the harness depicted in cats 146 and 151.

163
Pair of stirrups

16th century
Turkey; Chater Manuk bequest, 1948
Inlaid and gilded red-lacquered iron
H 15 cm, W 14 cm, D 5.5 cm
BM 1948,1020.1.a-b

These stirrups are flat at the bottom with a broad base for the foot and oval loops for suspension at the top. There is floral decoration on the sides.

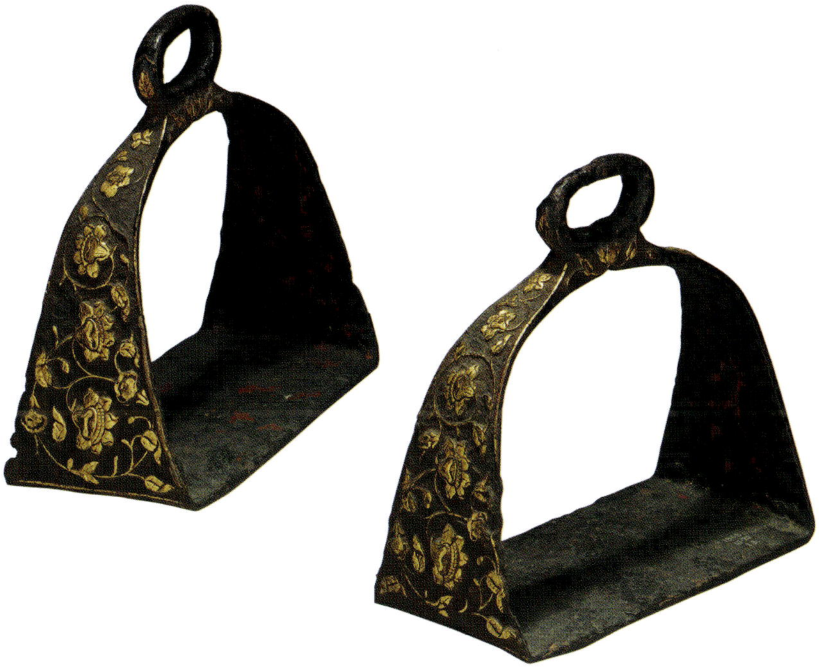

164

GigaPan images of rock drawings

The petroglyph project aims to record rock drawings throughout Saudi Arabia, particularly those featuring horses using GigaPan photography. This is a system developed by Carnegie Mellon and NASA, using very large format digital images in extremely high resolution, which is finding increasing application as a means of recording, sharing and studying sites and objects across a variety of disciplines.

Directed by Sandra L. Olsen, curator of anthropology at Carnegie Museum of Natural History, and paleontologist Chris Beard of Carnegie Museum of Natural History and Majeed Khan of the Ministry of Tourism and Antiquities in Saudi Arabia, the petroglyph project (made possible through the cooperation of the Saudi Commission for Tourism and Antiquities, with the support of the Layan Foundation) has used GigaPan photography to document sites of ancient rock art in Saudi Arabia in unprecedented detail.

Rock drawings from a number of periods have been recorded, showing chariots, horsemen and horses and scenes of hunting and warfare, many inscribed. The example illustrated here shows a remarkable rock formation at Al-Naslaa, near Taima in Saudi Arabia with a pecked and engraved representation of a man standing in front of a large horse on the right-hand sandstone block and holding it by a rein. The horse is shown with a concave face, forelock, arched neck and a high arched tail. There is an inscription in a circle above and to the rear of the horse.

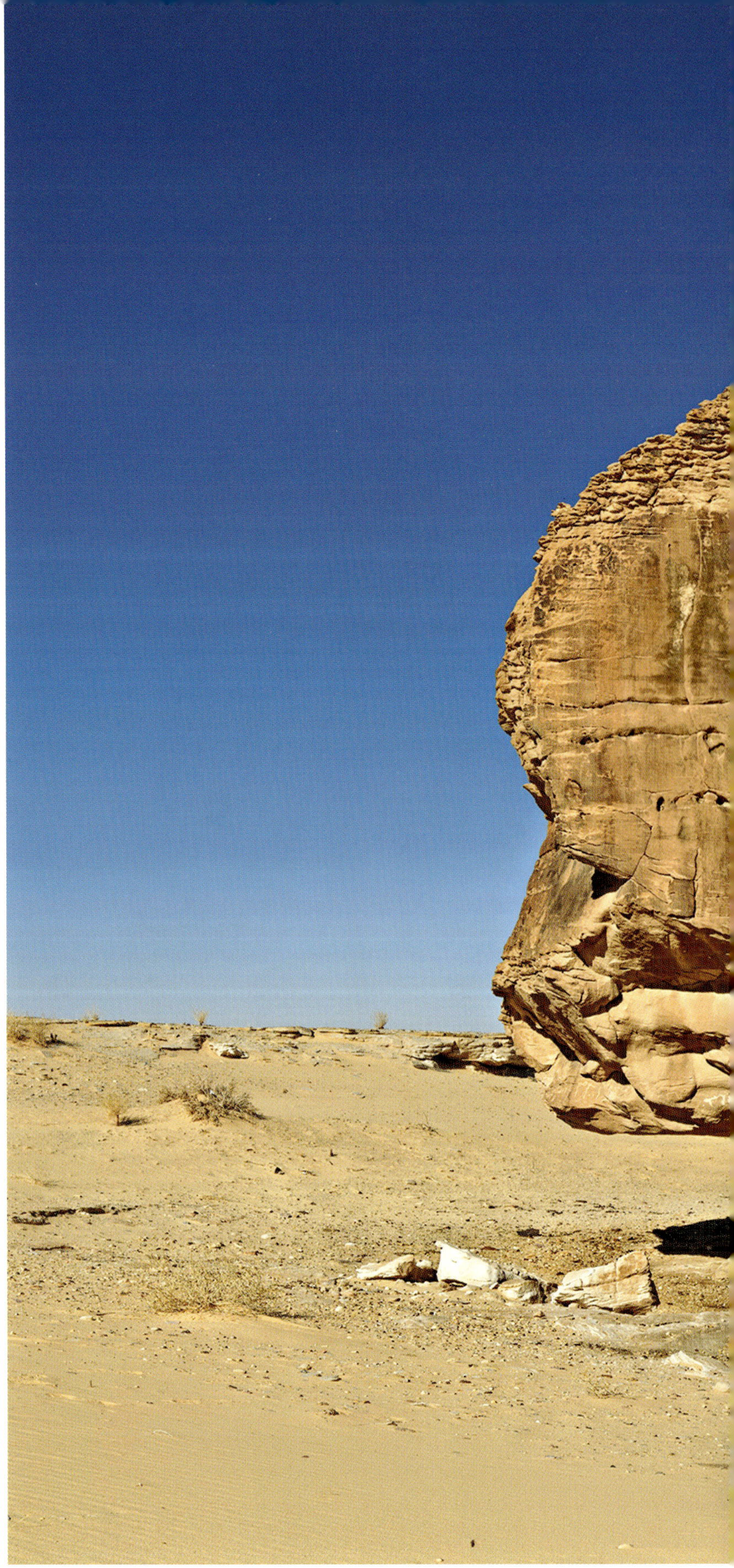

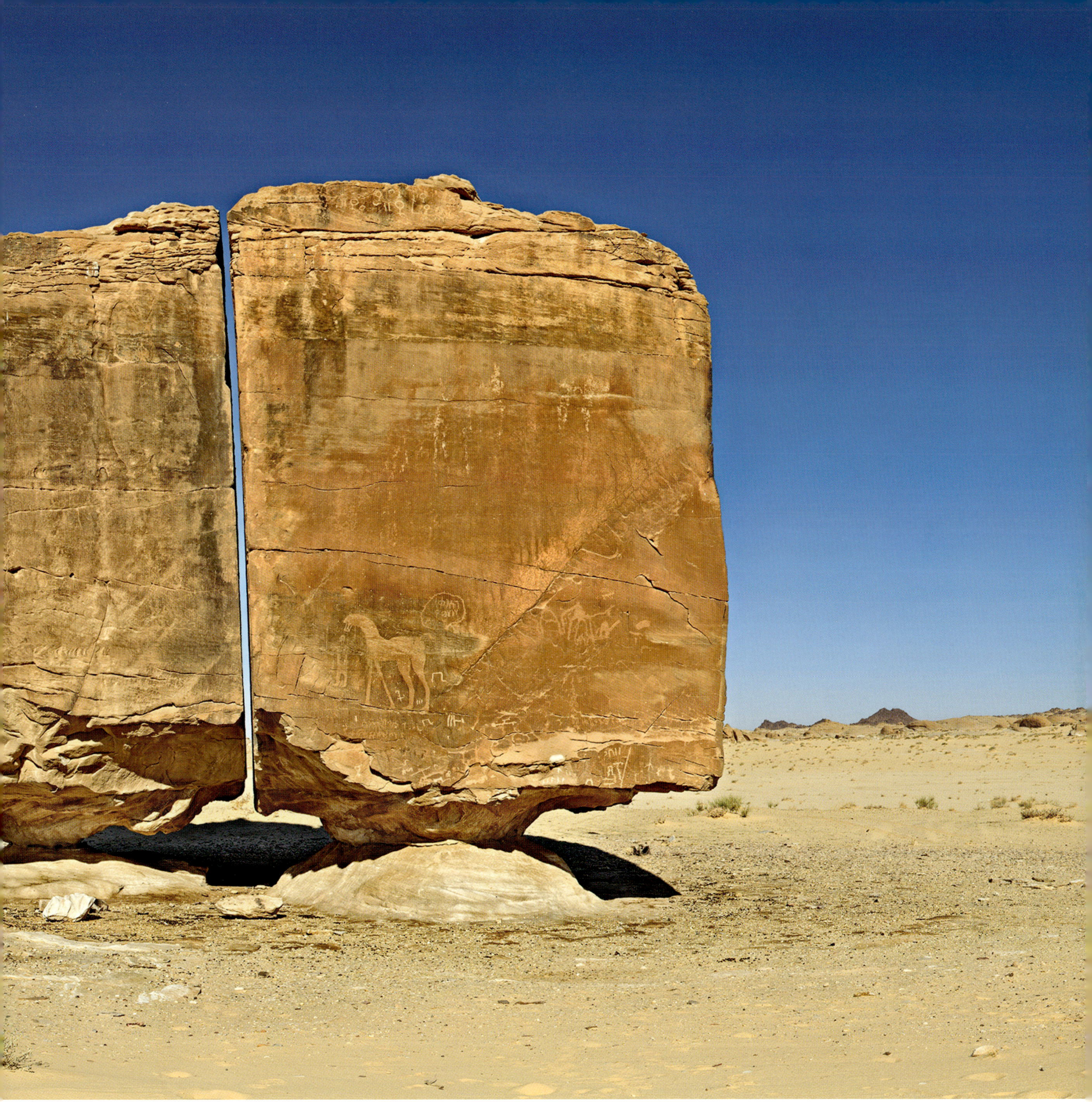

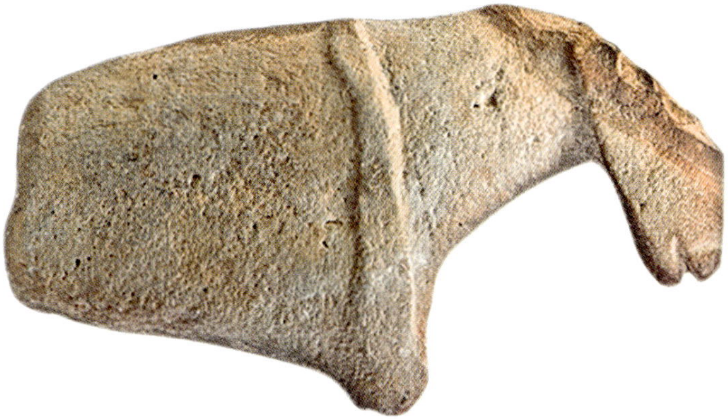

165

Stone carving in the form of a horse (?)

Prehistoric?
Al-Maqar, Saudi Arabia
Stone
H 86 cm, W 52 cm, D 18 cm
National Museum of Saudi Arabia, 3172

This carving shows the head and front part (minus legs) of an animal that bears some resemblance to a horse. The animal has a long head of equine shape and a vertical rib at the base of its neck that possibly represents a halter or harness element.

This stone carving was found together with cats 166–7 at the same site as the arrowheads, scrapers, vessels and loom-weight (cats 168–80). The arrowheads and scrapers can be dated to the Neolithic period on typological grounds, and this dating is confirmed by C-14 analysis (radiocarbon dating). However, the association of the stone statues with the Neolithic material is not clearly established and work is ongoing to determine the exact date of the three stone carvings shown here.

166

Stone carving in the form of a bird of prey (?)

Prehistoric?
Al-Maqar, Saudi Arabia
Stone
H 24 cm, W 18 cm, D 6.5 cm
National Museum of Saudia Arabia, 3181

This carving shows what appears to be the head and neck of a bird of prey such as an eagle or a falcon.

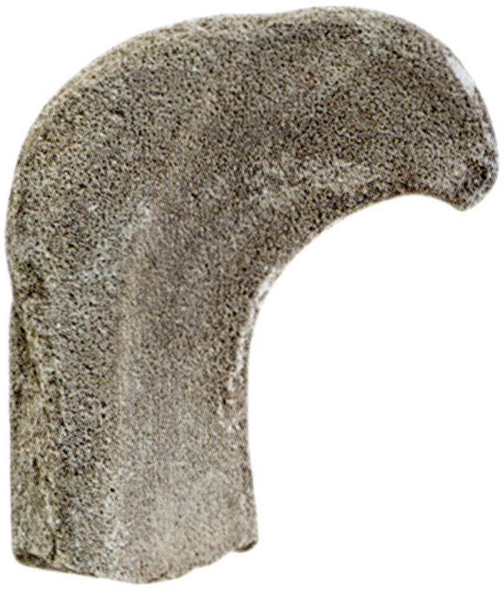

167

Stone carving in the form of a dog (?)

Prehistoric?
Al-Maqar, Saudi Arabia
Stone
H 40 cm, W 12 cm, D 5.5 cm
National Museum of Saudi Arabia, 3176

This carving shows the head, neck and chest of an animal resembling a dog. It has a thin, pointed nose and a graceful, arched neck that are reminiscent of a saluki or hunting dog.

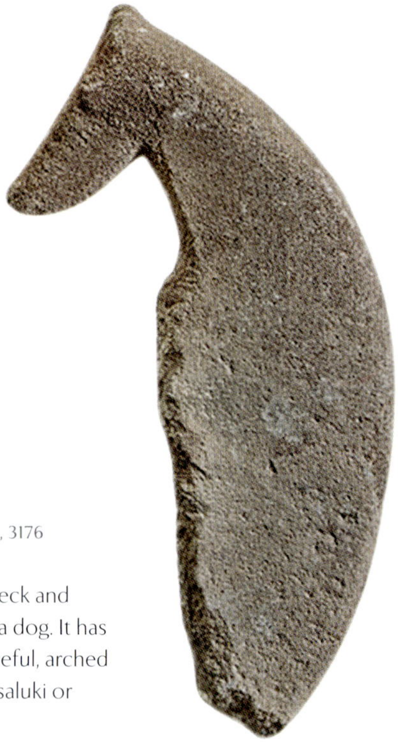

168–72

Group of flint arrowheads

5th millennium BC, Neolithic
Al-Maqar, Saudi Arabia
Flint
L 2.5–5.5 cm, W 1.2–2.3 cm, Th. 0.3–0.7 cm
National Museum of Saudi Arabia, H 4/1281, H 5/1281, H 1324, H 6/1281, H 9/1281

Five bifacial arrowheads with barbs and tang.

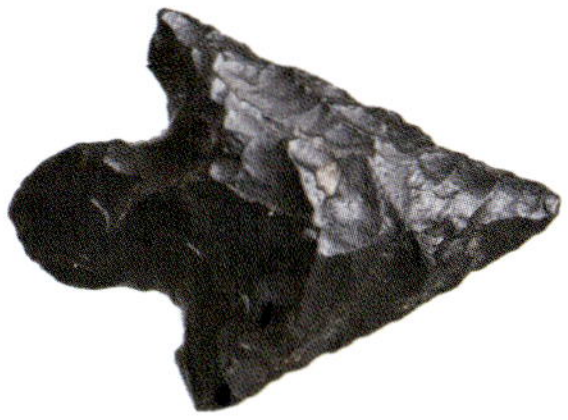

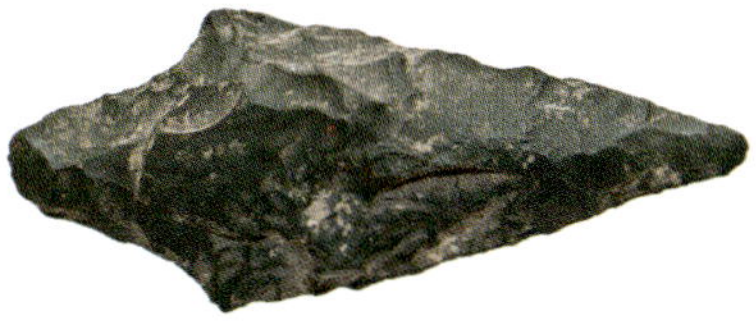

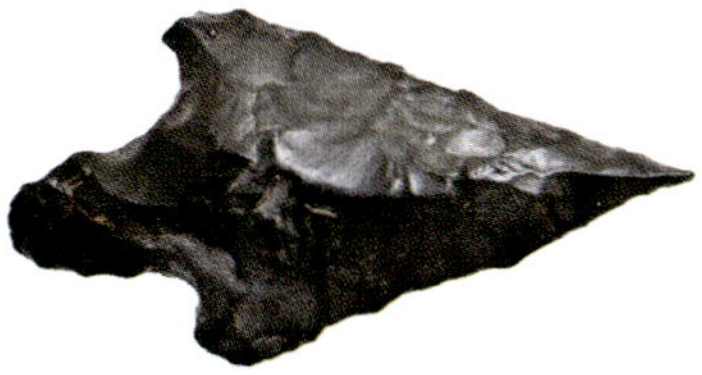

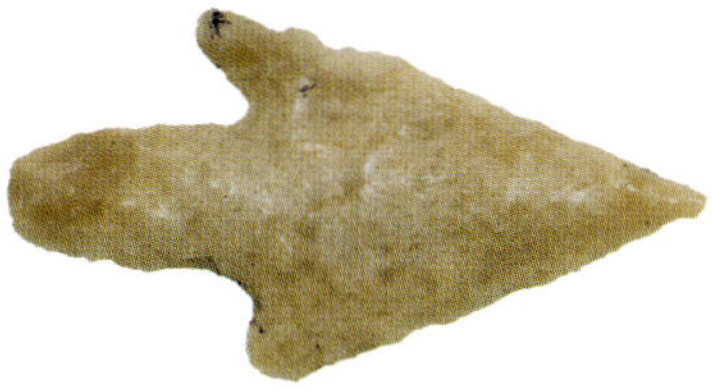

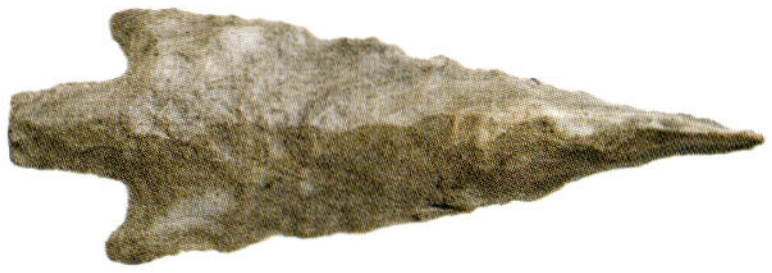

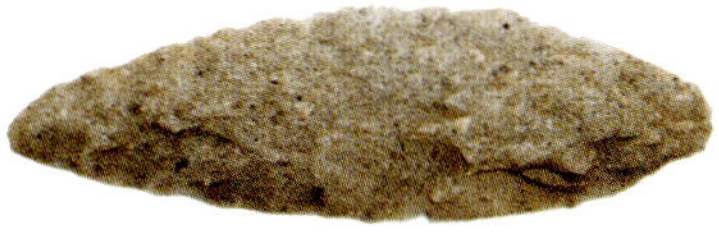

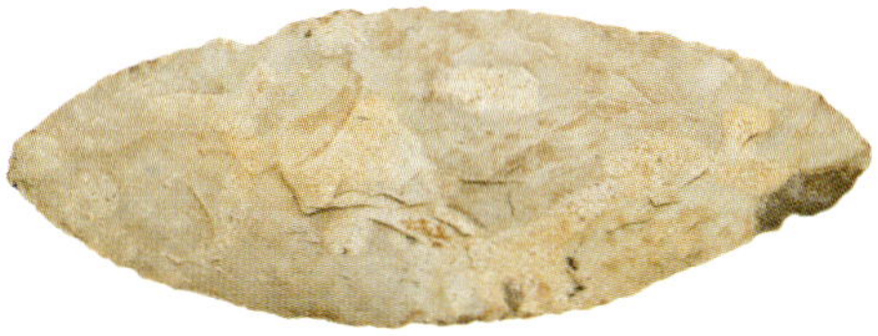

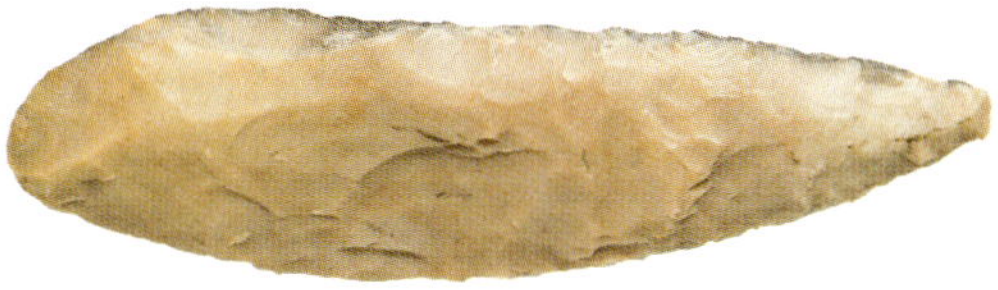

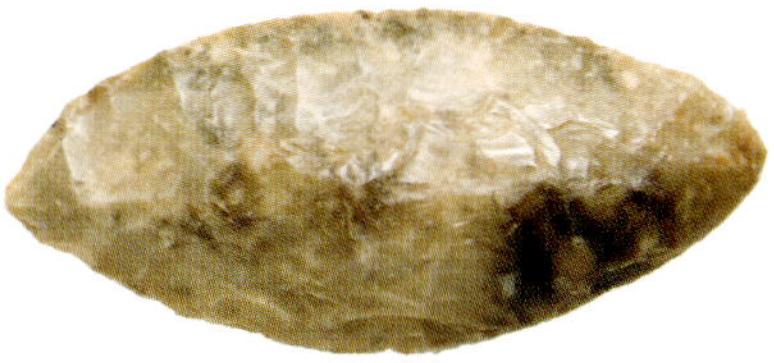

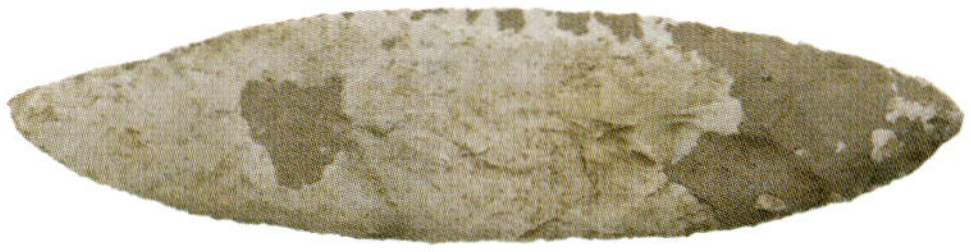

173–7

Group of scrapers

5th millennium BC, Neolithic
Al-Maqar, Saudi Arabia
Stone and flint
L 2–19.2 cm, W 0.8–4.7 cm, Th. 0.2–1 cm
National Museum of Saudi Arabia, H 4/1283, H 3/1284, H 2/1283,
H 1/1284, H 1288

One stone and four flint scrapers with pointed ends and sharp edges.

178

Pulley-wheel (?)

Prehistoric (?)
Al-Maqar, Saudi Arabia
Stone
Diam. 5 cm
National Museum of Saudi Arabia, 3299

A circular disc with a central hole and groove around the edge that may have been used in weaving.

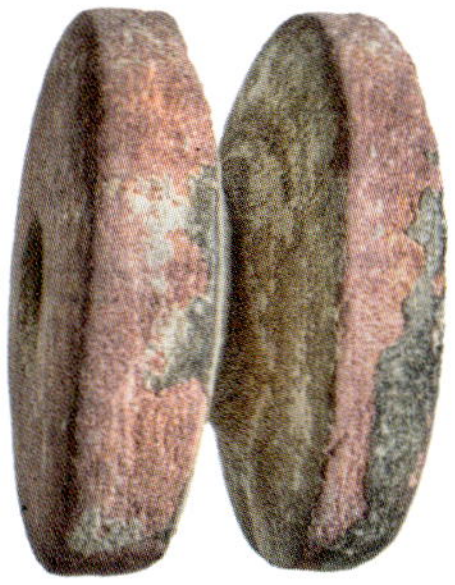

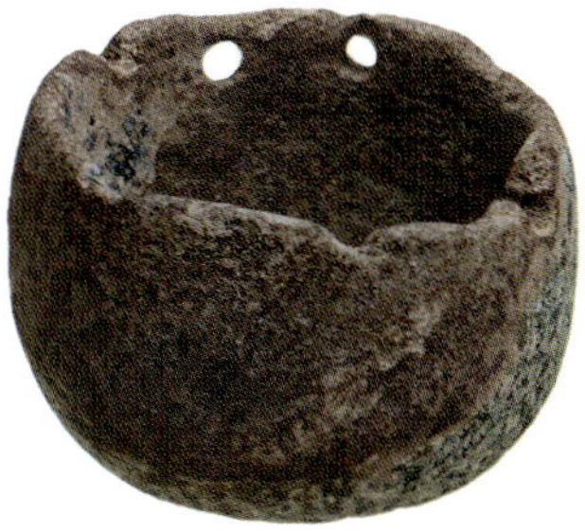

179–80

Soapstone bowls

5th millennium BC, Neolithic (?)
Al-Maqar, Saudi Arabia
Soapstone (?)
H 2.4–4.6 cm, Diam. 4.2–9 cm
National Museum of Saudi Arabia, 3362, 3301

Two small circular bowls made from soft stone (possibly soapstone). One of them has a pair of holes drilled just beneath the rim.

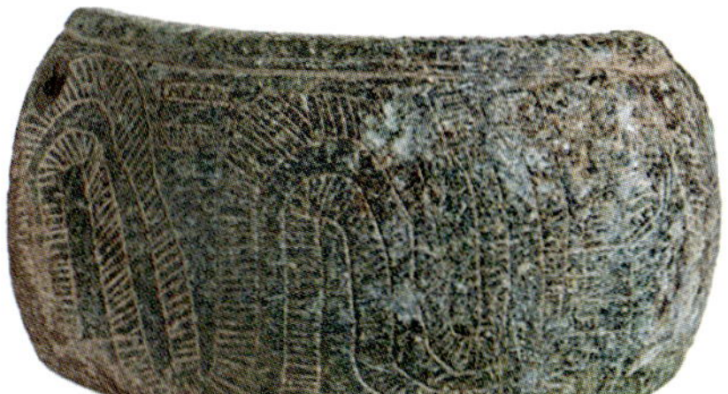

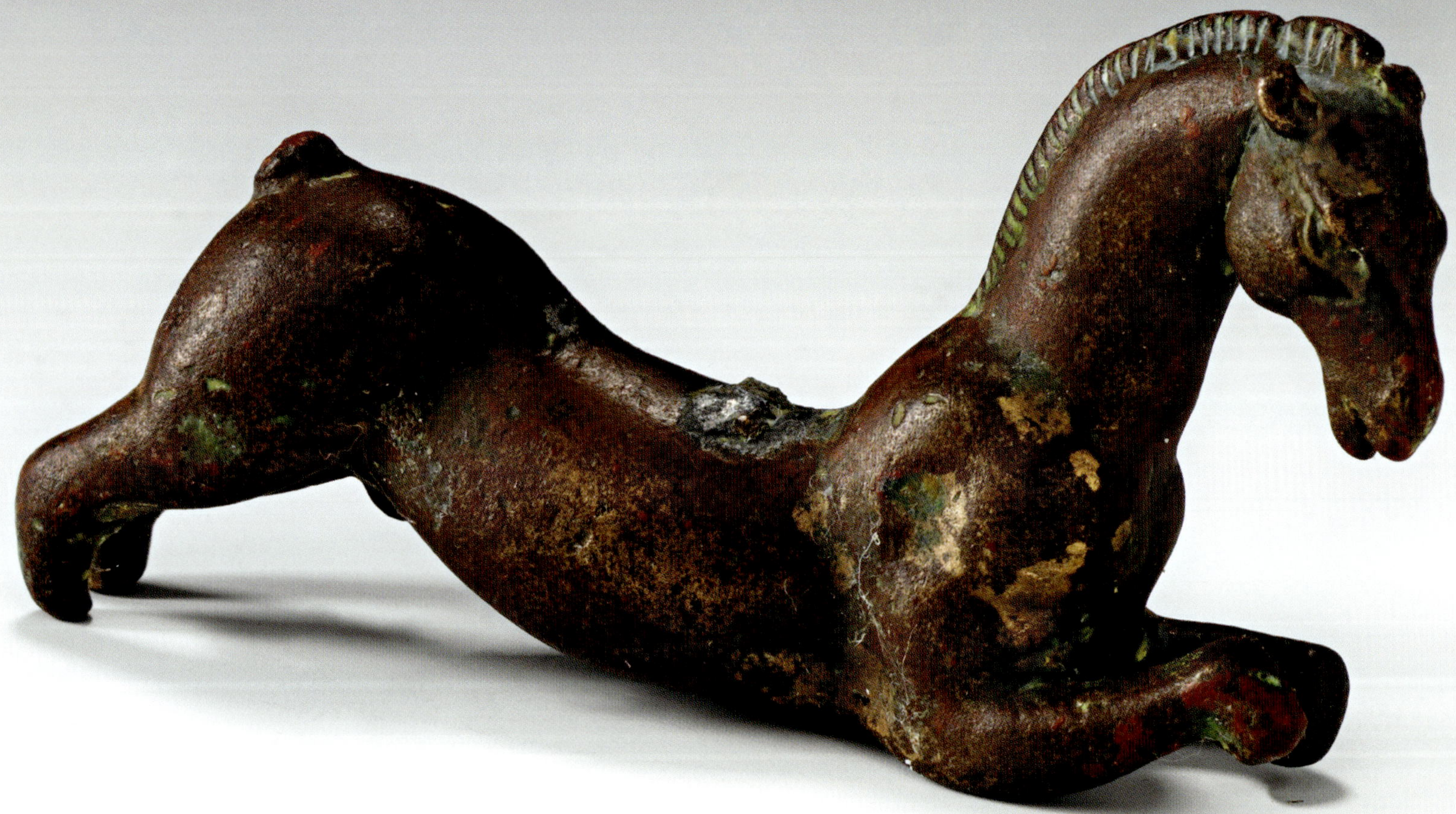

181

Rearing horse figurine

c. AD 200
Qaryat al-Fau, Saudi Arabia
Bronze
L 8.7 cm
King Saud University Museum, F16-18

This lifelike bronze figurine of a rearing stallion was discovered in Tomb H, 6, at Qaryat al-Fau. Created using the lost-wax casting method, it still has traces of gilding around the face and mane. The mane is cropped and the forelock was possibly bunched into a ball. Qaryat al-Fau is an ancient caravan town located at an oasis on the north-west edge of the Rub'al-Khali (Empty Quarter) in southern Saudi Arabia. The site was first occupied between the second century BC and the third century AD and was therefore partly contemporary with the Roman empire. The excavations here have provided much information for the use of horses in this region.

182

Fresco showing horses fording a stream

1st–2nd century AD
Qaryat al-Fau, Saudi Arabia
Painted gypsum plaster
H 44 cm, L 101 cm
National Museum of Saudi Arabia, F6-650

A fragment of fresco that is part of a larger scene showing horses crossing a stream. The hoofs of two horses can be seen, with fish swimming in the water. There is a band of inscription contained within a red border, beneath which are leaves on a yellow background. This fresco was found in the great temple at Qaryat al-Fau.

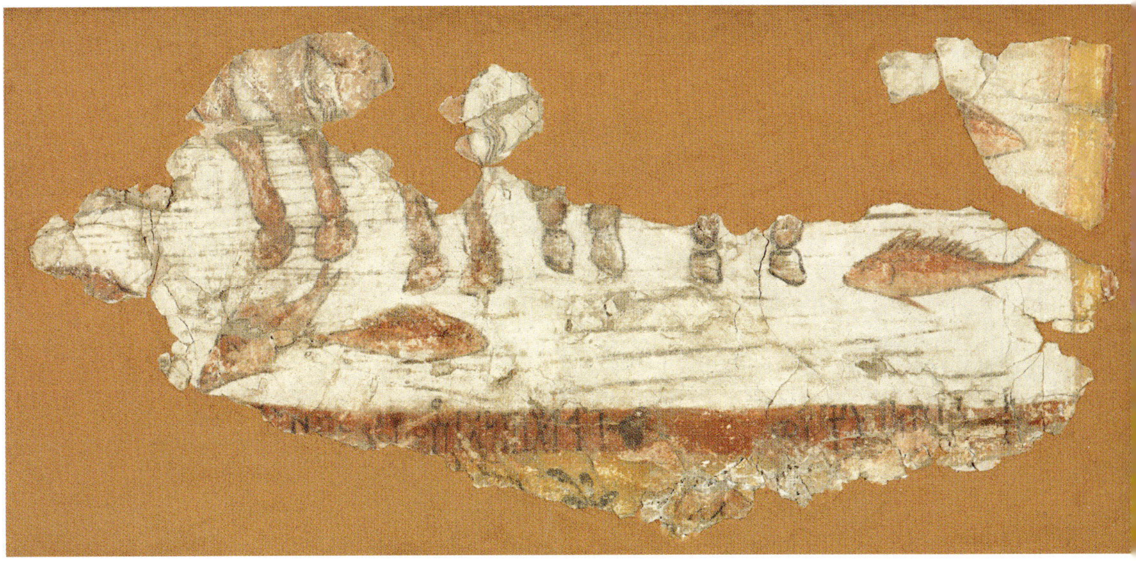

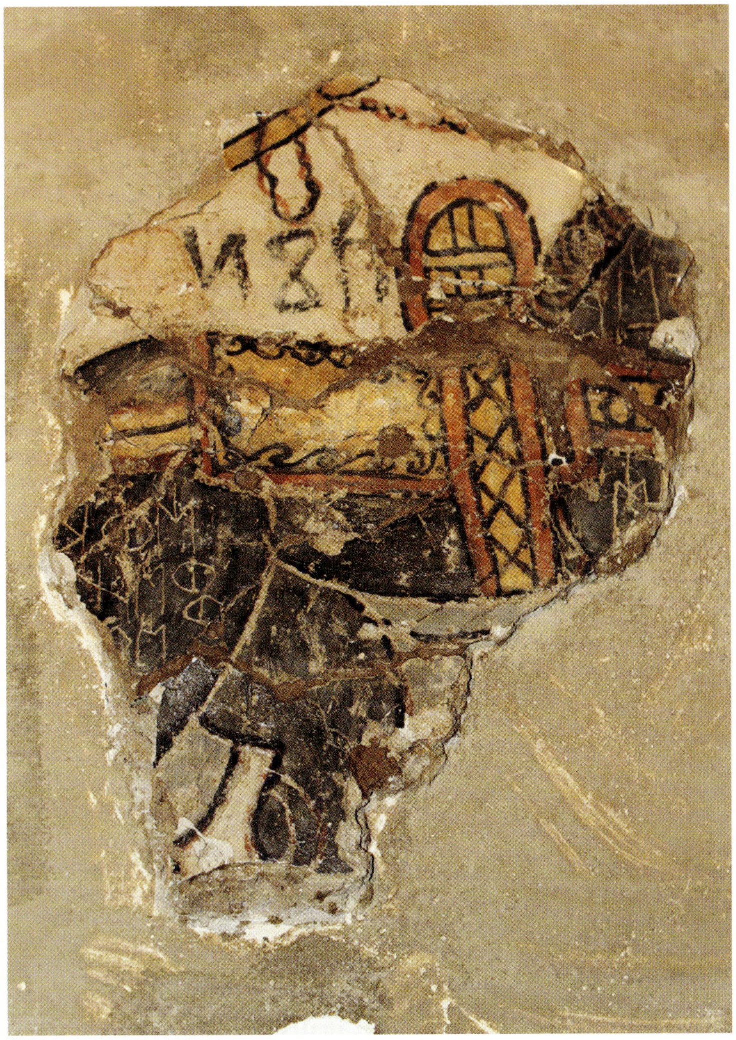

183

Fresco showing a saddled horse

1st–2nd century AD
Qaryat al-Fau, Saudi Arabia
Painted gypsum plaster
H 32.5 cm, W 24 cm
King Saud University Museum, F7-65

Some frescoes found at Qaryat al-Fau show scenes of hunters on horseback with long lances chasing camels, as well as inscriptions in the *Musnad* script, a pre-Islamic South Arabian alphabet.

This fragment of a fresco from a Qaryat al-Fau shows the neck, back and flank of a black horse. The saddle or saddle-blanket is yellow with a black and red border. A yellow girth strap and possible rounded saddlebow are crosshatched in black and outlined in red. A multi-coloured breast strap and crupper are also depicted. The horse is tethered by rope to a pole suspended above its back. The name *Kazim* is written above the horse in the *Musnad* script. This is probably part of a scene showing a hunter on horseback with a long lance, perhaps chasing camels.

184

Basalt stela showing a mounted warrior

4th–5th century AD
Qanawat, Syria; acquired 1972
Basalt
H 72 cm, W 44 cm, D 16 cm
BM 135708

This carved stela shows a mounted figure who has braided hair, wears a long, belted tunic and holds a spear and shield. It is carved in high relief on basalt. The horse has his left foreleg raised and his bridle, breast strap and crupper are depicted.

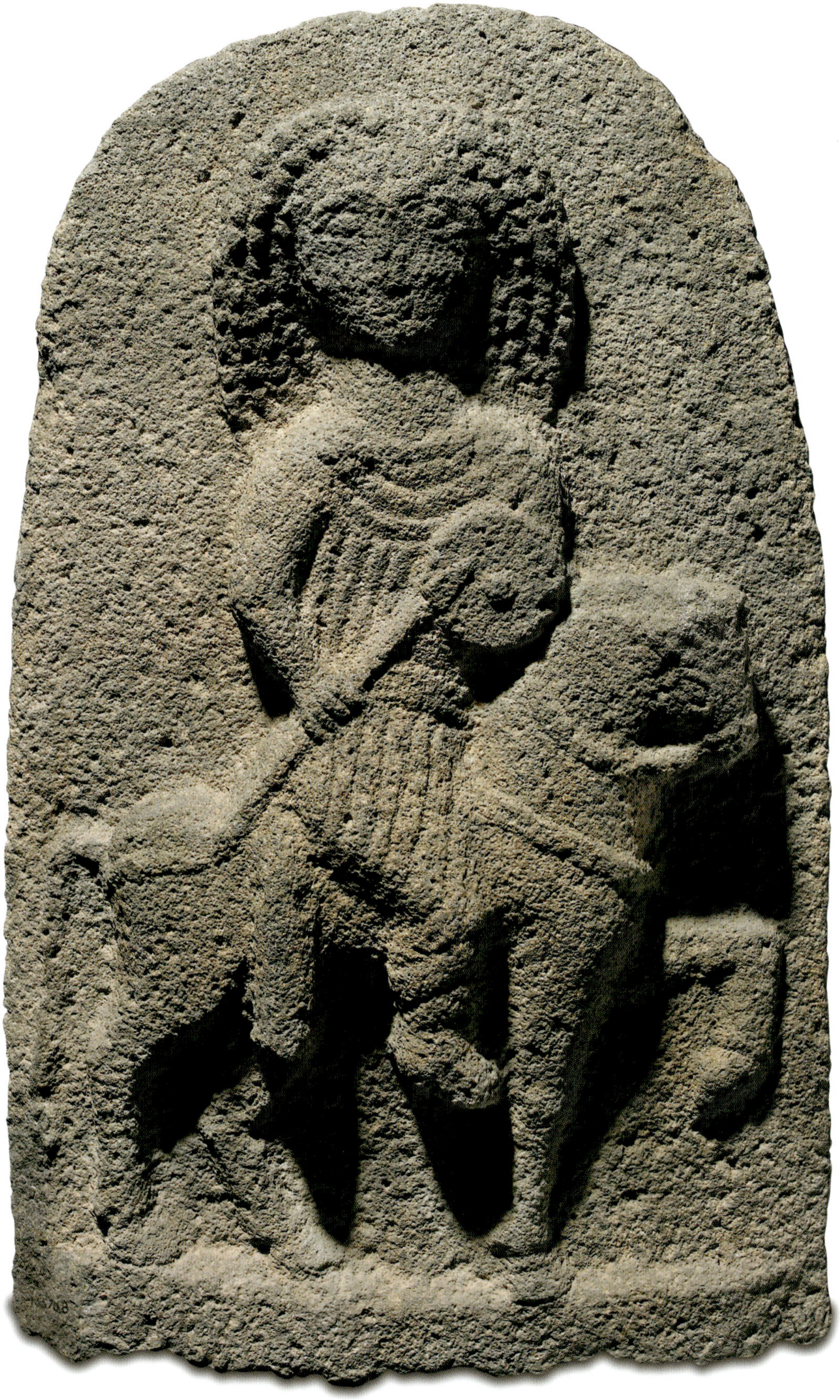

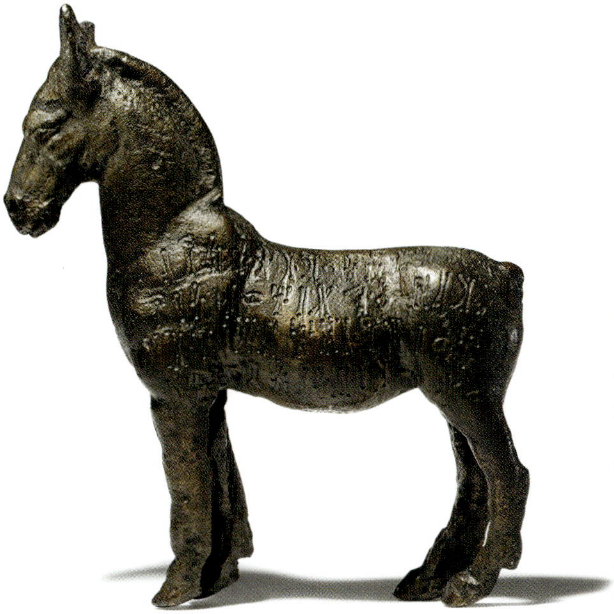

185

Figure of a donkey with Sabaean inscription

2nd century AD
Yemen; acquired 1961
Bronze
H 7.1 cm, L 6.3 cm, W 1.8 cm
BM 132932

This statuette of a donkey was made using the lost-wax casting method. The four lines of Sabaean inscription cast into the surface on both sides have not yet been translated.

186

Bronze lamp with horse-head handle

50–150 AD, Roman
Qasr Ibrim, Egypt; acquired 1962
Bronze
L 17.5 cm, H 11 cm
BM 66576

This elegant bronze lamp has an elongated body and circular wick hole. The top is sunken, with a raised edge and flat rim around the body and nozzle. The filling hole is shaped like an ivy leaf, with an engraved stem. At the rear is a handle which curves forward and ends in a beautifully modelled horse's head. Although this particular example was made in Egypt, it may be compared with bronze lamps with zoomorphic handle terminals that have been found in Arabia.

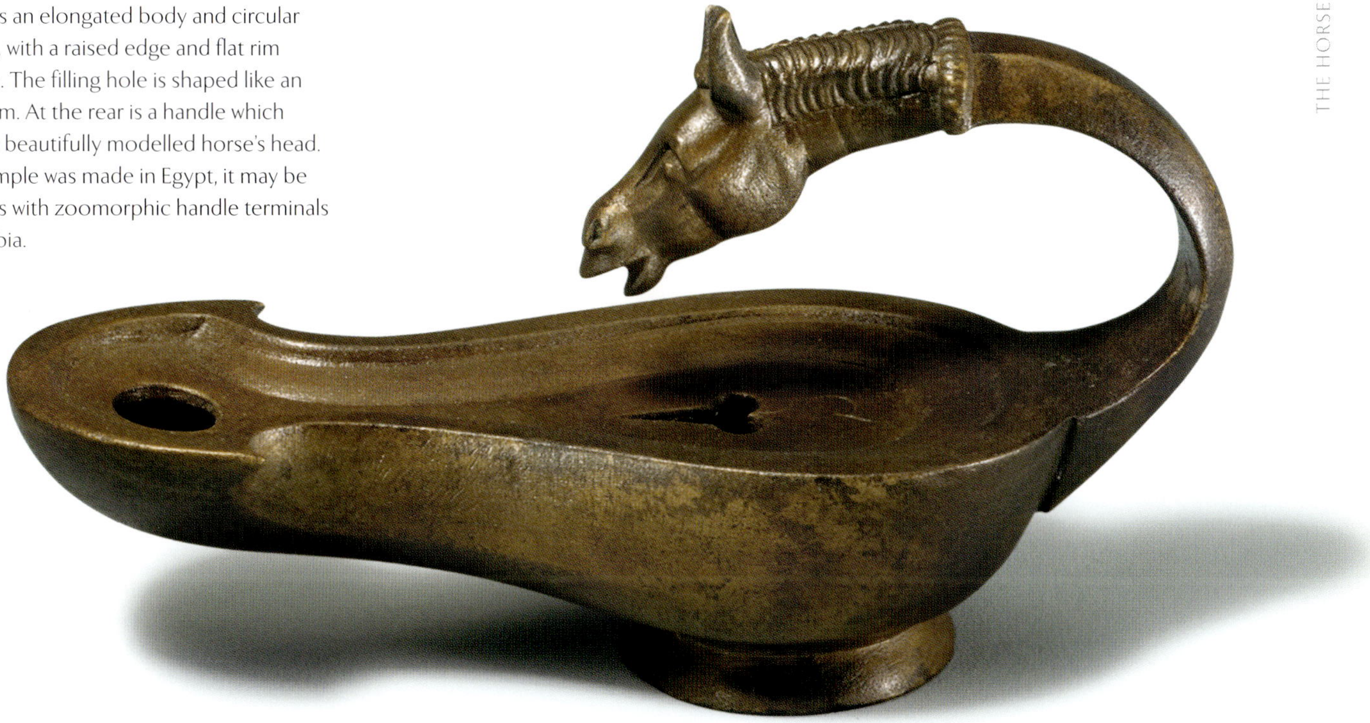

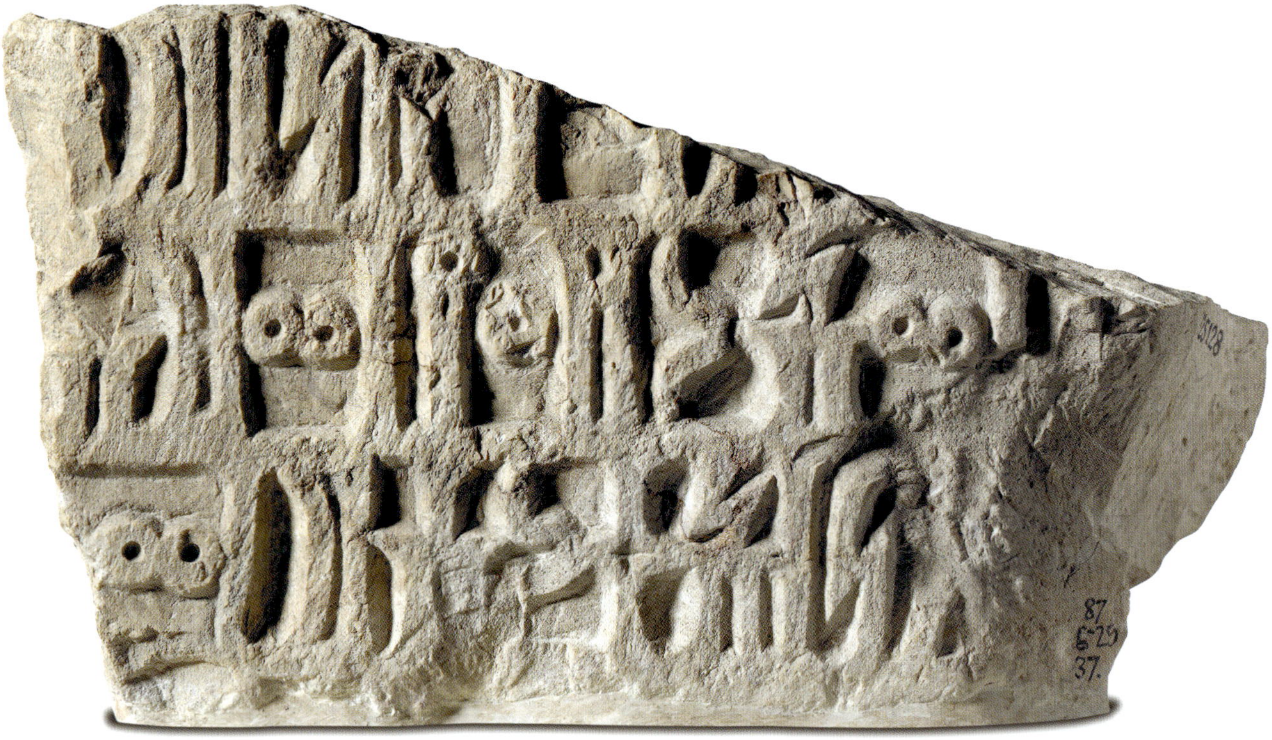

187

Stone fragment with three lines of Sabaean inscription

1st–3rd century AD
Zafar, Yemen; acquired 1887
Stone
H 14.8 cm, W 27 cm, D 9.6 cm
BM 125128

This stone slab fragment bears a three-line Sabaean inscription referring to horses.

188

Basalt boulder showing two horsemen

1st–2nd century AD
Azraq-Asqwafeh ridge (100 miles east of Askar), Jordan; acquired 1931
Brown basalt
H 34 cm, W 36 cm, D 15 cm
BM 122182

The decoration on this boulder was created simply by pecking figures on its smooth, unprepared face, revealing the lighter rock matrix below the natural desert polish. The figures are filled in with cross-hatching. The scene shows two horsemen, one above the other, both facing towards a camel with an exaggerated hump. Both riders are sitting in the middle of their horses' backs, with their legs fully extended and hands in the air. There are three vertical inscriptions written in Safaitic script dedicating the boulder to various deities. Safaitic, an Old North Arabian script, accompanies scenes of rock art in Syria, Jordan, Lebanon and northern Saudi Arabia drawn by the local Bedouin nomads.

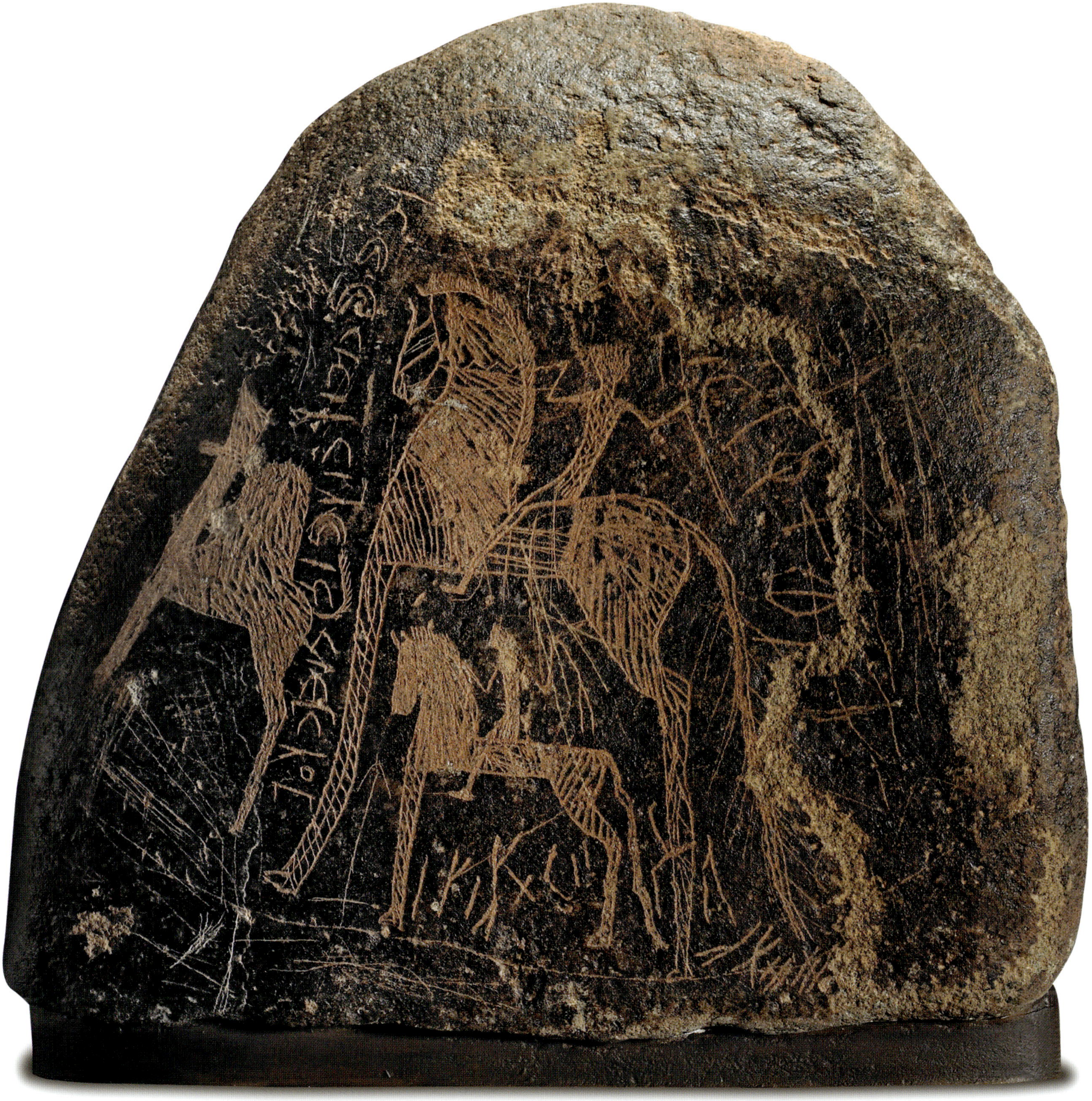

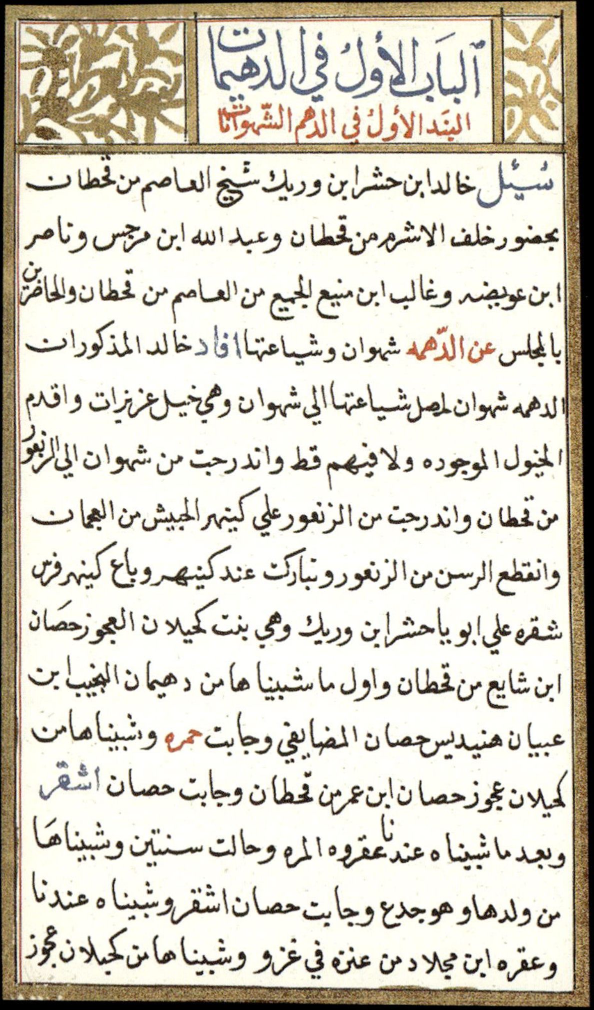
الباب الأول في الدهيمات

البند الأول في الدهم الشهوانات

سُئِل خالد ابن حشر ابن وريك شيخ العاصم من قحطان
بحضور خلف الاشرم من قحطان وعبد الله ابن مرجس وناصر
ابن عوبضه وغالب ابن منيع لجبيع من العاصم من قحطان والحاضرين
بالمجلس عن الدهمه شهوان وشياعتها افاد خالد المذكور ان
الدهمه شهوان لحصل شياعتها الي شهوان وهي خيل عزيزات واقدم
الخيول الموجوده ولا فيهم قط واندرجت من شهوان الي الزنعور
من قحطان واندرجت من الزنعور علي كينهم الجبيش من العجمان
وانقطع الرسن من الزنعور وتباركت عند كينهم وباع كينهم فرس
شقره علي ابو يا حشر ابن وريك وهي بنت كحيلان العجوز حصان
ابن شايع من قحطان واول ما شبيناها من دهيمان النجيب بن
عبيان هنيديس حصان المضايفي وجابت حمره وشبيناها من
كحيلان عجوز حصان ابن عمر من قحطان وجابت حصان اشقر
وبعد ما شبيناه عند عقروه المرء وحالت سنتين وشبيناها
من ولدها وهو جدع وجابت حصان اشقر وشبيناه عندنا
وعقره ابن مجلاد من عنزه في غزو وشبيناها من كحيلان عجوز

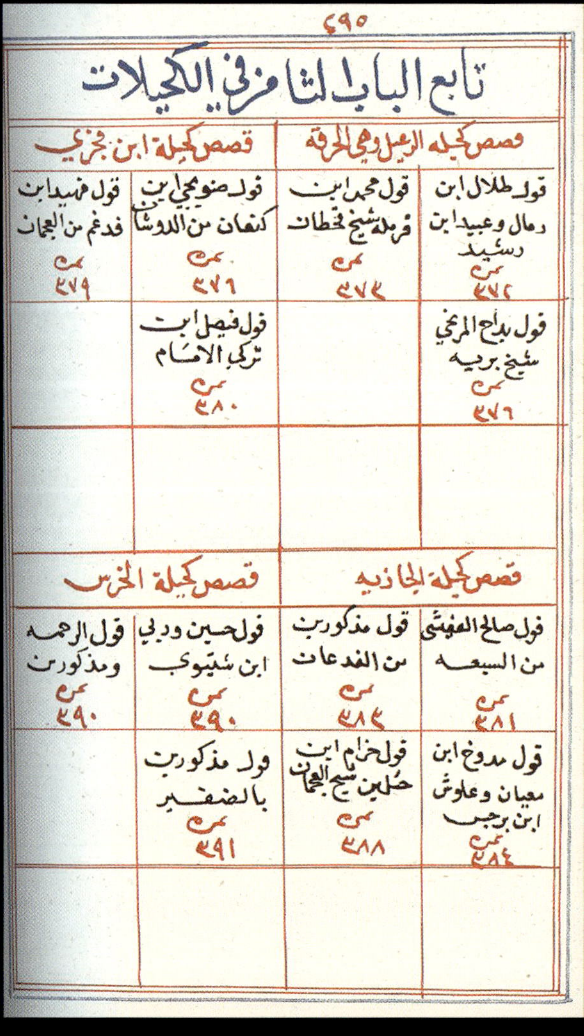
٢٩٥

تابع الباب الثامن في الكحيلات

قصص كحيلة ابن جزري		قصص كحيلة الرعل وهي الحرقه	
قول فهيد ابن فدغم من العجمان ص ٢٧٩	قول صنوبحي ابن كنعان من الدوشان ص ٢٧٦	قول محمد ابن فرمله شيخ قحطان ص ٢٧٢	قول طلال ابن رمال وعبيد ابن رشيد ص ٢٧٢
	قول فيصل ابن تركي الامام ص ٢٨٠		قول بداح المريخي شيخ بريه ص ٢٧٦
قصص كحيلة الخرس		قصص كحيلة الجاذيه	
قول الرحمه ومذكور ابن ص ٢٩٠	قول حسين ودبي ابن شيبوب ص ٢٩٠	قول مذكور ابن من الفدعان ص ٢٨٤	قول صالح العفيشي من السبعه ص ٢٨١
	قول مذكور ابن بالضفير ص ٢٩١	قول خزام ابن حلين شيخ العجمان ص ٢٨٨	قول مدوخ ابن معيان وعلوش ابن برجس ص ٢٨٤

189

Abbas Pasha Manuscript

19th century
Egypt
Manuscript
H 27 cm, W 19.5 cm (closed), W 39 cm (open)
King Abdulaziz Public Library, 2513

This handsome book documents the ancestors of the Arabian breed through horses acquired by Abbas Pasha I, Viceroy of Egypt from 1848–54. Vividly described are the Bedouin tribes who bred the horses, as well as European royalty who concurrently established stud farms from them which endure today. The manuscript itself, narrated in almost biblical prose by the Bedouins to Abbas Pasha's scribes, recounts colourful Arabian horse histories, poetry, tales of blood feuds, raids, hospitality and chivalry. It derives its importance from the historical, literary and geographical information contained in it about the era of the Imam Faysal b. Turki which was collected from the oral reports. Moreover, it is useful for the pedigrees it provides for Arabian horses which left Najd to Egypt, and some of which later made their way to Europe and America.

190

Horse and Horseman

Ahmed Moustafa
1996–8
Mixed oil and acrylic on canvas
H 200 cm, W 162 cm
King Abdulaziz Public Library

Although it bears a superficial resemblance to equestrian portraits in the European tradition, this remarkable painting by Ahmed Moustafa is a unique work of art in a genre invented by the artist. The whole composition consists of Arabic letters derived from literary works which have inspired the artist, including poems in praise of the horse by Imru' al-Qays and Al Muzarrid ibn Dirar and poems in praise of King Abdul Aziz ibn Saud by Abbas Mahmud al-Aqqad and Ibn al-Uthaymin. Although this painting is not intended as a formal portrait, it was inspired by the achievements of King Abdul Aziz ibn Saud who is often regarded as the last person to unite a kingdom on horseback. This culminated in the creation of the State of Saudi Arabia in 1932. In the words of Jeremy Henzell-Thomas who has written a booklet about this painting based on an interview with Ahmed Moustafa, 'This is the portrait not of a historical monarch exulting in his own triumph, but an idealized representation of an archetypal horse and horseman expressing the universal attributes associated with the Arab horse, that aristocrat of horses, and its noble rider, who epitomises manliness (*muru'ah*) and chivalry (*futuwwah*).' The same composition has also been reproduced on a tapestry woven in France.

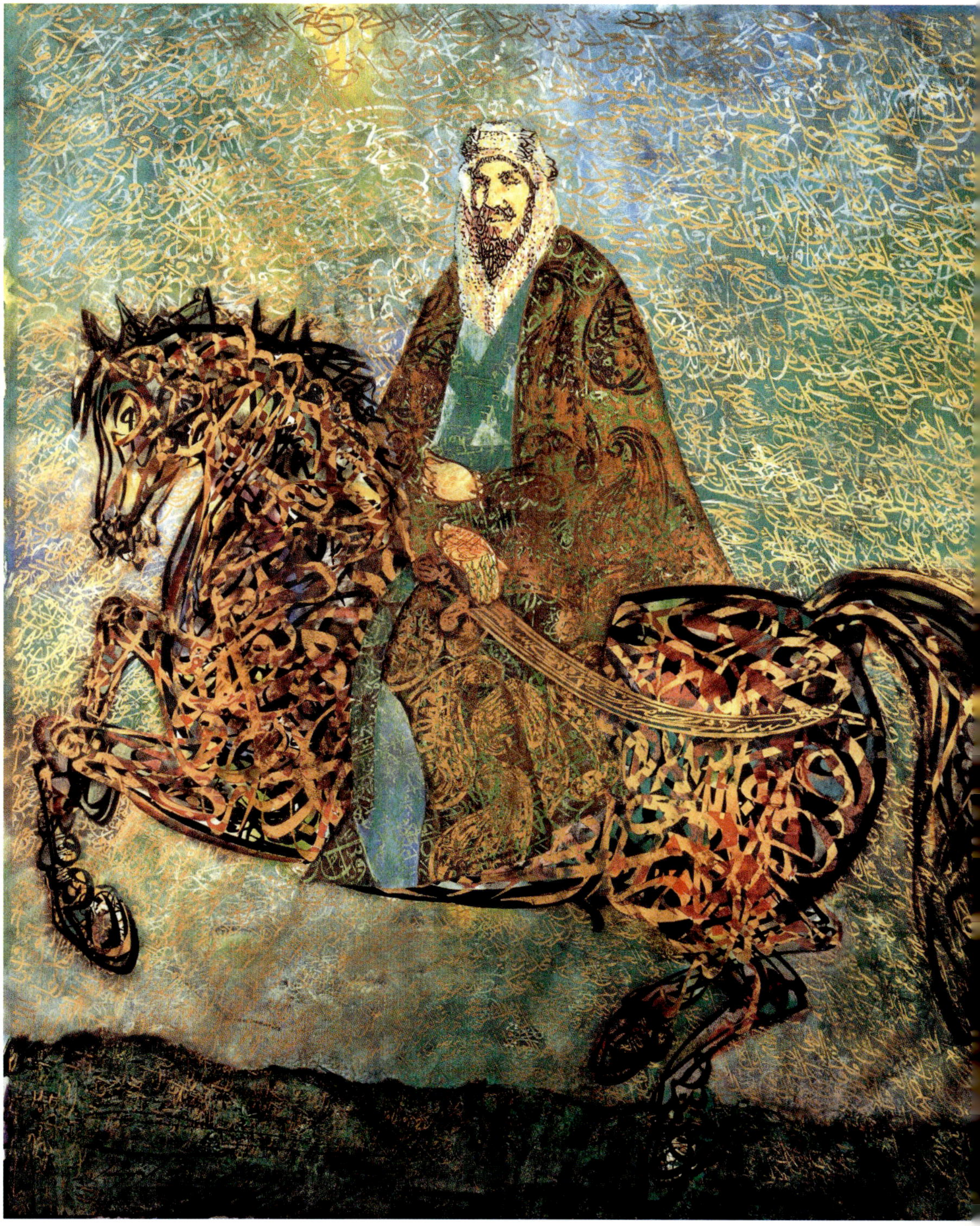

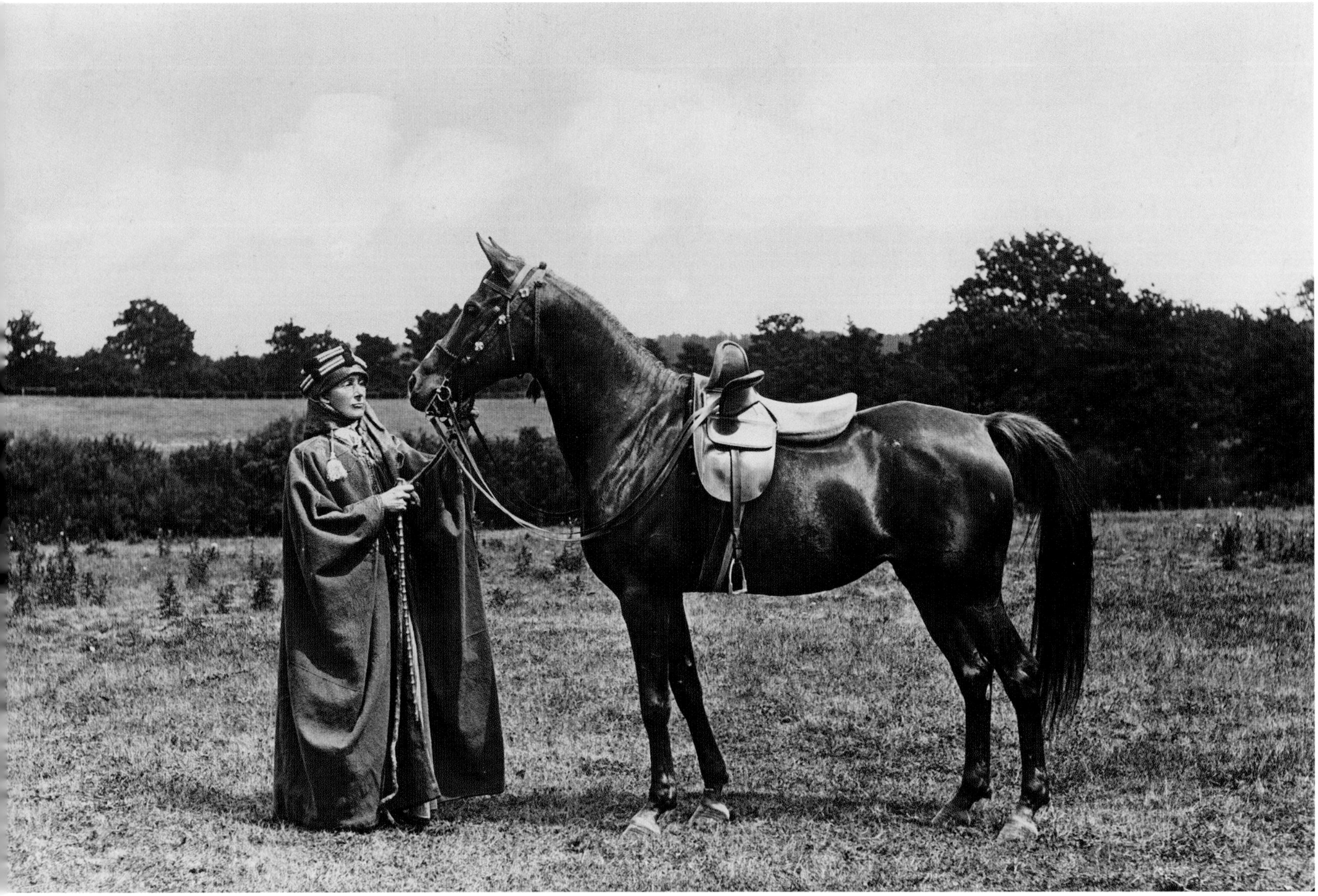

191

Photograph of Lady Anne Blunt

H 11.5 cm, W 17.5 cm
Fitzwilliam Museum, PH 27-2004

In this photograph Lady Anne Blunt is shown in Arabian dress standing at the head of her dark-coloured Arabian mare Kasida at her home, Crabbet Park.

192

Crabbet Park Stud Book

1878–88
Notebook
H 24 cm, W 16 cm, Th. 2.8 cm (closed)
British Library, Wentworth bequest, Add MS 54131

This is the earlier volume of stud notes from Crabbet Park in Sussex, listing in detail the pedigrees, acquisition and disposal of the Arabian horses collected and imported by Lady Anne Blunt and Wilfrid Scawen Blunt from 1878. It was the Blunts' careful documentation of their Arabians, both purchased and bred, and the purchase and retention only of Arabians of exceptional quality, which was to be crucial in establishing the reputation and legacy of Crabbet Park. This unwavering attention to detail was almost certainly one of the key contributions of Lady Anne to the success of Crabbet.

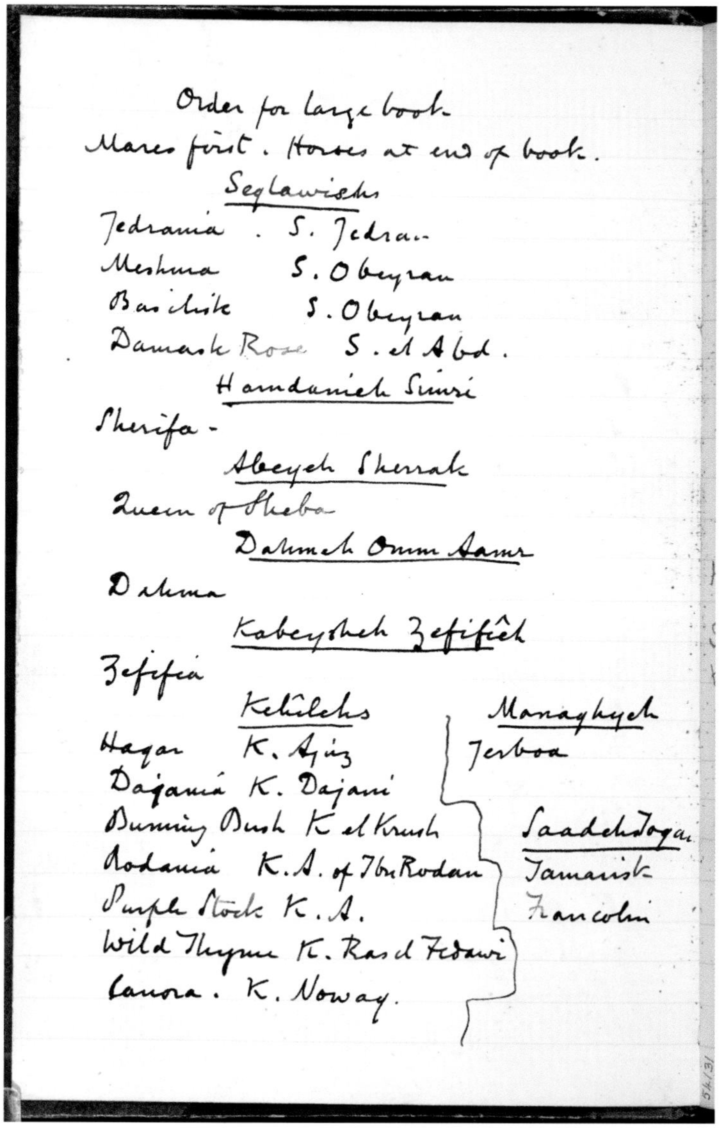
Order for large book
Mares first. Horses at end of book.
Seglawiehs
Jedrania . S. Jedran
Meshura S. Obeyran
Basilisk S. Obeyran
Damask Rose S. el Abd.
Hamdanieh Simri
Sherifa -
Abeyeh Sherrak
Queen of Sheba
Dahmeh Omm Aamr
Dahma
Kabeysheh Zefifieh
Zefifia
Kehilehs — Managhyeh
Hagar K. Ajuz — Jerboa
Dajania K. Dajani
Burning Bush K. el Krush — Saadehtogan
Rodania K.A. of Ibn Rodan — Tamarisk
Purple Stock K.A. — Francolin
Wild Thyme K. Ras el Fedawi
Canora. K. Nowag.
54131

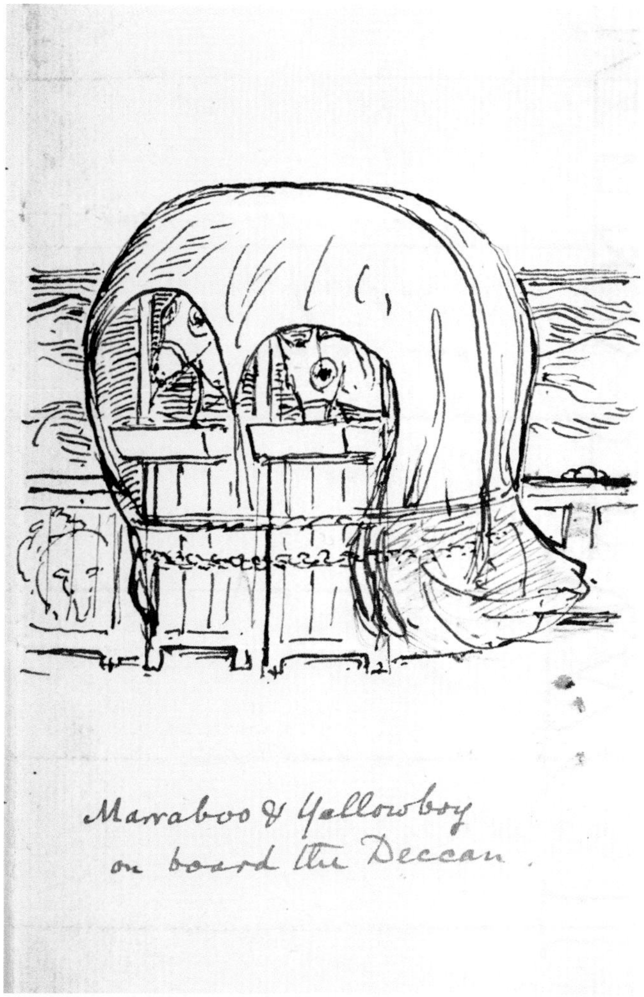

193

Lady Anne Blunt's letter to Judith, 4 January 1877

1877
Ink on paper
H 14.3 cm, W 8.9 cm
British Library, Wentworth bequest, Add MS 54109

In this letter to her only child, her daughter Judith (here called Beebee), Lady Anne describes an eventful and uncomfortable sea voyage with Wilfrid to Gibraltar on board the *Deccan*. Lady Anne wrote to Judith every two or three days composing letters full of amusing incident and enlivened with little sketches. Sometimes there is gentle complaint over the short replies or lack of letters in return, which seems only natural until one realises that Judith was only four in 1877.

This sketch shows the horses the Blunts had brought for the intended riding holiday, Marraboo and Yellowboy, wrapped in blankets in horse boxes stowed next to the livestock on the deck: 'The poor horses are still alive though the captain said that they ought to have been killed. They are each in a box with a great tarpaulin over both.'

194

Lady Anne Blunt's letter to Judith, 17 December 1877

1877
Ink on paper
H 18 cm, W 11.2 cm
British Library, Wentworth bequest, Add MS 54109

In November 1877 the Blunts began their first ambitious journey in the Middle East in search of the purebred Arabian horse. They embarked via Marseilles for Alexandretta and Aleppo on the *Alphee*, ultimately heading for Baghdad since, as Lady Anne explained to Judith, 'people tell us that the best Arab horses are to be got at Baghdad'.

By the 17 December the initial rather vague plans had been modified through discussion with James Henry Skene, the British consul in Aleppo, who planned their route and gave them letters of introduction to the sheikhs of the Anaiza tribes. While explaining her remorse at missing Christmas with Judith, Lady Anne explained that 'Papa has now arranged a plan to go to a place called Deir on the river Euphrates, & to buy some horses there to bring home. The Arabs we want to see at Deir are probably not yet there and we must wait to hear when they are coming & also when it is convenient.'

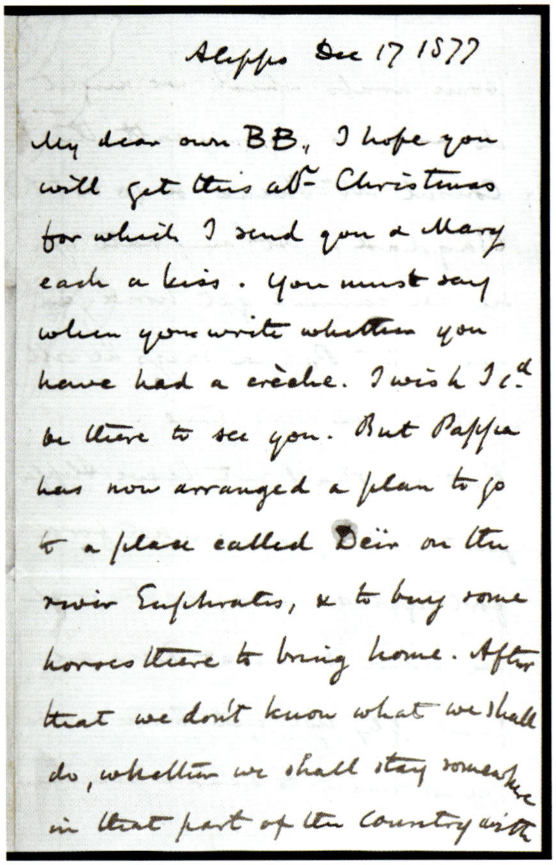

Aleppo Dec 17 1877

My dear own BB, I hope you will get this at Christmas for which I send you & Mary each a kiss. You must say when you write whether you have had a crèche. I wish I c.d be there to see you. But Pappa has now arranged a plan to go to a place called Deir on the river Euphrates, & to buy some horses there to bring home. After that we don't know what we shall do, whether we shall stay somewhere in that part of the country with

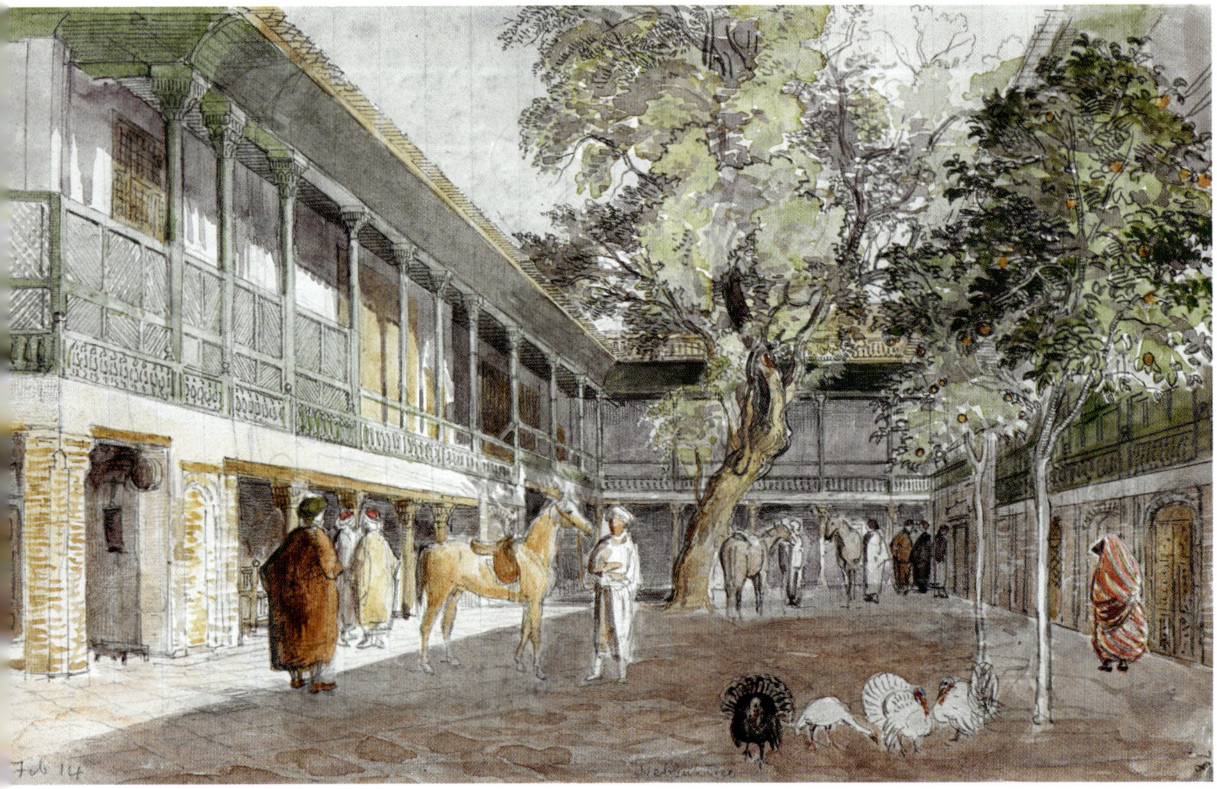

195

Watercolour in Lady Anne Blunt's diary

1878
Watercolour on paper
Diary H 24 cm, W 16 cm, Th. 2.3 cm (closed)
British Library, Wentworth bequest, Add MS 53890

Lady Anne had received instruction in drawing as part of the expected accomplishments of an educated young woman, and in Anne's case it was from Ruskin personally. She illustrated her journals of these travels with expressive watercolours suffused with the light and shade of the Middle East. Here she shows the spacious courtyard of the house of Nawab Ahmed Aga, which the Blunts visited while staying in Baghdad to see his horses.

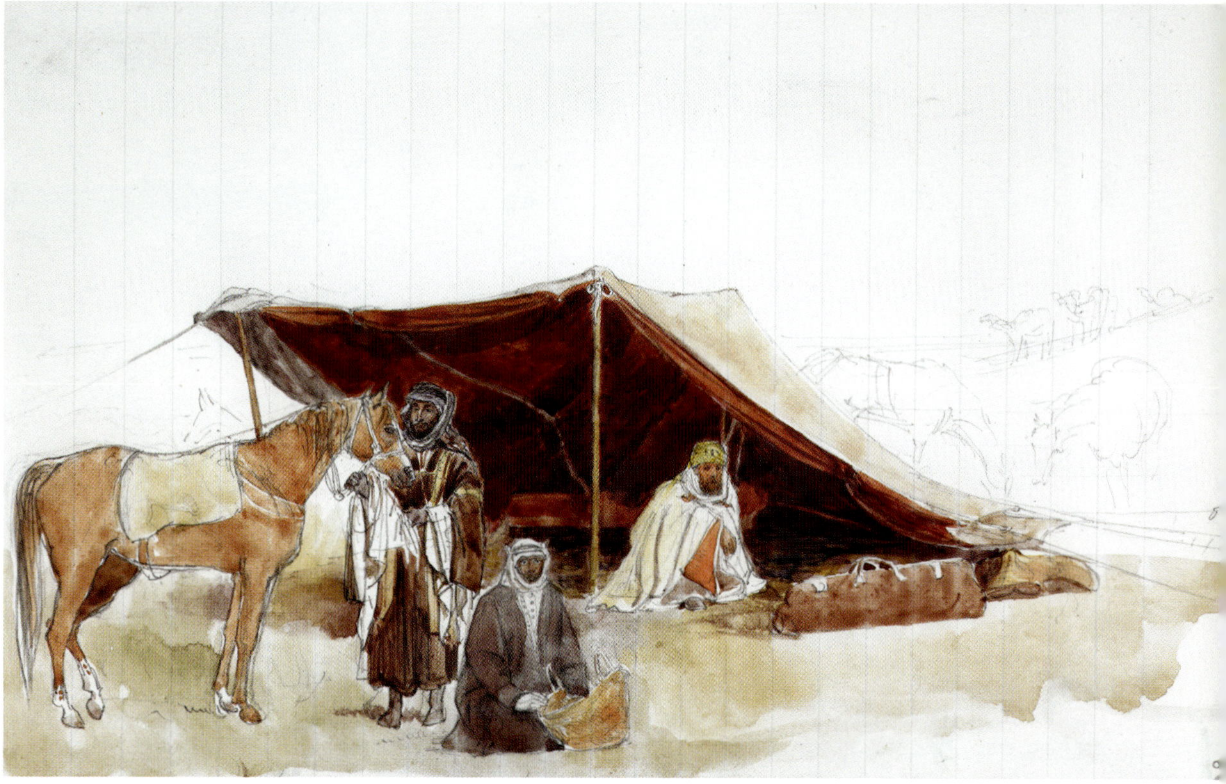

196

Watercolour in Lady Anne Blunt's diary

1878
Watercolour on paper
Diary H 23.8 cm, W 15.6 cm, Th. 2 cm
British Library, Wentworth bequest, Add MS 53893

This scene shows the tent used by the Blunts on their travels. It was specially designed by the Blunts and hand sewn by Lady Anne herself.

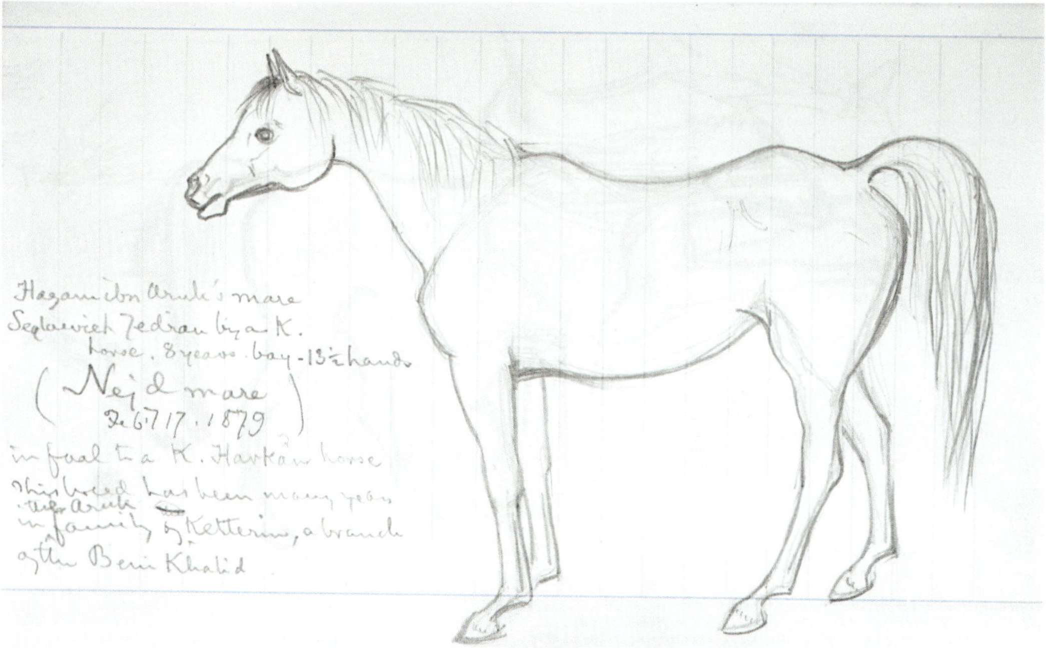

197

Sketch in Lady Anne Blunt's diary

1878–9
Pencil on paper
Diary H 18 cm, W 11.7 cm, Th. 1.6 cm
British Library, Wentworth bequest, Add MS 54076

This was one of the first glimpses the Blunts had of a horse from the Nejd in the heart of Arabia, and so it received special attention in Lady Anne's diary of December 1878 to early February 1829.

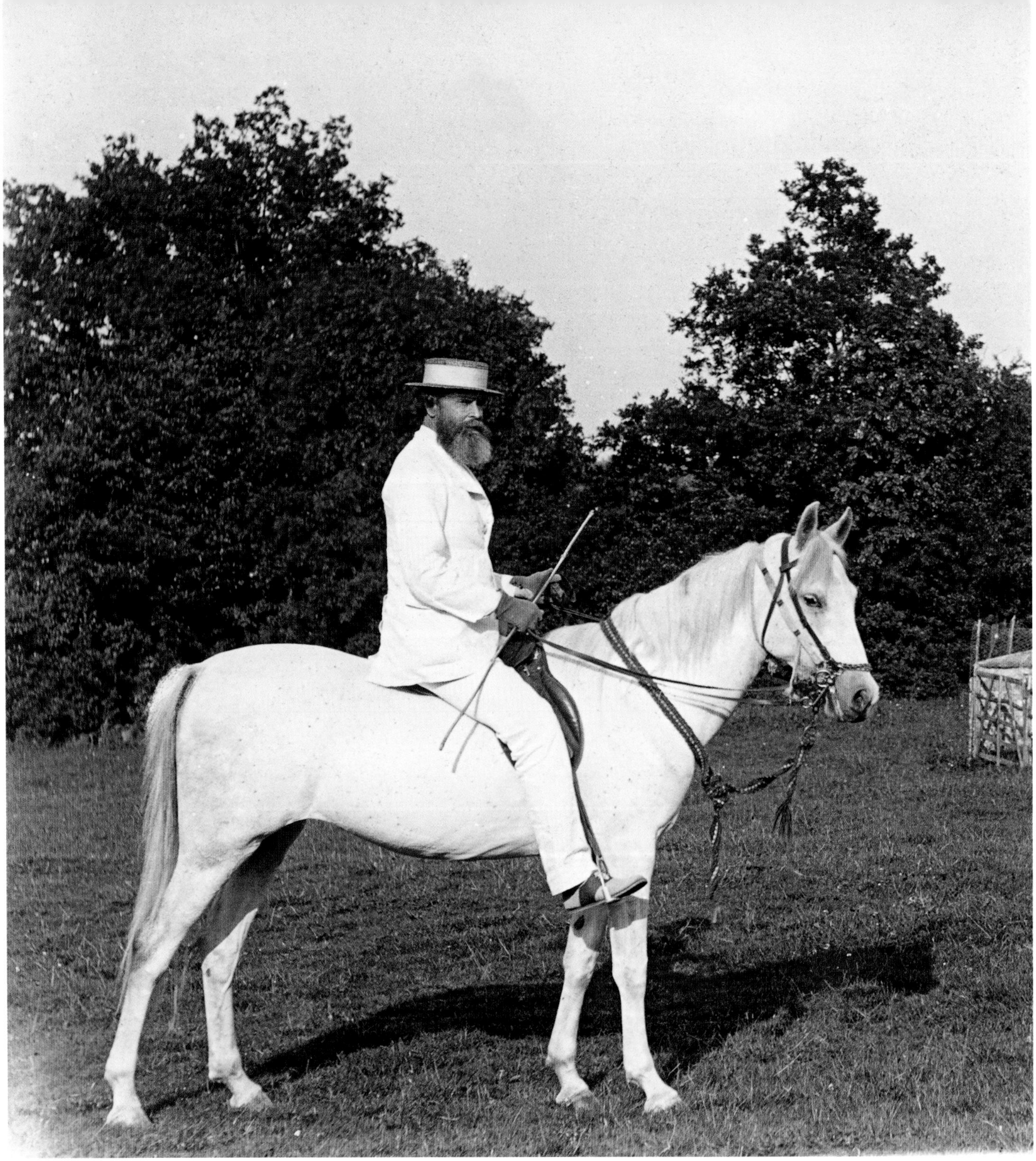

198

Photograph of Wilfrid Scawen Blunt

H 9.5 cm, W 10.5 cm
Fitzwilliam Museum, PH 16-2004

In this photograph Wilfrid Scawen Blunt is shown on the white mare Shieha at Crabbet Park. Sherifa was bought by Skene at Aleppo from 'the executors of the late Sheykh Takha' on the Blunts' behalf in March 1878. Notable for her fine head and her considerable speed and endurance, Sherifa was one of the first Arabian mares imported by the Blunts and a great favourite much missed on her death in 1892.

199

Copy of a print of Crabbet Park

1901
H 23 cm, W 32 cm
Fitzwilliam Museum PH124-2004 (1-2)

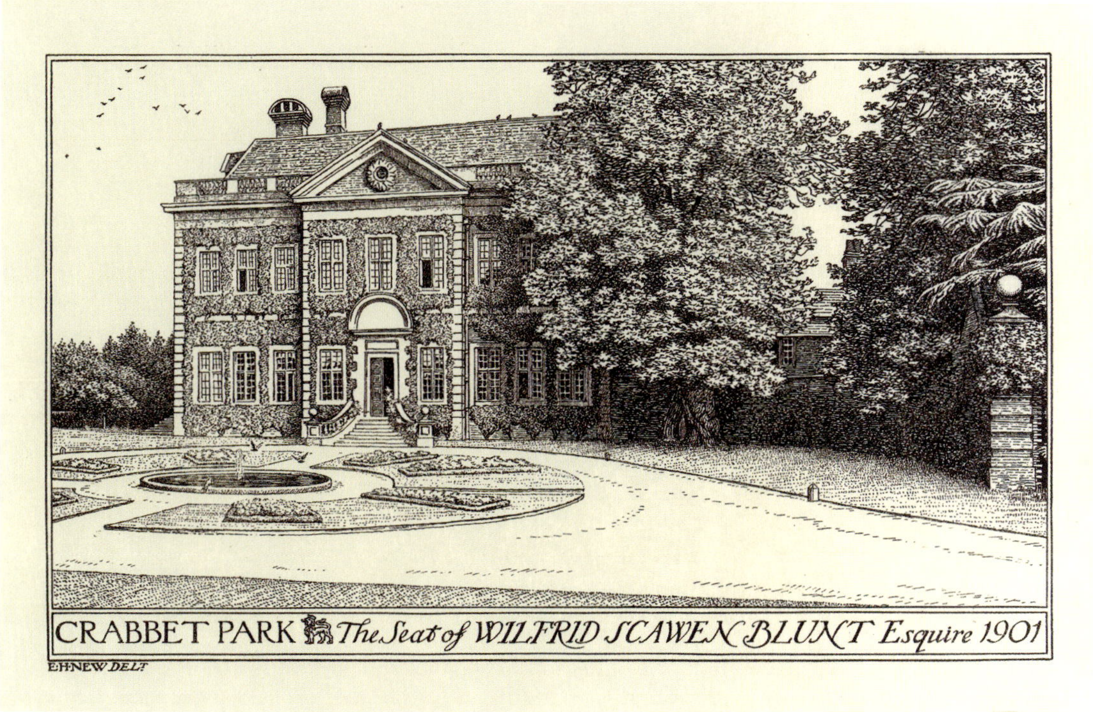

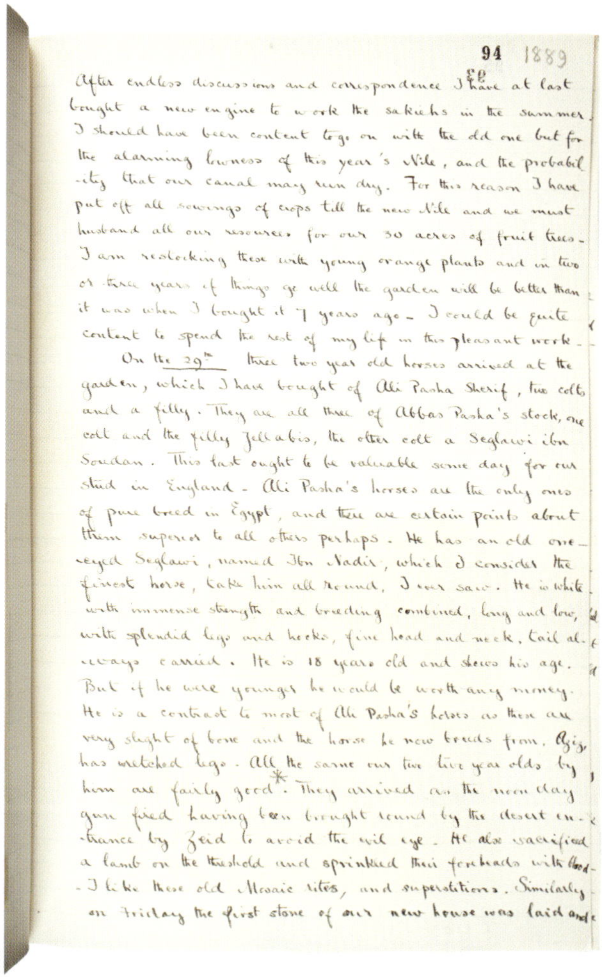

94 1889

After endless discussions and correspondence I have at last bought a new engine to work the sakiehs in the summer. I should have been content to go on with the old one but for the alarming lowness of this year's Nile, and the probability that our canal may run dry. For this reason I have put off all sowings of crops till the new Nile and we must husband all our resources for our 30 acres of fruit trees. I am restocking these with young orange plants and in two or three years if things go well the garden will be better than it was when I bought it 7 years ago. I could be quite content to spend the rest of my life in this pleasant work.

On the 29th three two year old horses arrived at the garden, which I have bought of Ali Pasha Sherif, two colts and a filly. They are all three of Abbas Pasha's stock, one colt and the filly Jellabis, the other colt a Seglawi ibn Soudan. This last ought to be valuable some day for our stud in England. Ali Pasha's horses are the only ones of pure breed in Egypt, and there are certain points about them superior to all others perhaps. He has an old one-eyed Seglawi, named Ibn Nadir, which I consider the finest horse, take him all round, I ever saw. He is white with immense strength and breeding combined, long and low, with splendid legs and hocks, fine head and neck, tail always carried. He is 18 years old and shews his age. But if he were younger he would be worth any money. He is a contrast to most of Ali Pasha's horses as these are very slight of bone and the horse he now breeds from, Aziz, has wretched legs. All the same our two five year olds by him are fairly good*. They arrived on the noon day gun fired having been brought round by the desert entrance by Zeid to avoid the evil eye. He also sacrificed a lamb on the threshold and sprinkled their foreheads with blood. I like these old Mosaic rites, and superstitions. Similarly on Friday the first stone of our new house was laid and

200

Wilfrid Blunt's memoirs

Notebook
Album H 32 cm, W 21 cm (closed)
Fitzwilliam Museum, MS 30-1975

Written in longhand by his secretary, these journals were intended as Wilfrid's memoirs. Their candid revelations concerning his many loves and affairs, written in a sometimes charged and poetic style, coexist with detailed descriptions of places and events, and especially of horses.

'On the 29th three two year old horses arrived at the garden, which I have bought of Ali Pasha Sherif, two colts and a filly. They are all three of Abbas Pasha's stock, one colt and the filly, Jellabis, the other colt a Seglawi ibn Saudan. This last ought to be valuable some day for our stud in England. Ali Pasha's horses are the only ones of pure breed in Egypt, and there are certain points about them superior to all others perhaps. He has an old one-eyed Seglawi named Ibn Nadir, which I consider the finest horse, take him all round, I ever saw. He is white of immense strength and breeding combined, long and low, with splended legs and hocks, fine head and neck, tail always carried. He is 18 years old and shows his age, but if he were younger he would be worth any money.' (Wilfrid Scawen Blunt, *Secret Memoirs*, vol. XIII, p. 94.)

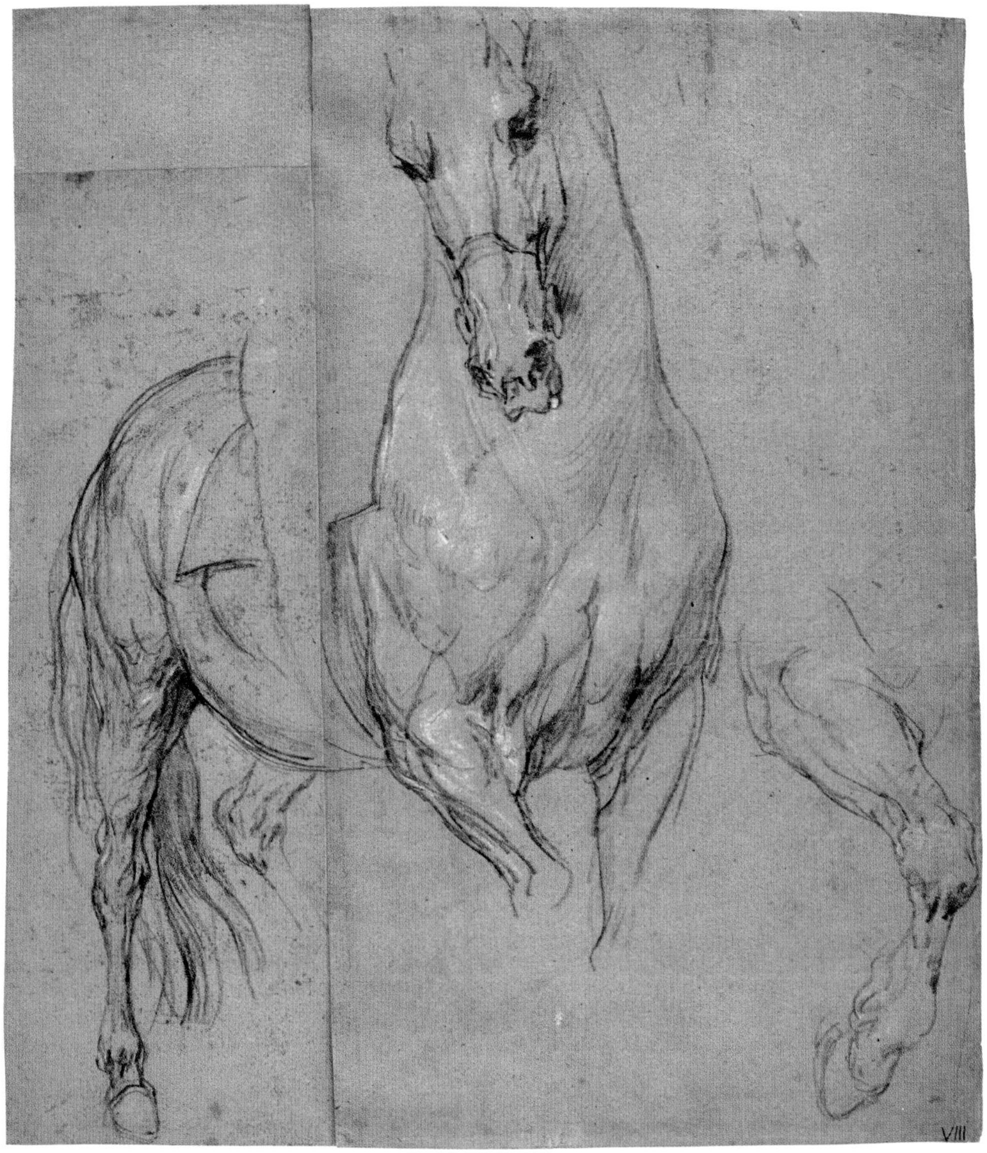

201

Studies of a horse for the portrait painting of Charles I on horseback

Anthony van Dyck (1599–1641)
1633; acquired 1874
Black chalk on blue paper
H 43 cm, W 37 cm
BM 1874,0808.22

Drawn on three overlapping sheets of paper, the horse is shown with the back legs shortened, probably in order to accommodate them on the sheet. A separate study of the foreleg has been included on the right. This study was almost certainly made in connection with the equestrian portrait *Charles I with M. de St Antoine* (see fig. 37) in the Royal Collection, executed in 1633 for the Gallery at St James's Palace. The arrangement of horse and rider advancing towards the spectator derives from the type of equestrian portrait first established by Rubens in his portrait of *The Duke of Lerma* (Prado, Madrid), painted in 1603. The painting would have been seen by Charles on his visit to Spain in 1623 and may have provided the source of inspiration. This type of painting showing a ruler on horseback epitomized the exalted image of royalty at this time.

202

Medal showing Emperor of Byzantium on horseback

1438–42
Ferrara, Italy
Bronze
Diam. 10.3 cm
BM G3,NapM.9

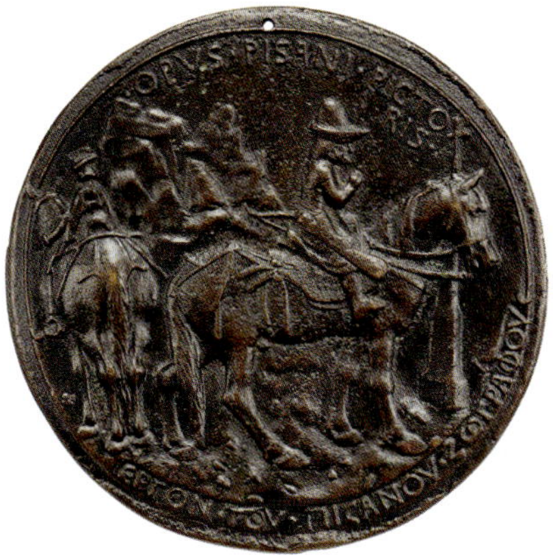

On the reverse of this medal the Emperor of Byzantium is shown on horseback. He wears a hat, has a bow at his left side and a quiver at his right side and he raises his hands as he passes a wayside cross. Behind him is a page on horseback and in the background are some rocks. According to art historical tradition, this is the first true portrait medal of the Renaissance.

The medal commemorates the visit of the Emperor John VIII Palaeologus (1392–1448) to Ferrara in October 1438 at the invitation of Pope Eugenius IV, for the Council intended to unite the Greek and Latin churches. Plague in the city forced the council's removal to Florence in February 1439. The emperor is shown equipped with a bow in the eastern tradition, but riding a powerful western warhorse (which can be compared with the identical mount of Sir John Hawkwood on his monument in Florence by Paolo Uccello of 1436).

203

William Cavendish performing a dressage movement

Abraham van Diepenbeeck (1596–1675)
c. 1657; Sloane bequest 1753
Pen and brown ink with grey wash
H 39.1 cm, W 52.6 cm
BM SL,5236.112

This print shows William Cavendish, first Duke of Newcastle, on horseback performing a dressage movement, 'croupade'. The Duke holds a whip aloft in his right hand, and Bolsover Castle is in the background.

This is the preparatory drawing for the engraved illustration of the same size by Peeter van Lisebetten for the Duke of Newcastle's manual of horsemanship. The manual, 'La methode et invention nouvelle de dresser les chevaux', contains a series of forty-two engravings (plus the frontispiece) illustrating horse dressage. It was published in Antwerp in 1657.

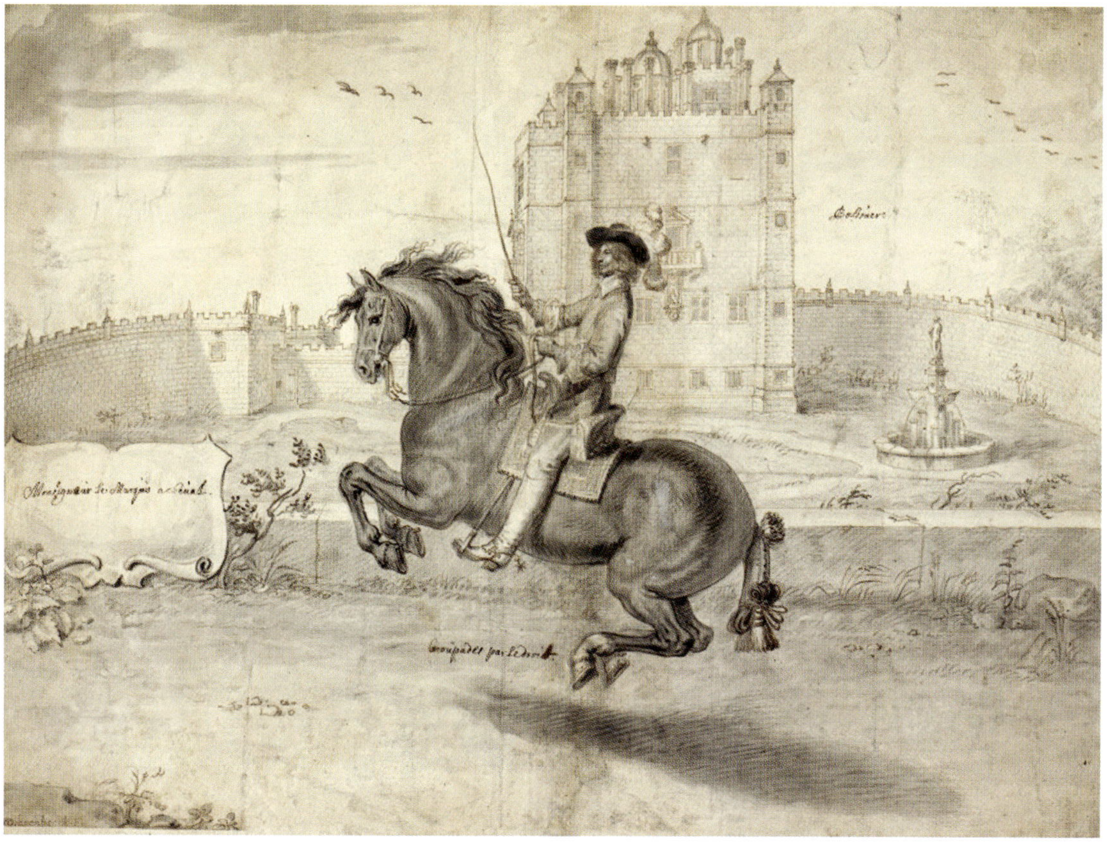

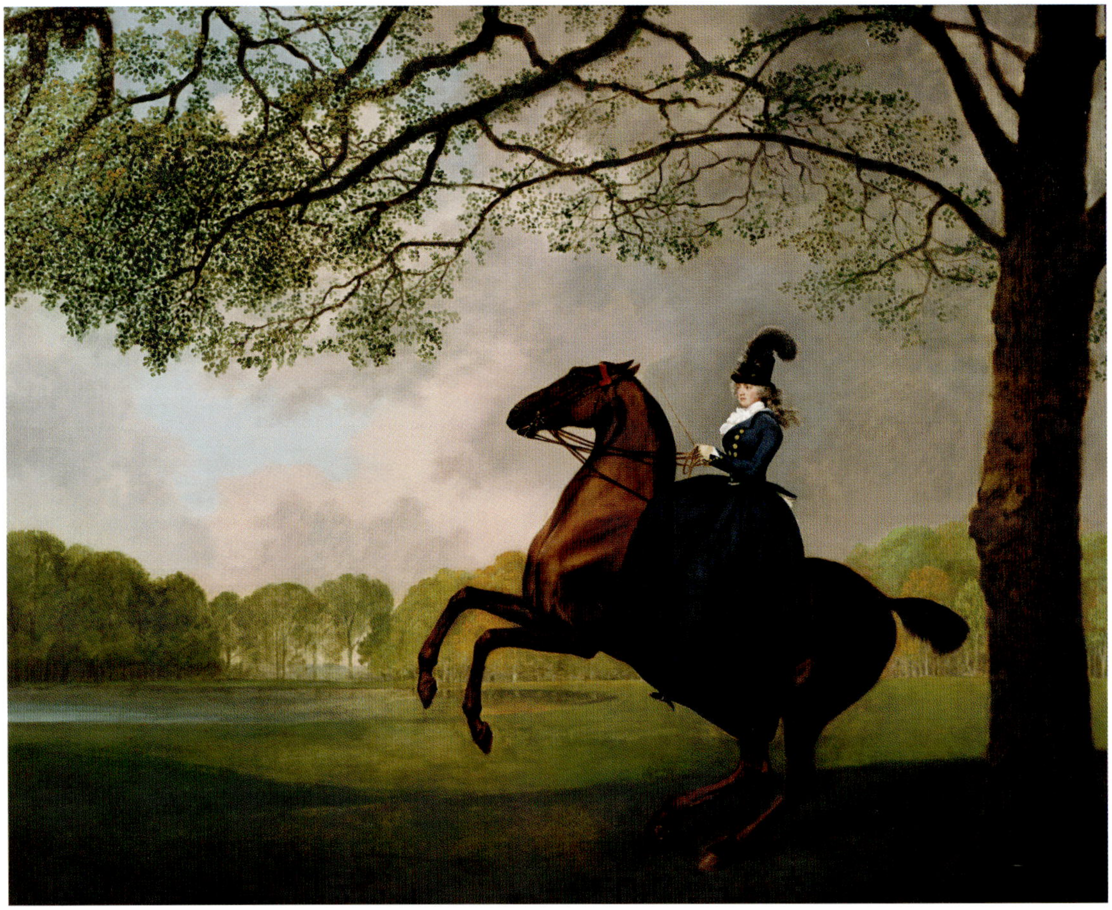

204

Laetitia, Lady Lade

George Stubbs (1724–1806)
1793
Oil on canvas
H 102.5 cm, W 128.2 cm
The Royal Collection, RCIN 400997

Lady Lade (d. 1825) was a woman of humble origins who before her marriage was the mistress of the highwayman 'sixteen string Jack Rann' and of the Duke of York. In 1787 she married Sir John Lade (1759–1838) who was a crony of the Prince Regent (later George IV). Lade was a very wealthy racehorse and stud-farm owner, who was famous for his skill and daring in carriage driving, notably between London and Brighton. His heavy drinking and gambling eventually led him to a debtor's prison. Lady Lade was notorious for her colourful language, and the Prince Regent is alleged to have said of someone that 'he swears like Lady Lade'. Both she and her husband were also painted by Joshua Reynolds.

This portrait by Stubbs was commissioned by the Prince Regent to hang in his chambers. The name of the horse is unknown but probably belonged to Sir John Lade. As he was a racehorse breeder, this could be a Thoroughbred horse.

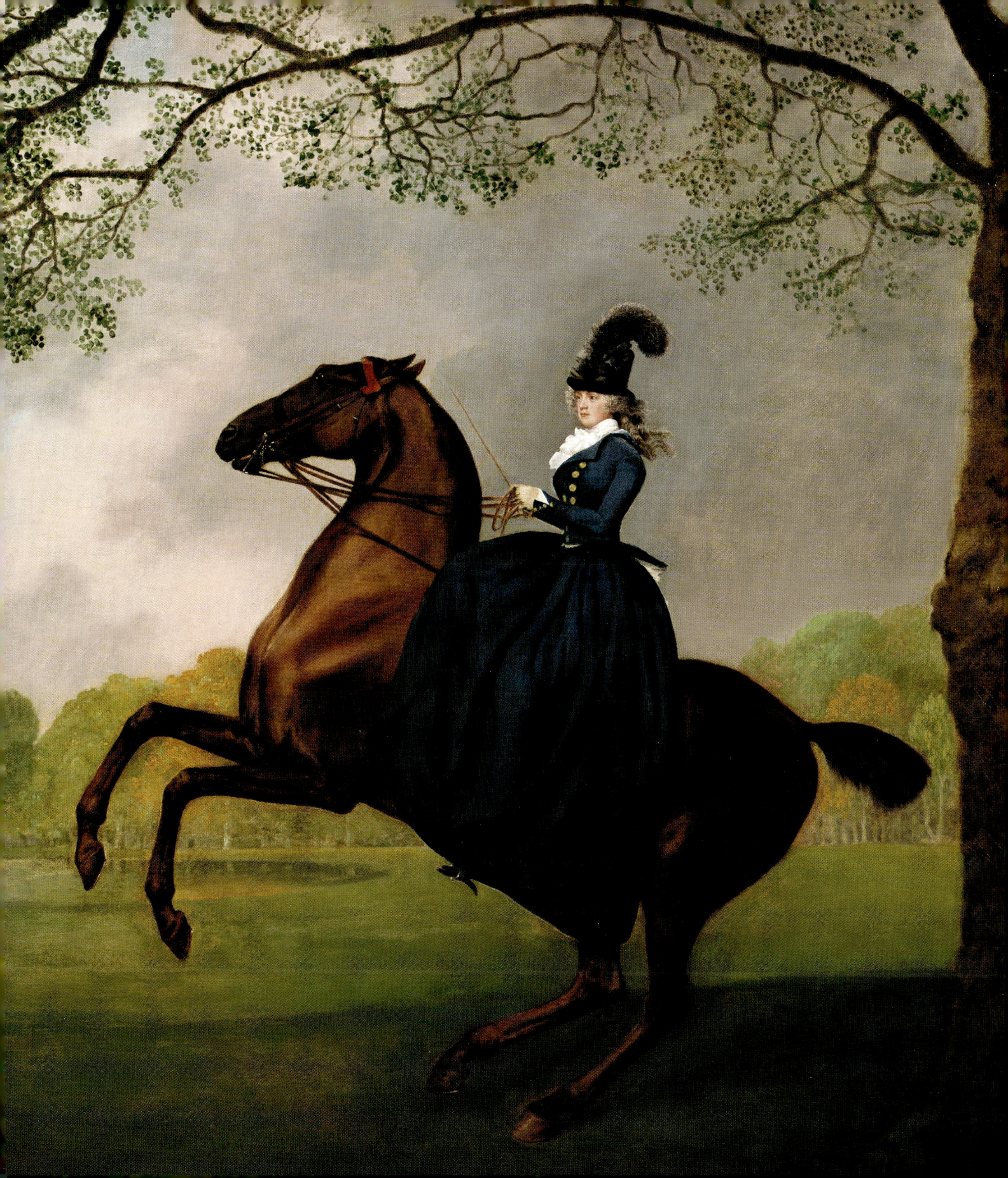

205

Miseries of London

Thomas Rowlandson
1807
Hand-coloured etching with stipple
H 27.5 cm, W 37.1 cm
Collection of Nicholas Knowles

A street-scene based on Beresford's *Miseries of Human Life* (1806), illustrating lines which follow the title of the design: 'In going out to dinner (already too late) your carriage delayed by a jam of coaches – which choak up the whole street and allow you at least an hour or more than you require to sharpen your wits for table talk.'

Coaches are shown in a traffic jam on a busy London street, with a carriage driving to the right, tipping to one side, to the consternation of the passengers, the driver raising his whip against the driver of a carriage travelling in the opposite direction, whose passenger is a buxom woman, leaning out of the window in distress. The spire of St Giles can be seen in the distance on the left. At this time horses were extensively used to pull carriages and cabs in the streets of London.

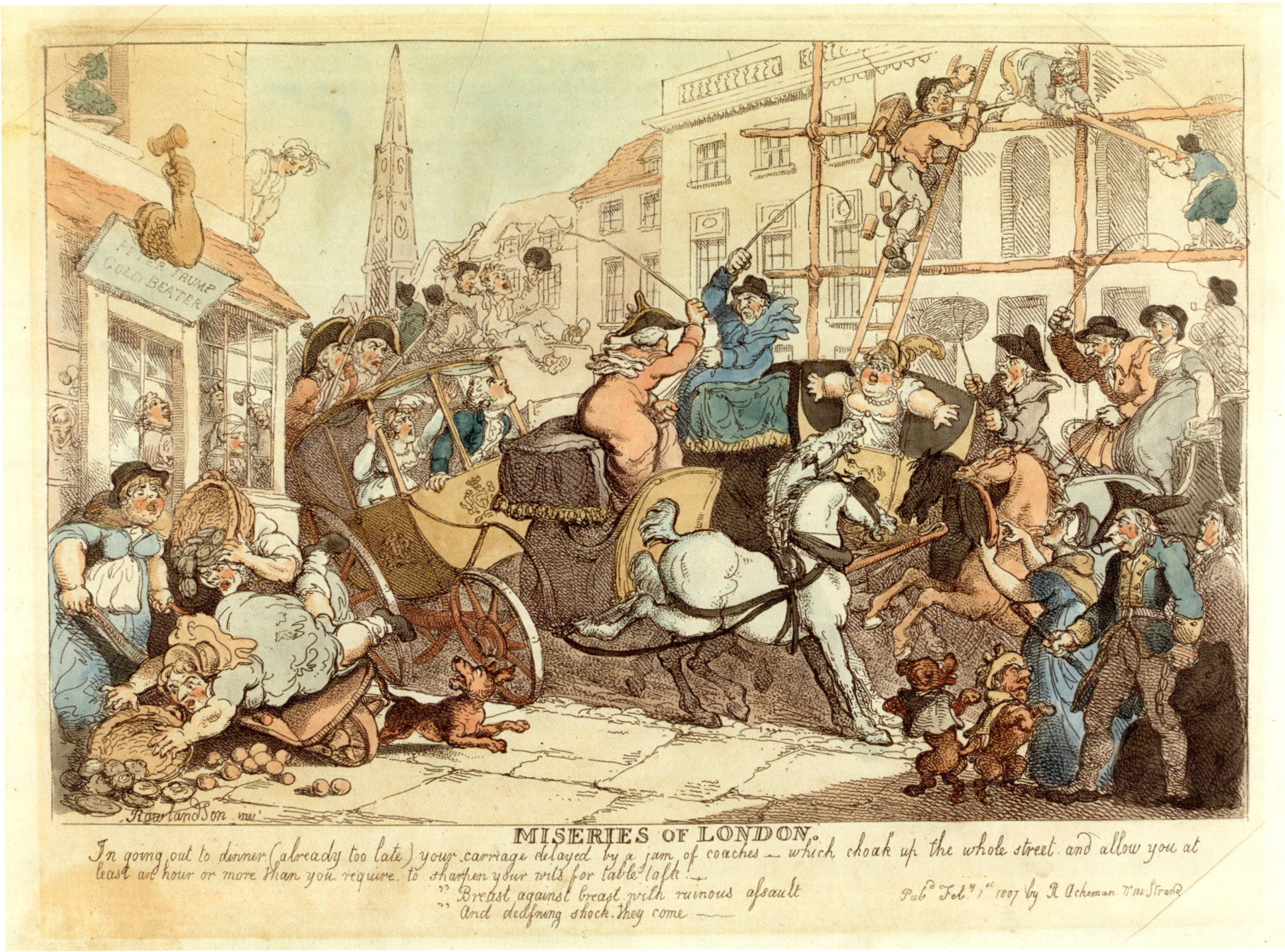

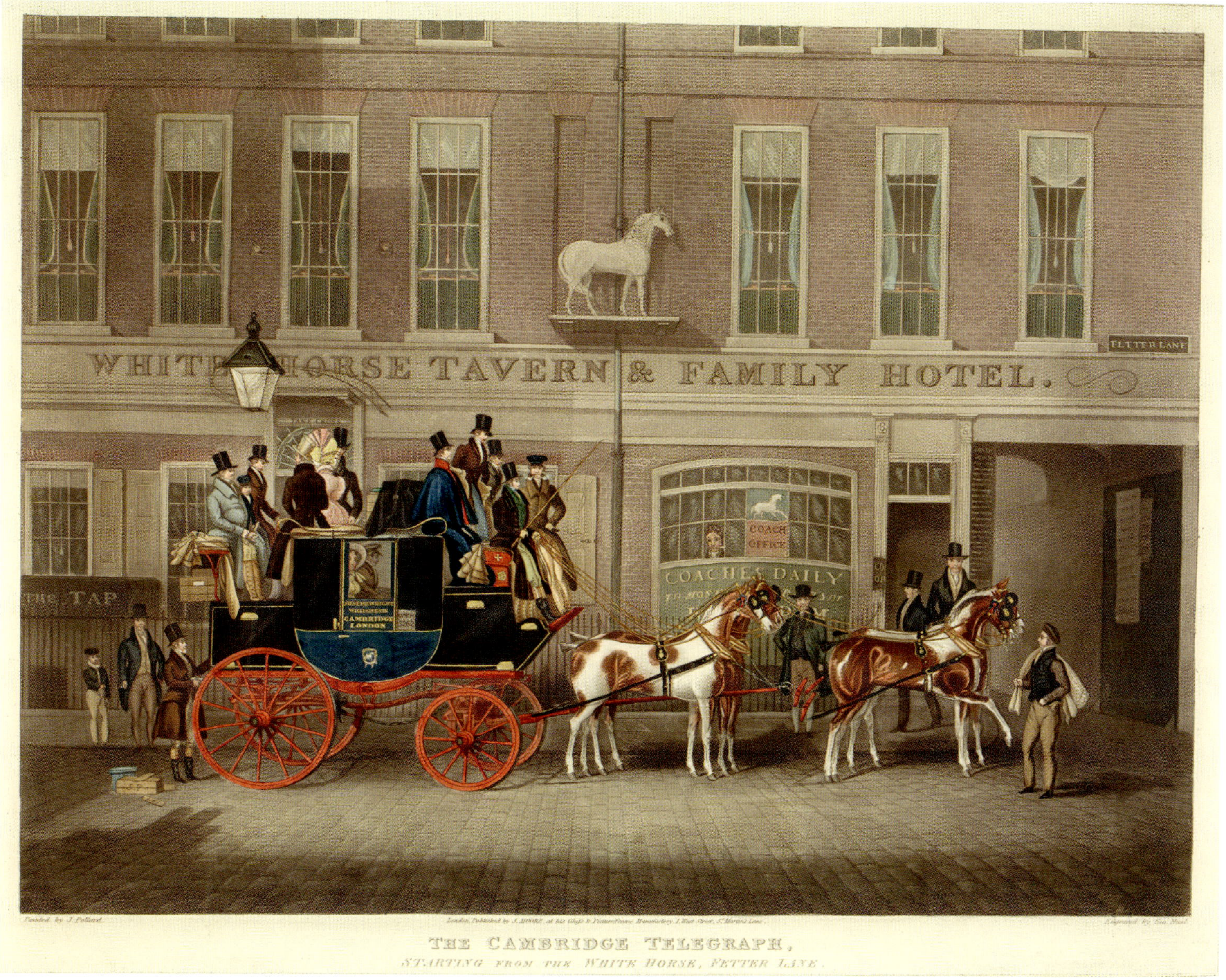

206

The Cambridge Telegraph

George Hunt
1825–36
Hand-coloured aquatint with etching
H 43.6 cm, W 55 cm
BM 1880,1113.4311

A view of the London to Cambridge mail coach about to depart outside the White Horse Tavern at night, with passengers on top and inside the carriage.

Horses were yoked in teams of four to pull mail coaches over long distances. At this time, the journey from London to Cambridge took about five hours. The use of horses for travel and mail delivery was essential until the late 1830s, when the rail network was widely developed, providing faster journey times. The last regular national mail coach delivery was made in 1846, from London to Norwich, via Newmarket.

207

A Representation of the Persians in the Costume of their Country, Attending at Carlton Palace, with portraits of the horses presented to His Majesty by His Excellency the Ambassador from the Emperor of Persia

Henry Bernard Chalon (1770–1849)
1819
Oil on canvas
H 101 cm, W 144 cm
Tate, T02357; presented by Paul Mellon through the British Sporting Art Trust, 1979

Chalon exhibited a picture with this title at the British Institution in 1820. The exhibited picture is likely to have been the more highly finished version signed and dated 1819, reputedly commissioned by George IV (at that time Prince Regent) but not paid for, and subsequently purchased by Major Bower, by whose descendants it was sold at Sotheby's on 17 November 1976. This painting may be either a preliminary version or a replica painted for an unknown admirer of the exhibited picture.

The painting shows eight Arabian horses to be presented to George III by the ambassador of Fath-'Ali Shah of Persia in 1819. The purpose of the mission was to discuss with Lord Castlereagh certain aspects of the Anglo-Persian treaty concluded by Sir Gore Ouseley in Tehran in 1812. During his visit, the Persian Ambassador was taken to Epsom races.

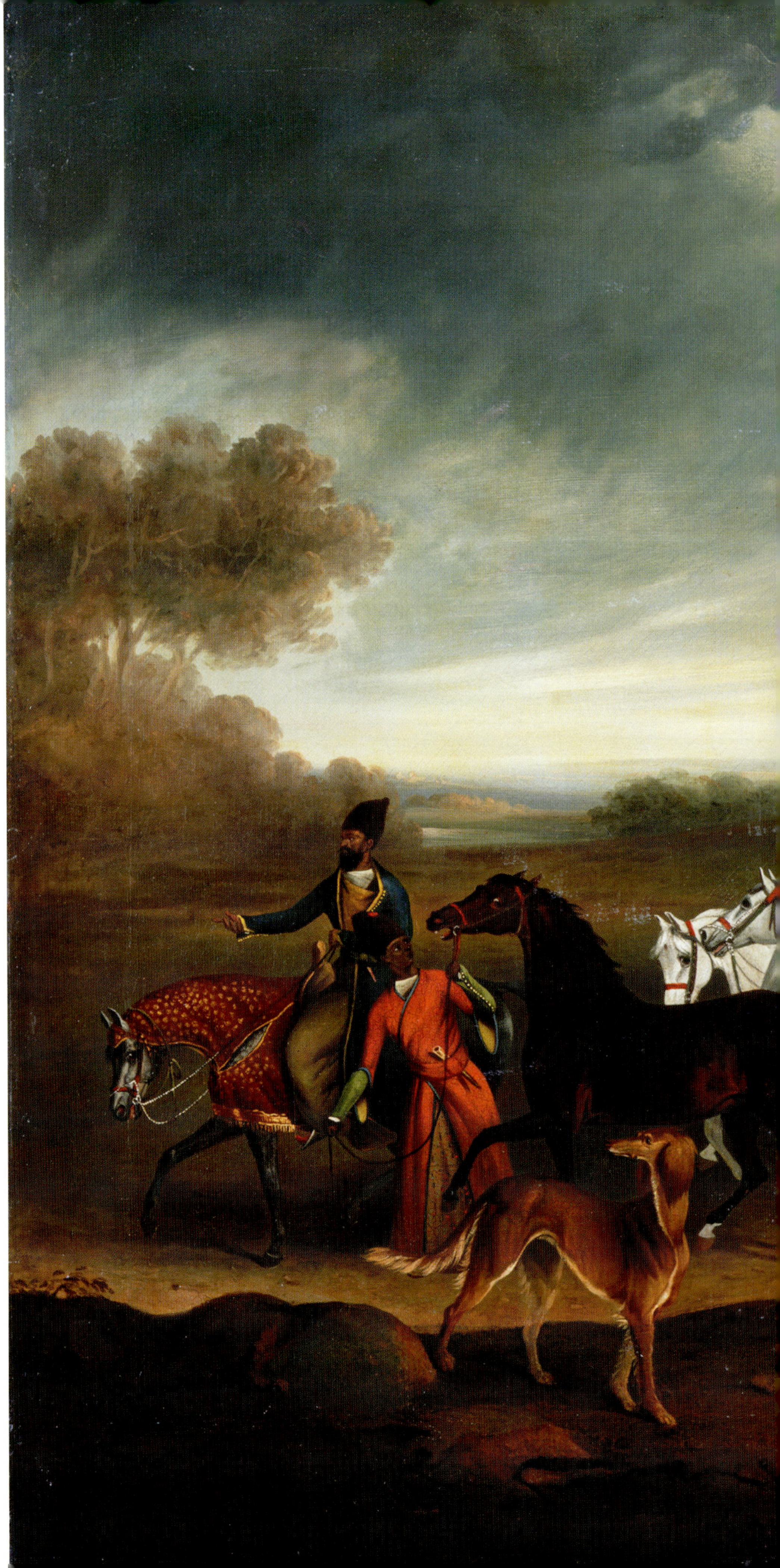

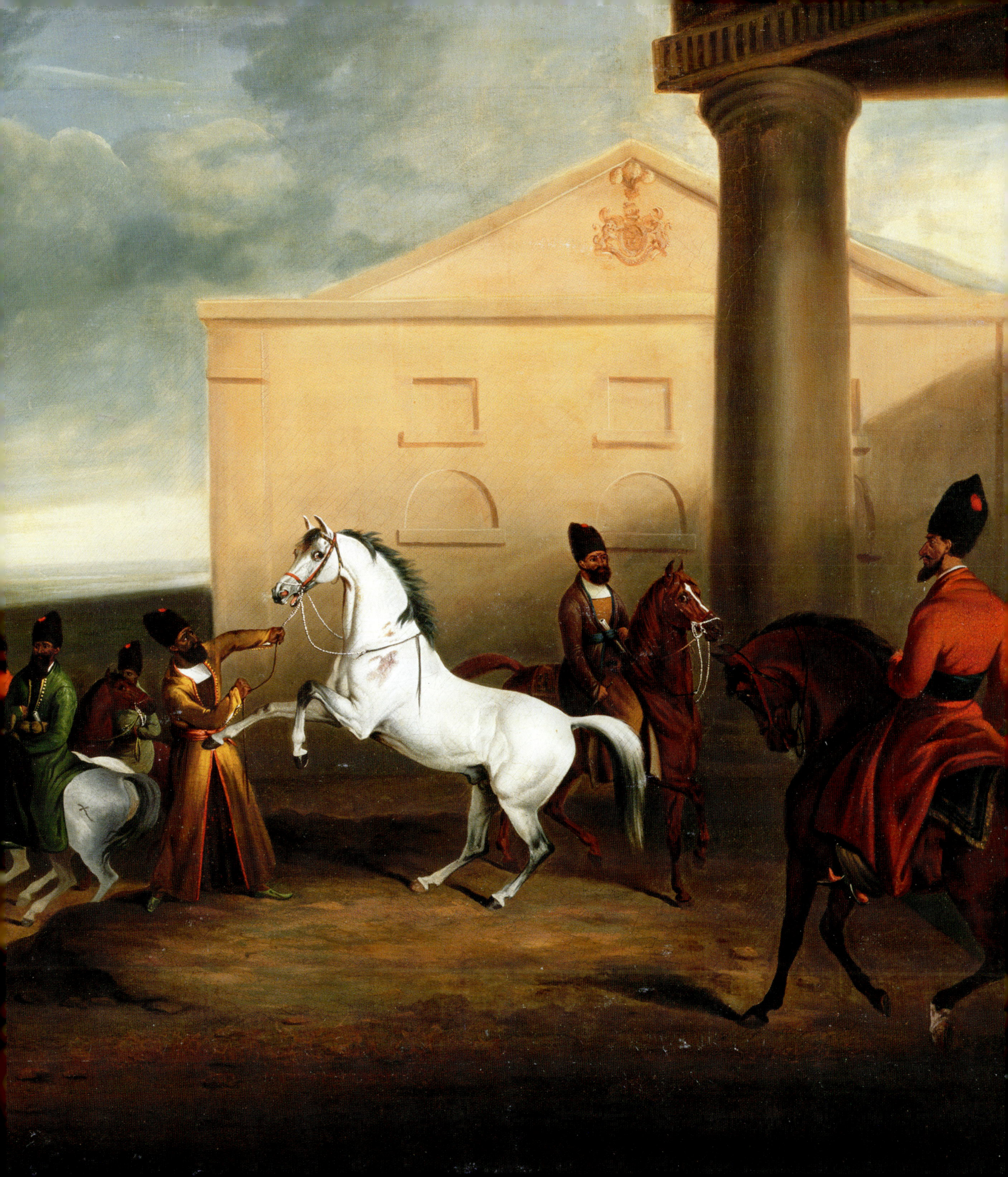

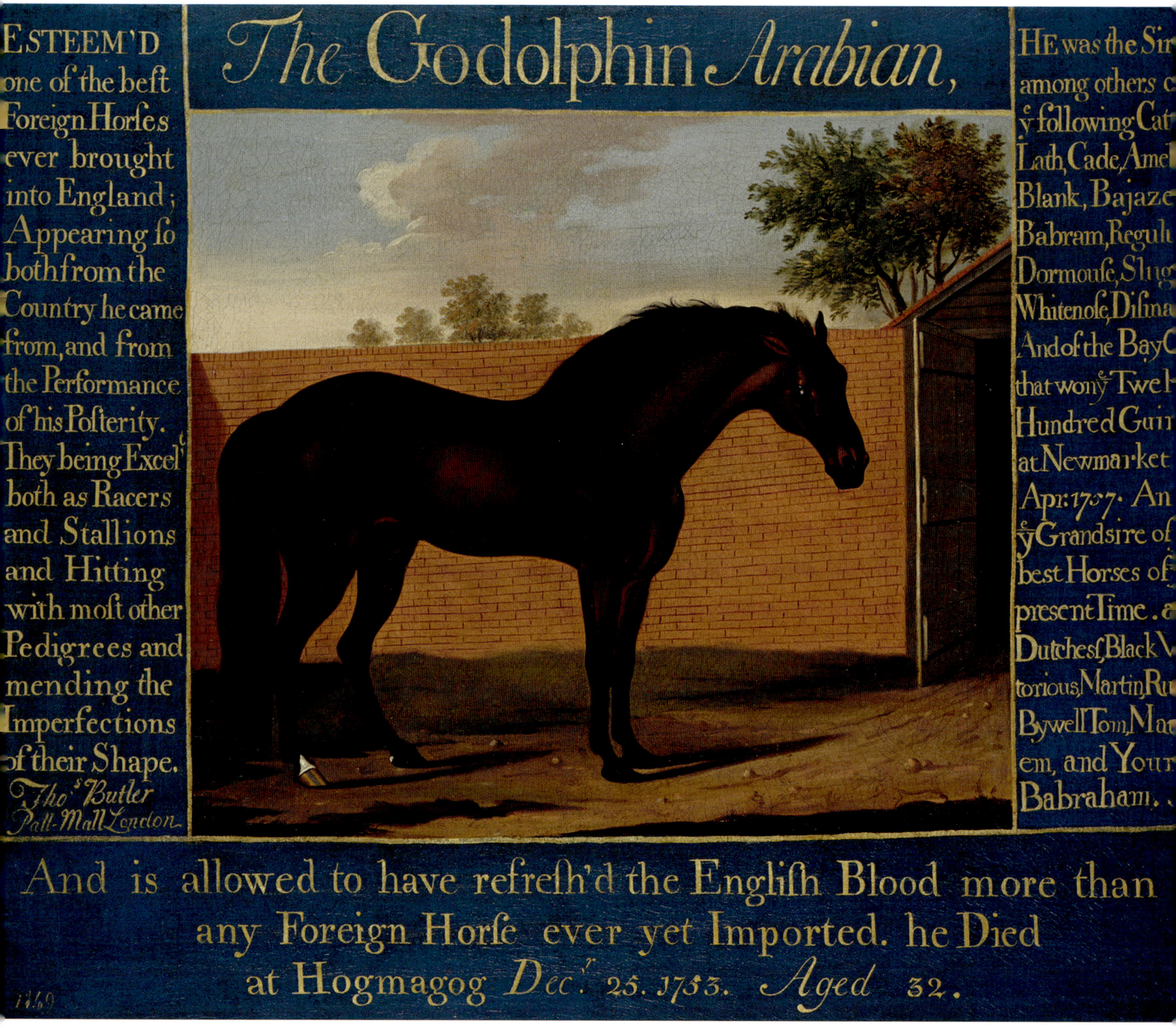
The Godolphin Arabian,
ESTEEM'D one of the beſt Foreign Horſes ever brought into England; Appearing ſo both from the Country he came from, and from the Performance of his Poſterity. They being Excel^t both as Racers and Stallions and Hitting with moſt other Pedigrees and mending the Imperfections of their Shape.
Thos Butler
Pall-Mall London
HE was the Sir
among others o
ye following Cat
Lath, Cade, Ame
Blank, Bajaze
Babram, Reguli
Dormouſe, Slug
Whitenoſe, Diſma
And of the Bay C
that won ye Twel
Hundred Gui
at Newmarket
Apr: 1757. An
ye Grandsire of
best Horses of
present Time. a
Dutcheſs, Black V
torious, Martin, Ru
Bywell Tom, Ma
em, and Your
Babraham.
And is allowed to have refreſh'd the Engliſh Blood more than any Foreign Horſe ever yet Imported. he Died at Hogmagog Decr 25. 1753. Aged 32.

208

The Godolphin Arabian

Thomas Butler (*c.* 1730–*c.* 1760)
c. 1750–5
H 63.6 cm, W 76.4 cm
Oil on canvas
The Royal Collection, RCIN 406001

The Godolphin Arabian was imported from France in 1729 by Edward Coke. After Coke's death in 1733, he was taken to the stud of the 2nd Earl of Godolphin at Babraham, Cambridgeshire, where he remained until his death in 1753. Most known portraits of the Godolphin Arabian were painted after the death of the horse.

This painting by Butler is inscribed:

ESTEEM'D/one of the
best/Foreign Horses/ever brought/into England;/Appearing so/both from
the/Country he came/from, and from/the Performance/of his Posterity./They being Excel'nt/both as Racers/and Stallions/and Hitting/with most other/Pedigrees, and/mending the/Imperfections/of their Shape./
He was the Sire/among others of/ye following
Cattle./ Lath, Cade, Amelia,/ Blank, Bajazet,/Babram, Regulus/Dormouse, Slugg,/Whitenose, Dismal./And of the Bay Colt/ that won ye Twelve/Hunderd Guin's./at Newmarket/Apr. 1757. And/ ye Grandsire of ye/ best Horses of ye/ present Time. As/ Dutchess, Black Vic-/torious, Martin, Ruby, Bywell Tom, Matchem, and Young Babraham./
And is allowed to have refresh'd the English Blood more than/any Foreign Horse ever yet Imported. He Died/at Hogmagog Dec'r. 25. 1753. Aged 32.

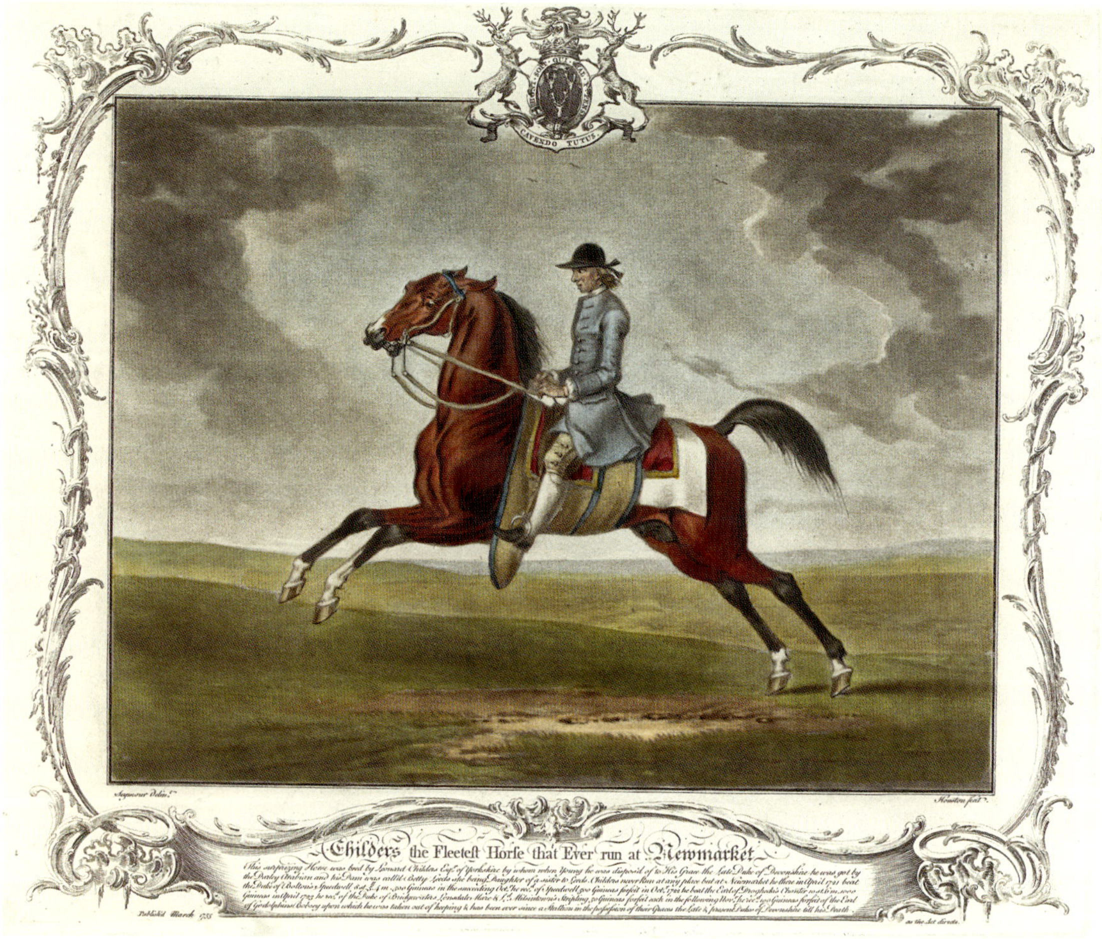

209

Childers the Fleetest Horse that Ever run at Newmarket

Richard Houston (*c.* 1721–1775), after James Seymour (1702–1752)
1756; acquired 2010, with assistance of NHMF, Friends of the BM, the Art Fund, Mrs Charles Wrightsman, the Michael Marks Charitable Trust and individual donors
Hand-coloured mezzotint and etching
H 30.2 cm, W 35.2 cm
BM 2010,7081.2369

Flying Childers, after whom the Flying Childers Stakes at Doncaster are named, was sired by the famous Darley Arabian, one of the three founding sires of the Thoroughbred breed. He is widely considered the first truly great racehorse in Thoroughbred history. He came to the races at the age of six, competing in three races in 1721, and winning all of them. The first was on 26 April, at Newmarket, the second was also at Newmarket in October, where he scared off all comers and won in a walkover. In the third race, he defeated Almanzor, also sired by the Darley Arabian, and Brown Betty, in a three-horse match.

His owner, the Duke of Devonshire, was given many offers for the horse, including one reportedly of the horse's weight in gold crowns, which was refused. He retired unbeaten, and died in 1741, aged twenty-six.

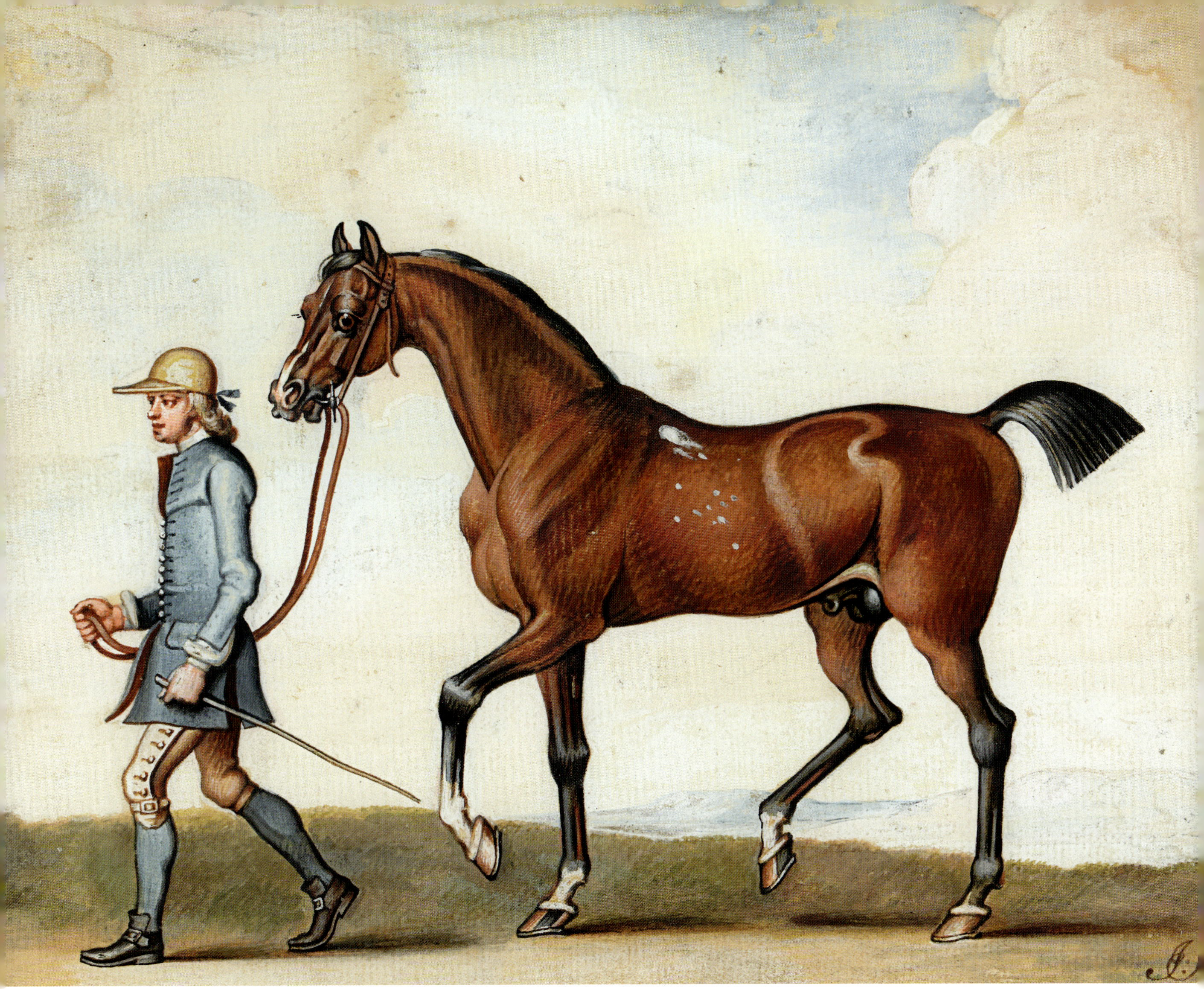

210

Flying Childers with a groom

James Seymour (1702–1752)
n.d.
Watercolour
H 13.3 cm, W 17 cm
BM 1881,0611.186

A bay horse is being led by a groom who wears a buff cap, light-blue coat, buff breeches and blue stockings. This horse has been previously identified as possibly a son of the famous Flying Childers, owing to its colourings, but it is more likely to be Flying Childers himself. His distinctive white spots on his withers, narrow stripe, pastern, stocking and two socks are clearly shown here, and he looks similar to other portraits of the famous racehorse (such as cat. 209).

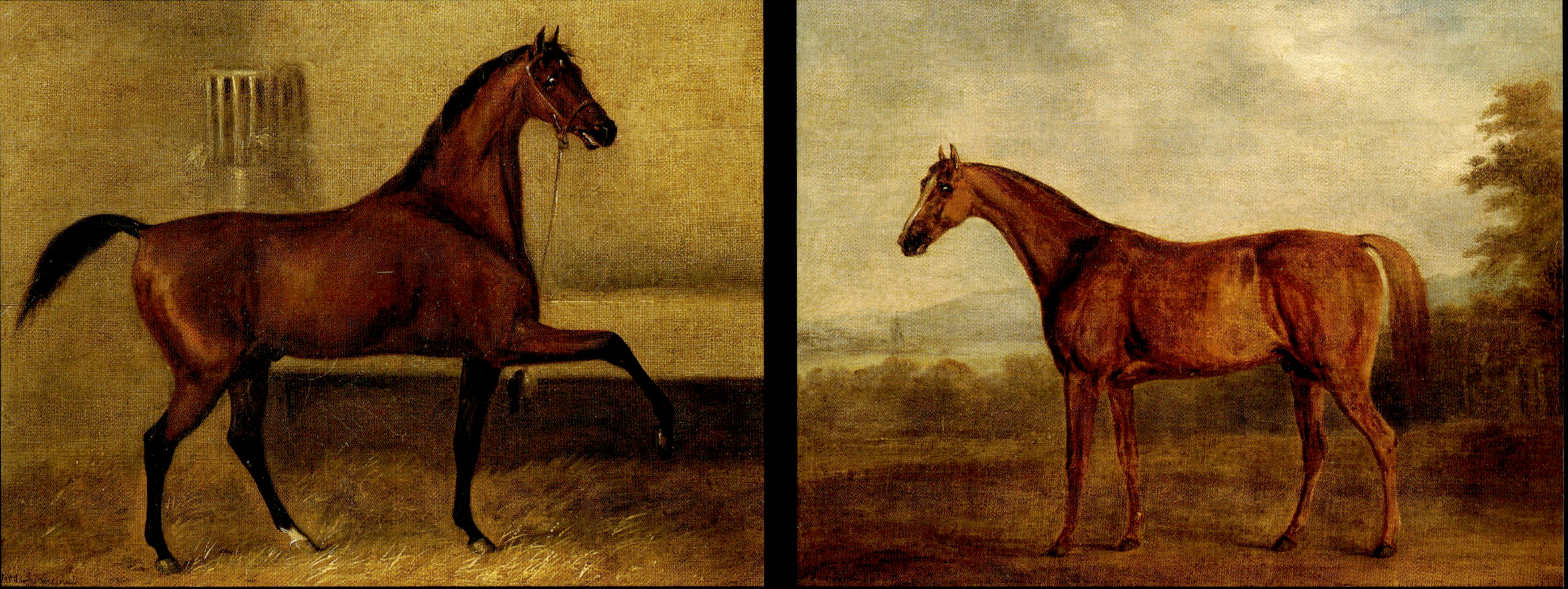

211

Portraits of Herod, Pot-8-os, Flying Childers and Grosvenor's Arabian

John N. Sartorius (1759–1828)
n.d.
Oil on canvas
H 30 cm, W 115 cm
Mrs A.A. Edmunds, on loan to the National Horseracing Museum

These four portraits of famous early racehorses have been mounted together in a horizontal frame. A prolific portraitist of horses who specialized in paintings of racing and hunting, John N. Sartorius was the son, grandson and brother of artists. Portraits of celebrity horses, like these, were of course unlikely to be from the life, but the best of Sartorius's horses can show more

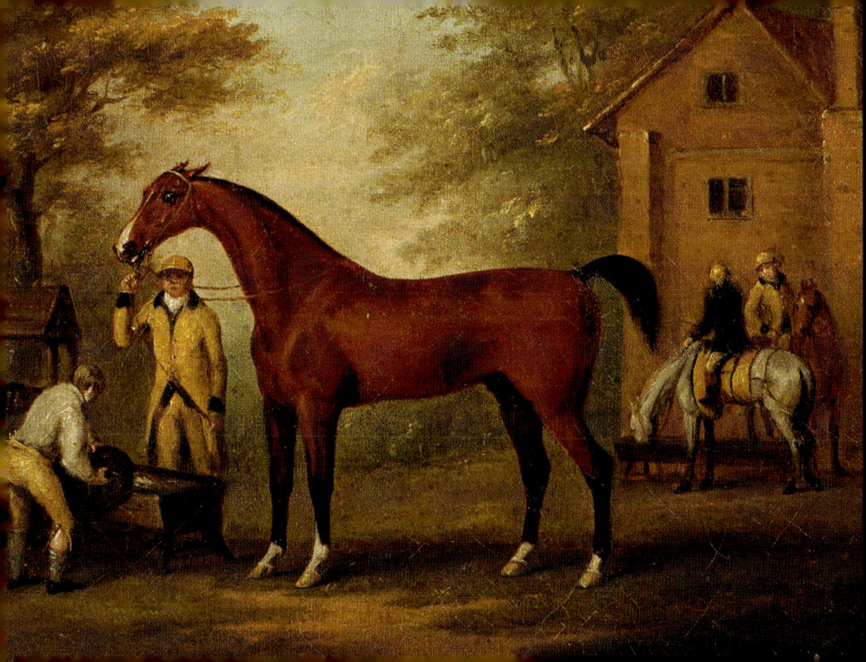

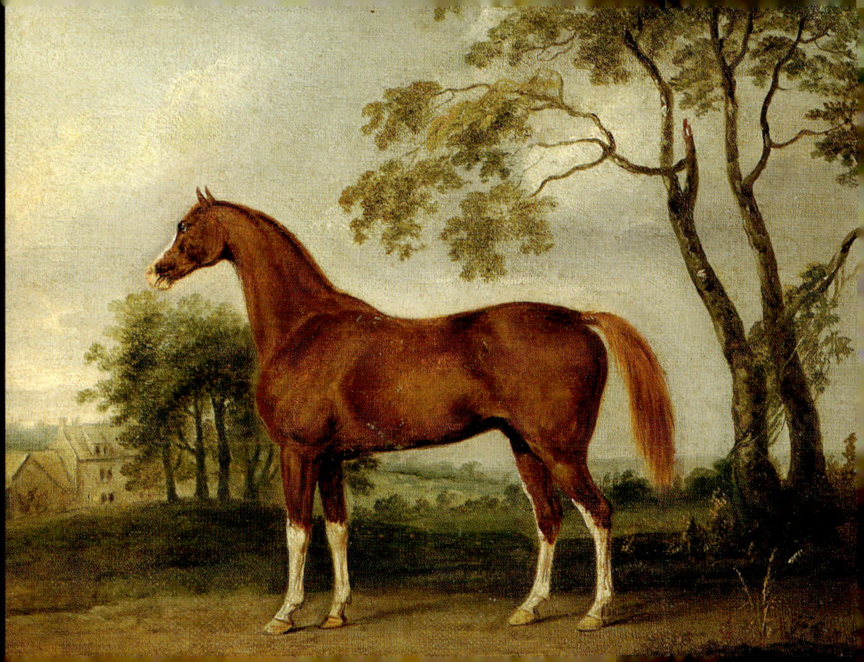

212

Eclipse

John N. Sartorius (1759–1828)
1790
Oil on canvas
H 71 cm, W 92 cm
Jockey Club Estates

This portrait was painted a year after the death of Eclipse, probably based on a drawing by Francis Sartorius, the artist's father. Eclipse (1764–1789) was an undefeated Thoroughbred racehorse who was also distinguished as a sire. He is sometimes referred to as the greatest horse ever to appear on British turf.

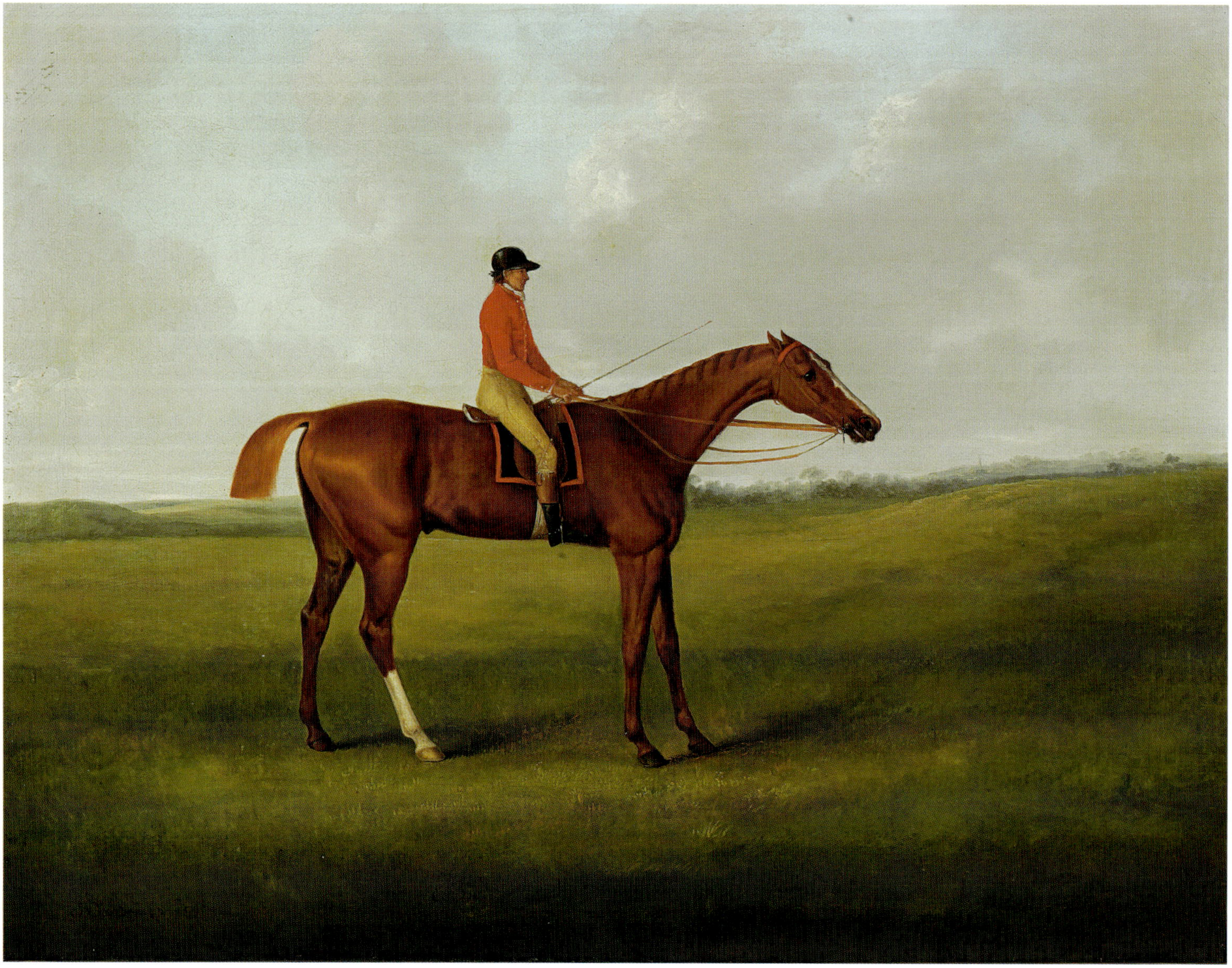

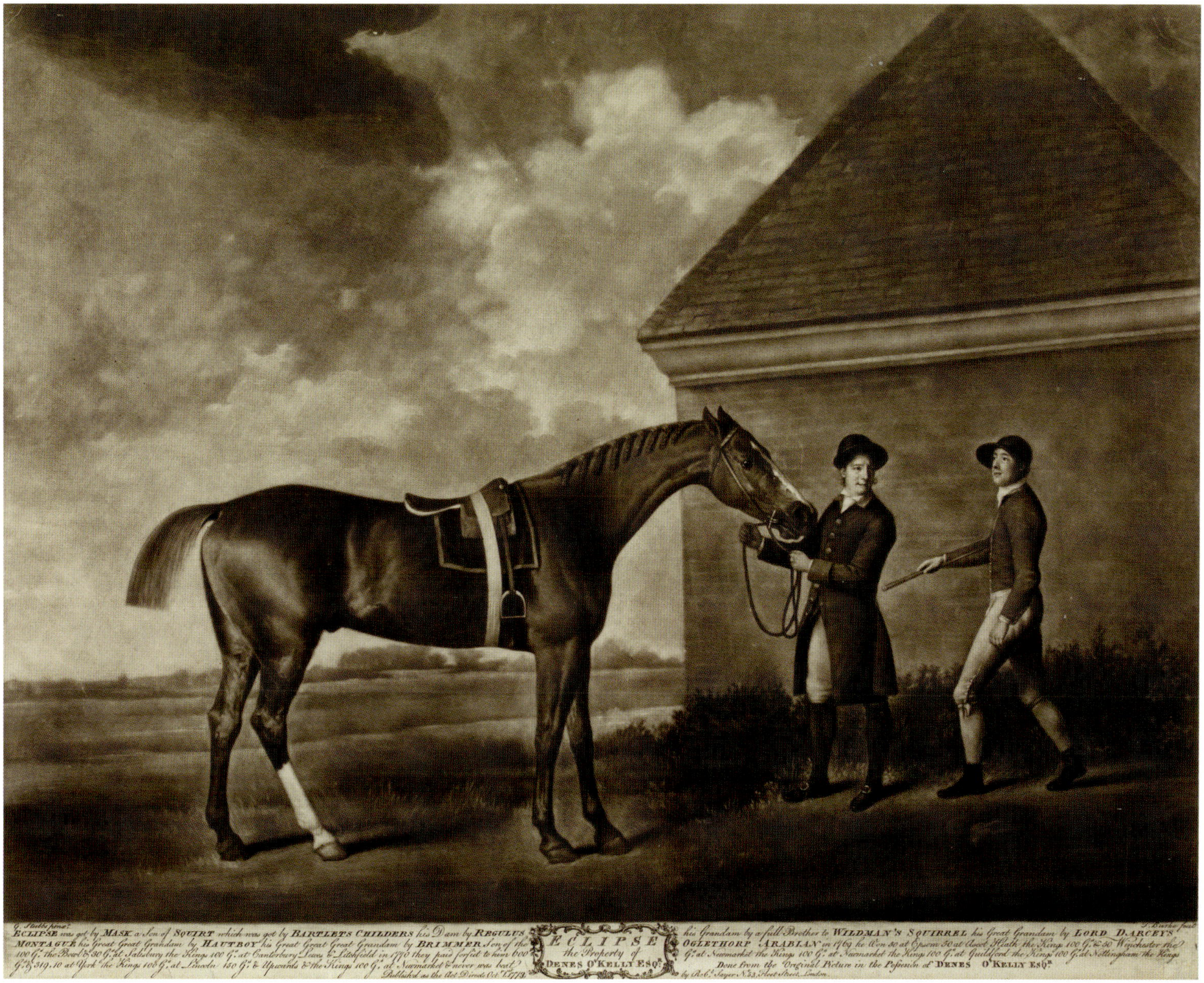

213
Eclipse

Thomas Burke (1749–1815), after George Stubbs (1724–1806)
1772
Mezzotint
H 46 cm, W 56.5 cm
BM 1854,1020.26

This print is after a painting by George Stubbs (*c.* 1770) and shows Eclipse being held by a groom, as his jockey, John Oakley, approaches. They are standing outside one of the four 'rubbing-down houses' that stood at Newmarket Heath during the eighteenth century. These houses were used for rubbing down sweaty horses with pieces of straw or cloths after exercising or racing, as seen in another of Stubbs's paintings, *Hambeltonian, Rubbing Down* (1800).

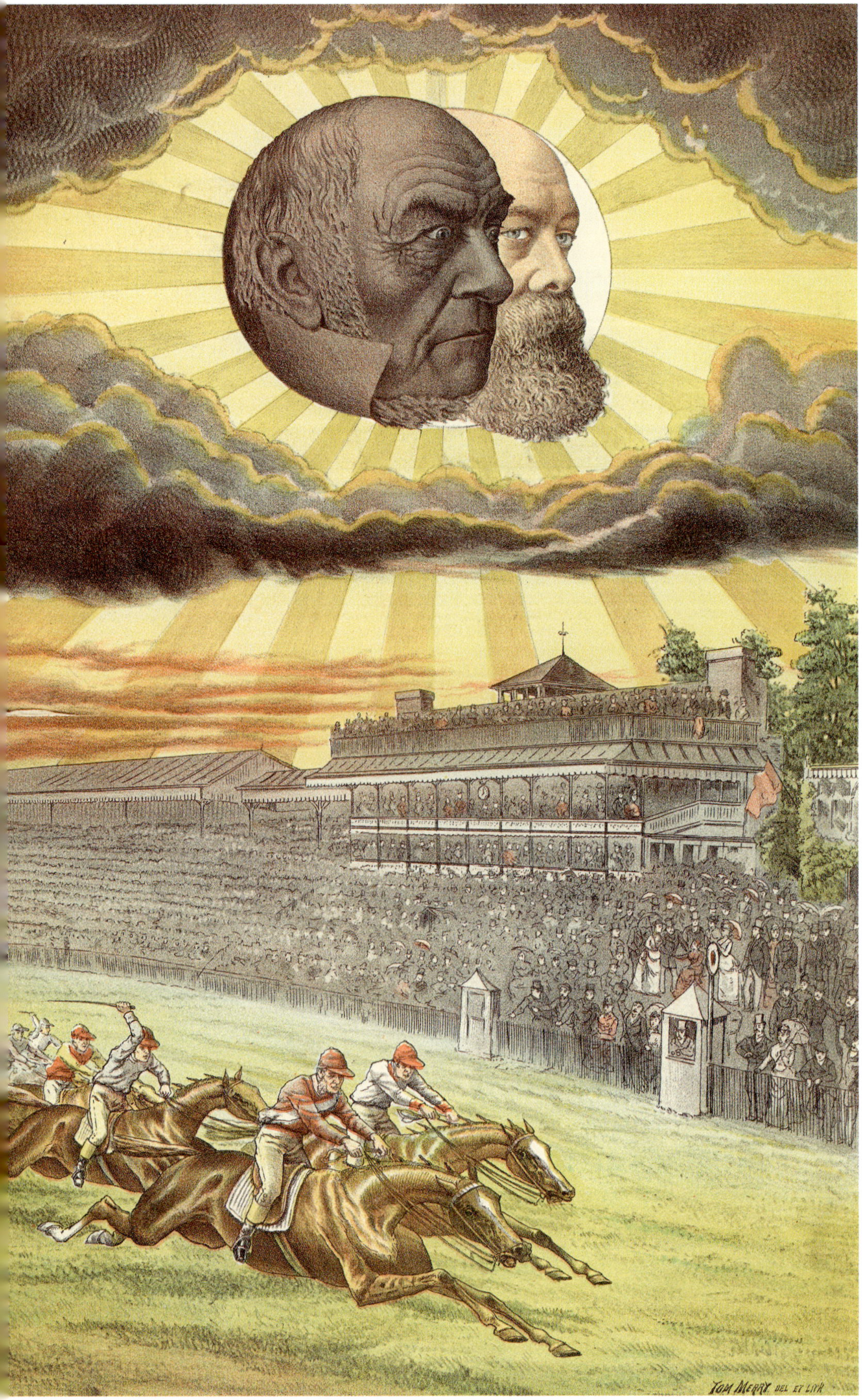

214

The Eclipse Stakes: The Finish

Tom Merry (pseudonym for William Mecham, 1853–1902)
1886
Lithograph
H 47.4 cm, W 30 cm
BM 1945,0109.38

The bottom of this print shows the finish of the first ever Eclipse Stakes, named after the racehorse Eclipse, held at Sandown Park on Friday 23 July 1886. This race was attended by HRH the Prince of Wales, later Edward VII. At the top of the print we can see a rather stern-looking William Ewart Gladstone depicted as the moon and Lord Salisbury (Robert Gascoyne-Cecil) depicted as the sun. It is written in the accompanying text that: 'it has since transpired that just as the race was being run HRH had seen a vision in the sky – of a luminous body emerging from behind the eclipsing shade of a black and opaque mass. These bodies had shaped themselves, as he thought, into the faces of leading statesmen.' Thus, Salisbury is here seen as the sun emerging from the darkness of Gladstone, a prediction that pre-empts his re-election as Prime Minister a month later in August that year.

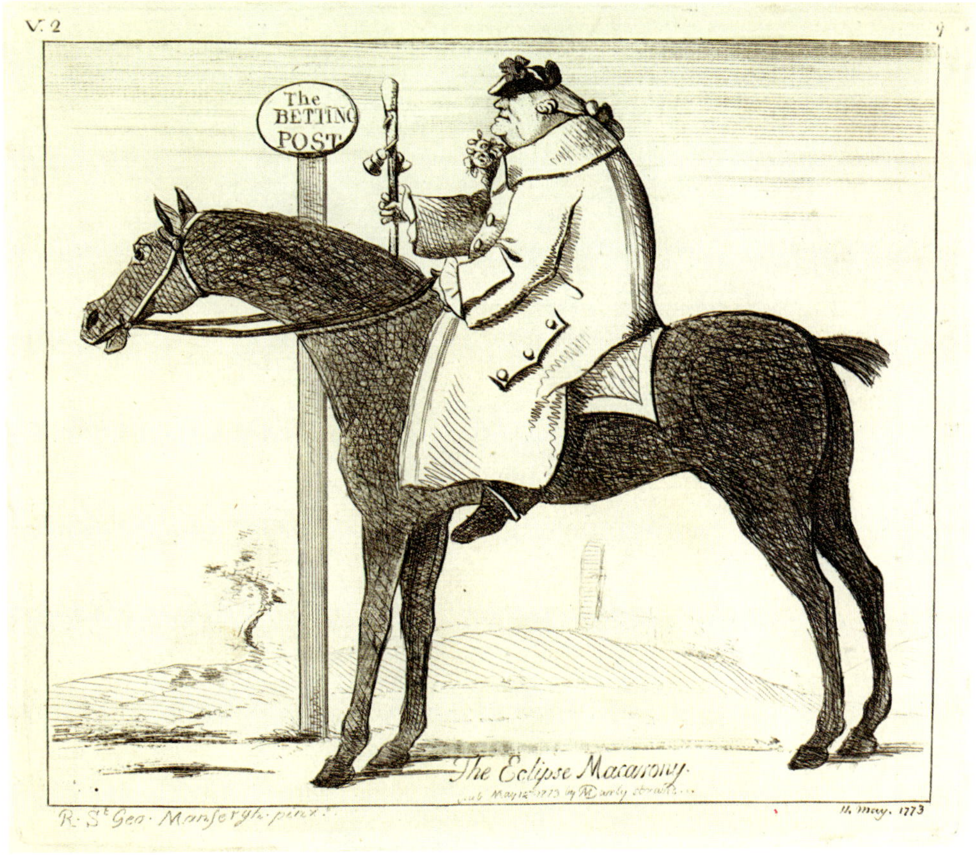

215

The Eclipse Macarony

Published by Matthew Darly
1773
Etching
H 18.5 cm, W 21.2 cm
BM 1867,0309.750

This Darly cartoon shows Colonel Dennis O'Kelly, who owned the racehorse Eclipse, satirically described as an ultra-fashionable 'macaroni' and mounted by 'the Betting Post'.

216

Pot oooo oooo

Charles Howard Hodges (1764–1837), after Sawrey Gilpin (1733–1807)
1790; acquired 2010, with assistance of NHMF, Friends of the BM, the Art Fund, Mrs Charles Wrightsman, the Michael Marks Charitable Trust, and individual donors
Mezzotint
H 43 cm, W 50.7 cm
BM 2010,7081.2498

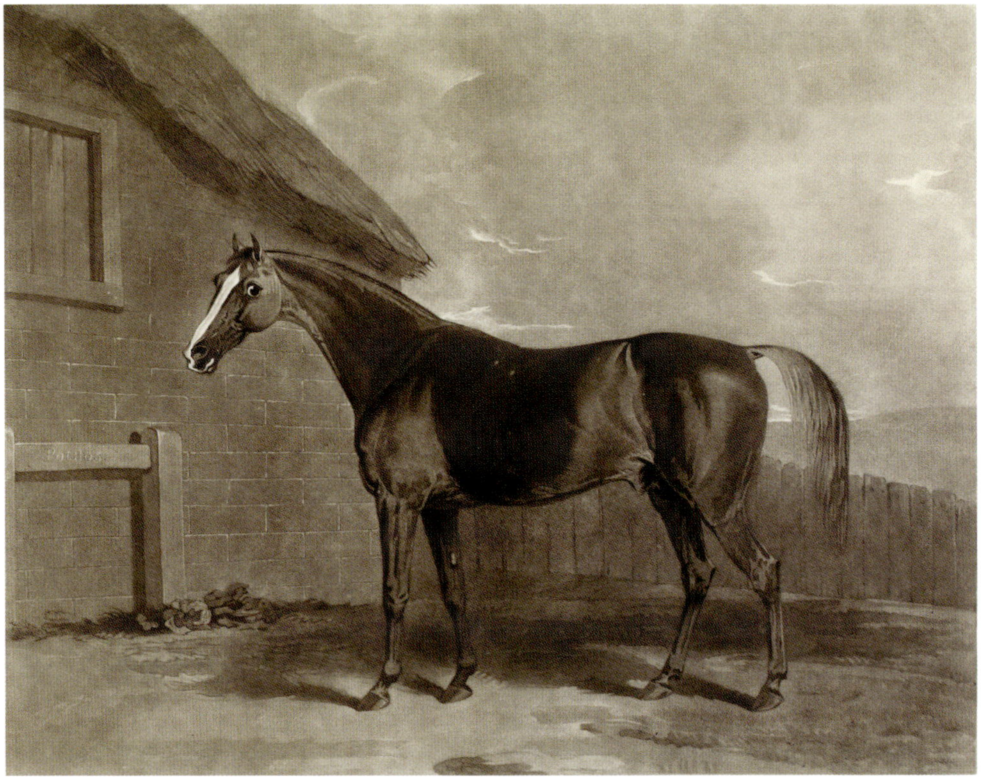

This portrait shows the racehorse Pot oooo oooo, or Pot-8-os, who was sired by Eclipse, standing in the stable yard. He was a very successful and well-known racehorse of his time, and went on to become an important stud.

The origin of his name, it is said, came about when the stable boy was asked to write the horse's name, Potatoes, on its feed bin or stall door and he wrote 'Potoooooooo'. The Earl of Abingdon, who owned the horse, apparently found this amusing and kept this version as its name, which then became shortened to Pot-8-os, as can be seen on the fence post in the print.

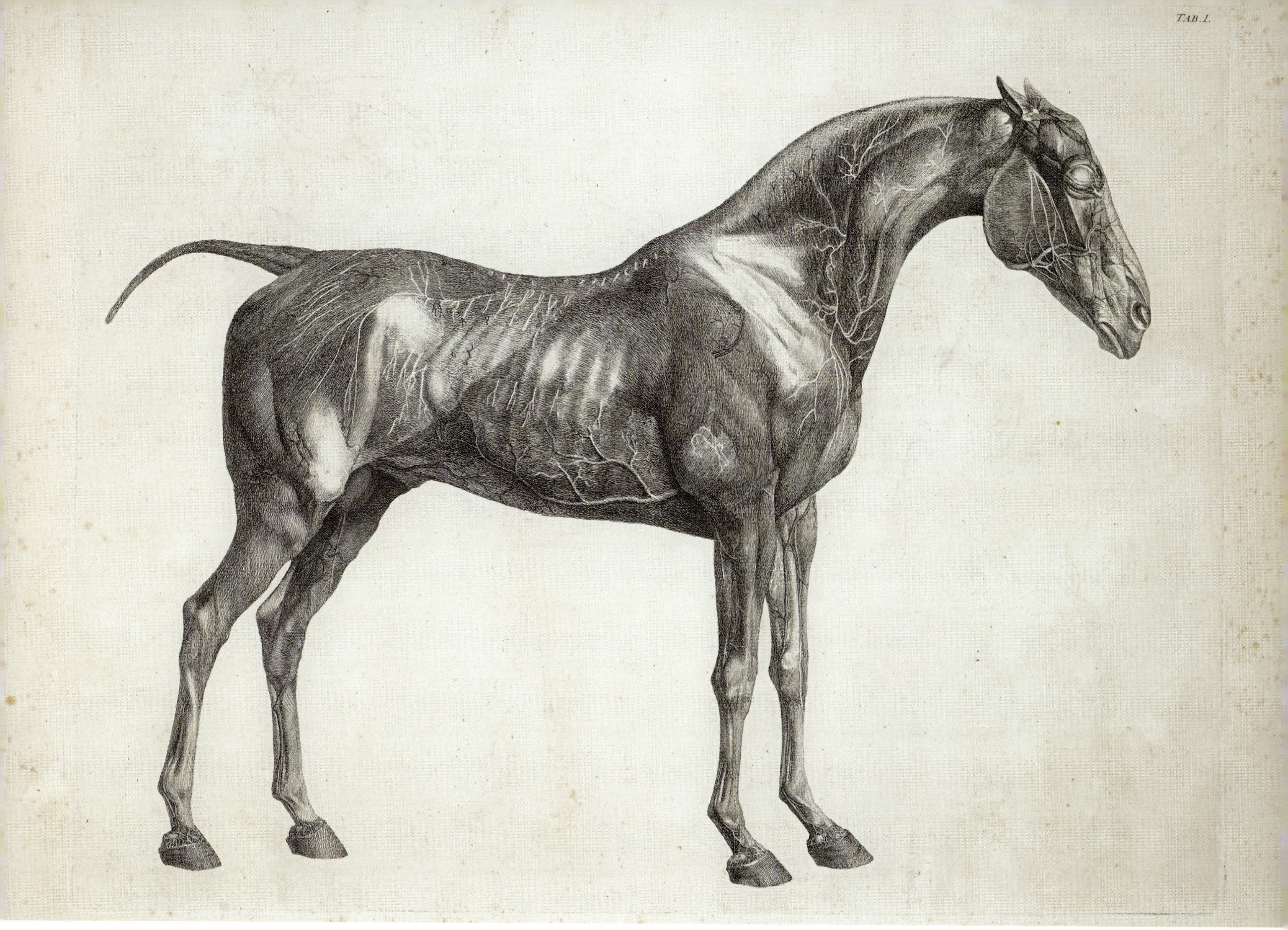

217

The Anatomy of the Horse

George Stubbs (1724–1806)
1766
Etching
H 45.8 cm, W 58 cm
BM 1914,0228.3013.1-24

The famous equestrian artist George Stubbs was much interested in the anatomy of horses, and in 1756–7 he spent eighteen months dissecting and drawing the corpses of horses. These drawings were published in 1766 in a volume entitled *The Anatomy of the Horse*. These studies were of great help to Stubbs in informing his paintings of horses and they also helped to attract commissions for horse paintings.

218

Gimcrack with John Pratt Up on Newmarket Heath

George Stubbs (1724–1806)
c. 1765; acquired with subscriptions led by their Majesties the Queen and Queen Elizabeth, the Queen Mother and contributions from the NHMF, the V&A Museum Grant-in-Aid, the National Art Collections Fund, the Pilgrim Trust and the British Sporting Art Trust, through Michael Tollema
H 100 cm, W 124 cm
Oil on canvas
Fitzwilliam Museum, PD.7-1982

Gimcrack is one of the most famous racehorses of the eighteenth century, here painted by George Stubbs on Newmarket Heath – still an important centre for horseracing in Britain. In the background is the rubbing-down house where the animals would be dried with straw or cloth after their exertions.

Whereas previous horse painters had concentrated on recording distinctive markings, Stubbs wanted his portraits to capture the unique character of each animal. Here he captures a quiet moment between Gimcrack and his jockey, removed from the hustle and bustle of the racecourse. John Pratt sits, relaxed but alert, in the saddle, wearing the colours of Gimcrack's wealthy owner, William Wildman, who commissioned the painting in 1765.

Stubbs draws on his work on the anatomy of the horse (cat. 217) to suggest the underlying skeleton, musculature and ligaments of this powerful thoroughbred animal, defined by the dazzling sheen of his coat.

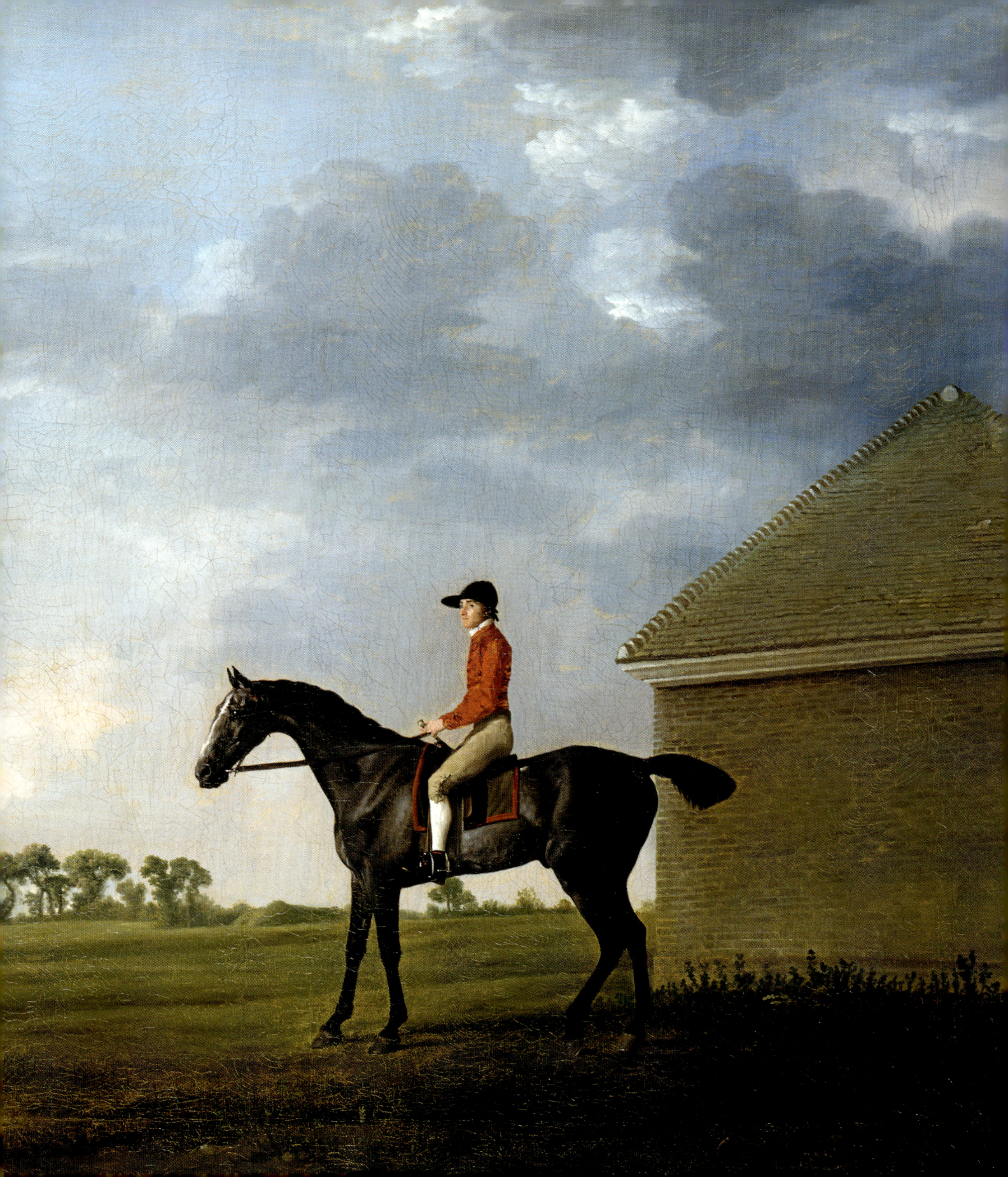

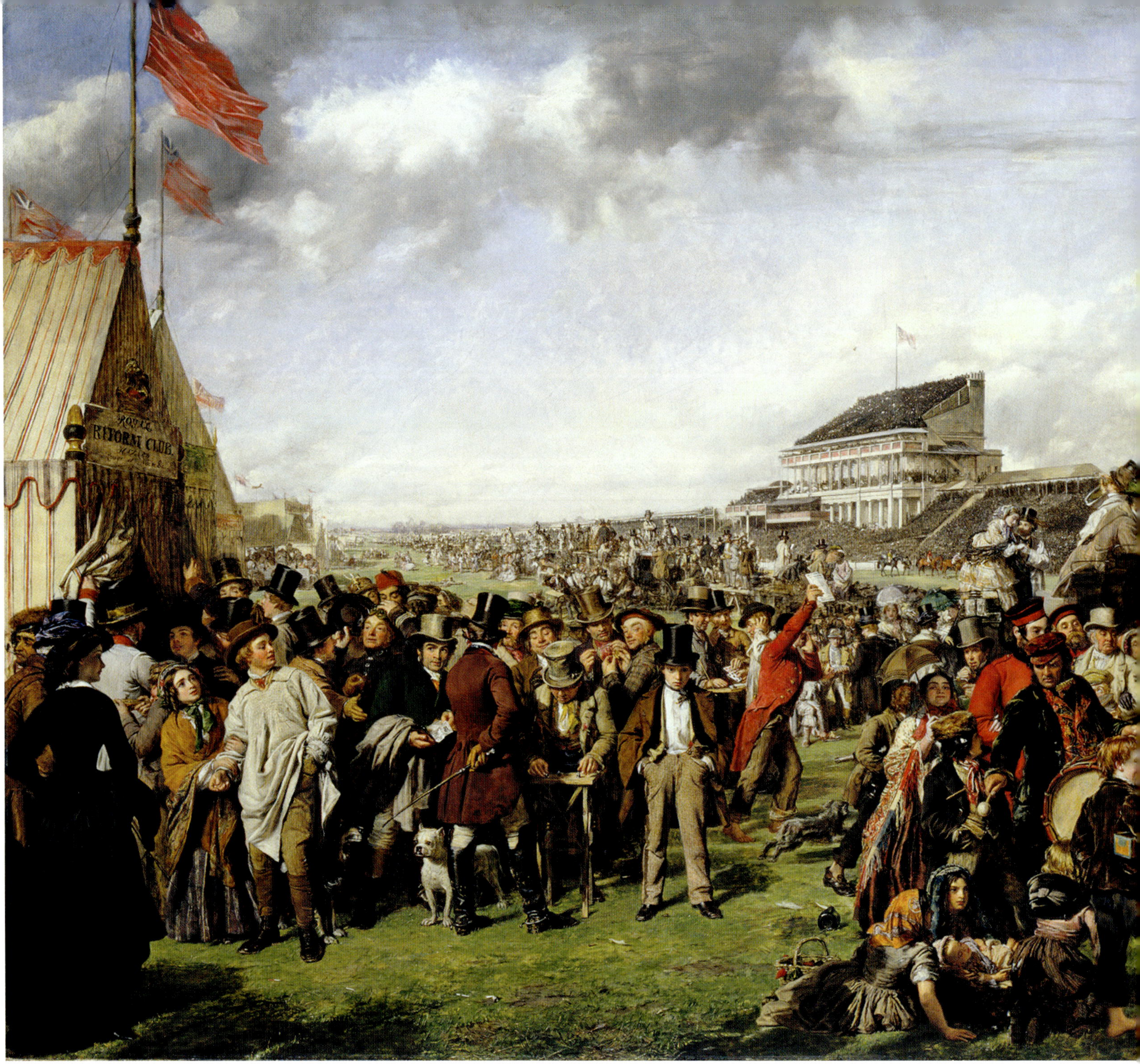

219

The Derby Day

William Powell Frith (1819–1909)
1856–8
H 101.6 cm, W 223.5 cm
Oil on canvas
Tate, N00615; bequeathed by Jacob Bell, 1859

Even within the seemingly limitless quantity of nineteenth-century sporting art, William Powell Frith's *The Derby Day* is unrivalled both for its visual impact and for illustrating the immense popularity and appeal of horseracing across all sections of Victorian society.

Frith's achievement in this multi-layered work, cast within the popular genre of a panorama of contemporary life, is in highlighting current social and moral concerns and themes through a partly documentary and partly satirical approach, while simultaneously celebrating the phenomena of racing as a great event unifying all people and classes. Through easily recognizable stereotypes of simple countryfolk led astray, ordinary racegoers and outsiders on the fringes of acceptable society (travellers, acrobats, wealthy

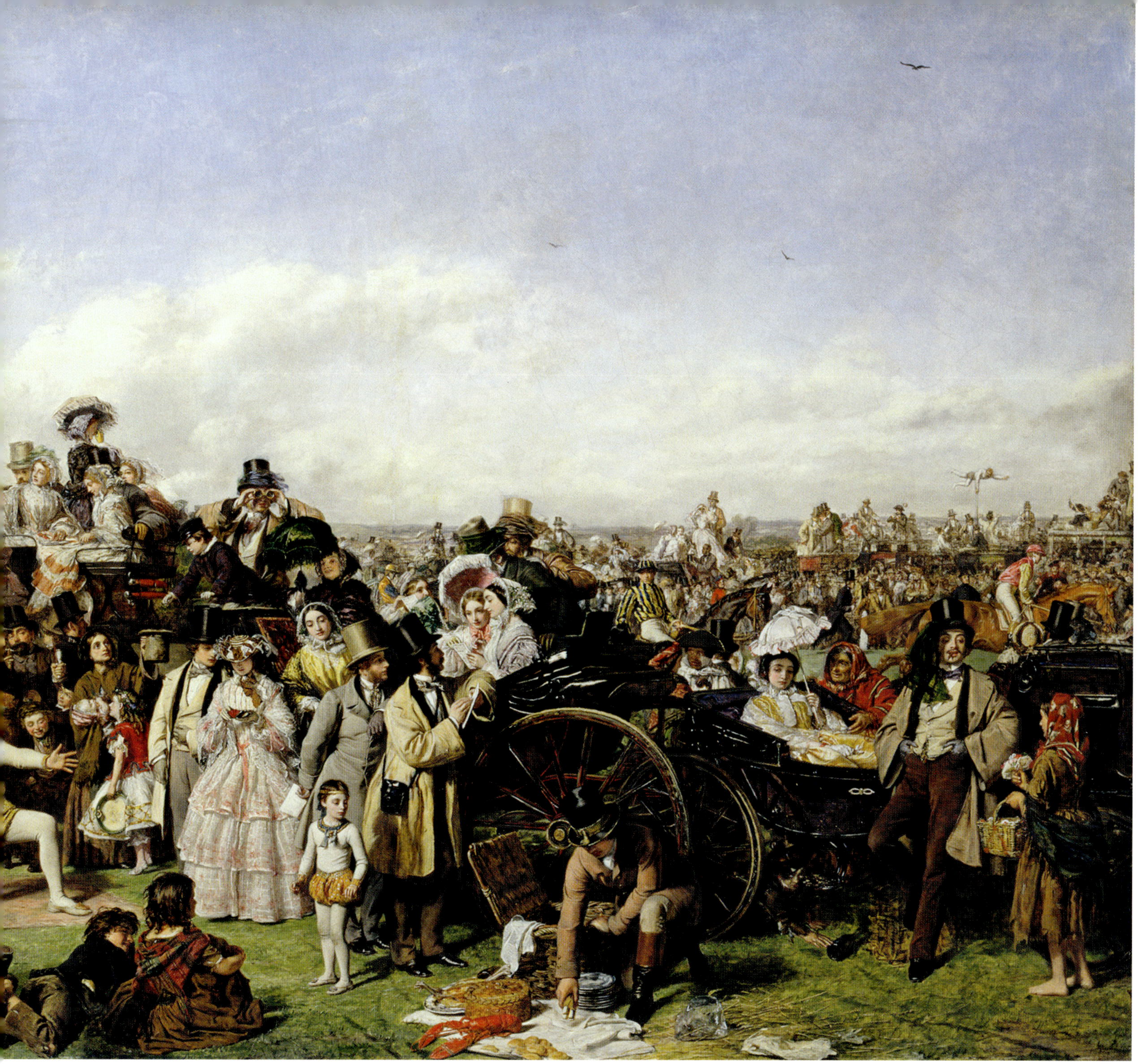

transgressors and courtesans) Frith both reassured and challenged his audience.

Remarkably, the painting's history mirrors these same themes, illuminating what may now seem the unexpectedly interlocking social networks within Victorian society. The painting's origin and success linked artists, the world of business and politics, equestrian sport and royal circles, and the growing popular interest in contemporary art (and the new fortunes to be made from it). *The Derby Day* was commissioned by Frith's close friend Jacob Bell (1810–1859) for £1,500 on the basis of an unfinished sketch. Bell, a Quaker by upbringing, was the owner of an established pharmaceutical business, a founder of the Pharmaceutical Society of Great Britain and a sometime MP (whose normal for the time but unfortunately inept bribery to secure his St Albans seat precipitated eventual bribery reform). Yet Bell was also an enthusiast of art and the turf who had attended the same art school as Frith, who procured Frith's female models, and acted as the unofficial business agent of his great friend Edwin Henry Landseer (1802–1873), the immensely popular animal artist and royal favourite. The dealer Ernest Gambart bought the copyright and exhibition rights anticipating the immense popularity of the subject and the sale of engravings in large numbers.Such was the enthusiasm for the painting when it was shown at the Royal Academy in May 1858 that a rail was erected to keep the crowds away from it.

220

Grand Stand Ascot: Gold Cup Day 1839

Charles Hunt (1803–1877), after John Frederick Herring (1795–1865)
1839; acquired 1949, gift of Edward Croft-Murray
Hand-coloured engraving and aquatint
H 62 cm, W 79.5 cm
BM 1949,0217.31

The black horse in the foreground appears to be being prepared for the race, with his jockey standing behind it carrying the saddle and a groom removing the horse's blanket, while another groom holds it steady. The movement of the other horses in this scene indicates the tension and energy before the race begins. In the background is the Grand Stand and enclosure, packed with racegoers. To the right of the Grand Stand is the Royal Box, which is flying the Royal Standard, indicating Queen Victoria's presence at the race.

The first Grand Stand at Ascot opened in 1839, after a year of construction, and it was able to hold up to 1200 people on the ground floor and 1800 on the roof. The winner of the Gold Cup that year was Caravan, a descendant of Eclipse and the Darley Arabian.

This print is after John Frederick Herring who counted Queen Victoria as his patron.

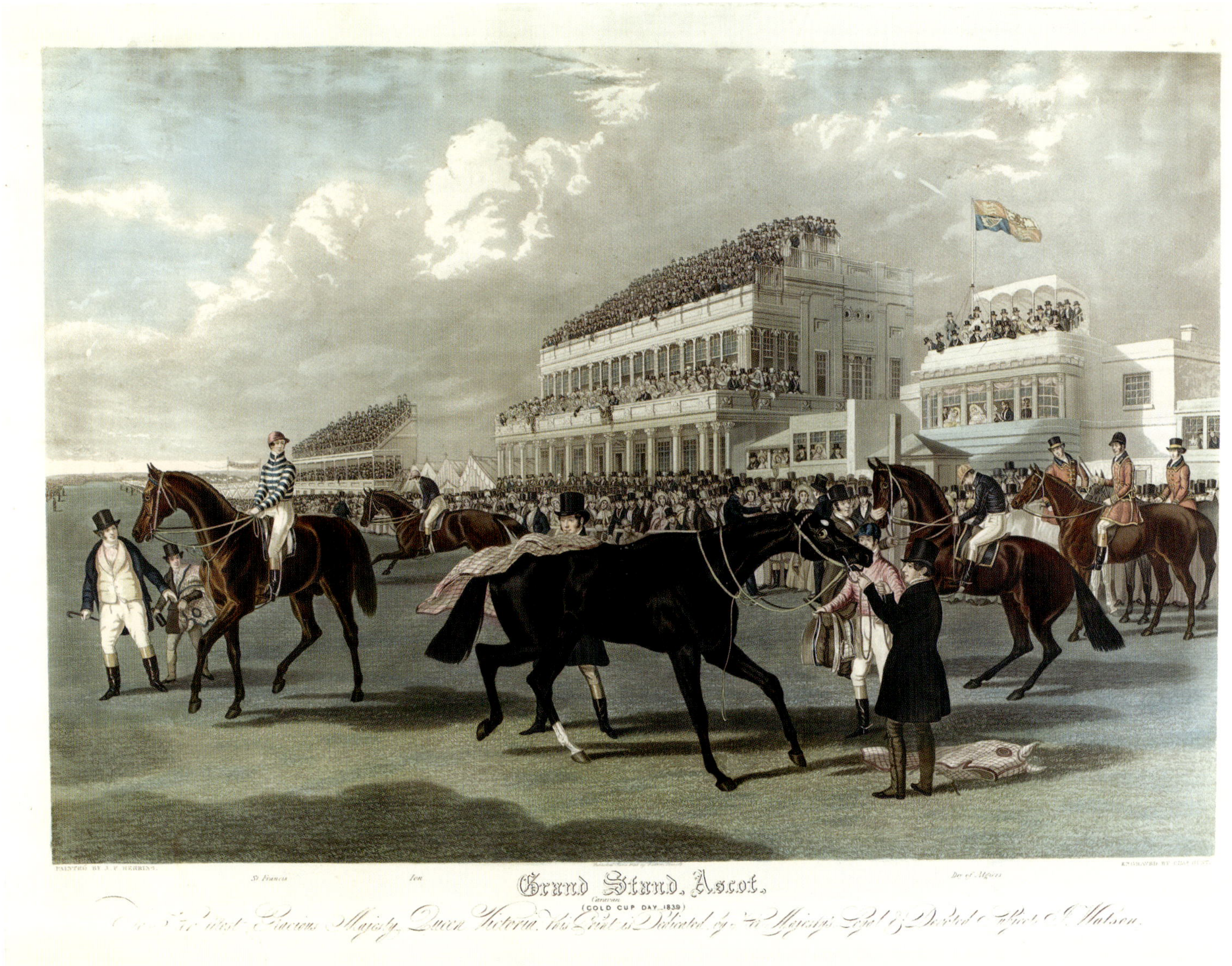

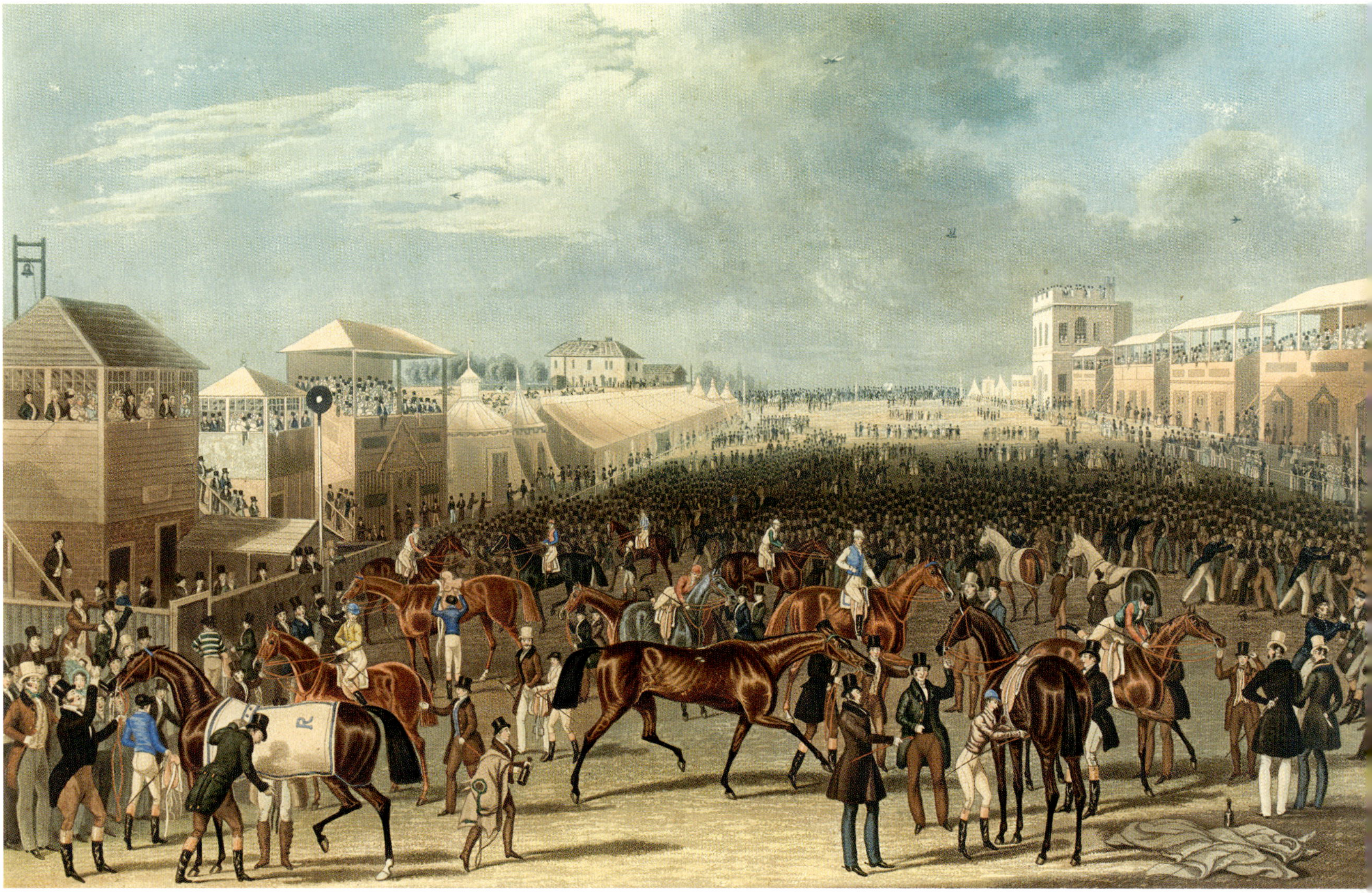

221

Epsom: The Race Over

Charles Hunt (1803–1877), after James Pollard (1792–1867)
1836; acquired 1933, gift of C.F.G.R. Schwerdt
Hand-coloured etching and aquatint
H 33.6 cm, W 46.2 cm
BM 1933,1014.103

The scene here shows the end of the race, with jockeys dismounting their horses and removing their saddles in the foreground. In the background is a large crowd, being kept back by men in dark coats and white trousers. Either side of the centre are stands and enclosures, still crowded with people.

The Epsom Derby in 1836 was won by Bay Middleton, a descendant of Herod and the Byerley Turk.

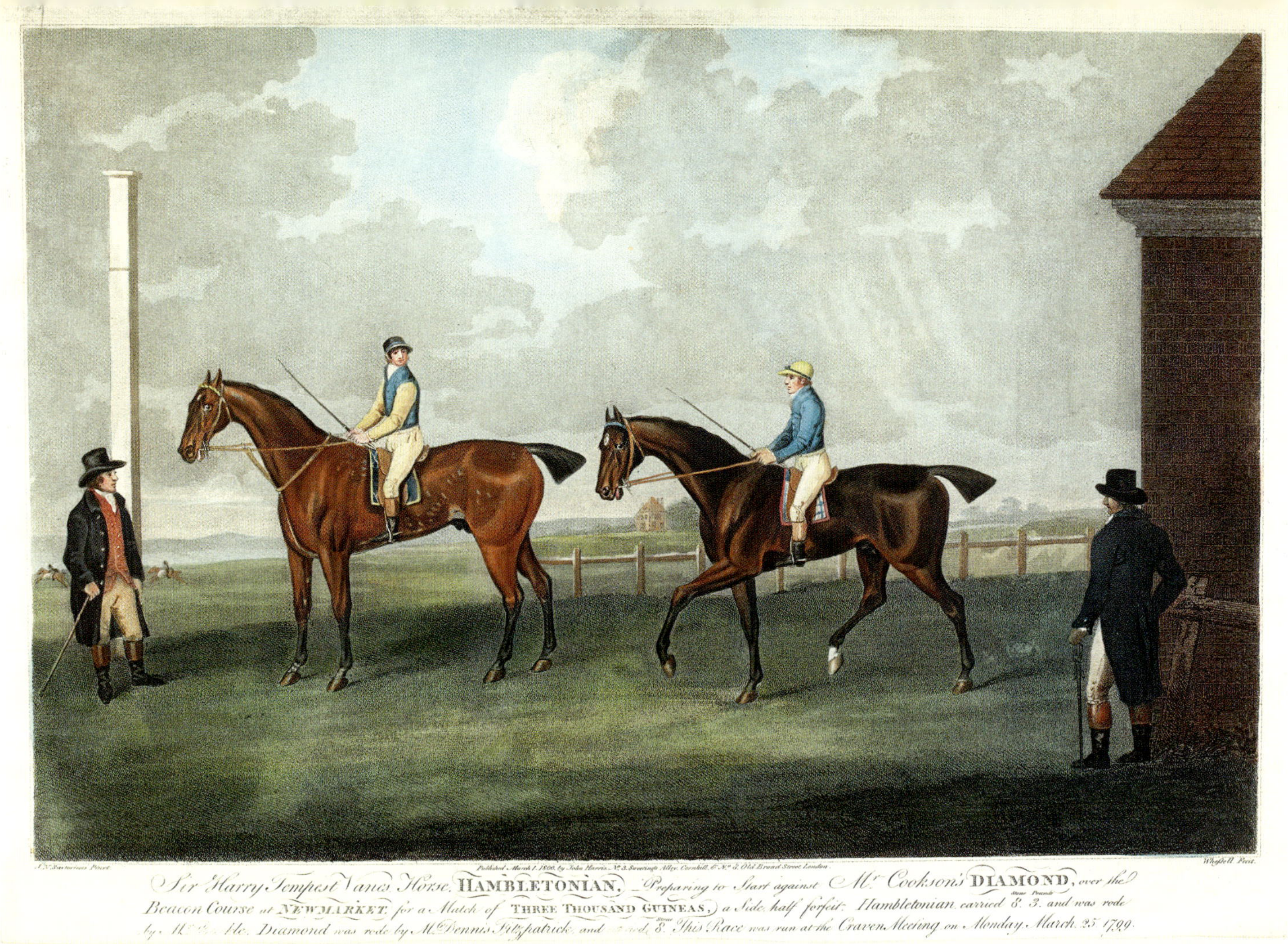

222

Hambletonian and Diamond at Newmarket

John Whessell (*c.* 1760–1806), after J.N. Sartorius (1759–1828)
1800; acquired 1917, gift of N.I. Cooper in memory of A.T. Herbert
Hand-coloured stipple and etching
H 38.9 cm, W 53.8 cm
BM 1917,1208.2434

This print shows the moments before the famous Craven Meeting between Hambletonian, owned by Sir Henry Tempest Vane, and Diamond, owned by Mr Cookson. The two horses are seen making their way to the starting post on the left, with their jockeys mounted, and to the right is the rubbing down-house. Hambletonian, on the left, is ridden by Mr Buckle, who wears a dark hat, white breeches and a blue jacket with yellow sleeves, while Diamond's jockey, Mr Fitzpatrick, wears a yellow hat, white breeches and a blue jacket.

At this early stage in horseracing, matches were often arranged between pairs of horses rather than a group of them. The text below the scene states that this race took place on 25 March 1799 at the Beacon Course and was for the sum of three thousand guineas. Hambletonian, whose grandsire was Eclipse, narrowly beat Diamond, whose grandsire was Herod, to the finish.

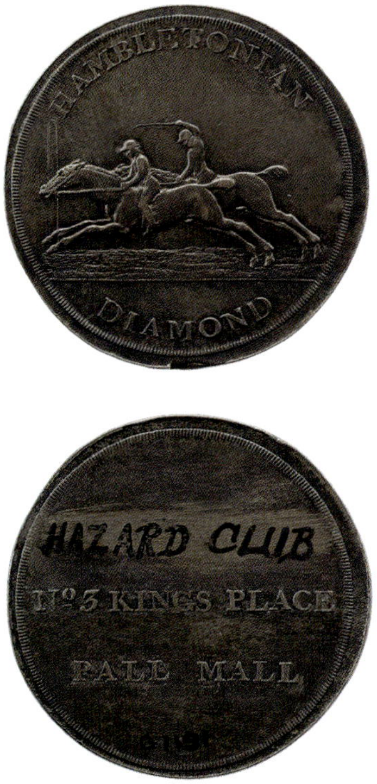

223

Commemorative token

1799; acquired 1907, gift of Montague Guest
Silver
Diam. 3.6 cm
BM MG.1191

The obverse shows two racehorses with the inscription 'Hambletonian Diamond'; and the reverse has the inscription 'No. 3 King's Place, Pall Mall'. This counter commemorates the famous race between Hambletonian and Diamond in 1799 (see cat. 222).

224

Pass for Doncaster Races

19th century; acquired 1907, gift of Montague Guest
White metal
Diam. 3.2 cm
BM MG.1182

The obverse shows the facade of a building with the inscription 'New betting rooms Doncaster'. The reverse shows two racehorses, with the inscription 'Established 1800'. This token was used as a pass by which the bearer might gain access, during the race, to the course or Grand Stand.

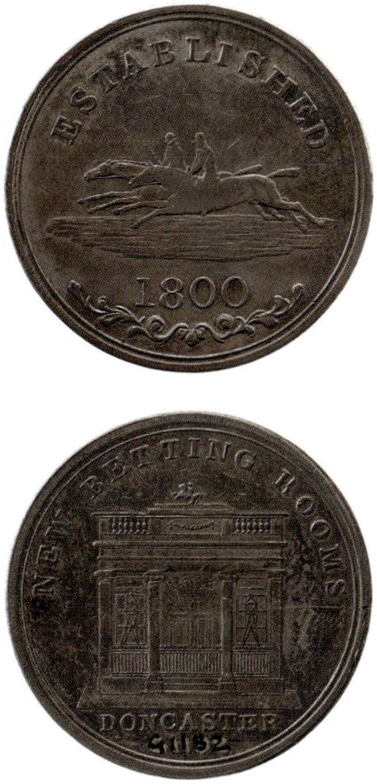

225

Fabergé statuette of Persimmon

Henrik Wigström (1862–1923)
1908
H 24.3 cm, L 31.2 cm, D 9.6 cm
Silver, nephrite
The Royal Collection, RCIN 32392

Persimmon, owned by the Prince of Wales (Later King Edward VII), was bred at the Sandringham Stud and won the Derby and the St Leger in 1896 and the Ascot Gold Cup and Eclipse Stakes in 1897. Fabergé's statuette was probably completed after Persimmon's death in February 1908, and cost Edward VII £135. He also bought six bronze copies of the model at a cost of £63 each.

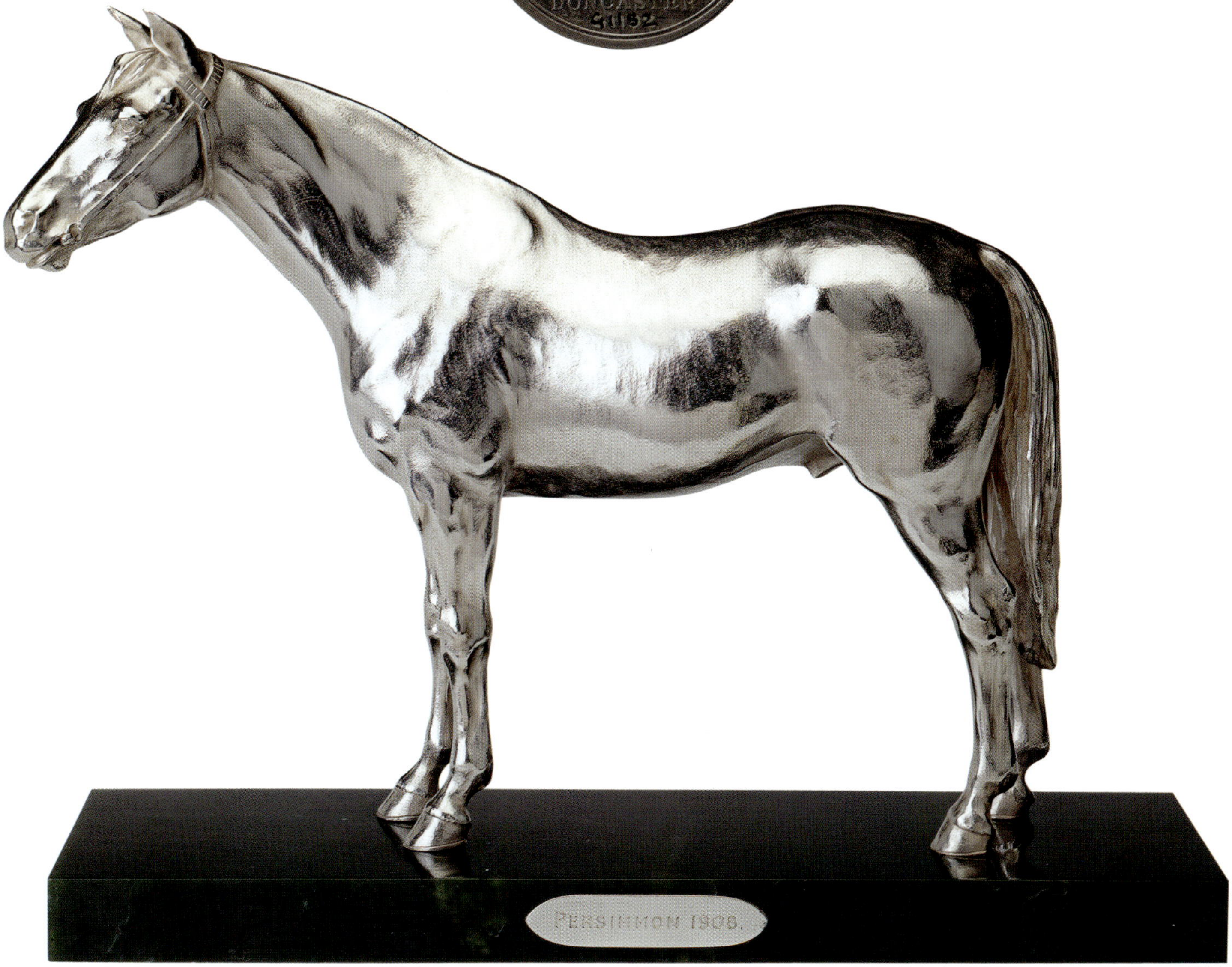

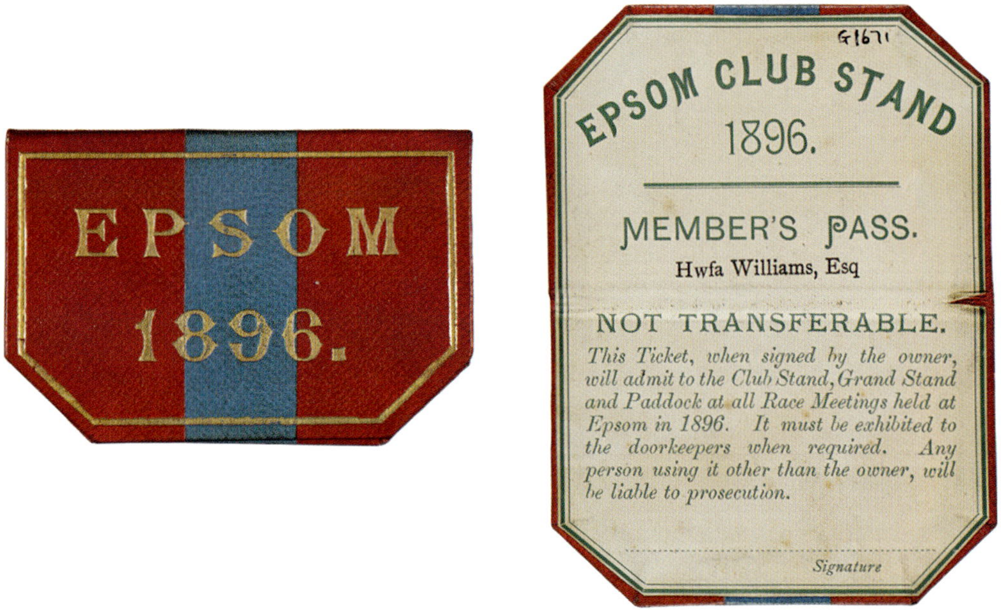

226

Member's season ticket for Epsom

1896; acquired 1907, gift of Montague Guest
Cardboard
L 7 cm
BM MG.1671

This season ticket is from 1896, the year in which Edward VII's horse Persimmon (cat. 225) won the Derby at Epsom.

227

Tickets to the Grand Stand

1904; acquired 1907, gift of Montague Guest
Cardboard and string
H 7 cm
BM MG.1761, MG.1760

Two oval tickets to the Grand Stand at a racecourse in 1904.

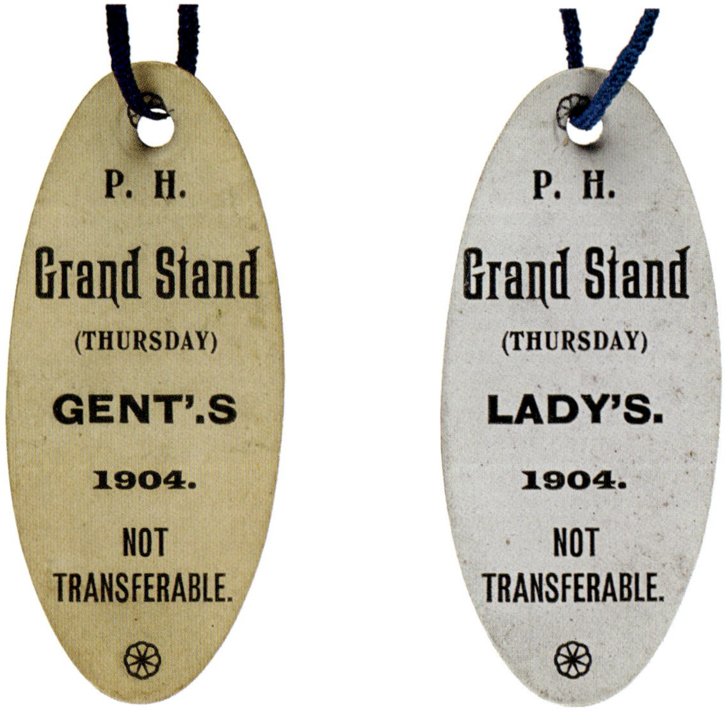

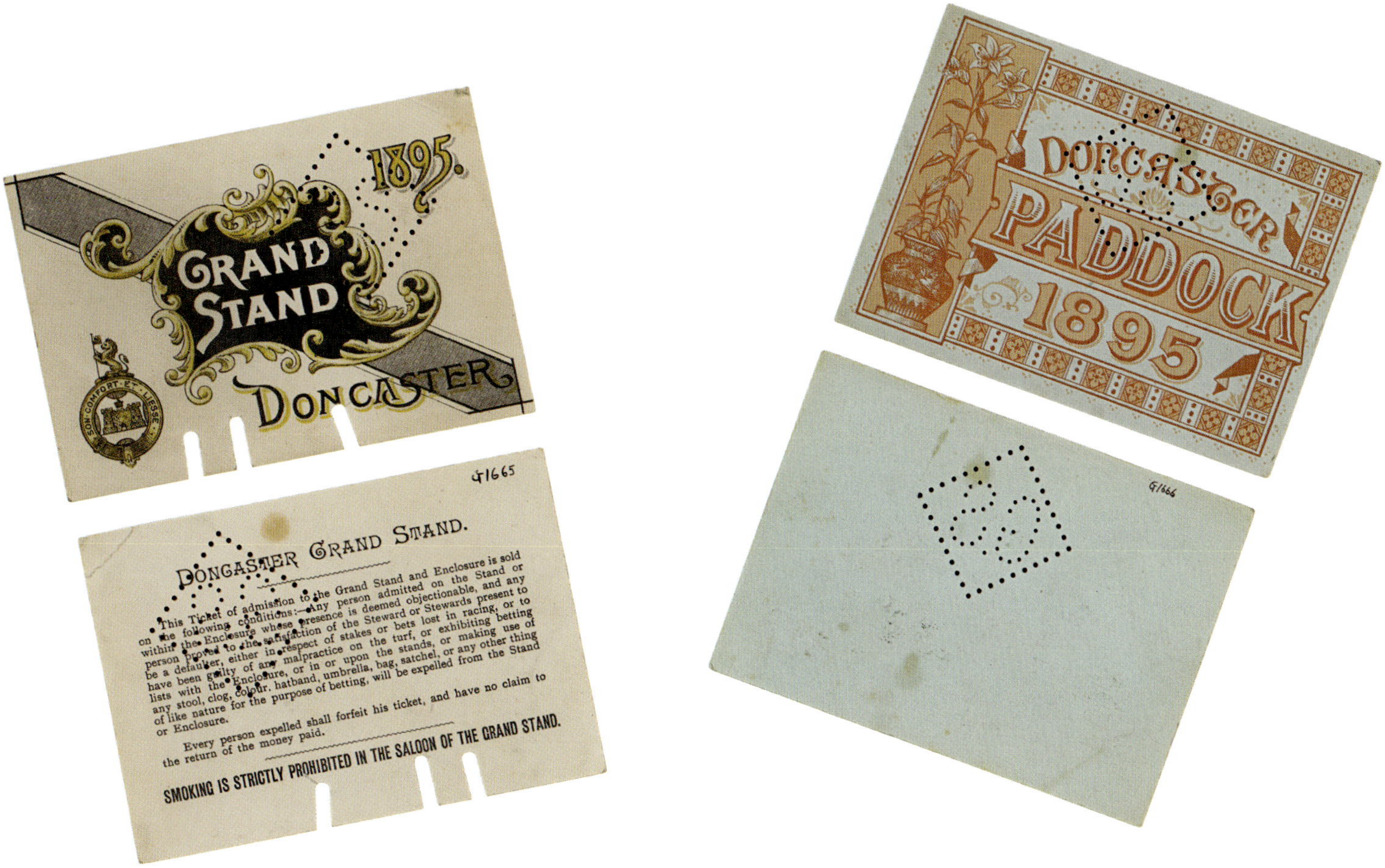

228

Racecourse tickets

1895, 1898; acquired 1907, gift of Montague Guest
Cardboard
W 11.5 cm
BM MG.1665, MG.1666

Two tickets to Doncaster races in 1895, one for entry to the Grand Stand and the other for the Paddock, and one ticket for the Derby November meeting in 1898.

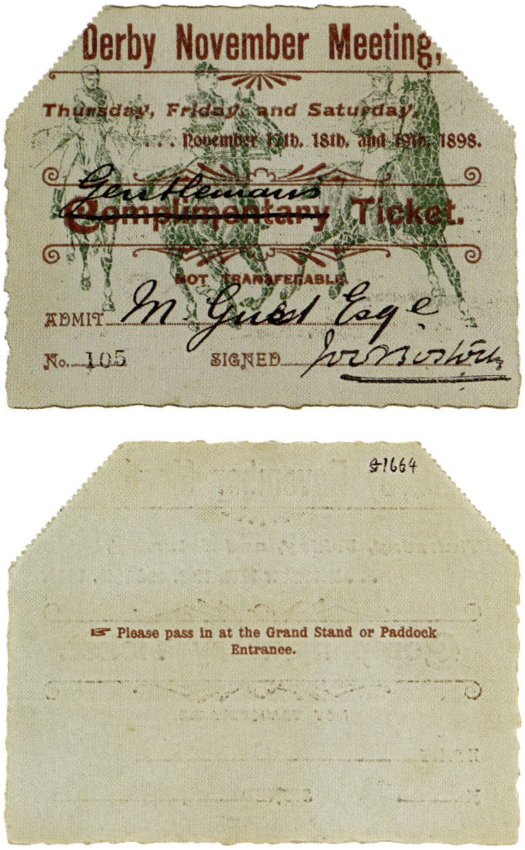

229

Racecourse ticket

1898; acquired 1907, gift of Montague Guest
Cardboard
W 11.5 cm
BM MG.1664

Gentleman's ticket to the Derby November meeting for three days, 17 to 19 November 1898.

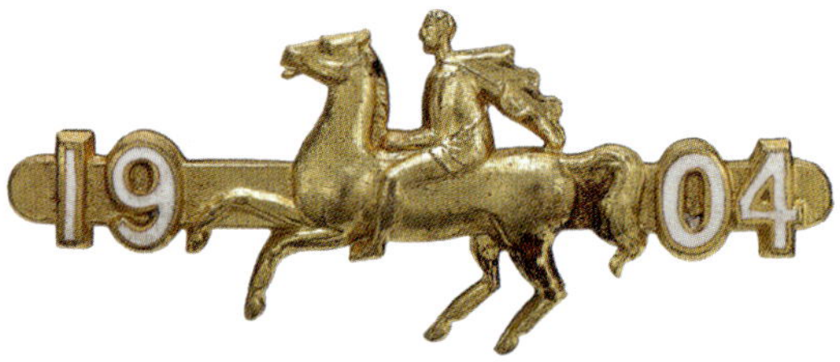

230

Badge with pin

1904; acquired 1907, gift of Montague Guest
Metal
W 4.3 cm
BM MG.1998

Golden metal badge with a pin, showing a classical design of horse and rider, with the date 1904 picked out in white. On the reverse is engraved 'Sandown', indicating that this is a member's badge for Sandown Park.

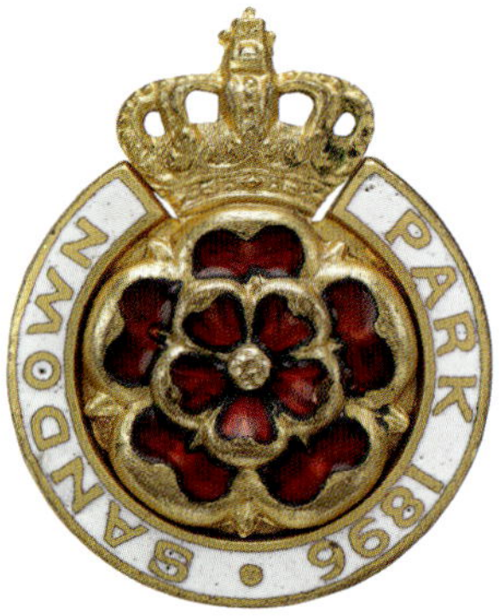

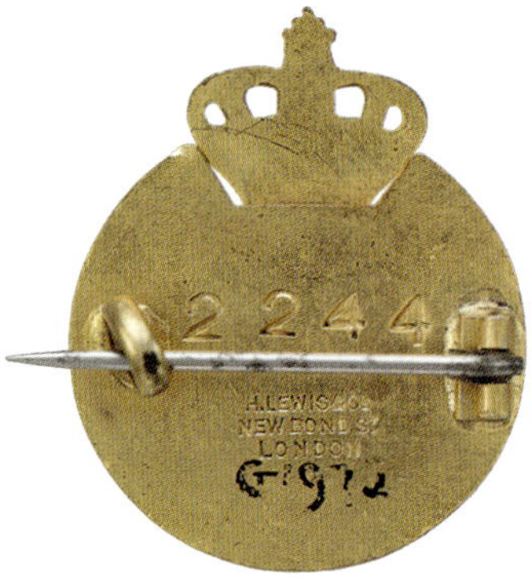

231

Badge with pin

1896; acquired 1907, gift of Montague Guest
Metal
H 2.8 cm
BM MG.1972

Golden metal badge with a pin with a central red rose and surmounted by a crown. Inscribed around the rose Sandown Park 1896.

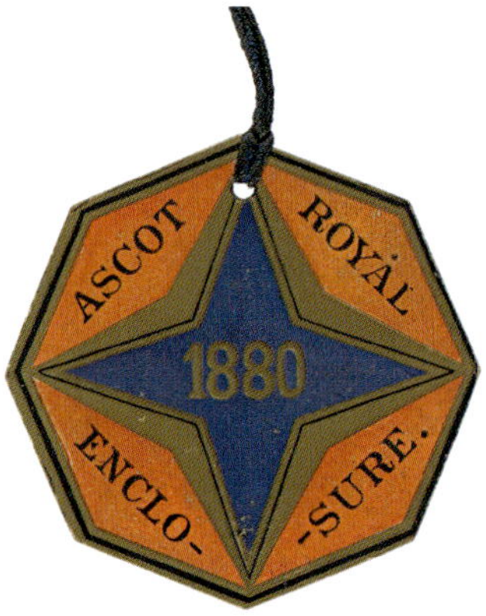

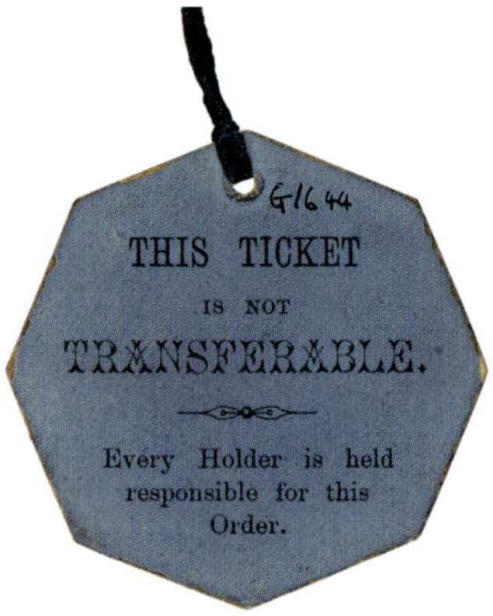

232

Ticket to Royal Enclosure at Ascot

1880; acquired 1907, gift of Montague Guest
Cardboard
L 3.6 cm, W 2.4 cm
BM MG.1644

Octagonal-shaped badge with a blue star and the date in the centre.

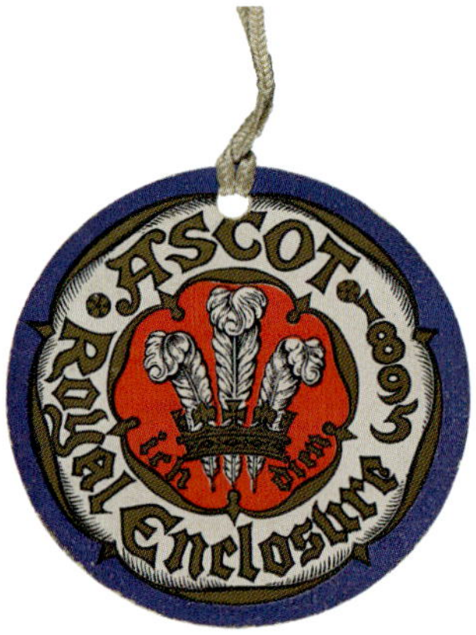

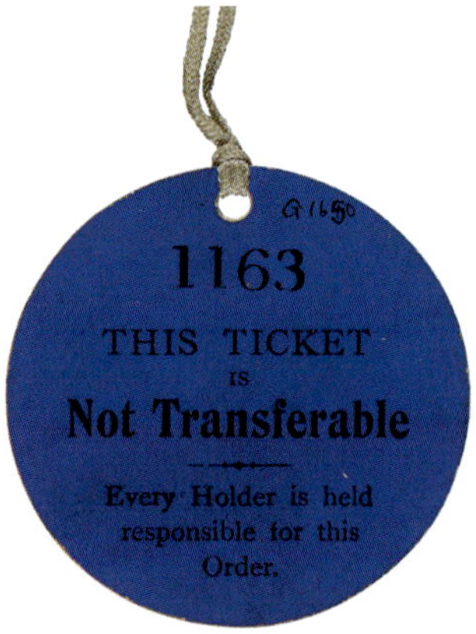

233

Ticket to Royal Enclosure at Ascot

1895; acquired 1907, gift of Montague Guest
Cardboard
Diam. 5.5 cm
BM MG.1650

Circular badge showing the feathers of the Prince of Wales and inscribed Ascot Royal Enclosure 1895.

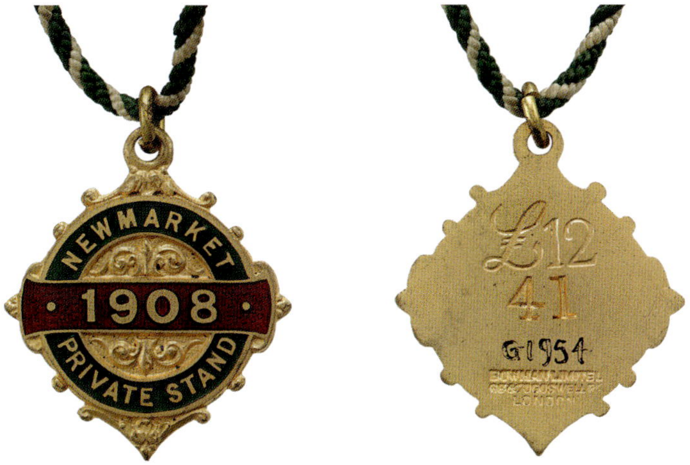

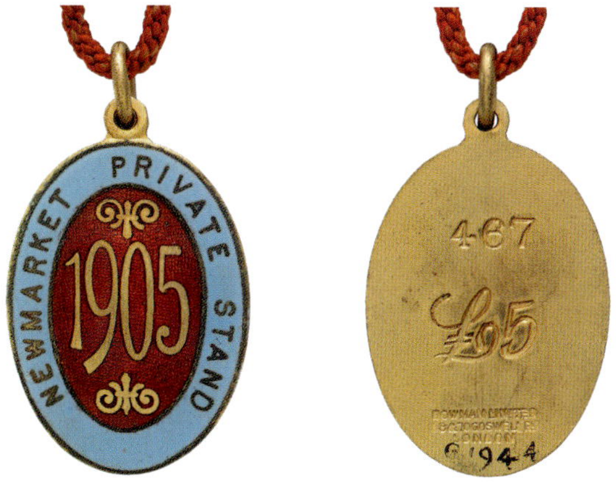

234
Metal Badge

1908; acquired 1907, gift of Montague Guest
Metal
W 2.8 cm
BM MG.1954

Metal badge inscribed 'Newmarket Private Stand 1908'. This is presumably a season ticket for 1908 and cost £12.

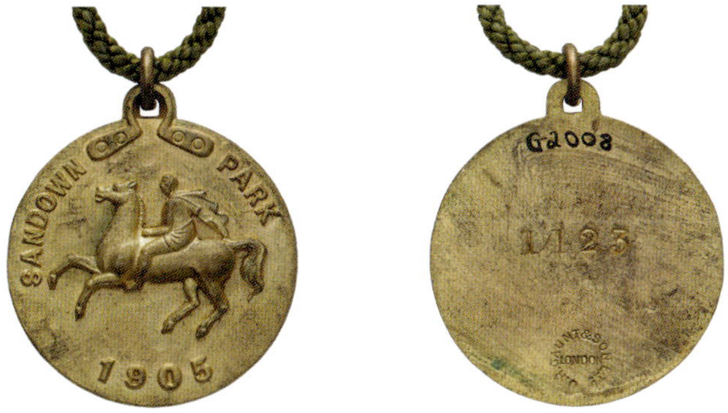

235
Metal Badge

1905; acquired 1907, gift of Montague Guest
Metal
D 3.2 cm
BM MG.2008

Circular gold-coloured badge suspended on a green cord showing on the obverse a classical horse and rider and inscribed Sandown Park 1905.

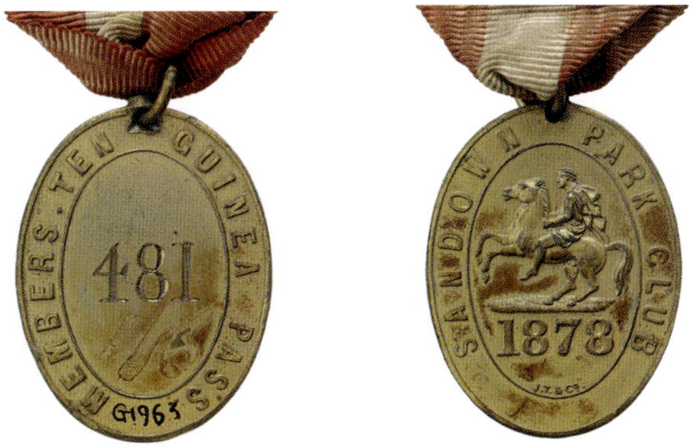

236
Metal Badge

1878; acquired 1907, gift of Montague Guest
Metal
H 3.8 cm
BM MG.1963

Oval metal badge with a red and white ribbon. On the obverse is a classical horse and rider above the date 1878, and around the edge is inscribed 'Sandown Park Club'. Around the edge on the reverse is inscribed 'Members Ten Guineas Pass'.

237
Metal Badge

1905; acquired 1907, gift of Montague Guest
Metal
H 3.6 cm
BM MG.1944

Oval metal badge suspended on a red cord with blue and red enamel on the obverse and inscribed 'Newmarket Private Stand 1905'. On the reverse it is inscribed £5.

238

Cigarette cards

1933

Cardboard

H 3.5 cm, W 6.7 cm (each card)

Private collection

Set of cigarette cards showing Derby and Grand National winners. Issued by John Player and Sons in 1933. Such cards, covering a wide range of subjects, were included singly in packets of cigarettes and were collected in sets of twenty-five or fifty.

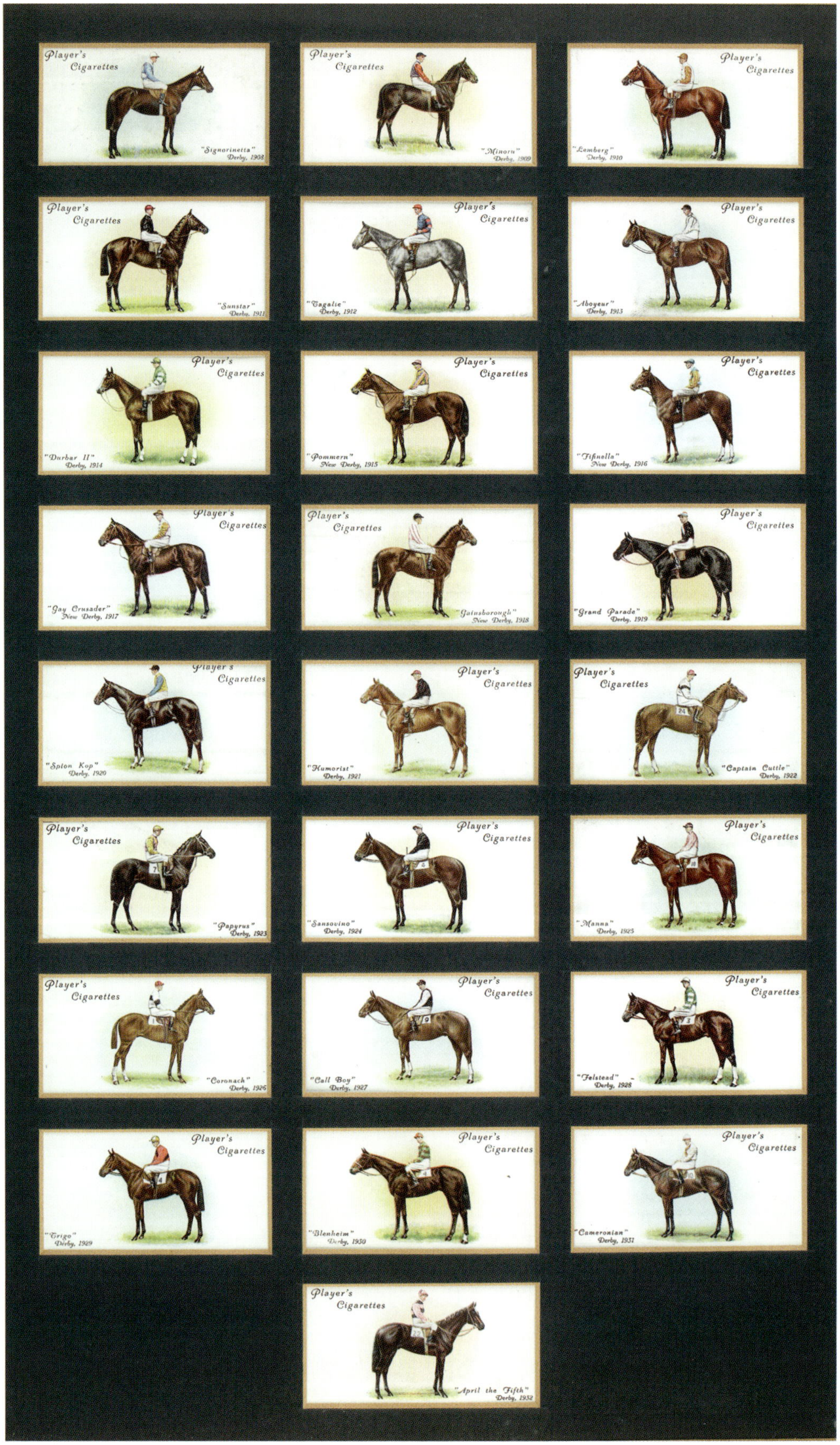

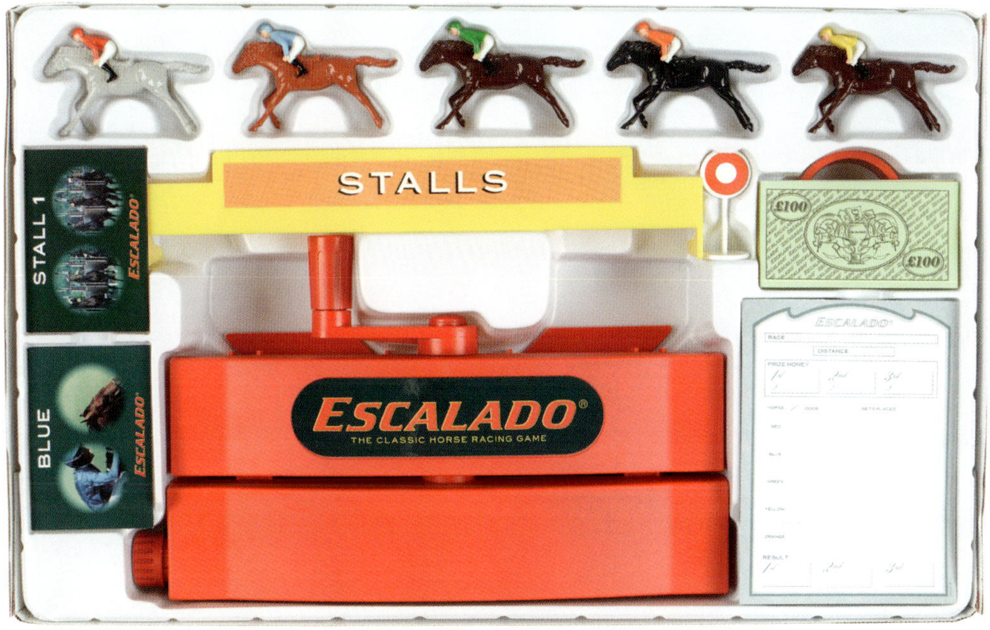

239

Escalado horseracing game

1997
Plastic, cardboard and paper
L 48 cm, W 30.5 cm
BM EPH-ME 636

Escalado is a horseracing game that was made by the Chad Valley Toy Company of Birmingham from 1928 onwards, and later by Waddingtons. In this game model horses race down a track which is made to vibrate by turning a handle. Players bet on the different horses, and the player who has the highest amount of token money at the end of an agreed number of races is the winner.

240

Ascot board game

c. 1950, French
Plastic, cardboard and paper
L 50.5 cm, W 36 cm
BM EPH-ME 637

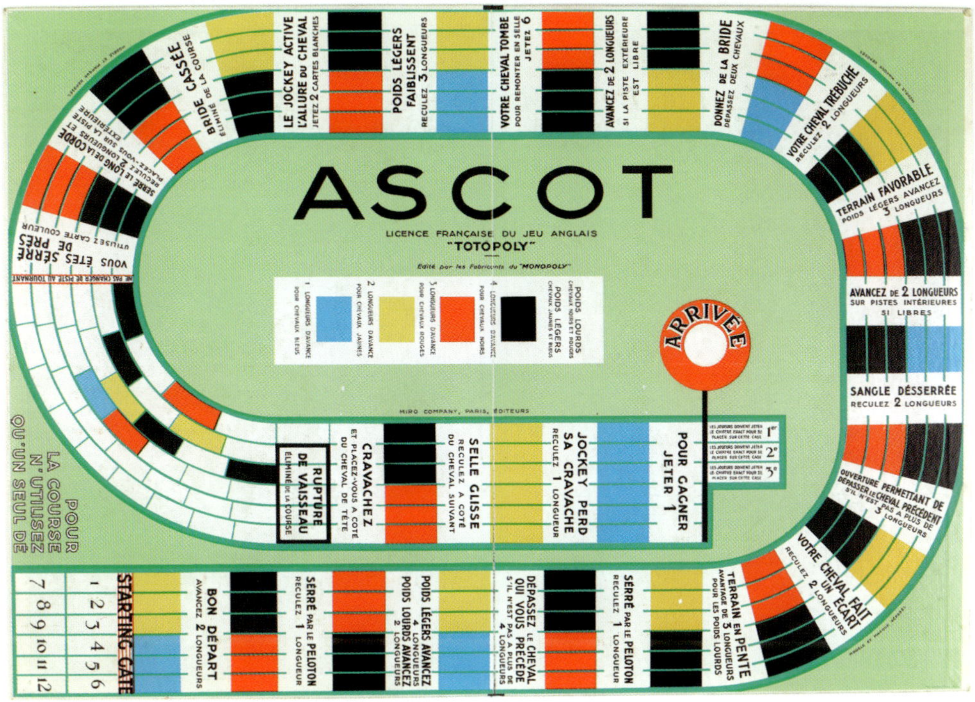

The board game Ascot is a French version of the English board game Totopoly. The English version was manufactured by John Waddington of Leeds from 1938 until about 1984. Several different editions were made abroad under licence, such as the present French example. Totopoly is a horseracing game which involves moving horses around a board according to a throw of the dice. Bets may be placed on the horses with the paper money supplied with the game, and paper prize money is also paid out to the winning horses. In the English edition the horses are named after the winners of the Lincolnshire Handicap between 1926 and 1937.

Although Totopoly never attained the popularity of its sister game Monopoly, it was widely distributed and well known and reflects the keen interest in horseracing in northern Europe.

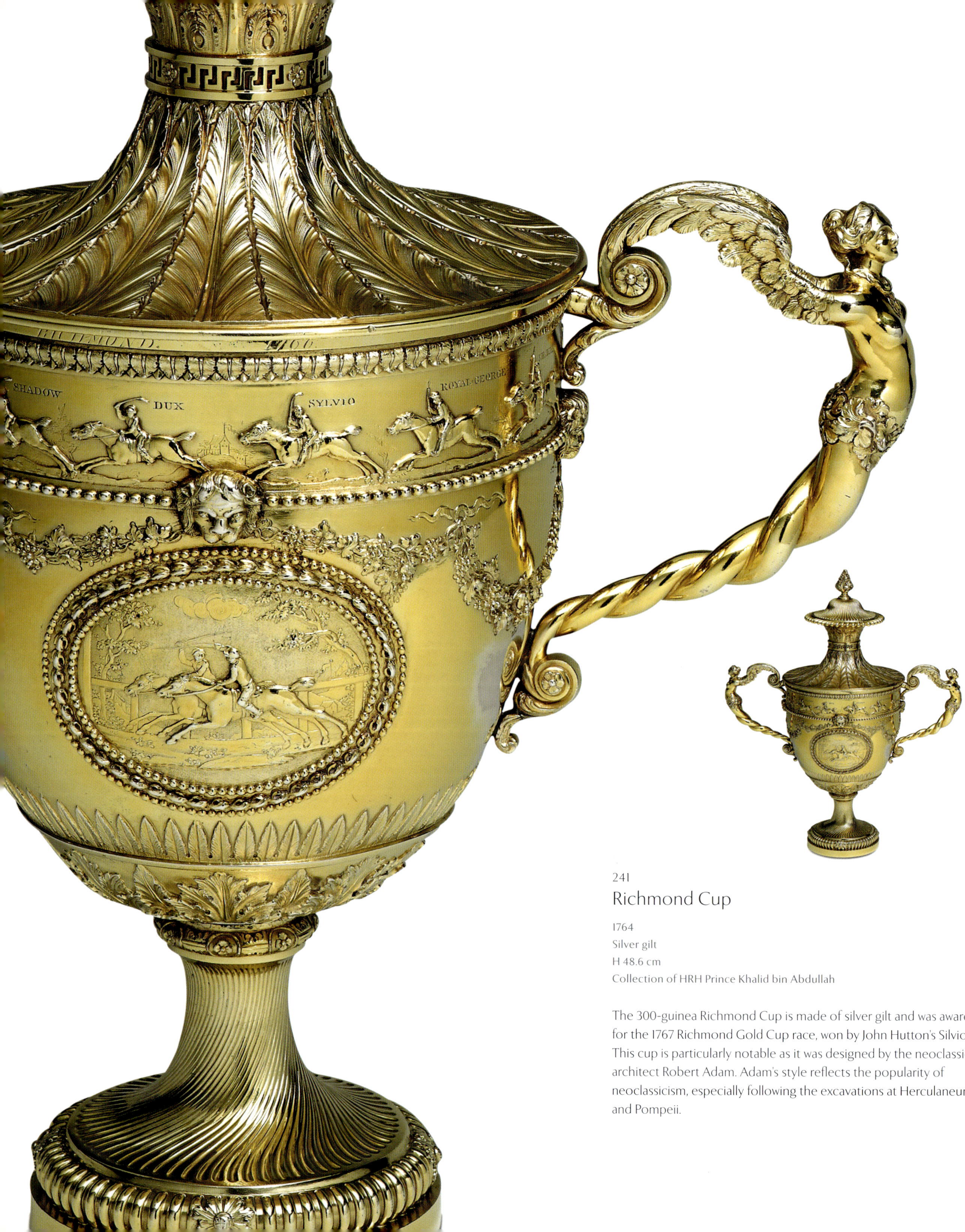

241

Richmond Cup

1764
Silver gilt
H 48.6 cm
Collection of HRH Prince Khalid bin Abdullah

The 300-guinea Richmond Cup is made of silver gilt and was awarded for the 1767 Richmond Gold Cup race, won by John Hutton's Silvio. This cup is particularly notable as it was designed by the neoclassical architect Robert Adam. Adam's style reflects the popularity of neoclassicism, especially following the excavations at Herculaneum and Pompeii.

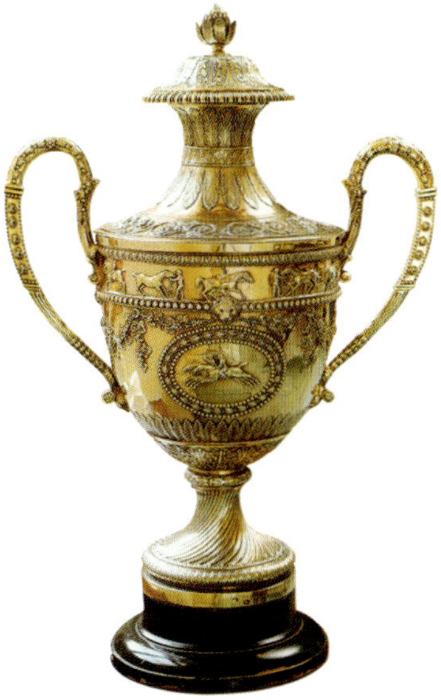

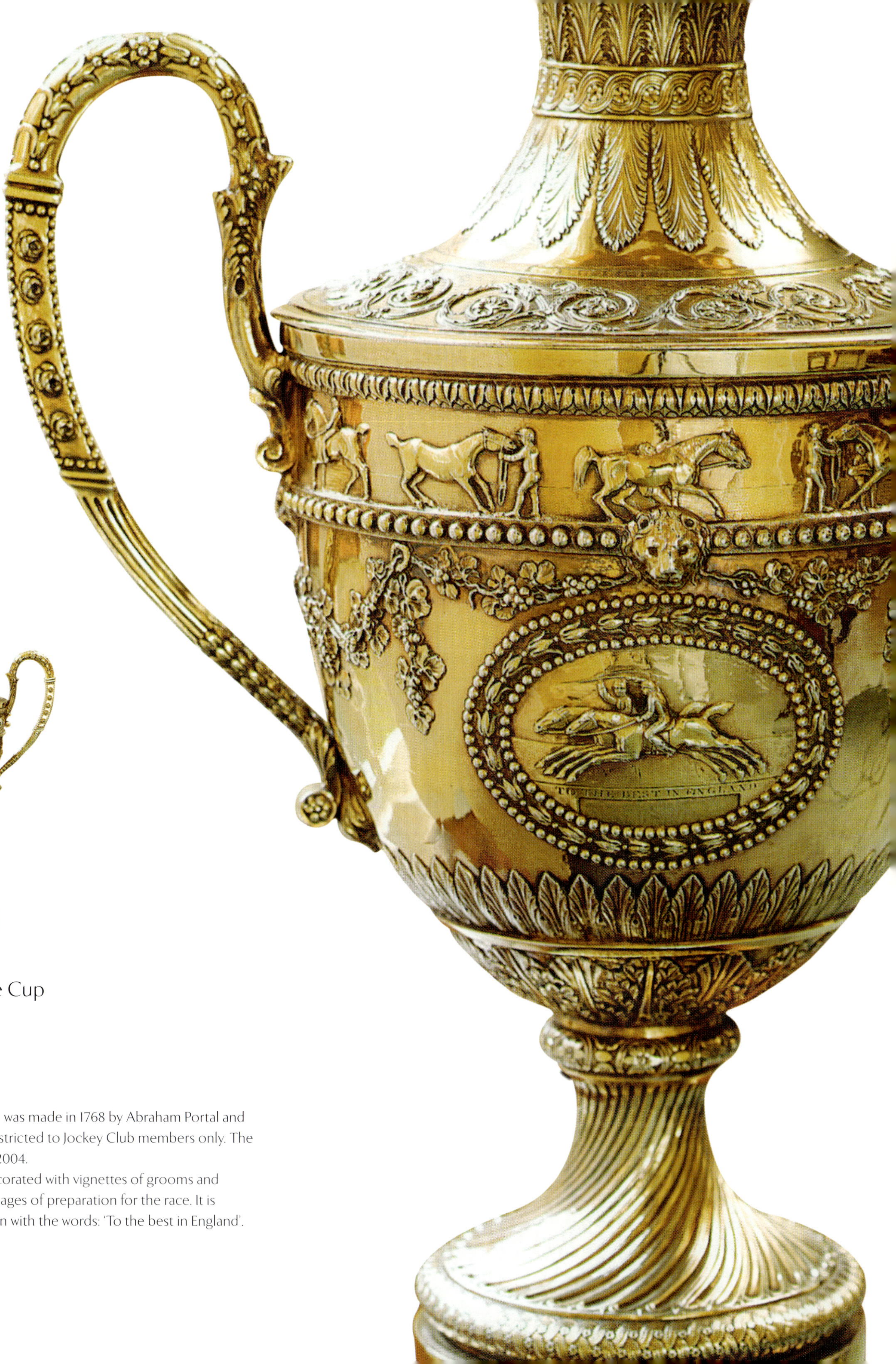

242

Newmarket Challenge Cup

1768
Metal
H 51 cm
Jockey Club Estates

This elaborate two-handled cup was made in 1768 by Abraham Portal and entry for the race was initially restricted to Jockey Club members only. The last race run for this cup was in 2004.

The brim of the cup is decorated with vignettes of grooms and jockeys with horses at various stages of preparation for the race. It is inscribed in the centre medallion with the words: 'To the best in England'.

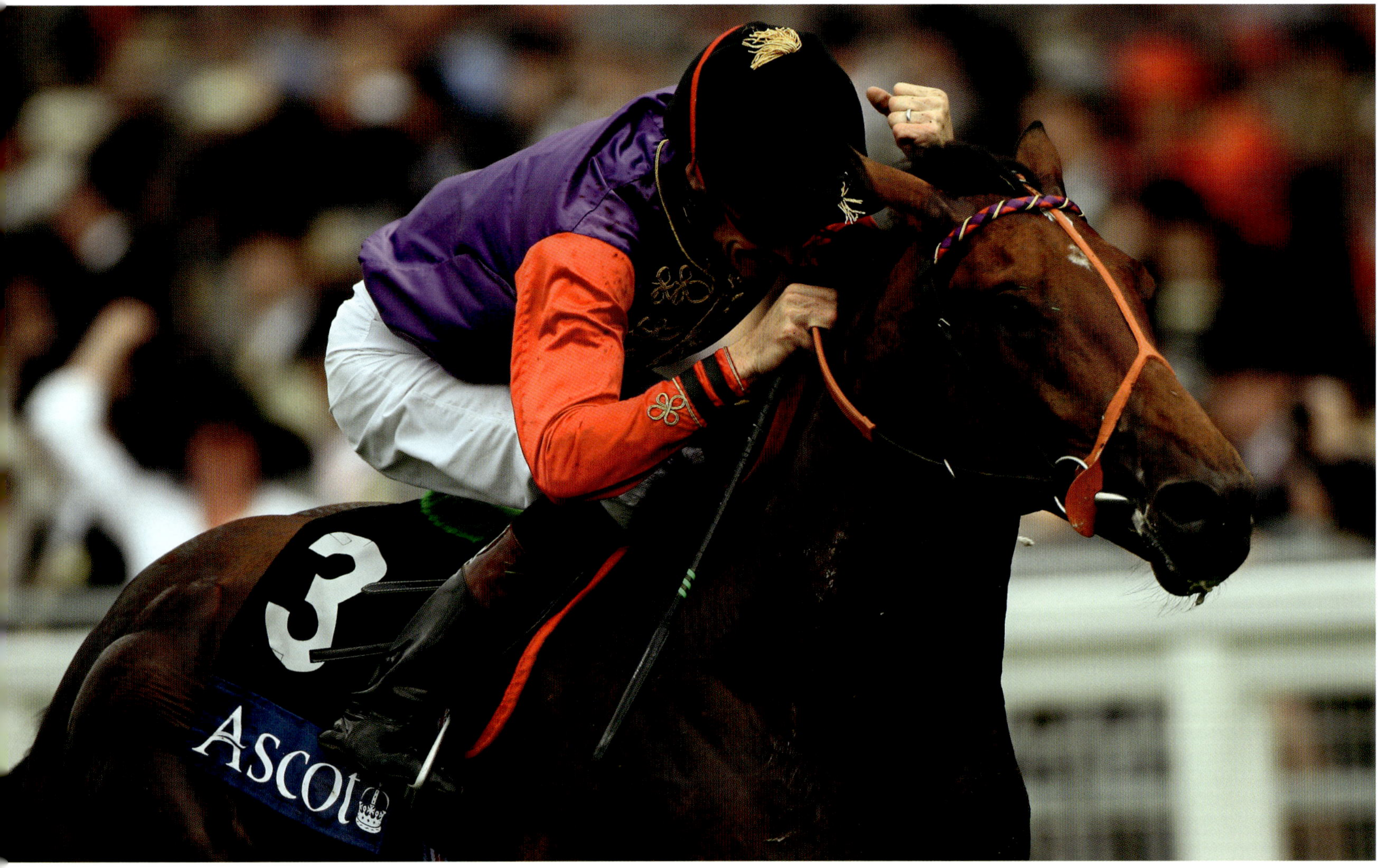

Fig. 48
Queen Elizabeth II's horse Free Agent wins the Chesham Stakes at Royal Ascot on 21 June 2008, ridden by Richard Hughes.

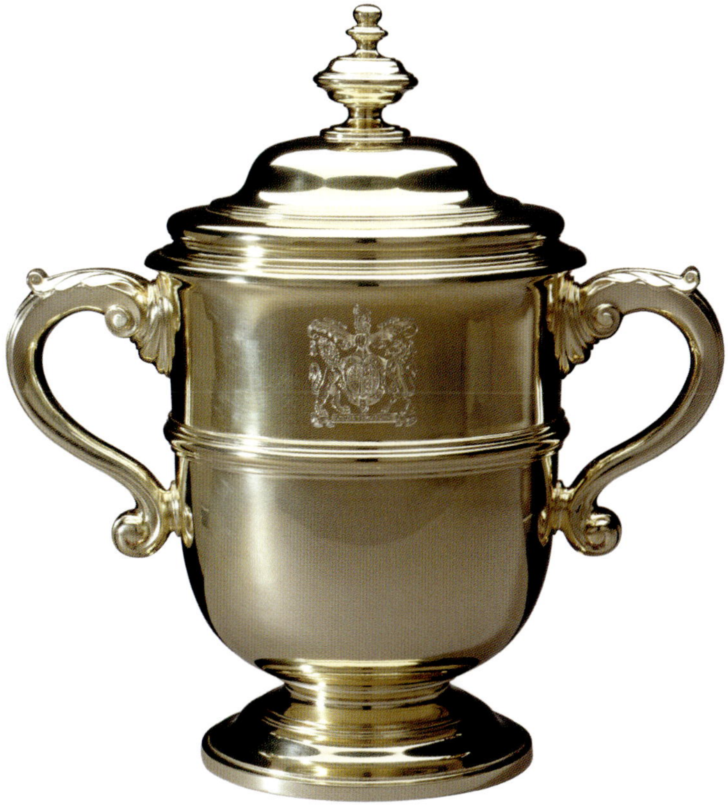

243

King George VI and Queen Elizabeth Stakes Cup

1954
Silver gilt
H 30.6 cm
The Royal Collection RCIN 50532

This cup, made by Richard Comyns, was won by the Queen's horse Aureole in the King George VI and Queen Elizabeth Stakes at Ascot in 1954. This was Aureole's last race.

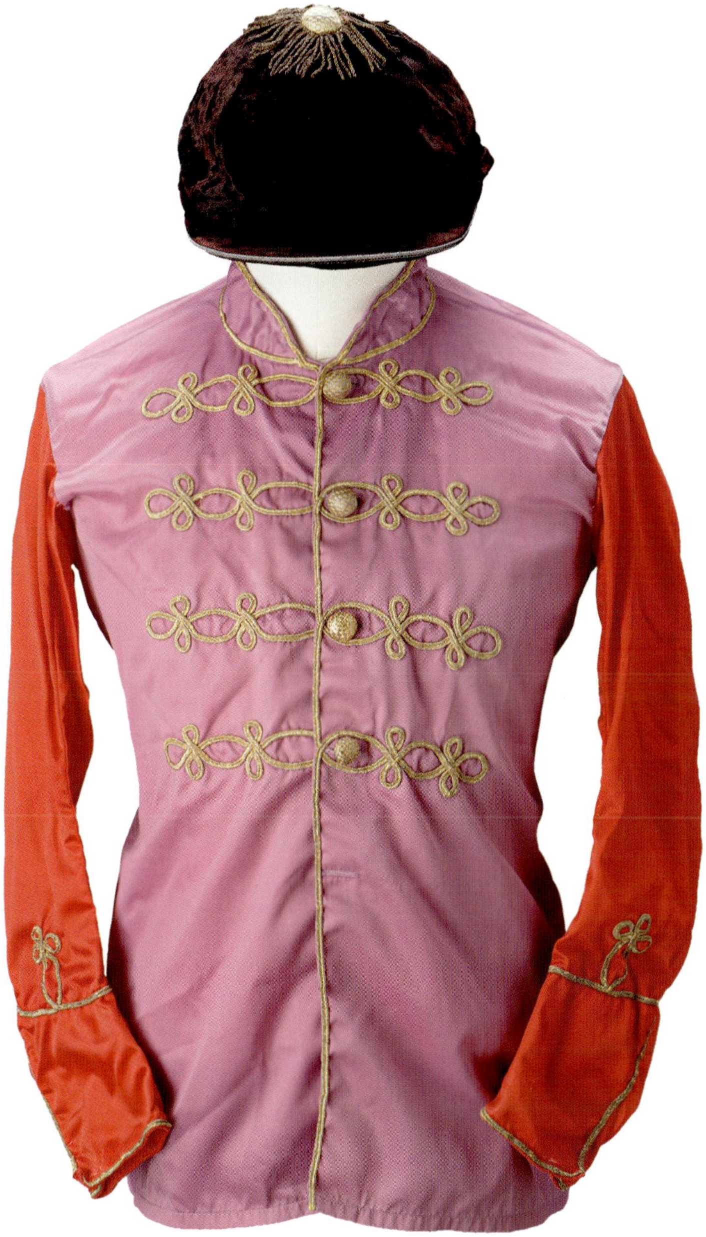

244

Her Majesty the Queen's Racing Colours

Silk and velvet
The Royal Collection

Her Majesty's colours of purple, gold braid, scarlet sleeves and a black velvet hat with a gold fringe have been in use since the time of Edward VII.

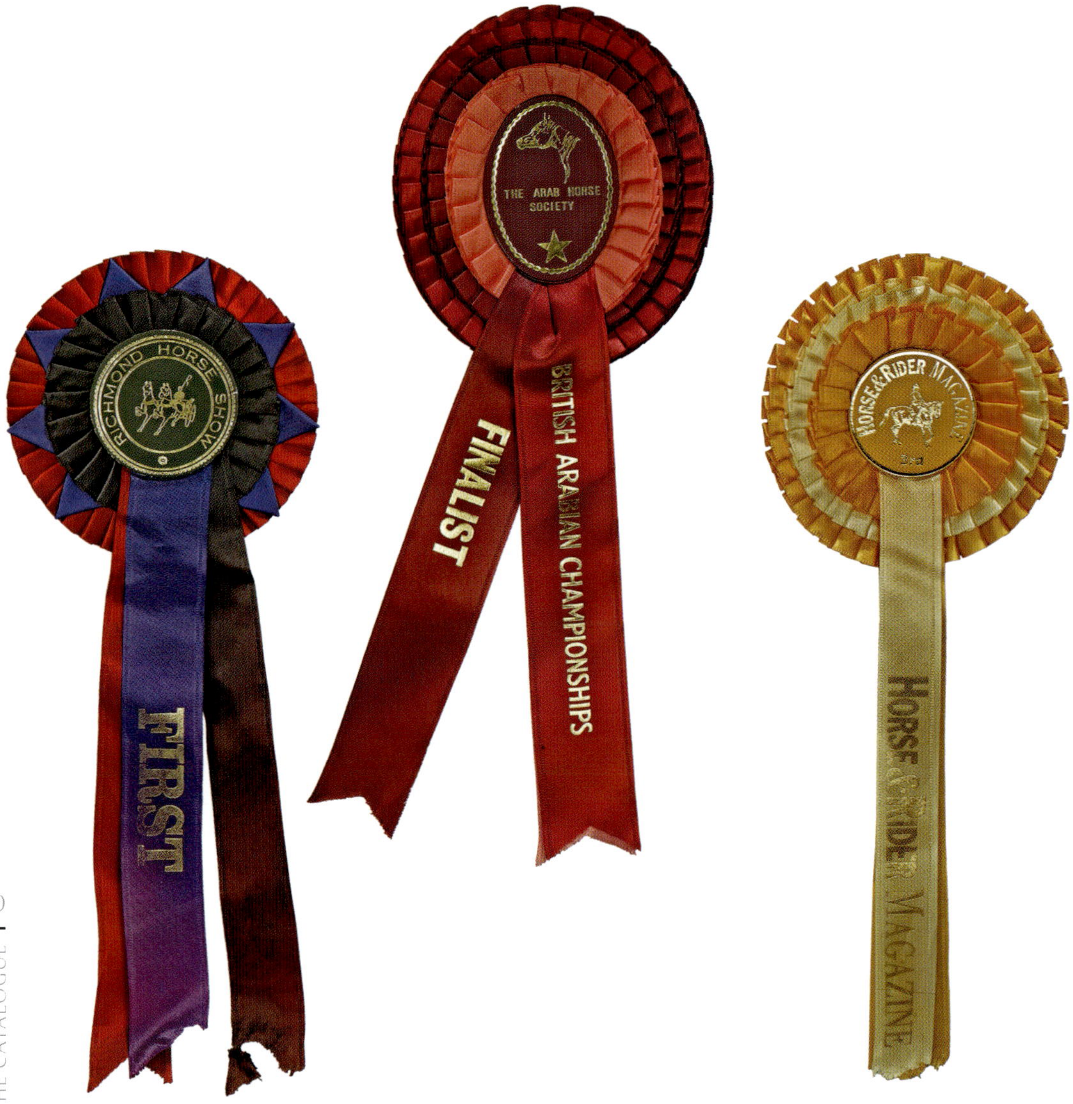

245

Rosettes

1998–9
Cardboard and ribbon
L 40 cm, W 12 cm approx.
Collection of Alice Rugheimer

Rosettes awarded to the Arabian horse Darona at different equestrian events between 1998 and 1999. There is a long tradition of awarding such rosettes at horse shows.

246

Sculpture of Tarfa

Karen Kasper
Late 20th century
Bronze
H 40 cm, W 50 cm, D 12 cm
The Layan Foundation

This bronze cast sculpture is of Tarfa, an Arabian mare. She was sired by an Abbeyan al Hamra and is one of the most well-known mares in Saudi Arabian history. She was presented as a coronation gift to King George VI in December 1937 by King Abdul Aziz al-Saud. Tarfa was later purchased by Henry Babson and became a part of his famed breeding program in the US.

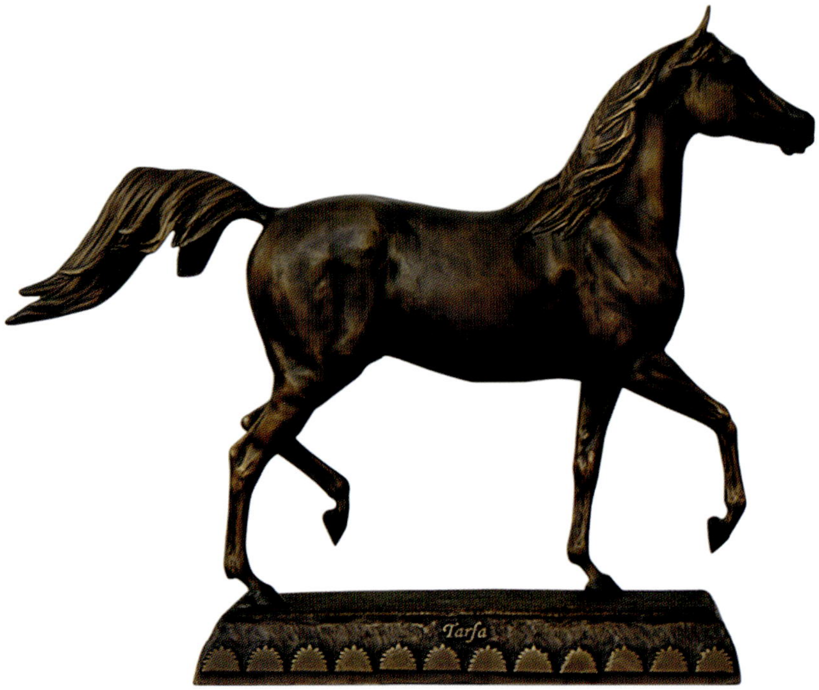

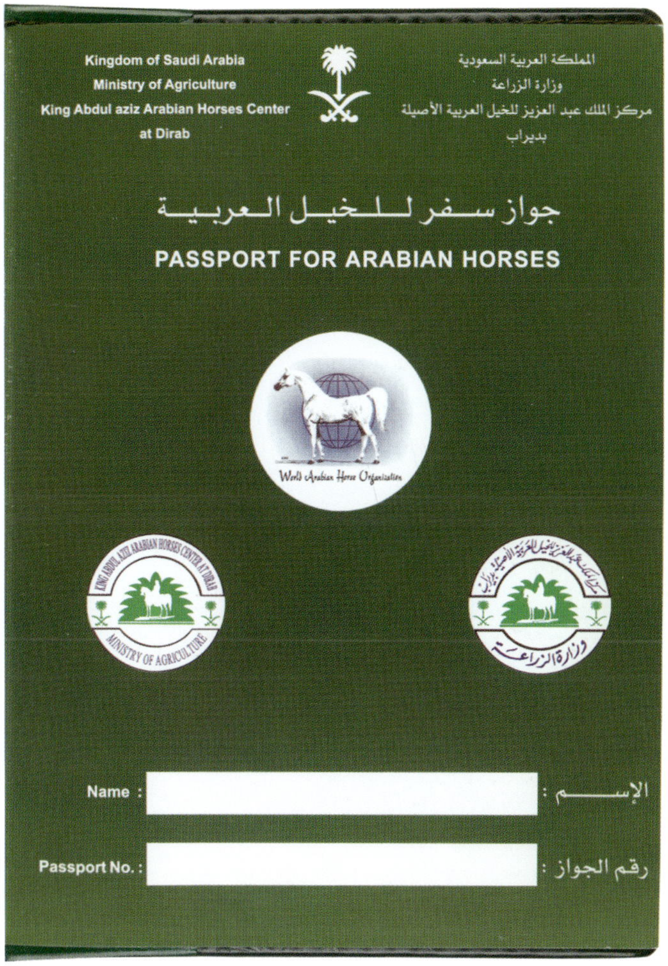

247

Passport for Arabian horses

2011
Issued by the King Abdulaziz Arabian Horse Centre at Dirab, Saudi Arabia
Paper, plastic
H 21.5 cm, W 15 cm (closed)
BM EPH-ME 638

Today, the purity of the Arabian breed is carefully preserved through registration and the tracking of exports and imports around the world. In the kingdom of Saudi Arabia, for example, all purebred Arabian horses are registered at the Ministry of Agriculture King Abdulaziz Arabian Horse Centre at Dirab, 35 kilometres south-west of Riyadh. Each horse is registered with a passport issued in accordance with the regulations of the World Arabian Horse Organisation (WAHO), giving full details of identification.

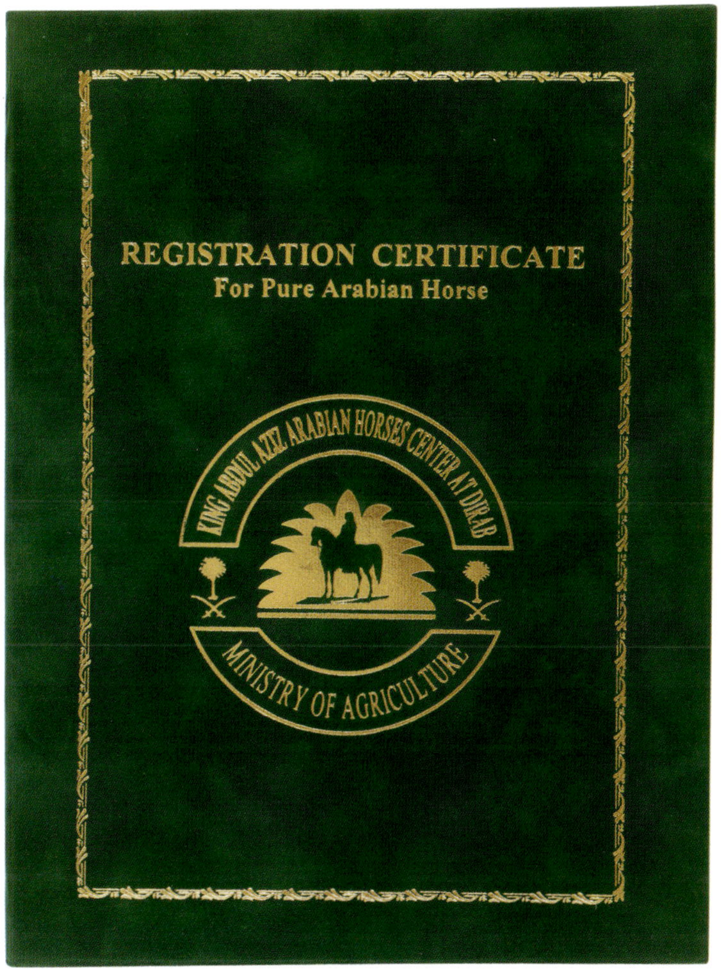

248

Registration certificate for a pure Arabian horse

2011
Issued by the King Abdulaziz Arabian Horse Centre at Dirab, Saudi Arabia
Paper, plastic, velour
H 31 cm, W 23.2 cm (closed)
BM EPH-ME 639

In addition to a passport, each registered purebred Arabian horse receives a registration certificate and a pedigree chart.

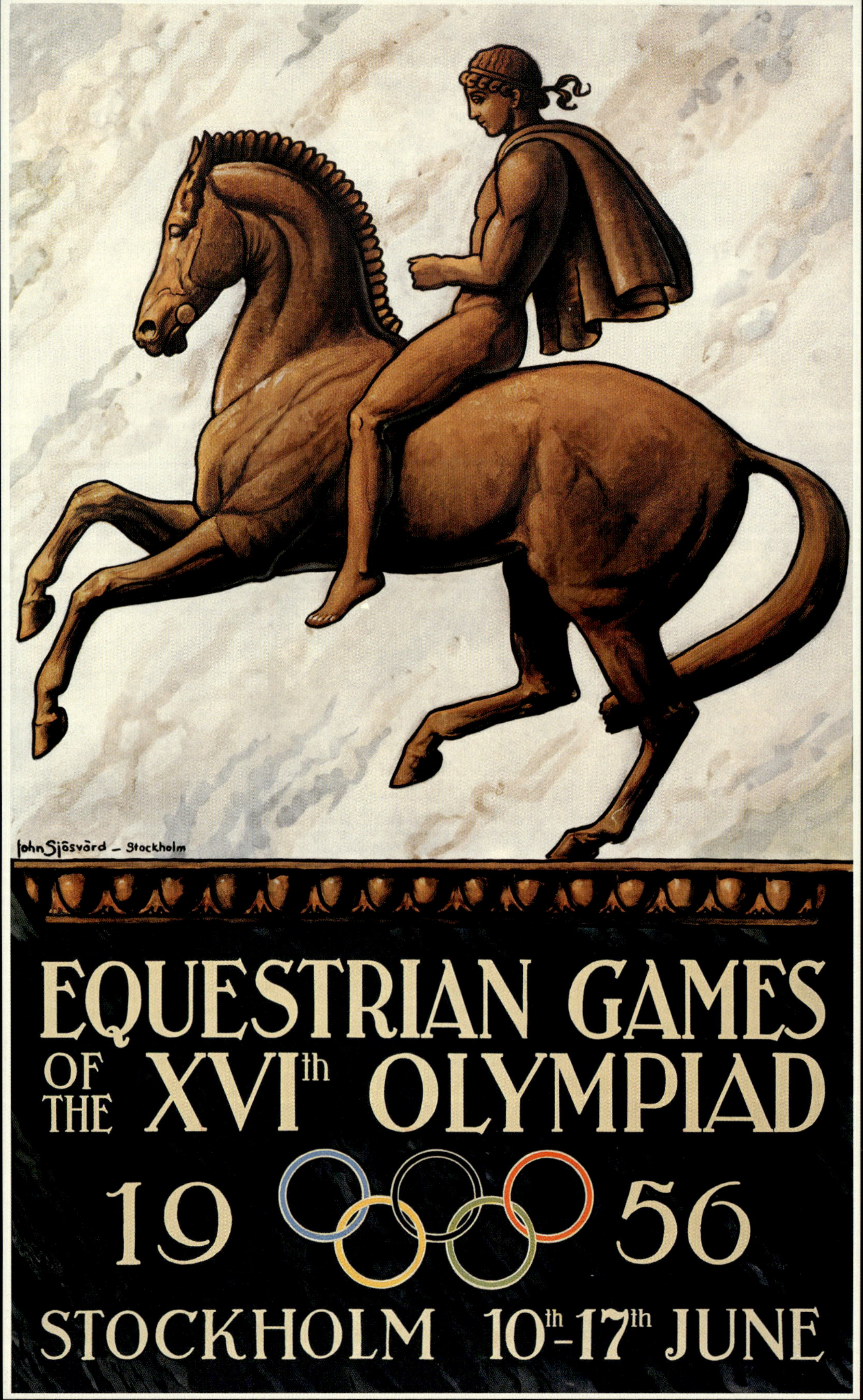

249

Olympic poster

1956
Paper
H 99 cm, W 61.8 cm
Olympic Museum Lausanne, 105806

Official poster for the equestrian events at the XVIth Olympic Games in Stockholm, 10–17 June 1956.

250

Olympic Prize Medal

Bertram Mackennal
1908
Metal
Diam. 3.2 cm
BM 1908,0903.5

This medal shows on the obverse three classical figures and on the reverse St George on horseback fighting a dragon. His bridle is held by a winged Victory.

251

Olympic commemorative medal

Bertram Mackennal
1908
Metal
Diam. 5 cm
BM 1908,0903.2

This medal was issued to commemorate the Olympic Games held in London in 1908. On the obverse is a symbol of a winged victory and on the reverse is a classical chariot and horses. It was designed by Bertram Mackennal. This was the first time horses were shown on Olympic medals.

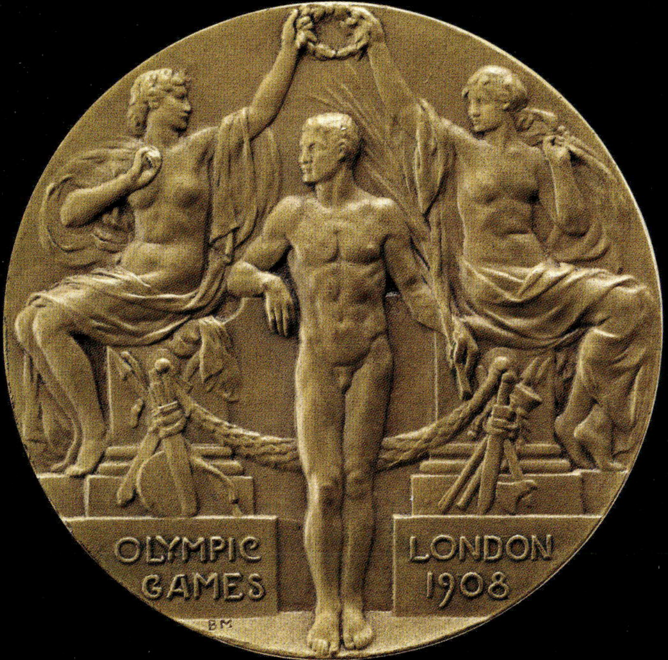
OLYMPIC
GAMES
LONDON
1908
BM

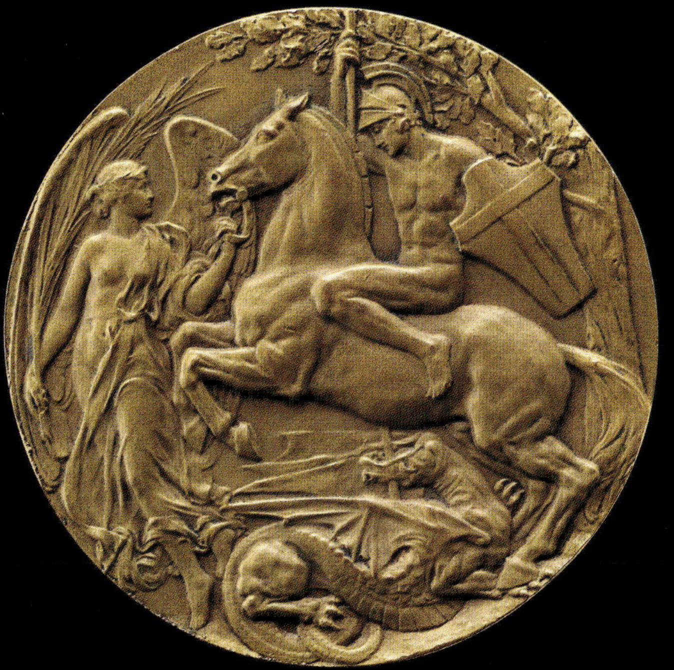

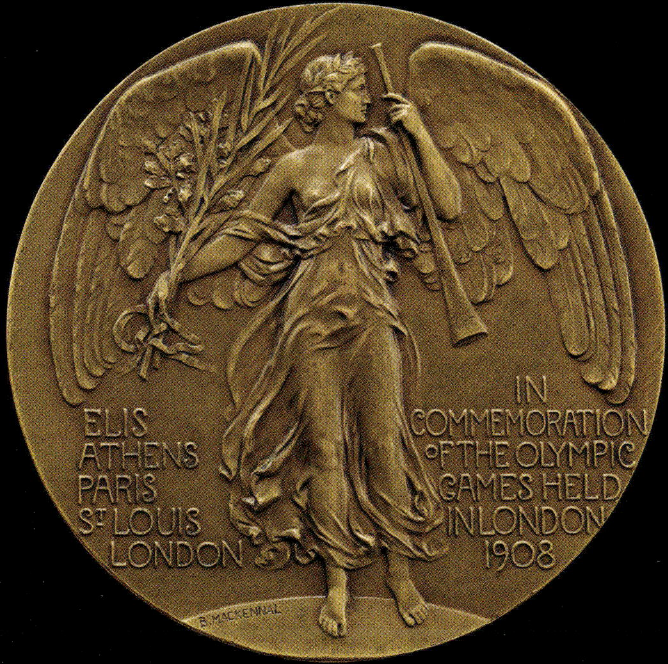
ELIS
ATHENS
PARIS
St LOUIS
LONDON
IN
COMMEMORATION
OF THE OLYMPIC
GAMES HELD
IN LONDON
1908
B. MACKENNAL

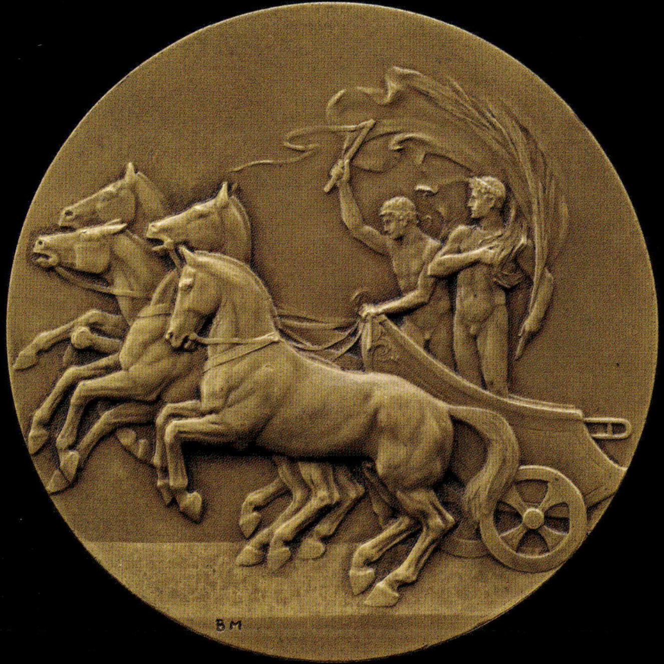
BM

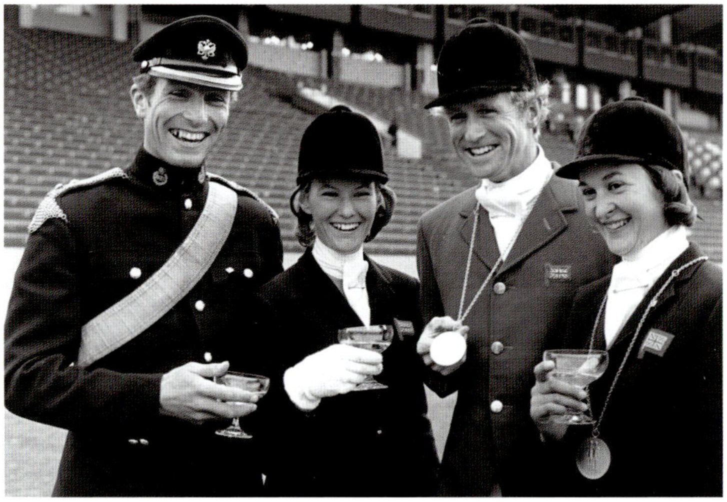

252
Winning medals from 1968 and 1972 Olympics

1972
Metal
Private collection

Richard Meade shows his gold medal, won on Laurieston at the 1972 Munich games, as part of the eventing team. Other team members were Mary Gordon-Watson (on Cornishman V), Bridget Parker (on Cornish Gold) and Mark Philips (on Great Ovation).

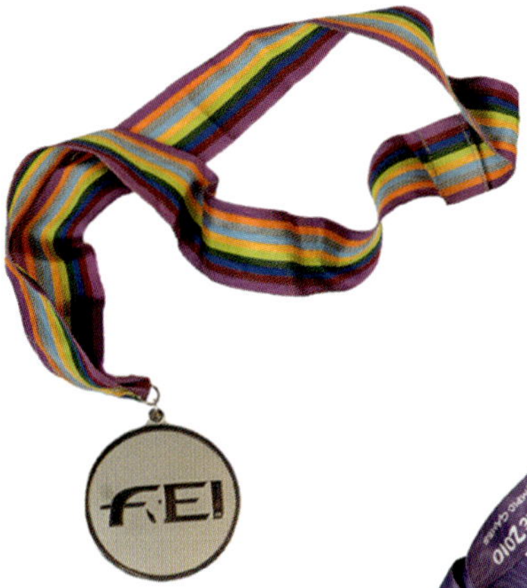

253
FEI Alltech silver medal

2010
Metal
H 7 cm, W 6.2 cm
Private collection

Silver medal from the 2010 FEI Alltech World Equestrian Games in Kentucky, won by Abdullah Waleed al-Sharbatly.

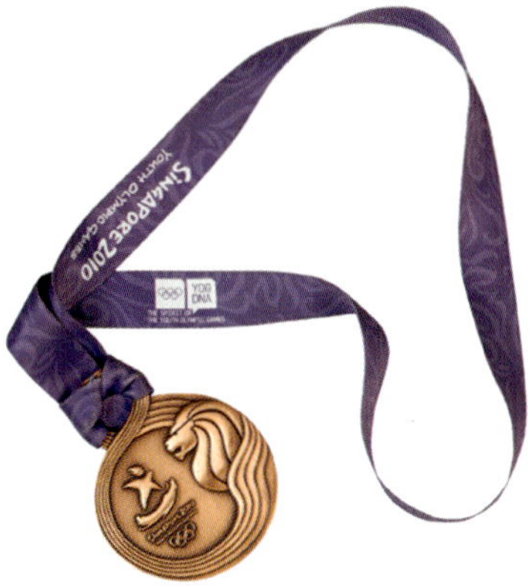

254
Youth Olympics bronze medal

2010
Metal
H 10 cm, W 8 cm
Private collection

Saudi Arabia's bronze medal from the inaugural Youth Olympic Games in Singapore 2010, won by Delma Rushi Malhas for the individual show jumping.

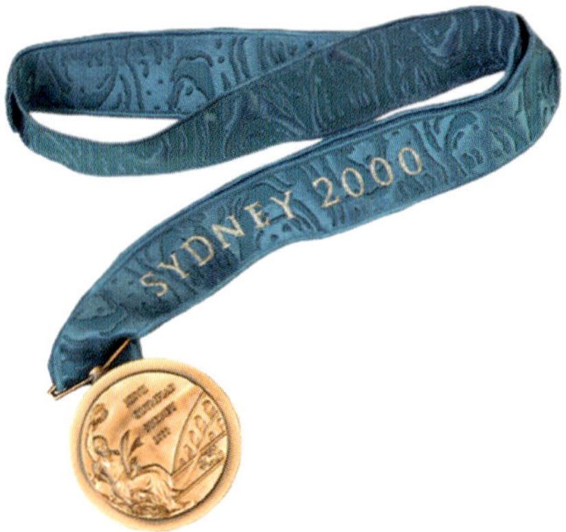

255
Olympic bronze medal

2000
Metal
H 7.7 cm, W 6.2 cm
Private collection

Saudi Arabia's bronze Olympic medal from the 2000 Sydney games, for the individual show jumping, won by Khaled Abdulaziz al-Eid (on Khashm Al Aan).

256
Queen Elizabeth II Stakes Cup

2011
Metal
H 35.6 cm
Collection of HRH Prince Khalid bin Abdullah

This cup of elegant modern design was won by Prince Khalid Abdullah's horse Frankel trained by Henry Cecil and ridden by Tom Queally in the Queen Elizabeth II stakes at Ascot on Inaugural Champions Day (15 October 2011). Frankel, at present unbeaten, is one of the most famous Thoroughbred racehorses of modern times.

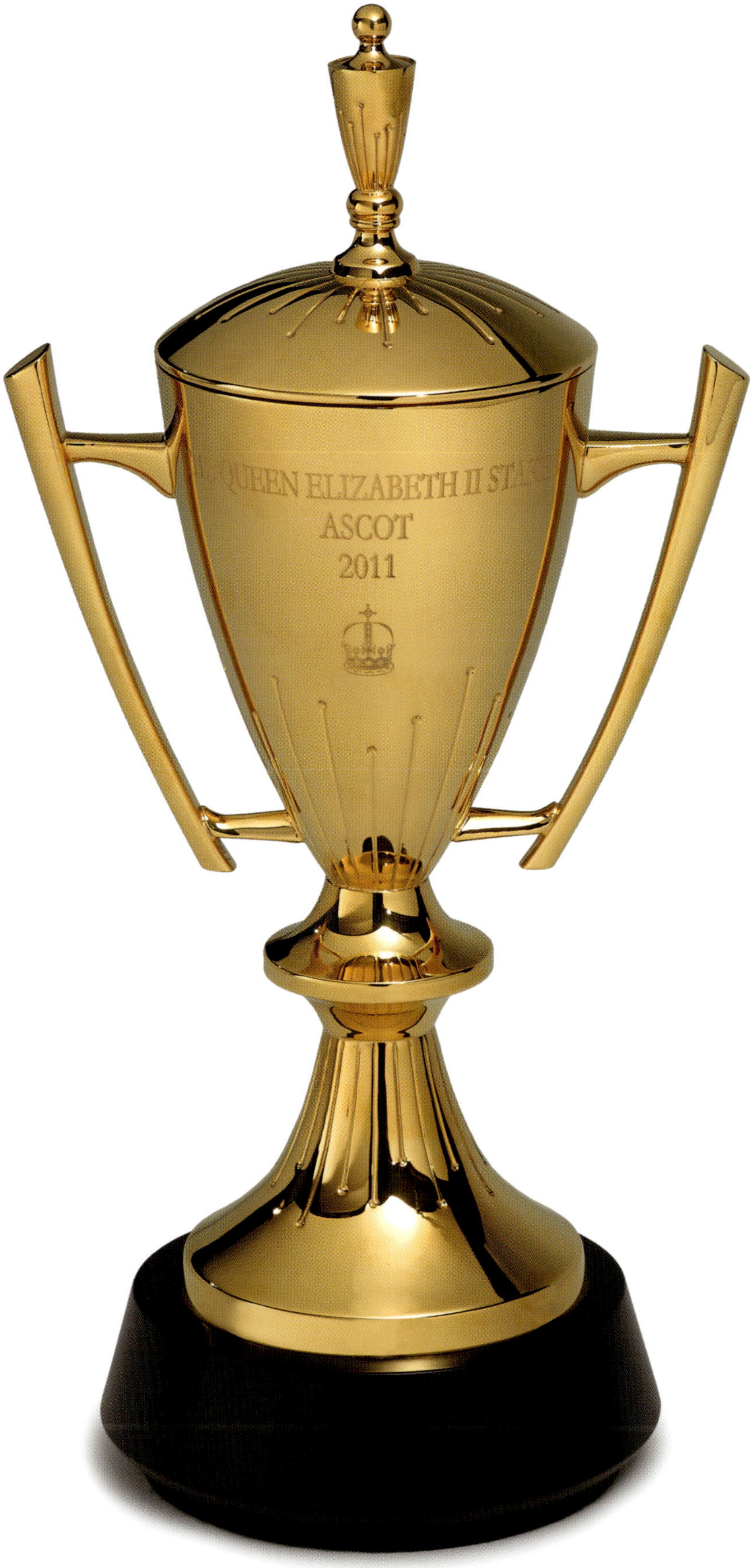

Notes

CHAPTER 1

1. R.G. Kent, *Old Persian: Grammar, Texts, Lexicon*, 2nd edn (New Haven 1953), p. 140.
2. Epitome of the *Philippic History* of Pompeius Trogus, translated with notes by the Rev John Selby Watson (London 1853).
3. Dio's *Roman History*, Book XL, translated by E. Cary, Loeb Classical Library, vol. III (1914).
4. Plutarch's Life of Crassus, *Plutarch's Lives*, Everyman's Library (London 1910).
5. See note 2.

CHAPTER 2

1. Malik's *Muwatta*, Book 21, No. 21.1.3; Vol. 3, Book 40, no. 559; Vol. 4, Book 52, no. 105; Vol. 4, Book 52, no. 112; Volume 6, Book 60, no. 486.
2. Malik's *Muwatta*, Book 21, no. 21.19.44; Vol. 4, Book 52, no, 102; Sahih Muslim, Book 20, no. 4614.
3. Malik's *Muwatta*, Vol. 4, Book 52, no. 115.
4. Malik's *Muwatta*, Book 21, no. 21.19.47
5. *Gift of the Desert*, p. 63.
6. In her introduction to *The Arabian Horse of Egypt*.
7. Vesta Sarkhosh Curtis, *Persian Myths* (London 2009), p. 45.
8. Michael Rogers in David Alexander (ed.), *Furusiyya* vol. 1 (Riyadh 1996), p. 176.
9. William Heude, *A Voyage up the Persian Gulf and a Journey overland from India to England in 1817* (London 1819), pp. 133–4.
10. A.H. Layard, *Discoveries in the Ruins of Nineveh and Babylon* (London 1853), pp. 329–30.
11. T.H. Ward, *Humphry Sandwith, A Memoir compiled from Autobiographical Notes* (London 1884), p. 65.
12. Thérèse Bittar in David Alexander (ed.), *Furusiyya* vol. 1 (Riyadh 1996), p. 161.

CHAPTER 3

1. Charles F. Horne (ed.), *The Sacred Books and Early Literature of the East*, Vol. V: *Ancient Arabia* (New York 1917), pp. 24–5.
2. Ammianus Marcellinus, *Res Gestae*, Book XIV, 4.
3. Dennis, George T, *The Taktika of Leo VI*, Dumbarton Oaks Texts (Harvard 2010), 18.129.
4. George T Dennis, *Three Byzantine Military Treatises*, Dumbarton Oaks Texts (Harvard 1985), PM II 104–11.
5. George T Dennis, *Three Byzantine Military Treatises*, Dumbarton Oaks Texts (Harvard 1985), *Attaleiates* 117.17-18; 114. 16–19.
6. William Heude, *A Voyage up the Persian Gulf and a Journey overland from India to England in 1817* (London 1819), p. 183.
7. William Gifford Palgrave, *Narrative of a Year's Journey through Central and Eastern Arabia 1862–63*, vol II (London 1865), p. 92.
8. Johann Ludwig Burckhardt, *Notes on the Bedouins and the Wahabys collected during his Travels in the East by the late John Lewis Burckhardt*, vol II (London 1831), p. 51.
9. Lady Anne Blunt, *A Pilgrimage to Nejd, the Cradle of the Arab Race*, vol II (London 1881, 2nd edn), pp. 13–14.

CHAPTER 4

1. Wilfrid Scawen Blunt, *The Poetical works of Wilfrid Scawen Blunt* (London 1914), p. 64.
2. H.V.F. Winstone, *Lady Anne Blunt, a Biography* (Manchester 2005), p. 96.
3. Winstone, op. cit., p.146.

Other quotations from unpublished diaries and correspondence in the Wentworth Bequest, British Library.

CHAPTER 5

1. William Osmer, *A Dissertation on Horses* (London 1756).

Further reading

Penguin Classics translation of the Koran by N.J. Dawood (1956)

David Alexander (ed.), *Furusiyya, vol. 1, The Horse in the Art of the Near East*, vol. 2, *Catalogue* (Riyadh 1996).

HRH Princess Alia al Hussein and Peter Upton, *Royal Heritage: the Story of Jordan's Arab Horses* (Newport, Isle of Wight, 2011)

Hossein Amirsadegeh (with an introduction by HH Sheikh Zayed bin-Sultan al-Nahyan), *The Arabian Horse: History, Mystery and Magic* (London 1998)

Lady Anne Blunt, *Bedouin Tribes of the Euphrates* (London 1879)

Lady Anne Blunt, *A Pilgrimage to Nejd* (London 1881)

Johann L Burckhardt, *Travels in Arabia* (London 1829)

J. Clutton-Brock and S. Davies, 'More donkeys from Tell Brak', *Iraq* LV (1993), pp. 209–21

J.E. Curtis and J.E. Reade (eds), *Art and Empire: Treasures from Assyria in the British Museum* (London 1995)

J.E. Curtis and N. Tallis, *Forgotten Empire: the World of Ancient Persia* (London 2005)

Geoff Emberling and Helen McDonald, 'Excavations at Tell Brak 2001–2002: preliminary report', *Iraq* LXV (2003), pp. 1–75

Judith Forbis and Gülsün Sherif, *The Abbas Pasha Manuscript and Horses and Horsemen of Arabia and Egypt during the Time of Abbas Pasha 1800–1860* (Mena, Arkansas, 1993)

Robert G Hoyland, *Arabia and the Arabs* (London 2001)

M.A. Littauer and J.H. Crouwel, *Wheeled Vehicles and Ridden Animals in the Ancient Near East* (Leiden/Köln 1979)

Elizabeth Longford, *Pilgrimage of Passion: The Life of Wilfrid Scawen Blunt* (London 1979)

Nasr Marei and Cynthia Culbertson, *The Arabian Horse of Egypt* (Cairo 2010)

David Oldrey, *The Jockey Club Rooms: a Catalogue and History of the Collection* (London 2006)

S.L. Olsen and C. Culbertson, *A Gift from the Desert: The Art, History and Culture of the Arabian Horse* (Lexington, Kentucky 2010)

William G Palgrave, *Personal Narrative of a Year's Journey through Central and Eastern Arabia (1862–1863)* (London 1865)

Carl R. Raswan, *Drinkers of the Wind: the Amazing Story of the Steeds of the Arabian Desert* (London 1938)

Fred Rice, Chestnuts, *Greys and Rodeo Days: My Life at Crabbet Park* (Worth, Sussex 1993).

G. Rex Smith, *Medieval Muslim Horsemanship: a Fourteenth-Century Arabic Cavalry Manual* (London 1979)

Keith Thomas, *Man and the Natural World: Changing Attitudes in England 1500–1800* (London 1984)

Peter Upton, *Out of the Desert: the Influence of the Arab Horse on the Light Horse and Native Pony Breeds of Britain* (Newport, Isle of Wight, 2010)

Peter Upton, *The Arab Horse* (Newport, Isle of Wight, 2012)

Malcolm Warner and Robin Blake, *Stubbs and the Horse* (New Haven and London 2004)

Judith, Baroness Wentworth (1945) *The Authentic Arabian Horse and his Descendants* (London 1945)

H.V.F. Winstone, *Lady Anne Blunt: A Biography* (London 2003)

Illustration acknowledgements

The publishers would like to thank the copyright holders for granting permission to reproduce the images illustrated. Every attempt has been made to trace accurate ownership of copyrighted images in this book. Errors and omissions will be corrected in subsequent editions provided notification is sent to the publisher.

All photographs of British Museum objects are © The Trustees of the British Museum, courtesy of the Department of Photography and Imaging. Map artwork © The Trustees of the British Museum (artwork by Matt Bigg at Surface 3)

Half-title page: Supplied by Royal Collection Trust / © HM Queen Elizabeth II 2012
Fig. 8 © Superstock
Fig. 10 John Curtis
Fig. 14 Private Collection / Archives Charmet / The Bridgeman Art Library
Fig. 16 The British Library Board (Add 18866)
Fig. 17 The British Library Board (Add 18866)
Fig. 20 Richard T. Bryant
Fig. 22 Richard T. Bryant
Fig. 23 Richard T. Bryant
Fig. 24 © Latif Al Obaida
Fig. 25 © Latif Al Obaida
Fig. 26 The British Library Board (Add 53893)
Fig. 27 The British Library Board (Add 54055)
Fig. 28 The British Library Board (Add 54085B)
Fig. 29 From C.R. Raswan, *Drinkers of the Wind* (London 1938), facing p. 224
Fig. 31 The British Library Board (Add 54085B)
Fig. 32 The British Library Board (Add 54085B)
Fig. 33 Peter Upton
Fig. 34 The British Library Board (Add 54141)
Fig. 35 The British Library Board (Add 54085B)
Fig. 36 Alan Crowhurst / Getty Images
Fig. 37 Supplied by Royal Collection Trust / © HM Queen Elizabeth II 2012
Fig. 38 Tate, London 2012
Fig. 39 Christie's Images Ltd, 2012
Fig. 41 The Bodleian Library, University of Oxford (Harding B 25 [1784]; Harding B 6 [54])
Fig. 42 Supplied by Royal Collection Trust / © HM Queen Elizabeth II 2012
Fig. 43 Press Association
Fig. 44 Carl Court / Getty Images
Fig. 45 Reproduced by permission of the Vorderasiatisches Museum, Berlin.
Cat. 3 Drawing after S. Smith, An Early Painted Vase from Khafaji, *British Museum Quarterly*, VIII, 1933–4, p. 39, fig. 1
Cat. 37 © The Trustees of the British Museum (artwork by Kate Morton)
Fig. 47 Drawing after R. Campbell Thompson and R. W. Hutchinson, 'The Site of the Palace of Ashurnasirpal at Nineveh, excavated in 1929–30 on behalf of the British Museum', in *Annals of Archaeology and Anthropology*, vol. XVIII, 1931, pl. XVIII.
Cat. 47 Drawing © The Trustees of the British Museum (drawing by Ann Searight)
Cat. 105 Drawing © The Trustees of the British Museum (drawing by Ann Searight)
Cat. 106 Drawing after O.M. Dalton, The Treasure of the Oxus (London, 1964), p.15, Fig. 49
Cats 129–32 King Abdulaziz Public Library
Cat. 133 King King Abdulaziz Public Library
Cat. 134 The British Library Board (Add 18866)
Cat. 145 The Bodleian Library, University of Oxford (MS Douce Or. a. 1: fol. 25.a)
Cat. 155 Image courtesy of Jila Peacock
Cat. 157 Bridgeman Art Library / Royal Armouries, Leeds
Cat. 159 Royal Armouries, Leeds
Cat. 164 Richard T. Bryant
Cats 165–80 National Museum of Saudi Arabia
Cat. 181 King Saud University Museum
Cat. 182 National Museum of Saudi Arabia
Cat. 183 King Saud University Museum
Cat. 189 King Abdulaziz Public Library
Cat. 190 King Abdulaziz Public Library
Cat. 191 © The Fitzwilliam Museum, Cambridge (PH 27-2004)
Cat. 192 The British Library Board (Add 54131)
Cat. 193 The British Library Board (Add 54109)
Cat. 194 The British Library Board (Add 54109)
Cat. 195 The British Library Board (Add 53890)
Cat. 196 The British Library Board (Add 53893)
Cat. 197 The British Library Board (Add 54076)
Cat. 198 © The Fitzwilliam Museum, Cambridge (PH 16-2004)
Cat. 199 © The Fitzwilliam Museum, Cambridge (PH 124-2004 (1-2))
Cat. 200 © The Fitzwilliam Museum, Cambridge (MS.30–1975)
Cat. 204 Supplied by Royal Collection Trust / © HM Queen Elizabeth II 2012
Cat. 205 Reproduced by permission of Nicholas Knowles
Cat. 207 Tate, London 2012
Cat. 208 Supplied by Royal Collection Trust / © HM Queen Elizabeth II 2012
Cat. 211 © Private Collection at the National Horseracing Museum
Cat. 212 Jockey Club Estates
Cat. 218 © The Fitzwilliam Museum, Cambridge (PD 7-1982)
Cat. 219 Tate, London 2012
Cat. 225 Supplied by Royal Collection Trust / © HM Queen Elizabeth II 2012
Cat. 241 Courtesy of Prince Khalid Abdullah
Cat. 242 Jockey Club Estates
Fig. 48 (p. 258) Julian Herbert / Getty Images
Cats 243–4 Supplied by Royal Collection Trust / All rights reserved
Cat. 246 The Layan Foundation
Cat. 249 IOC
Cat. 252 photo McCabe / Getty Images
Cat. 256 Courtesy of HRH Prince Khalid bin Abdullah